Torchbearers of Democracy

The John Hope Franklin Series in African American History and Culture

WALDO E. MARTIN JR. AND PATRICIA SULLIVAN, EDITORS

Torchbearers

AFRICAN AMERICAN SOLDIERS

of Democracy

N THE WORLD WAR I ERA

Chad L. Williams

The University of North Carolina Press Chapel Hill

Set in Minion Pro and Onyx by Tseng Information Systems, Inc. Manufactured in the United States of America. The paper in this book meets the guidelines for permanence and durability of the Committee on Production Guidelines for Book Longevity of the Council on Library Resources. The University of North Carolina Press has been a member of the Green Press Initiative since 2003.

Library of Congress Cataloging-in-Publication Data
Williams, Chad Louis, 1976–
Torchbearers of democracy : African American soldiers and the era of the First World War / Chad L. Williams.
p. cm. — (The John Hope Franklin series in African American history and culture)
Includes bibliographical references and index.
ISBN 978-0-8078-3394-0 (cloth : alk. paper)
1. World War, 1914–1918—Participation, African American. 2. World War, 1914–1918—African Americans. 3. African American soldiers—History—20th century. 4. African Americans—Social conditions—20th century. 5. African Americans—Civil rights—History—20th century. 6. Racism—Political aspects—United States—History—20th century. 7. Citizenship—United States—History—20th century. I. Title.
D639.N4W497 2010
940.4′03—dc22

2010006647

A version of chapter 7 was previously published as "Vanguards of the New Negro: African American Veterans and Post–World War I Racial Militancy," *Journal of African American History* 92, no. 3 (Summer 2007): 347–70. Used by permission of the Association for the Study of African American Life and History.

cloth 14 13 12 11 10 5 4 3 2 1

for Madeleine, Gabriel, & Michael

Contents

Illustrations

Acknowledgments

This book began some twenty-five thousand feet in the air, on a red-eye flight from San Francisco to Newark, New Jersey. With a good five hours to spare and unable to fall asleep, I figured I would try to get some work done, or, at the very least, organize my thoughts for the upcoming week. In doing so, I kept returning to a book I had recently read—*The Unknown Soldiers: African-American Troops in World War I* by Arthur Barbeau and Florette Henri—and a question that continued to swirl in my mind: "Why are there so few studies of African Americans and the First World War?" I pulled out the cheap blue-lined notebook tucked away in my carry-on bag. I began to write. I attempted to answer this question and, with my curiosity now fully sparked, scribbled others onto the paper. Before I knew it, I had filled several pages with ideas that still remain at the core of this book. Occasionally I will look at these notes, now somewhat tattered but still in decent enough condition, and smile at my good fortune in gravitating toward a subject and historical era that continues to captivate my interests.

I may not have become a historian if it were not for Brenda Stevenson, who exposed me to the joys of research and the craft of scholarship as an undergraduate at UCLA. Colin Palmer, Elizabeth Lunbeck, James McPherson, and Daniel Rodgers have also been wonderful teachers, asking all the right questions and inspiring me to push my intellectual boundaries. I could not ask for a better mentor than Nell Irvin Painter. From day one, she has been a rock of both personal and professional reinforcement, instilling in me the confidence to vigorously pursue my historical visions.

Initial funding for this project was provided by the History Department, the Center for African American Studies, and the Graduate School at Princeton University. A research grant from the George C. Marshall Foundation was greatly appreciated. Several fellowships made the final completion of this book possible. A Ford Foundation Postdoctoral Fellowship gave me valuable time away from the classroom, as well as the opportunity to join a wonderful family of young scholars. I am thankful to Sylvia Sheridan, Richard Hope, and Bill Mitchell for their leadership with the Woodrow Wilson Career Enhancement Fellowship. I owe a special debt to Craig Wilder, a brilliant historian and dedicated mentor, who not only read the entire manuscript but gallantly endured a cross-Atlantic flight from England to attend the fellowship retreat. My time at the Schomburg Center for Research in Black Culture Scholars-in-Residence Program made much of the revision process a wholly enjoyable experience. I am grateful to Howard Dodson, Diana Lachatenere, and Colin Palmer for giving me the opportunity to complete my book at one of the world's finest research facilities and, at the same time, mature as a scholar. I benefited from the feedback, intellectual exchange, and camaraderie of Valerie Babb, Lisa Gail Collins, Sylviane Diouf, Johanna Fernandez, Nicole Fleetwood, Venus Green, Kali Gross, Shannon King, Barbara Krauthamer, Malinda Lindquist, Ivor Miller, Raphael Njoku, Kezia Page, Carla Peterson, Evie Shockley, and Jon-Christian Suggs. Hillina Seife never ceased to amaze me with her skills as a research assistant.

The true heroes of this book are the librarians and archivists who provided invaluable assistance. I extend my gratitude to Emily Belcher at Princeton University's Firestone Library and George Deyo of the Calhoun County Historical Society in Anniston, Alabama, and the staffs of the United States Army Military History Institute, the Moorland-Spingarn Research Center, the Schomburg Center for Research in Black Culture, the Library of Congress, the Kautz Family YMCA Archives at the University of Minnesota, the Smithsonian Archives of American Art, Burke Library at Hamilton College, and the special collection departments at Cornell University and the University of Massachusetts at Amherst. A huge *merci beaucoup* goes to the archivists at the Service Historique de l'Armée de Terre at the Château de Vincennes, France, who understood enough of my painfully limited French to steer me toward essential military documents. I am also thankful for the generosity of the staff and guards at the Service des Archives de l'Assemblée Nationale in Paris (especially for recognizing my embarrassment upon realizing I had mistakenly taken a fellow foreigner's passport from the Archives de France!). Navigating the labyrinth of records at the United States National Archives at College Park, Maryland, is no easy task. This would not have been possible without the skill of Mitch Yockelson, Richard Boylan, and, most important, the late Walter Hill Jr., whose legacy will be long remembered.

The relationships forged in the making of this book are ultimately more meaningful than the finished product itself. The friendship and collegiality of Tammy Brown, Anastasia Curwood, Crystal Feimster, Cheryl Hicks, Barbara Krauthamer, Drew Levy, Malinda Lindquist, Kenneth Mack, Keith Mayes, Samuel Roberts, James Wilson, and Eric Yellin made my time at Princeton memorable. My colleagues at Hamilton College have been extremely welcoming. I am thankful for the support of my fellow historians, Doug Ambrose, Esther Kanipe, Shoshana Keller, Al Kelly, Robert Paquette, Lisa Trivedi, Thomas Wilson, and especially Kevin Grant and Maurice Isserman, who both took the time to read the entire manuscript and offer helpful suggestions. I am particularly grateful to the Dean of the Faculty Office for crucial financial assistance that allowed me to complete my research. Many friends and fellow scholars have read either all or parts of this project, in various forms and incarnations. I have presented my work at several conferences over the years and profited from the insights of my co-panelists. I am deeply appreciative of the collegiality of Davarian Baldwin, Nikki Brown, Christopher Capozzola, Adam Green, Robert Hill, Jennifer Keene, Adriane Lentz-Smith, David Levering Lewis, Pellom McDaniels III, Minkah Makalani, Saje Mathieu, Koritha Mitchell, Tiffany Patterson, Kimberly Phillips, Steve Reich, Mary Lou Roberts, Jeffrey Sammons, Naoko Shibusawa, Tyler Stovall, William Tuttle Jr., Cornel West, and Robert Zeiger.

The stellar editorial staff at UNC Press has patiently steered this project, and me along with it, through the publication process. I received constructive feedback from John Morrow Jr. and a second anonymous reader, whose meticulous attention to language strengthened this book immensely. Sian Hunter has been a wonderful editor, providing much appreciated encouragement and understanding.

As in all things, I would not have come this far without the support and love of my family. Thank you to the Lopez family, especially my brother Lenny, one of the most gifted minds I know. From New York to Alabama to California, a seemingly always expanding network of aunts, uncles, and cousins has provided me with both inspiration and deep pride in my family history. My research has led to unexpected genealogical discoveries, including at least two relatives who served in World War I. I have been blessed with two unconditionally supportive parents, Jayne and Carl Williams, and an amazing sister, Kelli Williams, who together keep me grounded and mindful of what is truly important in life. My two boys, Gabriel and Michael, are an everyday source of joy, wonder, and pure love. Madeleine has accompanied me along this journey, every step of the way. Words cannot express how lucky I am to have you by my side.

Torchbearers of Democracy

Introduction

James Preston Spencer was born on June 15, 1888, in Charlotte Court House, Virginia. The small town, nestled in the heart of Charlotte County, drew its name and claim to historical significance from the red-bricked, white-columned courthouse designed by Thomas Jefferson in 1823. James's parents, William and Bettie Spencer, raised an impressive young man. He graduated from high school and, by the spring of 1917, had enrolled as a student at Virginia Normal and Industrial Institute in Petersburg, Virginia, founded in 1882 as the nation's first fully state-supported college for African Americans. He received a solid education and even gained a bit of rudimentary military instruction, mostly likely in the form of basic drilling. The college experience also sharpened Spencer's racial consciousness and political awareness. The tension between loyalty to race and loyalty to nation Spencer and so many other African Americans struggled to reconcile became potentially a matter of life or death when, in the summer of 1917, he received a draft notice. His choice was clear. "I felt that it was my patriotic duty to serve my country at the most critical hour in the Nation's history," Spencer reflected, "though my Race had not been given the proper rights."[1]

Spencer carried this attitude into his October 16, 1917, induction at Camp Lee, where, at the age of twenty-nine, he became part of the 155th Depot Brigade.[2] While he may have received some limited training, Spencer, like most black soldiers in the American army during the war, worked, toiling at Camp Lee for six months under strenuous conditions that made him "mentally more alert to the political social patterns of the day." Spencer's fortunes changed, however, when he received orders to join the 370th Infantry Regiment, formerly the Eighth Illinois National Guard, one of the four regiments of the all-black Ninety-third Division, as it prepared to depart for France. Spencer left Hoboken, New Jersey, aboard the SS *Finland* on April 30, 1918, and arrived on May 12 at the French port city of St. Nazaire, crowded with thousands of African American stevedores, as well as laborers from Africa, Southeast Asia, and other parts of the globe. War had taken James Spencer far from Virginia and transplanted him in a new world of different people, languages, customs, and ideas.

Spencer spent only a few days at St. Nazaire before proceeding to the town of Grandvillars near the French-Swiss border. St. Nazaire and other port cities in France, however, remained home to thousands of black Services of Supply troops, consigned to labor duties for the duration of their time in the army. Jim Crow segregation defined many of their experiences, from the quarters they slept in to participation in Young Men's Christian Association (YMCA) recreational activities. But unlike the majority of African American soldiers in France who shouldered shovels instead of rifles, Spencer actually fought. The Ninety-third Division was one of only two black combat divisions established by the War Department. The other, the Ninety-second Division, reached France in June of 1918. Orphaned by the American army, the Ninety-third had the dubious honor of being the lone American combat division fully incorporated into the French fighting forces, and as such saw extensive action on the western front. After a period of training under their French commanders, Spencer and the 370th by early July found themselves in the fray, engaging German forces in the treacherous terrain of the Argonne Forest. After a disillusioning beginning to his military experience, Spencer was on the front lines, proving his manhood and demonstrating both his personal valor and that of his race more broadly. He proudly recalled an incident where his battalion "once marched to the Argonne under shell fire from the German artillery which caught the range of the road over which we passed for a distance of six miles." In the face of an intense barrage, Spencer and the men in his unit pressed forward, and "instead of getting to the designated position behind time we got there two hours ahead of time, and not an officer or man lost his courage under such a trying situation." Fully aware of critics within and outside of the army who asserted African Americans would not make good fighting men, Spencer, the 370th, and other black troops determined to prove these skeptics wrong.

While Spencer and his regiment braved combat in the Argonne, back in the United States W. E. B. Du Bois, the influential editor of the National Association for the Advancement of Colored People's journal of news and opinion, the *Crisis*, received a letter. It was from a black man—we do not know his name—who wanted to inform Du Bois about a captain and recruiting officer in the 370th Infantry Regiment, Leonard W. Lewis.[3] Du Bois, who had championed the cause of black officers by supporting the creation of a segregated training camp at Fort Des Moines, Iowa, viewed men like Captain Lewis as models of "Talented Tenth" manhood and racial leadership, and thus read the letter with interest. Lewis, according to the letter writer, felt "supremely optimistic on the outlook of the Negro in America both during and after the war," and he observed that black men of the 370th currently stationed in France "went over very sanguine to do their bit for their country and their people." He went on to describe Lewis, other soldiers of the 370th such as James Spencer, and all African American servicemen more generally as "'*Torch Bearers*' to make the world safe for democracy and America especially by being men in the truest sense of the word compelling a reluctant recognition from both friend and foe." With African American soldiers fighting not only to make the world safe for democracy but to make democracy a reality for some ten million oppressed citizens in the United States, black people had to, in his estimation, "forget and temporarily overlook every thing tending to bar progress." Many African Americans, including a significant number who donned the uniform of the United States, refused to accept such a bargain. Nevertheless, while not always treated accordingly, African Americans remained citizens, a status rife with both contradiction and democratic possibility. Reflecting this tension, the letter ended with a strong declaration, one that African Americans hopefully and painfully grappled with throughout the war and in its aftermath: "This is *Our* country right or wrong."[4]

Torchbearers of Democracy is about this moment, a crucial period in African American history when, during the First World War and its immediate aftermath, black people engaged in a fierce struggle to infuse personal and collective meaning into the ideals and everyday realities of democracy. More specifically, it is about James Preston Spencer, Leonard Lewis, and the nearly 400,000 African American soldiers who served in the United States Army during the war. *Torchbearers of Democracy* explores the complex place and meaning of black soldiers in wartime American society, with all of its ironies. For many African Americans, black servicemen stood as harbingers—torchbearers—of a new dawn of democratic freedom and opportunity reminiscent of Reconstruction following the Civil War. Conversely, for many white Americans, black soldiers represented a distinct threat to prevailing social hierarchies and white supremacist visions of American democracy. These symbolic constructions were directly informed by the presence, thoughts, and deeds of African American troops themselves. Through their participation in the army, black soldiers wrestled with what democracy meant to their individual lives and, increasingly, what it meant for black people more broadly. The actions of African American soldiers and veterans and their everyday engagements with the challenges of military and civilian life, both during and after the war, stood at the heart of an era when the very future of peoples of African descent appeared to be at stake. By recentering the First World War as a turning point in the struggle for African American freedom, citizenship, and self-determination, *Torchbearers of Democracy* reflects the hope and threat, the potential and betrayal, and the fulfillment and disillusionment of democracy for black people during this time.

"The world must be made safe for democracy," President Woodrow Wilson dramatically pronounced in his legendary war address before the U.S. Congress on the evening of April 2, 1917. When he uttered these fateful words, Wilson surely did not anticipate the ideological forces they would unleash and the diverse assortment of social groups they would inspire. Indeed, democracy, as the keyword of the war and its aftermath, reverberated with profound domestic and global ramifications.[5] Democracy, however, was at the time and has always been a vigorously contested term. It has meant different things to different people in different contexts. Most simply, democracy is a political process and system of fundamental rights predicated upon the concept of rule by the people. It is comprised of various institutions designed to ensure that all citizens have the opportunity for effective participation in the political process, the right to vote, the ability to gain enlightened understanding, the chance to exert final control of the political agenda, and, lastly, to have full inclusion in these opportunities. But democracy, particularly throughout American history, has been a work in progress. It has been deeply flawed, inconsistent, and all too often blatantly contradictory. Democracy is therefore more than just a way of governing; it is an ideal, something to be strived for and constantly perfected. It is a way of thinking about the world, one's place in it, and the desire to fully realize one's human potential.[6]

Through the trials of slavery, Reconstruction, and the rise of Jim Crow, democracy existed for African Americans as both a powerful ideal and an elusive reality. When the clouds of war finally reached American shores in the spring of 1917, many black people skillfully juxtaposed the Wilsonian democratic ambitions of the war against their own racially marginalized social and political conditions. At the same time, they exploited the broadened rhetorical terrain created by Wilson to assert their own vision of democracy, one in which black people not only would have political equality and the full rights of American citizenship but would be treated and respected as human beings. Established prewar organizations, such as the National Association for the Advancement of Colored People (NAACP), the National Association of Colored Women (NACW), and the Negro Fellowship League (NFL), as well as a host of postwar "New Negro" groups, such as the League for Democracy (LFD) and the Universal Negro Improvement Association (UNIA), provided African Americans and other peoples of African descent of various ideological persuasions with opportunities to challenge racial oppression. The exigencies of the war likewise emboldened black people at the everyday level to resist white supremacy, affirm their citizenship, and assert their basic humanity. Most notably, the migration of some 500,000 black southerners during the war era to the urban North and Midwest reflected their desires for social, political, and economic equality.[7] By staking claim to democracy as both an effective relationship with the state and an imaginative ideal, African Americans viewed the war as a potentially defining moment in their history of racial progress and struggle for freedom.[8]

But if history provided a lesson, expanding the boundaries of American democracy would not materialize from the benevolence of the Wilson administration or suddenly racially enlightened white citizens. African Americans would have to fight. As in the Civil War, if African Americans truly sought freedom, they had to be prepared and willing to pay the cost with their blood. The approximately 187,000 black men who donned the Union blue after the Emancipation Proclamation were the face of an army of liberation and the ultimate destruction of slavery. As they triumphantly marched through the South following the Civil War, black troops became both symbols and living embodiments of freedom and the hopes of a new era characterized by the full incorporation of black people as citizens into American democracy.[9] This legacy and its social reverberations continued with the exploits of the "Buffalo Soldiers" in the Regular Army and was carried into the twentieth century. Military service and the presence of African American soldiers thus emerged as the central issue shaping how black people viewed, interpreted, and internalized the contested meanings of democracy and citizenship during the years of the First World War.[10]

The historical experiences of African American soldiers constitute an important part of the broader story of American participation in the First World War. Arthur Barbeau and Florette Henri's *The Unknown Soldiers* (1974) remains the lone study of black troops, although several other important works have recently added to our knowledge of the subject.[11] Nevertheless, the place of black soldiers in the war has too often been treated as tangential to the larger history of American involvement and the place of the conflict in American memory. The war experience of black soldiers, and African Americans more generally, has been characterized as one of disillusionment and dashed expectations because of the resilience of white racism. This view has contributed both to the historiographical marginalization of black soldiers and to a failed appreciation for how their presence shaped the war as a seminal moment in the history of African Americans, the United States, and the African diaspora.[12] Moreover, scholars have yet to examine the legacy of African American soldiers in the war beyond the constraints of discriminatory military policy, thus leaving crucial aspects of their individual and collective experiences unexplored, as well as their significance in the broader context of wartime and postwar African American history.[13]

African American soldiers were a diverse lot. They came from all walks of life, regions of the country, and social backgrounds, from affluent members of the "Talented Tenth" to poor sharecroppers from the southern Black Belt. The

Regular Army contained some 10,000 African American soldiers, many with extensive prior service, who stood poised to carry on the proud tradition of the "Buffalo Soldiers" on the battlefields of France. In addition to their presence, a select number of African American National Guard companies quickly filled their volunteer quotas and became some of the first black units mobilized for combat. The majority of black servicemen entered the army through the draft, for which an estimated 2.3 million black men registered and nearly 370,000 ultimately served. The bulk of these men came from the South, which, despite wartime northern migration, continued to serve as the regional home for most black people.

They entered a racist army. The military has historically functioned as a mirror of American society and the political status of African Americans in particular. This held true during the First World War. The "race question" informed the thinking of white politicians and military officials and dictated their actions in regard to black servicemen. Black men were excluded from the marines and limited to only menial positions in the navy. War planners deemed racial segregation, just as in civilian life, the most logical and efficient method of managing the presence of African Americans in the army. Fully aware of the potential of military service to transform the terms of citizenship and the relationship of African Americans to the state, military officials attempted to replicate the practices, customs, and hierarchies of white supremacy as closely as possible in the army. A combination of biological racism and historical fears of armed black men shaped army policy and the decision to consign the majority of African American draftees to labor and service units. For black soldiers and officers in the Ninety-second and Ninety-third Divisions, the two all-black combat units, the army went to great lengths to reinforce their marginalized role in the American Expeditionary Forces and larger Allied war effort. The select number of African American officers fortunate enough to earn commissions had few opportunities for upward advancement and coped with unrelenting hostility from their white counterparts and superiors. Whether at domestic military installations or in the trenches of France, African American soldiers faced constant reminders of the army's ingrained racism.

While acknowledging this reality, the story of African American servicemen in the war does not end here. African American soldiers, as combatants and noncombatants, made important and in many instances truly heroic contributions to the war effort. Most significant, black soldiers were complex men, with complex identities, and as such responded to military service in a variety of ways that did not always hinge exclusively on race and their confrontations with racism. Race constituted one dimension of black soldiers' ideological worldview and did not function independently of the contours of their gender, class, political, regional, international, and diasporic identities.[14] Their experiences were extremely personal and variegated and cannot be generalized through the narrow lens of racist military policy. Using a broad range of methodological tools, a central aim of *Torchbearers of Democracy* is to demonstrate the diversity of African American soldiers, their breadth of experience, and how the war shaped their lives and identities in ways large and subtle, negative and positive.

The service of African American troops uniquely captured the connections between race, nation, manhood, and the obligations of citizenship in the context of the First World War. The patriotic demands of the war forced African Americans to try to make sense of their conflicted status as American citizens. This was especially imperative for the thousands of black men called upon to potentially give their lives for the nation. African American soldiers, by fulfilling the civic obligation of military service, consciously staked claim to their citizenship, manhood, and place in the body politic.[15] Without question, the democratic framing of the war and its racial politics profoundly affected many black soldiers, who linked their service to larger questions surrounding the future of the race and its condition. But the obligations of citizenship for most black servicemen assumed more personal dimensions. As their experiences revealed, African American soldiers did indeed see themselves as American citizens, and participation in the army presented a rare opportunity to infuse this essentially moribund political status with life and effective meaning. Black soldiers, in particularly those from disadvantaged backgrounds, reaped important tangible benefits from their service, such as financial allotments and improvements in health and education, that tightened both the material and imaginative bonds between African Americans and the nation-state. It also offered black people an opportunity to challenge pejorative conceptions of black masculinity, while at the same time upholding and vindicating the broader manhood of the race through the heroic valor of military service. With an internalized sense of civic obligation, as well as an expectation for democratic reciprocity, many African American soldiers came away from their service, in spite of systemic racial discrimination, convinced they had successfully fulfilled their patriotic duties, affirmed their citizenship, and proved their worth as men.

On and off the battlefield, African American servicemen literally fought for democracy, their manhood, and rights as citizens. Many white Americans saw black soldiers as a menace, a threat to an idea of democracy rooted in longstanding racial and gender hierarchies. Domestic training camps, cross-Atlantic transport ships, French cities and towns, and numerous American communities both during and after the war emerged as sites of violent social and political conflict due to the physical presence of black servicemen. With the specter of interracial sex frequently lurking in the background, black soldiers and veterans regularly clashed with both white soldiers and civilians, confrontations that blurred distinctions between comrade and enemy. All too often, many black soldiers saw white Americans as no different, if not worse, from the German "Hun." Following the armistice, many black veterans refused to accept a continued second-class citizenship status, after having sacrificed their blood and sweat for the nation and the cause of democracy.

As *Torchbearers of Democracy* demonstrates, the presence of African American soldiers and veterans was, in part, so volatile because of what they symbolized. When the author of the before-mentioned letter to W. E. B. Du Bois described black soldiers as "torch bearers," he invoked a powerful trope of black soldiers as symbols of racial pride, manhood, and citizenship. African American servicemen embodied the inherent tensions of fighting for a country that denied democracy to its own citizens and the dilemma of remaining loyal to both nation and race. The symbolic meanings of black soldiers during the First World War, while informed by Civil War and postbellum antecedents, were historically and contextually specific. Both white and black Americans viewed and utilized black soldiers and their symbolisms in various and often competing ways as determined by their respective racial, class, gender, and regional ideologies. The First World War and the mass mobilization of military manpower brought the symbolic meanings of black soldiers to the forefront of the nation's racial consciousness and in turn impacted the course of wartime social relations within and outside of the army itself.

The symbolic power of African American soldiers informed the tenor of and provided crucial organizational fuel for civil rights activism and struggles for democracy during the era of the First World War. Race advocates, male and female, shaped a public discourse linking black military service to specific claims for expanded citizenship rights and broader demands for self-determination.[16] Black journalists, clergymen, intellectuals, and soap-box orators used African American soldiers to unequivocally demonstrate the manhood, loyalty, bravery, and respectability of the race and their importance to the regeneration of democracy. One could not pick up an issue of the *Crisis*, the *Chicago Defender*, the *New York Age*, or any black newspaper during the war without reading about African American soldiers. Activists ranging from Ida B. Wells-Barnett to Marcus Garvey employed African American soldiers and their various symbolisms as part of their strategic arsenal to organize African Americans against specific instances of racial discrimination as well as to create broader movements challenging white supremacy. The war, black soldiers, and the political meanings of their service became a central theme for "New Negro" radicals who espoused a distinct postwar militant racial consciousness in meeting halls and on street corners in Harlem, Chicago, Washington, D.C., and other black communities throughout the country. The figure and very idea of the African American soldier profoundly influenced the nature of war-era black protest.

In the end, black soldiers themselves made the war and postwar period one of the most significant moments in African American history. The eight chapters of *Torchbearers of Democracy*, divided into two parts, chronicle the domestic and international experiences of black soldiers and veterans through the social, political, military, and cultural history of the World War I era. We begin Part 1 with American entry into the war, its democratic framing, and what this meant for African Americans broadly and for those black men called upon to fight for the nation in particular. The experiences of African American soldiers, officers, and draftees at Houston, Texas, Fort Des Moines, Iowa, and induction centers across the country foreshadowed the extent to which wartime democracy would be contested and potentially explosive. From here we explore the incorporation of African American soldiers into the nation's army, setting our sights on how the Wilson administration struggled over the "question" of African American soldiers, the efforts of race advocates to influence the government, and the experiences of black troops in training camps across the country. We then delve into the service of African American soldiers, combatants and noncombatants, in the United States and in France, and their struggles both within and against a racist military power structure. Our voyage with black soldiers during America's short participation in the war concludes in France, the central geographic and imaginative terrain upon which the black press discussed the global implications of the war, and where African American soldiers through their social interactions with French citizens and African soldiers experienced these implications firsthand.

Part 2 commences with the armistice and the ironies of peace. African American hopes for postwar democratic change, as seen in the pages of black newspapers and journals, as well as within black communities throughout the country, hinged on the experiences of African American soldiers and the power of their service to expand the boundaries of American democracy. We travel with African American veterans through the racial battleground of postwar American society, back to their homes in the South, as well as to cities like Washington, D.C., Chicago, and Tulsa, where they confronted a wave of lynchings and race riots that challenged the meaning of all they had fought for. Many African American veterans did not passively accept a devaluation of their citizenship, manhood, and very lives. They fought back and, as we see through the participatory presence of several former soldiers in various postwar "New Negro" organizations and movements, were determined to remake American democracy on their own terms. We fittingly end our journey with the place of black soldiers and the legacies of their service in African American history and historical memory, itself a dynamic arena of both individual and collective intellectual, political, and cultural representation.

The era of the First World War represents a defining moment in American history. It likewise marks a critical juncture in African American struggles for freedom, citizenship, and true democracy. *Torchbearers of Democracy* demonstrates that the history of African Americans during the First World War, and the very meaning of American democracy itself, is incomplete without the history of African American servicemen.

PART I War

Negro Soldiers

These truly are the Brave,
These men who cast aside
Old memories, to walk the blood-stained pave
Of Sacrifice, joining the solemn tide
That moves away, to suffer and to die
For Freedom—when their own is yet denied!
O Pride! O Prejudice! When they pass by,
Hail them, the Brave, for you now crucified!

These truly are the Free,
These souls that grandly rise
Above base dreams of vengeance for their wrongs,
Who march to war with visions in their eyes
Of Peace through Brotherhood, lifting glad songs,
Aforetime, while they front the firing line.
Stand and behold! They take the field to-day,
Shedding their blood like Him now held divine,
That those who mock might find a better way!

—Roscoe C. Jamison (1917)

> If America truly understands the functions of democracy and justice, she must know that she must begin to promote democracy and justice at home first of all.
>
> —Arthur G. Shaw, New York City, May 31, 1917

1

DEMOCRACY AT WAR

African Americans, Citizenship, and the Meanings of Military Service

August 1914, in many ways, told the story of African Americans in the early twentieth century. It was a month mixed with both the glimmer of progress and the pain of disappointment. On August 14 the National Association of Colored Women (NACW) held its annual meeting at Wilberforce, Ohio, where delegates representing clubwomen from throughout the country reelected Margaret Murray Washington, the wife of Tuskegee founder and principal Booker T. Washington, as their president.[1] One week later, the National Negro Business League (NNBL) convened at the Muskogee, Oklahoma, convention center, bringing together thousands of black entrepreneurs and race men.[2] For African American communities, in the North and South, small but meaningful local happenings continued to hold tremendous importance, such as the dedication of a new $12,000 library provided by the Carnegie Foundation for the black residents of Savannah, Georgia, or an August 27 ninth-inning, 10–8 victory of the Cuban Giants over the Bronx Athletics in New York.[3] But August also brought with it reminders of the long road that lay before black people in their quest for freedom. The black press still fumed over the decision of the Wilson administration to require photo identification of all potential Civil Service Commission applicants.[4] This paled in comparison to the threat of racial violence black southerners continued to face on a daily basis. During a bloody five-day span, between August 5 and August 9, lynch mobs in Louisiana took the lives of five black men. In the small town of Monroe, the *Chicago Defender* reported, four perished at the hands of "bloodthirsty 'crackers.'"[5]

An ocean away, blood also spilled. This was no ordinary month. In August

1914 Europe descended into the abyss of war and transformed the fate of the modern world. The June 28 assassination of Austrian archduke Franz Ferdinand and his wife by a Serbian nationalist was only the pretext for a conflict many saw as inevitable. German war plans had been long in the making, as Europe's preeminent industrial power saw territorial expansion and the subjugation of its French and British rivals as a matter of national survival. Germany poked and prodded Austria-Hungary's emperor Franz Joseph to declare war on Serbia, and when he did on July 31, 1914, one by one the dominoes of a precarious national alliance system fell. Russia mobilized in support of Serbia. On August 1 Germany declared war on Russia and, two days later, on France. On the basis of the "Schlieffen Plan," the kaiser and the Central Powers had a straightforward strategic aim: encircle and crush the French army with a combination of brute force and blinding speed; continue the counterclockwise sweep into Russia; and end the war within a matter of months. Doing so necessitated the invasion of neutral Belgium, an act of aggression that brought international condemnation and led to Great Britain's entrance into the war on the side of the Allies. Nevertheless, the massive German military machine, acclaimed as the finest in the world and further inspired by a belief in Teutonic racial supremacy, swelled with confidence and believed no force could stand in its way.

This self-assurance proved illusory. The French buckled but, in the end, failed to break at the crucial battle of the Marne in September 1914, ultimately pushing back with the aid of British forces a German offensive that at one point stood within a mere thirty miles of Paris. The best chance for a German victory thus came and went in these pivotal, early days of the war. The ensuing result was the entrenchment of armies along the western front and a bloodletting unparalleled in modern history. The battle of Verdun between February and December 1916, an ultimately futile German offensive, resulted in over 400,000 casualties. The Allied Somme campaign from July to November 1916 proved even more catastrophic. The British, which led the operation, lost more than 60 percent of their troops to death or injury in the initial advance. A total of 419,654 British soldiers alone died by the end of the five-month battle, and the final dead and wounded on both sides reached well over one million.[6] As the war bogged down on the western front, Russia and the Central Powers battled in the East, where the fighting was much more fluid but nevertheless equally devastating. The number of Russian combat deaths surpassed one million. Such incomprehensible loss of life and destruction shattered Europe's image of Enlightenment civilization and rationality. By the spring of 1917, some three years after the buoyant summer of 1914, when young German, Russian, Austrian, British, and French men marched off to war filled with nationalistic pride, the European combatants found themselves exhausted and in search of any and all advantages to bring the conflict to an end.[7]

Most Americans initially observed the European war with a mixture of dismay and stunned detachment. If anything, the war offered final confirmation for descendant Europeans of the historical and evolutionary distance between the United States and "old world" Europe. For millions of recent immigrants with direct ties to the conflict, their response was understandably more emotional and immediate. While some support for the Central Powers existed in German American and Irish American enclaves, American public sentiment overwhelmingly favored the Allies, shaped in large part by Germany's invasion of Belgium and widely reported atrocities. Although the United States government clearly leaned toward the side of the Allied forces, providing material support and generous credits to Great Britain, President Woodrow Wilson firmly adhered to a policy of American neutrality.[8] Despite the sinking of the *Lusitania* in 1915 and the pleas of Britain and France for the United States to intervene, the carnage occurring on the European battlefields served as a strong deterrent to American military involvement. Events occurring south of the U.S. border in Mexico, where American troops were busy chasing the insurgent forces of Francisco "Pancho" Villa, actually elicited greater immediate concern than those across the Atlantic. By the beginning of 1917, however, circumstances had dramatically changed, and the United States faced the troubling reality of fighting in a war of unprecedented magnitude and scope. Formal American entrance into the war on April 6, 1917, demanded the creation of an army capable of ensuring an Allied victory and positioning the United States as the central player in the peace process.[9] Such an undertaking required the mobilization of all financial, material, human, and ideological resources at the government's disposal.

This mobilization included African Americans. Considering the social, political, and economic obstacles black people faced on the eve of the war—segregation, disfranchisement, job discrimination, racial violence—they had every reason to dismiss the significance of the war to their lives. Many, in fact, did. Nevertheless, most approached the war with guarded optimism, and placed faith in the ability of loyalty and patriotic duty, specifically regarding military service, to infuse life into the moribund condition of African American citizenship. The democratic framing of American participation in the war played a significant role in why many African Americans felt this way. Wilson asserted that the country entered the war not for territorial gain or national aggrandizement but for the singular purpose of making the world "safe for democracy," of ensuring that the cherished American principles of freedom, self-determination, personal liberty, and peace became the hallmarks of a new postwar global community. African Americans were no strangers to the ideals of democracy. They had intimate, painful experience with both its inspiring possibilities and its cruel disappointments. As an ideological struggle, with the future of democracy purportedly at stake, the war suddenly bore greater relevance to the everyday realities of black people. The United States could either live up to its potential as a model of democracy and freedom by supporting the rights of its African American citizenry or demonstrate its hypocrisy to these principles on a global stage.[10] The choices were clear.

African American soldiers and the contested meanings of black military service shaped the historical and ideological context within which the United States mobilized for war. As arguably the most sacred obligation of citizenship, military service for black people became a highly contentious issue. The organization and participation of African American soldiers in the war, many race spokesmen and -women perceived, represented an opportunity for the race to demonstrate its loyalty to the country in its hour of need. Black soldiers became potent, albeit unstable, symbols of African American patriotism, racial pride, manhood, and citizenship. They had the power, many African Americans hoped, to challenge white supremacy and make democracy a reality.

Questions concerning what role African American soldiers would have in the war were extremely volatile. The government had little time to waste, as thousands of black soldiers in the Regular Army readied themselves for battle, while millions of civilian black men awaited the possibility of induction. Democracy, race, manhood, citizenship, and obligation made for a combustible combination, one experienced by African American soldiers and draftees in various forms, moments, and places in the earliest stages of American participation in the war. There was Houston, Texas, where black soldiers declared war on white supremacy as an assertion of their manhood and human dignity. There was the struggle for black officers, exemplified by the contentious Des Moines training camp and the tragedy of Charles Young. And, perhaps most significant, there was the draft, an unprecedented reconfiguration of the relationship between the nation-state and its citizens, which eventually pulled close to 370,000 black men into the army. Although Wilson and the American military set their focus on Germany and the French western front, in the summer and fall of 1917 the United States became the crucial battleground in the fight for the meaning of democracy and its viability for black people. African American soldiers and civilians, literally and figuratively, prepared for war.

ON THE EVE OF AMERICAN entry into the First World War, democracy had become increasingly severed from the lives of most African Americans. Black people were citizens in name only, as one by one, the achievements of Reconstruction faded into memory. Millions of black farmers in the South remained trapped in slavery-like conditions, shackled by the debt and crushing poverty of a sharecropping system that provided little hope for economic freedom.[11] The challenges confronting black workers went hand in hand with the rise of Jim Crow. While segregation was not a new phenomenon, the 1896 *Plessy v. Ferguson* Supreme Court decision legally sanctioned a system of de jure racial separation that soon pervaded southern social and cultural life.[12] For African Americans residing in northern and midwestern cities, de facto segregation, particularly in housing, education, and employment, became the norm. The steady stripping of African American voting rights left black people with little political recourse to address these problems. State governments employed a variety of tactics—"grandfather" clauses, poll taxes, literacy tests—all geared to deprive African Americans of access to the ballot. Pockets of black electoral participation still existed in some upper South communities, as well as in northern cities where white politicians courted African American patronage. Nevertheless, the ability of African Americans to exert political power through the ballot, arguably the most cherished privilege of democracy, was considerably weakened.

What white supremacists intent on driving African Americans from the political sphere could not accomplish through deceit they achieved with raw violence. The bloodshed of the 1860s and 1870s spilled into the post-Reconstruction era and, in many respects, worsened. The efforts of African Americans to assert their citizenship were often met with fierce resistance, as witnessed in the 1898 Wilmington, North Carolina, riot, which effectively stamped out one of the last remaining vestiges of black political participation in the state.[13] However, racial violence and the general disregard for black life went far beyond strictly politics and infected the entire social, economic, and cultural fabric of the nation. In the South, where the stakes of white supremacy ran highest, violence served as a tried-and-true strategy for maintaining a sense of stability to a precarious racial hierarchy. Lynching became a deadly method of social control and regulation of the codes of racial etiquette. Between 1882 and 1916, at least 2,833 African Americans lost their lives by extralegal violence, perpetrated by "persons unknown" who rarely received punishment for their actions.[14] As the number of lynchings increased during the 1890s, so too did their carnivalesque character. Many were advertised in advance and attended by sometimes thousands of people, who shot, stabbed, burned, and mutilated black men and women as a grisly form of public entertainment and cultural bonding.[15] Racial violence was not exclusive to the South. Race riots erupted in New York City in 1900 and in

Springfield, Illinois, in 1908, demonstrating that in various regions of the nation, black people lacked the fundamental civic expectations of safety and equal protection under the law.

African Americans did not quietly acquiesce to the assault on their democratic rights and humanity. Despite the erosion of black citizenship in the aftermath of Reconstruction, African Americans continued to build upon existing social, religious, and educational institutions, while also establishing new vehicles for political activism and agitation. The 1915 death of Tuskegee Institute president Booker T. Washington marked a shift in the landscape of black political ideology.[16] The Tuskegee "Wizard" had effectively shaped the terms of debate on the "race question" with his controlling grip of crucial philanthropic financial resources, the black press, and access to white political elites. Washington's politics of appeasement and conciliation to the logic of racial segregation, while influential, did not go unchallenged. The "Tuskegee machine" encountered vocal and at times fierce opposition from individuals such as Ida B. Wells-Barnett, the vociferous antilynching activist and founder of the Negro Fellowship League; William Monroe Trotter, the pugnacious head of the National Independent Equal Rights League and editor of the *Boston Guardian*; and W. E. B. Du Bois, the Harvard-trained scholar-activist widely recognized as the leading intellectual voice of his day.[17] In 1905 Du Bois, Trotter, and other progressives disenchanted with the course of racial progress convened to establish the Niagara Movement on a platform of unyielding advocacy for the full rights of African American citizenship. Although accomplishing little, the spirit behind the Niagara Movement gave birth to the National Association for the Advancement of Colored People (NAACP), founded in 1909 in the wake of the Springfield riot by a diverse group of black and white reformers, including Du Bois, Wells-Barnett, Florence Kelley, Mary White Ovington, John Dewey, and Oswald Garrison Villard. Throughout its infancy, the organization, capitalizing on the void left by Washington's death, slowly grew in size, stature, and influence, due in large part to its journal of news and opinion, the *Crisis*, edited by Du Bois.[18]

The membership of the NAACP reflected the growth of a politically engaged black middle class, which saw itself as the vanguard of racial progress. Black colleges such as Howard, Fisk, Hampton, and Tuskegee furnished a new generation of young race men and women, many with a sharpened racial consciousness and sense of political purpose. This expanding "Talented Tenth" of lawyers, doctors, educators, and entrepreneurs established viable black economies and provided crucial social services for black communities neglected by the state. Middle-class African Americans envisioned themselves as harbingers of social change and racial uplift by serving as examples for working-class black people to emulate. At the same time, they presented white America with a new image of blackness, one not rooted in negative stereotypes.[19] This emphasis on respectability allowed middle-class black women to exert their public voice. They used the church and a plethora of social and political clubs, many falling under the umbrella of the NACW, founded in 1896, to address issues affecting black people and women in particular.[20] A vibrant black press served as the voice of the black middle class, as papers such as the *Chicago Defender*, *New York Age*, *Washington Bee*, *Baltimore Afro-American*, *Pittsburgh Courier*, *Savannah Tribune*, *Norfolk Journal and Guide*, and *Cleveland Advocate* reported, chronicled, and debated the status and future of the race.

Charles Hamilton Houston epitomized this growing black middle class. Charles was born on September 3, 1895, in Washington, D.C., to William and Mary Houston. Houston's father was a well-known attorney, and his mother worked as a hairdresser for many of the city's political elite. They unashamedly doted on their only child, laying a strong foundation for their son's academic success and sense of racial purpose. Houston attended the exclusive M Street High School in Washington, D.C., where he learned Latin, French, Greek, history, math, and the arts from many of the finest black instructors in the nation. While not stellar, his grades were strong enough to earn him a scholarship from Amherst College. In the fall of 1911, he stepped foot on the picturesque New England campus, the only black student in his class. He studied hard, stayed mostly to himself, and graduated in 1915 Phi Beta Kappa. When he returned home to Washington, D.C., Houston had not yet settled on a firm career path but, with the help of his father, received an appointment as a replacement instructor in English at Howard University's Commercial Academy.[21] At the tender age of nineteen, he was a faculty member of black America's most prestigious institution of higher learning, and well positioned for future great accomplishments.

The challenges confronting Charles Houston and his middle-class brethren paled in comparison to the daily struggles faced by the majority of working-class black people. These were the men and women who, in the North, battled against job discrimination and the racism of labor unions. These were the folk who, in the South, adopted various strategies to cope with the rigors of work and family, the burdens of poverty, and the threat of racial violence. In ways overt and subtle, black workers fought against the racial status quo and preserved their dignity. Working-class black men and women participated in formal civil rights organizations, like the NAACP, but also engaged in small, hidden, everyday acts of protest, such as refusal to yield one's place to a white passer-by on a city sidewalk, or a black laundress's ruining a load of wash for a white client.[22] Institutions such as the church provided much needed spiritual sanctuary, while at the juke joint and after-hours spots, black workers could sing, dance, and cavort free from the judgmental eyes of white people. Through this rich culture of opposition, black people, against all odds, successfully reclaimed and expressed their humanity.[23]

Most significant, African Americans during the war years challenged white supremacy with their feet. The Great Migration became one of the largest internal mass movements of peoples in American history. The war brought European immigration to major northern and midwestern cities to a virtual standstill, creating a pressing need for industrial manpower. Larger global and domestic economic forces may have created the opportunity for black southerners to migrate, but it was their fundamental desire for social freedom that drove the exodus. "[I] am in the darkness of the south and i am trying my best to get out," one aspiring black migrant from Alabama poignantly stated in May 1917.[24] "I still have a desire to seek for myself a section of this country where I can poserably better my condishion in as much as beaing asshured some protection as a good citizen under the Stars and Stripes," another migrant from Florida declared the same month.[25] Potential migrants relied on family and community networks to aid their journey, while the influential *Chicago Defender* actively encouraged black southerners to cast off the shackles of their oppression and relocate to the "promised land" of the North. "I bought a Chicago Defender," a black man from Memphis, Tennessee wrote, "and after reading it and seeing the golden opportunity I have decided to leave this place at once."[26] By the end of the decade, an estimated 500,000 black people had reshaped the demographics of cities such as New York, Milwaukee, St. Louis, Detroit, Cleveland, and Chicago. While black relocation to the North generated the most attention at the time, major southern cities also experienced significant increases in their black populations. Big-city life, whether in the North or the South, was not the panacea many African American migrants envisioned. They still had to contend with job discrimination, family separation, poor housing, and frequent hostility from older black residents. Migration nevertheless provided those men, women, and children who bravely packed their bags, boarded trains, and determined to start anew with a constellation of social, economic, and political possibilities, allowing them to exert greater control over their lives and destinies.[27]

THE GREAT MIGRATION DEMONSTRATED that the war, while an ocean away, still had direct bearing on the lives of African Americans. This became more evident as America's involvement in the crisis deepened. Following his hotly contested reelection in November 1916, Woodrow Wilson turned his focus almost exclusively to the European conflict. On January 22, 1917, he stood before the

United States Senate and outlined his vision of "peace without victory" and a postwar world predicated upon the principles of diplomacy and international cooperation.[28] Germany, however, had become increasingly desperate and, in an attempt to turn the tide of the war in its favor, tested Wilson's pacifist resolve. Disregarding its pledge made in the aftermath of the 1915 *Lusitania* sinking, German military forces resumed a campaign of unrestricted submarine warfare, commencing on February 1, 1917, in hopes of crippling the British army by cutting off crucial supplies. Two days later Wilson severed diplomatic relations with Germany but still stopped short of declaring war, opting instead for a policy of "armed neutrality." The United States remained on the sidelines while U-boats wreaked havoc in the Atlantic, and, at least for the moment, the German gamble appeared to pay off. This changed with the dramatic March 1 public release of the "Zimmerman Telegram." In the January 16, 1917, communication, which was intercepted and decoded by British intelligence, German foreign minister Arthur Zimmerman pledged to help Mexico reacquire territories annexed by the United States in 1848 if it entered the war on the side of the Central Powers. Germany, by attempting to exploit tensions between the United States and Mexico, had now gone too far. With the majority of his cabinet and significant portions of the nation in favor of war, Wilson felt compelled to act.

As Wilson prepared to throw the United States into the European cauldron, his relationship with African Americans lay in ruins. Frustrated with the Republicans' inability to halt a steady erosion of African American citizenship rights, some black leaders approached Wilson's 1912 election with guarded optimism, thinking at the very least matters could get no worse under a Democratic president. Instead, the native Virginian ushered in the return of southern-style white supremacy to the White House. Following his inauguration, Wilson appointed a slew of southerners to prominent posts in his administration. Most disconcerting was his institution of racial segregation in government agencies, such as the Department of the Treasury and the Post Office, which had historically employed large numbers of African Americans. Wilson famously clashed with William Monroe Trotter at a November 12, 1914, White House meeting over the continued segregation of black federal employees. "We are sorely disappointed," Trotter challenged Wilson, "that you take the position that the separation itself is not wrong, is not injurious, is not rightly offensive to you. . . . Why, Mr. President, two years ago, among our people, and last year, you were thought to be perhaps the second Abraham Lincoln." Trotter's passion so unnerved Wilson that he vowed never again to meet with the National Independent Equal Rights League unless its spokesman conducted himself with proper deference.[29] Wilson's racial paternalism carried into his foreign policy, specifically regarding the

1915 occupation of Haiti by U.S. Marines, an act of imperial aggression vigorously protested by the black press. Black opinion of Wilson was solidified with his White House screening of *Birth of a Nation*, D. W. Griffith's 1915 epic film adaptation of Thomas Dixon's novel *The Clansman*. While the NAACP and other organizations staged protests at movie houses throughout the country, Wilson, a historian of the Reconstruction era, gave the inflammatory film his ringing endorsement.[30] African Americans thus had just cause to suspect American entry into the war as being yet another extension of Wilson's commitment to white supremacy.

On the evening of April 2, 1917, as throngs of flag-waving supporters stood in the rain, cheering his motorcade, Woodrow Wilson made the short trip up Pennsylvania Avenue to the Capitol. At approximately half past eight, he took his place behind the rostrum of the House chamber. The applause showered on the president from the joint session of Congress lasted for two minutes before he began his speech. Up to that very moment, Wilson's intentions remained a mystery. With a solemnity of purpose and resolve, holding the typewritten speech with both hands, rarely making eye contact with his transfixed audience, Wilson spoke in careful and measured tones, summarizing the German government's transgressions and concluding that "armed neutrality, it appears, is impracticable." "We will not choose the path of submission," Wilson declared to a roar of approval, and asked Congress, on the behalf of the nation, to "accept the status of belligerent which has been thrust upon it." The costs and sacrifice would be tremendous. In addition to increasing the level of taxation, Wilson called for an enlargement in the size of the army to at least 500,000 men, raised "on the principle of universal liability to service." More forebodingly, he also demanded absolute loyalty from all Americans, firmly stating that, "if there should be disloyalty, it will be dealt with with a firm hand of stern repression."

But what would the United States fight for? In his "peace without victory" speech, and again in his inaugural address, Wilson had been compelling in why the United States should avoid the European maelstrom. Now, in framing the justification for war to the American public, it was necessary for Wilson to again reshape the malleable rhetoric of progressivism to suit his needs.[31] He expounded on his "peace without victory" speech and further projected his vision of progressive internationalism, highlighted by the creation of a league of nations.[32] Referring to the January 22 address, Wilson stated, "Our object now, as then, is to vindicate the principles of peace and justice in the life of the world as against selfish and autocratic power and to set up amongst the really free and self-governed peoples of the world such a concert of purpose and of action as will henceforth ensure the observance of those principles." The war would thus be an ideological conflict as much as a military one, fought for the broader principles of self-determination and freedom from militarism and autocracy.

To make his case, Wilson invoked the most deep-seated, emotionally evocative, and politically contested ethos at the core of the American historical experience: democracy. "The world must be made safe for democracy," Wilson proclaimed. The *New York Times* in its reporting of the speech provided a particularly dramatic retelling of the moment Wilson delivered the celebrated phrase: "This sentence might have passed without applause, but Senator John Sharp Williams [Mississippi] was one man who instantly seized the full and immense meaning of it. Alone he began to applaud, and he did it gravely, emphatically—and in a moment the fact that this was the keyword of our war against Germany dawned on the others, and one after another followed his lead until the whole host broke forth in a great uproar of applause."[33] The peace of democracy, Wilson continued, "must be planted upon the tested foundations of political liberty. We have no selfish ends to serve. We desire no conquest, no dominion. We seek no indemnities for ourselves, no material compensation for the sacrifices we shall freely make. We are but one of the champions of the rights of mankind. We shall be satisfied when those rights have been made as secure as the faith and the freedom of nations can make them." While lamenting the decision to wage war, Wilson nevertheless asserted that the nation had a providential duty to "fight for the things which we have always carried nearest our hearts—for democracy, for the right of those who submit to authority to have a voice in their own governments, for the rights and liberties of small nations, for a universal dominion of right by such a concert of free peoples as shall bring peace and safety to all nations and make the world itself at last free."[34] In his thirty-six-minute speech, Wilson had set the ideological course for the nation's entry into the war and simultaneously raised the expectations of its outcome to soaring heights.

When Wilson spoke of "democracy," "rights and liberties," "peace and safety," he referred explicitly to Europe and did not have Americans of any background, much less African Americans, on his mind. The president, however, created an opening for black people to appropriate the ideological impulses driving America's involvement in the war and apply them toward the cause of racial equality and justice.[35] African Americans promptly seized upon the irony and hypocrisy of Wilson's famous pledge to make the world "safe for democracy," while in the United States democracy remained a distant ideal for some ten million black citizens. "The preachments in the behalf of democracy and human rights abroad," Joseph Manning from Alabama wrote in the *Washington Bee*, "must go far to convince the people of this nation that it is not consistent to advocate government with the consent of the governed, and democracy for other lands without applying the principle everywhere in our own land."[36] Abstract, dynamic, and open to reinterpretation, the keyword of democracy became a rhetorical and ideological weapon in the hands of African Americans.[37]

The editors of the *Baltimore Afro-American* provided one of the most thoughtful deconstructions of Wilsonian democracy. An April 28 editorial titled "Democratic Government" opened with a standard dictionary definition of democracy as a "political system in which government is directly exercised or controlled by the people collectively" and "a state of society without class distinction made or favored by law of custom." "This is a beautiful theory," the *Afro-American* sarcastically mused, and went on to ask, "Will some one tell us just how long Mr. Wilson has been a convert to TRUE DEMOCRACY?" The systemic disenfranchisement and segregation of black people stripped the president of any credibility to speak on the meaning of democracy, much less to advocate for its expansion around the world. "It does seem that we ought first set at liberty our own slaves before recommending liberty for the slaves of other countries," the *Afro-American* suggested. "Let us have a real democracy for the United States and then we can advise a house cleaning over on the other side of the water."[38]

A number of African Americans, recognizing these hypocrisies, explicitly opposed the war and black participation in it. In churches, beauty parlors, and on street corners in communities across the country, black people discussed the coming war. Many saw little reason to offer their support. A black man in Harlem, when asked by the patrons of a neighborhood barbershop engaged in a vivid conversation about the war if he planned to join the army, replied, "The Germans ain't done nothin' to me, and if they have, I forgive 'em."[39] Skeptics such as this had a voice in Hubert Harrison, the brilliant organic intellectual from the Caribbean island of St. Croix, who had earned a reputation throughout Harlem as a fierce critic of white supremacy and unyielding advocate of black self-determination.[40] A. Philip Randolph and Chandler Owen, editors of the New York–based socialist news magazine the *Messenger*, also championed the antiwar cause. The pair, who became acquainted in 1915 while Randolph attended City College and Owen took classes at Columbia University, were conscientious objectors who believed African Americans should not sacrifice their lives for a nation that denied true democracy to its own citizens.[41] The *Messenger* served as an outlet for their political views, as well as a forum for critical commentary on the war, global race relations, and the ineffective state of bourgeois black leadership. "Let Du Bois, Kelly, Miller, Pickens, Grimke, etc., volunteer to go to France to make the world safe for democracy," Randolph and Owen retorted in the November 1917 issue. "We would rather make Georgia safe for the Negro."[42]

Their outspokenness carried considerable risk. The war produced a social and political atmosphere in which American nationalism became increasingly repressive. The Wilson administration did not view its goal of "100% Americanism" as a natural process but, instead, one that demanded coercive measures.[43] The fears of many progressive opponents of the war came to fruition, as reform gave way to suppression of freedom of speech, censorship of the press, and the creation of a federal intelligence bureaucracy designed to eliminate domestic radicalism and subversion. The government imposed its own vision of the war and patriotism through a deluge of propaganda, coordinated by the Committee on Public Information (CPI) and its leader, George Creel.[44] The Espionage Act, passed by Congress on June 15, 1917, made interference with recruitment and the draft as well as refusal to submit to military duty federal crimes, punishable with a maximum fine of ten thousand dollars and twenty years in prison. In May 1918 Congress amended the Espionage Act with the Sedition Act, which criminalized spoken or written criticism of the government. To further restrict the freedom of the press, U.S. postmaster general Albert S. Burleson wielded unilateral authority to ban mail deemed as antiwar. To guard against potential radicalism, the government established the Military Intelligence Branch (MIB), a precursor to the modern CIA. Empowered by new wartime legislation, the MIB and the Justice Department, led by Attorney General A. Mitchell Palmer, arrested more than two thousand peace advocates, suspected German sympathizers, and labor organizers.[45] The government could not eliminate all dissent, but, with the aid of civilian vigilante groups such as the American Protective League (APL), it certainly tried. A November 1917 article in the *Messenger* ironically noted, "Suppression of free-speech and free-press in the United States is making the world safe for democracy."[46]

The government's net of suppression predictably ensnared A. Philip Randolph and Chandler Owen. In the summer of 1918, the duo set out on an antiwar speaking tour. On August 4 they addressed a Socialist street-corner rally in Cleveland, exhorting the crowd to oppose the war while two colleagues sold issues of the *Messenger*. An undercover agent who had infiltrated the gathering purchased a copy. After skimming through the paper, the agent, already disturbed by Randolph and Owen's fiery rhetoric, waited for the rally to conclude and promptly arrested both men on charges of treason and violation of the Espionage Act.[47] They spent two days in jail before they were brought before a judge. The judge looked at Randolph and Owen, who appeared younger than their twenty-nine years of age, read what they had written in the *Messenger*, and became convinced that they had been taken advantage of by white Socialists. These two fresh-faced bombastic Negroes, he surmised, could never produce such a sophisticated paper, and ordered the pair released. Randolph and Owen quickly left Cleveland and, flaunting the possibility of future arrest, continued their tour, lambasting Woodrow Wilson and his war at every stop.[48]

The federal government feared that individuals like Randolph and Owen were only the tip of a much larger iceberg of black antiwar sentiment. Could African Americans, with their long list of grievances, be trusted to patriotically support the war effort? Black people may have been Americans, but were they truly American enough? Anxious white citizens asked similar questions, and remained convinced of the susceptibility of African Americans to German propaganda.[49] Rumors of black people attending meetings of Germany sympathizers and planning violent uprisings circulated throughout the South. Intelligence agents busied themselves trying to separate fact from fiction. Elisa Belle Withers, a white woman from Midway, Kentucky, informed investigators that one of her black neighbors, Robert Withers, was making statements to the effect that "if he were over in Germany he would fight the Americans." She believed that the residents of a German settlement located near Withers's home were to blame for his reckless talk.[50] Agents explored the claim of a Sarasota, Florida, woman, who suspected a German superintendent of "endeavoring to persuade the negro population to consider the white Americans as their enemy . . . and that the negroes should consider the Germans his friends."[51] A "Texas Citizen" from Longview wrote an urgent letter to Woodrow Wilson, dripping with violent sexual panic, warning him that "the negro's of this city are plotting and planning to do something awful. The negro men claim that if war comes and all of the young white men go off to the war that they (the negroes) will kill off all of the old white men and women also the children and take the pretty white maidens for wives."[52] While in the end the government gave little credence to such claims, its heightened level of insecurity spoke volumes to its concerns regarding African American loyalty.

Unwilling to risk the lash of government repression, most African American political leaders and much of the black press vigorously proclaimed the patriotic fidelity of the race. It would not take much, they reasoned, for the government and vigilante groups like the APL to view and treat black people with suspicion. "The bald truth is that the Negro cannot afford to be rated as a disloyal element in the nation," James Weldon Johnson, the acclaimed author, NAACP official, and contributor to the *New York Age* wrote in the newspaper shortly before America entered the war. "Imagine the results if he should for an instant arouse against himself the sentiment which is now directed against the pro-German element."[53] The *Norfolk Journal and Guide* ran a story under the headline "Richmond Negroes Pledge Loyalty" only days after Wilson's war address.[54] The influential *Richmond Planet* instructed in an April 21, 1917, editorial, "Colored folks should be patriotic. Do not let us be chargeable with being disloyal to the flag simply because a Democratic administration is in control at Washington. . . . Above all, be loyal! If you wish to express your feelings, do so behind closed doors."[55]

These declarations of black loyalty rested on more than mere pragmatism. Black spokespersons tapped into a post–Civil War political tradition that linked patriotism with nationhood and civic belonging. In doing so, they hoped to reconcile the paradoxical nature of American nationalism with a racially inclusive vision of democracy.[56] Just as James Weldon Johnson proclaimed the loyalty of black people, at the same time he asserted that "the Negro" would perform his civic duty "not stupidly, not led by any silly sentiment, not blindly, but with his eyes wide open," while "repeating his demand that this nation do its duty by him."[57] Patriotic loyalty demanded reciprocity on the part of the government and the recognition of African Americans as equal citizens. "What the colored man wants," the *Savannah Tribune* asserted, "is reasonable and equitable consideration in all the affairs of our government. . . . There is nothing withheld; we have kept nothing back; we have stated our case, freely, frankly and devoid of temper. Give us justice."[58]

Justice would be hard fought. In July 1917, less than three months after Woodrow Wilson's declaration of war, black people were reminded of the battle they faced not in Europe but within the borders of the United States. The wartime expansion of industrial labor opportunities facilitated the dramatic increase in African American migration to northern cities. One of the most popular destinations was East St. Louis. Upward of ten thousand migrants swelled the city's black population, placing considerable strain on labor relations between white and black workers. Growing tensions between the races, exacerbated by a failed April strike at an aluminum plant that white union leaders blamed on black strikebreakers, culminated on July 2, 1917, following a shooting incident that left two white men dead. The city erupted into a storm of violence and racial cleansing. Burning, shooting, stabbing, and pummeling with impunity, white rioters killed between 40 and 125 African Americans—making no distinction between men and women or the young and the old—and injured hundreds more. By the end of the four-day pogrom, as bodies floated in the Mississippi River, thousands of surviving black residents had fled the city as refugees. Along with the dead, the riot left more than three hundred buildings in smoldering ruins at an estimated property loss of three million dollars. The nation was aghast.[59]

For African Americans across the country who read about the horrors of East St. Louis, the rhetoric of democracy and unconditional loyalty to the nation rang painfully hollow. How could black people muster the patriotic spirit and strength to fight for the nation, when the murder of innocent men, women, and children went unpunished? As East St. Louis made abundantly clear, loyalty did not and could not necessitate acquiescence to segregation, racial violence, and government discrimination. Editorials criticizing the violence filled the pages of black newspapers.[60] The *Norfolk Journal and Guide*, which had only recently boasted of the loyalty of Richmond's black community, boldly called upon the government to provide justice or "renounce its purposes for entering the world war and stand convicted among the nations of the earth as the greatest hypocrite of all times."[61] The *Cleveland Advocate* called upon Woodrow Wilson to denounce "the barbarity committed at East St. Louis" and questioned just how he could boast "to make 'democracy safe for humanity' when humanity is UNSAFE in our own country."[62] In addition to the fiery words of black editors, the East St. Louis massacre sparked collective political action. On July 28, 1917, the NAACP held a "silent protest parade" down Fifth Avenue in New York City in response to the riot and the continued terrorism of African Americans throughout the country. It represented a dramatic demonstration of black political fortitude and civilized respectability in the wake of raw barbarism. To the sounds of muffled drums, eight thousand African Americans, women dressed in white gowns, men dressed in black suits, marched and held signs of protest, many invoking Woodrow Wilson's own rhetoric. "Mr. President," one of the placards poignantly read, "why not make America safe for democracy?"[63]

While rhetorical appeals to the conscience of white America remained an important tactic for African Americans throughout the war, it was evident that black people would have to fight for democracy. As in the Civil War, racial progress would require African Americans to place their lives on the line. For this reason, African American soldiers and the meaning of military service, the highest form of patriotism and civic obligation, dominated public and private discussions concerning black participation in the war.

GEORGE SCHUYLER COULD NOT WAIT to get out of Syracuse. Although born in Providence, Rhode Island, he spent the bulk of his childhood and adolescence in the upstate New York city. Out of a population of 100,000 residents, only 1,000 were black. Despite the support of a loving family, Schuyler gradually became disillusioned with Syracuse's small African American community, one that, in his words, "was so fragmented by class divisions that any group unity was out of the question." As he entered his teenage years, Schuyler grew more and more restless in his search for racial inspiration. This changed when, in 1909, several companies of African American troops arrived in Syracuse for training maneuvers. They were the famed "Buffalo Soldiers," the label given to the roughly 12,500 African American troops of the United States Regular Army, which included the Ninth and Tenth Cavalries and the Twenty-fourth and Twenty-fifth Infantries. "The black infantrymen and cavalry were something else again," he recalled. "We were impressed by their superb order and discipline, their haughty and immaculate noncommissioned officers, and their obvious authority." The soldiers, legendary for their service throughout the American West, during the Spanish-Cuban-American War, and in America's recent imperial outposts in the Caribbean and Pacific, appeared, as Schuyler admired, "clean, upstanding, orderly" and, most significantly, "represented the power and authority of the United States."[64] Schuyler never forgot this experience. By the time he turned seventeen in 1912, Schuyler was convinced that he had no future in Syracuse and, remembering his encounter with black soldiers three years earlier, decided to enter the army. "In the army I could see the world I wanted to see and have a chance to advance myself," he reasoned.[65] With his mother's consent, Schuyler left home and traveled to Fort Slocum on David's Island, New York. After three weeks of training, he received an assignment to join the First Battalion of the Twenty-fifth Infantry.

Schuyler trekked by train to the West Coast, passing through Wisconsin, Minnesota, North Dakota, Montana, and Idaho before finally reaching Fort Lawton in Seattle, Washington. He felt at home with the Twenty-fifth Infantry and enjoyed hearing stories from seasoned veterans about fighting in the "Indian wars," guarding the Mexican border, and clashing with insurgents in the Philippines. Schuyler became a man with the Twenty-fifth, as military service fulfilled his thirst for adventure, camaraderie, and leadership. When war erupted in 1914, the Twenty-fifth had been transferred to Schofield Barracks in Honolulu, Hawaii, and Schuyler recalled that he and his regiment "were at the time excited by the prospect of entering the world conflict."[66] He reenlisted in November 1915 for a second tour of duty, became a noncommissioned officer the following year, and gained a reputation for the satirical skits he wrote for the weekly military magazine and the *Honolulu Commercial Advertiser*.[67] The war still loomed. After the 1916 presidential election, Schuyler suspected that, despite Wilson's claims to the contrary, it was just a matter of time before he and his comrades were called upon to fight. "It was evident to a cynical minority among us," he recalled, "that we would soon be in the war against the Central Powers."[68]

Another "Buffalo Soldier," Osceola McKaine, also stood ready to answer the call to war. McKaine was born in Sumter, South Carolina. At the age of sixteen, he bid Sumter farewell, got a job as a stevedore on a merchant freighter, and eventually settled in Boston, Massachusetts. He finished high school and, after graduating, occasionally took classes at Boston College. During his time in Boston, McKaine exhibited a strong race consciousness, sense of brotherhood, and penchant for political activism. He served as associate editor of the *Cambridge Advocate* and secretary of the Colored Progressive League of New England during the 1912 presidential campaign, and later became a founding member of the Omega Psi Phi fraternity Gamma chapter in Boston. Perhaps the same restlessness that prompted McKaine to leave Sumter drew him to the army. On October 15, 1914, he joined the Twenty-fourth Infantry and became a soldier.[69]

McKaine's three years of service reflected the complicated legacy of black men in the Regular Army. They were a source of tremendous race pride and historic accomplishment. But, however unwittingly, they also functioned as agents of empire, spreading the "White Man's Burden" and asserting America's hemispheric superiority.[70] McKaine himself served in the Philippines, where black soldiers had long been responsible for suppressing, in sometimes brutal fashion, insurgent forces following American acquisition of the former Spanish colony.[71] In early 1916, his regiment was called back to the United States to participate in the Mexican "punitive expedition," a fifteen-thousand-troop campaign ordered by Woodrow Wilson with the goal of capturing Francisco "Pancho" Villa, who had brazenly conducted a series of border raids against American civilians and soldiers. African American soldiers of the Tenth Cavalry and Twenty-fourth Infantry composed two of the units under the command of General John J. Pershing, derisively nicknamed "Black Jack" by his white peers for his prior experience commanding black troops. The expedition crossed the Mexican border on March 15, 1916, and traveled hundreds of miles over rugged terrain in its futile search of Villa, in the process clashing with Mexican troops at Santa Cruz de Villegas and Carrizal. After vigorous protests by the Mexican government, and with the European war on the horizon, Wilson withdrew the expedition, and the participating black units returned to the Southwest.[72] At their barracks in Columbus, New Mexico, McKaine and the rest of the Twenty-fourth Infantry waited to learn what role they would play in the war.

The historical significance of black soldiers like Osceola McKaine and George Schuyler influenced how African Americans approached the war. They symbolized freedom, manhood, and martial heroism. Most significant, they demonstrated the potential for citizenship and how military service in the war could expand its boundaries to fully include African Americans. The legacy of black soldiers thus received increased attention following the declaration of war. On

April 28, 1917, an article titled "Some Interesting Facts about Negro Soldiers" appeared on the front page of the *Savannah Tribune*, providing readers with an overview of the fighting record of black troops from the American Revolution to the Spanish-Cuban-American War.[73] In Norfolk, Virginia, black residents held a parade, only days after the American declaration of war, in honor of local veterans of the Spanish-Cuban-American War. Coverage of the parade by the *Norfolk Journal and Guide* constructed these veterans as historical antecedents of a new generation of black soldiers and visible reminders of African Americans' legacy of fighting for freedom and equal citizenship.[74]

African American soldiers also symbolized the possibility of violent resistance to white supremacy. Military training and access to firearms emboldened many black soldiers to stand up against racial abuse, with sometimes deadly results. Black volunteers of the experimental Third Alabama Regiment, created during the Spanish-Cuban-American War, clashed with white troops and civilians at Anniston, Alabama, culminating in an outburst on the night of November 24, 1898, that left one black soldier dead and a white soldier seriously wounded.[75] Numerous violent incidents involving black troops stationed in Texas and other parts of the Southwest occurred in the early twentieth century. African Americans did not forget the August 13, 1906, Brownsville shooting involving soldiers of the Twenty-fifth Infantry, as well as the injustice of then president Theodore Roosevelt's dishonorable discharge of 167 men without due process.[76]

White southerners did not forget Brownsville and other clashes either. Since the Civil War, white supremacists equated the presence of black soldiers in the South with potential violence. African American Union troops had sparked fears of racial unrest in the wake of emancipation and symbolized a social order turned upside down.[77] These memories continued to resonate, causing many southern white politicians and citizens to view the participation of black soldiers in the World War as an issue of deadly concern. Mississippi senator James K. Vardaman, an opponent of the war and outspoken critic of the use of African American soldiers, echoed this sentiment on August 16, 1917, in a vitriolic address on the senate floor.[78] Under no circumstances, Vardaman asserted, could black and white people live together on equal terms and that the introduction of African American servicemen to the South would "inevitably lead to disaster":

> It is a lamentable fact, and one we should be prepared to meet, that one of the horrible problems which will grow out of this unfortunate war, which the southern white people particularly must meet and overcome, is the training

> as a soldier which the negro will receive. Impress the negro with the fact that he is defending the flag, inflate his untutored soul with military airs, teach him that it is his duty to keep the emblem of the Nation flying triumphantly in the air—it is but a short step to the conclusion that his political rights must be respected, even though it is necessary for him to give his life in defense of those rights, and you at once create a problem far-reaching and momentous in its character.[79]

Vardaman gave voice to southern segregationists who saw black military service as a threat to the region's racial status quo.

The white South, however, did not have a solid attitude toward black soldiers. Many white people, cognizant of the financial rewards war mobilization could bring to the region, attempted to dampen outward expressions of racial tension and opposition to the idea of black men bearing arms. Business leaders, major newspaper editors, clergymen, and even prominent Democratic politicians at both the local and national levels openly applauded the enlistment of black soldiers and the loyalty of black people as a race, presenting an image of "New South" racial progress that meshed with declarations of southern support for the war as a final step toward sectional reconciliation.[80] An editorial in the *Atlanta Constitution* proclaimed, "The negro has no divided allegiance; he is plainly and entirely an American, with no blood qualms to influence his fighting against any race or nationality engaged as America's foe. He is loyal to his government, obedient to discipline, and, according to military men, when he gets into the fight is full of courage."[81] Southern white progressives touted black loyalty in comparison to the assumed divided allegiances of recent European immigrants. These statements, which fell far short of an endorsement of racial equality, reflected a paternalistic and naive belief that southerners "knew" their black folks. Nevertheless, they revealed that southern white people had a diverse range of opinions concerning wartime race relations. The sincerity of these demonstrations of support for African American soldiers would be severely tested as the sight of black servicemen in the South became more and more frequent.[82]

IN EARLY JULY, THE WAR DEPARTMENT ordered the Third Battalion of the Twenty-fourth Infantry from Columbus, New Mexico, to Houston, Texas. Its assignment: protect the construction site of Camp Logan, one of the army's sixteen National Guard training cantonments. The battalion had a long history, rich with tradition. However, this was not the same group of men that had charged San Juan Hill in 1898, trudged through the Philippine jungles, and, most recently, served along the Mexican border during the army's pursuit of

"Pancho" Villa. Although its historical stature remained, many of the battalion's vital noncommissioned officers had been transferred, and the unit received an influx of fresh recruits in the weeks leading up to its new assignment.[83] With its leadership destabilized and its ranks including a number of men unfamiliar with the volatile relationship between black soldiers and white Texans, the Third Battalion was entering dangerous waters.[84]

On July 28, the 645 men of the battalion settled into their quarters on the outskirts of Houston. From the onset of their duties, they endured the burning insults of white construction workers and the indignities of segregation in metropolitan Houston. Although eager to reap the economic benefits of the training camp, many of Houston's white residents feared the potentially troublemaking presence of black soldiers in their city. After all, a handful of soldiers from the First Battalion of the Twenty-fourth Infantry, assigned to guard the construction site of Camp MacArthur at Waco, had only recently engaged in a shootout with white military police following a confrontation between black soldiers and local white men over the protocols of racial etiquette. Conversely, Houston's sizable black community welcomed the soldiers, who, much like occupying black Union soldiers in the aftermath of the Civil War, empowered African Americans to test the boundaries of their freedom. They relished the arrival of the Twenty-fourth Infantry as a source of protection from the vigilante-like Houston police, composed of some 150 officers, only 2 of whom were black. White police officers, who refused to acknowledge the authority of black MPs, provoked the Buffalo Soldiers with verbal and physical abuse. In the weeks following their arrival in Houston, the frustrations of many of the battalion's men simmered and steamed.[85]

On August 23, tensions reached a boiling point. That morning, private Alonzo Edwards happened upon a pair of white police officers, Rufus Daniels and Lee Sparks, in the process of arresting a local black woman, Sara Travers. After shooting at and pursuing two black teenagers playing dice, Sparks stormed into Travers home looking for the suspects. The notoriously hot-tempered officer accused a stunned Travers of hiding the boys. She professed her innocence. Sparks responded by demeaning the womanhood and respectability of the hardworking mother of five children, railing, "You all God damn nigger bitches. Since these God damn sons of bitches nigger soldiers come here you are trying to take the town."[86] He then slapped Travers, forced her into the street only partially clothed, and placed her under arrest. Private Edwards, among the gathering crowd of black onlookers who witnessed the disturbing scene, came to Travers's defense. He confidently approached Sparks, questioned his actions, and requested that Travers be released to his care. With his authority threat-

Corporal Charles W. Baltimore. Portrait photo of Charles Baltimore, the soldier at the heart of the Houston rebellion. Source: Singleton, Autobiography of George A. Singleton.

ened, the white officer reacted violently, pistol-whipping Edwards and placing him under arrest. Sparks was not finished. When another black soldier, military policeman Corporal Charles Baltimore, later inquired about Edwards's whereabouts, Sparks struck Baltimore over the head and fired several shots at the unarmed soldier as he attempted to flee. Baltimore, bloodied and bruised, was captured and placed in jail. Word began to circulate among the black soldiers in camp that he had been killed.[87]

As day turned to night, rage continued to mount, and rumors continued to swirl. Charles Baltimore returned to camp in fact very much alive but, with his head bound in a white cloth, bore visible evidence of his abusive treatment. The anger of his comrades escalated.[88] After enduring weeks of disrespect, enough was enough. In the darkness, talk of revenge spread from tent to tent. Female visitors were ordered to go home.[89] Men started cleaning their rifles and stockpiling ammunition in preparation for an evening assault. Sergeant Vida Henry of Company "I" informed his white commanding officer, Major Kneeland Snow, that trouble was brewing. Snow canceled all evening leave passes and later assembled the battalion for a weapons check.[90]

Suddenly, a soldier shouted that a mob of white people was approaching camp. Pandemonium ensued. Men rushed to their tents to procure guns and ammunition. Some began firing wildly into the pitch-black night at the direction of the imagined mob. Most of the battalion stayed in camp, with a number of soldiers forming a defensive line, while the rest remained on hair-trigger alert. Other men, however, had different plans. "We are tired of this. We will take the law into our own hands!" one soldier allegedly shouted. "To hell with going to France. Let's go clean up that damned city," yelled another.[91] War had been declared. Sergeant Vida Henry, switching from peacemaker to rebel leader, ordered the men of Company "I" under his command to fall in and assume positions for the "serious business" they were about to undertake.[92]

Around 8:50 P.M., as a light rain fell, more than one hundred soldiers in military formation left Camp Logan and proceeded down San Felipe Road and into downtown Houston.[93] Before long, the crackling sound of gunshots pierced the evening summer air. Some detached groups of black soldiers attacked white residents with reckless abandon. The column led by Vida Henry, however, acted with a grim sense of purpose, striking down anyone who got in the way of its intended targets, the Houston police. In the span of under three hours, fifteen people lay dead, including four law enforcement officials.[94] Two black soldiers died that evening, one of them Vida Henry. "You all can go in, I ain't going in, I ain't going to camp no more," an injured Henry said to the men under his command before taking his own life.[95] Injuries claimed two more soldiers the following day. Never before in the history of the United States had black troops enacted such vicious retribution with such a heavy toll.

What happened in Houston was described alternatively as a riot and a mutiny. Both terms, while perhaps technically accurate, do not sufficiently reflect the actions of the Third Battalion and its motivations. They did not lash out against their superior officers, nor did they engage in completely indiscriminate violence and random acts of property destruction. What occurred on the fateful night of August 23, 1917, was a rebellion, a desperate revolt against a racial order, which had for too long degraded the manhood and dignity of black soldiers, and its perpetrators, embodied by the white residents of Houston and its police officers in particular. Some of the participants may have sincerely believed their lives were threatened by an approaching mob and therefore needed to take preemptive measures. Others found themselves caught in the heat of the moment and, out of a combination of camaraderie, fear, and intimidation, joined the uprising.[96] For most, their faith in the nation had been irrevocably destroyed; they had tolerated too much. Lacking security from the very flag they swore to protect, they would now make white America feel their pain. It was a nihilistic endeavor, with either lengthy imprisonment or death a virtual certainty. But if death came, it would be on their own terms, not from the hands of a white lynch mob or rogue police officers. They would die like men.

The Houston violence produced a seismic shift in national debate on the potential place of African American soldiers in the U.S. military. White supremacists now had irrefutable proof that black troops lacked discipline, threatened southern racial tranquility, and could not be trusted. In the aftermath of Houston, southern political leaders intensified their resistance to the stationing of African American soldiers in the region. U.S. congressman A. Jefferson McLemore of Texas introduced a House resolution condemning the offending black soldiers and declared that "the policy of sending negro soldiers to the South is detrimental to the best interests of the country and should at once be abandoned, that there may be no recurrence of the horrible crimes so recently perpetrated at Houston."[97] Senators from both Mississippi and Alabama appealed to Secretary of War Newton D. Baker to prevent black soldiers from being housed in their respective states.[98] Unless the military restricted the stationing of African American servicemen to northern camps, southern lawmakers reasoned, further violent conflict between black soldiers and white residents was all but inevitable. James Vardaman complained to a southern news magazine about the prospect of black troops, "inflated with military airs." In his judgment, he wrote, "the Houston, Texas, incident will be a trivial affair compared with the magnitude of the problems which the white man of the South will be called upon to solve," should black soldiers be stationed in their midst. Faced with the presence of thousands of African American troops, white southerners like Vardaman saw themselves as potentially "living upon a slumbering volcano."[99]

The Houston bloodshed and its reverberations put advocates of black enlistment on the defensive. Unwilling to risk being branded as disloyal, African American leaders and newspapers denounced the actions of the Twenty-fourth Infantry soldiers. At the same time, they remained critical of the conditions that had caused the revolt. "There are, of course, two sides to the Houston affair," James Weldon Johnson reasoned in a *New York Age* editorial. "One of these sides we need not consider here, because it will receive more than enough emphasis elsewhere. That side is the fault attributable to the soldiers. The other side, that is the provocation or rather the long line of cumulating provocations leading up to the outbreak, will not receive so much attention."[100] Martha Gruening conducted an investigation for the NAACP, which published her findings in the November 1917 issue of the *Crisis*. "The primary cause of the Houston riot was the habitual brutality of the white police officers of Houston in their treatment of colored people," Gruening concluded.[101] More than anything, the image of African American soldiers as loyal, disciplined, unwavering patriots had been shattered. African American spokesmen struggled to piece this symbolism back together, while confronted with the reminder that black soldiers were, in the end, only human and could tolerate only so much abuse. A. Philip Randolph best captured this conundrum, writing in the *Messenger*: "The Negro is probably the best and most loyal soldier in the United States. He does his duty in a fine, manly, courageous way. But the Government has failed too often to do its duty by the Negro soldier." He continued, "Do not expect the supernatural from the Negro soldier. He has feelings, race pride and ambitions like other men. If you prick him, he bleeds. If you tickle him, he laughs. In a few words, the Negro soldier is just Human."[102]

On November 30, 1917, in San Antonio, the first of three courts-martial proceedings involving sixty-three defendants concluded. After weeks of testimony, fifty-eight soldiers were found guilty of mutiny, assault, and murder.[103] Thirteen men, including Corporal Charles Baltimore, received sentences of death. In the early morning hours of December 11, 1917, at Fort Sam Houston, the condemned soldiers were marched out to hastily constructed gallows and hung in unison. In their eagerness to enact retribution, military authorities failed to inform the press and the Wilson administration when and where the executions were to occur. The ensuing controversy forced the War Department to institute a new policy requiring the suspension of a death sentence until the president fully reviewed all records pertaining to the case. But this came too late. The executed soldiers, buried in thirteen undistinguished graves, became instant martyrs, symbols of both African American resistance to racial abuse and the government's disregard for the welfare and legal rights of black servicemen. In the *Crisis* editorial, "Thirteen," Du Bois poignantly wrote, "They have gone to their death. Thirteen young, strong men; soldiers who have fought for a country which never was wholly theirs; men born to suffer ridicule, injustice, and, at last, death itself."[104]

The memory and cause of the Houston soldiers became a rallying cry for racial justice. Following the sentencing of five additional soldiers to death in the second court-martial, letters of protest from aggrieved African Americans flooded the White House.[105] "The hanging of the thirteen soldiers and the conviction of five more has pained the heart of the men and women of our race as it never was before pained," wrote a concerned black citizen from Atlantic City, New Jersey.[106] Jean O'Neill, a correspondent for the *Brooklyn Daily Times* who had interacted with the regiment in Columbus, New Mexico, during coverage of the "Punitive Expedition," implored Wilson: "Please be as merciful as you are wise and free the men of the 24th Infantry now under sentence and stop the trial that is today stirring the hearts of our colored people almost to the point of bursting with woe and indignation."[107] From Marion, Indiana, a group of black clubwomen demanded fairness, writing to Woodrow Wilson, "We the members of Eurydice Club—composed of thirty colored women of this city—that stand for uplift and the best in American citizenship beg of you to hear our plea."[108]

Similar to the clubwomen from Indiana, Ida B. Wells-Barnett viewed the executions with a mixture of sadness and outrage. The veteran journalist, antilynching activist, and race spokeswoman was determined to preserve the soldiers' memories and protest the indignity of their deaths. From the Chicago offices of her Negro Fellowship League, Wells-Barnett began efforts to organize a memorial service in their honor. In need of a venue, she approached the pastors of several large African American churches in Chicago for their cooperation, but they all refused her request, intimidated by the specter of disloyalty. While Chicago's "race men" meekly capitulated to the pressures of wartime nationalism, Wells-Barnett remained undeterred. She launched an individual protest through the Negro Fellowship League and, spending twenty dollars of her own money, created and distributed buttons with the inscription, "In Memoriam Martyred Negro Soldiers, Dec. 11, 1917."[109] Wells-Barnett's actions spoke to her personal integrity, as well as a growing militancy among black female activists sparked by the war.

However, by yet again challenging traditional notions of womanhood and patriotism, she placed herself at risk. Government investigators paid Wells-Barnett a visit and threatened her with arrest if she did not cease distributing the buttons. She refused.[110] "No one can criticize me as disloyal," she declared in a *Chicago Daily Tribune* interview. "I have helped to send hundreds of comfort kits to our Negro soldiers at Camp Grant."[111] Reflecting on this trying moment in her autobiography, she wrote, "I'd rather go down in history as one lone Negro who dared to tell the government that it had done a dastardly thing than to save my skin by taking back what I have said. I would consider it an honor to spend whatever years are necessary in prison as the one member of the race who protested, rather than to be with all the 11,999,999 Negroes who didn't have to go to prison because they kept their mouths shut."[112] Her statement reflected more than just her penchant to speak truth to power; she linked her fate with that of the martyred and persecuted Houston soldiers. The sacrifice of the Houston soldiers, and all black soldiers, would be her sacrifice as well.

THE HOUSTON UPRISING UNDERSCORED the volatility of debates concerning the place of African American men in the nation's military. The issue of black officers and their future in the new army further complicated matters. Since the Civil War, black combat soldiers had served almost entirely under the command of white officers. In the history of West Point Military Academy, only three black men, Henry Flipper, John Alexander, and Charles Young, had successfully graduated from the prestigious institution. The War Department believed that African Americans lacked the requisite attributes of manhood—mental sturdiness, self-control, objectivity—to become quality officers. Moreover, it paternalistically assumed that only white officers could effectively manage black troops and instill discipline.[113]

The preparedness movement rejuvenated discussions about what role, if any, African American officers should play in the wartime army. In the summer of 1915, preparedness advocates, led by Major General Leonard Wood, a onetime army chief of staff, and his fellow "Rough Rider," former president Theodore Roosevelt, established a reserve officers training camp at Plattsburgh, New York, exclusively attended by the cream of white middle-class gentility. One of its participants, Joel Spingarn, led the fight for African American officers. Spingarn, the eldest son of a Jewish immigrant and former professor of comparative literature at Columbia University, became a member of the NAACP board of directors in 1910 and assumed the chairmanship in 1914. Viewing patriotism as inextricably linked to democratic inclusion within the body politic, Spingarn embraced the civic obligation of military service as American involvement in the war became more likely, much to the chagrin of his antiwar NAACP colleagues. Spingarn approached the question of African American officers as, on the one hand, a test of the military's commitment to equal opportunity for black soldiers and, on the other, a demonstration of African American patriotism and potential for racial leadership.[114] He faced an uphill battle, in light of entrenched hostility within the military to the presence of black officers and the War Department's adamant rejection of the very thought of an integrated officers' training facility. Spingarn, however, found an ally in Wood, who, despite having explicitly barred African Americans from Plattsburgh, proposed in January 1917 the creation of a separate training camp for black officer candidates on the condition that at least two hundred supremely qualified men applied for admission.[115]

Spingarn quickly responded to Wood's challenge. He began open recruitment the following month with a letter that appeared in black newspapers throughout the country. Spingarn couched his call for officer candidates in the language of "Talented Tenth" manhood and racial leadership. Spingarn limited recruitment, in his words, to "educated colored men" of "intelligence, character, and ability," reasoning in Du Boisian parlance: "All of you cannot be leaders, but those of you who have the capacity for leadership must be given an opportunity to test and display it."[116] Spingarn surely recognized the perilous road he prepared to embark on by advocating for a Jim Crow camp, an idea that coming from a white man, irrespective of his progressive credentials, would be viewed by many black people with suspicion if not outright hostility. "I do not believe that colored men should be separated from other Americans in any field of life," he explained, "but the crisis is too near at hand to discuss principles and opinions, and it seems to me that there is only one thing for you to do at this juncture, and that is to get the training that will fit you to be officers, however and wherever and whenever this training may be obtained."[117] The highest obligation in a time of war, Spingarn asserted, was to the nation.

It did not take long for criticism to rain down upon Spingarn's head. Principles and opinions meant a great deal, and African Americans vigorously debated the merits of a segregated training camp or the alternative possibility of no training camp at all. The greater part of the black press, including the *Chicago Defender*, the *Baltimore Afro-American*, and the comparatively conservative *New York Age*, voiced their opposition to the proposal, arguing that the camp would represent an implicit endorsement of racial segregation in the military.[118] It was one thing to reluctantly accept the imposition of a segregated camp by the War Department, but another matter entirely to openly advocate for it. Black officers were needed, but what good, critics asked, could possibly come from a tantamount acceptance of arguments asserting the inherent inferiority of black men? Spingarn further provoked the ire of the black press with a vigorous response to his detractors that smacked of paternalism. "This project is intended to FIGHT segregation in the Army and not to help it," he declared, and further chastised, "will the leaders of the colored race help their Southern enemies by preaching treason and rebellion? Or will they face facts now, and prepare themselves to go as leaders and officers instead of followers and privates?"[119] *Chicago Defender* editor Robert Abbott fired back in an April 7 statement, asserting, "No one denies that we sorely need efficient military training for officers, privates and every citizen, but we do not want it, nor will we take it in a 'Jim Crow' way, if we never get it."[120] Spingarn, swept into the hypernationalist fever of the war, failed to fully appreciate how, for most African Americans, loyalty to the country in a time of war did not dictate an abdication of democratic principle on questions of civil rights.

W. E. B. Du Bois, black America's most eloquent voice on the problem of the color line and Spingarn's good friend, stepped into the firestorm. The camp controversy compelled Du Bois to sort out his thoughts on the meanings of national loyalty, obligation, and service and their compatibility with an uncompromising fight for black racial equality and democratic justice. Du Bois deliberated long and hard, but in the end sided with Spingarn, rationalizing that the opportunity to have black officers prevailed over the need to take an obstinate stand against racial segregation. In an April 1917 *Crisis* editorial appropriately titled "The Perpetual Dilemma," Du Bois argued that African Americans had in the past and continued in the present to painfully accept segregation in numerous aspects of social, political, and educational life as a matter of survival. True, in a democratically just society, black men would have the opportunity to train as officers alongside white men. But for that society to materialize, African Americans needed leaders, men who would demonstrate beyond reproach the manhood, loyalty, and advancement of the race, thus rendering justifications for the continued denial of equal citizenship obsolete. As Du Bois wrote, the stakes were clear, as was the only logical answer: "We must choose between the insult of a separate camp and the irreparable injury of strengthening the present custom of putting no black men in positions of authority. Our choice is as clear as noonday. Give us the camp."[121] It was a bold declaration, one that lacked complete support among the predominantly pacifist NAACP board of directors. The same month in which Du Bois's editorial appeared, NAACP secretary Roy Nash contacted Secretary of War Newton Baker to express his opposition to the "undemocratic" and "unnecessary" camp.[122] Foreshadowing the storm over the merits of segregation that prompted his departure from the NAACP in 1934, Du Bois, with eyes looking toward the future, urged African Americans to temporarily sacrifice principle for the long-term progress of the race.[123]

Despite the controversy, recruitment of potential officer candidates moved forward. Historically black colleges, composed of the best young manhood of the race, provided a groundswell of support. Due in large part to its Washington, D.C., location, Howard University became the epicenter of the officer camp movement. Howard had established a preexisting military training program in cooperation with the War Department, and several other black colleges likewise stressed the disciplinary benefits of army life, thus providing a ready-made pool of potential applicants for the officer camp. Howard supplied seventy-three of the initial volunteers, and Hampton Institute, the sister institution of Tuskegee, provided another forty-six.[124] By March 28 Spingarn boasted to Leonard Wood that he had 231 bona fide individuals of impeccable background ready to enlist. The campaign appeared headed for success.

The official April 6 entry of the United States into the war complicated the prospects of the officers' camp. Not unexpectedly, the War Department designated the fourteen officer training facilities established by Congress for white men only. The ultimate fate of the camp no longer rested with Colonel Wood, but with the War Department and Secretary of War Newton Baker.[125]

In response, black students and faculty at Howard established the Central Committee of Negro College Men (CCNCM), which was chaired by Thomas Montgomery Gregory. Born in Washington, D.C., in 1887, Gregory received an excellent education, attending the Williston Academy boarding school in Easthampton, Massachusetts, and then moving on to Harvard University. Gregory graduated from Harvard in 1910 and returned to Washington, D.C., to accept an appointment on the faculty at Howard, where he taught English and later dramatic arts.[126] His leadership quickly propelled the CCNCM into an extremely efficient operation. It set up headquarters in the basement of the university chapel and, on a twenty-four-hour schedule, coordinated activities on various campuses across the country to secure potential candidates and pressure both Congress and the War Department.[127] The CCNCM worked closely with local groups such as the "Committee of 100," a collection of prominent black residents in Washington, D.C., led by the Reverend J. Milton Waldron and Dr. George W. Cabaniss. Gregory and the CCNCM framed their efforts as essential to the success of the war effort. In a May 11, 1917, letter to Woodrow Wilson, Gregory asserted, "This opportunity for our representative young men to receive training as officers is not only necessary for the proper efficiency of the army but it is also essential to the active and hearty patriotism of ten million Colored citizens."[128]

Charles Hamilton Houston also became swept up in the excitement to establish the officers training camp. "The boys and young instructors at Howard university who were within the draft ages," Houston would later recall, "made up their minds that they were not going to be herded into the Army like sheep."[129] Houston served as chairman of the publicity committee of the CCNCM, spreading word about the camp and the need for potential recruits among similarly energetic aspiring race leaders on campuses ranging from Cornell University to Fisk University.[130] The efforts of Houston, Thomas Gregory, and the rest of the CCNCM paid immediate dividends. In the span of only one week, following its May 1 establishment, the committee had remarkably secured the names of fifteen hundred potential applicants.[131]

Secretary of War Newton Baker lent his support to the camp and, on May 19, issued a formal announcement of approval. Howard and Hampton both offered their campuses, but the War Department chose the remote location of Fort Des Moines, Iowa, as the training facility. One final hurdle appeared when the preferred minimum age for applicants was set at twenty-five, eliminating the vast majority of potential candidates already procured. The CCNCM expanded its efforts beyond the college campuses, enlisting the aid of fraternal organizations, churches, and other local black organizations. A widely disseminated broadside rallied black men to assume their racial duty. "Let us not mince matters: the race is on trial. It needs every one of its red-blooded, sober minded men. . . . Up! brother, our race is calling."[132] Organizers soon secured the requisite twelve hundred applications, well in advance of the camp's June 18, 1917, opening.[133]

Charles Hamilton Houston almost never made it to Des Moines. Despite his active role in securing the camp, Houston was only twenty-one years of age, and thus too young under the new requirements to enlist. He would not be denied. "I was determined that if I lived I was going to have something to say about how this country should be run and that meant sharing every risk the country was exposed to," he reflected.[134] Using his Washington, D.C., contacts, Houston secured a letter from Kentucky senator Ollie James on his behalf. Armed with the recommendation, he traveled to army headquarters at Governor's Island, New York, to plead his case for acceptance. When he arrived, the adjutant informed him that every vacancy had been filled, but if a cancellation arose, the spot was his. As luck would have it, that very same day, an applicant from New York withdrew his name in order to get married. Houston was on his way to Des Moines. Not wanting to risk his good fortune, the young Howard University instructor passed on the opportunity to join his fellow Washington, D.C., candidates on their specially chartered train and instead traveled to Des Moines alone, ahead of everyone else, stopping only briefly to tell his family goodbye.[135]

Houston was among 1,250 candidates assembled for the historic camp, officially designated the Seventeenth Provisional Training Regiment. Although many exceptional individuals had been eliminated by the revised age requirement, it was nevertheless an extremely impressive collection of men. College professors and instructors like Charles Houston and Thomas Gregory rubbed elbows with star athletes, such as Benjamin Hills of Danville, Kentucky, who before joining the camp had tied world records in both the fifty- and seventy-five-meter dash.[136] There were Ivy League students like Victor R. Daly, an undergraduate at Cornell University, who had managed to enter the camp despite being under the preferred age. He was a member of Alpha Phi Alpha, the black fraternity, founded in 1906 on the Cornell campus, which played an active role in the CCNCM and was well represented among the officer candidates.[137] There were policemen like James Wormley Jones, a twelve-year veteran of the

The First African American candidates enlisting for the officers' training camp at Fort Des Moines, Iowa. 165-WW-127 (212). Courtesy of National Archives and Record Administration, College Park, Md.

Washington, D.C., force, whose distinguished record of service earned him a recent promotion to detective.[138] There were business leaders, lawyers, physicians, government employees, and a host of other self-made "race men," most with some form of advanced education. The candidates also included men from more modest backgrounds, such as Walter Sullivan Ross, from Austin, Texas, a brick mason and plasterer, and Thomas Jefferson Wright, a letter carrier from Edwards, Mississippi.[139] For these individuals, the camp functioned as a rare opportunity to claim the status and privileges of black middle-class manhood.

George Schuyler became one of the 250 handpicked soldiers and noncommissioned officers joining Des Moines from the Regular Army. He was still stationed in Hawaii when the United States entered the war. "The most historic development," he recounted, "was the selection of some eighty noncommissioned officers from the Twenty-fifth Infantry to be sent to the separate Negro officers' training camp." After a "pleasant and uneventful" journey from Honolulu to Des Moines, Schuyler was assigned as a drill instructor for Company 12.[140] Osceola McKaine was also among the select group of Regular Army soldiers who attended the camp upon the recommendation of his commanding officer in the Twenty-fourth Infantry. He arrived at Des Moines with high hopes and aspirations for translating his service into racial progress.[141]

In early July, the War Department and the Office of the Surgeon General agreed to allow African American dentists and physicians to train for officer commissions in the Medical Reserve Corps. The camp was also held at Fort Des Moines, giving medical candidates already enlisted the opportunity to transfer. The first course of instruction ran from August 27 to September 30, followed by another session for new candidates, which began on October 1 and concluded November 3.[142] Dr. William Holmes Dyer trained in this second class. Dyer had recently completed his internship at Kansas City General Hospital and returned home to Lincoln, Illinois, to begin his medical practice when the United States entered the war. Upon learning about the new medical officers' camp, Dyer "decided to offer my life upon our nation's alter as a sacrifice, that Democracy might reign and autocracy be forever crushed." He passed his July examination and received word of his acceptance by telegram on September 21. Three days later, on an emotional Sunday afternoon, he departed for Des Moines, Iowa. "Mother and father standing there with tears in eyes were too full to speak when I kissed them and bade them farewell," Dyer remembered. He arrived at Fort Des Moines early the next morning and reported for duty. His living quarters were less than inviting, "a cold room in a stable," but the excitement of being part of a historic group of men more than made up for any disappointment. "Here was the best blood of the nation in that great school of the soldiers," Dyer reflected, "fitting themselves to become leaders of men in the army of our nation."[143]

"Race Leaders in the Making" headlined a July 28, 1918, story in the *Norfolk Journal and Guide*, echoing Dyer's sentiments.[144] Attendees and advocates alike saw the Des Moines camp as both a test of black leadership and a challenge to stereotypes of black male mental and physical inferiority. As the camp got under way, the men socialized largely along lines of their state, city, college, fraternal organization, or profession.[145] The brothers of Omega Psi Phi fraternity established a Des Moines war chapter; a group of black attorneys created the Fort Des Moines Lawyers' Association; and the Howard University contingent, composed of some two hundred students, faculty, and alumni, proudly boasted its presence.[146] John Cade, an enthusiastic Atlanta University student, enjoyed his assignment "in a company composed exclusively of and for Georgians."[147] Despite this factionalism, the officer candidates remained fully cognizant of their importance and trained with a shared sense of purpose. Thomas Gregory established the Seventeenth Provisional Training Regiment Association to further build camaraderie. The goal of the association was to "promote the efficiency of the colored soldier of our country by maintaining his highest standards and traditions, by fostering esprit de corps, by dissemination of professional knowledge, and by exchange of ideas as to the utilization of such knowledge with particular reference to the role of the colored soldier in modern war."[148] The camp bolstered the cadets' race and manhood consciousness. As candidate Leon Everett Proctor, a Lincoln University student from Jackson, Mississippi, stated, "It is the height of my ambition to do credit to my country and my race." He arrived at Des Moines determined to show that he and his fellow officer candidates were "real men having integrity."[149]

Lieutenant Colonel Charles Young was the person destined to whip the officer candidates into form and lead them in battle. As only the third black man to graduate from West Point Military Academy, Young held near-legendary status among African Americans, both within and outside the military.[150] Young had established an impressive military record as the lone black officer in the Regular Army, commanding black troops in the Philippines and throughout the West. His claim to fame took place during his service as a major with the Tenth Cavalry in the 1916 "punitive expedition" in Mexico, where he earned widespread respect for his leadership at Carrizal and a promotion to lieutenant colonel. He was black America's war hero, a patriot in the truest sense of the term, and functioned as a striking model of "Talented Tenth" manhood, leadership, and citizenship. W. E. B. Du Bois chronicled the career of his good friend in the pages of the *Crisis*, profiling him as a "Man of the Month" in the October 1916 issue.[151] Considering the rapid pace of wartime promotions, Young, at the prime age of forty-three, stood poised to assume the rank of brigadier general upon American entry into the war. But more than anything, he eagerly anticipated training the Des Moines officer candidates, preparing them for combat leadership in France, and shattering once and for all the myth that black men could not make quality officers and represent their country with distinction.[152]

Developments beyond his control soon tested Young's patriotic resolve. A routine May 7, 1917, physical for Young's promotion to colonel revealed high blood pressure. Although willing to advance Young irrespective of the diagnosis, on May 23, 1917, the examination board ordered him to report to Letterman General Hospital, located on the Presidio army base in San Francisco, for further tests.[153] He appeared before a second medical examining board on June 2, which again voted to approve his promotion. The chief medical examiner, however, intervened, asserting that Young possessed a debilitating condition and recommended his disqualification.[154] Young was ordered to remain at Letterman Hospital until resolution of the matter, much to his surprise and disappointment. Young did, in fact, have Bright's disease, but this went undiagnosed, and he at the time felt physically well, possessing in his words a "constitution of iron." Young saw no logic in the army not utilizing his services at a time when experienced officers were in short supply.[155] More pressing, the Des Moines candidates awaited his leadership. He voiced his frustrations in a letter to W. E. B. Du Bois, with whom he maintained a close relationship dating back to the doctor's brief tenure at Wilberforce. "Without an ache or pain," Young impatiently told Du Bois, he waited in San Francisco, losing precious days, "when I should this minute be at Des Moines helping to beat those colored officers into shape."[156] As word spread of Young's situation, the black press suspected foul play. In a June 14 article, the *New York Age* stated, "In sending Lieutenant Colonel Young to Presidio 'for observation,' some profess to see a move to retire the highest Negro officer in the army because of his color."[157]

The editors of the *Age* did not know how on the mark their suspicions were. Woodrow Wilson took an unusual interest in Charles Young, who, if he had white skin, would not have received any of the president's attention. In March 1917 Mississippi senator John Sharp Williams forwarded Wilson a letter from a white lieutenant, Albert Dockery, whom Young commanded in the Tenth Cavalry. Wilson wrote to Secretary of War Newton D. Baker on June 25, informing him that Dockery, "a Southerner," found it "not only distasteful but practically impossible to serve under a colored commander." Wilson requested that Baker look into transferring the white soldier in order to avoid "some serious and perhaps even tragical insubordination" on his part.[158] The next day, Baker notified Wilson that he, first, envisioned Young training the black officer candidates at Fort Des Moines and, two, that the colonel was apparently "not in perfectly good health," thus reassuring the president that Young would not be commanding white soldiers of the Tenth Cavalry in the foreseeable future. Before Young's fate had been officially determined, on June 29 Wilson wrote to Senator Williams that the black officer would no longer command the Tenth Cavalry because of "ill health" and, when he recovered, would likely "be transferred to some other service."[159] Young's promotion posed a serious threat, both real and symbolic, to the core tenets of white supremacist thought embedded in the American military. The southern-bred Wilson revealed his sensitivity to this problem, so much so that he ensured that Young would never again be in a position to issue an order to a white man.

Meanwhile, word of Young's prognosis, confinement to Letterman Hospital, and possible forced retirement from active service provoked growing outrage from black political leaders and the press. Du Bois wrote to Young, assuring his friend that the NAACP and the *Crisis* "will take all possible steps to bring your case to the authorities."[160] The *Chicago Defender* proclaimed, "It is the duty of every member of the Race to protest" to all relevant government departments and offices "to stop any high-handed methods which might be used in railroading this man from the army at this day when the nation faces a crisis simply because the man is not white."[161] The *New York Age* predicted that, in the eyes of African Americans across the country, the forced retirement of Young would constitute nothing less than "a racial calamity."[162]

On July 30 the War Department officially ordered Young's retirement from active duty as commander of the Tenth Cavalry and reassigned him to training duty with the Organized Militia of Ohio.[163] Although Young was promoted to colonel, the decision effectively ended his chance at training the Des Moines candidates, serving in France, and leading black troops into combat. Considering the fact that Young was indeed ill, the army's decision did have some merit. But for a man who based his entire career on placing nation before race, the unexpected decision was heartbreaking. Moreover, the chain of events surrounding the time of Young's examination, Woodrow Wilson's inquiries into the matter, and Young's ultimate retirement from active service paint a troubling picture of the president's complicity. To add insult to injury, Young would later find out that all National Guard units in Ohio had already been mustered into service, and his presence was unnecessary.[164] Not content to passively accept his fate, Young valiantly demonstrated his physical fitness by riding 500 miles from his Wilberforce home to Washington, D.C., on horseback to register a personal protest with the secretary of war. It was to no avail.

The seemingly unjust dismissal of the most prominent symbol of black patriotism and military accomplishment stung African Americans. Editorials and letters of protest filled black newspapers. Du Bois, taking the issue personally, openly questioned the motivations behind the War Department's actions in the *Crisis*.[165] Young continued to push for reinstatement, all the while remaining a loyal soldier and standing firmly by his country. From Wilberforce he wrote to W. P. Bayless, editor of the *Pittsburgh Courier*, "It seems regrettable for both the country and our people, for I could have done good work for both, but as the President willed it and ordered it, I submit cheerfully like a soldier."[166] With his military career cut short, he reluctantly accepted a seat on the NAACP board of directors. If he had served in the war, his presence would have undoubtedly had a strong positive effect on the morale and efficiency of African American servicemen. Instead, Young's marginalization ominously foreshadowed the military's concerted efforts to devalue and discredit African American officers and the soldiers under their command. In a cruel twist of fate, the army reinstated

Young five days before the November 11, 1918, armistice, deeming him healthy enough to serve in Liberia as an official American adviser following the war.[167]

The Young affair, for the many Des Moines candidates who either knew him personally or admired him from afar, was bitterly disappointing. Hoping to be trained by the legendary West Pointer, some openly wept upon hearing news of Young's confinement to Letterman Hospital. George Schuyler, who by chance encountered Young on a streetcar in Oakland, California, while traveling to Des Moines, remembered his anger when Young was "removed from the scene, a sacrifice on the altar of political expediency, a thorn in the side of the military hierarchy."[168] Young, despite his own misfortune, still felt a strong obligation to the officer candidates and accepted an invitation to address the men. When he arrived at the camp, emotions ran high. He received a hero's welcome, as the candidates showered him with applause. Young reciprocated with a moving speech, imploring the would-be officers to "prove your valor" and fulfill their duties "as finely, as splendidly, as any white man performed his duty."[169] In a moment of darkness, Young gave the Des Moines trainees reason for optimism.

However, like Charles Young, the Des Moines men also felt the brunt of institutional hostility toward the very idea of black officers. The War Department selected Charles Ballou, a former commanding officer of the Twenty-fourth Infantry, to oversee the camp because of his background leading black soldiers. He adopted a supportive, yet paternalistic view of African American soldiers and had little interest in broader questions of black racial progress. Although he knew from firsthand experience that black men made quality fighters, he questioned their ability to serve as effective officers. This view informed his initial impressions of the Des Moines candidates, whom he felt as a collective lacked the education and experience necessary for the highest officer positions. Based in large part on Ballou's recommendations, the army limited the course of instruction for the candidates to infantry training only.[170] Some of the black Regular Army noncommissioned instructors, like George Schuyler, noticed that the African American officer candidates were not receiving the same courses as their white counterparts and became suspicious. "This had every appearance of sabotage," Schuyler later wrote.[171]

The candidates also had to confront tense relations with white residents of nearby Des Moines. Des Moines had a small, yet vibrant black community of some six thousand people that provided important support for the black officers in training. African American residents welcomed the presence of the cadets, and the local black newspaper, the *Iowa Bystander*, chronicled their experiences. Although white civic leaders voiced their support for the black officers' camp, many white residents viewed the presence of African American soldiers in their midst with suspicion. A culture of de facto segregation determined relations between white and black people in Des Moines. As such, a number of the officer candidates, to their surprise, encountered various incidents of discrimination. "About three weeks after camp opened," Charles Hamilton Houston remembered how "a group of candidates had been refused service in a Chinese restaurant in Des Moines," although the state had a civil rights law prohibiting racial discrimination in public facilities. "The men refused to leave and a scuffle ensued when the proprietor tried to put them out," Houston wrote.[172] As race men, the Des Moines cadets internalized a responsibility to confront racial oppression whenever and wherever it reared its ugly head. Edgar Webster, principal of the Normal Department at Atlanta University, who remained in contact with a number of the candidates from his institution during their training experience, observed, "But on the question of the color line, men's minds have been changed out here, and when the men here who do not go to France, get back home, a mob in their vicinity will be in a danger zone without doubt. The camp has been worth while as an antidote to mob rule and lynch law in the South."[173]

Charles Ballou and other white officials feared the implications of this type of thinking. The Houston rebellion had placed the camp on edge. Charles Hamilton Houston and other trainees "all knew a crisis had come."[174] Ballou, with his career and hopes for advancement on the line as well, made it clear to the candidates that the military viewed the camp as an experiment whose outcome would determine the future presence of African American officers. This necessitated that they comport themselves in such as way as to avoid any friction with local white residents, regardless of the circumstances. Ballou was convinced, as he told Adjutant General W. T. Johnston, the men "could not ram social equality down the throats of the white population, but must *win* it by their modesty, patience, forbearance and character."[175] At Ballou's behest, the adjutant general addressed the camp and prohibited the officer candidates from defending themselves against the racial insults of hostile whites in Des Moines. "From the moment he spoke," Charles Houston reflected, "morale at Fort Des Moines died."[176]

As the ninety-day camp concluded, the military had not yet developed any formal policies concerning the use of black combat soldiers and officers. The Houston bloodshed and subsequent southern protests complicated War Department plans to draft and train black soldiers. As a result, the future of the Des Moines officer candidates remained in limbo. When the scheduled close date arrived, they did not have regiments to command and the War Department never considered the option of assigning them to white divisions. The adjutant general realized that if commissioned black officers were placed on inactive duty, they would "feel that they were not being given the same treatment as graduates of white Officers' Training Camps" and "immediately use all the 'influence' they could bring to bear on the War Department to have themselves put on active duty."[177] Still dousing the flames of protest sparked by Charles Young's retirement, the army needed no additional controversies. As a result of the uncertainty, military officials extended the camp for an additional four weeks, giving candidates the option to take a new oath for renewal of service or receive a discharge.

Some candidates welcomed and undoubtedly benefited from the extra month of training. George Schuyler surmised, with some truth, that the decision to extend the camp was not "entirely racism" and that "it would have been suicidal, in many instances, to just have men commanding regiments who had no training whatsoever."[178] Atlanta University student John Cade, like many of his comrades, remained "determined to see it out to the bitter end and find out the real motives of Uncle Sam," but others, he noted, "went home, disappointed, sick at heart, despondent."[179] One of these disappointed individuals, Edward Micksey, wrote to W. E. B. Du Bois, "Personally I would prefer to remain in for the general good of the cause, but my duty to my mother and sisters and the urgency of the call to my business compel me to leave at this time."[180] General Ballou vigorously defended the decision, lambasting critics as "trouble mongers," "whose one desire on learning of the extension of this camp was to twist the facts so as to create discontent and ill-feeling."[181] Thomas Gregory and other leaders encouraged the candidates, despite this latest hurdle, to press on. "I shall remain to the end," Gregory stated in a telegram to his mother.[182] They had come too far to quit now.

The camp closed on October 14, 1917. Six hundred thirty-nine men—nearly half of the original enrollees—earned commissions, most at the ranks of first and second lieutenant. The school for black medical officer candidates concluded the following month. Race leaders and the black press viewed the camp as a significant stepping-stone, if not an outright success. Many of the newly minted officers were proud of their accomplishment and enthusiastic about their future service. Victor Daly graduated along with thirty-two of his Alpha Phi Alpha brothers, receiving a first lieutenant commission. Osceola McKaine likewise was commissioned as a first lieutenant and looked forward to representing his race in France. "I am eager for the fray," he selflessly wrote to his friend and famed portrait painter Orlando Rouland. "Death does not matter, for it will mean life for thousands of my countrymen, and for my race, for right must triumph."[183] Although still skeptical of the army's intentions regarding black officers, George Schuyler accepted his first lieutenant commission with pride. James Wormley Jones was among the 105 men to earn a commission at the rank of captain. The newly minted officers received a roughly two-week furlough—October 15 to November 1—to gather their personal effects and report to their designated training camp.[184] Whom they would command remained a mystery.

ON THE EVE OF THE WAR, the U.S. military had an available land force of just over 220,000 men, composed of the Regular Army, the National Guard, and the marines.[185] To put this number in perspective, the European Allied forces endured just under 624,000 casualties in the 1916 battle of the Somme alone. If it was to have any discernible impact on the course of the war, the army needed men, and needed them in a hurry. While proponents of preparedness had advocated various programs of conscription and universal military service as early as 1914, viewing participation in the nation's army as a fundamental obligation of American citizenship, entry into the war brought a sense of immediacy to the debate.[186] An assortment of groups—socialists, populist-oriented southern politicians, antiwar progressives, feminists, agrarian radicals—frowned upon the idea of compulsory military service for a variety of reasons. Opponents viewed the draft as a tool of big business and the economic elite, an infringement on personal liberties, a blood tax on the poor, and a death knell to any hopes of continued progressive reform.[187] Proponents argued that conscription was not only a military necessity but an opportunity to forge a new "unhyphenated" national identity and shared sense of civic belonging among an American populace increasingly fractured by racial, ethnic, and religious difference. Compulsory military service, military officials, business leaders, and northern and southern elites argued, would function as an engine of Americanization and nationalism.[188]

The Selective Service Act, passed on May 18, 1917, required all men between the ages of twenty-one and thirty-one to register for possible induction. The creation of the Selective Service System marked a defining moment in U.S. history. Even more so than the Civil War draft, it represented a significant expansion of the state and its incursion on the lives of individual citizens. More specifically, it shifted the authority to mobilize military manpower resources from the local and state levels to the national. This process also redefined the meaning of citizenship and the relationship between citizens and the nation. The federal government enhanced the social and political value of citizenship during the war by linking it to the obligation of military service, an act that empowered those compelled to serve to demand the fruits of their civic sacrifice.[189]

This made the potential inclusion of African Americans into the Selective Service System a highly contentious issue, particularly in the South. White southern planters opposed the drafting of their labor force, arguing that the region's agricultural economy, already destabilized by northern migration, would be adversely affected by the removal of thousands of African Americans for military service. Some politicians, like James Vardaman and Ben Tillman, voiced their opposition to compulsory military service for African Americans as an issue of regional safety.[190] Advocates, conversely, argued that white men alone should not have to shoulder the burden of conscription while black men remained at home. This was couched as a matter of principle but also of regional safety, as the wives and daughters of white soldiers would be left vulnerable to malingering black men.[191]

The military rejected arguments opposing black conscription on the grounds that the loyalty of black people had never been in question and their manpower would be needed. A total of 290,527 African American men registered for military duty on the two draft calls of June 2 and September 12, 1917. They represented 9.6 percent of the nation's potential soldiers.[192] Despite professing their commitment to racial equality, Provost Marshal General Enoch H. Crowder and those who devised the draft did not go so far as to institute a colorblind system. Draft board officials carried instructions to tear off the lower left-hand corner of all selective service forms submitted by African Americans, laying the administrative groundwork for a segregated army.[193]

With the draft under way, the War Department debated how best to use the anticipated influx of black men deemed eligible for military service. On August 24, 1917, army chief of staff Tasker H. Bliss submitted a memorandum to Secretary of War Newton Baker concerning the use of African American draftees in the military. Bliss offered six potential plans to Baker, providing his opinion on the practicality of each one. He gave his personal endorsement to the final option, seen as "the preferable plan with respect to the object of preventing racial trouble." It entailed, first, suspending the number of African American draftees. With a more limited pool, the army would then begin "to call these men out as they are required for service with the Quartermaster Corps, Engineers," and other labor organizations, providing them with "preliminary instruction in the localities where raised." When ready, they would finally be shipped abroad "as rapidly as possible."[194] The recommendation reflected a belief that just as in civilian life, black men, especially southerners, were best suited for work that maximized their supposed natural physical abilities. Bliss and like-minded military officials also saw the employment of African American draftees for menial labor duties as the ideal way to both postpone addressing the use of black soldiers for combat service and avoid potential racial conflict with white troops and civilians. Although the War Department drew up these plans before the Houston bloodbath, the incident and its reverberations undoubtedly informed Baker's decision making. The secretary of war unconditionally supported Bliss's proposal, and, with his stamp of approval, the use of African American draftees primarily as laborers became embedded into official military policy.

The actions of the War Department conveniently dovetailed with the racism of draft boards. In order to personally invest American citizens in the war effort and avoid the perception of conscription as an attack on personal and civil liberties, the federal government placed administrative control in the hands of local communities. The sensitivity of the South to federal incursion made the issue of communal control an even greater necessity. Enoch Crowder explained in his December 1918 postwar report, "In framing the selective service act Congress definitely decided to entrust the draft directly to the people, and to enlist their full confidence by placing upon them the fullest responsibility. . . . To effectuate the ideal of localizing the draft, it seemed necessary to have it administered by committees of men intimately acquainted with the lives and circumstances of the people of their communities."[195]

This decision ultimately had negative repercussions for African Americans and working-class whites, particularly those in the South, who represented the majority of the region's population and eligible inductees.[196] Wealthy and influential white men, the political appointees of state governors, controlled county induction and exemption boards, thus leaving the process open to corruption resulting from class and racial biases. The implementation and execution of the draft followed the racial conventions of each particular locality and the individuals who oversaw the process. This frequently translated into draft board administrators carrying Jim Crow customs into examination facilities. One black soldier, after his induction into the army at a segregated center where posted signs separated "white" and "colored" draftees, vented his anger in a passionate letter to W. E. B. Du Bois. "Thus the initial step in my military career and of the military career of every colored man examined at this place was blotted by the accursed stigma of race prejudice, and segregation," he wrote. The democratic framing of the war made the hypocrisy of his experience all too glaring. "Picture yourself an American citizen of color standing before an examination where you risk the highest thing this world affords, your life to make Democracy safe for the world, and such humiliating signs displayed. I doubt whether Prussianism can be much worse."[197]

The combination of endemic poverty, especially in the South, and the discriminatory nature of the draft resulted in draft boards inducting black men in disproportionate numbers. Ten percent of the total national population, African Americans nevertheless made up 14 percent of the country's drafted men. The military inducted 36 percent of Class I African American draftees and whites at a rate of 24 percent.[198] Racial bias embedded within the draft took multiple forms. Envisioning most draftees serving in the capacity of laborers, physical examination boards consistently inducted black men who were deemed ineligible for combat duty. Medical examiners determined 74.6 percent of the total number of African Americans drafted eligible for general military service, compared to 69.7 percent of white draftees.[199] In the case of African American conscripts, examiners regularly ignored physical debilitations that would have excluded many draftees from the army altogether, while others rejected African American claims for the explicit purpose of lessening the enlistment burden on white men.[200] Discrimination of this sort prompted the removal of the entire draft exemption board of Fulton County, Georgia, which exempted only 6 of the 202 African American applicants, as opposed to 526 of the 815 white applicants.[201]

Black men also received subjective dependency exemptions at a far lower rate than whites. Draft boards initially linked dependency claims to marriage, but the pressing need for soldiers compelled boards to closely consider the financial conditions of draftees and their families. Boards based qualifications for exemption on whether a draftee's family was financially dependent on his regular employment and whether military service would adversely impact its economic stability. Because the vast majority of black men in the South earned less than thirty dollars a month, the standard allotment under the War Risk Insurance Act, passed by Congress in October 1917, all-white exemption boards routinely denied claims of family dependency, regardless of marital status. Although this practice impacted poor whites as well, the general dismissal of African American exemption claims masked a deeper disregard for black families, and black women in particular. Boards used the fact that many black women turned to domestic work as a source of supplemental income as a rationale for denying the dependency claims of their husbands, reflecting how race shaped conflicting notions of domesticity and respectability.[202]

Many African American draftees were unwittingly caught between the competing agendas of white southerners. As the draft pulled more and more black men into the army, white landowners and employers suddenly found themselves with a shrinking labor force. Compounded by preexisting black migration, the drafting of black men had the potential to wreak havoc on the southern economy. As a result, crafty white landowners attempted to favorably mold the malleable category of dependency regarding their black tenants and employees by submitting petitions of exemption on their behalf, on the grounds they represented essential labor. This provided an opportunity for some African Americans to avoid induction, although they still remained tied to servitude to their employer. By and large, the efforts of white landowners proved futile in the face of racially subjective induction boards. Cornelius Bridgeforth, a black farmer from Virginia, actually wanted to enlist in the military, despite the objections of his employer. When he was drafted, Bridgeforth recalled that his employer "tried to get me exempted but could not."[203]

With the odds stacked against them, it is no wonder that many black men opted to avoid military service altogether. African Americans constituted 22 percent—105,831—of the 474,861 reported draft deserters.[204] These numbers reflected a particularly high level of draft evasion among southern African Americans, who made up more than 60 percent of reported deserters from the former Confederacy. Many southern black men understandably had little interest in the war and consciously ignored their call, taking their chances against local enforcement agents. Future sociologist and Howard University professor E. Franklin Frazier, living in Georgia at the time, avoided induction by traveling from job to job from June to September 1918, until he found employment as a YMCA secretary at Camp Humphreys, Virginia.[205] More common, however, were the thousands of black men who, lured by the promise of jobs and social freedom, gathered their belongings and migrated from their southern homes, leaving behind their induction notices in the process. Black people relocated to the urban North and Midwest during the World War I era for a host of political and ideological reasons, some of which were undoubtedly related to an aversion to military service.[206] Migration was oftentimes an act of political expression, one that in the context of the Selective Service System and its coercive power, spoke to how many black men felt about the war and the prospect of entering the army.

Draft officials and local southern politicians looked for excuses to explain the discrepancy between black and white deserters. They continued to blame "outside agitators" and German agents for stirring up unrest among an easily gullible African American population. Provost Marshal General Crowder latched onto the stereotype of black inferiority as his rationale, writing, "With striking unanimity the draft authorities replied that this was due to two causes; first, ignorance and illiteracy, especially in the rural regions, to which may be added a certain shiftlessness in ignoring civic obligations; and secondly, the tendency of the Negroes to shift from place to place." Crowder pointed to the "natural inclination" of African Americans to "roam from one employment to another" and confidently boasted that "willful delinquency or desertion has been almost nil."[207] He fell back on an old antebellum trope of the happy-go-lucky black southerner, content with his station in life, absolutely loyal, and posing no threat to the social and economic stability of the region. His reasoning disregarded any political motivations southern African Americans may have had for rejecting military service and masked fears regarding the loyalty of African Americans, which pervaded the South.[208]

The statistics of the provost marshal actually contradicted his own characterization of black desertion as a principally southern problem. African American desertion rates in northern states with sizable African American populations surpassed those of southern states with the largest populations. For example, Georgia, the state with the highest number of African American registrants, had an 8 percent desertion rate in comparison to Pennsylvania, which had a black desertion rate of 16.8 percent for its 39,363 registrants. With 25,974 African American registrants, New York State had a black desertion rate of 15.6 percent.[209] These numbers reinforce the fact that many black people in northern cities did not regard the war and potential military service enthusiastically. As the populations of New York, Chicago, Milwaukee, and other cities swelled in size from the newly arrived presence of black migrants, many having escaped a life of virtual bondage and unwilling to enter another form of servitude, hostility toward and resistance to military service became more and more common.

While not resisting military service outright, a much larger segment of draft-eligible African Americans reflected the general attitude of most other Americans, especially from the South, and approached induction and the prospect of dying for the United States with a discernible sense of apathy.[210] The responses of African American veterans to the Virginia War History Commission questionnaire, which was distributed beginning in 1919 and continued throughout the mid-1920s, offers a unique opportunity to explore how a sizable number of black men, and those from the South in particular, responded to the call. Farmer Mac Tidsdale said that he felt "rather indifferent to military service" before receiving his draft notice.[211] George Wyche, a student at the Hampton Institute, had little enthusiasm for military service as well, responding that he "did not care much about it personally."[212] While hoping to avoid the call, a number of apathetic men nevertheless acknowledged the power of the state and the inevitability of their induction. Twenty-one-year-old George Thomas Clark, a farmer and sawmill worker from Runnymede, Virginia, declared that he "did not desire to enter military service and would not have done so if possible to avoid it."[213] Howard Garrett, who worked on his father's farm in Buckingham, Virginia, similarly felt, "I was at my country's call though not particularly anxious."[214]

Other men offered much more explicit responses, reflecting a strong political consciousness and critical view of democracy on the part of many African American southerners. A number of individuals expressed a clear reluctance to join the army because of the nation's undemocratic treatment of black people. This sentiment cut across class lines but was especially pronounced in the responses of college-educated black men. Twenty-one-year-old Howard University graduate Herbert Ulysses White from Norfolk, Virginia, despite the overall enthusiastic participation of his alma mater in the war mobilization effort, eloquently stated, "I did not feel justified in going into the service to fight for so called democracy which I could not myself enjoy as an American citizen."[215] Luther Robinson, a thirty-one-year-old graduate of the Hampton Institute at the time of his induction who received some military training while a student, bluntly reflected that he "never cared for military service," principally because "I never thought that I had any country to fight for."[216]

The perverse logic of fighting for a nation that denied African Americans their basic citizenship rights obviously weighed heavily on the minds of many draftees as they confronted military service. Black men, however, had the same reservations as other citizens, regardless of color, when their draft call arrived. The uncertainty of many drafted men, for example, revolved not around the future of the race but the future of their families and loved ones. Moses Randolph, born on August 28, 1892, to Kit and Rose Randolph, remembered that he "did not mind going except that it left my aged mother alone."[217] Albert Johnson "was willing to go," although he worried about leaving behind his wife, Emma, and their newborn son, Eugene, only two weeks old at the time of his induction.[218] Royal Lee Fleming, a railroad worker from Henrico, Virginia, also did not explicitly oppose entering the military but still "hated to leave my family."[219] In the case of other draftees, a natural fear of dying fueled their apathy. Ernest Bartee, from rural Cumberland County, Virginia, admitted, "At first it was more a dread or fear than pleasure as I had never had any military training or recognition."[220] African American draftees were complex human beings, with complex identities, who experienced love, sadness, and fright just like anyone else.

As American citizens, they also experienced the patriotic excitement of participation in the war and serving on the behalf of the nation. While resistance and apathy ran high among black men facing the possibility of military service, the majority of draft-eligible African Americans answered their call and did so with a strong measure of patriotic enthusiasm. Wartime conceptions of citizenship opened new possibilities for African Americans to reimagine their relationship with the nation.[221] While often denied their full rights, a significant number of African Americans drafted for military duty saw themselves as citizens nevertheless. A clear sense of civic obligation therefore shaped the responses of many African American men who ultimately served in the army. By entering the army and fulfilling the obligation of military service, African American men had the opportunity to establish a tangible relationship with the nation and make a direct claim on the citizenship and manhood rights denied to them as civilians. This held true even in the South. Although black resistance to the draft ran high in many areas, and apathy was widespread, military service provided the chance for poor rural black men to escape the clutches of southern racial oppression. As such, a significant number of draftees approached induction with feelings of excitement, possibility, and, most of all, responsibility to meet their duty as citizens to the nation. Just as some African Americans used the draft to express their displeasure with the facade of American democracy, many more approached it as an opportunity to express their belief in its transformative potential.[222]

When it came time for Thomas Clary to enlist, the twenty-year-old blacksmith from Brunswick County "thought over it" and "considered it an honor as well as a great privilege to go and fight or die for my country."[223] Highly personal, yet intensely political responses such as this were common among black men drafted from Virginia. "Perfectly willing to do any bit for my country" was how draftee Stanley Hammon, a twenty-four-year-old farmer from Daugherty, Virginia, who had never had the opportunity to vote, responded when asked if he was ready to answer the call.[224] Tonias Thomas White, a railroad employee with no education, felt "willing to enter the service and to do what I could for the interest of my country."[225] They had every reason to denounce the government on the basis of its lack of reciprocity in fulfilling the social contract of American citizenship, but they still embraced and affirmed their relationship to the state. Charles Brodnax, a farmer from Brunswick County, Virginia, stated with confidence that he "belonged to the Government of my country and should answer to the call and obey the orders in defence of Democracy."[226] Paul Washington Alexander, a longshoreman in Norfolk at the time he received his notice, similarly reflected, "My attitude was patriotic and I felt that my call to the colors was a blessing from God to give me a chance to serve my Government and country in its greatest crisis." Floyd Bishop viewed his call to the colors not as an imposition, but as a right and privilege of citizenship, one that he was determined to take advantage of. "I felt that as an American citizen," Bishop asserted, "I was as entitled to service as any other citizen and that so long as my country needed me I was willing to serve." As indicated by the frequent appearance of "my" in their responses, these black men, and countless others like them, internalized a strongly possessive conception of American citizenship and the potential of democracy that held valuable personal meaning.

The idea of obligation fundamentally shaped definitions of citizenship during the First World War, and likewise informed how African Americans approached the draft. The bureaucratic expansion of the nation-state, combined with the broadened ideological and rhetorical space created by the democratic framing of the war, allowed many politically marginalized groups to stake claim to their citizenship rights through the obligation of conscription.[227] Many black draftees who served saw it as their responsibility and civic duty to follow through with induction. Hatcher Mack, a twenty-seven-year-old waiter, believed, "As an American born citizen I felt it my indispensable duty to perform honest and faithful such duties as were my lot to perform."[228] "As an American citizen, I felt it my duty to go," declared Walter James Lethcoe, who made a living before the war cleaning and pressing clothes in the town of Glade Springs, Virginia.[229] Citizenship and duty reinforced one another, causing a significant number of black draftees to view military service as a long-sought-after opportunity to assert their rightful place in the nation.

In addition to the powerful ideological currents steering African Americans into the army, important practical reasons also existed why black men would not be averse to receiving their draft call. Most black draftees, especially those from the South, may have had only a vague conception of the army they were soon to enter. They did, however, have a clear historical and material appreciation of the potential of military service to enhance the quality of their lives. The army offered a chance for both economic and social upward mobility. In large part because of its historical connection with emancipation, donning the uniform carried a measure of honor and status prestige within African American communities. Earnest Burwell, who worked for a steel company in Philadelphia before receiving his call, saw the army as "a noble work."[230] Elija Spencer stated that he "believed in military service," while Clarence Bailey saw the military as a "great institution."[231] The opportunity for travel, adventure, and, possibly, the emotional rush of combat appealed to young black men seeking to affirm their manhood. Perhaps most significant, military service was a job, offering a form of steady employment and financial stability that many African Americans sorely lacked. The prospect of at least thirty dollars a month appealed to thousands of men trapped in the perpetual debt of sharecropping and other forms of economic exploitation. Additionally, dependency benefits from the War Risk Insurance Act provided meaningful relief for thousands of impoverished black households.[232]

Race, however, still influenced motivations for joining the army. Men such as Solomon Spady viewed induction and military service as a duty to both race and nation. A YMCA secretary and graduate of the Hampton Institute and Virginia

Union University, Spady recalled that he was "in general very favorable" to the idea of military service and added, "My own call seemed to me the opening of an opportunity for me to be of service to humanity and to my own people."[233] While educated men such as Solomon Spady may have been more inclined to see military service in racial terms, race consciousness crossed class boundaries. Aaron Jones, who worked as a stevedore before being drafted, stated, "My attitude toward the military service received, is that we as members of the colored race, need better educational advantages in order that we can be more able to appreciate our country."[234] As the war progressed, the relationship between race, nation, and obligation would become even more pronounced, and increasingly complex.

IN THESE EARLY DAYS, weeks, and months of the American war mobilization effort, the nation found itself not just in a titanic battle with Germany and the Central Powers but in a struggle over the very meaning of democracy. Woodrow Wilson had provocatively framed the question of why the United States entered the war, and what its citizens must fight for as a struggle for global democracy. African Americans, with a deep and often painful appreciation for the ideals of democracy, quickly recognized the larger historical significance of the war moment as a potential turning point in their continued struggle for freedom and citizenship. Democracy was worth dying for, and the United States emerged as a literal and figurative battleground. As black and white Americans of various ideological persuasions dug in and established positions, questions surrounding black military service and the presence of African American soldiers in the nation's army dominated racial politics and social relations. The violence at Houston dramatically revealed the extent to which African American soldiers would go to defend their dignity and manhood, while the struggle over black officers demonstrated the inextricable relationship between military service and wartime notions of racial leadership and progress. Moreover, the Selective Service System compelled thousands of African American men to contemplate their relationship as citizens to the nation. Some explicitly opposed military service, more viewed the prospect of enlistment apathetically, while most approached their call as an opportunity to affirm and stake claim to their citizenship. As they entered the United States Army, African American servicemen embodied both the personal and political dimensions of democracy in the context of a racially volatile social climate. In the days ahead, their physical and ideological presence would become even more central to shaping how the United States went about waging war and the place of black people in it.

> There is no intention on the part of the War Department to undertake at this time to settle the so-called race question.
>
> —Secretary of War Newton D. Baker, November 20, 1917

THE "RACE QUESTION"

The U.S. Government and the Training Experiences of African American Soldiers

On Saturday, October 13, 1917, the black community of Winnfield, Louisiana, gathered to honor their local heroes. Winnfield was the seat of Winn Parish and would later become famous as the birthplace of three future governors of Louisiana, Huey Long, Earl Long, and Oscar Allen. Life was hard for African Americans in Winnfield, the small yet bustling town nestled in the heart of the lush Kisatchie Forest. Black residents, like African Americans throughout the South in the early twentieth century, experienced the everyday realities of segregation, poverty, and disfranchisement. They also had to contend with the legacy and constant threat of racial violence; terrorist groups such as the Ku Klux Klan and the White League had a long history in Winn Parish dating back to the turbulent years of Reconstruction. But despite these challenges, black people in Winnfield had successfully created a community for themselves, and Saturday, October 13, was a night for celebration. At five o'clock, nineteen draftees marched from the town courthouse to a popular restaurant for supper. Afterward, joined by more than five hundred African American residents, the men went to the local Odd Fellows Hall. The soon-to-be soldiers listened to patriotic speeches, danced to piano music, and enjoyed treats of sandwiches, cake, punch, and smokes. The festivities continued the following morning. At the train station, 350 friends, family members, and well-wishers cheered their departure to Camp Pike, Arkansas, where they hoped to represent their town with pride.[1]

Throughout the fall of 1917, and continuing well into the summer of 1918, African American families and communities across the country sent their young men off to war. Parades and festivities, large and small, ranging in mood from solemn to euphoric, took place in major cities and nondescript towns alike. In April 1918, "practically every colored inhabitant" from Crawford County, Arkansas, packed the city of Van Buren for a send-off parade honoring 28 men headed to Camp Pike.[2] The same month, some 15,000 black residents of Memphis, Tennessee, cheered 250 drafted black men off to Camp Lee and Camp Meade with a parade down Main Street, replete with banners reading, "To Hell with the Kaiser" and "Black Faces but Red Blood." The parade concluded with a raucous farewell at Union Station, where the "laughing, shouting, dancing" crowd watched their sons, brothers, and husbands depart to the sound of "Beale Street Blues."[3] These were local affairs, reflecting the community's demographics and politics. In several instances, white people also cheered the soldiers along in a heartwarming display of patriotic solidarity. In other cases, as in Winnfield, Louisiana, black residents organized celebrations without white support.[4] These events, however, did share a common feature: black draftees, with the rare exception, departed for training alone. They were called to serve the same flag and sacrifice for the same cause. But as black and white inducted men marched off to camp, segregation and the politics of race remained inescapable, and placed them on different paths. North and South, the so-called race question, the dilemma of the place and future of black people in American society, shadowed the entry of black men into the wartime army.

The "race question" also loomed large as government leaders, military officials, self-appointed race spokesmen, and African American activists battled over the place of black soldiers in the U.S. Army. During the explosive summer and fall months of 1917, approaches to the "race question" hinged on how various individuals, white and black, male and female, viewed the relationship between African Americans, citizenship, and military service. War planners grudgingly acknowledged that citizen-soldiers had the power to negotiate the extent to which the army exerted absolute power over their lives and thus the nature of their incorporation into the American military.[5] The Wilson administration, however, was by no means prepared to treat African American soldiers, regardless of their sacrifice, as equal citizens. White military officials, some paternalistic, others unashamedly racist, approached the "race question" as the "problem" of incorporating black men into the army and training them for duty.

"How does it feel to be a problem?" W. E. B. Du Bois painfully queried in his 1903 classic *The Souls of Black Folk*.[6] Still confronted with this question during the war, African Americans, in and outside of the army, struggled against their imposed problematic status and attempted to pressure, mold, and reap gains from the government reflective of their individual and collective visions of democracy. The American military and the numerous civilian agencies under its purview tried as best they could to replicate the racial dynamics of everyday life in the army. Race "leaders" and activists, men and women, hoped that by assisting the government and joining various social welfare organizations, their contributions to the war effort would translate into better conditions for African American soldiers. Black men drafted for military service and headed for training camp encountered a segregated army, but one that also served as a site of social and political activism reflective of the powerful symbolic meanings ascribed to African American soldiers. Black troops, fully cognizant of the discriminatory nature of their treatment and how it contradicted the supposed democratic objectives of the United States in the war, therefore could not escape being drawn into the "race question." This did not mean, however, that it defined their training experience. Entering the army with democratic ideals and aspirations, many black soldiers approached their service as a potentially transformative opportunity and therefore took advantage of the benefits before them, however limited or racially circumscribed they may have been. The battle lines in African Americans' war for democracy had been drawn. Black soldiers, before even setting foot on European soil, found themselves in the trenches.

WHEN CONFRONTED WITH THE question of African American soldiers in the army, the War Department found answers hard to come by. The army was an institution steeped in traditions of white supremacy, a reality war planners remained well aware of as they grappled with how best to employ black troops. Instituting policies that promoted full equality for African American servicemen would create a furor among white soldiers and officers, many of whom came from the South. The torpedoed promotion of Charles Young illustrated the depths to which racial intolerance undergirded American military culture. At the same time, openly endorsing the marginalization of black troops and officers not only would contradict the supposed democratic motivations behind the nation's entry into the war but would also more hauntingly provoke potential racial unrest, which the military, in the wake of the East St. Louis and Houston mayhem, hoped to avoid at all costs. Moreover, the army *needed* African Americans and could not afford to disregard this vital source of manpower.

This placed Secretary of War Newton Baker in a precarious position. Baker embodied the contradictions of most white progressives when it came to matters of race and questions of African American social and political advancement. He acknowledged the importance of incorporating African Americans into the nation's war effort but only within the ideological and structural framework of Jim Crow. Informed by Progressive Era notions of social efficiency, the former Cleveland mayor pragmatically accepted a racially segregated military as the best way to avoid clashes between white and black soldiers that could undermine the pace of the war mobilization effort and hamper the effectiveness of the army. He therefore attempted to walk the fine line between addressing the demands of African Americans for fair treatment and preserving the white supremacist customs and hierarchies of the army. Baker could point to his support for the Des Moines officers' training camp, his dismay at the forced retirement of Colonel Charles Young, and his success at persuading Woodrow Wilson to commute the sentences of ten of the remaining sixteen soldiers scheduled for execution for their involvement in the Houston rebellion.[7] Conversely, he knew the true power of the army rested with its officers on the ground and made little effort to encroach upon their autonomy to run their units as they saw fit. On August 17, 1917, Baker wrote to Woodrow Wilson, "In general I have a feeling that this is not the time to raise the race issue question and I am trying to preserve the custom of the Army."[8] Such a commitment did not bode well for African American servicemen.

With the Des Moines officers' training camp under way and the employment of most African American draftees for labor purposes a foregone conclusion, arguably the most vexing question facing Baker as war mobilization proceeded concerned the use and organization of black combat soldiers into the army. The Buffalo Soldiers of the Twenty-fourth and Twenty-fifth Infantries and the Ninth and Tenth Calvary Regiments represented the most experienced and combat-ready collection of black troops at the army's disposal.[9] Baker had personal familiarity with the Tenth Cavalry and Twenty-fourth Infantry because of their participation in the 1916 "punitive expedition" in Mexico, which he authorized. Moreover, they held deep historical and symbolic meaning for black people as embodiments of African American citizenship, manhood, and martial heroism. These considerations did not factor into the decision of the War Department to redeploy the African American regulars for garrison duty in Hawaii, the Philippines, and along the Mexican border throughout the duration of the war. They would not see combat service in France. With their history of challenging white supremacy in Texas and throughout the southwest, the last thing the army needed was the burden of incorporating battle-hardened and racially conscious African American soldiers into the American Expeditionary Forces.[10] Many ultimately did serve in the wartime American army via the Des Moines officers' training camp and transfers to various African American units, both combat and noncombat, as noncommissioned officers. Nevertheless, the army's decision foreshadowed a consistent willingness to put the racial status quo ahead of sound military logic.[11]

Despite this setback, African Americans still fully expected that their men would be represented on the front lines. African American political leaders and newspaper editors demanded that black soldiers receive the opportunity to fight, prove their manhood, and demonstrate the patriotic valor of the race. "The Race throughout the country has made up its mind to one thing," the *Chicago Defender* declared, "and this is the men drafted, if called into the service of the country, must be called into the army and not to farm."[12] James Weldon Johnson appreciated the fact that, "some time ago," Newton Baker had "said some complimentary things about the Negro's record as a soldier" but emphasized that "what we want is the practical recognition of those qualities."[13]

The War Department implicitly acknowledged the military and political impossibility of assigning every African American draftee for labor duties and thus began floating various ideas for establishing combat units composed of black men procured through the Selective Service System. One option proposed the creation of sixteen black infantry regiments dispersed to various training camps. Incorporating these hypothetical units into divisions containing white regiments was out of the question, and so the idea of an exclusively black combat division, comprising conscripts and the Des Moines officers, gained momentum within the War Department and Army War College.[14] The aftershocks of the Houston cataclysm, however, empowered southern politicians to argue against placing guns in the hands of black men. By October 1917 the War Department had yet to reach a clear decision on the creation of a separate combat division of black draftees and how it should be constituted.

The additional month of training for African American officer candidates bought the military extra time to assemble the conscript division. Having already delayed the African American draft call and facing increased pressure from the black press and civil rights advocates, Baker signed off on the creation of one black combat organization, officially designated the Ninety-second Division, on November 29, 1917. The War Department selected Charles Ballou to serve as major general on the basis of his five years of past duty with the Twenty-fourth Infantry and recent command of the Des Moines officers' camp. The division crossed regional boundaries and brought together black men from throughout the country; the 365th Infantry Regiment contained drafted men predominantly from Texas and Oklahoma, the 366th from Alabama, the 367th from New York, and the 368th from Tennessee, Pennsylvania, and Maryland.[15] The War Department assigned the graduates of the Des Moines camp to the Ninety-second, while white officers, many with experience in the black Regular Army regiments, completed the division's command hierarchy.[16]

It was a victory but a hollow one. The military had demonstrated its reluctance to having African American men bear arms, and now black draftees would serve in a Jim Crow division. It would have black officers, but racial policy limited their possibilities for promotion and ensured that white men always outranked them.[17] From its birth, the Ninety-second Division bore the mark of political concession.

This elevated the importance of the African American National Guard. On the eve of American entrance into the war, upward of five thousand African Americans served in various National Guard units, almost exclusively located in the North and Midwest. The Eighth Illinois National Guard, based in Chicago, had a rich historical legacy, with many of its veterans having served in the Spanish-Cuban-American War and most recently in the Southwest in 1916. Most significantly, the Eighth's officer corps and commanding colonel, Franklin Dennison, were black, distinguishing it from other African American National Guard regiments. The men of the Eighth and Chicago's black community took tremendous pride in this fact. The New York Fifteenth National Guard, organized in 1916 and led by Colonel William Hayward, a white native New Yorker, quickly came to rival the Eighth Illinois in notoriety. By the spring of 1917, the regiment had reached full wartime strength, fueled by a strong response from the Harlem community and the publicity generated by its world-class band, led by the acclaimed ragtime conductor James Reese Europe. The six-hundred-man-strong Washington, D.C., First Separate Battalion was federalized on March 25, 1917, and had the distinction of being deployed to protect vital facilities around the nation's capital against potential sabotage following Woodrow Wilson's declaration of war.[18] Other black militia organizations included Company L of the Sixth Massachusetts Regiment, the Ninth Ohio Battalion, the Maryland First Separate Company, Company G of the Tennessee National Guard, and the First Separate Company from Connecticut. All eight black National Guard units quickly secured their required number of enlistees, reflecting a strong spirit of civic obligation among many African Americans eager to serve their country.

Rayford Logan was determined to fight for democracy. Born and raised in Washington, D.C., he attended the prestigious M Street High School, where he took French classes from Carter G. Woodson and Jessie Fauset. After graduating, he spent a year at the University of Pittsburgh before transferring to Williams College, located at the foothills of the Berkshire Mountains in western Massachusetts. In April 1917 Logan, who had served four years in his high school Cadet Corps, was just months away from receiving his degree in history when the United States entered the war. "War fever was high at Williams," Logan remembered in his unpublished autobiography. He participated in the campus Reserve Officers Training Corps, but despite his prior training was appointed only to the rank of corporal, a disappointment Logan described as his "first foretaste of my bitter experiences in the Army." He badly wanted to attend the Des Moines officers' camp, but at twenty years and nine months, fell short of the age requirement. Like Charles Houston and Victor Daly, Logan could have tried to enroll regardless, but received word that if he left Williams early he risked not receiving his diploma. He stayed and, on June 25, took the stage as one of three seniors to speak at the Class of 1917 commencement ceremony. He titled his address "The Consent of the Governed," referring to a line in Woodrow Wilson's January 22, 1917, "Peace without Victory" speech.[19] Logan boldly challenged the premise of Wilson's claim, pointing out that "this country has the problem of woman suffrage just as England had, has labor questions almost as menacing as those in Germany and Russia, and finally, has the problem of a subject people, a race governed without its consent." He provided examples of racial progress to argue why African Americans were worthy of full political rights, challenged his fellow graduates to help solve the race question, and asserted that, in the present crisis, black people would do their part in the "battle of democracy." "In spite of opposition by the government," Logan exhorted, "in spite of German plots to incite rebellion, the Negroes almost to a man, while not forgetting their grievances, have looked forward to defend the only flag they have known, a flag hollowed by the blood of the black man from Boston Commons to Carrizal."[20] His moving address beat out the other two orations for top prize. The patriotic spirit and determined, yet critical, belief in democracy internalized by many black people to whom Logan gave voice likewise shaped his decision to fight in the war. "Carried away by my own eloquence," he recalled, "I enlisted on July 10, 1917, as a buck private in the First Separate Battalion of District Columbia National Guards."[21]

Patriotism and civic obligation formed only part of the reason why black men volunteered for service in the black National Guard. Just as, if not more, important was the spirit of racial pride, camaraderie, and male bonding the black militias promoted. These were exclusive groups, in many ways mirroring African American fraternal societies, like the Elks and Freemasons. Similar to these organizations, the black National Guard, in equating manhood with discipline, respectability, and leadership, nurtured both the race and the gender consciousness of their members.[22] Moreover, they had a significant communal importance. The *Chicago Defender* featured regular stories of the Eighth Illinois, just as the *New York Age* did with the Fifteenth and the *Cleveland Advocate* did with the Ohio Ninth Separate Battalion. The lure of the New York Fifteenth National Guard enticed Harlem native Arthur Davis to enlist along with three of his brothers. Davis had previously evaded the draft, but he knew that "to be a somebody, you had to belong to the 15th Infantry or jealously look at them in uniform. . . . So, to be a somebody, I joined up."[23] Twenty-nine-year-old Horace Pippin, a part-time coal yard worker, furniture packer, and iron molder, traveled the roughly seventy miles south from his hometown of Goshen, New York, to volunteer for service in Company K of the 369th as well. "I liked and stayed with it all through the big war," he remembered. "I did not care for any others, for every man in that co. were a man."[24] Membership in the black militias, with their rich history, functioned as a marker of social status and respectable manhood.

This is why Harry Haywood chose to join the Eighth Illinois. Born Harry Hall in Omaha, Nebraska, Harry grew up listening to his father's stories of black troops who gave their life for freedom in the Civil War and the legendary "Buffalo Soldiers." A picture of the Twenty-fifth Infantry and the Tenth Cavalry at San Juan Hill prominently adorned a wall in their living room. Harry and his family were forced to flee Omaha in 1913 after a gang of Irish immigrants attacked his father, demanding that he leave town or face even more dire consequences. The family relocated to Minneapolis and later to Chicago in 1915, where Harry got a job as a busboy. As he settled into big-city life, Harry befriended several veterans of the Eighth Illinois National Guard, who captivated him with their tales of service along the Mexican border in support of the 1916 "punitive expedition." In early 1917, at the age of nineteen, Harry enlisted in the regiment. The fact that the Eighth Illinois was "officered by Blacks from the colonel on down (many of them veterans of the four Black Regular Army regiments)" and possessed "a high esprit de corps which emphasized racial solidarity" gave him a "feeling of pride." Patriotism and the opportunity for wartime adventure were secondary to the privilege of being part of a race-conscious organization made up of the best of black manhood. "I didn't regard it just as a part of a U.S. Army unit," Harry reflected, "but as some sort of a big social club of fellow race-men."[25]

Enlistment in the National Guard represented a significant individual opportunity for many black men but also a chance to channel their democratic sensibilities into a broader collective struggle for racial progress. An African American lieutenant, also of the Eighth Illinois, related to the *Cleveland Advocate* his response to a fellow soldier, when asked why he joined the army despite being over the maximum draft age. "I told him I was fighting because I know the meaning of democracy and envy it." The soldier continued, "I told him that millions of Americans fought for four years for us Negroes to get it, and now it was only right that we should fight for all we were worth to help other people get the same thing. I told him that now is our opportunity to prove what we can do." The war was about much more than individual valor; the manhood of the race, its political status, and the future of democracy were at stake. "If we can't fight and die in this war just as bravely as white men," he proclaimed, "then we don't deserve an equality with white men, and after the war we had better go back home and forget about it all."[26] For African American guardsmen such as this, obligation to the nation and obligation to the race went hand in hand.

Having agreed to create the Ninety-second Division, the War Department hesitated to establish an additional African American combat force. But it faced yet another dilemma. The white National Guard units had been among the first collection of men organized into combat divisions, federalized as a result of the 1916 National Defense Act.[27] Not utilizing the African American National Guard would surely incite outrage from black social and political leaders. In a November 1917 memorandum to Chief of Staff Tasker Bliss, the Army War College presented a convenient solution. It suggested maintaining the Ninety-second Division at maximum strength for the duration of the war and not pulling any more African American combatants from the draft until absolutely necessary. Concerning the African American National Guard, the memo recommended the creation of a provisional division: two infantry brigades, one composed of the New York Fifteenth and the Eighth Illinois, and the second composed of the undersized District of Columbia, Ohio, Tennessee, Massachusetts, Connecticut, and Maryland National Guard units and a South Carolina regiment of draftees. In order to alleviate any domestic friction, the War College urged sending the two brigades to France as soon as possible for training as replacement troops.[28] The National Guard units were then organized into regiments—the New York Fifteenth became the 369th Infantry Regiment, the Eighth Illinois became the 370th Infantry Regiment, the remaining guard units were combined to form the 372nd Infantry Regiment, and the still unorganized regiment of South Carolina conscripts became the 371st Infantry Regiment. On January 2, 1918, for administrative purposes, these troops officially became the Ninety-third Division (Provisional), the last numerical division assembled for the American Expeditionary Force (AEF).[29]

The "race question," as the decision-making processes regarding the Ninety-second and Ninety-third Divisions demonstrated, proved extremely challenging for the War Department and its leadership to grasp, much less to solve. For all their efforts at diffusing possible racial strife, American war planners knew very well that their policies had the real potential of adversely affecting the morale of black soldiers and sparking conflict. Newton Baker and the War Department lacked confidence in their balancing act of maintaining white supremacy, while outwardly professing equality of opportunity for black troops. Without the cooperation of African American leaders and white race advocates, the "race question" would continue to stump army officials and limit their ability to establish any semblance of military effectiveness. This provided an opening for a number of individuals, professing their expertise with the "race question," to gain favor with the American government and engage in efforts to shape from within the direction of its policies concerning African American soldiers, and black people more broadly.

EMMETT J. SCOTT BECAME THE most influential black person in Washington, D.C., during the war. Educated at Howard University, Scott served as Booker T. Washington's personal secretary at the Tuskegee Institute until the Wizard's death in 1915. Scott was diligent, moderate, and nonconfrontational; Newton Baker could not have asked for an individual better suited to address the growing apprehensions of intelligence officials regarding potential black unrest and susceptibility to German propaganda. He appointed Scott as his special assistant on October 5, 1917, following an August 31 meeting with Tuskegee president Robert Russa Moton and Chicago philanthropist Julius Rosenwald, where they discussed "the need and necessity of having in the War Department a colored man in touch with Northern and Southern white people and colored people, who could advise whenever delicate questions arose affecting the interests of the colored people of the United States."[30] While longtime rivals such as W. E. B. Du Bois and William Monroe Trotter viewed the decision with skepticism, much of the black press praised Scott's selection. The *Cleveland Advocate* hailed Scott as "every inch a man," with "every fibre of his anatomy . . . inoculated with race loyalty," while the *Richmond Planet* exclaimed, "When Secretary of War Baker gave Hon. Emmett J. Scott an appointment in Washington, he did about the best thing he could have done."[31]

In his role as confidential adviser, Scott assumed responsibility for addressing all issues relating to African Americans and the war effort. This mammoth and wholly unrealistic task consisted of settling complaints of racial discrimination by black draftees and soldiers, as well as fostering African American enthusiasm, both within and outside of the military. Assembling a staff of loyal assistants and secretaries, Scott worked directly with various government agencies, including George Creel's powerful Committee on Public Information.[32] Scott reveled in the stature afforded by his new position, upholding himself as a testament to the government's commitment to racial equality and fairness for African American servicemen. He approached his work seriously and took pride in the modest accomplishments achieved through his office. His role in the War Department, however, remained largely symbolic and was used by the government to boost the fragile patriotic spirits of African Americans, as opposed to truly addressing their concerns.

While Scott roamed the corridors of the War Department, Walter Loving, the Military Intelligence Bureau's most prized African American agent, worked in the trenches of African American social and political wartime discontent. Loving was a soldier and approached his position as such. He had joined the Twenty-fourth Infantry in 1893 and received an honorable discharge in 1901. He subsequently served as a bandmaster of the Philippines Constabulary Band, achieving the rank of major.[33] After unsuccessfully applying for a commission to command black volunteers when the United States entered the war, Loving accepted an assignment with the MIB in October 1917 for the purpose of monitoring African American loyalty and, specifically, the morale of African American soldiers. Loving served as the MIB's first line of defense against the possibility of racial turmoil within the military, alerting his superiors to instances of discrimination that did or potentially could push African American troops past their limits of toleration. His presence seemed ubiquitous, as he kept his finger on the pulse of African American's political sentiments and activities throughout the country, in the process earning the complete trust of white military officials.[34] "I am most loyal to the race with which I am identified," Loving declared in a November 1917 memorandum, "but not to the extent that I would see the blood of thousands of American soldiers shed upon a foreign battlefield, before I would consent to lend my assistance either by deed or pen to help win the struggle."[35] While Loving did not hide his racial allegiances and commitment to African American social advancement, he firmly believed in placing American nationalism and, in his case, military obligation before political agitation. Loyalty to race did not supersede loyalty to nation.

In May 1918 a threat to Loving's privileged position within the MIB appeared in the form of Joel Spingarn. Health issues prevented Spingarn from receiving an overseas officer's commission, so the former NAACP chairman instead opted for a position with the MIB and an opportunity to influence government racial policy. Upon reporting for duty on May 27, 1918, he quickly laid out an ambitious self-formulated "programme for work in Negro subversion."[36] His first effort along these lines entailed proposing a conference of major black newspaper editors and race spokesmen. Its goal was to alleviate any perceptions of African American disloyalty and to establish a unified patriotic front for shaping, in Emmett Scott's words, "Negro public opinion."[37] While Spingarn did the organizational legwork, Scott presided over the conference, held in Washington, D.C., from June 19 to 21, 1918. Thirty-one editors and representative race men listened to speeches from Baker, George Creel, Assistant Secretary of the Navy Franklin D. Roosevelt, and several other American and French military and government officials. The attendees vented their frustrations and endorsed a general statement drafted by W. E. B. Du Bois calling for the elimination of lynching, Jim Crow in public travel, and discrimination against government employees, while professing their loyalty to the government and support for the war effort.[38]

Along with promoting African American patriotism, Spingarn prodded the government to address the scourge of lynching, the most debilitating influence on black morale.[39] On June 6, 1918, Spingarn testified before the House of Representatives Committee on the Judiciary to push for passage of the Dyer antilynching bill as a wartime measure.[40] His agitation made inroads within the War Department, as Secretary of War Baker, in a July 17 letter, encouraged Woodrow Wilson to openly declare "that military necessity, no less than justice and humanity, demands the immediate cessation of lynching."[41] The president responded on July 26 with a carefully crafted public statement that, while denouncing mob violence, made no specific mention of African Americans, an omission designed not to enrage his fragile southern support base.[42] Spingarn and the black press hailed Wilson's words as a potential turning point in the battle against lynching. The next day, July 27, a white mob killed Gene Brown in the small town of Benhur, Texas.

Needing a team of intelligent, patriotic, and trustworthy colleagues, Spingarn solicited Thomas Montgomery Gregory to join him in his work on "Negro subversion." Spingarn considered Gregory a good friend, as the two had worked closely together in the fight for the Des Moines officers' camp. Gregory was a first lieutenant with the 349th Field Artillery Regiment of the Ninety-second Division at Camp Dix, New Jersey, when he received a letter from Spingarn informing him of the MIB's need for an "Intelligence Officer of ability, discretion and indubitable loyalty for special work in the colored field." "I feel that there is no place where your particular abilities could be of greater service to the Government than in this Branch," Spingarn pressed in his June 4, 1918, note.[43] Gregory submitted an application, was accepted, and got to work the same month. He began by investigating rumors of unrest among African Americans in Washington, D.C., and focused his attention on Emanuel Hewlett, a well-known black lawyer. Hewlett, described by Gregory in a June 29 report as "a radical on race matters," had given a number of "fiery" speeches which aroused concern. Gregory received assurances that Hewlett was nevertheless loyal and "would be careful not to give further cause for any complaint as to his actions or speech." Gregory attributed the rumors of black discontent in the city, centered "in the Georgetown section," to "largely the loose and ignorant talk prevalent among the lower classes."[44]

Along with Gregory, Spingarn recruited another close friend to his exclusive section of the MIB, W. E. B. Du Bois. Spingarn knew that the fifty-year-old Du Bois had little reason to actively seek a position in the War Department, but the lure of an army captaincy might do the trick. Du Bois claimed to be "more than astonished" when he received the offer.[45] The combined pressures of allegiance—to the nation in a time of war, to the race and its advancement, and to his most trusted confidant—prompted Du Bois to accept Spingarn's invitation. White intelligence officers within the MIB expressed deep concern over the possible trouble-making presence of the outspoken *Crisis* editor, prompting a June 8 statement from Spingarn to MIB head Colonel Marlborough Churchill assuring him of Du Bois's cooperation and intentions to "make his paper an organ of patriotic propaganda."[46]

The following month, not coincidentally, "Close Ranks" appeared front and center in the opening editorial section of the *Crisis*. "This is the crisis of the world," it began. In succinctly direct prose, Du Bois presented the stakes involved in the war and their direct relation to the future of African Americans and other people of African descent. "We of the colored race have no ordinary interest in the outcome. That which the German power represents today spells death to the aspirations of Negroes and all darker races for equality, freedom and democracy." He then offered his prescribed course of action. "Let us not hesitate," Du Bois implored. "Let us, while this war lasts, forget our special grievances and close our ranks shoulder to shoulder with our own white fellow citizens and the allied nations that are fighting for democracy. We make no ordinary sacrifice, but we make it gladly and willingly with our eyes lifted to the hills."[47]

"Close Ranks" unleashed a firestorm of controversy across the African American political spectrum. Young radicals like A. Philip Randolph and Chandler Owen of the *Messenger* lampooned Du Bois, while the influential Washington, D.C., branch of the NAACP openly revolted against the editorial and demanded an explanation for Du Bois's apparent conciliation. "DUBOIS' 'SURRENDER' EDITORIAL CAUSES RUMPUS IN N.A.A.C.P.," blared a front-page *Cleveland Advocate* headline.[48] Criticism toward Du Bois only increased when word of his efforts to secure a captaincy became public. Harlem radical Hubert Harrison, in the devastating article "The Descent of Dr. Du Bois," deftly recognized "Close Ranks" as having "a darker and more sinister significance" linked to Du Bois's "being preened" for the military intelligence post. "For these reasons," Harrison wrote, "Du Bois is regarded much in the same way as a knight in the middle ages who had his armor stripped from him, his arms reversed and his spurs hacked off. This ruins him as an influential person among Negroes at this time, alike whether he becomes a captain or remains an editor."[49] Stunned by the outcry, Du Bois attempted to regain the offensive and fiercely defended himself in the next issues of the *Crisis*. The situation only grew more contentious when Du Bois refused to resign his editorship and requested the NAACP supplement his military salary in the event he did receive the commission, prompting a sharply divided board of directors to vote against Du Bois's accepting the captaincy.[50] What began as an opportunity, filled with grandiosity, to influence the government and demonstrate through African American loyalty the race's fitness for equal citizenship, had rapidly devolved into a miscalculation of epic proportions.

It was not white army officials but, surprisingly, Walter Loving who drove the final nail into the coffin of Du Bois's captaincy and Spingarn's "constructive programme." Perhaps threatened by Spingarn's influence and worried about being overshadowed by Du Bois's towering presence, Loving used the "Close Ranks" controversy to push both men out of the MIB. Hubert Harrison had in fact penned "The Descent of Dr. Du Bois" at the request of Loving, who then used it as evidence for why Du Bois had no future in military intelligence. With Harrison's blistering assessment in hand, Loving wrote to Major Nicolas Biddle of the MIB, "It is my personal opinion that Dr. Du Bois should not be commissioned in the army but that he should continue to edit the Crisis," based on the premise that the uproar caused by "Close Ranks" had seriously damaged his credibility as a race leader. "A man cannot desert overnight the principles he has followed for twenty-five years without incurring the suspicion and mistrust of his people," Loving deftly concluded.[51] Validation from his most valued African American agent provided MIB director Churchill with all the justification necessary to reject Du Bois's captaincy application and, on July 30, terminate Spingarn's "constructive programme," thus bringing an end to his brief but dramatic two-month career as an intelligence officer.

Discussions of "Close Ranks" have overwhelmingly focused on the furor generated by the editorial, Du Bois's angling for the MIB captaincy, and the statement's place in a broader wartime context of African American racial accommodation.[52] Evidence supports the contention that Du Bois crafted "Close Ranks" to gain favor among military intelligence officials as the fate of his commission hung in the balance.[53] Preoccupation with this intrigue, however, has overshadowed the evocative message of the editorial and its candor in striking to the heart of African American opinions about the war and, more broadly, the conflicted nature of African American racial and national identity. The fact that Du Bois, the previously unimpeachable voice of black intellectual militancy, wrote "Close Ranks" in part accounts for the widespread debate it generated. But it was the *words* of the editorial, not solely its author, that made it so explosive at a time when African Americans continued to struggle with their wartime support for a country that cast them as second-class citizens. "Close Ranks" hit such a sensitive nerve because, by polarizing race from nation, it suggested that African Americans had to make a choice between the two.[54] While Du Bois and other similarly pragmatic African Americans may have been able to rationalize such a divorce of their identity, the vast majority of black people, soldiers included, felt no need to sacrifice their sense of self. It was indeed a "damnable dilemma," to use Du Bois's words, exacerbated by the war, but one that African Americans had confronted in the past and would continue to confront in the future.

The actions of Emmett Scott, Walter Loving, Joel Spingarn, Thomas Gregory, and W. E. B. Du Bois and their relationship with the government were not simply cases of political conciliation or co-optation. Black wartime activism spanned a broad ideological and tactical spectrum. These individuals, and others, believed in the transformative potential of the war and the need for African Americans to assert their rightful place in the government's decision-making institutions. The war inspired the optimism of many African Americans and race activists, stoked the fires of their democratic sensibilities, and gave them hope that through patriotic sacrifice reform was indeed possible. Their methods may have been at times elitist and shortsighted. And surely not every recently drafted African American shared the lofty idealism of Du Bois and his visions of a world transformed by the inevitable march of democracy. But many soon-to-be soldiers did approach their service with a strong sense of civic obligation and faith that, on both an individual and a broader collective racial level, participation in the army would change their life for the better. Indeed, the true test of the nation's democratic war ideals would take place not in the halls of the War Department, the pages of black newspapers, or the offices of the NAACP, but in the army's thirty-three training camps and various other army establishments, where African American men, by the thousands, arrived to begin their transformation into citizen-soldiers.

SAMUEL BLOUNT AWOKE AT SEVEN o'clock on the morning of Tuesday, October 30, 1917, to the sound of driving rain and howling wind. The patriotic spirits of the Brooklyn native had been lifted by a send-off celebration for local black draftees the previous night, but now he just wanted to stay in bed. He nevertheless willed himself up and, after a quick breakfast, left with his father to the local induction board. At nine o'clock, Blount, along with twenty-four other men, marched behind a band to the tune of "Over There" toward the Long Island Railroad Freight Yard, where hundreds of additional draftees awaited their departure to Camp Upton, the army's central training facility for the New York metropolitan area. The men crowded into the coaches—Blount secured a seat by a window—and they soon pulled out of the freight yard, as throngs of enthusiastic well-wishers, cheering loudly and waving flags and handkerchiefs, sent them off to war. It was a tranquil, even picturesque three-hour train ride through the countryside of Long Island, marked by scenes of woods, fields, farmhouses, and meadows that would belie the environment Blount witnessed when the conductor finally cried out "Camp Upton! Camp Upton!"[55]

Rain continued to fall. Blount and hundreds of similarly anxious men, with suitcases by their sides or clothes tucked underneath their arms, poured from the trains and were assembled by marshals in the middle of the muddy, unprotected station. "The more I penetrated the camp," Blount recalled, "the better the picture I obtained and stronger became my dislike for my now home-to-be. Everything appeared to be so improvised . . . the streets, the barracks, the warehouse, the stables, repair shops and whatnot." In the face of pelting rain and a cold, driving wind, he plodded to the barracks and his new home. Soaking wet and chilled to the bone, Blount and his fellow soldiers huddled around a furnace in the center of the room. A number of men who had arrived with only the clothes on their backs hung their now drenched garments to dry over the furnace. But when it quickly got too hot, Blount humorously reminisced, "These unfortunate owners were forced to go about with scorched or burnt clothing and some of them were minus a trouser leg, a coat sleeve or had a hole burnt somewhere in something."[56] After a few hours at Camp Upton, Blount must have felt like he had seen enough and longed to be back in his bed in Brooklyn. While Blount's introduction to army life was of course distinct, thousands of other recently drafted black men similarly experienced the physical dislocation and emotional upheavals of being transplanted into what often seemed like a different world.

From the perspective of the army, the military world newly minted African American soldiers entered would, like the civilian world they left behind, remain racially segregated. The War Department rationalized its decision to segregate black and white troops within military cantonments on the overarching necessity of maintaining racial tranquillity and discipline. This policy, however nobly intentioned, created additional complications for the training of black draftees and the organization of the camps in general. For reasons of custom, convenience, and building morale, the military strove to first assign conscripted soldiers to facilities in their home states. A colorblind adherence to this plan would have produced significant majorities of African American draftees at most southern camps. At the same time, many southern racists, from local citizens to state governors, opposed the stationing of African American soldiers in the region altogether.[57] War planners attempted to resolve this problem by mandating that all training camps maintain a "safe" ratio of two white soldiers for every black soldier. This necessitated the arrival of white draftees at southern training camps ahead of black soldiers and then, when the proper ratio had been determined, sending a certain number of African American soldiers from southern states to northern camps in order to maintain racial balance.[58] By the fall of 1917, the military's racial policies had aggravated an already chaotic process.

African American draftees, 83,400 from the delayed September 22 induction, began pouring into training camps and cantonments throughout the fall of 1917, and continued to arrive well into the summer of 1918.[59] Hastily thrown together, the sites reflected their rushed construction. Some camps had the luxury of wooden barracks, whereas others had only canvas tents in which soldiers uncomfortably slept. Discrimination exacerbated these already harsh conditions. Just as in civilian life, the doctrine of separate but equal failed to become a practical reality in wartime training facilities. This was particularly true for the vast majority of African American draftees whom the government had no intention of placing anywhere near the front lines, unless to perform manual labor. Charles Arnold of the 325th Field Signal Battalion stationed at Camp Sherman, Ohio, informed W. E. B. Du Bois in a July 1918 letter he hoped to have published in the *Crisis*, "Some of the Negro drafted men who came to the camp during the week have been quartered in stables which are in close proximity to other stables which are occupied by horses and mules."[60] Charles Williams of the Hampton Institute, who surveyed conditions at training camps for the Committee on Welfare of Negro Troops of the War Time Commission of the Federal Council of Churches, reported that during the winter of 1917–18, black soldiers at Camp Alexander, Virginia, "died like sheep in their tents," because of "insufficient clothing, shortage in supply of overcoats, inadequate bedding, and tents without flooring and oftimes situated in wet places, where ice formed."[61] Exposure to harsh weather conditions also resulted in higher than average influenza rates among African American soldiers as the global pandemic continued to spread.[62] Even the defining moment of a new soldiers' experience—receiving the uniform of the United States Army—was often bitterly disappointing. Instead of new fatigues, black labor troops stationed at Camp Hill in Newport News, Virginia, were given old Civil War–era uniforms left over from the Union army.[63] The discarded uniforms of soldiers at Camp Sevier in Greenville, South Carolina, arrived especially marked for the "current colored draft."[64] Many soldiers did not even receive uniforms, only work overalls, reflecting the army's intention to employ them strictly as laborers.

As drafted black men flooded into training facilities, the War Department continued to ponder the contentious issue of deploying the black National Guard regiments to the South. The War Department's initial plan of sending northern African Americans to southern cantonments stoked the ire of several governors and congressmen. They argued that northern-bred African American soldiers would not conform to southern racial customs, while white southerners would inevitably resort to the only solution they deemed practical to address this problem: violence. South Carolina governor Richard Manning, for example, visited Washington, D.C., for the specific purpose of convincing Baker to reconsider the War Department's policy on the grounds that the black national guardsmen would clash with local white citizens.[65] In July 1917 U.S. senator John Sharp Williams expressed concern at the prospect of the New York Fifteenth being sent to Camp Beauregard, Louisiana, to augment white soldiers of the New York Eighteenth National Guard Division.[66]

It was clear that race would be at the heart of any decision the War Department made regarding where to train the African American National Guard units. "The race question is also involved," William A. Mann, chief of the Militia Bureau, bluntly noted in a July 31, 1917, memo to the adjutant general. "As a matter of policy, it is believed that organizations composed of colored men should be segregated in camps apart from white organizations, and these camps should be located in communities where the race question is not acute." He therefore reasoned that until the military established separate training camp sites for black soldiers, National Guard units should remain in their home states in order to avoid potential friction with racist southerners.[67] Joseph Kuhn, chief of the War College Division, echoed these sentiments in a letter only weeks later to the assistant chief of staff: "It is realized that it would be unwise to send National Guard regiments, composed of colored personnel, outside the States in which they were raised."[68]

Secretary of War Baker, resisting the pressures of southern demagogues, remained committed to stationing northern African American soldiers in the South. The Eighth Illinois departed for Camp Logan in Houston on October 17, 1917. The August rebellion of the Twenty-fourth Infantry had delayed their mobilization, and the regiment stood on edge. Harry Haywood and his comrades "left Chicago in an angry and apprehensive mood which lasted all the way to Texas."[69] The New York Fifteenth arrived at Camp Wadsworth in Spartanburg,

South Carolina, on October 10, and the Ninth Separate Battalion of the Ohio National Guard was sent to Camp Sheridan in Montgomery, Alabama.[70] On Christmas Eve, 1917, Rayford Logan and the Washington, D.C., First Separate Battalion boarded a train and left for Camp Stuart at Newport News, Virginia.[71] For most of these men from the North, they were entering foreign territory.

The fate of the Ninety-second Division still remained undetermined. The very idea of some twenty-five thousand black combat soldiers in one location sent chills down the spines of war planners. Joseph Kuhn, chief of the War College Division, recognized in a July 1917 memo that "there would doubtless be objection if an entire division of colored troops be stationed in any one cantonment, whether North or South."[72] Because of the "impracticability" of assembling the entire division in one training cantonment, in early October 1917 the army recommended, "All colored units will be organized and equipped and then training begun at cantonments where the proportion of white troops to colored troops will be at least three to one." Additionally, black soldiers drafted for the Ninety-second Division would only be trained in northern camps, where racial discrimination was presumed less acute, "thereby reducing the chance of friction between the civil population and the colored troops."[73]

Organizational problems plagued the Ninety-second from its inception. Unlike other combat divisions of the AEF, the Ninety-second never had the opportunity to develop cohesiveness by training as a unit before its departure for France. Heeding Joseph Kuhn's warning, the War Department parceled the division's regiments among seven military training facilities: Camp Dodge (Iowa), Camp Grant (Illinois), Camp Sherman (Ohio), Camp Meade (Maryland), Camp Dix (New Jersey), Camp Upton (New York), and Camp Funston (Kansas). Camp Funston served as the division's headquarters. Remarkably, the various regiments of the Ninety-second would not assemble as a complete division until after the armistice, in France, as it prepared to return to the United States. The actions of the War Department severely curtailed the development of individual morale and a collective divisional identity. Charles Hamilton Houston, who after receiving his commission at Des Moines had been sent to Camp Meade, Maryland, with the 368th Infantry Regiment, reflected, "This policy all but destroyed the efficiency of the 92nd Division from the start."[74]

George Schuyler's time in the Ninety-second was short-lived. Schuyler had grown increasingly disillusioned with the army, and with America itself, throughout his experience at the Fort Des Moines training camp. Suspecting that African American officers were being groomed for failure, he "personally lost interest after the first month."[75] Nevertheless, he accepted his first lieutenant commission and, on November 1, 1917, reported for duty at Fort Dix in New

Jersey. He spent four idle months at Fort Dix, awaiting command of a training battalion of the 153rd Depot Brigade that never arrived. With nothing to do and frustrated by his "disappointing state of affairs," Schuyler "got into the habit of going to the city quite often and I traveled a little swifter pace than I should have." He soon found himself in serious debt. Schuyler received a transfer to the 368th Infantry Regiment at Camp Meade but still remained in urgent need of money. On April 1 he went to Philadelphia, "with the intention of borrowing the amount I needed and returning to Camp the next afternoon." He was unsuccessful and, with limited options, made the desperate decision to seek assistance among old friends in California. Schuyler's plan, by his own admission, "failed miserably." He reached California but, lacking money for return train fare back to Camp Meade, found himself stranded out west for more than two months. A career soldier with a previously stellar record, Schuyler felt ashamed by his evasion of responsibility. "Therefore, on the 1st of July, I wired the Adjutant General of the Army, informing him of my whereabouts and requesting advice." He surrendered himself on July 10 to authorities at Fort MacArthur in San Pedro, California.[76] On August 30, army officials charged Schuyler with being absent without leave.

Court-martial proceedings took place on September 26, 1918, at Camp Meade. Schuyler pled guilty. "This is the first time I have been in any trouble whatsoever since I've been in the service," Schuyler offered in a written statement explaining his actions. The court sentenced the disgraced officer to be dismissed from the army and "confined at hard labor at such place as the reviewing authority may direct for ten (10) years."[77] After an examination of the trial record, the judge advocate at Camp Meade recommended lowering the sentence to five years on the basis of Schuyler's prior service and two honorable discharges with the Twenty-fifth Infantry.[78] Woodrow Wilson further reduced his time to one year following a review by Secretary of War Newton Baker.[79] In early December 1918, Schuyler arrived at the Atlantic Branch United States Disciplinary Barracks on Governor's Island, New York, where he would eventually spend seven months in jail.[80]

This was the darkest secret of George Schuyler's life. He revealed this slice of his past to no one except the black inventor Solomon Harper and his wife, Josephine Cogdell. And even then he told a quite different story. Schuyler, as he recounted to Cogdell years later, had indeed gone to Philadelphia after his transfer to the 368th Infantry Regiment. But, while at the train station and dressed in his full officer uniform, a Greek shoe shiner refused to serve him because of his race. Schuyler, or so he said, reached his breaking point with this final indignity. "I'm a son-of-a-bitch if I serve this goddamn country any longer!" he exclaimed,

Portrait photo of First Lieutenant George Schuyler, taken before he went AWOL, *ca. 1917. Schuyler Family Photograph Collection. Courtesy of the Photographs and Prints Division, Schomburg Center for Research in Black Culture, The New York Public Library, Astor, Lenox and Tilden Foundations.*

and with that deserted the army. After eluding authorities in Chicago, the veteran soldier remained on the lam for three months in San Diego, working as a dishwasher. After hearing that his old regiment from Hawaii intended to station at the city and fearing he might be recognized, only then did he decide to surrender himself to authorities.[81] The court-martial record and other official documents regarding Schuyler's arrest, trial, and imprisonment, including his own statement, make no mention of this version of events. The cause of his AWOL offense is listed as "fast living."[82] While possible, it is highly unlikely, especially considering his guilty plea, that Schuyler would risk further punishment by perjuring himself. What remains clear, however, is the once proud officer's shame regarding this episode and his desire to bury it from all personal and public knowledge.

George Schuyler was unique. The vast majority of African American draftees and officers had a much different training camp experience and shared certain commonalities. Upon arrival, many were initially struck not by the inequality of army policy but by the sight of hundreds of black men from various social backgrounds and walks of life. "Heavens! what a collection and assortment of men," remarked Samuel Blount, who was joined at Camp Upton by an assortment of "rogues, 'pimps,' cut-throats, longshoremen, hod carriers, tramps, thieves, students, professional men, business men and men who were just plain nothing!"[83] Training camp marked a unique moment for black soldiers to experience both the differences and commonalities between themselves and other black men from throughout the country. Walker Jordan described the 351st Field Artillery Company of the Ninety-second Division, stationed at Camp Meade, Maryland, as "most heterogeneously composed, incorporating men from North and South, East and West, and ranging in its educational scope from the occasional illiterate to men fresh from the walls of Brown, Howard and Union Universities and the Philadelphia Academy of Fine Arts, and any number of Normal, Business and High School graduates."[84] "Meeting all types of men of various backgrounds which was an experience I had never confronted" was the highlight of 367th Infantry Regiment soldier Walter Robinson's introduction to military service at Camp Upton.[85] Many servicemen valued the rare opportunity to learn from and interact with black men from various social standings. George Robinson, a student from Virginia Union University, wrote of his training camp experience at Camp Upton, New York, that "it gave me a chance to study different classes which I never realize I would come in contact with."[86] Orville Webb, a volunteer from Tuskegee who was stationed in Columbus, Ohio, at Camp Sherman, observed, "On many things I find very little difference between the educated Negro and the average plantation Negro. Each seems to be equally as jealous and fussy about things which ought not to be taken seriously as the other."[87] Class hierarchies remained and shaped how black soldiers viewed themselves and each other. The "gross ignorance" of black draftees surprised the Atlanta University–educated John Cade, an officer in the 366th Infantry Regiment at Camp Dodge, Iowa.[88] The camp experience, at the same time, often challenged the significance of these divisions.

Just as black soldiers learned about class in army training camps, they also learned about race, and how it differed from region to region. The military's efforts to preserve racial balance resulted in African Americans from different areas of the country being transplanted to northern and southern training cantonments. Camp Grant in Illinois housed the state's own black draft quota, along with black soldiers of the Ninety-second Division and conscripts from North Carolina. At Camp Dodge in Des Moines, black draftees from Iowa trained alongside men from Alabama.[89] The impressions of southern-born black servicemen who arrived at northern and midwestern camps undoubtedly mirrored those of African American migrants who experienced a sense of liberation upon leaving the South. Attempts by the army to replicate Jim Crow challenged romanticized visions of northern racial utopia, but soldiers from the South nevertheless enjoyed a previously unattainable semblance of freedom.

For many transplanted northern black soldiers, conditions in the South shocked their racial sensibilities. They had heard and read stories of life in the South, but seeing and experiencing it for themselves was truly eye-opening. An African American lieutenant, referring to the southern draftees under his command, wrote, "They tell me of conditions out of which they have come that are largely those of slavery. I was disposed not to believe, but others confirmed the facts."[90] Many northern soldiers endured the humiliation of Jim Crow firsthand and did not adjust well. According to Rayford Logan, with the 372nd Regiment in Virginia, "Patterns of racial discrimination in Newport News, Portsmouth, and Norfolk irked most of the colored officers and soldiers."[91] For a group of northern African American servicemen, their experience at Camp Jackson, South Carolina, proved unbearable. "We the negro soldiers from the north are treated like dogs down here," they stated in an anonymous letter. The men told of "sleeping out doors" with insufficient shelter and clothing, being "cursed at every turn we make," and facing the wrath of white officers with the authority to "kill the first nigger that don't do as he is told." "We would like for the war department to transfer us back north if possible," they pleaded, "because we can't stand the treatment here."[92] Harry Haywood and the soldiers of the 370th Infantry Regiment (the former Eighth Illinois) made a pointed effort to be "at their provocative best" and confront southern racism. As they traveled to Camp Logan, the men brazenly challenged Jim Crow and southern codes of racial etiquette, going so far as to vandalize stores practicing segregation, blow kisses to white girls, and taunt local whites into verbal and physical confrontations.[93] The 370th viewed their small acts of resistance and assertions of manhood as retribution for Houston, East St. Louis, and the countless number of racial atrocities black people in the South had endured over the years.

Challenging white supremacy, as Charles A. Tribbett learned, came with potential consequences. Tribbett was an exemplar of racial progress. A native of New Haven, Connecticut, and graduate of Yale University in electrical engineering, he had received a commission as first lieutenant from the Des Moines officers' camp and an assignment with the 367th Infantry at Camp Upton. His time at Camp Upton was cut short when he received a recommendation for training with the embryonic Army Signal Corps Aviation Section, an impressive achievement. On March 1, 1918, while en route to Fort Sill, Oklahoma, as per his orders, Tribbett's train stopped at the town of Chickasha. Apparently alerted to Tribbett's presence, the chief of police and a party of several other white men approached the uniformed black officer and told him to move to the colored section of the Pullman. Tribbett stood silent, collected his thoughts, and responded by saying, "Sir, I have fully decided not to enter your separate coach, but I want you to know that I am entirely at your service." Tribbett offered no resistance as the chief of police placed him under arrest. A number of African Americans in the Jim Crow section witnessed the incident and immediately offered to help Tribbett secure legal representation. The local police took considerable pleasure in their attempt to strip Tribbett of the dignity of his officer status, while other onlookers viewed his boldness as an unpardonable offense of racial protocol. While the police debated how to handle the repercussions of his actions, someone casually threatened, "He will smell like brimstone before he reaches Fort Sil."

Law enforcement officials brought Tribbett before a county judge, who ordered him held on bail of $50.00. Although Tribbett had the money, he opted to remain in jail to protest the injustice of his arrest. After an hour, apparently satisfied he had made his point, Tribbett decided to post bail and spent the night with the Colored Red Cross Ladies of Chickasha. The following morning, on the advice of his attorney, Robert Fortune, he pled guilty, paid a fine of $24.90, and left to resume his military duties at Fort Sill. Emmett Scott referred this seemingly flagrant transgression of federal jurisdiction on the part of the local Chickasha authorities to the Department of Justice, but no immediate action was taken.[94]

Another incident involving an African American officer and the color line sparked what became a defining moment in the contentious history of the Ninety-second Division. The War Department selected Camp Funston in Kansas as headquarters for the division specifically because of its location and laws prohibiting racial discrimination. However, as a border state, many of Kansas's white citizens internalized the Jim Crow customs of their southern brethren. This reality apparently did not dawn on L. E. Mathis, a black sergeant of the 317th Sanitary Train, when he obtained a pass to visit the neighboring town of Manhattan, roughly eight miles from the camp. While attempting to go into the Wareham Theatre, Mathis was barred from entering by the theater owner, who reasoned that the officer's presence would potentially hurt business. Insulted, Mathis complained to Ninety-second Division commanding general Charles Ballou with the expectation of redress.

In response, on March 28, 1918, Ballou issued Bulletin No. 35, outlining in stark terms how he expected the black men under his command to comport themselves. Referring to the offended officer's decision to attend the theater, the bulletin began, "It should be well known to all colored officers and men that no useful purpose is served by such acts as will cause the 'color question' to be raised." "It is not a question of legal rights," Ballou rationalized, "but a question of policy, and any policy that tends to bring about a conflict of races, with its resulting animosities, is prejudicial to the military interest of the 92d Division, and therefore prejudicial to an important interest of the colored race." Despite being within his legal rights to enter the theater, the officer of the Medical Department was, as stated in the bulletin, "guilty of the greater wrong in doing *anything*, no matter how *legally* correct, that will provoke race animosity." As a result, Ballou insisted that the men of the Ninety-second observe some basic rules: "Avoid every situation that can give rise to racial ill-will. Attend quietly and faithfully to your duties, and don't go where your presence is not desired." The bulletin included an ominous threat if this did not occur: "White men made the Division, and they can break it just as easily if it becomes a trouble maker."[95]

Bulletin No. 35 had a devastating impact on the morale of the soldiers of the Ninety-second Division and confidence in their commanding officer. It was a stunning insult to their rights as citizens, their status as soldiers, and their dignity as men. Black soldiers of the 367th Infantry Regiment stationed at Camp Upton, New York, responded with pure anger. They repeatedly tore down the directive whenever it was posted, resulting in their confinement to the base.[96] The volatile atmosphere prompted the respected army general J. Franklin Bell, commander of the Seventy-seventh Division also at Camp Upton, to assemble the regiment for a confidence-boosting speech. "This is the best disciplined, the best spirited, and the best drilled regiment I have had under my command in this cantonment," Bell asserted, "and as long as you are under my command I will see that you get a square deal." Walter Loving of the MIB hoped that other cantonment commanders would follow Bell's example to help alleviate the sting of Bulletin No. 35, "which had such a demoralizing effect upon the morale and spirit of these soldiers as well as the colored people in general."[97] Serious damage had been done.

The blunt tone of Bulletin No. 35, coupled with its not so veiled threat, served as a flashpoint for the black press, civil rights leaders, and ordinary black citizens. In an April 11 letter, NAACP secretary John Shillady demanded immediate clarification from the War Department.[98] African American newspapers throughout the country vehemently protested against the humiliating bulletin and the military's apparent endorsement of racial discrimination. "Will the Negro be made a better soldier by subordinating his manhood rights and catering to prejudiced white Americans who have no respect for him even when in the uniform of 'Uncle Sam,' although ready to die, if necessary, to uphold the honor and good name of the United States?" questioned the *New York Age*.[99]

The *Cleveland Advocate* was much more direct. "General Ballou's order, in effect, is to MAKE THIS DEMOCRACY BUT A DISCRIMINATORY AUTOCRACY," the paper railed. "We cannot bring ourselves to believe that when the government is calling for men—STRONG MEN, BRAVE MEN, LOYAL MEN, HEROIC MEN to help put down barbarous Prussianism that this government will disband army divisions composed of just such men."[100] As such commentary illustrated, the dignity and manhood of black soldiers and, through them, the entire race had been challenged and degraded. Ida B. Wells-Barnett, under the auspices of the Negro Fellowship League, continued to defend the honor and manhood of African American servicemen. Wells-Barnett fired off a scathing letter to Woodrow Wilson, excoriating Ballou and Bulletin No. 35.[101] "No order so vicious or undemocratic has been issued in any armies fighting in Germany," Wells-Barnett exclaimed, and ended her letter with a demand that the president, "Protect American soldiers in Democracy at home before sending them abroad in Democracy's War."[102]

The bulletin, most significantly, galvanized African American citizens in communities across the country to rally and organize in defense of their black soldiers. Representatives of the Citizens' Forum in Kansas City, Kansas, declared in a letter to the War Department, "As American citizens we regard the spirit of this bulletin, not only humiliating and insulting, but unjust and un-American."[103] Groups and individuals such as this used Ballou's directive to demonstrate the loyalty of the race by bringing to light the fundamentally undemocratic actions of the army and the American government. African American pastors read Bulletin No. 35 to their congregations, turning Sunday worship into protest meetings. The fifteen-hundred-member congregation of Zion Baptist Church in Philadelphia, "as an aid to democracy and as an inspiration to the fighting forces," sent a letter of protest to Secretary of War Baker.[104] As they would in future civil rights struggles, black churches functioned as staging grounds and sites of political mobilization.

On April 22, 1918, more than four hundred black New Yorkers filled the Concord Baptist Church in Brooklyn to capacity to voice their indignation. The outspoken Reverend George Frazier Miller of Brooklyn, a contributing editor to the *Messenger* and member of the Socialist Party who was in the midst of a campaign for Congress on the party ticket, presided over the meeting. A twenty-four-year-old Walter White, who had recently moved to New York from Atlanta to begin his career with the NAACP, served as its secretary.[105] NAACP executives Mary White Ovington and John Shillady addressed the crowd, as did George Miller, who declared, "The black man has won many a victory. The negroes saved Roosevelt and his Rough Riders at San Juan Hill. They fought at Carizal. Now they are asked to fight to make the world safe for democracy and still they are denied the privilege of enjoying this democracy right here at home."[106] Miller, never shy to use the pulpit to voice his political beliefs, had previously spoken out against the execution of the thirteen black soldiers involved in the Houston rebellion and opposed the war because of his religious and socialist beliefs.[107] The resolutions adopted from the meeting and sent to Secretary of War Newton Baker, however, were not a statement of opposition to the war but instead constituted a critique of the government's hypocrisy. Describing Ballou's declaration as "the most un-American and un-democratic; the most humiliating, injudicious and unjust, the most potent agency in promoting and fostering the very friction and opposition which the general order was avowedly given to prevent," participants of the mass meeting registered their "righteous protest" and stated their belief that "as our country is the professed champion of a world democracy based upon justice, fellow feeling and equality, that its first and most binding obligation is to safeguard every man within its own domain—black and white alike—and to accord and protect all men in the enjoyment of every proper dignity appertaining to their manhood."[108] At the local level, African Americans demonstrated their mastery of the rhetorical weaponry of democracy and would not let an attack upon black soldiers pass without retaliation.

Beneath the broader rhetoric on manhood and rights Bulletin No. 35 unleashed, the order reflected the tensions between black soldiers and local white citizens in cities adjoining military training camps. As in Houston and Des Moines, relations between local whites and African American troops were often rife with tension, particularly in the South. The chairman of the Operations Branch recommended that, because of white hostility toward black labor troops at Camp Johnston in Florida, the army transfer the black soldiers to a northern cantonment.[109] The combination of white racism and African American rights consciousness fueled by military service led to numerous instances of racial violence involving black soldiers and local whites who objected to their presence.

On October 18, 1917, Joseph B. Saunders returned home to Vicksburg, Mississippi, for the first time in fourteen years. Only four days earlier, the veteran soldier of the Twenty-fifth Infantry had received a second lieutenant commission from the Des Moines officers' training camp. As he stepped off the train, he encountered a group of white soldiers from the 155th Infantry also at the station. "They did not make any attempt to render any military courtesy whatsoever, but that was all right," Saunders accepted. He passed them without a word, but again crossed paths with the soldiers on the street. "[T]hey called me all kinds of names and said I need not look at them for a salute, for I would not get it. I was knocked off the sidewalks on several occasions and then 'cussed.'" Saunders, hoping his ordeal was over, went to the home of his parents. Two police officers soon arrived. Upon the sheriff's orders, they instructed Saunders to remove his uniform and leave town. "I started, at first, to refuse," he recounted, "but when I noticed that a mob was forming to lynch me I decided to leave for fear my parents' house would be burned down." Saunders changed into one of his father's old suits, and escaped through the back door. He traveled to Greenville, where his mother later met him and returned his uniform. He then left for St. Louis to resume his military service.[110] The local *Vicksburg Herald*, while admitting that Saunders's reception "may have been somewhat inhospitable," vigorously refuted the claim he was forced from the city and that a lynch mob threatened his life. The paper, nevertheless, lauded the actions of the local authorities and asserted that "the best and only, sure way of avoiding such race clashes is prevention as far as possible of contact of negro soldiers with Southern whites."[111]

Apparently white soldiers in Vicksburg had not learned their lesson, because the following month another black officer almost lost his life. Lieutenant George W. Lee, a native of Memphis, Tennessee, who received his commission along with Joseph Saunders, was accosted by several white servicemen while walking down the street. Lee's uniform was like a red flag, and the soldiers, according to the *Cleveland Advocate*, "threatened to tear his clothes off if he did not leave the city." Terrified, Lee fled into a local movie theater and hid in the "Colored" section. Outside, an angry crowd of white soldiers promised that when the "dammned nigger came out they were going to take his uniform off him and throw him in the river." Authorities eventually escorted Lee out of the theater.[112]

Hostile white soldiers and civilians often acted as aggressors. But when violence did erupt, it was not always one-sided. Houston had vividly demonstrated that African American soldiers would not passively submit to racial abuse. Although race wars on the scale of Houston did not reoccur, small skirmishes took place with disturbing regularity. On September 24, 1917, African American troops clashed with local white men just outside of Camp Meade, Maryland, after receiving a flurry of racial insults. During the confrontation, the group of white men beat a black soldier with a brick. Approximately twenty black soldiers later returned to seek retribution.[113] The streets of local towns and cities often became theaters of war for African American soldiers and lessons in combat.

The training camp experience of the 369th Infantry Regiment from New York proved to be particularly harrowing. Whites in Spartanburg, South Carolina, including the city's mayor, vigorously protested the stationing of the 369th at nearby Camp Wadsworth to no avail. Upon their arrival, the soldiers of the regiment encountered intense racial abuse, which included, according to acclaimed vocalist and 369th member Noble Sissle, "verbal insults and unwarranted arrests by city police."[114] Tensions soon reached a boiling point. On October 20, 1917, Sissle entered a hotel in downtown Spartanburg to purchase a New York newspaper. Seemingly out of nowhere, the proprietor grabbed Sissle by the neck, knocked his hat off, and uttered, "Damn you and the government too, no nigger can come into my place without taking off his hat." He proceeded to kick Sissle several times, as the stunned soldier attempted to pick his hat up from the floor. After learning of the incident, a number of enraged men from the 369th immediately headed toward the hotel, accompanied by white soldiers of the New York Twelfth National Guard regiment who had witnessed the assault. In this particular case of interracial solidarity between the black and white New York guardsmen, regional and local pride trumped white supremacy. Not a moment too soon, bandleader and officer James Reese Europe arrived on the scene and successfully persuaded the heated group of black and white soldiers to return to camp.[115]

Emotions, however, remained high. The following night a group of black soldiers prepared to storm Spartanburg in retaliation for the steady stream of racial insults. The first combat experience of the 369th appeared destined to occur in the American South, not France. Fearing a replication of Houston, or worse, Colonel Hayward informed Secretary of War Baker of the situation, who dispatched Emmett Scott to the scene. Scott addressed the men of the 369th, some, in his words "with tears streaming down their faces," and encouraged them to bury their frustrations for the good of the race and the reputation of black soldiers. The men grudgingly heeded Scott's advice, a testament to their discipline. In order to diffuse the growing hostilities and avoid a calamity of catastrophic proportions, the War Department, with Scott's approval, pulled the 369th out of Spartanburg on December 2, 1917, after only two weeks of training and hastily shipped the regiment to Camp Whitman, New York, in advance of its embarkation to France.[116]

Southern racism trailed the 369th back to New York. White soldiers of the 167th Infantry Regiment of the Alabama National Guard, also stationed at Camp Whitman, greeted the 369th with racist taunts and slurs. One afternoon, white officer Hamilton Fish learned that the regiment of southern whites intended to attack. Fish informed his soldiers, procured firearms, and along with other officers ordered them to fight back if they were ambushed. At midnight, revolver by his side, Fish convinced three white officers of the Alabama regiment that the men of the 369th stood fully prepared to retaliate and that a racial massacre was not in the best interests of the soldiers and the nation. No violence ensued.[117] After several delays, the 369th departed for France on December 14, 1917, trading one combat zone for another. Without having yet crossed the Atlantic, the 369th was seasoned, having already faced battle in both northern and southern training camps.

The experience of the 369th at Camp Whitman demonstrated how, even in the confines of northern cantonments, racial violence hovered as an always-present possibility. Southern white soldiers took umbrage at the permeability of the color line in the North and black soldiers' receiving even a semblance of equal treatment. Violence between black and white soldiers over access to contested spaces, where the strict regulation of segregation proved impossible, occasionally resembled pitched battles.

A particularly serious confrontation took place at Camp Merritt, New Jersey. The embarkation facility housed, at a given time, upward of fifty thousand white and black soldiers from various parts of the country as they prepared to set sail from Hoboken for service in France. The transitory nature of the camp and its occupants made for volatile racial conditions. The site's YMCA huts were sources of tension, where, as African American YMCA secretary William Lloyd Imes noted in a report to Emmett Scott, "outbursts of friction" occurred with disturbing regularity. Southern white soldiers, unaccustomed to the laxity of Jim Crow in the North, frequently insulted black soldiers who were trying to take advantage of the YMCA's services. On August 16, 1918, Imes stated, a camp YMCA secretary received a threatening message from white soldiers of the 155th Infantry from Mississippi. "You Y.M.C.A. men are paying entirely too much attention to the niggers, and white men are neglected," it read. "Because of this, if it is not corrected by sundown, we are coming to clean this place out." The note bore the signature, "Southern Volunteers."

The next day twenty-five of the self-proclaimed "Southern Volunteers" from the 155th Infantry entered the YMCA hut. They spotted five black soldiers purchasing money orders and writing letters to their loved ones, and promptly assaulted them. Trouble spilled over to the camp barracks. News of the incident spread, and other African American servicemen prepared for a confrontation. The mob of white soldiers continued to roam the camp's buildings, determined to impose segregation by force. Camp Merritt was on the verge of a full-scale riot. One black soldier attacked by the mob responded by cutting a white assailant on the neck in self-defense. Black and white troops continued to clash in the barracks. In the midst of the chaos, shots rang out. Without hesitating to distinguish aggressor from victim, white military police opened fire on the barracks housing black soldiers, killing one man and wounding three others. Military officials quickly moved black and white soldiers to opposite ends of the camp, thus reducing the possibility of further violence. William Imes bitterly reported to Emmett Scott, "All the bullets were of the regular steel-jacket, high-power sort, meant for Germans, not for Americans."[118] Such incidents blurred the meaning of the war for many African American soldiers, as training camps became literal battlefields, and their fellow white soldiers played the role of the Hun.

As the Camp Merritt melee demonstrated, the space and services provided by the Commission on Training Camp Activities (CTCA) often became flash-points of racial conflict. The CTCA was established on April 17, 1917, and chaired by veteran reformer Raymond Fosdick. An extension of war planners' progressive ideals, the CTCA functioned as the military's primary tool for regulating the moral and social behavior of its soldiers. Training camps, from the CTCA's perspective, represented a grand experiment in social engineering. Military officials and social reformers, ensconced in a white middle-class position of privilege, employed various strands of progressive ideology with the goal of promoting order within the army by creating new men, ethnically unhyphenated and morally upstanding. The CTCA's responsibilities entailed providing a wide range of educational, recreational, and religious services in order to occupy soldiers' idle time and prevent potential malfeasance. A host of volunteer social welfare organizations fell under the umbrella of the CTCA, including the YMCA, the YWCA, the Red Cross, the War Camp Community Service (WCCS), and the Knights of Columbus.[119]

The CTCA, like the War Department, viewed Jim Crow as wholly compatible with its conception of social and organizational efficiency. This logic squared with mainstream progressive thought concerning the "race question." Efficiency, however, came at the cost of quality services for black soldiers. By the time African Americans began arriving at training camps in September 1917, the CTCA had already made significant progress in establishing recreational programs and facilities for white soldiers, but Jim Crow equivalents did not exist for black troops. Improvised efforts by the CTCA to accommodate black soldiers resulted in a chronic shortage of "colored only" buildings, inadequate staff, and all-around substandard services. This was reflected in the policy of the Red Cross regarding its convalescent homes. In a memo to the army chief of staff, D. W. Ketcham committed the Red Cross to providing "various forms of amusement, recreation and opportunities for social enjoyment for the benefit of convalescents" and pledged to build separate facilities for black troops with "no discrimination as regards desirability." Ironically, in the very same sentence, Ketcham stated, "The houses may necessarily be smaller and operated on a smaller scale." He confidently asserted, "It is believed that the colored soldiers themselves will prefer to have their own place rather than to mix with the whites," but he revealed his true motives by noting that "the proposed arrangement will avoid friction." His plan received War Department approval.[120] Policies such as this extended beyond the training camps and into neighboring communities. The WCCS, established to promote healthy relations between soldiers and civilian communities, neglected the needs of black troops and local black residents alike.[121] Despite a pledge that the services afforded to African Americans would be equal to those of white soldiers, the CTCA, displaying a paternalistic confidence that it "knew" black people, consistently treated African American enlisted men as social inferiors who needed to be controlled, as opposed to being molded into effective citizen-soldiers.

The YMCA wielded the most influence of all the organizations grouped within the CTCA during the war. The first civilian organization admitted under the banner of the CTCA, the YMCA assumed responsibility for providing a significant amount of the social, educational, recreational, and religious services afforded to American soldiers. Jesse Moorland, whose affiliation with the YMCA began in 1891, held the post of senior secretary of the Colored Work Department. Following American entry into the war and the mobilization of African Americans for duty, Moorland faced the challenges of limited staff, inadequate resources, and disinterest from white YMCA leaders regarding their responsibilities to black soldiers. While the organization recruited 12,971 white secretaries during the war, the number of African Americans stood at a paltry 300.[122] Moorland and his peers in the Colored Work Department nevertheless remained optimistic that they could make a difference and fulfill its commitment to equal services irrespective of race.

Moorland, however, remained very much aware that the YMCA as an organization failed to, in his own words, "fully live up to this ideal resolution."[123] At training camps across the country, YMCA secretaries frequently ignored the needs of black soldiers, and huts established specifically for black soldiers were often of poor quality. After visiting a YMCA tent at Columbus Barracks in Ohio, former Tuskegee student Orville Webb wrote, "Apparently there is quite a bit of prejudice here and the officers in charge have done a lot to increase it. For in the 'Y' and other public places, colored folks are permitted only at the most unfavorable hours."[124] Jesse Moorland acknowledged the existence of widespread discrimination within the YMCA concerning its relationship with black soldiers but maintained that under the circumstances he and his fellow black secretaries did the best they could. Unfortunately, it was not enough for many black soldiers, who naturally began to question the meaning of their service. As one soldier said, "Just as I begin to feel patriotic and clamoring to do my bit, along comes something which makes me feel as no citizen wishes to feel toward his country."[125]

A closer examination of the CTCA's impact on black soldiers reveals a more complex picture than one of blanket discrimination and subsequent civic disillusionment. Many African Americans had positive recollections of their training camp experience, in spite of racial segregation, abuse, and unequal distribution of services. The Anglo-Saxon Protestant background of most CTCA officials made working with soldiers from various ethnic, religious, and racial backgrounds a challenge. But their program, as a whole, positively affected American soldiers, including black troops.[126] For working-class black soldiers from poor, rural areas of the South, the medical, recreational, and educational services provided by the YMCA and other organizations under the umbrella of the CTCA were greatly welcomed and significantly improved the quality of their lives. Middle-class black troops often relished similar opportunities as well. For these soldiers, institutionalized discrimination failed to diminish the very real benefits of camp life, suggesting that racism cannot function as the sole interpretive framework for understanding how African American soldiers internalized the meaning of their service and ultimately its memory.[127]

Many southern black trainees pointed to health care as a much-appreciated aspect of their camp experience. African Americans, particularly from the South, suffered disproportionately higher rates of malnutrition, tuberculosis, and venereal disease.[128] A significant number of the draftees drawn from the region therefore required some form of medical attention upon their arrival to training camp.[129] The treatment they received commonly reflected the dubious racial theories of the Office of the Surgeon General and its doctors. Two white physicians, in a postwar study, blamed a lack of natural resistance for the high infection rate of tuberculosis and other respiratory diseases among African American servicemen, while "difference in ability to control the sexual instinct" were thought to account for divergent rates of venereal disease infection among black and white soldiers. At the same time, medical personal perceived uninfected African American troops as "constitutionally better physiological machines than the white men" because of a more stable nervous system and efficient metabolism, a view that conveniently meshed with the army's decision to employ the majority of black draftees as manual laborers.[130] Such assumptions translated into African American servicemen frequently receiving inferior treatment in comparison to their white counterparts at a time when the influenza pandemic ravaged army training camps in the spring and fall of 1918. Black soldiers had a lower hospital admission rate for influenza infection than white troops, but a higher rate of pneumonia mortality, indicating that inadequate medical care exacerbated the treatable disease.[131] Moreover, the poor conditions black troops endured in many camps and the backbreaking labor they often had to perform made them even more susceptible to life-threatening illness.

Despite these circumstances, in the larger context of the camp experience and the CTCA's recreational program, many black soldiers could proclaim notable improvements in their personal health. Considering that a large body of African American troops had never before received formal medical treatment, the camp services were extremely valued. Veteran Hezekiah Lofland, a farmer before being drafted, stated that while at Camp Humphreys, "through extra treatment, I was greatly improved."[132] Better health resulted from more than solely access to medical services. Although exceptions existed, many black soldiers received three meals a day and ate a relatively balanced calorie-high diet for possibly the first time in their lives.[133] Douglass Baskerville, a farmer from Bracey, Virginia, "came out of service twenty pounds heavier, and felt better."[134] Moreover, an estimated 125,000 black troops participated in YMCA-sponsored physical and recreational programs, increasing their strength and overall health condition through regular calisthenics and sports activities, such as boxing, baseball, and wrestling. These benefits cut across class lines. Chesleigh Franklin, assigned to duty at Camp Lee, Virginia, was a student of Virginia Union University in Richmond and an Alpha Phi Alpha fraternity member. With access to at least basic medical care at his university, Franklin most likely entered the military in much better condition than many of his fellow soldiers who labored alongside him in the 155th Depot Brigade. He nevertheless remarked after the war, "Physically, I enjoyed good health. The outdoor life of the army taught me the value of fresh air and exercise to good health."[135] Willie Anderson Chambers, a native of Pamplin, Virginia, split his time in the army between Camp Upton and Camp Lee. The former farmer, in his words, enjoyed "keeping free from filth and breathing pure air, and many other things that help make a sound body."[136] Clarence Bailey, a Howard University–trained dentist, had a particular appreciation for the health benefits of his service, admitting that the physical effects of his time at Camp Meade were "very good" and that he gained weight.[137] African American soldiers from various backgrounds and life experiences often viewed their time in camp, while not equal to that of white soldiers, as nevertheless positive toward their overall physical improvement.

Countless black soldiers especially valued educational opportunities. Specious intelligence testing, popularized by army-employed psychologists, attributed the lower scores of African Americans to innate mental difference between the races, ignoring the embarrassing fact that illiteracy rates among many white soldiers from the South almost equaled those of black soldiers.[138] A significant number of black men did, however, enter the military lacking the ability to read or, in numerous instances, simply write their name. Army officials estimated the overall percentage of illiterate African American soldiers at 50.6 percent, compared to 21.5 percent for white troops.[139] One black officer observed of the soldiers in his unit, "We have 153 men and among them is one man only who has had any college training (this is the writer). One other has had high school, and only from 15 to 20 have had grammar school education." The poor educational condition of African American draftees was not limited to just those from the South. A black officer who commanded mostly draftees from the Northeast wrote, "The situation really surprised me, especially here in the East where schools and colleges are to be had for the asking."[140] The military saw illiteracy as an embarrassment to the image of the U.S. Army and a potentially debilitating hindrance to the effectiveness of its soldiers.

Many African Americans took advantage of the broad educational program the army, through the CTCA, instituted for its soldiers. The services of the YMCA, in cooperation with the American Library Association, provided illiterate soldiers, black and white, with a rudimentary education. Mandatory classes focused on developing essential reading and writing skills. The YMCA conducted approximately two hundred monthly lectures, attended by some ninety thousand black soldiers.[141] John Cade observed that "within three months" of their arrival at Camp Dodge, Iowa, black draftees from Alabama "were writing letters home."[142] For a number of soldiers with little or no educational base, learning to read and write proved liberating. Jesse Moorland of the YMCA witnessed how "some men, after having learned to write their names, have actually shouted for joy over the new found power which at last had released them from the shackles of an oppressing ignorance."[143] The camp services benefited literate black soldiers as well, allowing them to become more knowledgeable of the technical aspects of warfare. Charles Arnold of the 325th Field Service Battalion, in a letter to W. E. B. Du Bois regarding the conditions of black troops at Camp Sherman, Ohio, reported that no racial discrimination existed at the camp library. "It is a most pleasing and inspiring sight," he wrote, "to see the Negro troops in the library, reading not only magazines and works of fiction but technical books on war tactics, engineering, electricity, radio telegraphy and the like."[144] Combined, the classes, library facilities, and other social programs provided by the CTCA contributed to the educational and mental development of tens of thousands of black soldiers. Peter Beverley, who entered the army with some education, enjoyed his time at Camp Meade and Camp Humphrey. He particularly appreciated the "movies, sight seeing and lectures" offered to the men at camp,

Class of illiterates. African American soldiers of the 165th Depot Brigade at Camp Travis, Texas, receiving a lesson from a black YMCA *secretary. Courtesy of the Kautz Family* YMCA *Archives, University of Minnesota.*

which increased his "knowledge along several lines."[145] Albert Johnson, a self-employed farmer in Prince Edward County, Virginia, who by way of education had nothing more than "3 or 4 sessions," felt the same way. Stationed at Camp Lee the duration of his six months in the army, Johnson "was glad after I went as I learned right smart."[146]

For servicemen like Albert Johnson who tasted their first extensive dose of education, the knowledge they received was life altering. Looking back on his camp experience, Page William West, a farmer from Bridgetown, Virginia, with no prior education, stated, "Mentally it created a more ardent spirit to conquer disadvantages."[147] With access to a broadened world, large numbers of African American soldiers emerged from training camp with a new feeling of pride and self-worth.

With improved health, education, and self-confidence, many African American soldiers saw themselves as better men. The CTCA set out to create new men along the lines of a white late-Victorian conception of manhood rooted in notions of discipline, bravery, controlled aggressiveness, physical prowess, mental fortitude, and high morality. These represented traits that white racists asserted black men inherently lacked the ability to possess. Military service allowed black troops to reconstitute their sense of manhood in such a way that both challenged negative constructions of black masculinity and affirmed their identity as true men.[148] Eules Bracey, a self-described "common laborer" and farmer from La Crosse, Virginia, with no education before his induction, believed that "the mental and physical effects of my camp experience in the United States Army tended to make me a better and more useful man."[149] Time at Camp Lee led Walter Allen of Guinea Mills, Virginia, to state, "I think I am a better man than before the training."[150] The moral reformers of the CTCA would have been quite pleased with the impact of their services on Roy Fleming, who came away from his camp experience "a better man" and "stopped gambling."[151] Educated black soldiers and those with professional backgrounds particularly welcomed the opportunity to validate their manhood as a simultaneous affirmation of their class status. Waverly Lee Crawford, a student at Howard University with aspirations to attend medical school, trained from January to June 1918 at Camp Sherman in Ohio. He reflected, "My training at Camp Sherman made me a better man mentally and physically than before."[152] For these individuals and others, the training camp experience represented a rite of passage into manhood.

Black women played a crucial role in this process. The politics of the war drew notions of black manhood and womanhood even closer together as mutual aspirations for both individual and collective racial advancement. Black women assertively entered the public sphere to profess their commitment to the race, through their aid to African American soldiers and to the nation, by lending their patriotic support for the war effort, and to their gender, by demonstrating that women were essential to victory. In doing so, they revealed how the war created new opportunities for black female social and political engagement. Black women joined with black soldiers to broaden the meaning of democracy. The war and military service may have privileged black men, but African American women made it their war as well.[153]

African American women and their activism provided important emotional and material sustenance to black servicemen as they adjusted to military life. In the case of middle-class black women, their support was tightly bound to a gendered political agenda aimed at using the organizational and ideological space created by the patriotic exigencies of the war to both promote racial uplift and assert the civic value of black women in the public sphere. To this end, national organizations such as the National Association of Colored Women (NACW) and its membership of some fifty thousand women representing various clubs throughout the country transferred private-sphere notions of womanhood to their work on the behalf of African American soldiers. To ensure that black draftees had at minimum basic living necessities when they arrived at their respective training camps, clubwomen knitted everything from caps to socks and put together comfort kits composed of essentials such as soap, toothbrushes, handkerchiefs, drinking cups, paper, pencils, envelopes, needle, thread, and scissors.[154]

Complementing existing clubs, black women created new organizations to address the specific needs facing the African American soldiers of their communities. On May 2, 1917, the Woman's Loyal Union, New York's oldest black women's club, officially became the Women's Auxiliary of the New York Fifteenth National Guard regiment. The group, led by Susan Elizabeth Frazier, had more than one hundred members, who equipped soldiers of the New York Fifteenth with comfort bags.[155] A similar organization existed for the Chicago Eighth Illinois National Guard.[156] African American activists also collaborated across the color line, as in the case of the Circle for Negro War Relief, an organization designed to provide material support for black soldiers and their families. Although established in August 1917 by a white woman, New York reformer Emily Bigelow Hapgood, and having an executive board of prominent white and black men, African American women served as the foundation of the Circle for Negro War Relief and represented its most active participants. The organization quickly established sixty branches across the country within a few months of its creation, providing a host of services.[157] Black women mobilized to assert their place in the public sphere and ensure that black soldiers knew they had not been forgotten.

The relationship between African American women and the various government and social welfare agencies engaged in war work was often contentious. While the government provided opportunities for black women to demonstrate their patriotic fidelity to the nation and to uplift of the race, they consistently confronted an institutional belief that the needs of black soldiers, and black people more broadly, were at best secondary. Alice Dunbar-Nelson, who began her wartime activism with the Circle of Negro War Relief, remained the lone African American field agent for the Woman's Committee of the Council of National Defense. Although the Woman's Committee professed its commitment to fostering patriotism among black women, the singular appointment of Dunbar-Nelson reflected the organization's lack of sincerity. In her capacity as field agent, Dunbar-Nelson conducted an investigation of conditions among black women in eight southern states, where she found multiple networks of self-sustaining black women's war work, the majority functioning independently of white women's activities. Her travels also revealed a dramatic surge in labor activism and union organizing among working-class southern black women, most notably revolving around domestic work.[158] Her position abruptly ended along with the Women's Committee itself, which disbanded in October 1918, thus yielding little in the form of tangible results.[159] Another prominent female African American activist, Mary Church Terrell, worked with the War Camp Community Service, but not until after the signing of the armistice in November 1918. Appointed as director of the Colored Girls and Women's Work Program, the former inaugural president of the NACW in a postwar report exposed the failures of the WCCS, which forced black women at the local level to organize their own activities for black soldiers. The Red Cross treated African American women particularly poorly, explicitly rejecting the volunteer services of black nurses until the fall of 1918, when the influenza pandemic compelled a reconsideration of its policy.[160] While black women provided crucial assistance to black soldiers, they did so while struggling against both racism and sexism.

The YWCA offered the greatest opportunity for women to involve themselves in the government war effort. African American women welcomed the autonomy the YWCA's policy of separate black chapters afforded. However, the fact they still had to operate under the national jurisdiction of the organization and its discriminatory allocation of resources proved a constant hindrance to their effectiveness. Eva Bowles served as executive for colored work in the YWCA throughout the duration of the war and sought to confront this dilemma head on. With a shoestring wartime budget of $200,000, out of a total YWCA fund of $5 million, Bowles coordinated the efforts of black YWCA workers across the country, many with NACW affiliations.[161] By carving out institutional space within the YWCA, Bowles and her colleagues asserted their leadership capabilities. Throughout the war, Bowles struggled to convince white YWCA officials that black women were capable of and, most importantly, ideally suited to addressing the needs of black men in the nation's training cantonments. "Most exasperating of all the prejudices to overcome," Bowles wrote after the war, "was the calm assurance of officials that they, being white men, understood the negro race as no colored women could."[162] She also directly challenged the legitimacy of white women in the arena of interracial social work. "The war has given opportunity to the colored woman to prove her ability for leadership," Bowles perceptively reflected. "She had her chance and she made good. With all the strength of having suffered, she will be able, through the patience born of suffering, to lead the women and girls whom only she can lead. The time is past for white leadership for colored people. As white and colored women, we must understand each other, we must think and work and plan together for upon all of us rests the responsibility of the girlhood of our nation."[163] Cooperation across the color line remained important, but, as Bowles asserted, the war had created momentous social and political opportunities for black women to demonstrate their independence.

Along with supporting African American soldiers, black female activists used the war to prioritize social and moral reform issues specifically concerning black women. Black women working with the YWCA, for example, devoted just as much attention to the "problem of the black girl" as they did to the problem of the African American soldier. Their attempts to alleviate the negative moral, health, and social impacts of the war, migration, and industrial labor on young black women reflected a middle-class ideal of racial and gender uplift characteristic of late nineteenth- and early twentieth-century African American women's club work.[164] At the same time, black female activists provided important services for a much neglected segment of the American populace.

The YWCA's most important contribution to this end was the creation of fifteen hostess houses at various training camps. These functioned as places where soldiers could relax, enjoy entertainment, and socialize with members of the opposite sex. The racial policies of the War Department and the CTCA, however, limited the number of available hostess house facilities and hindered the quality of service black women could reasonably provide. The first hostess house opened in November 1917 at Camp Upton for black troops of the 367th Infantry Regiment. The men of the regiment assisted Executive Hostess Hannah Smith in renovating the facility, a dilapidated, windowless building with a leaky roof, and clearing its surrounding grounds. Facilities at other camps did not open until April 1918, nearly five months after the arrival of most African American troops, and were of similarly poor condition.[165] The hostess houses for black soldiers, as well as the barracks for hostesses, at Camp Pike and Camp Logan were converted barns, open to wind, rain, and snow.[166] Despite these difficulties, black women gritted their teeth and remained committed to their work and its larger political significance. "We are doing all that is possible to help each other overcome the little things that hurt and look forward to the time when real democracy will have reached our land," proclaimed YWCA volunteer May Belcher.[167] The houses played a crucial role in sustaining the morale of black soldiers by providing both a sense of community and interaction with the opposite sex, albeit within a controlled environment.

This spoke to a second purpose of the hostess houses, that of providing a safe space for young black women of local communities. By bringing them into the camps, YWCA workers hoped to shield black women from the potential sexual aggressions of soldiers, dissuade prostitution, and promote a vision of black female respectability and virtue.[168] At Camp Funston, Kansas, more than four thousand black people, including twelve hundred women, used the hostess house in August 1918 alone.[169] Lugenia Burns Hope, wife of Atlanta University president John Hope, praised the hostess house at Camp Upton, remarking, "The hostess house is a great blessing to women and certainly men are more contented when their women are happy."[170] Activists such as Hope and other YWCA secretaries, through their politics of respectability, appropriated the organizational and ideological space created by the war and its focus on the manhood of American soldiers to prioritize the progress of black womanhood as well.

THE INITIAL EXPERIENCES OF African American soldiers revealed the U.S. Army to be a physical and ideological battleground. For the War Department, the mobilization of African American soldiers represented a perplexing question in need of answering, while their very presence constituted a troublesome problem to be managed with as much efficiency as possible. Secretary of War Newton Baker, military officials, and the leaders of wartime civilian agencies viewed the segregation of black soldiers as the ideal solution, but this proved far from perfect. Enduring physical and psychological abuse from both white soldiers and citizens, black servicemen fought a war, often for their very survival, before even setting foot on European soil. They managed to take advantage of the opportunities, however limited, provided in domestic training facilities and received morale-boosting assistance from black female activists. But, if anything, these early experiences of African American servicemen in the wartime army demonstrated that the individual and collective racial aspirations of expanded citizenship rights and democratic opportunity would not easily materialize. As the participation of African American soldiers in the war deepened, the stakes and costs associated with black military service became even higher.

> Today there are thousands of colored boys fighting for the same thing white boys are fighting for, but the question is: Will we get our share? Every mother who has a son, every sister who has a brother, and those who have loved ones fighting for democracy should pray to God that we receive what is due us after the war is over.
>
> —Unnamed African American soldier, 372nd Infantry Regiment

THE HELL OF WAR

African American Soldiers in Labor and Combat

"They are not treating me right," Private Silas Bradshaw declared in a pained June 1918 letter to his former commanding officer. Bradshaw had recently been transferred from Camp Dix, New Jersey, to Camp A. A. Humphreys, Virginia. And, while thousands of American troops were pouring into France, he remained in the United States, laboring in Company C of the 522nd Service Battalion. He was in the South, and life at Camp Humphreys, Bradshaw quickly learned, was far different from life at Camp Dix. The camp's white officers subjected him and other black soldiers to numerous indignities. "We hafter eat in the rain nowhere to wash out cloths and no where to take a bath only the Macomack River no latrine and sleeping in tents with no floor and nothing to sleep under only what we brought with us." His captain was a "hard task master," Bradshaw stated. "He knock one of our men down and cursed him because he was sick and not able to double time and made him chop wood all day." Bradshaw may have entered the army with high expectations, but now he desperately needed help. "If you can do anything for me please do so for I don't want no trouble with these white officers."[1]

Sergeant Matthew Jenkins and Company F of the 370th Infantry Regiment were on the front lines near Mont des Singes when he received orders to move forward with a detachment of thirty-two men and rendezvous with fifty-seven troops of the French 59th Division. Their mission was to capture the "Hindenburg Cave," a much fought-after depot, located along the notorious "Hindenburg Line," that was large enough to hold a regiment of soldiers and substantial caches of ammunition. German commanders had used the cave to plot strategy and plan attacks against Belgium, France, and England. Early in the war French troops had gained control of the cave, only to have the Germans recapture it. It now fell on Jenkins and the black soldiers of the 370th to take it back.[2] Their task would not be easy; German shells had already killed three men en route to their position. But at nine o'clock on the morning of September 19, 150 yards from enemy lines, they attacked. "Shouting, and yelling, and firing our guns at the same time rushing like mad men we went for our objective," Jenkins recalled. Inside the cave, they met 275 Germans, who threw up their hands in surrender, screaming, "Kamrad!, Kamrad! [*sic*]." The men of Jenkins's detachment looked at him for direction. "I told them we did not have time to take prisoners." Nothing more needed to be said, and the men fixed bayonets. "Of course we thought of home, German mustard gas, German torpedoes, ruthless submarine, Belgian horrors, raped women, murdered babies, the desolation of France, atrocities in German Africa—and behind each thrust of the bayonet was the spirit of a wronged civilization."[3] They had taken the cave, but holding it proved to be their greatest challenge. "We remained in the cave for 48 hours without food or water to drink," Jenkins recounted, "and the worst of all we could not get a message back to my regiment until the third day." His company repelled three counterattacks, using the machine guns and ammunition they had seized from their German foes. Losses were heavy, but when reinforcements arrived three days after the initial attack, Jenkins and his company had achieved their objective. "The Germans could not get near the cave. We captured it and we held it."[4] For his heroics, Jenkins received the French Croix de Guerre and the American Distinguished Service Cross.

> Black man fights wid de shovel and de pick—
> Lordy, turn your face on me—
> He never gits no rest 'cause he never gits sick . . .
> Lordy, turn your face on me. . . .[5]

As they labored in France from daybreak to sundown, African American soldiers regularly droned songs such as this. Tens of thousands of black stevedores, engineers, cooks, mechanics, and other service troops constituted the vital, yet often unacknowledged, cogs of the overseas American military effort. They loaded and unloaded ships. They built roads and dams. They dug trenches. They handled dangerous armaments. They buried the rotting corpses of dead soldiers and animals. And they often sang, invoking the field songs that sustained black farmers on plantations in the Deep South, and adapting them to the hardships of war. In these lyrical moments, with their promise of deliverance, army life became just a little more tolerable, the work a little less tedious, the aches and pains a little less agonizing. But African American laborers had no misgivings: this was not what it meant to be a soldier. No wonder some sang a more somber tune:

> I gave myself to Uncle Sam—
> Now I'm not worth a good goddamn—
> I don't want any more France. . . .
> Jesus, I want to go home.[6]

For many African American soldiers, in the United States and in France, as laborers and as combatants, this was war. From their entrance into the army and throughout their training camp experiences, black servicemen had grappled with the personal and larger political meanings of democracy, both to their own lives and to the future of the race. The tangible and intangible opportunities black soldiers reaped from the army, however limited, reinforced a belief that the war represented a transformative individual moment. Race spokesmen and women had thrown their lot with black troops, rallied behind their symbolism, and envisioned an Allied victory, due in no small part to the vital contributions of black servicemen. Indeed, any hopes for change, of convincing the Wilson administration and white America more broadly that African Americans deserved the full rights of citizenship and national belonging, hinged on the performance of black soldiers in the war and the eventual place of their performance in the historical record of American participation. Having fought to assert their place in the U.S. Army, African American soldiers anxiously awaited the chance to demonstrate their valor on the battlefields of France, and to win the democracy they had so longingly strived for. The stakes were high.

African American soldiers and officers, both domestically and in France, fought a war within the war. They struggled to break free from the tenacious grasp of institutionalized racial discrimination. Much to their disappointment, the majority of black servicemen found themselves employed as noncombatants, performing manual labor that blurred the lines between civilian and soldier. Though essential to the war effort, their roles within the army reflected how military officials consciously sought to strip them of the status and dignity of being a soldier. Nevertheless, black noncombatants resisted attempts to marginalize their place in the military. Despite treatment to the contrary, they remained soldiers, held firm to this status, and performed their duty. African American combatants in the Ninety-second and Ninety-third Divisions, while able to stake claim to a warrior tradition of manhood and martial heroism, likewise faced an enemy in the form of institutionalized racism that in many respects proved as resolute as German forces. African American officers, potent symbols of racial leadership and respectable manhood, came under particularly harsh attack. The consequences were real, as the experience of African American servicemen in the Meuse-Argonne Offensive proved to be a moment with profound implications for the place of black soldiers in the history and memory of the war. The efforts of racist white military officials, however, could not fully undermine the numerous acts of bravery and heroism black combatants displayed on the battlefield, and the admiration African Americans at home had for their contribution. African American soldiers, personally and collectively, sacrificed with their sweat and blood for both the nation and the race. They labored and fought for democracy, an ideal that, while holding out the promise of a better day, seemed increasingly elusive and distant as the war dragged on.

FROM THE MOMENT AMERICAN troops began arriving overseas, the War Department intended to keep the vast majority of black soldiers serving in a noncombatant capacity. The implications of this decision became evident as the Ninety-second Division reached its quota, and the second draft registration of September 12, 1917, promised to bring additional black servicemen into the national army by the thousands. The War Department remained committed to only one conscripted African American combat division and saw fit to use the surplus of black draftees for work-related duties. As Colonel E. D. Anderson, chairman of the Operations Branch, wrote in a May 1918 memo, the army believed that with the exception of "the cream of the colored draft," most black men lacked the inherent capability of being effective combat soldiers. "The poorer classes of backwoods negro," Anderson surmised, "has not the mental stamina and moral sturdiness to put him in the line against opposing German troops who consist of men of high average education and thoroughly trained."[7] The racist logic of military officials complemented the actions of draft board personnel, who determined African Americans in disproportionate numbers physically or mentally unfit for combat service, yet healthy enough to be denied exemptions, serve in labor units, and perform the dirtiest work of the war. In justifying this philosophy, Anderson explained, "In these days of conservation, when every rag and bone and tin can is saved, human beings cannot be wasted."[8] The army, however, did not view the average black soldier as a human being but as a material cog in the machinery of war. Unlike for its white drafted men, military officials saw little need to invest time and resources into developing most African Americans into combat troops.[9]

Roughly 170,000 of the 370,000 African Americans drafted for military service remained in the United States, where they performed an assortment of labor duties at training camps throughout the country. Visitors to northeastern sites such as Camp Devens in Massachusetts, embarkation centers like Camp Dix in New Jersey, and Deep South facilities like Camp Travis in Texas would have encountered black draftees, from various backgrounds, constructing buildings, chopping wood, loading ships, hauling materials, and doing all other sorts of manual work. With little prospect of ever seeing combat, they received minimal to no training. Orville Webb, a Tuskegee Institute student who toiled in Camp Sherman, Ohio, for the duration of the war, wrote in his diary, "How long are we to be kept here doing nothing while the countries of Europe are crying to us to train men and send them over to help end the war? Apparently there is some confusion in the direction of the war activities in this country. We have been here almost two months and have not been taught to 'squads right' or 'catch step.' These things I learned in school at Tuskegee."[10]

African American noncombatants in the South felt the brunt of this policy. Southern military camps and installations, reflecting national demographics, housed the largest numbers of black servicemen. The War Department had few qualms about stationing African American labor troops in the South, reasoning that stripped of the prestige—and guns—associated with combat, they posed no real threat to the region's racial hierarchy. In response to a memo concerning the possible relocation of black laborers from Camp Johnston, Florida, and the military's general policy toward noncombat soldiers, Colonel Anderson revealed, "While it is known that the prejudice against colored troops exists more or less in southern states, it is believed, in view of the fact that these men are nothing more than laborers in uniform, that they do not have colored officers and that they come from the state within which they are mobilized, their mobilization and organization in the labor and service battalions at the points now designated should be continued."[11] The perception that the vast majority of black draftees were merely "laborers in uniform" reinforced the military's attempt to replicate the occupational stereotypes and limitations black men faced as civilians within the wartime army. Corporal John L. Jordan of the 154th Depot Brigade stationed at Camp Meade, Maryland, notified the NAACP that he and other black soldiers were "nothing but servants to the white men of the company," forced to clean their barracks, make their bunks, oil their floors, and cook their food.[12]

Many African American labor battalions in the South more closely resembled convict-lease labor gangs as opposed to military units.[13] The War Department reserved noncommissioned officer positions in labor battalions for white men with backgrounds in "handling" African American workers. The *New York Age* received a circular distributed among recruiting stations throughout Florida that read: "Non-Commissioned Officers Wanted. White Men. Married or single.

Experienced in the Handling of Colored Men."[14] Colonel Anderson remarked that, "Colored foremen for colored troops is not logical. A colored man, unless he be one who has been trained as a non-commissioned officer in the Regular Army for a number of years is utterly incapable of handling men of his race." Because African American labor and service units were often quickly sent overseas without extensive training, Anderson asserted, "the white men in such colored battalions must be the class of men who can get work out of colored men."[15] The military therefore granted white officers absolute authority to drive black labor troops to the brink of their physical limitations. Most telling, black men rejected for overseas service and assigned to domestic labor duty regularly did not receive uniforms but instead were provided with blue overalls similar to those of black civilian laborers. Army officials did this in order to distinguish African American noncombatants from white troops who had to perform similar duties and to avoid potential disturbances with local white citizens by denying black labor soldiers the status of the military uniform.[16] "Many do not know why they are in camp and think it a 'chain-gang,'" Edgar Webster of Atlanta University disturbingly observed.[17]

Work conditions were often eerily similar. Without worry of accountability or consequence, white noncommissioned officers used violence as a means to enforce discipline and productivity. On several occasions, Orville Webb witnessed white officers beating African American soldiers, leading him to conclude, "People who labor under the illusion that army life is free from the use of brute force are deceived."[18] Sergeant Bernard Henderson alerted W. E. B. Du Bois to the plight of black stevedore and labor troops at Camp Alexander in Virginia, who were "cursed, kicked and often beaten" by their white noncommissioned officers.[19] Pervasive abuse of this sort sapped many black soldiers of morale and patriotic fervor. Stanley Moore, who served in the 165th Depot Brigade at Camp Travis, Texas, desperately wrote to his sister in September 1918, "I can't say that I like the Army life, it is a hard life to live and they are so mean to the colored boys here. They curse and beat them just like they were dogs and a fellow can't even get sick. Oh! it is an awfully mean place. I will be so glad when they send me away from here."[20]

African American troops rejected for overseas duty endured particularly harsh conditions at Camp Jackson, South Carolina. The complaints from several soldiers sent to Emmett Scott described a camp that resembled a prison farm more than a military facility. "The Lieut and Capt walk about on the drill field with a whip in his hand like the boys were convicts on state farm," one man wrote. He asked Scott to quickly intervene before the abused soldiers took matters into their own hands, emphasizing, "We have stood it just as long as we can."[21] A comrade echoed these sentiments: "We are Negro and are in the army and want to be treated as soldiers and not dogs." He did not sign his name on the letter "for fear they get hold to it."[22] Yet another soldier detailed the malicious behavior of the camp's white officers, writing that they, "even down the Captain beat us with sticks and whip and give the non-commission officers the authority to beat or kill any of us negro that don't do what they say and they will give him a five or ten day furlow for doing so . . . our captain told us that we were not soldiers, that all niggers are made to work." The soldiers indicated they stood prepared to desert if military officials did not immediately investigate their plight. African American servicemen like these resisted being demeaned as "niggers" and treated as less than human. But upholding their manhood and dignity came with tremendous risk. All of the soldiers who wrote to Emmett Scott withheld their names out of fear of punishment from their commanding officers.[23] The most challenging feat faced by thousands of African American labor troops unable to fight on the battlefields of France entailed reclaiming the meaning of their service and its personal significance in the United States.

For many black noncombatants, their domestic travails were only a precursor to their overseas experience as part of the Services of Supply (SOS). This was the official label given to the logistical system of operations that facilitated the movement of people and materiel from various French port cities, through the interior base sections, and ultimately to the combat front.[24] A total of 602,910 men, and an additional 30,593 officers, composed the SOS.[25] An estimated 160,000 African American soldiers sent overseas toiled in the SOS, nearly one-third of all such soldiers.[26] The disproportionate representation of African Americans reflected how the army attempted to link black military service exclusively with labor, as opposed to combat. With sometimes less than one month of training before shipping overseas to France, black SOS troops performed a wide variety of tasks, such as constructing base facilities, delivering mail, building roads, feeding horses and mules, cleaning latrines, salvaging battlefields, and burying the dead. While essential to the war effort, this type of work did not meet the heroic expectations of army life.

Stevedores constituted the largest segment of African American SOS troops and, in many respects, became the black face of the American army. The first African American stevedores were contracted by the army and reached France in June 1917. As America's presence in France increased, so too did the numbers of black stevedores stationed at port cities such as Brest, St. Nazaire, Bordeaux, and Le Havre.[27] At a given time, Brest contained upwards of forty thousand black laborers, a number that swelled during peak shipping times.[28] The first sight of most American troops upon their arrival in France was of African

American stevedores loading and unloading ships, and preparing food, clothing, ammunition, and other crucial supplies for transportation from the port base sections to the front lines.

African American stevedores endured the stigma of inferiority associated with their service. For white soldiers, stevedore work became a wartime racial stereotype, a caricature in the model of the cheerful antebellum slave. The official AEF newspaper, *Stars and Stripes*, regularly featured stories and the occasional cartoon of smiling, singing, hard-working black stevedores, replete with negro dialect and minstrel tropes.[29] In a March 1918 article on the creation of a gardening branch of the Quartermasters Corps, the paper joked, "Negro stevedore regiments will, however, be kept as far removed as possible from the watermelon patches."[30] Even the lowest-ranking white soldier could take comfort in these images, knowing that his place on the racial hierarchy and his sense of whiteness remained secure. Black labor troops, conversely, struggled to reconcile their high aspirations for army life with the cold reality of their present condition. Eighth Illinois chaplain William Braddan remarked that "the most dejected looking men I ever saw in uniform, and the most unsoldierly are the Stevedores. Truly, I would rather be a dog than such a soldier."[31] "I don't want to stagger under heavy boxes," one wistful stevedore lamented. "I want a gun on my shoulder and the opportunity to go to the front."[32]

The physically exhausting conditions African American noncombatants labored under made their plight all the worse. Many stevedores and black SOS troops worked upward of sixteen hours a day, were quartered in substandard housing, and received little opportunity for recreation. This unhealthy environment spiked influenza infection and fatality rates. The commanding officer of the 304th Labor Battalion reported the deaths of ten soldiers in his unit since reaching France in the fall of 1918, six from pneumonia and one from bronchitis.[33] Enduring such conditions, some men undoubtedly wondered if they had in fact entered a second slavery. War veteran Enoch Dunham, who served as a mechanic, was "forced to work rain or shine and a good many times without food." He related an incident where 75 to 100 of the men of his company defied their officers and refused to work as a result of not being fed for several days. The protest resulted in the imprisonment of six of the men. Dunham reflected, "We were doged and cursed and treated worst than prisoners."[34]

The racial hostility of white soldiers and military police made St. Nazaire, Brest, Bordeaux, and other port areas virtual racial battlegrounds. Charles Dawes, the white major of the Seventeenth Engineers and future vice president of the United States under Calvin Coolidge, recalled an all-too-common incident where a "very much intoxicated" Marine policeman was found "beating a

Two African American labor troops at the captured town of Malancourt after the Meuse-Argonne. RG 111-SC 33783. *Courtesy of National Archives and Record Administration, College Park, Md.*

negro" on the docks of St. Nazaire.[35] Charles Green, a white soldier of the Twentieth Engineers, testified before Congress after the war about a gruesome encounter he had working in St. Nazaire. Passing by the morgue, he saw the bodies of two dead black troops "lying on the slab." He asked a soldier on detail what happened to the men. "The nigger killer got them last night," Green learned. "The nigger killer," an MP notorious for his brutality, had shot one of the black servicemen through the eye, and the other through the chest. "Oh, every time he goes on guard, we get some up here," Green was casually informed. Army physicians used the corpses of the two soldiers for medical research.[36] The taxing work African American SOS troops performed went hand in hand with frequent mistreatment and racial terror.

African Americans assigned to one of the thirteen all-black pioneer infantry units confronted some of the most difficult obstacles of all SOS soldiers.[37] Pioneer infantry men labored immediately behind the front lines, building roads, salvaging battlefields, constructing ammunition dumps, and reburying the dead. The units were commanded by white men but did contain noncommissioned black officers. One of these officers was a young aspiring sociologist named Charles Spurgeon Johnson. When the United States entered the war, Johnson had just moved to Chicago, where he studied at the University of Chicago under the mentorship of the famed Robert E. Park. He quickly made a name for himself in social science circles, establishing a research department in the Chicago Urban League and studying the causes of black migration with a grant from the Carnegie Foundation. In June 1917, at the age of twenty-five and, as he remembered, with "no deep hatred of the Germans," he registered for the draft. He was eventually assigned to Camp Grant, Illinois, with the 803rd Pioneer Infantry, made up of black men from Illinois, Minnesota, Iowa, and Wisconsin.[38] After a month of training, the 803rd was shipped overseas to France, where Johnson's leadership and intelligence led to a promotion to regimental sergeant major.[39] It was challenging and oftentimes dangerous work. Despite their proximity to the front, few black pioneer infantry regiments received proper combat training.[40] Robert Stevens of the 801st Pioneer Infantry had a typical experience: "We marched for a couple of week and practice shooting a couple of week then went (shipped out) over seas."[41] They faced the twofold obstacles of racially demeaning labor and work conditions and the possibility of death from German shell and gas attacks.

Unlike other SOS troops, black pioneer infantrymen could at least claim to have been under fire. The army, for example, used black pioneer infantrymen extensively in the fall 1918 Meuse-Argonne offensive.[42] Charles Johnson and the 803rd Battalion dodged incoming artillery for twenty-two consecutive days during the operation, reconstructing damaged roads and performing other monotonous tasks, such as "rescuing and preserving the exposed books in the shattered libraries of wartorn French towns."[43] Alfred Allen arrived in France in January 1918 as part of the 808th Pioneer Infantry. He spent nearly four months on the front lines near Metz, hauling ammunition and cutting barb-wire entanglements, among other perilous duties, and returned home shell-shocked as a result.[44] German shelling and gas attacks killed and injured several African American Pioneer Infantry soldiers, the result of inadequate preparation and a lack of defensive support. J. A. Toliver of the 808th Pioneer Infantry informed W. E. B. Du Bois after the war that his unit survived a gas attack and did not receive instructions on how to use their masks until they were within enemy range.[45] Jerry Marton, also a veteran of the 808th Pioneer Infantry, stated honestly that he was "scared all the time I was there."[46] Although not actual combat, it was nevertheless close enough to provide an affirmation for many African American pioneer infantrymen that they did indeed deserve the title of soldier.

Kathryn Johnson and Addie Hunton, two of only three black women employed with the YMCA overseas before the armistice, empathized with the predicament of black noncombatants. Johnson and Hunton were "new women," embodying transformations in notions of modern womanhood that began at the turn of the century and continued during the war.[47] Johnson graduated from Wilberforce in 1902 and went on to become an accomplished teacher at various institutions. An activist at heart, she served as the first field worker for the NAACP in 1909, organizing new branches throughout the South and West. Staff conflicts within the NAACP led to her departure in 1916, and she subsequently served as associate editor of the *Half-Century* magazine. Johnson followed the war with keen interest and in the spring of 1917 joined the YMCA, hoping to better the lives of black servicemen and further the democratic aspirations of the race.[48] Addie Waites was born in Norfolk, Virginia. In 1893 she married William Alphaeus Hunton, the first director of the YMCA Colored Work Department, and moved to Atlanta. Far from a mere appendage of her husband, Hunton exhibited a strong level of independence and constantly pushed against the boundaries of a woman's proper place in the public sphere. She became an active member of the NACW and YWCA, and contributed articles to several popular African American journals on the unique role of black women in struggles for racial progress. Having traveled with her family to Germany, where she enrolled in classes at Kaiser Wilhelm University, Hunton possessed a global awareness that complemented her race and gender consciousness. Hunton continued to champion the work of her husband after his death in 1916 and leapt at the chance to go overseas with black soldiers as a YMCA secretary when the United States entered the war.[49]

As they did in the United States, social service agencies such as the YMCA had a problematic relationship with black soldiers in France. Paralleling the military's hesitancy to employ African American soldiers for combat duty, the Red Cross and the YMCA restricted the opportunities of black men and women to work overseas. Emmett Scott estimated that only three hundred African American Red Cross nurses reached the French battlefields, forced to provide medical care and convalescence within the confines of a War Department–approved system of racial segregation.[50] The YMCA, with an equally bleak record, employed only sixty black secretaries to meet the needs of some 200,000 African American troops. The lack of black secretaries and the hostility of white secretaries translated into neglect of crucial recreational services. At Is-sur-Tille, a town located approximately fifteen miles north of Dijon, only a single YMCA hut existed for 15,000 black soldiers.[51] The situation was particularly bad at Brest, where the YMCA did not establish a hut for black soldiers until the spring of 1919.[52] Relations between white and black secretaries were often characterized by racial conflict and tension more so than Christian brotherhood. African

Kathryn Johnson. Courtesy of the Kautz Family YMCA *Archives, University of Minnesota.*

American secretary James Wiley took umbrage at white secretaries' assuming credit for his hard work and complained to Director of Colored Work Jesse Moorland, "If this kind of treatment is to be meted out to us Secretaries in France it will kill our spirit and naturally our influence with the men."[53]

In the face of these obstacles, Addie Hunton and Kathryn Johnson committed themselves to alleviating the sting of racial discrimination inflicted upon black soldiers. Throughout the war Johnson and Hunton worked primarily with black stevedores and other SOS troops at St. Nazaire.[54] During their time at the bustling port facility, the two women shouldered the monumental task of attending to more than twenty thousand black soldiers, working most days from nine in the morning to nine at night.[55] They encountered challenges of all sorts, the most striking being the sin of injustice. "The colored women who served overseas had a tremendous strain placed upon their Christian ideals," Johnson wrote.[56]

Addie Hunton. Courtesy of the Kautz Family YMCA *Archives, University of Minnesota.*

Nevertheless, Hunton, Johnson, and their YMCA colleagues provided important benefits to black noncombatants in France. In cooperation with the Army Educational Commission and the American Library Association, they offered rudimentary educational courses for soldiers lacking the ability to read or write. Similar activities took place at other camps housing significant numbers of black noncombatants, like Camp Pontanezen at Brest, where local military officials instituted a program of mandatory education for illiterate troops.[57] Hunton and Johnson spent much of October 1918 tending to black stevedores at St. Nazaire who were ravaged especially hard by the influenza pandemic as a result of their poor living conditions and lack of proper medical treatment.[58] In addition to their company, Hunton and Johnson gave sick men candy, reading materials, oranges, and lemons and, for the gravely ill, their prayers. A soldier stationed in St. Nazaire "desperately sick with 'Flu' in October, 1918" confided in a letter to Addie Hunton, "You and Miss Johnson came with oranges and that most prized thing in all the world at that time—lemons. Oh, how good you did look to me!"[59] Seemingly small acts of kindness made a world of difference for black noncombatants and kept many from completely slipping into a state of despair. And sometimes it was just enough for them to maintain a tenuous grasp on the transformative democratic potential of the war and military service. Inspired by the bravery and resilience of the black noncombatants they got to know so well, Hunton and Johnson acknowledged that "through these men we came into an abiding belief that the colored man was in the war to justify his plea for democracy."[60]

The relationship between Hunton, Johnson, and African American SOS troops highlighted the connection between war-era notions of black womanhood and manhood. While ostensibly framing their service within the bounds of a traditional role of racial motherhood, Hunton and Johnson, by their very presence in France, offered a new vision of modern black womanhood.[61] At the same time, Hunton's and Johnson's race and gender consciousness buttressed the efforts of black noncombatants, stripped by the indignities of labor and white supremacy, to reclaim their sense of manhood. Hunton and Johnson saw it as their responsibility to uphold the self-respect and manhood of black SOS soldiers by transferring a sense of domestic maternalism to France. "True, these are not colored boys we are serving, but what matters that—they are soldiers all, and every lad of them a mother's son."[62] Hunton and Johnson affirmed that black SOS troops were indeed both soldiers and men, not merely "boys" and "niggers" whose sole purpose was to work. Many African American servicemen thus saw and treated Hunton and Johnson as saviors, some even weeping in their presence. Johnson could not forget the profound love black soldiers had for black women war workers, writing, "Their attitude of deep respect, often bordering on worship, toward the colored women who went to France to serve them only deepened this impression."[63] Unable to demonstrate their manhood through traditional means on the battlefield, black noncombatants relished their all too brief moments with Hunton and Johnson, which temporarily reconnected them with their mothers, wives, sisters, and daughters, and provided a reminder of who and what they were fighting for.

While African American noncombatants struggled to redefine what it meant to be a soldier and affirm their contribution to the war effort, African American combatants faced a host of challenges particular to their place and status in the American army. Combat held both personal and political meaning for African American servicemen. For those who envisioned the achievement of full democracy through the demonstration of African American's martial heroism and sacrifice in blood, the estimated thirty-seven thousand soldiers of the

Ninety-second and Ninety-third Divisions carried the hopes and aspirations of a race with them on the battlefield.[64] The weight of their symbolic burden was made even heavier by the policies of the American army and the hostility of white officials, some of whom saw no place for black men in the United States' overseas fighting forces. These combined factors shaped the combat experiences of African American soldiers but did not necessarily define them. In the end, they had a job to do, a duty to perform, and thus focused on demonstrating their competence, bravery, and manhood to the best of their abilities. They adjusted to the harsh life of combat, made more challenging by the ubiquitous presence of race, and attempted to make a name for themselves, all the while cognizant that the record of African American participation in the war would be judged on their service.

THE FATE OF THE NINETY-THIRD Division remained a mystery as late as February 1918. American military officials on both sides of the Atlantic debated how to best utilize the black national guardsmen. The 369th Infantry Regiment arrived in France on December 27, 1917, greeted by snow and freezing temperatures. Instead of heading off for the front, the regiment received orders to proceed from Brest to Camp Coëtquidan at St. Nazaire, where the soldiers performed SOS duties, much to their surprise and dismay. "Our soldiers' trusty Springfield rifles were taken from them," Noble Sissle recalled, "and in their place they were given picks, shovels and each one a pair of hip-length rubber boots."[65] In light of the hostility experienced at Spartanburg and Camp Whitman, the relegation to a glorified labor battalion represented a painful insult. For two months, the 369th laid hundreds of miles of railroad tracks, dug ditches, and waded in the mud of St. Nazaire harbor building docks and dams. Colonel Hayward and other white officers pressured Emmett Scott and the War Department to have the regiment reassigned.[66] The 369th band kept up the morale of the regiment during these trying early days of its experience in France. They would play an uplifting ragtime tune for the men as they trudged off to work at the crack of dawn, and greet them when they returned back to camp at the end of the day, emotionally and physically drained.[67]

After giving serious consideration to utilizing the entire Ninety-third Division as pioneer infantry, the War Department incorporated the 369th, 370th, 371st, and 372nd Infantry Regiments into the French military.[68] France desperately needed fresh troops and, having used African soldiers from Algeria, Morocco, and West Africa since the start of the war, cared little about race. "To meet the need for replacements in their units," AEF general John Pershing wrote in his memoirs, "I consented to send temporarily to the French four colored Infantry regiments of the 93d Division."[69] Assigning the division to the French army allowed Pershing simultaneously to fulfill his pledge to provide France with American combat regiments when the United States entered the war and to free himself from the dilemma of how to use the African American fighting regiments of the provisional Ninety-third. They now became France's problem, an act that cast African American troops as outside the U.S. Army, and, in a symbolic sense, outside of the nation itself.

On March 12, the 369th left for Givry-en-Argonne, a small town in the Champagne section of France, and reported for field training duty with the French Sixteenth Division. The regiment entered its new assignment reenergized but nevertheless seriously underprepared for combat, having wasted precious time that could have been devoted to learning crucial infantry tactics and skills such as artillery and gas defense. Mastering the fundamentals and subtleties of modern warfare became even more challenging for the 369th because of the replacement of its American equipment and weapons with French gear, much of it, especially the rifles, of inferior quality.[70]

The other three regiments of the Ninety-third Division, which reached France in April 1918, experienced a similar sense of dislocation. Harry Haywood and the bulk of the 370th Infantry Regiment stepped off the converted passenger liner the USS *Washington* at Brest on April 22, 1918, exhausted after a turbulent sixteen days at sea. "We were so weak on landing that one-half of the regiment fell out while climbing the hill to the old Napoleon Barracks where we were quartered," Haywood remembered. After the soldiers gathered themselves, the regiment began the long journey to eastern France, traversing almost the entire country on its way to the town of Grandvillars, located in the Vosges region next to the Swiss border. The French Seventy-third Division received the 370th upon its arrival, the first step in a process of incorporation and adjustment into the French army and its customs. "The American equipment with which we had trained was taken away," Haywood wrote, "and we were issued French weapons—rifles, carbines, machine guns, automatic rifles, pistols, helmets, gas masks and knapsacks." With a long-standing admiration for the French, Haywood did not seem to mind, but other soldiers of the regiment took the disconnection from the American army as a personal affront. "The men were greatly chagrinned when they were ordered to turn in their American equipment and were issued French equipment instead," 370th chaplain William Braddan observed. "This man's army certainly doesn't want us, was heard on all sides."[71] Many soldiers in the 371st and 372nd Infantry Regiments of the Ninety-third Division, which reached France in April, shared this sentiment as well. Charles Robinson, a first lieutenant in the 371st, described the French weapons the men of his regiment received as "not as accurate or effective as ours."[72] Even the food rations of the French army, consisting of soup and two quarts of red wine, differed dramatically from those of the AEF. From the guns they wielded down to the food they ate, the black soldiers of the Ninety-third Division had to confront the reality of being in, but not of, the U.S Army.

However, from a military perspective, the training black soldiers in the Ninety-third Division received probably surpassed what they would have otherwise been afforded in the American army. Their French instructors imparted valuable lessons learned from more than three brutal years of combat, such as how to distinguish between various poison attack gasses by smell, how to recognize the sound of different types of explosives, and the best strategies for effectively attacking enemy trench fortifications. The language barrier presented a challenge, but one that African American troops and officers generally approached with patience and an eagerness to overcome. In spite of their marginalization from the American army, black soldiers of the Ninety-third received crucial training that made them better prepared for combat than many of their AEF divisional counterparts.

The Ninety-second Division almost met a similar fate as that of the Ninety-third. Like France, Great Britain clamored for American reinforcements, and the War Department selected the Ninety-second Division for "temporary service and training." However, the British military attaché in Washington, D.C., with direct orders from London, protested the decision. General Pershing, taken aback in light of France's eager reception of the Ninety-third, contacted Marshal Douglas Haig, commander of the British Expeditionary Forces. Expressing his dismay, Pershing wrote in the May 5, 1918, letter, "You will, of course, appreciate my position in this matter, which, in brief, is that these negroes are American citizens. My Government, for reasons which concern itself alone, has decided to organize colored combat divisions and now desires the early dispatch of one of these divisions to France. Naturally I cannot and will not discriminate against these soldiers." He implored Haig to reconsider and "overcome the objections raised by your War Office."[73] On May 13, Minister of War Lord Milner, the former British high commissioner in South Africa and committed white supremacist, offered a reply, bluntly stating, "I am rather hoping that this difficult question may not after all be going to trouble us. . . . I hope this is so, for, as a matter of fact, a good deal of administrative trouble would, I think, necessarily arise if the British Army had to undertake the training of a colored Division. Believe me."[74] Pershing should not have been surprised by this response, being that hard-line imperialists such as Milner composed much of the British War Cabinet and Great Britain had restricted its colonial black South African servicemen from bearing arms on the western front, using them in an exclusively labor capacity.[75] While both were deeply invested in the project of empire building and the exploitation of African peoples, France and Great Britain departed on the employment of black colonials as combat soldiers in the war.[76]

The Ninety-second Division, in the end, remained attached to the American army, with all of its inexperience in warfare, training deficiencies, and racial hostility. The scattered regiments of the Ninety-second Division reached France in June 1918. Samuel Blount and the 367th arrived on June 19 and set up tents in a field just outside of Camp Pontanezen, the main encampment for American soldiers at Brest. His regiment lingered there for three rainy, confusing days, as their rations got lower and lower. "Each day we were somewhat uncertain about the next meal; even water was scarce."[77] On June 22, Blount and the 367th departed Brest and journeyed four days aboard crowded coaches to the Haute-Marne department of the Champagne-Ardenne for field training. His company billeted at the town of La Rochere, "a quaint little village and one of the cleanest we had yet struck in France," while division headquarters were established some twenty miles west at Bourbonne-les-Bains.[78] As the dispersed regiments of the Ninety-second settled into the French countryside, the presence of the white Third Cavalry of the Regular Army at Bourbonne-les-Bains placed the division's commanding officers on alert for possible conflict.[79] Sure enough, the white Texans of the regiment began spreading disparaging rumors about the Ninety-second Division and its black soldiers and officers among the local French population, characterizing them as subhuman and with an insatiable lust for white women.

Already forced to navigate the minefield of race relations, the Ninety-second Division also had to contend with the haphazard training program undertaken by most American divisions in France. The field artillery regiments, for example, lacked essential equipment, and the commanding officers had no advance intelligence on the French geography in order to make necessary adjustments to the training regime. For roughly eight weeks after its arrival, the Ninety-second Division attempted to prepare for war in a climate of racial tension and military unpreparedness.[80]

As the Ninety-second Division struggled to train throughout the summer of 1918, the 369th had already been christened in battle. By mid-April the regiment was conducting selective raids with the French Sixteenth Division west of the Argonne Forest on German positions, gaining valuable experience, as well as the trust of its French commanders. On April 29 the 369th received command of a roughly five-mile stretch of the front, the first assignment of its sort imparted to African American soldiers, and a clear demonstration of the significant divide between French and American usage of black combatants. The French were far from colorblind, as evidenced by their treatment of African colonial troops. But most French military officials, their army stretched to its physical and operational limits after nearly four bloody years, saw making use of thousands of fresh combatants as opposed to managing the "race question" their top priority when it came to the employment of African American soldiers. Thrown into the fray, the 369th quickly became a seasoned unit with a strong regimental identity. By late May, the 370th, 371st, and 372nd had also tasted combat.

With the "race question" preoccupying the minds of the AEF high command, the Ninety-second Division entered the fighting much more hesitantly. After its period of training, the division relocated to the St. Dié sector, a twenty-five-kilometer area located in the Vosges mountain range.[81] Responsible for patrolling and conducting raiding parties, the division saw its first combat activity on August 25 and remained under constant German artillery and gas shellfire throughout the duration of its time in the region. "The sector is supposed to be a quiet sector, but to us it seems far from quiet," opined Samuel Blount, who vividly remembered the first moments of his baptism into trench warfare.[82]

Any lingering romanticized notions of battlefield life quickly vanished when black soldiers experienced their initial immersion into the trenches and the troglodyte life European combatants had experienced for more than three years.[83] "Well the French lived in them and i can live in it to," thought Horace Pippin, who, like most soldiers, gradually adjusted to the cold, cramped, wet, vermin-infested conditions.[84] Trenches averaged five to six feet in depth, and extended in a zigzag pattern to avoid direct German assaults. A well-constructed trench was floored with wooden duckboards, allowing water to drain underneath, but many lacked this amenity. The unremitting French rain led to flooding often several feet deep. Crumbling walls, usually reinforced with sandbags or other improvised materials, required regular maintenance. Support and reserve trenches were modified with latrines, space for provisions, and crude sleeping quarters. The ear-shattering noise of explosives and artillery fire, however, was unrelenting and made rest difficult, as did the squalid air which reeked of mold and rotting bodies. These discomforts paled in comparison to the ubiquitous presence of lice and swarms of rats, whose size and boldness became legendary. Harry Haywood was convinced that "[u]ndoubtedly there were more rats than men; there were hordes of them. Regiments and battalions of rats. They were the largest rats I had ever seen."[85] Presented with a steady buffet of human corpses, trench rats always sought out their next meal, making sleep itself a sometimes frightening prospect. "Should he lie down to sleep these precious little animals scurry over and over his body," Walker Jordan of the Ninety-second Division observed, "smell for his breathing, romp over his face and gnaw assiduously at the toes bursting from over worked hobnails."[86] As black soldiers soon learned, war on the western front lacked both comfort and glamour.[87]

For many individuals who fought across "no man's land," their most lasting trauma stemmed from combat itself. African American soldiers grappled with the same emotions of fear, uncertainty, and vulnerability characteristic of all front-line troops, irrespective of race and nationality.[88] Robert Lee Cypress, a private in the 367th Infantry Regiment believed that "the effect of the horrors of war will have a life-long effect."[89] Combat service in the war represented a jarring emersion into modernity and its terrifying potential, an experience no amount of training could prepare one for. The sheer ferocity of the fighting hit Edward E. Brown, a telephone and signalman in the Ninety-second Division, especially hard: "Those days of fighting were the same as a nightmare to me, and the word 'drive' will forever bring back to me the scenes I went through. Even if I were allowed I could not begin to describe to you the horror of it all—cannon, high explosives, machine guns, pistols, grenades, rockets, and the results of such modern implements of war—the dead and the wounded."[90] For soldiers like Brown and countless others, the psychological upheaval of war rendered language itself insufficient to accurately reflect their memories and range of emotions.[91] "Words fail me in the attempt to describe the awful carnage of human blood!" Sergeant Oscar Walker of the 370th Infantry reflected.[92] Many servicemen struggled to find logic in a seemingly illogical experience and expressed a sense of stunned disbelief that they somehow managed to survive. "I never expected to get back to America alive and don't see how I did get back," wrote a deeply shaken Erkson Thompson, also of the 370th. "I can hear them shells busting over my head right now. I have never been shell-shocked, boys, but I will be searched for a nickel if I have not been shell-scared."[93]

War may have exposed the raw humanity of many African American combatants, but they still remained important symbols in the larger wartime struggle for democratic rights and racial equality. Race advocates, both in France and at home in the United States, waited anxiously for proof of valor and heroism on the battlefield in order to definitively proclaim the patriotic sacrifice of African Americans in the war. On the night of May 13, 1918, two soldiers from the 369th Infantry Regiment provided a perfectly scripted moment.

Needham Roberts, a native of Trenton, New Jersey, and Henry Johnson, a former railroad porter from Albany, New York, made up part of an isolated five-man observation post assigned to guard against German ambushes. At half past two in the morning, Roberts heard a number of suspicious noises and, with the remaining three members of the observation group asleep, alerted Johnson. It was the snapping of wire cutters. Just as the two men sent up a warning flare, a German raiding party of at least twenty-four soldiers attacked with a volley of grenades, followed by rifle fire. The initial assault left Roberts seriously wounded, but he still managed to provide Johnson with grenades. Johnson hurled them at the oncoming Germans, absorbing several gunshot wounds while doing so. He grabbed his rifle and attempted to repel the approaching attackers, but could get off only three shots before his gun jammed. German soldiers were now inside the trench, so Johnson resorted to hand-to-hand combat. He wielded his rifle like a club and knocked one man unconscious. In the midst of the fighting, a group of German raiders attempted to take the injured Roberts prisoner and carry him off to their lines. Johnson rushed to the aid of his comrade, unsheathed his bolo knife, and killed one of the German soldiers with a vicious downward thrust through his skull. He killed a second German with his knife after sustaining yet another bullet wound. By this time the raiding party had seen enough and began to retreat with its wounded back to the safety of the German lines. Johnson continued hurling grenades at the Germans until, assured they had fled, he finally collapsed from his wounds and utter exhaustion. In staving off capture and death, Johnson and Roberts killed four Germans and seriously injured at least a dozen more.[94]

"The Battle of Henry Johnson" became front-page news in the United States. Seizing the opportunity to promote the regiment, 369th officer Arthur Little relayed the amazing story to the prominent journalist Irvin Cobb of the *Saturday Evening Post* and other white American war correspondents. "Our colored volunteers from Harlem," wrote Little, "had become, in a day, one of the famous fighting regiments of the World War."[95] Within a week the mainstream New York press ran stories of the incident, and other national papers quickly followed suit. Most white newspapers and magazines, while praising the exploits of Johnson and Roberts, nevertheless filtered the two men and their actions through a prism of racial stereotype and caricature. The *New York Times*, in its May 22, 1918, editorial "Privates Bill and Needham," described the two heroes as "demoniac"; Irvin Cobb resorted to dialect and minstrel stock characters to describe his encounters with the 369th and other black soldiers; and the *New York Herald* displayed a cartoon of Henry Johnson invoking images of African savagery, in spite of its assertion of Johnson and Roberts as "Two First Class Americans!"[96]

African Americans, however, read and interpreted "The Battle of Henry Johnson" much differently. In Henry Johnson, African Americans had found their modern-day Crispus Attucks. The legend of Johnson and Roberts would

"Two First Class Americans!" Cartoon of Henry Johnson and Needham Roberts by W. A. Rodgers of the New York Herald. *Source: Scott,* Scott's Official History of the American Negro in the World War.

be spoken in the same breath as the valor of the Massachusetts 54th Regiment at Fort Wagner and the Buffalo Soldiers at San Juan Hill. Johnson and Roberts were unqualified African American war heroes. The black press, hungrily waiting for just such a moment, instantly exalted Johnson and Roberts as symbols of African American bravery, manhood, and sacrifice.

Their symbolism cut two ways. On the one hand, Johnson and Roberts functioned as compelling examples of African American patriotism. "Not since the entry of the United States in the World War has such a glowing account of the bravery and daring of the American soldier on the French battle field been received on this side," boasted the *New York Age*.[97] In this sense, Johnson and Roberts transcended race and, by their heroics, demonstrated that patriotism and the obligations of citizenship knew no color. In the eyes of African Americans, Johnson and Roberts were indeed "Two First Class Americans," without qualification or ridicule, who embodied the Americanness of black people more broadly.

At the same time, Johnson and Roberts also stood as shining examples of

African American historical valor. The *Chicago Defender* featured a photo of Johnson and Roberts, describing them as two soldiers "serving their Race and their country 'over there,' who, displayed remarkable courage and bravery."[98] The fact that the *Defender* capitalized and positioned "Race" before "country" is significant, indicating an emphasis of Johnson and Roberts as symbols of racial pride first and foremost and as representations of American nationalism second. African American communities, particularly in New York, rallied around the metaphorical importance of Johnson's and Roberts's heroics. On July 5, an estimated two thousand well-wishers and admirers attended a ceremony at the Harlem Casino organized by the New York Fifteenth Women's Auxiliary in honor of Henry Johnson's wife and the parents of Needham Roberts. They received telegrams of praise from Theodore Roosevelt, Secretary of War Newton Baker, Governor Charles Whitman of New York, and Governor Walter Evans Edge of New Jersey. Perhaps most notably, all proceeds from the evening were donated to the dependents of African American soldiers serving in France, revealing how organizers used the symbolism of Johnson and Roberts to promote the larger collective welfare of black troops and their relatives.[99] The two valiant men held a deep communal and ideological significance for African Americans, irrespective of what white people thought. Even the *New York Herald's* cartoon representation of Henry Johnson, reprinted in the *Chicago Defender* and other black newspapers, assumed a different meaning when viewed through the eyes of African Americans who saw Johnson and Roberts as racial heroes. Johnson, standing triumphantly over a pile of dead and wounded Germans, signified a graphic inversion of racial hierarchy. With superhuman strength and courage, Johnson both literally and figuratively vanquished the myth of white supremacy and demonstrated the manhood of the race.

While the legend of Henry Johnson and Needham Roberts buoyed the morale of African Americans in the United States, racial conditions in France continued to test the resolve of black combatants. Moments of triumph were counterbalanced with reminders of the marginalized position African American servicemen occupied in the American army. An example of this fact came in the form of German propaganda distributed among black soldiers of the Ninety-second Division on September 12 in the St. Dié sector. After German forces learned the soldiers they faced on the other side of the line were black, they airdropped a barrage of circulars addressed "To the Colored Soldiers of the U.S. Army." Samuel Blount kept a copy, which began, "Hello boys! What are you doing over here? Fighting the Germans. . . . Why? Have they done you any harm?" Encouraging them not to be seduced by the hypocritical propaganda of the Allies and the U.S. government, the Germans urged African American soldiers to critically ponder, "What is Democracy? Personal freedom, all citizens enjoying the same rights, socially and before the law. Do you enjoy the same rights as the white people in America, the Land of Freedom and Democracy, or aren't you treated over there as second class citizens?" The circular demonstrated a remarkable awareness of racial conditions in the United States by juxtaposing American "democracy" with Jim Crow segregation in the South and "lynching and the most horrible cruelties there after." The Germans implored African American soldiers to stop being exploited and cease fighting for the United States, as well as the equally racist English. "To carry the gun in their service is not an honor," the circular stated, "but a shame. Throw it away and come over to the German lines! You will find friends who will help you always."[100]

Black soldiers, especially those in the volatile Ninety-second Division, did not need German propaganda to remind them of their racial status and the incongruities of American democracy.[101] A soldier who read the document said to one of his officers, "We know what they say is true, but don't worry; we're not going over."[102] African American soldiers did not desert but instead held firm to their civic obligation, military duty, and an increasingly fragile faith in the potential of their service to transform the democratic underpinnings of the nation. Doing so, however, became increasingly difficult in light of continued efforts by the American army high command to denigrate the abilities, achievements, and manhood of black soldiers, and officers in particular.

RAYFORD LOGAN LEARNED ALL TOO quickly what it meant to be a black officer in the American army. Despite his education and cadet training, he was sworn into the First Separate Battalion of the Washington, D.C., National Guard as a "buck private." But the hastily thrown together 372nd Regiment, which Logan's battalion became a part of, needed officers. Graduates from the Des Moines camp had been assigned to the Ninety-second Division, so the War Department authorized the issuance of qualifying exams to black soldiers for possible promotion. Logan leapt at the opportunity. He first had to overcome the prejudice of 372nd Colonel Glendie B. Young, whom Logan described as "a goddamned son-of-a-bitch . . . Negro-hater." "I wouldn't make a god-damned one of these black sons-of-a-bitch an officer if I didn't have to," Logan overheard Young curse in a conversation with a group of white officers. Despite this hostility, Logan passed his examination, thanks in large part to the fact he majored in history at Williams College. On January 28, 1918, he received a promotion to first lieutenant.[103]

Logan and the rest of the 372nd departed for France aboard the *Susque-*

hanna on March 30, 1918. The journey unfolded as "a beautiful illustration of the American democracy in war." Colonel Young reassigned black officers to the smallest staterooms and segregated them in the ship's dining facilities. For Logan, "fresh out of Williams where I had been treated as a human being," these insults grated hard on his sense of democracy and justice. Matters worsened when the regiment arrived at St. Nazaire on the evening of April 12. "The French people gave us rather hearty cheers as we marched to camp," Logan remembered, but conditions in St. Nazaire soon added to his "growing disillusionment."[104] Logan and the regiment's other black officers received assignments to "cramped" living quarters that soon became "intolerable." After protesting their conditions, some of the men relocated to barracks housing the regiment's white officers. "When we got there, we found a white curtain separating that part of the barracks which [we] were to use."[105] Unlike white officers, Logan and his fellow African American officers were forced to eat lunch with black stevedores. After being ordered to camp headquarters and "unmercifully bawled out" for their alleged violation of army regulations, a humiliated Logan "burst into tears."[106]

With the exception of the 371st regiment, which contained no African American officers, the units of the Ninety-third Division all, in various ways, felt the effects of the army's belief that officer stripes had no place on the arms of black men. Incorporation into the French military did not make the Ninety-third Division immune from the racist attitudes and policies of white American military officials toward its black officers. The 369th arrived in France with a meager five black officers and by the time of the armistice only one, James Reese Europe, remained.[107] A number of black sergeants from the 369th, such as Noble Sissle, attended officer training schools in France, but upon earning their commissions were promptly transferred to other black regiments such as the 370th.[108] The army denied qualified African American soldiers opportunities for promotion, and many of the regiment's white officers assumed an air of superiority over the men in their command.[109] Although officers such as Hamilton Fish exhibited a strong commitment to the black soldiers of the 369th, attitudes of racial paternalism proved hard to shake.

Unlike the 369th, the 370th Infantry Regiment arrived in France with a full contingent of black officers led by Colonel Franklin A. Dennison. Dennison's dignified presence formed a central part of the 370th's identity. As the only African American field-grade officer in command of an entire regiment, he functioned as a source of tremendous pride, for the men of the 370th, as well as for Chicago's black community, which closely followed the exploits of its local heroes. His presence, however, also flew in the face of established military racial hierarchies. This led to his removal from command on July 12, 1918, for alleged "health reasons."[110] For the first time in its celebrated history, the Eighth Illinois would now be led by a white man, Colonel T. A. Roberts. James Spencer, a 370th veteran, praised Dennison, describing him as "a Negro officer of rare intelligence and ability" and lamented his removal from the regiment "simply on prejudicial grounds."[111] The morale of the former Eighth Illinois received a serious blow, and several soldiers refused to acknowledge Roberts as their colonel. Roberts did not endear himself to the men under his command when a host of other black officers were demoted and transferred.[112] "What's coming off?" the men and remaining officers restlessly asked. "Is it the purpose of this hard boiled egg to slip a bunch of white majors over on us?"[113] Regimental chaplain William Braddan could not hide his hatred for Colonel Roberts, characterizing him as "the arch enemy, vilifier and traducer of the Negro soldier," and he eventually requested a transfer back to the United States, an order Roberts gladly endorsed.[114] Although a number of black officers remained in the regiment, most notably Lieutenant Colonel Otis Duncan, the actions of the army in removing Dennison constituted a flagrant disregard of the regiment's historical legacy and sense of racial camaraderie.

For Rayford Logan in the 372nd Infantry Regiment, the combined traumas of combat and racism had a devastating impact. On June 4, the 372nd moved into position on the Meuse-Argonne front with the French 63rd Division, engaging in heavy fighting. Logan, who had become fluent in French during his time at Williams College, was a liaison officer with Company M and translated orders between American and French commanders. From the outset of 372nd's time at the front, Germans had closely tracked the regiment's movements, even down to when the officers crossed a local road for lunch. Logan warned his captain that they risked subjecting themselves to an attack. Sure enough, on June 13, as he crossed the road to eat, a German artillery barrage struck Logan. "One shell took off my helmet. I lay on the ground covering my head with my arms." After the assault stopped, Logan picked himself up, seemingly unharmed, and went to have his meal. However, later that evening, shell shock and months of racial slights took their toll: "It seems that during the night I was walking around in the woods in my pajamas. My sergeant found me and sent for Lt. Janifer. He gave me a dose of morphine. I sent a message to the major asking him how many Negroes had been lynched the year before. When he came to see me, I am supposed to have tried to shoot him but the sergeant knocked the gun out of my hand."[115] After his convalescence, Logan went before the deputy chief of staff, who did not reduce his rank, but instead "decided to punish me by sending me to a stevedore camp near Bordeaux."[116] He would serve out the remainder of the war overseeing black stevedores of the 840th Transportation Company.[117]

Logan undoubtedly took pleasure in the July 1918 removal of "goddamned son-of-a-bitch" Colonel Glendie Young from command. His replacement, Colonel Herschel Tupes, however, proved to be equally hostile to the presence of black officers in the 372nd regiment. Tupes, along with other white officers, colluded to bar and systematically remove African American officers from the regiment by deeming them incompetent.[118] Tupes rationalized his request for the immediate replacement of all black officers on the view that "the racial distinctions which are recognized in civilian life naturally continue to be recognized in the military life and present a formidable barrier to the existence of that feeling of comradeship which is an essential to mutual confidence and esprit de corps." Far from natural, the "formidable barrier" of the color line imposed by Tupes and other white officers represented a conscious effort on their part to transplant American racism to French soil. Tupes further justified his actions by stating that black officers neglected the "welfare" of the black soldiers under their command and performed their duties in "a perfunctory manner," a continuation of arguments put forth by opponents of African American officers at the earliest stages of the war that only white men could effectively command and discipline black troops. He asked the War Department not to transfer any additional black officers to his regiment, and that if white officers of the same rank were not available to replace the black officers, those of a lower rank should be forwarded instead.[119]

The order placed General Mariano Goybet, commander of the French 157th Division, under which the 372nd served, in the awkward position of interpreting the uniquely American racial dynamics of the regiment and making an informed decision. "I do not intend here to discuss the negro question which so greatly interests the American people but which does not concern us," he said in an August 21, 1918, memo. Goybet's disingenuous statement reflected the continued efforts of French military officials to perpetuate the myth of a colorblind nation and minimize the depths of its own "negro question" concerning its African colonial subjects. The American situation, however, was indeed unique and, as Goybet noted, merited attention. After observing the 372nd, he concluded that "there is not, and there will undoubtedly never be, camaraderie between the white officers and the black officers." White officers despised taking commands from black officers, contributing to an environment where "camaraderie de combat" was not likely to develop. Additionally, Goybet observed that "the situation of French officers of the regiment in relation to their American comrades is delicate," as cordial relations between French and black officers upset many white American officers. He concluded that "the disadvantages which I have pointed out would disappear completely" if the 372nd, like the 371st Infantry Regiment also under his command, had exclusively white officers. Goybet, in the interests of military effectiveness, therefore concurred with Tupes's request to replace the black officers of the 372nd with white men.[120]

From Tupes's perspective, his request had nothing to do with regimental effectiveness, but everything to do with reasserting the military's traditional racial hierarchy. His actions in fact represented a dangerous disregard for the welfare of the regiment, as the demoralization of the men reached near mutinous levels. A total of seventy-seven black officers of the 372nd Infantry Regiment were brought before efficiency boards and transferred out of the regiment on spurious grounds.[121]

Some of the most trying experiences occurred for the few black officers commissioned in field artillery. White army officials viewed field artillery, an area requiring a particularly high level of technical expertise, as beyond the capabilities of black men to succeed in, regardless of their educational background. Black officers from Des Moines assigned to the field artillery regiments of the Ninety-second Division received inadequate training, providing a ready-made rationale for the division's white commanders to recommend their wholesale removal.[122]

Lester Granger was among a handful of black men who received a field artillery commission. After the close of the Des Moines camp, the army decided that all future black officer candidates would train at regular facilities alongside white students. Born in Newport News, Virginia, Granger at the time of American entry into the war attended Dartmouth College on an athletic scholarship. In April 1918, along with several of his classmates, he applied for and earned admission to officer candidate school. He left for the Seventy-ninth Division field artillery school at Camp Meade, where he joined a company of approximately 115 other black students from various regions of the country. Following a change in policy that established centralized officer training facilities, the army transferred Granger and the other black candidates to the field artillery officer training school at Camp Taylor in Kentucky, where they became part of the Twenty-second Training Battalion.[123] Raised in a family that refused to accept segregation, Granger never adjusted to the Jim Crow policies of the American army and struggled to maintain any semblance of patriotic spirit throughout his war service. In a camp with some sixty-five hundred white candidates at a given time, Granger and his company of fellow black students, despite the strong camaraderie they developed among each other, experienced severe social isolation and lived in the smallest barracks.[124] "They were out to get us," Granger recalled of the white instructors at Camp Taylor, who in addition to ostracizing the black students consistently manipulated their test scores.[125] Eliminations gradually whittled their numbers, and by the end of the camp in late August of 1918, only thirty-three black candidates, including Lester Granger, received commissions.

Charles Hamilton Houston was one of the thirty-three graduating field artillery officers. After achieving his first lieutenant commission at Des Moines, the army assigned Houston to the 368th Infantry Regiment at Camp Meade. His entire time there, Houston kept up a vigorous personal campaign for a transfer to field artillery, insisting that he serve in an area commensurate with his capabilities. His persistence paid dividends, and he joined the training program at Camp Meade and eventually Camp Taylor. Despite constant reminders of his marginalization, Houston considered himself among select company, a fact that he took pride in and which functioned as a source of motivation. Houston viewed his fellow "Talented Tenth" comrades as "some of the finest men I have ever been privileged to associate with."[126] They were indeed an impressive lot; although only thirty-three received commissions, five graduated in the top fifteen of their class, comprising twenty-five hundred students. Along with Lester Granger, Houston graduated on August 31, 1918, hopeful that he would no longer have to prove his worth, both as a soldier and as a man.[127]

Their battles, however, had only just begun. Following graduation, Granger, Houston, and the exclusive group of field artillery officers received orders to train replacement artillery soldiers for the Ninety-second Division at Camp Jackson in South Carolina. White South Carolinians had exhibited their distaste for the presence of black soldiers when the 369th trained in Spartanburg, and Camp Jackson became notorious for the poor treatment experienced by black draftees, many consigned to brutal work and living conditions. The black field artillery officers remained at Camp Jackson for only one week before, as Lester Granger recounted, the "intense hostility of the whole community, and the entire encampment," prompted their rapid deployment overseas. Granger "was glad to get overseas, glad to get anywhere out of the United States."[128]

American racism followed closely on their heels. For Charles Houston, his experience in France, as he wrote in his memoir, "destroyed the last vestiges of any desire I might have had to get in the front lines and battle for my country." The inadequacy of American training required all field artillery officers to undergo additional preparation under French instructors. Houston and his fellow black lieutenants were the only African American soldiers at Camp de Meucon, located near the town of Vannes, among two brigades of white officers from Tennessee and Kentucky who leapt at every opportunity to express their commitment to white supremacy.[129] Never before had Houston endured such hatred and humiliation. He ate his meals on a bench in an abandoned kitchen. He slept in segregated living quarters. He bathed alongside lower-ranked white enlisted men in showers that were soon boarded off so "we would not physically come into contact with them." "The treatment meted out to us violated every principle of Army regulations, Army procedure and tradition and was visited on us solely in an attempt on the part of the white officers to humiliate us and destroy our prestige as officers in front of the French instructors, the white soldiers and even the German prisoners," Houston noted with anger.[130] Lester Granger shared Houston's frustrations, which reached the point to where he "had to pull my gun on one of my fellow officers."[131] For these black officers, democracy became nothing but hollow rhetoric, as the "hate and scorn" exhibited by the white officers in his company convinced Charles Houston that "there was no sense in my dying for a world ruled by them. My battleground was America, not France."[132]

For many black officers of the Ninety-second Division, their battleground, both figuratively and literally, was France. Racial discrimination emerged as their most resilient foe. It began on the ships transporting the division across the Atlantic, as Jim Crow traveled like a germ, infecting all who came into contact with it. "The submarines do not divert the minds of the white officers enough for them to forget segregation," wrote division interpreter Captain Matthew Virgil Boute, whose diary entrusted to W. E. B. Du Bois after the war recounted instance after instance of racial discrimination.[133] He mused in Du Boisian parlance: "The colored officers were assigned to a table in a corner by themselves. How will it be when we get to France? Is it possible that the shadow will follow us there? Are we not posing as the champions of democracy?"[134]

Osceola McKaine, who graduated from the Des Moines camp brimming with optimism and patriotic fervor, pondered similar questions as well. Self-assured, articulate, and possessing a strong racial consciousness, McKaine, like many black officers in the Ninety-second Division, viewed his duty on the behalf of the nation and the race as inextricably connected. He served in the 367th Infantry Regiment and felt confident that a better day for African Americans lay on the horizon. In a letter published by the *New York Age*, he declared, "The free allied nations of the world will not condone America's past treatment of her colored citizens, in the future." Having "fought beside the best blood," having demonstrated the willingness of African Americans "to pay and pay dearly in our own blood for the right of peoples of the earth to share equally in its blessings," McKaine, in the face of considerable hardship, remained certain "that my people will share equality with Armenian and Serb in the fruits of the triumph of right over might and Democracy over Autocracy." As race men, officers like McKaine viewed protecting and fighting for the future interests of black people as an obligation. McKaine thus explicitly linked his fate, as a soldier and officer, with the broader democratic fate of African Americans. "Death is nothing," he bravely proclaimed, "for I love my race more than life itself."[135]

The race pride and political awareness of officers like Osceola McKaine presented a direct challenge to the authority of white officers and the AEF high command, which determined to put them back in their place. Throughout their time in France with the American army, the Ninety-second Division's black officers, upon official orders, billeted in separate quarters, remained segregated from white officers at restaurants and other local establishments, and were consistently denied opportunities for promotion.[136] Additionally, black officers faced the constant threat of army efficiency boards, which the division's white officers used as a racially motivated purging mechanism. "There are many officers in the Ninety-second Division who are doing excellent work," Major General Ballou began in a July 23, 1918, memo. "There are others," he continued, "who are not only not improving, but who show signs of deterioration as soon as they are relived from the immediate presence and supervision of a superior officer. Some are drinking to such an extent that their minds are more sluggish than usual. Others have become swollen with their ideas of their own importance." From Ballou's vantage point, the division's black officers had gotten too uppity and needed a stern reminder of their place. He encouraged senior white officers to "resort to proper corrective measures," which included efficiency boards, courts-martial proceedings, and recommendations for demotion, to ensure discipline and, most important, to keep the egos of African American officers in check.[137] This approach had a chilling effect. A September 7, 1918, memo from General Ballou detailed his reasons behind the recommended reassignment of forty-three black officers on grounds ranging from a shortage of necessary "energy and force" to lacking "the mentality necessary" to properly drill African American troops.[138] The percentage of black officers in the division plummeted from 82 to 58 by the war's end.[139] The poisonous environment made it challenging for African American officers to devote undivided attention to their work, much less maintain any confidence in their white commanders. As 367th Infantry Regiment officer William Colson recalled, even before reaching the front, the black soldiers and officers of the division "had lost all faith, military and moral."[140]

The mood of the division and its black men could not have been much worse as it prepared for the huge fall 1918 Allied offensive in the Meuse-Argonne. With

German forces reeling following successful British advances in the north, Marshal Ferdinand Foch, in concurrence with British commander Douglas Haig, saw the time as ripe for cracking the "Hindenburg Line," an imposing one-hundred-mile German defensive zone, in some places twelve miles deep, saturated with trenches, machine gun nests, masses of barbed wire, and artillery encampments. Foch hoped to attach the American army to his French forces, but AEF general John Pershing vigorously objected. He viewed the Meuse-Argonne operation as the decisive moment of American participation in the war, the last opportunity to demonstrate the strength of his army and his personal leadership and validate Woodrow Wilson's envisioned head position at the peace table. Moreover, the AEF had just completed its first successful independent offensive at St. Mihiel, and Pershing brimmed with confidence. He thus saw his forces as more than up for the task of traveling some sixty miles west of their positions as of September 16 and into the line only ten days later.

The Meuse-Argonne operation revealed Pershing to be both naive and dangerously overconfident in his handling of the AEF. The sector assigned to the AEF consisted of 150 kilometers of brutal terrain, with the rugged Argonne forest to the left and the Meuse River to the right. Launching an advance at this location was potentially catastrophic, considering advantages the geography provided German defenses, positioned on the high ground and dug in and refortified over the span of three years. These operational challenges beyond Pershing's control were compounded by self-made logistical complications. Coming so quickly on the heels of the St. Mihiel offensive, most of the American divisions lacked proper preparation for the difficult undertaking. The massive number of American troops clogged the few available roads and congested supply lines. Some units arrived to the front only hours before the commencement of the assault. Pershing hoped that the sheer size and vigor of his army would be enough to overcome its glaring weaknesses and tactical disadvantages.[141]

Escaping the chaotic mismanagement of the AEF, the 369th, 371st, and 372nd Infantry Regiments of the Ninety-third Division all participated in the Meuse-Argonne offensive with the French Fourth Army in the Champagne region, while the 370th remained engaged in the Oise-Aisne campaign further northwest.[142] Unlike the American forces, which preferred to keep the operation shrouded in secrecy, the French commanding officers provided clear instructions and goals to the leadership of the black regiments.

At 5:25 A.M. on September 26, the 369th, as part of the 161st Division, entered the offensive.[143] Horace Pippin found himself in the thick of the battle. Pippin and other soldiers of the 369th's Third Battalion charged a heavily defended sector, facing an onslaught of machine gun and shell fire. A German machine gunner zeroed in on Pippin and another soldier, causing them to duck for cover in a shell hole. Hoping to draw the gunner's fire, Pippin and his comrade split up, and Pippin dashed for another hole. Pippin would later write of his fateful decision: "I got near the shell hole that I had pecked out when he let me have it." A bullet grazed his neck, and two more ripped through his right shoulder and arm. Pippin, immobilized, hungry, and thirsty, attempted to dress the wound and received assistance from his buddy. But his comrade soon departed to continue the advance, and Pippin found himself alone, lying on his back, unable to move, as machine gun fire, artillery shells, and shrapnel burst around him. Hours passed. Later that afternoon a French sniper happened upon Pippin in his weakened state. But before the soldier could offer first aid or even speak a word, a bullet struck his head and he fell lifeless on top of Pippin. "I seen him comeing on but I could not move. I were just that weeke. so I hat to take him." Pippin foraged the dead Frenchman's bread and water, as day turned into night, and with it rain and plummeting temperatures. The next day, Pippin was still clinging to life after having survived an evening exposed to the elements when a French patrol found him, took him off the battlefield, and eventually transported the wounded "Hellfighter" to a field hospital.[144] He was one of a staggering 222 casualties experienced by the 369th in the first two days of the offensive.[145]

As the 369th fought, the 371st and 372nd Infantry Regiments moved into position with the French 157th Division. The 371st experienced the heaviest action. It was ordered to fill a gap between the 161st French Division and the Second Moroccan Division. Events moved quickly, and information was hard to come by. Scouts had been sent out, but when the regimental commander received his attack orders just after midnight on the 28th, he did not know the extent of the gap between the 161st French Division and the Second Moroccan Division, nor did he have accurate information on the location and strength of the German force his regiment was soon to encounter. They nevertheless pressed forward. Updated orders were received for the 371st to take Côte 188, a hill German forces had strongly guarded for its strategic advantages over the local terrain. A day earlier French troops had attempted to take the hill and suffered heavy losses. By 5:45 A.M. on the 28th, thick fog filled the surrounding valleys. Companies B, C, and D of the First Battalion would lead the charge. The battalion trekked up a dirt pathway from the town of Grateuil, reorganized, and at 6:45 A.M. attacked.

Heavy mortar and machine gun fire met the First Battalion's advance. But after only a few minutes, the barrage stopped. The German's threw up their hands in surrender. The men ceased firing and prepared to take prisoners. However, they had unknowingly been drawn into a trap. The Germans leapt back into their trench and, with the 371st only 100 meters away and fully exposed, unleashed a devastating machine gun attack. "The leading platoons of 'C' Company were almost annihilated," Major Joseph Pate recalled, and the platoon commanders were gravely wounded. Casualties reached near 50 percent. Company C squad leader Freddie Stowers, a twenty-two-year-old farm laborer from Sandy Springs, South Carolina, took charge. He selflessly rallied the surviving men, who rushed forward to the first German trench and took out a machine gun nest. Company D came to the support of Company C and enveloped both flanks of the enemy position. Stowers was hit by machine gun fire, but pressed on. Bloody and exhausted, Stowers encouraged his compatriots to continue fighting up the hill until his wounds finally took their toll. German forces, this time in earnest, offered their retreat, running downhill toward Bussy Ferme. They made easy targets. Those who remained fought desperately, but were dispatched with bayonets. "This final phase of this assault was extremely gruesome," Pate recounted, "as our men could not be restrained from wreaking their vengeance upon the enemy who had so shamefully entrapped their comrades earlier that morning."[146] They had lost many fellow soldiers and, in killing the surrendering Germans, perhaps lost some of their soul. But they had achieved their objective, doing so in heroic fashion, and, in the process, earned the respect of French and American army officials alike.

After its service patrolling the St. Dié sector, AEF commanders moved the Ninety-second into position to participate in the initial wave of the massive Allied offensive. Only the 368th Infantry Regiment received orders to proceed to the front, while the remaining three regiments were held in reserve. The 368th, along with a French cavalry regiment, formed part of a special brigade called the Groupement Durand, created in order to fill a gap and maintain liaison between the French Fourth Army and American forces, consisting of the Seventy-seventh Division's 308th Infantry. With only limited experience in the quiet St. Dié sector, its men tired and hungry from the rapid redeployment, and wracked by racial discord, the 368th probably had no business assuming control of a complex operation that required weeks of advance planning for even the best-trained regiments. To make matters worse, the regiment lacked crucial supplies and equipment, such as maps, signal flares, grenade launchers, and cutters necessary to advance through the years of accumulated German barbed wire. Nevertheless, on the night of September 25, there it was, on the line, faced with a daunting task in the imposing terrain of the Argonne, and with no advance preparation, literally blind to what lay before it.[147]

On September 26, at 5:25 A.M., the Second Battalion of the 368th attacked. Receiving no advance artillery support and short of cutters, the battalion struggled with excruciating slowness to navigate through the masses of barbed wire overlaying the battlefield. The men soon became disorganized and communications broke down. A similar scene played out the following day, as the wooded terrain and wire entanglements continued to stymie the progress of the regiment. By September 28, the entire operation devolved into confusion and chaos. Heavy German shelling and machine gun fire stalled the three battalions of the 368th on several occasions; orders to advance and requests to withdraw flew back and forth; misunderstanding led several individual companies commanded by black officers to retreat to the rear; liaison with the French Fourth Army and, more important, the vulnerable 308th Infantry of the AEF Seventy-seventh Division collapsed. Despite efforts over the next two days to make headway in their advance, the 368th received orders to withdraw on September 30. The remaining three infantry regiments of the Ninety-second Division remained in reserve. Word of the failed operation spread like wildfire through the division and the entire AEF. On October 1, Colonel James Moss of the 367th Infantry assembled his regiment's black officers and noncommissioned officers and, according to Samuel Blount, told them that "the 368th Infantry . . . failed in its mission, and that the colored officer is a failure."[148] On October 5 the entire Ninety-second division was removed from the front.[149]

The disastrous experience of the 368th took place among a seemingly endless array of blunders endured by the AEF throughout the Meuse-Argonne offensive. After a successful initial penetration of German forces, the American army virtually ground to a halt. Built for open warfare, the hulking AEF had difficulty traveling over the hilly, woody terrain.[150] Progress became incremental, as clogged roads hampered communication, prevented supplies and reserve troops from reaching the front, and delayed the transportation of the wounded to hospitals. Unable to move, the Americans made easy targets for the Germans, who inflicted heavy casualties. Pershing suspended operations on October 1 in order to regroup and resumed on October 4 with slightly better success. Compounding an already lengthy set of problems, the influenza pandemic ravaged the AEF and incapacitated nearly seventy thousand troops just when they were needed the most.[151] Lacking proper training and advanced preparation, American soldiers struggled with their crash course in the horrors of modern warfare and performed with mixed and sometimes outright disappointing results.[152] The 368th Infantry Regiment's misfortune was thus not an anomaly. The failure of the 368th certainly paled in comparison to that of the Thirty-fifth Division from Missouri and Kansas, which spent five disorganized days retreating in the face of German artillery fire and roaming aimlessly around the battlefield, all the while taking devastating casualties.[153]

But military officials did not attribute the failures of the Thirty-fifth Division to an inherent lack of mental resilience and constitutional fortitude characteristic of inferior white men from the Midwest. In the case of the 368th Infantry, blackness served as an explanation for perceived incompetence, as white commanding officers both within and outside the Ninety-second Division immediately cast blame for the regiment's poor performance on its African American officers. Major J. N. Merrill of the 368th's First Battalion wrote to his superior officer Colonel William Jackson, "Without my presence or that of any other white officer right on the firing line I am absolutely positive that not a single colored officer would have advanced with his men. The cowardice shown by the men was abject." Merrill punctuated his malicious letter by labeling the black soldiers and officers in his presence as "rank cowards, there is no other word for it."[154] Sentiments such as this prompted General Charles Ballou to have thirty black officers from the regiment immediately removed from service. In his request, Ballou labeled the officers "worthless," "inefficient," "untrustworthy," and "cowardly," among other insults, all the while ignoring the ineptitude of the 368th's white officers.[155] In fact, responsibility for much of the confusion that led to several companies of black soldiers and officers fleeing to the rear fell on the shoulders of Second Battalion major Max Elser. Elser, who arbitrarily replaced all of the battalion's black officers before the first day of the attack, got lost on September 26, resulting in a complete communication breakdown, and admitted to withdrawing his men against orders, explicitly contradicting the assumption that black officers retreated because of cowardice. He was hospitalized for "psycho-neurosis"—medical terminology for fright—but nevertheless dodged accountability for his battalion's disorganization, content to let black officers take the fall.[156]

James Wormley Jones escaped criticism stemming from the Meuse-Argonne campaign. Jones, whose background as a police officer worked to his advantage, excelled as a captain in the 368th. In August 1918 he was handpicked to attend infantry school and eventually recommended for promotion to divisional instructor. He stood out among a select group of captains who, according to his supervising officers, had "done very well in their work" and are "serious, dignified men of excellent caliber, and are fully able to maintain the positions of trust and confidence in which they have been placed."[157] Fighting with the Second Battalion in the Meuse-Argonne, Jones apparently distinguished himself, along with a handful of other officers, by not losing his cool under fire. Elser remarked in a September 30 memo, "Captain J. W. Jones and Lt. Anderson made the only advance as directed and then only with a portion of their companies."[158] Elser's compliments placed Jones in the awkward position of being praised while his fellow black officers were unmercifully disparaged.

The accusations levied by Ballou, Merrill, and other white officers quickly became about much more than just the conduct of the 368th. They used the incident as fodder to color the entire Ninety-second Division and its black officers as failures. With their poor display of manhood, black officers had exhibited the inferiority of their race and why it could never achieve full inclusion into American democracy. Manliness, in the context of war, equated to Americanness, and on the basis of the performance of their soldiers and officers, so reasoned white racists, black people possessed neither.

With broken morale and anger in their hearts, the black soldiers and officers of the Ninety-second Division attempted to finish out the war as best they could. After the Meuse-Argonne, AEF commanders pulled the 368th back from the front. From October 8 until the armistice, the remainder of the division served in the Marbache sector, conducting frequent patrols to keep German forces occupied to prevent a withdrawal.

On November 10, the division had a chance for redemption of sorts. The fall Allied offensive had pummeled the German forces, and now they were in full retreat. American and French military officials saw their opportunity to drive a final stake into the heart of the German army and end the war. The 183rd Brigade, made up of the 365th and 366th Infantry Regiments and the 350th Machine Gun Battalion, received orders to attack enemy positions along the Moselle River, south of the city of Metz. As a white major of the 365th Infantry Regiment, Warner Ross, remembered upon receiving his orders, "Here, before the expected armistice went into effect, was an opportunity to prove the Division's ability and worth and refute any whisperings that might be in the air."[159]

The attack began at 7:00 A.M. on November 10, a "beautiful day," Samuel Blount of the 367th Infantry reflected. The 367th did not engage in combat but instead patrolled the valley of Ruisseau Moulon and provided rear support for the white Seventh Division after its advance stalled.[160] The 365th and 366th Infantry Regiments and the 350th Machine Gun Battalion went over the top, encountering heavy machine gun fire and artillery and gas shelling. Nevertheless, they pressed forward, returning fire and advancing two and a half kilometers before nightfall. John Cade and the 366th, "with fearful hearts" and in the face of oftentimes "terrific artillery fire," successfully attacked and captured the sectors of Bois Voivrotte and Bois Cheminot.[161] "When darkness came the fighting slackened down and during the night the various units reorganized their forces and consolidated their positions and made ready to carry on the following day," Samuel Blount recalled of the operations. The assault continued at 5:00 A.M. the morning of November 11, with additional gains by the 365th and 366th toward Bouxières and along the Moselle River. It appeared that black soldiers of the

Ninety-second Division had finally hit their stride. But at 7:18 A.M., orders came in that the armistice had been signed and all firing must cease at 10:45 A.M. At 11:00 A.M., the war was over. The "Woëvre Plain Operation" briefly resuscitated the image of the Ninety-second Division. Despite sustaining heavy casualties—498 dead and wounded—all three combat units of the 183rd Brigade fulfilled their objectives and advanced more than three kilometers from their initial positions.[162] Mistakes had been made, but, as Brigadier General Malvern Barnum noted, they were due to a "lack of experience, rather than to lack of the offensive spirit." "These men were just finding themselves," he stated, and had shown marked improvement.[163]

These achievements, despite the persistent efforts of black soldiers and sympathetic white officers to ingrain them into the larger collective public and historical consciousness, would remain overshadowed by the concerted efforts of the army high command to use the 368th as ammunition to destroy the reputation of all black soldiers and officers.[164] The 368th functioned as a convenient symbol for racist white military officials to demonstrate the inability of black soldiers to serve as effective combatants in modern warfare when under the leadership of African American officers. Even white officers and military leaders who professed their confidence in black soldiers could not see past negative perceptions of African American officers and their ability. William Alexander Percy, who temporarily served as a brigade instructor with the Ninety-second, wrote of the division's black officers, "Those who came from the regular army, where they had been sergeants, made splendid officers; those who came from civilian life by way of training camps were lazy, undevoted, and without pride. Both dressed well, but the latter were peacocks in splendor and strut."[165] General Pershing's previous experiences with black troops and, more specifically, his command of them, informed his evaluation of the Ninety-second Division. While having faith in their inherent abilities, African American soldiers remained dependent for combat success on the leadership of white officers. Black officers could not be trusted. From this premise, the so-called failure of the 368th, while unfortunate, was wholly predictable. Pershing wrote following the war:

> It was well known that the time and attention that must be devoted to training colored troops in order to raise their level of efficiency to the average were considerably greater than for white regiments. More responsibility rested upon officers of colored regiments owning to the lower capacity and lack of education of the personnel. . . . It would have been much wiser to have followed the long experience of our Regular Army and provided these colored units with selected white officers.[166]

General Robert Lee Bullard, who rose during the war to command of the American Second Army, of which the Ninety-second Division formed part, took particular interest in the situation involving the 368th and its officers. Bullard had previously served as an officer in the Third Alabama Volunteers, the experimental black regiment created during the Spanish-Cuban-American War. On October 25, 1918, he wrote in his diary, "Today I've had a disagreeable reminder of the time when I commanded the '3d Ala. Vol. Inf.,' Negroes. It came in the court-martialing of five negro officers of the 92d Div. of my army for cowardice and in the feeling that these negroes can not be treated as white men would be treated because politics prevent."[167] He personally investigated the charges against the black officers, the status of the Ninety-second Division, and its mental state. In the end, he refused to intervene in the courts-martial proceedings of the five accused black officers, who were convicted of cowardice. Four of the officers received death sentences, and one life in prison.[168] Bullard wrote off the division, like the Third Alabama Volunteers, as a misguided experiment. "The negro division seems in a fair way to be a failure," he penned in a November 1 diary entry. "It is in a quiet sector yet can hardly take care of itself while to take any offensive actions seems wholly beyond its powers. I have been here now with it three weeks and have been unable to have it make a single raid upon the enemy. They are really inferior soldiers; there is no denying it."[169]

IF AFRICAN AMERICANS LEARNED a lesson from the experiences of black combatants and noncombatants, it was to never again underestimate the depths of white supremacy in the United States Army and its ability to pervert the ideals the nation supposedly fought for. African American soldiers continued to stand as embodiments of patriotism, sacrifice, and the prospect of social change, but this idealism was tempered by their constant battles with abuse, insult, and slander. The virulence of racial discrimination shocked many black servicemen to the core of their being, especially those who had internalized their symbolic status. They naturally questioned the value and purpose of potentially risking their lives for a country that dehumanized the very people who fought for and protected its freedoms, freedoms African Americans could themselves not enjoy.

In the face of hate and fear, black soldiers nevertheless refused to let their service be in vain. Combatants of the Ninety-second and Ninety-third Divisions fought with pride and valor, determined to demonstrate their worth as soldiers and as men. For those who did not reach the trenches, military service may not have lived up to expectations held before induction. However, just as the army used their labor, African Americans used the army to test the credibility of the nation's commitment to democracy and its applicability to black people. In doing so, the very idea of democracy as a nation-centered concept became increasingly less tenable. Investment in the nation generated only limited results, causing African Americans at home, as well as African American soldiers laboring and fighting in France, to cast their visions to a broader world.

You are not fighting simply for Europe; you are fighting for the world, and you and your people are a part of the world.

—W. E. B. Du Bois, "The Black Soldier," *Crisis*, June 1918

LES SOLDATS NOIRS

France, Black Military Service, and the Challenges of Internationalism and Diaspora

Thirty-two-year-old Henry Gilliam lived a quiet life as a farmer in Cumberland County, Virginia. Gilliam had only a fifth-grade education, so his social and economic circumstances more than likely never allowed him to experience a world beyond his rural southern community. That changed when the United States entered the war. Having "no objection" to military service, Gilliam answered his draft call "without complaint" on October 27, 1917. He traveled the roughly seventy miles to Camp Lee at Petersburg and settled into his assignment with the 155th Depot Brigade and new calling as a soldier. After six months of training and work at Camp Lee, Gilliam shipped off to France in April 1918 as one of the numerous replacement troops for the 369th Infantry Regiment. He left Newport News aboard the transport ship *President Grant* and arrived at Bordeaux in early May. With casualties in the 369th beginning to accumulate as its uninterrupted front-line service continued, Gilliam enjoyed only a brief period of training and incorporation into the regiment before experiencing his first taste of combat in July 1918.[1]

While at Camp Lee, Gilliam may very well have crossed paths with Gillespie Garland Lomans, a twenty-three-year-old native of the small town of Chilhowie in western Virginia. Lomans was enrolled as a student at West Virginia State College at the beginning of America's involvement in the war, a first step towards escaping the isolation of black life in Chilhowie. He received his draft call with enthusiasm, viewing his service as an opportunity to "help free the entire world; America included." Inducted in October 1917 and sent to Camp Lee, Lomans served along with Gilliam in the 155th Depot Brigade. He was then ordered to proceed to Camp Upton for training with the 351st Machine Gun Battalion of the Ninety-second Division. Lomans left Hoboken, New Jersey, aboard the *Orizaba* and arrived in Brest on June 19, 1918. He subsequently fought with the Ninety-second Division in the St. Dié sector and in the Meuse-Argonne.[2]

When Henry Gilliam reflected on his experience five months after his discharge, he wrote that because of his service, "my mind broadened and I had a greater vision of the world."[3] The war had a similar effect on Gillespie Lomans, who reenrolled at West Virginia State College after his discharge with a new perspective of the world and his place in it. He had "met and learned" the "customs of many nations French particularly." "Those experiences," he recalled, "have broadened my vision [I] am no longer a provincialist."[4] After crossing the Atlantic on their transport ships, passing through French and English ports, and laboring and fighting from Brest to the Rhine, African American soldiers like Gilliam and Lomans returned to their homes transformed. It was a transformation that connected them to a real and imagined global community that extended past the geographically and ideologically restrictive boundaries of the United States. They were no longer just two black men from rural Virginia, but soldiers with exposure to a world in the midst of revolutionary social, political, and economic change.

The First World War was, in part, a battle for European imperial supremacy and the right to control the human and material resources of Africa and beyond.[5] A handful of European intellectuals and political leaders, such as Vladimir Lenin and later Oswald Spengler, acknowledged this very fact.[6] But black people did not need these men to alert them to the reality that powerful forces had been set in motion that would potentially alter the course of history for the oppressed. They needed only to witness the ways in which most of the war's major participants—Germany, France, Great Britain, the United States—marshaled the manpower of peoples of African descent throughout the world for the war effort. Suddenly, with Europe aflame and black people fighting on multiple fronts, the idea of white supremacy seemed less tenable. For African Americans, and black soldiers in particular, domestic concerns regarding the impact of the war on the social and political future of the race were thrust into an international context.[7] The fight for democracy became not just a local struggle but a global one as well.[8]

France served as the central front of this struggle, the physical site where the demands of war mobilized the African diaspora by bringing together thousands of black soldiers, laborers, and intellectuals from the United States, Canada, the West Indies, and the African continent.[9] The term "diaspora" refers to the dispersal of people from their original homeland.[10] The African diaspora, as a geographic space, is composed of the millions of peoples of African descent scattered throughout the globe as a result of various streams of movement and resettlement.[11] It also speaks to the shared social, political, economic, and cultural conditions facing dispersed peoples of African descent, and the processes through which peoples of the diaspora constantly reinterpret their sense of self.[12] The First World War marked a seminal moment in the historical evolution of the modern African diaspora. This was due to the extraordinary relocation and demographic upheaval of peoples of African descent through migration and military service, combined with the politics of the era. Black people openly asserted that democracy, citizenship, self-determination, and freedom must apply not only to Europeans but to the racially oppressed as well. For this reason, the war and its immediate aftermath have been traditionally cast as the crucible giving rise to twentieth-century Pan-Africanism, along with a diverse ideological range of black internationalist movements.[13]

While it is tempting to romanticize this moment, how African Americans engaged with the diasporic and international dimensions of the war came with significant tensions.[14] The experiences and symbolic meanings of black soldiers demonstrated that diaspora was a process of contention, rife with political inconsistencies, cultural miscommunications, and historical fissures. Just as the war and military service brought various peoples of African descent together in unprecedented ways, it also exposed their differences. And just as questions concerning the relationship between race and democracy played out on a global stage, the domestic concerns of African Americans still remained paramount. The black press extolled with pride the contributions of African soldiers in the French army, while at the same time it juxtaposed them to African American troops as culturally inferior to emphasize the fitness of African Americans for equal rights.[15] Through their interactions with French civilians and encounters with African soldiers, African American troops experienced the rich possibilities and stark challenges of internationalism and diaspora firsthand. They struggled to balance a critique of and simultaneous investment in the United States and American democracy. They struggled to reconcile the vivid contrasts between their treatment by French civilians with that by their fellow white soldiers and officers. And they struggled with what it meant to be a person of African descent, while thoroughly immersed in the politics, institutions, and racial ideologies of the United States. The war opened the door to a broader world for African Americans, who, while still uncertain as to what lay ahead, nevertheless knew that their lives would never be the same.

"YET IN A VERY REAL SENSE Africa is a prime cause of this terrible overturning of civilization which we have lived to see." From the first gun blasts in August 1914, W. E. B. Du Bois had observed the war with close personal interest. Although he had studied in Germany and held a deep admiration for France, his allegiances ultimately rested with the oppressed darker races of the world. In the May 1915 *Atlantic Monthly* essay "The African Roots of War," Du Bois penned his thoughts on the war, challenging its European origins and casting the conflict in the expanded context of Africa and the African diaspora. The landmark article detailed the destructive history of Western imperialism in Africa, the complicity of the white working classes in this process, and how the furious dash to control the continent's resources lay at the heart of the European civil war. As the "Land of the Twentieth Century," Africa had driven the rival European powers mad with jealously and greed to the point where war had become all but inevitable. The future of modern civilization and any hope for peace thus hinged on the future of Africa and the spread of "a world-democracy" to the continent free from foreign domination. Make no mistake, Du Bois conveyed, this was a war about black people, and as such they had an important role to play in its eventual outcome.[16]

With European civilization in crisis and black people dying on the front lines, the war captivated the attention of the African American press. Editors of black newspapers and journals monitored the conflict and its global racial implications, but did so with one eye overseas and another eye firmly fixed on the domestic struggles of African Americans. The war and the actions of its European participants created an opportunity to recast critiques of American racial discrimination and white supremacist violence in an internationalist context.[17] James Weldon Johnson sardonically wrote in February 1915, "It is worth while to think about the hypocrisy of this country. Here we are holding up our hands in horror at German 'atrocities,' at what is being done in Belgium and at what is being done on the high seas while the wholesale murder of American citizens on American soil by bloodthirsty mobs hardly brings forth a word of comment."[18] In a similar tone, W. E. B. Du Bois compared the April 1915 sinking of the *Lusitania* to "the same sort of happenings hidden in the wilderness and done against dark and helpless people by white harbingers of human culture." When "Negroes were enslaved, or the natives of Congo raped and mutilated, or the Indians of the Amazon robbed, or the natives of the South Seas murdered, or 2,732 American citizens lynched," Du Bois boomed, "we civilized folks turned deaf ears."[19] The ongoing violence and suffering of black people in the United States took on new meaning, as violence and suffering now seemed to engulf the entire world.

More pointedly, black journalists and editors alerted their readers that, however disconnected from their everyday trials and tribulations, the war did matter for no other reason than it had the potential to alter the fates of millions of peoples of African descent. An October 1914 *New York Age* editorial speculated on the war's meaning for African Americans, as well as "those engaged in it who are racially and nationally in positions similar to our own." The *Age* wondered if "the oppressed peoples will come out of this titanic struggle as the only real victors."[20] In a similar vein, the *Baltimore Afro-American* reflected in December 1915, "There is but little doubt but greater recognition of the manhood of the darker races will be conceded by all parties after this war is over. Perhaps after all in the end the 'Fatherhood of God and the Brotherhood of Man' will be recognized as never before."[21] In speaking of the "oppressed peoples" of the "darker races," the African American press posited an abstract conception of diaspora, one in which the connections, real and imagined, between black Americans and their scattered descendants were predicated upon a shared, albeit vague, racial oppression. These initial musings framed the conflict for African Americans, alerting them to the fact that this was not simply a "white man's war," but a potentially significant moment in the larger history of black people throughout the globe.[22]

At the center of this evolving transnational view of the war stood France. The romance between African Americans and France began well before the First World War. The ideals of the French Revolution—*liberté, egalité, fraternité*—captured the imaginations of black people, enslaved and free, during the late eighteenth and early nineteenth centuries. The ideals of republicanism and democratic rights traveled across the Atlantic from France, through Saint-Domingue, and into the United States, where enslaved African Americans like Gabriel Prosser found ideological inspiration to test the limitations of white slaveholder power and strike out for freedom.[23] Ranging from nineteenth-century figures such as William Wells Brown and Frederick Douglass, to twentieth-century notables like Henry Ossawan Tanner, Mary Church Terrell, and Ida B. Wells-Barnett, a number of African Americans found both temporary and long-term political, social, cultural, and emotional refuge in France and its luminous capital of Paris. They spread an image of France as the singularly colorblind and authentically democratic nation among its Western counterparts, most notably the United States.[24] Thus, as the United States prepared to enter the war, France, as an embodiment of the transnational potential of democracy, served as a shining example for African Americans. As the *Baltimore Afro-American* wrote in May 1917, "The blessings of 'Liberty, equality and fraternity' which the French citizenry won in the memorable revolution of 1789 have been actually enjoyed by every Frenchman whether he is European or African. Every man in France is a Frenchman first and then afterwards white or black."[25]

Lost in the black press's romantic portrayals of a colorblind France was the nation's contradictory historical relationship with peoples of African descent. By the late 1880s, France had established a strong colonial foothold on the continent with its acquisitions of Algeria and Tunisia, ensuring control of vital Mediterranean commerce routes.[26] During the late nineteenth and early twentieth centuries, France's imperial vision extended into sub-Saharan and equatorial Africa, and by the time of the First World War the tricolor waved throughout the greater western and central parts of the continent.[27] France stamped out indigenous resistance through a combination of brute military force and efforts to impart French enlightenment culture upon what they saw as backward savages. If they had looked closely, African American journalists would have found in France's *mission civilisatrice* a logic rationalizing the domination of white Europeans over African peoples.[28]

FRANCE'S USE OF AFRICAN SOLDIERS as combatants in the war captured the attention and admiration of the black press. After enduring devastating loses at the onset of war in 1914, France wasted little time in turning to its reservoir of colonial manpower. While other European nations used their colonial subjects in the war effort, only France mobilized African soldiers for combat on the western front.[29] It was a bold move, considering the widespread belief among German and British leaders that the war in Europe should be fought among members of the white race exclusively. Colonial officials rationalized that as beneficiaries of French civilization and freedom, subject Africans had a reciprocal obligation to provide service in defense of the nation.

France's North African forces, consisting of the Tirailleurs Algériens and Tunisiens and the Tirailleurs Marocains, represented the most readily accessible contingent of colonial servicemen.[30] The first of what would ultimately be thirty-four thousand Moroccan soldiers left for France in August 1914. These troops were organized into five battalions attached to the French Sixth Army and participated in the crucial September 1914 battle of the Marne, which thwarted German hopes for a quick victory. Their fighting abilities so impressed French military officers that by the end of the war they considered the Tirailleurs Marocains among the most valued colonial soldiers in the entire French army.[31] The Tirailleurs Algériens and Tunisiens were France's most experienced and battle-tested collection of colonial soldiers. By November 1917 nearly 85,000 of these men had seen duty in Europe, where they distinguished themselves in several major battles, including at Verdun. In total, an estimated 206,000 Algerian troops fought for France during the war.[32] Despite the fact that parts of Morocco and Algeria remained "unpacified," French military officials viewed their North African soldiers as evidence of colonialism's success in breeding a spirit of loyalty and civic obligation among the native populations.

The use of the Tirailleurs Sénégalais, a generic label applied to soldiers from the French West African Federation (AOF), for service in Europe generated a much more vociferous debate.[33] In 1857 Louis Faidherbe, then governor of Senegal, established the first contingent of West African *tirailleurs*, which were used essentially as a police force to impose and further legitimize French imperial rule in the region. However, one French colonial officer, Charles Mangin, saw potential for the Tirailleurs Sénégalais beyond their limited domestic capacity and emerged as the most outspoken proponent of employing West Africans for expanded combat duties. In his influential 1910 book *La force noire*, Mangin argued for the use of "black" Africans in the increasingly inevitable event of a European war to counter the demographic imbalance between France and Germany.[34] As a limitless and ultimately expendable pool of manpower, the influx of thousands of African bodies would allow the military to spare precious French lives. Other motivations were also at play. In the context of the French civilizing mission, Mangin and his supporters contended, military service represented another potential step in the process of elevating Africans to a higher level of humanity. Republican universalism fused with colonial racial ideology to justify the employment of African troops.[35] Although French opinions of their West African subjects varied according to region and ethnic group—some populations were perceived as being more "warrior-like" than others—military officials rooted the decision to raise a "force noire" in a constellation of ethnocentric beliefs: African peoples possessed a natural proclivity to warfare; intrinsically had a higher physical tolerance for pain than Europeans; were culturally predisposed to the discipline and hierarchal nature of military life; and, because of their inherent mental inferiority, would unquestionably follow orders from their white commanders.[36]

In the years leading up to the war, Mangin and colonial military officials tested the fortitude of the Tirailleurs Sénégalais by using them to secure the AOF and, most notably, solidify France's imperial grip on North Africa by challenging Moroccan and Algerian resistance. The number of West African soldiers increased following a 1912 decree by Governor-General William Ponty expanding conscription in response to recruitment concerns. On the eve of war in 1914, the Tirailleurs Sénégalais consisted of more than seventeen thousand soldiers organized into six regiments, which the army immediately shipped to France.[37] But it was not until late 1915, as French casualties on the European front continued to mount, that plans to mobilize West Africans on a mass scale proceeded.

The expanded use of West African soldiers created the opportunity for the Senegalese *originaires*, inhabitants of the four communes of St. Louis, Dakar, Gorée, and Rusfisque, to link the war and military service to claims for greater citizenship rights.[38] The *originaires* enjoyed certain privileges—the right to vote in local elections, access to French legal institutions—but could not join the military under the 1912 conscription law because they lived under a Muslim religious code. Blaise Diagne, the Senegalese deputy from the four communes to the French Assembly elected in 1914, had his vision set squarely on using the war and military service to expand the boundaries of French citizenship and forcefully advocated for the right of colonial Africans to bear arms in defense of the motherland. Diagne determined to make the *originaires* eligible for military service in the French regular army, as opposed to the *tirailleur* army of conscripts, which he accomplished with legislation in 1915. With the 1916 "loi Blaise Diagne," soldiers of the four communes and their descendents received full French citizenship.[39] The appeal of securing formal legal status served as a motivating force in causing *originaires* to enlist, which many did with enthusiasm.[40] The politicization of the war for the Senegalese *originaires* transformed it into a test of their future social and political status within the French empire.

Diagne, advocating first and foremost on the behalf of the cosmopolitan Senegalese elite, did not fundamentally challenge the French imperial system and how the military viewed African troops. French colonial officers saw the Tirailleurs Sénégalais as fierce, yet undisciplined fighters who required white leadership in order to grasp the complexities of modern warfare.[41] As a result, white units always held positions directly behind and to the side of regiments composed of African soldiers to supposedly check their inclination to retreat in the face of intense assaults.[42] Moreover, the French military used the Tirailleurs Sénégalais primarily as "shock troops," resulting in disproportionately higher causality rates than for white French soldiers.[43]

By late 1917 their numbers had been significantly depleted, necessitating an influx of new soldiers. French prime minister George Clemenceau, despite considerable opposition from white colonial officials, selected Diagne to lead a recruitment campaign throughout the AOF in 1918. Commissioned with much pomp and circumstance, Diagne enthusiastically exhorted the benefits of military service as a path to greater social and political rights.[44] Diagne's message proved remarkably effective, and, with the assistance of local chiefs, he recruited an additional sixty-three thousand men into the French army. While Diagne's success elevated his personal stature, as well as that of his fellow *originaires*, the promise of expanded rights for the majority of *tirailleurs* remained chimerical at best.[45] Beneath the lofty rhetoric of republicanism, colonial benevolence, and civic reciprocity espoused by French military officials and Senegalese elites alike, the history of West African participation in the war exposed cleavages between France and its colonies.

FROM ACROSS THE ATLANTIC, the black press viewed the exploits of African soldiers in the war as further evidence of France's commitment to racial equality. Black newspapers and journals, by focusing their attention on soldiers of African descent serving in the French military, reframed a debate on the meaning of race and democracy in a broadened internationalist and diasporic context. Stories on France's African servicemen appeared in black newspapers in the months preceding American entry into the war, presenting another Western nation that, unlike the United States, saw black people as playing an important role as combatants in the defense of the nation. "Whenever and wherever black soldiers are placed they fight with the same steadiness and intelligence as white soldiers," the *New York Age* proclaimed in September 1914, and continued, "The French is the only government in Europe that appreciates this fact and makes the most of it."[46] In September 1916 the *Crisis* reported on the presence of French "colored troops" "mixed with white troops from the finest regiments" engaged in fighting at Verdun.[47] These articles swelled African American racial pride and challenged the democratic legitimacy of the United States in comparison to France.

Black America's most influential newspaper, the *Chicago Defender*, chose pictures over words to convey the contribution of African peoples to the French war effort. Between the spring of 1916 and 1917, the *Defender* featured several photographs of African soldiers in the French army on its front pages. The power of photography made the images appearing in the *Defender*, with its circulation that reached into the Deep South, ripe with symbolic meaning.[48] Viewed one way, they functioned as a visual education for dispersed African Americans about the participation of African peoples in the war and its global reach. The images of Algerian and West African soldiers could invoke feelings of transnational racial pride by highlighting their military achievements. One of the earliest photos, appearing in April 1916, showed a contingent of unspecified "African" soldiers traveling through Bordeaux on its way to the front. The accompanying caption read, "These Stalwart Men Are Relied upon for Their

Tirailleurs Sénégalais. French West African colonial troops. Source: Scott, Scott's Official History of the American Negro in the World War.

Courage and Valor."[49] A subsequent June 3 photo was more specific, depicting two Algerian soldiers on horseback above the statement, "These Brave Troops Have Meant Much to the French in Their Success around Verdun."[50]

The photos visually refuted negative stereotypes of African people and black manhood in particular. Several images emphasized the essential humanity of African peoples by showing the soldiers eating and engaging in moments of relaxation.[51] These were not savages but civilized men. Moreover, the *Defender* used African troops to critique arguments that positioned African peoples, and black men specifically, outside the bounds of modern civilization. An extremely compelling photo appeared in the January 27, 1917, issue. Under the heading "Picking Off Germans," the picture displayed a group of African soldiers manning machine gun turrets and included a statement alerting readers to "notice the latest model of machine guns these troops are using."[52] The editors of the *Defender* seemed aware of colonial propaganda asserting that African soldiers lacked the mental capacity to master the use of sophisticated weapons. They challenged such claims with visible evidence to the contrary, and in the process provided their readers with a positive image of Africa and its contributions to the war.

"Picking Off Germans," Chicago Defender, *January 27, 1917.*

The photos, however, also served the more narrow purpose of specifically highlighting African American racial injustice. Just as significant as how these images were framed was how they were not framed. Notably, they appeared alone, with no accompanying articles. As a result, the images stood completely removed from the colonial context in which African soldiers fought, thus reinforcing a misleading view of France's relationship with its subject populations. The paramount goal of the *Defender* was not solely to celebrate the contributions of African servicemen or glorify France as a uniquely democratic and racially egalitarian nation but also to critique the U.S. government by positioning it in dialectical opposition to France.

On the front page of its July 22, 1916, issue, the *Defender* featured a picture with the heading "Wounded French Troops." It depicted several Algerian soldiers, wounded in combat against Germany, "sunning themselves on the balconies of the leading hotels in Paris." Also in the photo was an African American expatriate named Bob Jones, who, according to the *Defender*, left the United States when the state of Georgia refused to allow black men to enlist in its National Guard. "He went to France," the underlining caption bluntly stated.[53]

The message was clear: in the United States, African Americans in most sections of the country lacked the opportunity to defend their country, and, because of Jim Crow segregation, the sight of several black men casually relaxing on the balcony of a prominent hotel was unimaginable. In comparison to France, as the photo and its accompanying caption made explicit, the hypocrisy of the United States was glaring. But this provocative image left many signifi-

"Wounded French Troops," Chicago Defender, *July 22, 1916.*

cant questions unaddressed: who were these Algerian soldiers, and what were the conditions under which they fought? How did they get to Paris, and what type of reception did they receive? Who was Bob Jones?[54] How did he get to France, where did he fight, and how did he end up in Paris? How well did Jones know these Algerian soldiers? What type of exchanges occurred between them? The paper left these questions for the imagination, thus missing an opportunity to investigate a potentially dramatic moment of diasporic unity for the chance to critique the United States and American racial attitudes through a glorification of France. Considering the domestic political focus of the *Defender* and its primary reading audience, this decision is not altogether surprising. The war and the participation of African people in it provided the *Defender* with an expanded range of journalistic possibilities to cast critiques of American racial inequality in a transnational and, more specifically, diasporic context. But the paper remained first and foremost committed to a nation-centered agenda of African American democratic rights, as opposed to a broader critical interrogation of the statuses of and relationships between various peoples of African descent, African Americans included.[55]

The priorities of the black press became more transparent when the United States entered the war. African American soldiers expectedly became the main focus. In the *Chicago Defender*, photos of African American soldiers, and the Eighth Illinois National Guard in particular, replaced photos of African soldiers in the French army and elsewhere. Interestingly, several stories about African Americans in the French Foreign Legion appeared in other papers, including profiles of Bob Scanlon, a middle-weight prizefighter who served in the French Foreign Legion from the outset of the war and won numerous medals for bravery, and the famous Eugene Bullard, an expatriate from Georgia, three-year veteran of the legion, and the world's first black fighter pilot, who came to be known as the "Black Swallow of Death."[56] Their romantic stories reflected a sustained fascination by the black press in France as a symbol of racial equality in opposition to the United States, but also an elevation of African Americans over African soldiers. When the black press did mention African soldiers, it regularly occurred in the context of discussions of African American military service and the domestic racial politics of the war. The *Richmond Planet*, for example, preached a gospel of unconditional African American loyalty and in a June 1917 editorial upheld the historical record of black soldiers. The paper invoked France's African soldiers to underscore its argument, writing, "If the French Senegalese are the terror of the enemy, the well-trained Southern Negro will make a soldier worth while. We believe it without qualification!"[57]

The fact that the *Richmond Planet* even mentioned France's Senegalese troops is itself significant and reflective of the growing war-inspired interest in Africa among the black press. Unpacking this statement, however, reveals much about not only how the black press viewed African soldiers but also how it employed them to further stress the need for expanded African American democratic rights. With the label "French Senegalese," the *Planet* empowered France with ownership of Senegalese, tacitly accepting and legitimizing a hierarchy of West African subjugation to French colonial benevolence. Describing the Senegalese as "the terror of the enemy" likewise reinforced a stereotypical construction of the inherent warrior-like nature of West Africans. It also created a stark contrast between Senegalese soldiers and African Americans. Whereas the Senegalese were naturally fierce fighters, African Americans, even from the South, had progressed beyond such an evolutionary state, responded to training, and would make equally, if not more effective soldiers than their African counterparts. As newspapers like the *Richmond Planet* continued to invest in the service of African American soldiers, they positioned African Americans as occupying a higher rung than France's African colonial soldiers on the ladder of modern civilization.

In one especially revealing case, the black press, in its haste to promote African American enthusiasm for the war, served as a partner with French military officials in propagandizing the imperial civilizing mission. Well before America's official entry into the war, France had taken active steps to cultivate fruitful relations and open lines of communication with the United States by sending several key officers of the French High Command to its embassy in Washington, D.C. One of these men, Lieutenant Colonel Édouard Réquin, was a close confidant of both Marshal Joffre and Marshal Foch with past experience commanding Senegalese soldiers in North Africa. Joel Spingarn, as part of his "constructive programme" in Negro subversion with the Military Intelligence Branch, and Emmett Scott, in his capacity as special assistant to the secretary of war, saw Réquin as a potentially valuable resource for increasing black support for the war. Réquin attended and spoke at the June 1918 Washington, D.C., editors' conference, and the following month, Spingarn requested that he compose a statement regarding France's employment of African soldiers in its army.

Réquin's extraordinary statement, titled "Emploi des troupes des couleur dans l'armée française" (Use of Colored Troops in the French Army), read as a glowing tribute to the success of French colonialism in rescuing Africans from barbarism, providing them with the civilizing benefits of military service, and granting them the ultimate privilege of defending the motherland. Réquin explicitly stated the utilitarian purpose African troops served before the war, writing, "They have been the best instrument of our colonial expansion." He went on to single out the service of Algerian and Moroccan troops as prime examples of the civilizing mission's positive effects, asserting, "If one considers that in North Africa the Mohammedan group has been essentially refractory to all foreign intervention, the voluntary participation of colored men in the defense of French soil consecrates definitely the motivating principles of our expansion." The most glaring aspect of Réquin's article was his characterization of the Tirailleurs Sénégalais, which placed the views held by French military officials of West African soldiers on full display. Completely devoid of self-conscious agency and autonomous thought, they exhibited a blind devotion to their white officers and disregard for their own bodily safety. Unable to master the complexities of modern warfare, such as use of the machine gun, the Tirailleurs Sénégalais were "particularly apt for attack and counter-attack," a euphemism for their crude battlefield utilization as shock troops. This was of no consequence because, as Réquin rationalized, these Africans felt "equally devoted to France, whom they serve most loyally, and to the flag which represents France," and "so that just as we have delivered these black men from African barbarism so we have given them civilization and justice; it is their duty in turn to defend among us that justice and that civilization against Prussian barbarism." Perhaps Réquin had forgotten his article was intended for African Americans who might take offense at his troubling choice of words. But the French officer in fact remained fully cognizant of his audience and made it clear that his characterizations of African soldiers did not apply to African Americans. "But they are primitive men," Réquin wrote of France's West African soldiers, "without civilization—men who cannot be compared from this point of view with colored Americans."[58] In one eye-catching sentence, Réquin provided African Americans with an opportunity to distance themselves from African soldiers, West Africans more broadly, and proclaim their superiority.

A classic piece of French propaganda from Réquin's perspective to promote France's colonial *mission civilisatrice*, the article also gave credence to the idea held by many African Americans that they were superior to other peoples of African descent. Réquin forwarded the article to Joel Spingarn, who saw no problems with his observations and translated the document, without revision, into English. After receiving the translated copy from Spingarn, Emmett J. Scott similarly expressed his pleasure with the article's content, its potential to "cheer and hearten the colored people generally," and promised to have it disseminated to "some of our more important colored newspapers."[59] One of these papers was the influential *New York Age*. The *Age* featured Réquin's article on the front page of its August 10, 1918, issue, under the subheading "French Officer Says Colored Soldiers of France Are Received Exactly the Same as White Soldiers—Foreign Colored Troops Cannot be Compared with Colored Americans who are Products of Civilization."[60]

The *Age* wanted its readers to come away with these two central points of Réquin's article. The subheading framed and positioned France in ideological opposition to the United States and its racially segregated military, a consistent theme throughout much of the black press in its coverage of African soldiers. Second, it reinforced a civilizationist hierarchy of African peoples by portraying African Americans as having a superior mental, cultural, and historical development, thus justifying their full social and political inclusion into modern democracy. This revealed much about the place of Africa in the African American imagination both before and during the First World War.[61] Just as coverage of the war, France, and African soldiers could forge a broadened awareness of the diaspora among African Americans, it also functioned to illuminate significant difference in how African Americans saw themselves in relation to other peoples of African descent. This same tension manifested itself in the experiences of African American soldiers in France.

COLONEL LOUIS ALBERT LINARD served as head of the French Mission, a liaison between the French and American forces specifically concerning the translation and communication of orders and directives.[62] Attached to the American General Headquarters, Linard was responsible for managing coordination between the AEF and the French army regarding the Ninety-third Division. Much of this work was logistical and relatively mundane. But as reports of cordial relations that African American soldiers of the Ninety-third Division enjoyed with their French officers and, most troubling, French civilians increasingly unsettled the racial sensibilities of the American High Command, Linard found himself in the role of both translator and transmitter of American white supremacy.

On August 7, 1918, at the behest of American military officials, he issued one of the most infamous memos of the entire war pertaining to African American soldiers in France. Titled "On the Subject of Black American Troops," marked "confidential," and distributed to French officers of the Ninety-third Division, the article began, "It is important for French officers who have been called upon to exercise command over black American troops, or to live in close contact with them, to possess an exact idea of the situation of Negroes in the United States." Linard presented the "Negro question" as no longer open for debate, stating that "American opinion is unanimous," and that French "indulgence" and "familiarity" were matters "of grievous concern to the Americans." Throughout the memo, Linard took for granted that "American" equated to "white" Americans. "Although a citizen of the United States, the black man is regarded by the white American as an inferior being," whose "vices" made him a "constant menace to the American who has to repress them sternly," Linard claimed. He moved beyond a coded language of rape and lynching to link this staple trope of American white supremacy to the presence of African American soldiers in France. "For instance, the black American troops in France have, by themselves, given rise to as many complaints for attempted rape as all the rest of the army," Linard wrote, although he provided no actual evidence in support of this inflammatory claim. He concluded, "We must prevent the rise of any pronounced degree of intimacy between French officers and black officers." This goal especially applied to relations between African American soldiers and French civilians. He thus encouraged French officers to "make a point of keeping the native cantonment population from 'spoiling' the Negroes," as "the Americans become greatly incensed at any public expression of intimacy between white women with black men." This likewise held true for France's African colonial soldiers, whose relations with white women represented "a considerable loss to the prestige of the white race."[63] Almost in passing, Linard linked African American soldiers and French African colonials through a sexualized language of racial hierarchy and national purity. With stunning bluntness, the directive offered a primer in American racism and how to apply its logic to the treatment of black soldiers in France.

As the Linard memo reflected, the social experiences of African American soldiers in France occurred within an extremely volatile racial, political, and sexual environment. Traveling outside of the United States for the first time, thousands of black soldiers began to move beyond the local and national boundaries of their lives. France and its people offered an oftentimes stark contrast not only in language and culture but in racial customs as well. With eyes blurred by the sting of American racism, African American soldiers relished their cordial and even intimate interactions with French civilians, encounters that served to reenergize their democratic aspirations. American white supremacy was no longer absolute, and the nation itself no longer entirely stable within the minds of many black troops.[64] But, try as they might, African American troops could not escape the reality that, as soldiers, they served on the behalf of the United States. This undeniable connection meant that black soldiers had to contend with the dogged presence of American racism and its influence on army policy. The nation may have been increasingly destabilized for many African American soldiers, but transplanted American racism ensured that it remained present. Through the experiences of African American troops in France, the inspiring hopes and painful limitations of democracy in the international context engaged in a dramatic struggle for legitimacy.

By the time of Linard's memo, African American soldiers had been in France for several months. Having read or heard about men like Bob Scanlon, Eugene Bullard, the exploits of the Senegalese, Algerian, and Moroccan troops in the French army, and the democratic spirit of France, many black servicemen arrived with romanticized impressions of the country and its people. Harry Haywood, at the young age of twelve, became a "Francophile" through an avid reading of French history and the novels of Alexandre Dumas.[65] Other African American soldiers, as they neared the shores of France, looked forward to a respite from the racism of the United States after their often degrading training camp experiences. Lester Granger and his fellow field artillery officers "were all sick of the USA." While realizing that overseas he faced exposure "more than ever to tyrannical authority," Granger could look forward to the prospect "that at least we'd be among friendly people—the French."[66] Many soldiers like Walker Jordan of the Ninety-second Division's 351st Field Artillery Regiment regarded France as a nation "whose regard for class and color worship was shorn away with the guillotine in 1789."[67]

African American soldiers stepped off their transport ships on the docks of Brest, St. Nazaire, and Bordeaux and into a different world. They were initially comforted by the sight of hundreds, thousands of black stevedores busily transferring the American war machine to French soil and ensuring that it ran smoothly.[68] But as they traveled from the port cities and into the French interior, that comfort gave way to the realization of being in a foreign country, with little grasp of the language and only an idealized image of its peoples. Simultaneously, the French citizenry had never seen, much less personally interacted with, black men from the United States, and thus had a frame of reference shaped largely by racial stereotypes of their own African colonial subjects.

Not surprisingly, then, many of the initial interactions between African American soldiers and French women and children were fraught with tension. African American troops, fully cognizant of the rules of racial etiquette that dictated social interactions across the color line in the United States, but yet unaware of how these rules applied to France, approached French women and children with caution. From the perspective of the French, the sight of a black person, and one from the United States at that, often came as a shock and sometimes elicited emotions bordering on racial panic. A French woman named Jeanne Barques recalled in a letter the reactions of the inhabitants of a small town upon the arrival of a contingent of African American soldiers. "How can these dark-faced troops come from America?" the townsfolk wondered. "The people question each other in excitement," Barques wrote. "Some women grow frightened. One tells me mockingly that she is beginning to feel sick at the stomach."[69] Similar to their initial views of African *tirailleurs*, French locals relied upon racial preconceptions of African peoples to interpret the curious presence of African American troops. Harry Haywood remained struck by how the French peasants he encountered, "hearing our strange language and noticing our color, would often mistake us for French colonials. Not Senegalese, who were practically all black but Algerians, Moroccans or Sudanese."[70]

White soldiers of the AEF often went out of their way to educate the French on the subtleties of American racism. Either dead, maimed, or at the front, combat-age men were virtually absent from most French towns. African American soldiers therefore interacted with a disproportionately female French civilian population. White troops injected American ideas of race and sex into this social dynamic.[71] On numerous occasions, they warned the French to avoid black troops because of their natural impulse to commit rape. They often went so far as to characterize African American servicemen as diseased and less than human. Walker Jordan, with a mixture of offense and bemusement, witnessed "groups of school children" who would "slip behind colored soldiers and peer to see if, indeed they wore tails like monkeys."[72]

After interacting with African American soldiers, many French civilians began to discard these racial stereotypes. In a letter to W. E. B. Du Bois, Enoch Dunham of the 324th Labor Battalion noted, "When we did get a chance to go out we proved to the people just the other way and they were not long to find that these statements were false."[73] Indeed, a consistent theme in the testimonies of African American veterans is their positive impression of the French people. Louis Pontlock was "glad the people found us different and learned to love us.

The same thing happened in other town[s] when Negro troops first entered."[74] "As for the nature of the inhabitants themselves," John Cade concluded, "we found them a simple lot, loving peace among themselves and having an abiding tolerance and kindness for the stranger within their gates."[75] Lester Granger and his fellow officers "had very pleasant relations with the French all the time we were there."[76] Richard Hall of the 804th Pioneer Infantry Regiment acknowledged how this treatment was often better than what the black troops received from their fellow white soldiers and officers in the American military.[77] With some irony, 803rd Pioneer Infantry Regiment veteran Robert Stevens remembered, "They treated us with respect. Not like the white American soldiers."[78]

The flattering anecdotes of black soldiers like Robert Stevens must be viewed critically. The French were certainly far from colorblind. Working-class French citizens reacted violently to the presence of colonial laborers from Africa and other parts of the French empire who flooded the metropole during the war, viewing them as a source of labor and sexual competition.[79] Even after interacting with African American troops, stereotypes often held sway, especially the image of black soldiers as rapists propagated by Linard and other American military officials. A French report on relations between American soldiers and the French civilian population made note of an alleged rape committed by a black soldier in the town of Sapois, which as a result made the residents of the community "very nervous and worried about the presence of black soldiers on their territory."[80]

Black troops, however, viewed the French from a perspective warped by American racism and segregation. African American servicemen interpreted their encounters with the French in juxtaposition to their interactions with, and treatment by, their fellow white American soldiers. Black soldiers therefore did not see racism but instead were transfixed by the extent to which their French hosts exhibited little racial prejudice in contrast to white Americans.[81] The glowing accounts of the French stemmed not so much from perceptions that the French lacked racist sentiments but from the fact that white soldiers and officers of the American army regularly acted with such hatred.

Nevertheless, the reality that many French civilians did indeed establish cordial relations with African American soldiers is significant and demands closer inspection. The generally fond view the French had of African American soldiers did not come from a natural proclivity toward racial equality on their part. A number of alternative reasons therefore account for why the French citizenry by and large embraced African American servicemen.

One the most significant factors in shaping how the French interacted with and viewed African Americans was their contentious relationship with white

American soldiers. White soldiers, especially after the war, held French civilians in low regard. They accused French merchants of intentionally inflating prices and, even more unsettling, refusing to conform to American racial customs.[82] The behavior of some white Americans reflected their national and racial arrogance, causing many French merchants and hostesses to prefer the *soldats noirs*. Lester Granger observed, "The French liked the Negro officers better than they did white American officers, because . . . we were 'plus gentil.' The average white American in France in that day—so far as I could see—was the advance cartoon of the bumptious American overseas today. Almost none knew any French. A number of us did know quite a bit. Almost none was interested in the culture, in the history, in the monuments of France. They herded around in public places and made remarks and made passes."[83] Walker Jordan took pleasure in watching a French shopkeeper refuse to serve a group of white soldiers, firmly dismissing them by saying, "Allez! Allez! Le blanc soldat no bon—ugh!" (Go! Go! The white soldier no good—ugh).[84] Charles Hamilton Houston remembered how he and other black officers made a concerted effort to communicate in French: "The general contrast between our attitude and the typical attitude of the white officers was so great that the townspeople took our side and after we had been in the district a month all the lies the white officers tried to spread about us fell on deaf ears."[85] As black soldiers self-consciously demonstrated their best manners, French civilians, contrasting their behavior to white American soldiers, reciprocated and treated them with respect.

The French, however, embraced African American troops not simply because they were polite but in large part because of their perceived unique status as black *Americans*. Many French people assumed that physical and temporal distance from Africa, because of the Atlantic slave trade and successive generations born in the United States, had benefited African Americans by allowing them to attain a higher level of acculturation into Western civilization.[86] African Americans, and black soldiers specifically, represented what France hoped their own colonial subjects would become through their *mission civilisatrice*. They embodied the ideal "noire évoluée," an evolved black man, who had overcome the legacy of African barbarism and successfully adapted to modernity.

This was evidenced by the military participation of African Americans in the war but most prominently by their cultural aesthetic. The French approached African Americans as racial exotics, a view informed by their fascination with "primitive" culture. The destructiveness of the war led to an increased interest in primitivism and the simplistic sensuality of African culture among French intellectuals.[87] The presence of African American soldiers allowed the French to temporarily reconcile their conflicted identity as colonizers. They could embrace

African American troops as the stereotypical racial "other," while extolling their culture as proof of the West's positive civilizing influence.

African American musicians played a significant role in the fetishization of blackness that emerged during the war and flourished during the postwar period.[88] Black regimental bands took France by storm and became almost singularly responsible for the international spread of jazz during the war and in its immediate aftermath.[89] Their abilities captivated the French populace, who had never heard traditional and relatively bland military tunes infused with the "jazz" flair of African American ragtime syncopation and improvisation. Most of the black combat regiments contained their own bands, some led by professional musicians. James Tim Brymn, an acclaimed composer from Philadelphia, directed the 350th Field Artillery Regiment band made up of seventy soloists. Described as "a military symphony engaged in a battle of jazz," the band won rave reviews throughout France.[90] Alfred Jack Thomas, a veteran bandleader of the Tenth Cavalry, led the 368th Infantry Regiment band. Thomas, well known throughout New York and New England, received one hundred applications to join his ensemble, ultimately made up of forty top musicians. Before heading to France, where it gave numerous performances, the band played before Woodrow Wilson and other government leaders at a huge April 6, 1918, parade featuring more than twelve thousand American soldiers from Camp Meade, which included the 368th Infantry Regiment.[91]

And there was James Reese Europe's 369th band, consisting of the best talent from black America and Puerto Rico, which made its presence felt the moment the regiment reached France. When the ship carrying the 369th arrived at the port of Brest on January 1, 1918, Colonel William Hayward immediately had the band whip out its instruments. "Jimmy" Europe appropriately ordered his men to strike up "La Marseillaise," the French national anthem. When the band started playing, according to Noble Sissle, the French soldiers and sailors milling around the docks failed to stand at attention, much to his surprise. But as the "Hellfighters" ensemble continued, the French servicemen realized they were indeed listening to their national song, but being played in a way they had never before experienced. As Sissle proudly recalled, "It was the unaccustomed interpretation of their anthem that caused the French soldiers and sailors to be so tardy in coming to the salute." When they finally recognized it, "there came over their faces an astonished look." By the time the 369th departed France, their "jazzed" version of "La Marseillaise" had become wildly popular, putting the staid French version to shame.[92] In addition to keeping up the morale of the 369th, Europe's band served as the official representative of the U.S. Army and, by extension, the American nation, playing concerts large and small, from venues in the Parisian capital to nondescript French villages, and before audiences that ranged from the highest French dignitaries to elderly French women.[93] African American bands satisfied French cravings for both American popular culture and African primitivism, as well as providing a much needed emotional release for the war-torn nation.[94] At the same time, they demonstrated the profound democratic possibilities of jazz to challenge racial, linguistic, and national barriers.

For many African American soldiers, their interactions with French civilians had a deep impact on their racial consciousness and appreciation of democracy. Black servicemen bore the emotional and psychological scars of their battles with the color line and thus found a sense of both comfort and hope in the potential of interracial democracy through their contacts with French civilians. Suddenly, America and its undemocratic treatment of black people ceased to be the norm. Alternate visions of democracy existed. Lieutenant Osceola McKaine, for these reasons, could hardly contain his effusive admiration of the French. "We have received a most wonderful reception everywhere we have gone," McKaine wrote. Referring to his fellow soldiers in the 367th regiment, he continued, "The Buffaloes have been tres polit and have made friends," and have treated their "new freedom" with respect and responsibility. McKaine spoke of a broadening of the collective racial and political consciousness of the black soldiers in his regiment who enjoyed a level of "freedom" in their social relations with white people on French soil that did not exist in the United States. The deepened internationalism of black soldiers, however, was fundamentally personal and struck at the heart of their political, racial, and gender identities. "As for myself," McKaine declared, "I have never before experienced what it meant to be really free—to taste real liberty—in a phrase to be a man. I love the French."[95]

Arthur George Gaston had a similar experience. Before the war, Gaston dreamed of traveling to France and visiting "Gay Paree." When he received the opportunity as a regimental supply sergeant of the 317th Ammunition Train of the Ninety-second Division, his first sight of the war-torn city, "sand-bagged, blacked-out and scarred from enemy attacks," momentarily dashed his romantic expectations. Gaston's adoration of France was restored by his interactions with the French citizenry, whom he described as "exceptionally kind to us" and accepting of "Negro soldiers as equals of any other soldiers and of themselves." Gaston loved being overseas, where it was "different for a Negro," and he "could be accepted as an equal, as a friend." Visiting the homes of French families for dinner and wine, the playfully confusing conversations in broken English and tattered French, "the marvelous aromas that rolled from the kitchens," "the wonderful feeling of camaraderie and warmth," all had a visceral impact on

Gaston. "I could feel it surge in me," he exclaimed, "this new sense of confidence, of being equal."[96]

But the white supremacist realities of American democracy nevertheless remained vividly present throughout the experiences of African American soldiers in France. The American military viewed the egalitarian treatment of black troops like Osceola McKaine and Arthur Gaston as a matter of grave concern. White American officers, as Linard articulated, remained all too aware of the implications of black soldiers returning to the United States with a new conception of democracy and the threat this posed to the stability of American racial hierarchies. For African American troops, traveling to France was important, but had limitations. After all, they were in the army, an institution that replicated many of the same patterns of dominance, control, and violence that characterized race relations in the United States. While experiencing new possibilities for the expansion of democracy, black soldiers still had to contend with their identity as soldiers of the United States military and as agents of American nationalism. This was further reinforced by the systemic racism that accompanied their service and assumed the same ferocity as its domestic manifestations.

As was the case in the United States, the racism of the American military in France contained a strong sexual element. The specter of sex between black soldiers and white French women was ubiquitous. The protection of white womanhood, central to white male southern identity, traveled across the Atlantic and, with it, fears of black male sexuality as a threat to the stability of the domestic color line. The army energetically attempted to regulate the color line in France and control the interactions between African American soldiers and French women on the basis of American racial customs.

After an alleged wave of rapes and attempted rapes committed by black soldiers enflamed the sensitivities of American army officials, the Ninety-second Division came under obsessive scrutiny. The division, with its contingent of black officers and rigorously trained fighting men, became a potent symbol of black manhood and, as such, was cast as a threat to white womanhood. The burden of proof consistently rested on the Ninety-second Division to provide evidence exonerating black soldiers from involvement in cases of sexual assault, even in situations where a white soldier had been identified by the victim. The largely unsubstantiated charges, nevertheless, had a profound impact on the treatment of the division, its enlisted men, and the broader perception of it among the high command of the American army. Within the gossip circles of the AEF's white officers, the Ninety-second became derisively labeled "the rapist division."[97]

Less than two weeks after Linard's meditation on the acceptable boundaries of racial contact involving African American soldiers, Major General Charles Ballou, commander of the Ninety-second Division, produced an explicitly restrictive memo directed at his own men. "On account of the increasing frequency of the crime of rape, or attempted rape, in this Division, drastic preventative measures have become necessary," the August 21, 1918, memorandum began. Ballou placed sole responsibility for the situation on the shoulders of the division's African American servicemen, firmly stating that "all resulting hardship has been brought on themselves by their failure to themselves observe and report suspicious characters." As a result, Ballou ordered a periodic one-hour check of all troops between reveille and 11:00 P.M., the establishment of a strictly enforced one-mile-limit regulation for leaving camp, and a requirement that leave passes would be issued only to "men of known reliability." If, by Ballou's standards, conditions failed to improve, specific companies and regiments would be placed under armed guard.[98] It was a blatant attack on the manhood of the Ninety-second Division's African American soldiers and an implicit rebuke of the ability of black officers to control the men under their command.

The following day, August 22, 1918, Ballou issued a memo to the white commanding generals of the 183rd and 184th Brigades, this one with an ominous threat. According to Ballou, General John Pershing himself stated that if measures to address "the crime of rape" were not taken seriously, "he will send the 92d Division back to the United States, or break it up into labor battalions, as unfit to bear arms in France." It is unclear whether Pershing actually spoke these words, but authentic or fabricated, the threat served Ballou's purpose of striking fear into the officers and men of the division. Ballou couched the threat and the need of the division's white officers to take action "in the broader interest of the colored race." "*All* are expected to pull together to prevent the presence of colored troops being a menace to women," he concluded.[99] Ballou's memo demonstrated how the army transported white supremacy and the criminalization of black manhood to France.[100] His actions served as a painful reminder that the freedom and sense of internationalism experienced by African American servicemen had its boundaries.

A similar racial and sexual panic swirled within the Ninety-third Division. One particular unit, the 371st Infantry Regiment, became a source of considerable controversy. A memo written in August 1918 by the 371st Regimental Intelligence Officer Ernest Samusson to the town mayors of Marat la Grande, Marats la Petit, and Rembercourt aux Pots warned of "an undesirable relation" existing between "certain individuals of the French population" and African American soldiers. The tone and message closely mirrored the Linard memo and may have in fact been influenced by it. Samusson urged local civil authorities to actively prevent interactions between French women and black servicemen by "enlightening the residents in the villages concerned on the gravity of the situation and by warning them of the inevitable results." While assuming that the issue was "of great importance to the French people," he stressed that it was "even more so to the American towns, the population of which will be affected later when the troops return to the United States."[101] Having enjoyed sex with white French women and assuming that relations across the color line were acceptable, demobilized black soldiers would, in his logic, spark a rape epidemic in the South. The 369th, 370th, and 372nd Infantry Regiments did not receive similar directives. The fact that draftees predominantly from South Carolina, not national guardsmen, made up the 371st and that, unlike the other three units of the Ninety-third Division, most of the men in the regiment would indeed return to the South made the regiment a cause for potential concern from the perspective of its white commanders. In their eyes, southern black men possessed a higher propensity for sexual violence than northern black men. Samusson thus advanced several overlapping myths regarding black masculinity and rape.

Despite being heavily policed and closely monitored, black soldiers continued to fraternize with French citizens, often against direct orders. American military racism only served to increase the admiration black soldiers had for the French. When billeting, visiting, or passing through a town, black troops made a conscious effort to refute the racial propaganda of white military officials and make a good impression upon their hosts. The best attempts of white officials also did not prevent interracial sexual relations. In a July 23, 1918, letter to his church in Chicago, 370th Infantry chaplain William Braddan wrote that some of the regiment's men had "fell willing victims to cupid and married even though they knew no more about the French language than I do about an Aeroplane."[102] In his reply to the United States Military History Institute survey question "was there much consorting with local women," a black veteran of the 317th Ammunition Train responded: "Yes a plenty. Nature must take its course."[103]

Sleeping with a white woman was not an inherently political act. Black soldiers were after all men, irrespective of race and, like many American soldiers, had sexual urges.[104] But for those African American servicemen who did engage in sexual relations with French women, their actions contained an undeniable symbolic potency. Within the United States, the color line and notions of democracy itself were inextricably bound to the protection of white womanhood. White women functioned as symbols of the nation and an idea of democracy characterized by racial purity. By having sex with white French women, black soldiers not only consciously violated the most explosive racial taboo in the United States but made a statement about the fallacy of the color line and the potential of white and black people to interact with each other on the most intimate of levels. Black soldiers, consciously defying their superiors, found interracial democracy, so to speak, in the company of French women.

Their actions, however, also increased the potential of violent confrontation with white American soldiers and officers, who cringed at the sight of a French woman on the arm of a black soldier. Charles Hamilton Houston knew this from personal experience. One evening, while stationed in Vannes, a medieval town located in southern Brittany, Houston found himself at the explosive intersection of race, class, sex and violence. Two French "sporting girls" had spurned their white American officer companions for a black officer who drew their interest by his ability to speak French. The white captains, incensed, confronted the uppity black lieutenant. Houston and another officer happened to be passing by and observed the argument. Seemingly out of nowhere, two trucks "loaded with white enlisted men," led by one of the aggrieved white officers, arrived on the scene with orders to lynch the African American officers.[105] It was around 10:30 or 11:00 at night, in a deserted plaza save for the presence of four black officers and a mob of white soldiers, and southern-style racial justice had again reared its head on French soil. "The officer who led the mob," Houston vividly remembered, "began to yelp about 'niggers' forgetting themselves just because they had a uniform on, and it was time to put a few in their places, otherwise the United States would not be a safe place to live in after they got back." Houston and his comrades refused to back down. One of the African American officers invoked his authority, stating that "he was an officer and was not going to have anything to do with enlisted men, but that there were four white officers and four of us, and they could either fight it out one by one or all together so long as it was an officers' fight." Before an all-out brawl erupted, an American military police captain intervened, defusing a perilous situation.[106]

The scales of military justice, however, leaned heavily against black soldiers when it came to matters involving sexual relations with French women. For nineteen-year-old William Buckner this lesson had tragic consequences. Buckner served as a private in Company B of the 313th Labor Battalion. What truly happened between the young soldier from Henderson, Kentucky, and Georgette Thiebaux, a French woman from the town of Arrentières, on July 2, 1918, remains contested. No doubt exists that the two had sex in a local wheat field, and the episode ended badly. Thiebaux, in a panic, flagged down a pair of French soldiers, screaming that the black soldier had raped her. After his arrest, Buckner steadfastly proclaimed his innocence, asserting that their encounter was consensual, and Thiebaux became upset only when he refused to give her his watch. William Buckner was charged with violation of the Ninety-second Article of War—rape—and the court-martial began on July 27, 1918.[107]

For three days, the court heard from a long list of witnesses consisting of Thiebaux's family, town residents, French soldiers, white American officers, and several of Buckner's fellow black servicemen in the 313th Labor Battalion. The most dramatic testimony came from Thiebaux and Buckner themselves. The twenty-three-year-old victim made a riveting witness, describing in emotional detail through a translator how Buckner violated her despite a valiant attempt to resist his aggressions. "My head was on the ground," she testified. "He was carrying me by all manners, while I was screaming and he looked very angry." Throughout the ordeal, the young woman could not even bear the sight of Buckner's face. "He was so ugly that I would not look at him." When asked under cross-examination to explain how she did not see her assailant's face, but knew he was ugly, Thiebaux emphatically responded, "I say he is ugly because he is a nigger and niggers are disgusting." The prosecution used Thiebaux's mother, father, local acquaintances, and the two French soldiers who assisted her to bolster the case against Buckner. But their presentation, effectively contested by the defense, left considerable room for doubt. The available physical evidence was thin, black soldiers in Buckner's unit supported his story, and—perhaps most damning—the physician who conducted the medical examination on Thiebaux could not conclusively state that she had been raped. Buckner felt confident enough to take the stand on his own behalf. He presented a much different image of Georgette Thiebaux, that of a fast woman, with the ability to speak English, who had no reservations about having sexual relations with him on two prior occasions.

In the end, Buckner's testimony did not carry enough weight. Similar to accusations in the American South, a charge of rape when substantiated by the privileged voice of the white female victim amounted to a fait accompli for the alleged black perpetrator. Two-thirds of the court found the evidence compelling enough to render a verdict of guilty and sentence Buckner to death. The far from unanimous conclusion prompted the Office of the Judge Advocate to exhaustively review the case. It upheld the decision, General John Pershing concurred, and President Woodrow Wilson gave final approval for Buckner's execution.[108]

The last moments of his life would be a public affair. Army officials obtained permission from the mayors of Arrentières and neighboring Bar-Sur-Aube to erect a scaffold in a nearby field. "I am not guilty of raping Georgette Thiebaux. She consented to the intercourse," Buckner insisted up to the evening before his execution. At 5:50 A.M. on the morning of September 6, 1918, Buckner arrived in an ambulance to the site of his execution. A crowd had already gathered. He walked up the scaffold, escorted by two guards. When offered the chance to make a final statement, he replied, "No, Sir." He had already said enough. A black hood was placed over his head. The noose was adjusted around his neck. At 6:00 A.M., the trap door under Buckner's feet sprung open and he dropped six feet, six inches. Fourteen minutes later, a medical examiner pronounced Buckner dead.[109]

Eight of the eleven American soldiers sentenced to death by courts-martial and officially executed in France during the war were black. All of the cases involved charges of rape, and three incidents included charges of murder.[110] Moreover, persistent rumors, both during and after the war, of executions without trial—lynchings—suggest that vigilante justice disproportionately targeted African American soldiers as well.[111] Philip Bell, a black soldier from Memphis, Tennessee, who served in the 336th Labor Battalion, testified before Congress after the war about the lynching of another black servicemen at Is-sur-Tille. A mob of white troops hung the man from a tree limb for associating with a white French woman. When asked why he did not report the incident, Bell replied, "I was afraid I might git the same thing."[112] In mid-August 1918, as Harry Haywood and the 370th Infantry Regiment prepared to billet in a French town in the Meuse department, the battalion commander gathered the men. Only weeks earlier, Haywood was told, "a Black soldier from a labor battalion had been court martialed and hanged in the very square where we were standing. His crime was the raping of a village girl. His body had been left hanging there for twenty-four hours, as a demonstration of American justice."[113] A black soldier had indeed been executed on July 13, 1918, at the town of Bazoilles-Sur-Meuse, but his alleged crime was the rape of a sixty-eight-year-old French woman.[114] It is more likely that fact and rumor conjoined to distort Haywood's memory. Nevertheless, he did not stand alone among black troops who believed such stories and viewed "American justice" in France through the lens of domestic racial violence.

For every moment of affection, cordiality, and intimacy African American soldiers experienced with French officers and civilians, the U.S. Army provided a counterbalance and reminder of how a broadened international consciousness would have to be forged through discriminatory military policy and violence. The illuminating experience of travel to France and interaction with French men and women shaped the racial, political, and gender awareness of many African American soldiers. The United States and its racism, however, continued to loom large, constantly shocking black troops back to the reality that, for whatever it was worth, they remained Americans.

THESE TENSIONS BETWEEN nationalism and internationalism had significant implications for how African American soldiers viewed and saw themselves in relation to other African servicemen. The war brought previously disconnected peoples of the African diaspora together on the docks, streets, and battlefields of France. It also revealed the depths to which peoples of the African diaspora, African Americans included, struggled to forge a shared sense of connection through the entanglements of race, nation, empire, language, ethnicity, class, and history itself. The war and military service created unprecedented opportunities for African American and African soldiers in the French army to interact, communicate, and learn from one another. But this was far from a seamless process. African American soldiers remained historically tied to and often politically invested in the United States. And as Americans, they had internalized many of the stereotypes and misconceptions of African peoples popularized by the West. Their exchanges with other African troops, indeed how they experienced diaspora, were full of both fertile possibility and deep misunderstanding.

Combat and labor brought both African American and African colonial soldiers into oftentimes close contact. An estimated 135,000 Africans, largely from Algeria, Tunisia, and Morocco, arrived in France during the war as laborers, employed to fill the severe shortage of male workers lost to the army.[115] More than 160,000 African American soldiers attached to the American forces, many performing similar duties, complemented their presence. Both physical proximity and the racialized nature of their labor linked these soldiers together.

Service on the front lines likewise presented opportunities for African American troops to cross paths with other soldiers of African descent. This was particularly true for the Ninety-third Division. Black soldiers of the Ninety-third Division's four regiments—approximately 11,000 men—often fought side by side with thousands of African colonial troops from the AOF, Algeria, and Morocco in the French Fourth Army. The first assignment for the 369th Infantry Regiment took place in a region dubbed the "Afrique" sector because of the extensive service and presence of French colonial troops.[116] The war and military service created the physical conditions for African American and African soldiers to share the same space and frequently interact with each other.

African American soldiers took particular interest in the sight of African colonial troops. Coming upon other black men, other black soldiers, dressed in foreign garb and speaking different languages, must have been a remarkable experience. Many African American servicemen, however, could not help but notice how strange and exotic the French colonial troops appeared. William Dyer graduated as a medical officer from Fort Des Moines and received an assignment with the 317th Ammunition Train of the Ninety-second Division. He reached France on June 27, 1918, and spent much of his first month in France en route to the Ninety-second Division's headquarters at Bourbonne-les-Bains. Along the way he stopped at the bustling Mediterranean port city of Marseille, which he described as "the most cosmopolitan city on earth," filled with "people of every nation with their most peculiar dress and customs." The sight of whom he perceived to be Algerian soldiers struck Dyer and made a lasting impression. "The Algerians wearing their little red skull caps, many of whom were black as tar, were the strangest looking," he wrote. "These men all being soldiers, I cannot to this day see how with such clothing and peculiarities of dress, they could be of best service on the Western Front where small neat fitting garments seem essential."[117] The soldiers Dyer came into contact with were probably not Algerian, but West African *tirailleurs* from the AOF. Like most African American soldiers, Dyer still had much to learn about the history of French colonialism, the diversity of African peoples, and their cultural customs.

Language and problems of translation played a key role in the cultural disjuncture between African American servicemen and African soldiers.[118] African American soldiers could not speak Arabic, Wolof, Mandé, Bamanankan, or any of a host of West African dialects. Nor could African colonials speak English, a fact that surprised many African American soldiers who had never before encountered a black person outside of the United States.[119] A postwar report on American-Franco relations had little to say on the relations between African American soldiers and the French, but stated, "We find merely such inconsequential items as one concerning the astonishment of U.S. Colored troops at the inability of French Colored Colonials to speak English."[120] While white military officials may have found this issue "inconsequential," it was crucial in shaping the nature of interactions between African Americans and Africans, who quite literally spoke past each other. The *Cleveland Advocate* featured a slapstick story of "a genuine Negro from a Southern cotton plantation," who during his time in France "had seen many other black men" and "naturally figured them all members of the same race." However, when this soldier encountered "a French Algerian" and asked him for a light, "the Algerian looked at the American while he was repeating his requests and then walked away." The *Advocate* viewed the incident as worthy of a vaudeville comedy with stock minstrel characters. The surprised African American soldier complained to a fellow comrade, "Lordy,

Lordy, man; doan it beat all how some of dese kin fight so long heah in dis country dat they clean fergit dere own languidge?"[121]

Private Julius Paul, a soldier in the 371st Infantry Regiment had a more serious, but equally frustrating first encounter with a Senegalese soldier. Karl Bardin, a white first lieutenant, recounted how Paul's inability to speak French and the Senegalese soldier's lack of English hindered their initial attempts to communicate with each other. The fact that Paul approached this Senegalese soldier and made the effort to talk with him is itself remarkable, reflecting the potential power of blackness to forge connections between dispersed peoples of African descent. Blackness, however, had its limitations. Having never, in his words, seen "a nigger before that couldn't talk United States," Private Paul assumed that the Senegalese soldier was crazy and reported him to Lieutenant Bardin. To Paul's relief, Bardin explained to him, "Why Paul, that is one of your real Brothers from Africa. He is just as same as you are, but he only speaks French and his own African dialect." Although Bardin may have seen Paul and the Senegalese soldier as "just as same," they were in fact quite different. Paul's comment about talking "United States" revealed the linguistic and cultural divide between the two black soldiers, and how the identities of African American soldiers remained rooted in a strong, yet wholly predictable, connection to the nation.[122]

But diaspora was a process, and as such, the relationship between African soldiers and African American soldiers evolved with the course of the war and their service in France. Over time, the sight of African soldiers became less of a shock. As many African American soldiers developed a better grasp of the French language, and African soldiers did the same, their familiarity and interactions with each other increased. A correspondent embedded with the AEF reported with some amazement how many African American soldiers had "become fluent French talkers," engaging in "animated conversations" with "the Senegalese who chanced to be passing."[123] Military service itself functioned as the most important link in the evolving relationship between African American and African soldiers. Black troops, particularly those close to the front lines, developed an impression of their African counterparts as fierce and heroic fighters. Horace Garvin, a private in the 801st Pioneer Infantry, "came in contact with Algerians," who, in his view, "seemed to be good soldiers."[124] James Reese Europe informed readers of the *New York Age*, "It is glorious to see the French regiments intermingled with black boys, and I wish to state here of all the black French troops I have seen over here, I have never seen one without some sort of decoration and I have met thousands."[125] African soldiers became a source of racial pride for African American servicemen, many struggling against an army power structure that attempted to devalue their sacrifice.

Gradually, some African American soldiers began to see not only how they differed from their African counterparts but what they had in common as well. Most striking, they both occupied marginalized positions and endured similar discriminatory treatment in their respective armies. The training of both African colonial troops and African American combatants in the Ninety-second Division suffered as a result of shared assumptions by French and American military officials that black men could not grasp the complexities of modern warfare.[126] Both French West African *tirailleurs* and African American labor troops regularly endured substandard camp and living conditions. In early November 1918, the army stationed black servicemen of the 813th Pioneer Infantry in camps and huts also occupied by Senegalese soldiers of the Second Colonial Army Corps. "Attention is drawn to the fact that in most of these camps," an officer of the French Mission noted, "huts and dugouts are in area of former first line of defense and are in poor condition."[127] Shared racial oppression thus acted as an important foundation for African American soldiers to view their relations with African troops in a more explicit political context. Just as military service politicized African American soldiers and broadened their global awareness, it also did the same for many African soldiers in the French army. Exposure to metropolitan democratic ideals of the rights of man and expectations of citizenship based on the "dette du sang" (blood debt) caused many African *tirailleurs* to question their colonial subjugation.[128] They also became familiar with the issues and struggles of African Americans. In a letter to W. E. B. Du Bois, an unnamed African American serviceman admitted his surprise when a French African soldier asked him if the American army intended to hang the remaining men convicted in the Houston uprising. The soldier wrote of the French Africans, "They know everything and what they don't know we will tell them."[129]

Explicitly political exchanges between African and African American soldiers, while significant, were nevertheless rare. In spite of the eye-opening effect of interacting and communicating with African soldiers, African American servicemen struggled to completely break free from the controlling grip of American nationalism and dominant perceptions of African peoples. The fact remained that fundamental cultural, social, and political differences existed between African American and African soldiers rooted in their particular historical experiences and contemporary realities. Lacking a familiarity with the histories of North and West African soldiers, as well as the impacts of French colonialism, African American servicemen often continued to fall back upon stereotype, caricature, and exoticization. Pervasive notions of African inferiority, held by white and black Americans alike, proved difficult to overcome. Americanness regularly trumped Africanness.

The stumbling block of language and translation again played a significant role in preventing African American soldiers from developing a more nuanced view of their African counterparts. Horace Pippin described the Algerian soldiers fighting alongside him and the 369th Infantry Regiment as "a good lot" and observed that "they did not care for the French mutch." "If we were with one of them," Pippin noticed, "and a French men came by us the algerian would say Pare-Bon Dar French Par-Bon he ment that the French were no good for him."[130] Although Pippin clearly understood some French, a considerable communication barrier still existed between him and the Algerian soldiers he encountered. This was linguistic and, at the same time, historical. Pippin's understandable lack of knowledge and limited language skills prevented him from asking a crucial question: *why* did this Algerian soldier dislike the French? Pippin could not fully appreciate the rare firsthand lesson he received in the contentious colonial relationship between France and Algeria. Embedded within the seemingly flippant statement of this Algerian soldier lay a volatile history of French colonial aggression and Algerian resistance that defined the relationship between the two nations.

The same linguistic and historical disjunctures shaped interactions between African American and West African servicemen. In speaking French with these troops, African American soldiers lacked a full understanding of the regional, social, and cultural cleavages within West African societies exacerbated by the war.[131] In Senegal, for example, many of the *originaires* from the communes, and Dakar in particular, attended colonial schools and learned to speak, write, and read French fluently. This constituted an important part of the French civilizing mission, which was based on a belief in the ability of urbanized Africans to potentially attain a higher level of cultural evolution, thus warranting their label as *évolués*.[132] Consequently, the Senegalese *évolués*, similar to the African American bourgeoisie, internalized their elevated social and political status, which translated into a hierarchical relationship with rural and village Senegalese peoples. Outside of the communes, where the French army recruited and conscripted most of the *indigenes* into service as *tirailleurs*, they were educated in local schools and did not speak fluent French. During their time in the French military, most *tirailleurs* spoke a pidgin form of French—*petit nègre*—that provided just enough vocabulary to allow communication with their French officers.[133] Therefore, if an African American soldier encountered a Senegalese soldier fluent in French or, more rarely, English, he most likely came from the communes and approached military service with a different set of social and political sensibilities than other *tirailleurs* of the French army.

Most frequently, African American soldiers resorted to racially charged generalizations of African soldiers as fierce fighters. Horace Pippin may have indeed admired the Algerian soldiers he interacted with, but his impressions focused on their ruthless fighting ability, use of crude weaponry, and lack of compassion for their German adversaries. Pippin came away from the war convinced that "they were a bad lot to their foe, for they would not gave a foe a chance. I have seen them go over the top mineys a time and they never have a prisoner but his knife would have fresh blood on it, when he came back." Pippin, like many other African American soldiers, remained fascinated with the *tirailleurs'* use of the bolo knife, their purported weapon of choice in lieu of the rifle or machine gun. "They would cairy this knife in their belt all the time," Pippin continued, "but when they would go over the top they would put this knife in to thir mouth and no rifle at all with them. I have seen them do it. But when they come back do not look for a Germen, for they would not have any with them, that is the way they would handel the Germans."[134] A fellow veteran of the 369th Infantry Regiment similarly believed the soldiers he encountered "were game and they wouldn't take no prisoners." He went on to state how the Moroccans did not take German prisoners, but instead "cut their ears off and strung 'em on a string and tied around their waist."[135]

There is little evidence to support the idea that African soldiers routinely engaged in such acts. Moreover, both France and Germany propagandized competing myths about the ruthlessness of African soldiers, albeit for very different reasons. Whereas France hoped to strike terror into the hearts of their German foes, Germany constructed the presence of African troops as a threat to white civilization, and women in particular.[136] Pippin and other black troops may have seen a Senegalese or Moroccan soldier using the bolo knife to attack and kill Germans, but their embellishment reflected just how deeply certain national and international stereotypes of African peoples had been internalized by some African American servicemen. A black soldier of the 370th had never seen the "French black troops" drill but had heard that "they sure is fighting people." He relayed a wild story of two thousand African troops who had captured fifty thousand Germans in a single night. "They say they must gets crazy like in battle and throws away their rifles and goes after them boches with knives." But he was not finished. "We hear that they can't keep 'em in rest camps long or they go crazy. Just wants to be killing Germans all the time. Seems like they just got to see blood. If they ain't killed a German for some time, they takes a knife and cut themselves on their hand. They ain't no other way 'bout it. They sure is fighting people. They calls 'em Samboleese."[137]

The exaggerated and overtly stereotypical observations of African American soldiers were also influenced by, and continued to reinforce, a perception of Africans as lacking the capacity to master the sophistication of advanced weaponry, placing them outside the boundaries of modernity. Monroe Mason and Arthur Furr, two black soldiers who served as historians of the 372nd, described the participation of the regiment in the Meuse-Argonne offensive. They were especially impressed by a group of African troops, most likely from Morocco, manning huge artillery guns. Mason and Furr wrote that the African troops "took delight in explaining some of the important features" of these weapons of modern warfare to "interested and curious spectators."[138] It must have been an extraordinary sight for them to witness African soldiers educating white people on the use of complicated war machinery.

For Mason and Furr, however, these Moroccan soldiers still did not measure up to African American troops. The two African American authors simply described them as "African" and made no effort to acknowledge their nationality or ethnicity. They observed that "a marked impatience and fierceness prevailed among the African troops, whose valor as assaulting forces were unsurpassed by any of the Allies," a simultaneous compliment and civilizationist critique of the Moroccans.[139] When fighting commenced at daybreak on September 26, "Never was there a more appalling sight. The furious Africans plunged onward waving their arms and huge knives with fiendish glee, charging German machine-gun nests with absolute disregard of death and injury. Although their ranks were seriously depleted by the unerring machine-gun fire of the Huns, they drove on taking one position after another, leaving nothing but the wounded and dead, and utter destruction in their wake." The participating African American soldiers, however, "advanced in a more scientific manner, using the wave formation, which made it appear that there were double the number of men."[140] The crux of their juxtaposition of the Moroccan soldiers against African American soldiers paralleled the August 1918 statement of Colonel Réquin, in which he described France's African *tirailleurs* as "without civilization—men who cannot be compared from this point of view with colored Americans." The observations of Mason and Furr spoke to their political goals in writing a history of the 372nd, replete with glorification of the regiment's achievements as proof of African American's contribution to the war. They also reflected how many African American soldiers viewed their African counterparts with an internalized sense of cultural and evolutionary superiority.

Diaspora, as African American troops demonstrated, was a process, one characterized by cultural, linguistic, and ideological tensions between African Americans and various African peoples that would take time and experience to understand. Service in France provided opportunities for black soldiers to broaden their views of the world and the place of peoples of African descent in it. By interacting with troops from West Africa, Morocco, and Algeria, many African American soldiers learned important lessons about the global reach of the war and its impact on the diaspora. But African American troops could not simply disregard their attachment to the United States. The stumbling blocks they encountered and articulated during their interactions with other African soldiers confirmed that service in France had the power to both unsettle and reaffirm the racial and national identities of African American soldiers.

ON NOVEMBER 16, 1918, five days after the armistice, Blaise Diagne sent an impassioned letter to French prime minister George Clemenceau. The Senegalese deputy had learned of the August 7, 1918, memo issued by Louis Linard informing French officers of the Ninety-third Division how to treat African American troops. Shocked by the presence of the circular and its distribution by a French officer, Diagne wrote to register his protest against what he saw as an act of humiliation toward "the race to which I personally belong." Diagne expressed concern over the circulation of the memo and its impact on the minds of Frenchmen for whom, he disingenuously asserted, such audacious prejudices were completely foreign. Most interestingly, he accused Linard, in his claim "of a unanimous American opinion on the 'Negro question'" of being ignorant of "the evolution which has occurred in American opinion on the 'Negro question' and that the war has caused." He thus took it upon himself to provide Clemenceau with evidence of this development by including, along with his memo, a document entitled "The Impact of the War on the Negro Question in the United States and the Measures Taken to Improve the Condition of Negroes." Composed of information gathered from the *Literary Digest* and other northern periodicals, the document detailed the causes and implications of black migration, the responses of both southern and northern white people to the exodus, and various actions taken by the government, such as the creation of the Des Moines officers' training camp, to placate African American political demands. Diagne, exhibiting impressive knowledge of racial conditions in the United States, used the Linard memo as an opportunity to critique American white supremacy and challenge its importation to French soil. He requested that Clemenceau launch an investigation into the origins of the circular and what influence it may have had within the French army and take steps to have it invalidated, so that "nothing remains of the ideas which have inspired it."

While Diagne's words in defense of African Americans and in condemnation of Linard were sincere, his letter to Clemenceau most pointedly reflected a concern with the Tirailleurs Sénégalais and the implications of the memo regarding France's colonial policies. Diagne focused on the single sentence of Linard's directive alluding to France's colonial troops and their relationships with French women, blasting it as explicitly contradicting "the inviolable principles of our colonial policy" and slandering the good name and loyalty of the colonial troops who, in "sharing the same sufferings and the same dangers" as other soldiers, had the right to be treated with respect. To invalidate the memo, Diagne included within his letter excerpts of a statement from the minister of the colonies, which lauded France's *mission civilisatrice*, the expansion of conscription throughout the AOF, Diagne's role in promoting the war effort among his countrymen, and the reciprocal obligation of France to ameliorate the social, political, and economic conditions of West Africans as a result of their loyalty. Diagne was firmly invested in this French colonial project and thus demanded assurance that Linard spoke as a lone individual corrupted by American prejudices and not on the behalf of the government. The reputation and legacy of the Tirailleurs Sénégalais remained inextricably tied to his own personal political legitimacy, in the eyes of both French government officials and the Senegalese *originaires*. Diagne therefore took active measures to discredit the Linard memo and its association with France's colonial policies.[141] His letter to Clemenceau captured the complex dynamics of diaspora as a process shaped by the experiences of African American soldiers, and soldiers of African descent more broadly, and characterized by moments of racial fraternity and simultaneous ideological discontinuity.

Diagne's communication also speaks directly to the emergence of a distinct form of Pan-African politics informed by the war and the military participation of soldiers of African descent. Diagne's impassioned letter to Clemenceau likely played a role in the French prime minister's decision to allow Diagne and W. E. B. Du Bois to hold a Pan-African congress three months later in February 1919. With the backing of the NAACP, W. E. B. Du Bois proposed the congress as a direct response to the anticipated exclusion of peoples of African descent from the Versailles peace proceedings. Despite Du Bois's initiative, the congress would not have occurred without the influence of Diagne, who ensured Clemenceau that the meetings would not be a source of disruption. Similar to how Du Bois linked military service with "Talented Tenth" leadership and

African American citizenship, Diagne owed his reputation to an investment in the participation of black soldiers as a strategy to procure increased rights for the Senegalese *originaires*, first and foremost, and for colonized Africans more broadly. The Pan-African Congress, from this perspective, emerged as a direct outgrowth of the participation of African American and West African soldiers in the war but also of the respective political agendas of Du Bois and Diagne. The first session of the three-day conference opened in Paris on February 19, 1919, with Diagne serving as president and Du Bois as secretary. Attended by fifty-seven delegates from Africa, the West Indies, and the United States, the historic gathering dramatically demonstrated the potential for peoples of African descent emerging from the war to speak with a collective voice in challenging Western white supremacy and European colonial rule.

But it also demonstrated the challenges of practicing a certain type of diasporic politics within the French imperial context. Competing ideological agendas, conflicting political priorities, and divergent historical realities severely circumscribed the impact of the Pan-African Congress and its tangible achievements. The meetings left much to be desired in terms of political self-determination and true Pan-African representation, as continental Africans represented only a small minority of the delegates. Moreover, internal divisions and difference of opinion between Du Bois and Diagne wracked the proceedings. Diagne muted critiques of French colonial rule, and nothing resembling Du Bois's proposed independent Central African state, first posited in the January 1918 issue of the *Crisis*, appeared in the resolutions presented to the European and American representatives of the Versailles peace conference, who paternalistically dismissed its relevance.[142] While Du Bois pushed for a more aggressive challenge to European imperial hegemony, Diagne wielded his authority to ensure that France and its image of colonial benevolence remained untarnished. The two men and the Pan-African Congress they led symbolized how even in a moment of triumph, finding common ground and forging diasporic solidarity proved easier said than done.

BLAISE DIAGNE'S COMMUNICATION with Prime Minister Clemenceau and the 1919 Pan-African Congress demonstrate that wartime engagement with questions of internationalism and diaspora by black people had profound consequences. The issues articulated by the African American press, and later experienced firsthand by African American soldiers in France, shaped a broader political dynamic within which peoples of African descent began to rethink and reimagine their place in the world and their relationships to each other. The war fostered social and ideological conditions that proved fertile for broadening the international and diasporic consciousness of African Americans, both within and outside of the army. Through words and actions, African Americans idealistically latched onto France as a site where democracy and aspirations for freedom could become a reality, and where creating bonds, however tenuous, of diasporic unity were indeed possible. The military participation of black people in the war drove this process but, at the same time, halted and stalled its development. Army racism infected the experiences of African American soldiers and provided a cruel reminder of their Americanness, however devalued it may have been. This continued historical, social, and existential attachment to the nation shaped the interactions between African American and African soldiers, interactions that, while pregnant with considerable cultural and political opportunity, were characterized by gulfs of misunderstanding. The war and the experiences of African American soldiers laid a crucial foundation for the future development of black internationalism and diasporic mobilization, processes that would continue to evolve and mature during the postwar period and throughout the twentieth century.

PART II Peace?

The Goal

("To make the world safe for democracy")

Exalted goal! Oh, coveted ideal,
Which but to contemplate, causes to steal
Within the heart, the sting of ecstasy!
Oh, fateful words! Oh, potent prophecy,
Which yet shall make entrenched wrong to reel
And stagger from the place of power—to feel
The odium of men, outraged, set free!
Tho' *now* the words are empty, void of life,
And smoothly uttered to allay the strife
And discontent with which the world is rife,
These words shall yet become a fervent creed,
And vivified to meet The Peoples need,
Shall fructify into heroic deed.

—Carrie Williams Clifford (1922)

> And what of the colored soldier of America? Over 300,000 strong, despite the persecutions which he has undergone in times past; did go over the top with valor and determination to win for his country, which he believed the freedom of all men. Now that war is ended what has been his reward.
>
> —Unnamed African American soldier, 425th Reserve Labor Battalion, to the NAACP

WAGING PEACE

The End of the War and the Hope of Democracy

While combat hostilities ended with the November 11, 1918, armistice, the meaning of democracy in postwar American society remained far from settled. With the coming of peace, a mixture of optimism and uncertainty swept the American public. Progressives hoped the war would usher in an era of domestic and international reform. Able to point to the patriotic contributions of women to the war effort, the suffrage movement reached its pinnacle with the Nineteenth Amendment, passed by Congress on June 4, 1919, and ratified by the states the following summer.[1] Organized labor, most notably the American Federation of Labor led by Samuel Gompers, had achieved unprecedented gains during the war and fully intended to push for the expansion of "industrial democracy."[2] While President Woodrow Wilson set his sights on Europe and the upcoming Versailles peace conference, where he planned to present a bold agenda of international reform highlighted by the creation of a League of Nations, the domestic ramifications of the Allied victory and the ideological forces it unleashed demanded immediate attention. The Russian Revolution put military and government officials alike on edge, causing them to view expressions of postwar change voiced by soldiers and civilians through the specter of "Bolshevism." As it approached, 1919 had all the makings of a turbulent year.[3] Throughout the country, and the world, people anxiously wondered what impact the war, with its promise of increased democracy and self-determination, would have on their lives.

This was particularly true for African American soldiers and civilians. After laboring and fighting for months, both in the United States and overseas, for the cause of preserving the principles of global democracy, black servicemen began to take stock of their experience and make sense of its individual and collective meanings. The days and weeks following the end of the war were crucial moments, when African American soldiers and their advocates sought to gauge the results of their sacrifice, patriotism, and loyalty on white racial attitudes and, more specifically, the government's commitment to effective African American citizenship. Black soldiers' experiences and their record of service stirred the deep democratic sensibilities of African Americans throughout the country, revealing that democracy was not merely an abstract concept but a social and political ideal contested by both black soldiers and their supporters. With a strong sense of pride and an abiding faith in the fundamental tenets of democracy, African American soldiers, and black people more broadly, envisioned the end of the war as the dawn of a new era in United States history, where their place as citizens in the social, political, and economic fabric of the nation would be both acknowledged and affirmed.

From the end of combat, throughout the demobilization process, and upon their return to the United States, African American soldiers tested the viability and meaning of postwar democracy. Black troops serving overseas enthusiastically welcomed the armistice and, while reveling in the gratitude of their French hosts and status as military heroes, nevertheless looked forward to reuniting with their loved ones. Their fortitude would be tested by the dogged presence of American racism. The same was true for black soldiers in the United States, who continued to toil in labor battalions and desperately wanted out of the army. Throughout the demobilization process, black soldiers confronted the possibility, even likelihood, that the discrimination they faced foreshadowed postwar racial conditions and a delegitimization of their service.

Black people were determined to not let this happen. African American intellectuals and activists, male and female, saw an opportunity to use the record of black soldiers in the war to pressure the government and make their case for full inclusion in the nation's democracy. They sought to entrench the contemporary and longer historical contribution of African American soldiers in the nation's collective memory, thereby framing the successful fulfillment of their civic obligation as justification for the expansion of democratic citizenship rights. This view was shared by many African American soldiers as well, who, despite the challenges of racial discrimination that followed them throughout their overseas experience, returned home proud of their service. They had indeed affirmed their citizenship and, from an individual perspective, infused democracy with real meaning. The streets of American towns and cities, North and South, emerged as physical sites where returning black veterans and their communities staked claim to their citizenship and democratized the public sphere. The homecoming parades and celebrations, which occurred throughout the country, reflected the collective will of African Americans to demonstrate their civic belonging by organizing and congregating by the thousands around their returning heroes. Black people were not blind to the challenges that lay ahead. Racism and white supremacy had proved to be increasingly malignant throughout the war, and would possibly remain just as bad, if not worsen, during the postwar period. But they had survived. And now, with the wind of black soldiers' contribution to the war and physical return to the United States behind their sails, African Americans exuded a confidence that racial conditions would indeed change for the better. Anything else was simply unacceptable.

AT HALF PAST FOUR ON THE afternoon of November 11, 1918, Valdore Giles, a soldier in the Sanitary Detachment of the 349th Field Artillery, learned the war had come to an end. Giles was in the midst of a relaxing seven-day leave at La Mont Dore, a picturesque resort town in the Auvergne Mountains of central France. Taking in the scenery, frequenting the best hotels, he had temporarily forgotten all about the war. On the final day of his leave, Giles sat with a fellow soldier in the local casino, talking fondly of their lives back home. Suddenly, church bells began to ring. "Never in all my life, have I heard such tones from bells," Giles recalled. "I had heard them ring on the Sunday previous for church services, and they sounded as other bells, but this day, How they did ring!" Giles immediately knew that peace had finally arrived. "We ran around to the church," he wrote in a letter published by the *Savannah Tribune*, "and the people were coming from everywhere, young and old, women, children and men . . ." Children laughed and clapped their hands. But the sight of elderly French men and women, some openly weeping, had a particularly strong impact on Giles. "Was it for joy or sorrow, or was it for the ones lost in the war?" he wondered. "Some child of their heart, never to return again. Who knows? Jubilant over victory, yet tempered by the sight of these weeping ones, a prayer went from my heart to God. That day I can never forget."[4]

For Valdore Giles and other black soldiers, the end of the war was an emotional moment. Those at or near the front expressed their elation and divine gratitude at surviving the carnage of warfare. "When the guns ceased firing our boys sent up thanks to God by prayers and song," Garland Maddox of the 813th Pioneer Infantry wrote to his mother and sister.[5] "Happiness was abroad like a plague; everybody was glad and joyful," John Cade remembered.[6] Up and down the lines, German troops joined with their former adversaries in spontaneous celebrations. "The armistice!" Samuel Blount of the 367th Infantry Regiment exclaimed. "A band behind the German lines was heard striking up music. . . .

German soldiers started to come over to our lines and fraternize, but our officers turned them back."[7] Charles Reed and the 365th Infantry Regiment continued to engage the kaiser's forces until the armistice officially went into effect at eleven o'clock. "The Germans were happier than we," Reed stated in a letter, "for they gave a wild whoop and a yell, and from hidden dugouts and caves they came swarming and shaking hands with the American soldiers. A bunch of them came out in the opening and gave a wild war dance, or rather peace dance. They had a great time of it all day."[8] More than anything, African American soldiers, swept into the joy of victory, embraced their newly minted status as heroes and basked in the gratitude of the French citizenry. Robert Heriford, a mail orderly for the 370th Infantry Regiment, fondly reminisced how the French women of a town he passed through kissed every soldier in their sight—himself included—in euphoria upon learning of the war's end. "Armistice is not so bad after all," he coyly stated.[9]

Despite their jubilance that the war had come to an end, most black soldiers wanted to go home.[10] Sergeant John Williams of the Ninety-second Division witnessed how, "with the signing of the Armistice home-sickness broke out almost like an epidemic."[11] The rigors of war, labor, and racism exacted a heavy toll on black servicemen. However, their desires to be rid of the uniform as quickly as possible stemmed from much more personal and universally human motivations. Most African American troops had never traveled beyond their local communities, much less journeyed overseas, and as a result intensely missed their loved ones. "Gee, but I'd like to be back home now," lamented Harry Peyton, a corporal in the 350th Field Artillery, in a December 1918 letter to a friend. "We are all thinking about our return trip across the pond and wishing it was time to start right now. It kinder makes me blue to think of home when I am so far away."[12] Writing to his good buddy William Granger, Aldrich Burton of the 808th Pioneer Infantry confided, "How happy we feel when we receive news from home & our friends 'over there.' . . . although France is beautiful or at least was before the Germans (& Americans) marred the landscape & although her people are amiable still we miss our dear friends in America."[13] While many black soldiers embraced France and the democratic spirit of its people, America still remained first in their hearts.

For African American troops of the Ninety-third Division, formal congratulations from the French military for their service eased the pangs of homesickness. The French army honored the four regiments of the Ninety-third Division with commendation ceremonies before their reincorporation into the American forces. On December 13, 1918, the 369th reviewed before General Lebouc of the French 161st Infantry Division, who awarded the Croix de Guerre to each man in the regiment and lauded all the troops for their sacrifice. "Our men had tried to make history of honor to their race," wrote Arthur Little, "and their efforts had been recognized."[14] Four days later, despite rainy weather that limited the ceremony to only the presentation of medals, the French army bestowed the Croix de Guerre, the Distinguished Service Cross, and Médaille Militaire to men of the 372nd Infantry Regiment.[15] African American soldiers received similar praise from the local inhabitants of towns where they were billeted and temporarily stationed. Perhaps initially expecting trouble because of warnings from American military officials, town mayors applauded black troops for their behavior.[16]

Many black soldiers and officers of the Ninety-second and Ninety-third Divisions welcomed the opportunity before embarking for the United States to become tourists. Faced with a growing amount of idle time, American servicemen were understandably anxious to explore the French countryside and its cities.[17] African American troops saw through France's battle-scarred landscape and appreciated the beauty of the geography, the quaintness of its towns, and, more than anything else, the warmness of its people. Although the 808th Pioneer Infantry had received its embarkation orders, Aldrich Burton "wasn't exactly ready to leave France as yet." He "had saved up a few Francs and was anticipating a trip to Paris next month." Though he never made it to Paris, Burton "took a trip to St. Minnehould and had a very good time."[18] Some doughboys were more fortunate than Burton and found their way to the French capital. Harry Haywood, a self-described "old Francophile," had the good luck of convalescing at a Paris hospital and, when back on his feet, made sure to enjoy the city of lights: "I got a guidebook and spent days walking all over Paris, visiting all the historical places about which I had read."[19]

Black soldiers taking advantage of free time to travel and interact with French citizens presented the army with a serious problem. The War Department, in planning for a longer period of combat hostilities, failed to adequately prepare for the demobilization process. Army officials became increasingly concerned with incidents of lax discipline and a rise in immoral behavior. Determined not to have the AEF's performance tainted by malfeasance, the army attempted to implement a rigorous regime of drilling, expanded educational programs, and increased YMCA activities designed to keep soldiers busy and out of trouble. These efforts bred resistance among many soldiers, who felt a sense of betrayal. They had done their duty, and now it was the army's job to get them home as quickly as possible, not give them more work.[20] In the case of black soldiers, disciplinary concerns contained racial overtones. Throughout the war, the army viewed African Americans as having a natural aversion to following orders, unless strictly enforced by white men, ideally from the South and trained in the art of "handling negroes." This characterization underpinned the postwar anxieties of white officers and commanders, who feared the domestic implications of black soldiers returning to the United States, emboldened by their service and infused with a new sense of confidence and self-worth. They were determined to put them back in their place before they set foot on American soil.

With this goal, American military police received expansive authority to limit and control the interactions between black soldiers and French citizens. African American servicemen, as a result, were routinely denied leave passes as part of a concerted effort to confine them to their bases or towns of billet. Some refused to acquiesce. Harry Haywood's brother Otto Hall served in a stevedore battalion during the war and had his mind set on visiting Paris before returning to the United States. After military police refused to grant him an official pass, Hall visited the city nevertheless, joining the ranks of an estimated fifteen hundred deserters who did the same.[21] He was fully aware of the possible consequences of his decision to indulge in the Parisian nightlife and, in fact, was later arrested.[22] The military police wielded its far-reaching power with often repressive intentions. American military police regularly confronted African American soldiers with little to no provocation, which led to instances of physical brutality. The 369th Infantry Regiment, the most celebrated organization of African American servicemen, had a particularly contentious relationship with white MPs during its demobilization process. When the regiment arrived at the embarkation center of Brest from Le Mans, an MP assaulted a black private, "his head split open by a blow from the club." In what seemed destined to be a repetition of Spartanburg on French soil, fellow soldiers intervened on the man's behalf, and only the levelheaded reasoning of Arthur Little managed to prevent a more serious confrontation. A military police captain later informed Little that he had been warned the "Niggers" of the regiment were "feeling their oats a bit" and that he had orders to "take it out of them quickly, just as soon as they arrived, so as not to have any trouble later on."[23]

The policies of the American army and the actions of the military police, geared in the broadest sense to sap black soldiers of their self-confidence, possessed a more specific objective: eliminate contact between African American troops and French women. With more time on their hands, African American soldiers were seen as an even greater sexual threat. As they had throughout the war, American military officials viewed the presence of black servicemen in France after the armistice through a gendered and sexualized optic.

This included the Military Intelligence Division's (formerly the Military Intelligence Branch) most valued African American officer, Walter Loving.

Just over a week after the armistice, Loving sent a memo to his white MID superiors that undoubtedly struck a sensitive nerve. Loving warned that allowing black soldiers to remain in France for an extended period of time would promote the opportunity for interracial marriage, a red flag to American white supremacists. Perhaps realizing the implications of his statement, he attempted to shift focus by characterizing potential interracial unions as a problem negatively impacting black people, just as much as it did whites. "Already rumors are afloat that [a] number of negro soldiers are contemplating marriage in France," Loving reported, "and these rumors have given rise to much concern among the colored people of this country, and especially the women, who are looking forward to such opportunities themselves." Loving knew full well that the furor of white soldiers who encountered black servicemen socializing with French women could lead to "an American race war in France." In order to avoid such a calamity, Loving proposed that "no discharges be given colored soldiers in France," "all colored soldiers now in France be shipped home with the least possible delay," and the "strictest measures be taken to keep colored and white soldiers from meeting in places of prostitution while waiting for transportation home." These recommendations, in Loving's estimation, were "for the good of the service and to the best interest of the colored race in general."[24] Secretary of War Baker found Loving's memo "very thoughtful and judicious."[25] His warning confirmed the worst fears of many army officials and reflected a similar paranoia that gripped white officers commanding black soldiers in France after the war's conclusion.

Whether the military acted specifically upon Loving's recommendation is not clear, but only days later, on November 26, 1918, General John Pershing sent a pointed memo to Allied commander Marshal Foch. "My Government has directed me to give priority to colored soldiers in the return of my troops to the United States," Pershing stated, and requested that "the 92nd Division be prepared for shipment."[26] Foch apparently demurred. Pershing responded with another memo, pressing that "my government is very anxious to begin as early as possible the shipment of troops home, and wishes to give the colored troops the preference for various reasons."[27] These "various reasons" centered on the unsubstantiated rumors spread by white officers, at the highest levels of the army, that instances of rape involving black soldiers of the Ninety-second Division had reached epidemic proportions. Robert Bullard, commander of the American Second Army likewise pressured Foch to prioritize the Ninety-second Division, threatening that "no man could be responsible for the acts of these Negroes toward Frenchwomen."[28] Sure enough, as a result of Pershing's and Bullard's insistence, the Ninety-second, along with the Ninety-third Division, was among the first American combat troops scheduled to depart from France.

In the meantime, the army determined to control black soldiers as much as possible during the demobilization process. The Ninety-second Division again became a hypersexualized target. On December 16, 1918, James B. Erwin, a Georgia native, replaced Charles Ballou as brigadier general of the division. Ten days later, eager to assert his authority, Erwin issued General Order No. 40. The directive, along with mandating a strict work and drilling schedule during the embarkation process, granted virtually unlimited authority to military police to enforce discipline among black soldiers of the Ninety-second Division by preventing them from "addressing or holding conversations with the women inhabitants" of the towns where African American troops were billeted. Erwin saw these extreme measures as "necessary" to eliminate those black servicemen deemed as "a menace to the public and to the good name and reputation" of the division. The chief of staff, Lieutenant Colonel Allen Greer, concurred and interpreted the order as an explicit command to "prevent men coming into contact with white women."[29]

African American soldiers, in spite of the new regulations, continued to interact with French citizens. The men of the division "understood them all right," Samuel Blount admitted, but instead of obeying they "became very circumspect when visiting the homes of newly made friends." He continued to visit the home of a female acquaintance, Madame Augustin. On New Year's Day she allowed a group of black noncommissioned officers to use her dining room for a celebratory meal. After an evening of singing, poetry, and wine consumption, Blount and the other soldiers in attendance "returned quietly to their billets."[30]

Acts of defiance such this carried the risk of punishment. This was particularly true for African American officers of the Ninety-second Division, who directly felt the punitive brunt of General Order No. 40. As part of a broader smear campaign, white commanders such as Allen Greer attributed the perceived poor performance of the division's black officers to a compulsive preoccupation with French women. In a letter dated December 6, 1918, Greer wrote to Tennessee senator Kenneth McKellar concerning the anticipated reorganization of the army and the future use of African American soldiers and officers. He made direct reference to the actions of the 368th Infantry in the Meuse-Argonne operation, claiming that the black officers "failed there in all their missions, laid down and sneaked to the rear, until they were withdrawn." Greer provocatively claimed that instances of rape in the Ninety-second Division had become commonplace and that much of the blame lay at the feet of black officers. "The undoubted truth," Greer asserted, "is that the Colored officers neither control nor care to control the men. They themselves have been engaged very largely in the pursuit of French women, it being their first opportunity to meet white women who did not treat them as servants." In addition to having a lack of sexual control, black officers could not be trusted to tell the truth. "During the entire time we have been operating there has never been a single operation conducted by a colored officer, where his report did not have to be investigated by some field officer to find out what the real facts were. Accuracy and ability to describe facts is lacking in all and most of them are just plain liars in addition."[31] Merely criticizing the military performance of African American officers was insufficient. Commanders such as Greer felt obligated to attack their manhood as well. General Order No. 40 provided the perfect pretext.

Sergeant Charles R. Isum of the Medical Detachment of the 365th Infantry detailed to W. E. B. Du Bois his "personal experiences with the southern rednecks" in command of his division, brigade, and regiment. On January 21, 1919, Isum, along with four other black soldiers, attended the wedding of a French family he had befriended. A white soldier encountered Isum with the bridal party and reported him to regimental colonel George McMaster. McMaster promptly ordered military police to arrest Isum for violating General Order No. 40. Armed privates marched Isum, without respect to his rank, down the town's central street to the guardhouse, where he was sequestered, threatened with a court-martial, and promised a lengthy prison sentence. Isum, however, refused to be intimidated. Fully aware of his rights, he convinced the prosecuting major to release him from custody. Unsatisfied, Colonel McMaster issued new orders to arrest Isum the following day. He detained the sergeant for several hours before eventually releasing him the same evening. Nothing more came of the case, and Isum received an honorable discharge from the army when he returned to the United States.[32] Having no legal grounds to prosecute, the white officers of the regiment used the entire incident to humiliate Isum, strip him of the manhood associated with his rank, and make him an example for other African American servicemen to curtail their interactions with the French following the armistice.

The organized chaos of the demobilization process led to growing frustrations among black troops that the continued neglect of their physical, emotional, and psychological needs only compounded. American soldiers overwhelmed the Brest embarkation center, leading to a deterioration of social services and health conditions, most acutely experienced by the soon to be departing Ninety-second and Ninety-third Divisions. YMCA and Red Cross personnel did not waver in segregating black soldiers at their respective facilities. At the height of the embarkation process, Camp Pontanezen at Brest contained only one African American YMCA secretary to attend to the needs of some forty thousand black troops.[33] Addie Hunton and Kathryn Johnson remained steadfast in their heroic service, and, although the number of African American female YMCA secretaries eventually grew from three to sixteen following increased pressure from Jesse Moorland, the organization admitted it failed to meet the needs of black soldiers.[34] As resentment regarding the slow pace of demobilization grew, so too did tensions between black and white servicemen. "The negroes over here are certainly making the most of the military law of equality of all colors," a white soldier wrote from France to an acquaintance in Alabama. "They will certainly be taught a different tune when we all get back, am itching to get in the new Ku-Klux, it would be Heaven itself to become one of the instructors in the school of differentiation of the two colors. I would like to shoot down a few just to see them kick, they are getting too egotistical and important for me."[35]

FROM THE NAACP'S FIFTH AVENUE OFFICES, W. E. B. Du Bois followed the demobilization process with intense interest and palpable concern. Impatient to gauge the returns on his investment in the American war effort and the success of black soldiers, the *Crisis* editor persuaded the NAACP's board of directors to send him to Paris, where, he later stated, "the destinies of mankind" were being decided.[36] Du Bois provided a threefold justification for his trip: to represent the *Crisis* at the peace proceedings; to advocate on the behalf of peoples of African descent by holding a Pan-African congress; and to conduct research for a proposed historical study of the black war experience. These pretexts, however, masked deeper and significantly more personal motivations for Du Bois's sojourn in France. Having mortgaged his radical credentials on the democratizing potential of the war and, more specifically, the battlefield achievements of African American troops and officers, he needed firsthand validation, from the mouths of black soldiers themselves, that his political and moral sacrifice had not been in vain. Indeed, as black servicemen struggled against restrictive military policies, hostile white officers, and violent MPs, Du Bois felt a strong measure of responsibility for their fate.[37]

Robert Russa Moton, viewing unfolding global events from the confines of Tuskegee Institute, also had important reasons to go overseas following the armistice. Despite the death of Booker T. Washington in 1915, Tuskegee remained a center of sizable political, educational, and economic influence, and as its principal Moton wielded considerable national authority. He had used the opportunities provided by Emmett Scott's position in the War Department and its need to maintain black loyalty to demonstrate his abilities as both a legitimate spokesman for the race and a trusted ally of the federal government. The government acknowledged that the poor treatment of black troops had created potentially dangerous levels of disaffection. Only two weeks after the armistice, Secretary of War Baker and President Woodrow Wilson, upon Scott's encouragement, requested that Moton travel to France and meet with black soldiers in an attempt to boost their morale. Both Baker and Wilson felt "that the presence and words of a member of their own race would be particularly helpful," Moton would later write. Presented with an opportunity to further solidify his leadership, he readily accepted their offer.[38]

Du Bois and Moton were not the only African Americans who clamored to go to France. Between December 16 and 19, William Monroe Trotter's National Equal Rights League (NERL) convened at the Metropolitan AME Church in Washington, D.C., under the banner of the National Race Congress for World Democracy. Throughout the war, Trotter maintained his unequivocal commitment to black civil rights. He also continued to view the Wilson administration with contempt and dismissed its efforts to allay African American concerns as disingenuous acts of appeasement. With the signing of the armistice, and with Wilson's "Fourteen Points" serving as the foundation for peace negotiations, Trotter and the NERL insisted that the concerns of African Americans must be addressed. The 250 people at the meeting, after numerous speeches and lengthy discussions, adopted a "Fifteenth Point"—"elimination of civil, political, and judicial distinctions based on race or color in all nations for the new era of freedom everywhere." Trotter was one of eleven delegates, who also included Ida B. Wells-Barnett and the Harlem beauty product entrepreneur Madame C. J. Walker, selected by the NERL to travel to Versailles and deliver the message. In attendance to observe the proceedings was a young Jamaican immigrant named Marcus Garvey, president general of the upstart organization the Universal Negro Improvement Association (UNIA). Two weeks earlier, on December 3, a capacity crowd had gathered at the Harlem Palace Casino to witness Garvey nominate A. Philip Randolph and Wells-Barnett to represent the UNIA in Paris.[39] Soon, Garvey and the UNIA would be known well beyond just the streets of Harlem. But now Trotter was less concerned about the emergence of this new black radical voice than he was about reaching France. The State Department denied Trotter's visa request, along with those of every other black applicant with the exception of Du Bois and Moton. Wells-Barnett and Walker remained sidelined in the United States. Trotter, however, would not be deterred. After spending six futile weeks in New York attempting to secure passage across the Atlantic, in April he eventually got a job as a cook on the SS *Yarmouth*. He arrived in Paris on May 7, spending his first days in the city homeless, unkempt, and absolutely devoted to holding his nemesis Woodrow Wilson accountable to his democratic promises.[40]

Du Bois and Moton traveled more comfortably. The *Crisis* editor was a party of one. The Tuskegee president's entourage included two black men—his personal secretary, Nathan Hunt, and Lester Walton of the *New York Age*—and two white men—Thomas Jesse Jones of the U.S. Bureau of Education and Clyde Miller of the *Cleveland Plain Dealer*. Du Bois and Moton boarded the *Orizaba*, the official American press ship, on December 2, 1918, sharing a stateroom and conversing on various aspects of the Negro question throughout the duration of the transatlantic journey to Brest.[41] After disembarking at Brest, they boarded a train to Paris and then went their separate ways. Du Bois navigated through the hectic Gare Montparnasse station, settled into the city, and later used Moton's influence to secure a pass to visit the Ninety-second Division encampment. Both men had important and similar goals upon setting foot on French soil. They sought to uncover the depths of overseas racial discrimination, lay to rest rumors of rape involving the Ninety-second Division and the battlefield performance of its black officers stemming from the Meuse-Argonne, and ultimately emerge as the recognized spokesman for the interests of black servicemen. "I realized that the mission was a delicate one," Moton acknowledged.[42] While sharing some common ground, how they approached their objectives, the response they received from black troops and white officers, respectively, and what they ultimately did with their findings revealed the depths of the ideological and temperamental divide between Du Bois and his Tuskegee adversary. As Du Bois would write upon his return to the United States, "Our missions were distinct in every respect."[43]

After finalizing arrangements with Blaise Diagne and French government officials for the Pan-African Congress, Du Bois headed for the Ninety-second Division's encampment in Marbache sometime during the first days of January 1919. What Du Bois heard and witnessed during his visit with the division squared with the words of former 368th officer Louis Pontlock, who described the men by this time as "broken down with discouragement."[44] With military intelligence closely on his heels, and white officers greeting him with suspicion, Du Bois heard story after harrowing story of discrimination and abuse directly from the mouths of black soldiers themselves.[45] Throughout the previous year, Du Bois was well aware of rumors of gross mistreatment but, in the patriotic delirium of war, forced himself to not assume the worst. Now, faced with the harsh truth of the "hell" the Ninety-second Division experienced, Du Bois could not ignore the reality that American racism proved even more resilient than he ever imagined. In desperate need of an influential ally, black soldiers of the Ninety-second welcomed Du Bois and saw his visit as an opportunity to voice complaints that had fallen on the deaf ears of their white superiors. On several occasions, they implored the doctor to deliver a speech. But Du Bois bit his tongue, constrained by the "Visiting Correspondent's Agreement" he had to sign requiring that he "avoid all criticism of Allied Forces."[46] His presence offered a much-needed boost for many dispirited African American troops. The black officers whom Du Bois championed as the vanguard of the race were especially grateful for his investigative efforts and provided him with personal testimonies and official documents for the envisioned war history. Du Bois emerged from his time with the Ninety-second Division enraged.[47]

While Du Bois heard testimony and gathered evidence in preparation for his case against the army for its treatment of black soldiers and officers, Robert Moton proceeded with his parallel investigation. Having the full confidence of the government, Moton received unfettered access to the Ninety-second Division and, unlike Du Bois, traveled freely without the close monitoring of military intelligence.[48] After a disconcerting briefing from Atlanta University president and YMCA secretary John Hope describing the state of the division, he spoke directly with military personnel at AEF headquarters in Chaumont. From there he met with Major General Charles Ballou at Ninety-second Division headquarters in Marbache to discuss the unsubstantiated rumors of rape committed by soldiers in the division. He also spoke with commanding white officers, including General John Pershing, regarding the effectiveness of black officers and inspected the conditions of black Services of Supply (SOS) units located at Brest, Bordeaux, and St. Nazaire. Throughout the course of his investigation—which revealed charges of rape to be wildly inaccurate, claims of incompetence on the part of black officers overstated, and conditions facing black labor troops in many cases appalling—Moton was awakened to the poor treatment many black soldiers had endured during the war. However, unlike Du Bois, he had no intentions of embarrassing the government and placing his credibility with the Wilson administration at risk. Moton likewise had to consider issues closer to home; fears among southern whites regarding the return of black soldiers to the region had grown more intense in the days immediately following the armistice, as did the possibility of violent reprisals. In this context, knowing that his every word and action would be closely scrutinized by both government officials and Tuskegee's white benefactors, Moton had to tread with extreme caution.[49]

Moton highlighted his overseas experience by delivering a series of controversial speeches to African American soldiers. The new battle, in Moton's words, was "not against Germans, but against black Americans. This battle is against the men into whose faces I now look. It is your individual, personal battle—a battle of self-control, against laziness, shiftlessness and willfulness." He continued, "The best time to begin to show self-control is right here in France. Leave such a reputation here as will constrain our Allies, who have watched us with interest, to say forever that the American negro will always be welcome not only because of his courage but because of his character."[50] The Tuskegee president conveyed the same message wherever he went. Standing atop a truck at the Ninety-second Division's YMCA grounds, Moton began one of his addresses well enough by extolling the bravery, loyalty, and sacrifice of African American troops in the face of considerable hardship. His address took on a classic Washingtonian tenor, however, when he encouraged them to quickly find a job, a wife, conserve their money, and settle down upon their return to the United States, all in the hopes that, as Moton expressed, "no one will do anything in peace to spoil the magnificent record your troops have made in the war."[51] On other occasions Moton issued an explicit warning for the men not to return to the South "striking the attitude of heroes."[52] Many black soldiers, perhaps anticipating a more enthusiastic and morale-boosting rallying cry to lift their lagging spirits, walked away sorely disappointed. A number of servicemen openly heckled Moton and, during one speech, a particularly unruly black soldier expressed his contempt for the major's words. "Say, Moton, why in the hell did President Wilson send you over here to tell us how he honors the Negro?" Ely Green, a stevedore from Texas, shouted audaciously. "When he was here he didnt tell us, because he wouldnt dare quote the word Negro on French soil. We are represented as men to France. You are the only Negro slave on French soil. So go back to the States and teach that S.O.B. to the Halleluia Negro that dont know any better." Before he could continue his diatribe, guards promptly seized Green and led him away from the grounds. Although several soldiers chastised Green for disrespecting Moton, others undoubtedly sympathized with his rebuke.[53]

THE EFFECTIVENESS OF MOTON'S warning would be tested soon enough. Concerns regarding French–African American interracial sexual relations, and tensions between idle black and white soldiers and military police, prompted military officials to send black servicemen of the Ninety-second and Ninety-third Divisions back to the United States as quickly as possible. By the time they reached Brest and Le Mans, most African American troops had little desire to prolong their time in France. The combination of homesickness and racism had taken its toll. To make matters worse, overcrowding and the notoriously dreary French winter weather caused embarkation camps to become influenza breeding grounds.[54] No sooner had Harry Haywood rejoined the 370th at Brest following his recovery from the flu than he was struck with a reoccurrence of the deadly bug and hospitalized yet again.[55] A shortage of American transport ships added to the impatience of soldiers desperately waiting for their departure date. This, however, only provided army officials with yet another tactic to further enforce discipline among black soldiers, threatening that any misbehavior would result in their placement at the bottom of the embarkation list.[56] Stewing with anger, anticipation, and sheer exhaustion, black troops held their collective breath.

To their relief, within a span of three days the entire Ninety-third Division bid farewell to France. The men of the 369th Infantry Regiment, fearing a last-minute revocation of orders, nervously boarded the SS *Stockholm*, the SS *Regina*, and the SS *La France* on January 31 and February 1 for their journey back to New York. The Third Battalion reached New York on February 9, with the rest of the regiment arriving at Pier 97 three days later to a cheering crowd of relatives and friends.[57] The 370th Infantry Regiment pulled out of France on February 2 and arrived in New York on February 9. The 371st and 372nd Infantry Regiments departed from Brest the following day, reaching Hoboken on February 11. As for the Ninety-second Division, its first transports sailed from Brest on February 5 and continued throughout the month. The last ship carrying soldiers of the Ninety-second left France on March 12, 1919.[58]

Unlike their combat brethren, black Services of Supply soldiers continued to labor in France well after the signing of the armistice. The war had left France in shambles, and African American troops continued to function as the army's principal custodians. With the end of combat hostilities, black stevedores worked long hours on the docks during the chaotic embarkation process, while SOS soldiers assumed responsibility for salvaging battlefields, clearing barbed wire, filling trenches, and removing unexploded shells. African American SOS troops took on the unglamorous responsibility of reburying the dead and constructing cemeteries for the Graves Registration Service.[59] Black men of the 813th, 815th, and 816th Pioneer Infantry Regiments, as well as other labor battalions, built cemeteries and reinterred dead soldiers in varying states of decomposition for several months after the war. Addie Hunton of the YMCA, who continued to assist black soldiers in France after the armistice, described the work as "gruesome, repulsive and unhealthful." Feeling stigmatized as racially inferior by being assigned to such a macabre task, many African American service troops became increasingly hostile and overtly resistant. Hunton recalled the constant talk of mutiny among the soldiers because of the unremitting racial discrimination and insults.[60]

African American grave diggers. African American soldiers of the 322nd Labor Battalion removing dead bodies for reburial in the AEF *cemetery at Romagne.* RG 111-SC, 153215. *Courtesy of National Archives and Record Administration, College Park, Md.*

Rayford Logan similarly bore witness to how African American labor troops teetered perilously close to the edge of violent revolt. At a French café located just outside of Camp Ancona near Bordeaux, a drunk marine, stumbling out of the "white" section of the café, tripped over a black soldier sitting in the "colored" section. The aggrieved trooper, staking claim to his Jim Crowed territory, told the white marine to go back to his own spacious room. A fight ensued, with fists, bottles, and pool sticks flying about. Word of the melee spread, and soon most of the camp's black pioneer infantry soldiers and white marines had rushed to the scene. As marine officers intervened, a white MP grabbed an unsuspecting black serviceman from the floor of the café and placed him under arrest. His comrades stopped fighting and protested the injustice of his detainment while the white soldiers went free. One soldier took out a knife and lunged at the MP, who responded with gunfire. Nobody was hit, but tensions had reached a crisis point. Later, Logan's captain ordered him to investigate word of brewing trouble among the black pioneer infantry soldiers. The men in the camp, some eight thousand strong, had determined to kill every white officer and then punctuate their rebellion by shooting their way into nearby Bordeaux and burning the city to the ground. The task of averting a calamity that would have made Houston look trivial by comparison fell on Logan's shoulders. He acted quickly. "Go ahead," Logan told the men, but warned them that a regiment of marines was on its way to shoot any black soldier headed for Bordeaux. The ruse worked, and, as Logan reflected, "In about a half-hour I had them all back into the barracks."[61]

On the other side of the Atlantic, black servicemen in the United States faced similar challenges. The War Department, in theory, intended to release stateside soldiers from duty before overseas troops.[62] However, the dismantling of some training camp facilities, the continued upkeep of others, and the myriad tasks of menial labor required to maintain a functioning military necessitated a sizable reservoir of manpower. African American conscripts rejected for overseas duty, as well as those who missed the opportunity to serve in France because of the armistice, thus constituted an available and expendable labor force.

Charles H. Williams of the Hampton Institute continued to investigate the state of affairs at domestic encampments following the armistice. His findings revealed that, if only by default, the living conditions of most African American labor troops had generally improved. As white soldiers received their discharge, better living quarters became available, allowing black soldiers access to basic amenities such as working toilets, running water, and heated barracks. At Camp Humphreys, Virginia, Williams reported that "living conditions are excellent compared to what they were before the signing of the Armistice. The men now live in barracks, which are heated by stoves; they have good mess halls and sanitary latrines and hot and cold water for bathing."[63] Army life, at the minimum, became more tolerable and, at best, more personally meaningful. Moreover, by continuing to make use of YMCA services, religious meetings, educational lectures, and recreational activities, many African American servicemen reaped significant material and intangible benefits from their time in the army. While not what they might have expected when called to duty, for men who in civilian life were consigned to a destitute life as sharecroppers and lacked access to basic social services, their army experience had genuine value.

Nevertheless, the persistence of racial discrimination and outright abuse often outweighed any positives. Deprived of the dignities of military service—including the uniform itself—black labor troops continued to be exploited by the army in desolate camps throughout the country. Living conditions at Camp Humphreys may have improved, but soldiers of the 447th Reserve Labor Battalion continued to work from 7:00 A.M. to 4:00 P.M., six days a week, hauling coal and other materials, digging ditches, caring for livestock, and clearing ground. White sergeants, with their pistols drawn, treated the men of the encampment like prisoners. One officer shot a black man in the leg for not complying with an order quickly enough.[64] The distinction between military and civilian life was sometimes virtually indistinguishable. Black labor troops at Camp Meade and Camp Eustis in Virginia worked alongside hired hands who earned $3.80 a day.[65] Soldiers received substandard medical services at many facilities. But, despite suffering from tuberculosis and other chronic ailments, exacerbated by the often harsh climate conditions, they continued to work. The treatment of these soldiers demonstrated their vulnerability. The focus of the federal government, as well as most African American political leaders, was on the Paris peace proceedings and the conditions of demobilizing soldiers in France. As a result, their plight garnered marginal attention. Charles Williams's noble investigative efforts remained hidden away in the files of the Military Intelligence Division and generated no public outcry.

Many soldiers, however, refused to remain silent. With remarkable clarity, several black labor troops saw through the justifications for why they were being held in the army well after most white soldiers received their discharge. Lacking formal recourse, African American soldiers regularly took it upon themselves to ameliorate their conditions. Many of the black troops at Camp Eustis in Virginia, according to Charles Williams, felt "that they are being unfairly held simply to do the rough work." The men, as a result, determined that they would do as little work as possible as an act of protest. "When taken on details some slip away into the woods and return about time for mess call," Williams remarked.[66]

Some literate servicemen turned to letter writing, a potentially dangerous proposition if vindictive officers discovered their correspondence. The NAACP received several letters and petitions from black soldiers suffering in labor battalions after the war. They reflected an acute awareness of the incongruity of their treatment with the government's purported democratic principles. "We are being held here in this organization and treated like dogs," a soldier in the 416th Reserve Labor Battalion stationed at Camp Grant, Illinois, informed NAACP officials. "It is a shame that after our boys have gone to France and given their all for Democracy's triumph, that the survivals are treated the way they are treating us in the organization. We are under southern officers who have no feelings for colored men whatsoever."[67] Another soldier, who preferred to remain nameless for fear of retribution, described the state of affairs at Camp Upton, New York, writing, "We are forced to work 9 hrs a day, seven days a week. Therefore we do not have time to wash our clothes and keep clean. The sick men are given medical treatment but they are forced to work, in some cases, when they are not able. I would be pleased if you would help us out of this condition."[68] A group of servicemen, who suggestively identified themselves as "Soldiers of

America," informed the NAACP of the brutal environment they labored in at Camp Sherman, Ohio. The soldiers asked rhetorically: "Is a ware-house a fit place for men to sleep in, especially in these times when the government can well afford to provide barracks for its men. Such is the case here. Under such conditions that we have undergone for almost two months, we have often wondered whether we were in the army or in a penitentiary." Seeking immediate relief from the civil rights organization, the soldiers collectively reflected: "Really it doesn't seem possible that the country which we were ready and willing to die for, at a crisis should allow such conditions to go on."[69]

These men wanted to be released from service as quickly as possible. Even those not subjected to the most inhumane conditions grew increasingly restless as they continued to toil, day after day, in the postarmistice military. Reporting on black labor troops at Camp Meade, Charles Williams observed, "The soldiers are very much dissatisfied, not because of mistreatment in the way of being abused, but because they want to get out of the army."[70] The War Department routinely denied discharge applications, reasoning that the continued service of these soldiers was indispensable.[71] While this contained an element of truth—African American conscripts did indeed perform essential duties, providing a backbone of manual labor for the army to remain functionally effective—army officials saw these men strictly as workers, as opposed to citizen-soldiers. African American draftees, however, did not question their citizenship. They, along with other black soldiers, in the United States and France, laborers and combatants alike, emerged from the demobilization process optimistically clinging to the personally meaningful aspects of their time in the army, but yet all too aware that the democratic aspirations of their sacrifice, on both a personal and a collective level, remained unfulfilled. More work needed to be done.

W. E. B. DU BOIS RETURNED to the United States on April 1, 1919, invigorated and infuriated by his nearly four months in France. The Pan-African Congress, despite its limitations, had been a success. The disturbing testimonials of black soldiers, however, burned in his ears. In collecting research materials for the NAACP-sponsored war history, Du Bois had ample documentation to substantiate their claims and build a damning case against the army and federal government. In the March 1919 issue of the *Crisis*, he provided readers with a broad sketch of the historical study and a glimpse of his preliminary conclusions with the essay "The Black Man in the Revolution of 1914–1918," which asserted that "anti-Negro prejudice was rampant in the American army," and black soldiers returned home "at once bitter and exalted."[72] He could very well have been speaking for himself. Armed with a trunkful of letters, reports, confidential memos, and his editor's pen, Du Bois assumed the role of soldier and prepared to defend the honor and reputation of the black servicemen and officers in whom he placed so much hope.

Du Bois unleashed his passions in the May 1919 installment of the *Crisis*, arguably his finest piece of editorial work. The cover featured a black soldier, standing triumphantly in front of a shield emblazoned with the words, "The American Negro's Record in the Great World War: Loyalty, Valor, Achievement." Du Bois masterfully used the symbolism of black soldiers as racial heroes to launch an opening salvo against the U.S. government, the War Department, and all individuals, white and black, complicit in the insult of African American servicemen on and off the battlefield. Du Bois dismissed Tuskegee principal Robert Russa Moton's message to black soldiers as placating to southern racists and, more heatedly, accused Emmett J. Scott of deliberately concealing the true conditions black troops faced overseas from the African American public. His charges set off a firestorm of controversy in the black press.[73] Du Bois debunked the blanket accusation that African American soldiers were guilty of rape, providing statements from the mayors of twenty-one towns throughout France to corroborate his assertion. The "Documents of War" exposé provided tangible evidence that racial discrimination was official military policy and executed at the regimental level with debilitating efficiency. It featured copies of official directives, as well as Ninety-second Division chief of staff Allen Greer's inflammatory letter to U.S. senator Kenneth McKellar of Tennessee. Du Bois also included Linard's "Secret Information concerning Black American Troops" memo, revealing the army's efforts to instill American white supremacy among the French for the world to see. As a result of its provocative content, U.S. postmaster general Albert Sidney Burleson delayed distribution of the *Crisis* issue for six days.

The highlight of the May *Crisis* was "Returning Soldiers," a stirring editorial that joined African American servicemen and civilians in a mutual struggle for the achievement of democracy in the aftermath of the war. Du Bois succinctly framed black soldiers as vanguards of the race in a postwar battle for African American social and political rights. He began by boldly proclaiming, "We are returning from war! The Crisis and tens of thousands of black men were drafted into a great struggle," immediately connecting himself and his readers with black soldiers as joint combatants in the military conflict. He continued by asserting that African American troops fought gladly and willingly for France, which stood as a metaphorical beacon of racial equality, in stark opposition to the United States. For America, to the contrary, black soldiers fought with a mixture of "far off hope," "bitter resignation," and "vindictive fate." Having risked and given their lives for a nation characterized by lynching, disfranchisement, the denial of educational and economic opportunities, and racial insult, black servicemen returned singing: "This country of ours, despite all its better souls have done and dreamed, is yet a shameful land." Again using African American soldiers as symbols for the entire race as a whole, Du Bois declared, "This is the country to which we Soldiers of Democracy return." Du Bois, however, would not submit to abandoning a fundamental aspect of his identity. Two-thirds through the piece he reversed course and, instead of completing denouncing America, reasserted the fundamental right of black people to fight for their country, for better or for worse. Nevertheless, he made clear that in this new historical moment, black America had to commit itself to winning a more protracted and potentially painful war for full citizenship rights in the United States, lest their sacrifice in the war be in vain. He ended with a ringing call to arms:

> But by the God of Heaven, we are cowards and jackasses if now that that war is over, we do not marshal every ounce of our brain and brawn to fight a sterner, longer, more unbending battle against the forces of hell in our own land.
>
> We *return.*
> We *return from fighting.*
> We *return fighting.*
>
> Make way for Democracy! We saved it in France, and by the Great Jehovah, we will save it in the United States, or know the reason why.[74]

The power of Du Bois's words resonated with readers. "'Returning Soldiers' alone is worth many times the magazine's weight in gold," a loyal subscriber wrote to the *Crisis* the following month.[75] Arguably Du Bois's most famous *Crisis* editorial next to "Close Ranks," "Returning Soldiers" is rivaled only by Claude McKay's stirring poem "If We Must Die" as a literary representation of African American postwar political consciousness and racial militancy.[76]

The entire May 1919 issue of the *Crisis*, distinguished by "Returning Soldiers," persuasively conveyed the connection between black military service—and black soldiers specifically—and a continued struggle for postwar democracy. Black spokesmen and -women, espousing claims-making rhetoric, used the patriotic service and, in their view, untainted record of black soldiers to push for increased democratic rights and inclusion in the body politic. Still lacking formal political power in the aftermath of the war, African American activists pinned their hopes on the rhetorical and symbolic potency of black servicemen and their contribution to the Allied victory. They strenuously emphasized the unassailable link between military service and citizenship that formed the basis of their arguments for increased political rights and civic recognition. Patriotism necessitated reciprocity on the part of the government. Sacrifice demanded reward.[77] African American soldiers, and by extension the race, had proved their worth. And now they expected nothing less than full acknowledgment of their equal place in the nation's democracy.

"WHAT OF OUR HOPES?" the *Cleveland Advocate* pondered in a November 23, 1918, editorial. It was a question black people had asked themselves throughout the war. But with the armistice, it suddenly bore a greater sense of urgency. This was not a naive query. "We had hoped that the mighty convulsion would shake into new alignment the forces of mankind in America—in defense of human rights," the editorial continued. African Americans had broadened Woodrow Wilson's narrow view of democracy to encompass the rights of black people, in the United States and beyond. The hopes of the postwar moment were the hopes of oppressed peoples throughout the world.[78] A new era of freedom was at stake. "The black heroes who purchased anew our freedom with their life's blood, cannot 'sleep in Flanders' fields' if the great government under whose starry emblem they fought and fell 'breaks faith' with them—the hallowed dead." Indeed, the aspirations of a race following the war were grounded in the sacrifice of its soldiers. As the editorial concluded, "WHAT OF OUR HOPES?"[79]

In the days and weeks immediately following the armistice, as black soldiers slowly trickled home, African American periodicals and newspapers sang their praises. The black press, staking its ground on the crucial terrain of historical memory, characterized the participation of African American servicemen as an unqualified success. More pointedly, newspapers consciously constructed a heroic, triumphant symbolic black soldier, one who not only had been essential to the Allied victory but, most importantly, had vindicated the manhood, citizenship, and valor of the race as a whole. It was essential, in the face of growing criticisms of the battlefield performance of African American combat soldiers and officers, that their historical contribution be firmly established. African American newspapers and magazines thus glorified black servicemen and their military contribution, often portraying them as the most decorated soldiers of the war. "The Negroes were, perhaps, the most proficient bayonet fighters in the American army," the *Cleveland Advocate* asserted.[80] The *Washington Bee* went so far as to describe the First Separate Battalion of the District of Columbia, which formed part of the 372nd Infantry Regiment, as "the only heroes in the war."[81] Much of their reporting centered on the Ninety-third Division, which, in comparison to the controversial Ninety-second Division, had an irrefutable record of service and distinction. The African American press aggressively constructed a historical counternarrative of black heroism, loyalty, and sacrifice to unequivocally link the contribution of African American soldiers to the cause of global democracy.

While full of praise for black soldiers, the writings and speeches of African American journalists and intellectuals contained pointed criticisms. Speaking to white Americans as well, activists insisted the government uphold the civil rights of black people as just reward not only for their patriotic loyalty but also as compensation for the poor treatment of African American soldiers and officers, at home and abroad.[82] Stories of blatant racial discrimination targeting black troops appeared with increasing regularity in African American newspapers shortly after the armistice. With the restrictive thumb of military censorship lifted, whispers during the war about the army's racism were confirmed as fact from the mouths of black soldiers themselves. The front page of the November 30, 1918, issue of the *New York Age* featured the story of Corporal Charles Drysdale of the 369th Infantry, who told of being discriminated against by a white secretary at a YMCA restaurant in France. "I really felt hurt to think I had come all the way to France; in a land where the inhabitants know no discrimination, and then to be belittled by this official," Drysdale wrote.[83] Sergeant Greenleaf Johnson of the 372nd Infantry Regiment published an account of his experience in the *Washington Bee*. He told readers how black soldiers tolerated segregation, received second-hand clothing, performed the worst types of work, and endured constant slander from white officers. Johnson exclaimed, "No country has made the road of its Negro subjects more burdensome than America has, or bound about the brow of its Negro subjects and allies a crown more set with thorns of prejudice and persecution." He further questioned, "Will their country, after admitting them to full brotherhood in labor, sacrifice, suffering and death, continue to deny to them full heirship in the unmolested enjoyment of the pursuits of peace, happiness and the protection of its laws and guidance in the governing affairs of the nation?"[84]

The reports of Ralph Waldo Tyler carried considerable weight. Tyler was a veteran journalist from Columbus, Ohio, who had worked with many of the city's African American and general circulation papers. Politically, he sat firmly in the Tuskegee camp, maintaining personal relationships with both Booker T. Washington and Emmett Scott. From the time the United States entered the war until the summer of 1918, Tyler served as a contributing editor for the *Cleveland Advocate* and, with three of his sons in the army, acted as national secretary of the Colored Soldier's Comfort Committee. Howard University professor Kelly

Miller served as president of the organization, which raised money for African American soldiers and their families who needed assistance. A much larger and potentially rewarding opportunity soon presented itself. One of the demands made during the June 1918 Washington, D.C., editors' conference was that the Committee on Public Information (CPI) take active steps to disseminate information to the African American public on the activities of black servicemen, at home and overseas. Emmett Scott used this opening to pressure the CPI to enlist Tyler's services. CPI director George Creel and his assistant Carl Byoir agreed that an African American war correspondent could go a long way toward taming black dissatisfaction with the government. Upon Scott's recommendation, the CPI selected Tyler for the position, and he enthusiastically accepted. He departed for France on September 18 and arrived ten days later as the only accredited African American overseas reporter.[85] The *Cleveland Advocate* could barely contain its excitement, anointing Tyler as "The Man of the Hour" and confidently stating, "Readers of Colored newspapers throughout the country will await his reports from the front with the greatest expectancy, and they will devour them with avidity born of deepest interest."[86]

Tyler made the most of his brief two months with the AEF before the November 11 armistice. Heavy combat during the Meuse-Argonne initially confined him to Paris, but he later spent extensive time with both the Ninety-second and Ninety-third Divisions, as well as black SOS troops. Tyler remained keenly aware of censorship regulations and, while testing their boundaries, was careful to mute any explicit criticisms of the army. Indeed, much of his reporting during the war extolled the bravery of black soldiers and the loyalty of race.[87] In a statement appearing in the *Stars and Stripes*, Tyler proclaimed, "The United States is our country, its flag is our flag, the only country and flag we know, and for which we, as a race, stand ready and willing to mingle our last drop of blood with the blood of our white brothers."[88]

His postwar reports, however, pulled no punches. Freed from the restrictive oversight of the CPI and military censors, Tyler vividly detailed instances of discrimination practiced by white officers and social welfare organizations. In a December 1918 article appearing in the *New York Age*, Tyler wrote, "Had it only been the Boche colored soldiers had to fight against they would return to the States without a single complaint, but in not a few instances, I regret to admit, they have had to fight the Hun while at the same time they were enduring an infilading attack from those whom they had supposed were here to fight for the same thing they came oversea to fight for—world democracy."[89] He aggressively refuted charges of cowardice leveled against black officers of the 368th Infantry Regiment and defended their honor. "Colored officers never had a fifty-fifty break over in France," Tyler asserted in a February 15, 1919, article, "and now that hostilities are over, and the refusal to give them a fifty-fifty break can be easily established by the citation of General Orders, they should not be made the goats for inefficient white officers, or be permitted to become victims of race prejudice that was clearly discernable in our army over in France."[90] He even took Tuskegee president Robert Moton to task, writing that black soldiers found his "advice" to return home "modest and unassuming" "a gratuitous insult." Tyler declared that the "Colored heroes from France and their kinsmen just as effectively are serving notice on President Wilson's Colored 'special' emissary, Principal Moton, that they want the rights and privileges their services and blood purchased on the battlefields of France, and NOT a southernized democracy."[91] While continuing to praise the loyalty and bravery of African American soldiers and officers, Tyler made it clear that recompense was due for their disgraceful treatment.[92]

African Americans continued to sardonically appropriate the democratic rhetoric of President Wilson to ensure that the patriotic sacrifices of black soldiers and the race more broadly had not been in vain. Professor John H. Hawkins, financial secretary of the AME Church, utilized Wilson's Fourteen Point speech as the template for his pamphlet titled *What Does the Negro Want?* Drawing from an address he delivered to the Washington, D.C., branch of the NAACP, Hawkins enumerated fourteen specific articles for "democracy at home." "In the style of President Wilson," as Hawkins explained, he listed the points not as a definitive program but as the basis for a mutual understanding between white and black people following the war. Hawkins's fourteen points included calls for universal manhood suffrage, educational reform, the abolishment of Jim Crow, better sanitary conditions, removal of the South's peonage system, and enforcement of the right to a fair jury trial as opposed to lynching. He called for equitable military training for white and black soldiers without regard to race and the removal of the "dead line" in the promotion of black officers.[93] The democratic and overtly politicized language of the war remained a strategic rhetorical weapon in the hands of African American social commentators such as Hawkins who sought to reap tangible concessions from the government.

Other African American civic leaders deployed both the symbolism of black troops and the rhetoric of democracy to inspire postwar black political activism. At a Philadelphia community rally in honor of returning black soldiers, Reverend H. F. Butler, pastor of Zoar Methodist Episcopal Church, delivered a rousing speech in which he explicitly linked black military service with an expectation for democratic reciprocity on the part of the government. Butler proclaimed to his audience: "The war is over. We have met the Hun. We have come home, and we have come home to stay. Don't think we are going back to Africa or any other place. This is our land, because we have fought for it, spilled our blood for it and given our lives for it. We have made the world safe for democracy. We have 'cleaned up' over there, and now we are going to clean up home."[94]

Inspired by the record of African American soldiers, a handful of black intellectuals and race activists cautiously viewed the aftermath of the war as a period of national "reconstruction." By invoking this term, with its evocative historical connotations, they established a rhetorical connection between the vivid memory of Reconstruction following the Civil War, with the achievements of the Fourteenth and Fifteenth Amendments, and the end of the World War.[95] War, on a mass-mobilizing scale, was seen as an engine of social and political reform, and just as African Americans had emerged from the Civil War with tangible civic gains, black activists reasoned, the same should be true for the recently concluded conflict. Shortly after the armistice, Kelly Miller published the aptly titled *The Negro in the New Reconstruction*. While John Hawkins and other spokespersons enumerated specific material expectations from the war, Miller argued that any substantive and lasting reform must begin with a "reconstruction of thought." Reflecting on the record of African American soldiers, he adopted a tone of optimism, writing, "The gallant part which the Negro played in bringing victory to the side of liberty has also served to liberalize the feeling and sentiment in his behalf. The new reconstruction, therefore, in so far as it may effect [*sic*] the Negro, will grow out of this new attitude of mind."[96] From this, he anticipated the inclusion of black people into "the program of social justice and human opportunity."[97] William Pickens, in his postwar pamphlet *The Negro in the Light of the Great War: Basis for the New Reconstruction*, and Mary White Ovington, in a substantive *Crisis* article entitled "Reconstruction and the Negro," carried similar messages.[98] African Americans, in their estimations, stood at the dawn of a new era, brought about by the revolutionizing power of war and the inspiring sacrifice of African American soldiers.

James Weldon Johnson adopted a much more explicitly internationalist and diasporic view toward postwar conditions. In the *New York Age* editorial "The Battle Begins," Johnson reminded readers that the aims and ideals of Woodrow Wilson "aroused the nation" and "gave special hope and inspiration to the people of African blood in the United States and the world over." Nevertheless, the struggle over the implementation of true democracy and international self-determination remained unfinished. With the future of global race relations hanging in the balance, African Americans could not afford to be passive. "Now is the time," Johnson insisted, "for them [African Americans] to proclaim and insist upon the aims and ideals of America in the war, and not only for themselves, but for their brothers in Africa and the islands of the sea and for all the oppressed peoples of the world."[99] Johnson saw African Americans as having a responsibility to champion the cause of global democratic rights for peoples of African descent. The moment was ripe for them to assertively place their demands for equal citizenship on the world's stage.

Black and white intellectuals, journalists, activists, and community leaders pushed hard for the expansion of American democracy after the armistice. Skillfully intertwining history and symbolism, they crafted arguments that thrust African American soldiers and their loyal sacrifice to the center of the war, a war destined to bring about social, political, and economic reconstruction on a global scale. It is clear, in retrospect, that these men and women lacked crucial perspective of the actual limited impact of the war on transforming race relations and the American social structure for the better. The brevity of America's participation in the war and the fact that the political status of African Americans did not lay at the heart of the conflict as it did in the Civil War, despite vigorous attempts by African Americans to make this otherwise, failed to factor into their interpretations. While rhetoric was compelling, African Americans lacked formal political influence, and, for this reason, the federal government, unswayed by the moral legitimacy of their claims, had little reason to consider the demands of black activists and reformers.[100] Moreover, white supremacy remained thoroughly embedded into the social and political fabric of the nation, possessing a resilience that race spokesmen and -women underestimated. Nevertheless, theirs was not a blind optimism. African Americans sincerely believed that through their service and loyalty, holistic reform was not only likely but inevitable. With nothing less than the very meaning of democracy itself at stake, the record and civic obligation of black soldiers stood as the most persuasive evidence black intellectuals, writers, and civic leaders used to enhance their arguments compelling governmental action. But all they could do was wait, hope, and continue to fight along with the rest of the race for their words to ring prophetically true and aspirations for change to materialize.

ACTIONS SPOKE LOUDER THAN WORDS in African American struggles for postwar democracy. The physical return of black soldiers to the United States and their reception by African Americans nationwide dramatically reflected the collective determination of black people to assert their civic consciousness and stake claim to their rights as American citizens in the public sphere. In cities large and small, black communities throughout the country, North and South, welcomed African American troops home with meticulously organized celebrations. The parades, rallies, and festivities of the First World War and its aftermath were intended to display national cohesion and loyalty. The homecoming parades for African American soldiers, however, continued to invoke earlier traditions of civic pageantry by fusing war-era expressions of patriotism and nationalism with African American's particular sense of community and racial consciousness.[101] More than just parades, these were political gatherings, moments for African Americans to come together, proclaim victory, and assert that democracy would be theirs. By celebrating the return of African American soldiers, black people took advantage of the conditions of possibility created by the war to infuse the public sphere with an expressive, self-empowering, democratic ethos that recognized the legitimacy of their citizenship.[102]

If black servicemen felt devalued by the racism of the U.S. Army, their spirits were buoyed by the warm embrace they received in the parades and celebrations held on their behalf. Black communities coronated returning soldiers as heroes and vanguards of social change. At the same time, the parades offered a prescient moment for black soldiers to demonstrate their manhood and individual and collective civic worth in the public sphere before the eyes of black and white Americans alike. Uniformed, disciplined, and fiercely proud, in the early months of 1919 African American soldiers triumphantly marched through city streets across the country, basking in the praise of their fellow black citizens, and boldly declaring their place in the nation's democracy.

The homecoming parades that occurred in major northeastern and midwestern cities reflected the impact of war-era migration from the South. Cities that before the war had relatively small black populations found themselves by the time of the armistice with vibrant and rapidly expanding communities. After relocating to places such as Chicago, New York, Cleveland, and Pittsburgh, southern migrants had to reconstitute a sense of community and civic belonging. Familial networks, religious institutions, and various uplift organizations helped in this process, as did the postwar homecoming parades for African American soldiers. Returning African American soldiers embodied, from a symbolic perspective, the new realities many black migrants faced in the daunting environs of the urban North and Midwest. They encapsulated the challenges of modernity, cosmopolitanism, dislocation, and the search for democracy that shaped the lives of black people during the war. For African American migrants, the homecoming parades represented a moment for them to at least temporarily reconcile these conflicting aspects of their existence.

These were momentous occasions, attended by sometimes thousands of cheering people, black and white. Nearly ten thousand Cleveland residents welcomed the Ohio Ninth Battalion of the 372nd Infantry Regiment upon its return to the city.[103] Pittsburgh held multiple homecoming parades, highlighted by a rousing tribute to two hundred African American soldiers of the 351st Field Artillery attended by the majority of the city's black and white population.[104] Mayor Edward Babcock delivered an inspiring speech, proclaiming, "There is no creed or color in our patriotism" and commanded the industrial city to "open its arms" to the returning soldiers.[105] For more than two hours on March 11, 1919, downtown Buffalo, New York, rang with applause and cheers, as thousands celebrated the return of thirty-four local black soldiers from the 349th Field Artillery of the Ninety-second Division. "I want to say right here," Mayor George Buck affirmed, "that Buffalo is mighty proud of you."[106] The place of white people in the celebrations, as spectators and direct participants, spoke to the transformative potential of African American soldiers to reconstruct the very nature of American democracy. A mutual sense of patriotism allowed white and black people temporarily, if all too briefly, to see past racial difference and commemorate the service of their returning heroes. Even Rhode Island, a state that counted only 291 black men among its drafted soldiers, held a homecoming parade in Providence for its black veterans, attended by some four thousand people.[107] These events, along with functioning as communal and civic coalescing occasions for black people, were also moments that destabilized the color line.

February 17, 1919, marked one of the most dramatic moments of the postwar era for black America. On this day, both Chicago and New York welcomed the return of their respective National Guard regiments, the Eighth Illinois and the New York Fifteenth "Hellfighters." The simultaneous celebrations serendipitously linked Chicago, the "promised land" for thousands of black migrants from the South during the war, and New York, the increasingly recognized epicenter of African American political culture.[108] The return of Chicago and New York's black regiments unleashed the democratic energies of black people in the two metropolises, who rallied to actively reimagine their collective sense of race, nation, and community.

The 370th Infantry Regiment, more fondly referred to as the "Old Eighth," was the pride of Chicago's African American community. Black Chicagoans had followed its every move, both in the United States and in France, in the pages of the *Defender*, and now, on February 17, eagerly anticipated its arrival. The day of "wild rejoicing" began with a morning rally for the regiment at the Chicago Coliseum. An estimated sixty thousand residents swelled the venue, rendering the police helpless to control the "spirit of the carnival" as the "Old Eighth" "claimed the joy mad city." The regiment's officers addressed the raucous crowd, with deposed Colonel Franklin Dennison receiving a rousing ovation. Other speakers included *Chicago Defender* editor Robert Abbott and Mayor "Big Bill"

Thompson, who enthusiastically congratulated the men of the Eighth on their "distinguished service on the battlefield" and offered his wish that they receive "justice and equality of citizenship."

Following the jubilant reception, the regiment fell in line at 16th Street and Michigan Avenue for a parade through downtown Chicago. The police cordoned off all streets, and businesses officially closed for the day. Seemingly the entire city thronged to catch a glimpse of the "Black Devils," attired in their French combat apparel. The city's white and black civic and industrial elite looked on from a reviewing stand on the stairs of the Art Institute. Meanwhile, as the parade progressed, the crowd continued to swell and eventually surged into the street. Soldiers joyfully reunited with their loved ones. "Again and again the line of march was not distinguishable, girls carrying rifles and men carrying soldiers," reported the *Defender*. "Everywhere there was a riot of color, as all manner of persons waved the Stars and Stripes and French tricolor."[109] Upon the conclusion of the parade at Grand Central Station, the Eighth boarded trains to Camp Grant for final demobilization. It was an incredible day for both the regiment's black soldiers and the city's African American populace as a whole. Community and nation, race pride and patriotism, beliefs black people in the midst of American racism struggled to reconcile, united on this particular Chicago day as a result of the "Old Eighth"'s triumphant return.

On the same day as the homecoming of the Eighth Illinois, residents of New York City celebrated the much anticipated arrival of their "Harlem Hellfighters." At daybreak, the regiment left Camp Upton, where it had been sent for final demobilization procedures, for Long Island City, and then to lower Manhattan. At eleven o'clock, under a bright sun and cloudless sky, the 369th assembled at Madison Avenue and 23rd Street. Led by Colonel Hayward, the "Hellfighters," in perfect lockstep, began their triumphant march into midtown. A crowd estimated at 250,000, which included a host of prominent national, state, and city leaders such as New York governor Alfred E. Smith, former governor Charles S. Whitman, Secretary of State Francis Hugo, William Randolph Hearst, and Emmett Scott, poured onto the East Side to view the extraordinary spectacle. The proud men of the Fifteenth fully understood the gravity of the moment and carried themselves accordingly. "All the soldiers that had been complaining rheumatism and other ailments that heretofore had caused them to be limp and crippled, were now standing erect and in the best marching conditions," Noble Sissle remembered. The crowd showered the regiment with cigarettes, candy, and silver coins in a stunning outpouring of affection. Star attraction Henry Johnson rode in an open car, waving a bouquet of red lilies and proudly displaying his French Croix de Guerre. He stood throughout the entire parade, relishing the shouts of "Oh, you Henry Johnson," and "Oh, you Black Death." The men of the regiment, donning their French-issued helmets, rifle bayonets gleaming in the winter sun, and marching in a military formation perfected while serving with the French, made for an imposing sight. They conveyed an image of power, discipline, and aggressive black manhood. The *New York Times* was particularly fascinated by the regiment's impressive stature, commenting on the "bigness" and battle-scarred "grim visaged" demeanor of the men. The dramatic return of the Fifteenth represented a visually striking claim for full, inclusive citizenship in front of New York's most prominent white citizens.[110]

But this was a day for Harlem. As the soldiers marched uptown, the composition of the crowd gradually changed, until, by the time the regiment reached 110th Street, they were enveloped by a sea of black faces. Hayward reconfigured the men into a less impersonal formation, and Jim Europe's internationally acclaimed band switched from playing military marches to the swinging jazz tune "Here Comes My Daddy Now." Harlem overflowed with joy and excitement. People crowded rooftops and hung from windows and fire escapes to catch a glimpse of their returning heroes. American flags and banners welcoming the "Hellfighters" home adorned apartment buildings and local businesses. Black women and children, searching for their husbands, brothers, and fathers, joined the men of the regiment in the street. Much of the formality that distinguished the parade as it reviewed in front of white New York was now discarded as the regiment became swept into Harlem's euphoria. The festivities concluded with a dinner reception at the 71st Regiment armory for the men and their families.

In its report of the historic day, the *New York Age* stated, "The welcome given the 369th formerly the old 15th, in New York Monday should live long in the hearts and minds of the people. No one can deny that this colored regiment made history for the nation, the state and the city; for colored and white alike."[111] In a city accustomed to parades, the homecoming celebration of the "Harlem Hellfighters" was indeed a spectacle like nothing New York had ever witnessed. On the one hand, it represented an impressive display of the potential of civic interracial democracy on the grand New York stage. As Arthur Little surmised, "Upon the 17th of February, 1919, New York City knew no color line."[112] Black and white New Yorkers came together in an extraordinary moment of patriotic solidarity that empowered black soldiers and affirmed their citizenship in a way they had never before experienced. Following the dramatic parade James Weldon Johnson poignantly wrote, "We wonder how many people who are op-

James Reese Europe and 369th homecoming parade. 165-WW-127 (37). Courtesy of National Archives and Record Administration, College Park, Md.

posed to giving the Negro his full citizenship rights could watch the Fifteenth on its march up the Avenue and not feel either shame or alarm? And we wonder how many who are not opposed to the Negro receiving his full rights could watch these men and not feel determined to aid them in their endeavor to obtain these rights?"[113]

But the parade had other meanings as well. The inspiring presence of the Fifteenth, as James Weldon Johnson astutely captured, epitomized the urgent need to destroy the racial barriers that hindered the full potential of American democracy. Indeed, as it progressed up Fifth Avenue and into Harlem, the parade itself reflected the realties of segregation in New York and the physical divide separating the city's white and black residents; despite Arthur Little's claim, the color line remained well intact.[114] From the perspective of black Harlemites and the Fifteenth itself, however, the homecoming was not just about proving their civic worth and equality to white America. They just as importantly reaffirmed their own sense of community and racial pride around the regiment's historic record of service. White validation of the "Hellfighters'" heroism, while significant, was not entirely necessary. Whether or not the regiment's return in fact ushered in an expansion of African American citizenship rights, the Fifteenth would always be the pride of Harlem. It would never be forgotten.

The homecoming parades and celebrations held in the American South were particularly significant. Whereas the color line in the urban North was often fluid and less ubiquitous, Jim Crow segregation and the threat of racial violence cast a long shadow over the southern public sphere. But it also functioned as a space where white supremacy regularly demonstrated its malleability.[115] Late nineteenth- and early twentieth-century urbanization facilitated interactions between black and white southerners, as well as generated increased opportunities for African Americans' political expression.[116] New South city politics, the unique nature of southern white progressivism, and the patriotic exigencies of the war further combined to create spaces for both interracial cooperation and black activism. In this regard, the parades were political events.[117] By rallying around their veterans and celebrating their Americanness, black communities challenged the hypocrisies of segregation, disfranchisement, and lynching and confidently proclaimed their citizenship.

Homecoming parades took place throughout the South in the spring and summer of 1919. They shared a similar format: a parade featuring local African American veterans, followed by speechmaking and public festivities, usually at a central park. Most of the celebrations for black veterans occurred in major cities and were organized by local African American civic leaders. Both white and black people viewed the parades, but the concluding festivities, save for the presence of select white municipal leaders, were for the particular enjoyment of the black community. In Dallas, on April 22, 1919, white and black citizens came together to honor the city's recently returned African American servicemen. Mayor Frank Wozencraft, only twenty-six years of age and himself a veteran, declared the day an official holiday for the city's black residents and personally delivered a welcome address. Following the parade of black soldiers, the *Dallas Morning News* reported, several thousand people continued the festivities at Fair Park, highlighted by a baseball game and a feast of "barbecued beef, pork and mutton, with plenty of bread and cold drinks."[118] Over ten thousand black people from Mobile, Alabama, and surrounding areas turned out for a July 1919 homecoming parade, picnic, and barbecue.[119] The black veterans offered a stark contrast to the image of returning soldiers as a social and political menace. This held true even in the heart of the former Confederacy. Nearly all the residents of Richmond, Virginia, white and black, turned out for the July 8 welcoming parade for African American soldiers of the 808th Pioneer Infantry, described by a white newspaper as "the aristocrats of their race."[120] This event and others like it had the power to potentially shape white perceptions of black people, and soldiers in particular.

The parades and celebrations likewise served as important politicizing occasions to openly challenge white southern views of African Americans as noncitizens. On May 1, 1919, black residents of Jacksonville, Florida, held an elaborately planned victory celebration and welcome home parade for African American veterans, the largest event of its kind since the end of the Civil War. It was a principally black affair, with the governor and the local chamber of commerce intentionally left off the invitation list. All the African American residents of Jacksonville came together during an evening of pageantry, memorialization, and speechmaking to praise the heroism of their soldiers, as well as to stake claim to their rightful place as equal human beings in the South.[121] Similarly, in Bainbridge, Georgia, the "Home Coming Committee for Negro Soldiers" organized a day-long celebration for Decatur County's black veterans on April 14, 1919. Following a parade headed by returned soldiers, some five thousand people packed a local park for music, food, and speeches, including one by Henry Lincoln Johnson, a native of Atlanta and husband of acclaimed poet Georgia Douglas Johnson, who emphasized the patriotism and loyalty of African Americans in the face of segregation and lynching.[122]

One of the largest homecoming celebrations for southern black veterans occurred in Savannah, Georgia, a city whose segregated black neighborhoods, characterized by one of the highest death rates in the country, belied its carefully constructed image of southern gentility. A 1906–7 boycott of the streetcar system in protest against the passage of a segregation ordinance spoke to the political activism of Savannah's black community.[123] This carried over into the war and postwar periods. Led by Savannah's "Committee of One Hundred," preparations to commemorate Chatham County's estimated two thousand African American veterans began months in advance. The organizers selected May 7, 1919, as the date of the celebration to coincide with the one-year anniversary of a historic War Savings Campaign parade attended by some twenty-five thousand black people of the city. "Savannah is proud to welcome home her heroes, returned from the exploits and sacrifices of war," the *Savannah Tribune* wrote in advance of the festivities. "We have faith in the ultimate triumph of right, to bring a practical democracy to earth amongst men. And, then, we take fresh courage and march on to our tasks."[124]

The much-anticipated day began at eleven o'clock. Twelve hundred black veterans from various regiments and battalions formed six companies and marched in tight formation, receiving a steady shower of applause as they passed by the crowd of several thousand men, women, and children. They were followed by an assortment of African American fraternal, labor, religious, and civic organizations. Three black veterans of the Civil War marched in the procession, and a float depicting Revolutionary War hero Crispus Attucks was featured, linking veterans of the war to a longer historical legacy of African American patriotism and military sacrifice. Upon the conclusion of the parade, civic and religious leaders delivered speeches at the local park, including a speech by Pierce McN. Thompson, a first lieutenant and native of Albany, Georgia, commissioned at Des Moines.[125] Following a barbecue lunch, the day ended with the planting of an elm tree at the First Bryan Baptist Church in honor of the county's black servicemen killed in the war. "Savannah has the banner for entertaining the World War veterans," reviewed Ed Fleming. A soldier formerly of the 369th Infantry Regiment, he had marched in New York as well as in a Philadelphia celebration, and thus felt more than confident offering his expert opinion.[126] African American veterans, irrespective of rank and occupation, came away from the festivities with their contribution to the war effort validated and place as communal heroes and leaders confirmed. The planning, choreography, and emotion Savannah's black residents put into the day-long event was indicative of both their deep pride in the service of the country's African American veterans and determination to assert their rightful place as citizens in the postwar South.

Due in no small part to the buoyant reception from their fellow black citizens, many black servicemen returned to their homes emboldened. Elija Spencer, a farmer from Buckingham, Virginia, survived an arduous tour of duty with the 808th Pioneer Infantry. He labored dangerously close to the front lines during the Meuse-Argonne Allied offensive and, like other pioneer infantry units, continued to work long after the armistice. Reflecting upon his return to Buckingham and a life of farming, he declared, "I feel proud of the fact that I served my country."[127] Thomas Toney, a veteran of the 370th Infantry Regiment similarly stated that the war "made me a better American, more appreciative of my home country."[128] Having endured a life where the denial of citizenship occurred on a daily basis, many returned black soldiers, especially those from the South, felt a genuine sense of civic affirmation and national entitlement. Their postwar patriotism was not unconditional. Floyd Bishop, a veteran inducted into the 540th Engineers out of Norfolk, Virginia, stated in August 1919, "Before the war I was passive as to the treatment of the common people colored, in particular, but since the war I am constantly reminded that my people (colored) are not getting any of the things that i served in the war to help bring about—democracy."[129] For men like Floyd Bishop, democracy mattered on a broader racial level, as well as on a more personal level. African American soldiers and the communities they came home to emerged from the war transformed and committed to ensuring that the ideals championed by the United States in waging war would hold firm during the waging of peace.

THE DAYS IMMEDIATELY FOLLOWING the end of the war were pregnant with hope. Shaken by their discriminatory treatment throughout the demobilization process, black soldiers had every reason to be skeptical that the war had brought about any significant change in racial attitudes. Nevertheless, most held firm to the individual and collective meanings of their service. Black servicemen received further validation as African Americans sang their praises in the black press and celebrated their return in cities and towns across the country. The return of black soldiers, both figuratively and literally, represented a bold challenge to the meaning of postwar democracy. As many white Americans, even in the South, congratulated black veterans upon their return, African Americans hoped the record of their soldiers and the patriotic loyalty of the race signaled the arrival of a new era of race relations and democratic reciprocity in the United States. This optimism would be severely tested as the postwar period unfolded.

I went to war, served eight months in France; I was married, but I didn't claim exemption. I wanted to go, but I might as well have stayed here for all the good it has done me. . . . No, that ain't so, I'm glad I went. I done my part and I'm going to fight right here till Uncle Sam does his. I can shoot as good as the next one, and nobody better start anything. I ain't looking for trouble, but if it comes my way I ain't dodging.

—Anonymous veteran,
interview with the Chicago Commission on Race Relations

THE WAR AT HOME

African American Veterans and Violence in the Long "Red Summer"

Charles Lewis was finally home. The young black soldier had spent the war at Camp Sherman, Ohio. His services no longer needed, Lewis, carrying an honorable discharge, had returned to his humble shack in Tyler Station, Kentucky, a small town located just across the Tennessee-Kentucky border. It was a rough town, notorious for gambling and bootlegging. On the evening of December 15, 1918, a few days after Lewis's arrival, a deputy sheriff, Alvin Thomas, entered his home. Two local black men had recently been robbed, Thomas claimed, and Lewis fit the description of the assailant. He may have in fact been guilty as charged; Lewis apparently had a reputation for trouble before he went off to war. But now he was a soldier. Wearing his army uniform, Lewis asserted that his military status made him immune from arrest by a civil officer. When Thomas attempted to detain Lewis, he and another man reportedly in the house beat the deputy, stole his pistol, and immediately fled. A call went out for assistance. Police officers and local vigilantes soon captured Lewis in a nearby cornfield and charged him with assault and resisting arrest.

Police temporarily held Lewis in custody at Tyler Station. News of his brazen challenge to white authority and subsequent apprehension quickly spread. A line had been crossed, and now passions had been enflamed. Lewis was in great danger. A mob of seventy-five to one hundred people gathered as Lewis awaited transportation to the Fulton County Jail, located approximately fifteen miles east in Hickman, Kentucky. "Get a rope!" someone in the crowd shouted. They grudgingly adhered to the advice of officers to let the law take its course. Lewis's fortune did not last through the night. The mob had not dispersed but instead followed Lewis to Hickman. At midnight, the crowd of masked men stormed the Hickman city jail, smashing the locks with a sledgehammer and disregarding the protests of the police. They seized Lewis and pulled him out of his cell. The mob then tied a rope around the former soldier's neck, and hanged him on a nearby tree. Daybreak on December 16 brought with it the chilling sight of Lewis's suspended body, viewed by hundreds of white spectators, relieved that this "very dangerous character" had been disposed of.[1]

"Hoodlums Lynch Colored Soldier," the *Cleveland Advocate* headlined.[2] News of the Lewis lynching sent shock waves throughout black America. "Not since the East St. Louis riot have the colored people been so worked up as they are today," reported Walter Loving, impressing upon his superiors in the Military Intelligence Division (MID) that "the most rigid investigation should be conducted so that the guilty, who are well known to the Kentucky officials, may be brought to justice and punished to the fullest extent of the law."[3] An anonymous black serviceman from Hickman, who identified himself as "A soldier in uniform. A friend to the Race," encouraged the NAACP to investigate the incident because "it appears to be an effort made to keep it from being known outside of the community." The national office of the NAACP had in fact wasted no time in responding to the Lewis murder, recognizing the significance of the incident because it involved an American who "had at the request of the Government entered the service of the United States army, where he was prepared, if necessary, to lay down his life to see that the ideals of democracy were perpetuated."[4] They pressured a reticent Kentucky governor Augustus Stanley to act and spread news of the lynching through the press. A release issued by NAACP secretary John R. Shillady lamented, "Loyal Americans will be horrified to learn that one who offered his life for preservation of democracy and of America should thus be murdered for an offense that, if committed by a white soldier, would have been punished by a light sentence."[5] Scarcely a month after the conclusion of the war, a war in which African Americans fought to make the world "safe for democracy," the lynching of Lewis challenged the meaning of their sacrifice. As the *New York Evening Sun* questioned in its report of the incident, "And the point is made that every loyal American negro who has served with the colors may fairly ask: 'Is this our reward for what we have done?'"[6]

The lynching of Charles Lewis reflected the pervasive threat of violence African American veterans faced upon the conclusion of their service. The war inflated the hopes of African Americans that a new era of democratic opportunity lay on the horizon. Instead, these hopes were met by a wave of racial violence unmatched since the aftermath of the Civil War. The daily struggles of combating racism had in the past assumed a warlike quality for many black people. But the violence in the aftermath of the war was both qualitatively and quantitatively different from what had come before. An estimated twenty-five race riots, large and small, erupted throughout the nation; the number of lynchings increased from sixty-four in 1918 to eighty-three in 1919, counting seventy-six black victims; acts of individual vigilantism occurred daily. The violence formed part of a postwar global climate of unrest and upheaval, as peoples of African descent across the diaspora battled the forces of white supremacy and struck out for increased self-determination.[7] In the United States, African Americans found themselves, quite literally, engaged in a renewed struggle for their very survival, prompting James Weldon Johnson to label the bloody demobilization months of 1919 "The Red Summer."[8] At the heart of this maelstrom stood African American soldiers, returning in the thousands to a society seemingly on the verge of all-out racial warfare.[9]

From the end of the war up to contemporary historical accounts of the era, the image of the lynched, abused, and persecuted African American veteran has remained extremely potent. Indeed, the lynched African American veteran has functioned to symbolize the ferocity of the "Red Summer" and anecdotally highlight the depths of postwar racial injustice. This symbolic construction, however, was contextual and shaped by the actual presence and actions of African American veterans. Across the country, the vortex of racial tensions created by the war swirled around black veterans. This was particularly true in the American South, where the return of black servicemen contributed to a volatile social, political, and economic climate that produced a dramatic surge in racial violence, and lynching specifically, that claimed the lives of several African American veterans. Similarly, in cities throughout the country, from Washington, D.C., to Tulsa, Oklahoma, recently returned black soldiers on multiple occasions found themselves at the center of major race riots. In the context of a long "Red Summer," beginning with the end of the war and concluding with the 1921 Tulsa Riot, African American veterans, as both victims and aggressors, unsuspecting participants and conscious agents, profoundly shaped the history and meaning of postwar racial violence. For many ex-servicemen, their return to the United States and their homes marked both a continuation and an escalation of combat hostilities; seeking to reestablish some sense of normalcy, they unwittingly found themselves fighting for their lives. At stake in this new war was the future of American race relations, the legacy of black military service, and the very meaning of democracy itself.

WILL ALEXANDER EPITOMIZED the "new" white southerner. Although born in Missouri, Alexander spent most of his formative years in Tennessee, where he became a Methodist preacher. Struck by the forces of poverty and racial intolerance surrounding him, Alexander committed himself to the noble cause of interracial cooperation. During the war, he headed the Atlanta YMCA War Work Council and personally witnessed, with sanguine eyes, a spirit of patriotic unity and mutual sacrifice between white and black southerners. But, with the war now over, the South had become a powder keg of hostility. Racial tensions had, of course, existed in the South throughout the duration of war. The impending return of black veterans to the region, however, added a new and highly combustible element to an already explosive social climate. Alexander had hoped for a new era of race relations. To the contrary, "almost within forty-eight hours after the Armistice was signed," Alexander witnessed the "morale and spirit that had existed" begin "to disappear." "Within a very few weeks racial tensions mounted in almost every community in the South."[10]

Labor relations in disarray. Interracial sexual boundaries transgressed. Black-on-white violence leading to all out race war. All of these anxieties accompanied the return of African American servicemen to the South. The war and the reincorporation of black servicemen into southern society exposed the fragility of the often unspoken rules of racial etiquette, the customs of language and behavior that symbolically shaped relations and maintained boundaries between white and black southerners.[11] In the eyes of many white southerners, African American veterans epitomized a black population that had either forgotten or outright rejected its place in the region's racial hierarchy. Their presence, and the democratic sensibilities they represented, flew in the face of white supremacist constructions of black subservience and acquiescence to long-standing traditions of southern race relations. At the same time, the war had a significant impact on black veterans and black southerners more broadly, who were collectively less prepared to accept a prewar status quo. As Dr. Josiah Morse of South Carolina remarked during a meeting of the YMCA Inter-Racial Committee, "We have a new Negro with us, he has come back from the world war changed."[12]

African American veterans threw the South's economy and system of labor relations into a state of flux. Many black servicemen who returned to the South did so with a new sense of purpose and desire for a better life. Professor Benjamin F. Hubert of the State College in Orangeburg, South Carolina, who worked with African American troops through the auspices of the American Educational Corps, told the *New York Age* that hundreds of soldiers expressed to him the desire to improve their lives as well as those of their community upon returning to the United States. "We hear our boys in the army sing the song, 'How Are We Goin' to Keep 'Em Down on the Farm?,'" Hubert commented. "We smile and pass on, but have we ever thought seriously of all the heart-yearning back of the song? Do we wonder how hard it is for the boy from the country who has seen something of life in America and European cities to make up his mind to go back to a place where there is nothing going on?"[13] While no exact figures exist, the Inter-Racial Committee of the YMCA estimated that 100,000 discharged black servicemen relocated to northern cities after their demobilization.[14] Many returned black soldiers also abandoned plantation life for an opportunity to start anew in major southern cities like Atlanta and Birmingham, which experienced significant increases in their black populations during the war. In Louisiana, the state director of the United States Employment Bureau discovered that no discharged African American soldiers requested employment on farms; they claimed that they would rather find work in cities or return to the army.[15] A similar situation occurred in Clarke County, Georgia, where 70 percent of the county's white planters with black employees in the army reported that upon their return from service, veterans left the farm soon after. Those who did stay eventually became dissatisfied with their condition.[16]

The actions of black veterans presented white planters and industrialists with a problem. On the one hand, former soldiers represented a vital labor source and the region's economy could ill afford to lose their production. John Baker of the Jacksonville, Florida, Chamber of Commerce wrote to the Department of Labor, "We people of the south, understand the negro laborer, and the large employers of labor in this section of the country, prefer the working of the negro's to the white man." Facing a shortage of plantation, sawmill, and turpentine camp workers, he attempted to induce black servicemen back to the South, "where they really belong, and where they are better understood than they are in the north."[17] However, white planters, economists, and average citizens also remained extremely concerned about the potentially disruptive presence of black veterans on the region's system of labor relations, a system in which black workers were expected to accept their economic, social, and political position without question or protest. Returning African American servicemen seriously challenged this presumption. Would they demand an increase in wages? After all, the average soldier earned more money in the military—usually thirty dollars a month—than he did as a farmer. If their wages did not improve, would they become uncooperative? "Sometimes I very much fear that the return of the negro soldiers is going to be followed by trouble in the South," wrote a troubled white New Orleans resident in January 1919. "The negroes show a growing hostility and insolence to the whites, quite apart from their refusal to work for wages which we can afford to pay. This will probably be worse when the troops come home, flushed with the praises that they have received for their work in France."[18] White employers readied themselves for the distinct possibility of turmoil involving former soldiers throughout the region.

For many white southerners, the "problem" of the returning black soldier centered on the volatile issue of sex. The presence of black veterans in the South raised new concerns regarding the threat black men posed to the sanctity of white womanhood. Will Alexander attributed much of the postwar hostility to "the fact that some of these Negro boys had been to France, and, as most Southerners who talked about it said, had been accepted by French women."[19] Stories of liaisons between French women and black troops, sensationalized by white soldiers and officers, made their way back to the United States. French women, by welcoming black men into their homes and their beds, were cast as unrespectable whores, while African American soldiers emerged as opportunistic sex-hungry predators. Most egregious, however, loomed the possibility that this literal and symbolic blurring of the color line had deluded black soldiers into believing that after the war social equality and intimate interracial relations could become an accepted reality in America.

Charges that black soldiers, in particularly those under the command of black officers in the Ninety-second Division, had committed a disproportionate number of rapes increased white anxieties. These rumors had a powerful effect in the South, where the image of the "black beast rapist" remained a steady fixture in the white imagination.[20] The panic surrounding black veterans' masculinity and sexuality mirrored the aftermath of the Civil War, when white southerners expressed their alarm concerning Reconstruction-era citizenship rights gains for African American men in the form of a coded language of sexual fear regarding the danger black masculinity posed to white womanhood.[21] As a new generation of freeborn African Americans came to maturity in the 1880s and 1890s, the association between black men and rape reached hysterical proportions. The particular historical dynamics of the war and black military service thus account for the evolution of the "black beast rapist" into the black veteran. Rumors of rape, combined with the masculine attributes of military service itself, made African American veterans a sexual threat to be aggressively confronted. Former U.S. senator James Vardaman exhorted his fellow white Mississippians, whose daughters had been "outraged by the French-women-ruined heroes," to remain vigilant. These imaginary assaults, dramatized by Vardaman and others, linked African American veterans to a historical trope of hypersexual black masculinity that threatened the very sanctity of southern society and provided rhetorical and psychological legitimization for the region's lynching institution.[22]

The hypersexualization of African American veterans formed part of the broader association of returned black soldiers with potential violence in the South. This was not new. The legacies of occupying black Union soldiers in the aftermath of the Civil War, Brownsville in 1906, the still smoldering recent memory of Houston, combined with numerous other incidents of conflict between black servicemen and white southerners during the war, served to maintain a fresh connection between African American soldiers and violent unrest.[23] Underlying these fears was a relationship between black military service and a citizenship rights consciousness that ultimately challenged the tenets and very stability of the South's racial order. In this logic, black veterans, flaunting their service as proof of civic belonging, would provoke an inevitable violent response from southern whites. "The Negro ex-soldier wanted justice and a square deal and became everywhere a spokesman therefore," the YMCA Inter-Racial Committee observed.[24] Their minds full of talk of democracy and their egos swelled from praise, it was thought that black veterans would inspire other African Americans to strike back against enforcement of the color line and the region's unspoken codes of racial etiquette.

The fact that many black veterans returned to the South trained in the art of warfare and with extensive knowledge of handling weapons made white concerns even more palpable. Southern whites, always fearful of the specter of insurrection, had recognized the dangers of guns in the hands of African American men since the antebellum era. It was for this reason that southern states outlawed black National Guard organizations and vehemently resisted black soldiers being trained in the region's cantonments during the war. With the war over, the South faced the reality of thousands of African American servicemen, some increasingly politicized and others intensely embittered, returning to their homes as skilled marksmen. Whereas African American communities welcomed these soldiers as crucial protectors against the always-present threat of racial violence, many southern whites saw them as the tip of a potential regionwide black rebellion. Reports of black soldiers coming home carrying guns along with their discharge papers further fueled white apprehensions. One military intelligence officer gave credence to rumors of black veterans using firearms obtained during their service in "race or radical movements," being that it was a "well-known fact that there is a great deal of social and labor unrest among the Negro population of the United States, who are demanding social equality as well as other changes from their pre-war status."[25] As fears of bolshevism gripped the country, the prospect of a significant number of African American servicemen returning to their homes with weapons drew the immediate concern of military intelligence personnel and southern white citizens, the latter well seasoned in the ever-present possibility of racially charged violence.

Many southern whites prepared for war.[26] J. W. Sammons, an anxious white citizen from Georgia, wrote to Secretary of War Newton D. Baker that he had personally heard a leading Negro of his area say that "there would be a war between the negroes and white people before this year is out." Sammons added, "I fully believe that they mean to try to gain their wishes by force because some of the boys has had some military training they think that they can whip the white people because he said that there was ten thousand negro soldiers trained and ready that could whip every white man in the United States."[27] The YMCA Inter-Racial Committee investigated "a very serious situation" in Alexander City, Alabama, involving a white man and a returned black soldier that threatened to lead to "a serious race riot."[28] After a search, they found that 85 percent of the homes in the city had extra firearms and ammunition.

Black communities prepared themselves accordingly. Self-defense against white violence was by no means a new phenomenon. The determination of southern African Americans to protect their lives and property with arms, however, assumed an added intensity following the armistice, as rumors of an impending race war swirled throughout the region. Authorities in Harrison County, Texas, suspected local African Americans of purchasing "a great deal of arms and ammunition."[29] Reports of black people hoarding caches of guns and ammunition, while wildly exaggerated by white southerners, contained an element of truth. Emboldened by their patriotic sacrifice during the war and unwilling to be slaughtered without a fight, southern African Americans displayed a commitment to self-defense that transcended class lines. A statistician at the Tuskegee Institute, who held a Ph.D. in sociology from the University of Chicago, related to Will Alexander that "most colored people are feeling that they must arm, that we are in for bad times. I've been wondering if I ought to take steps to protect myself."[30] African Americans, realizing all too well the violent nature of southern white supremacy, refused to be caught off guard. Black southerners had no desire to instigate a race war. Nevertheless, they were more than prepared to defend themselves if one should occur.

Through outrageous stories in the southern press and word of mouth, talk of race war spread like wildfire.[31] The return of African American soldiers gripped white Texans with fear throughout the summer of 1919.[32] On August 1, 1919, federal agents in Galveston, Texas, reported that "considerable agitation and talk of race riots have been going on in that community for the past week."[33] In Columbia, South Carolina, rumors of planned organized attacks caused the city's white and black communities to mobilize for battle. Hoping to prevent a calamity, a white minister contacted a fellow black minister, who relayed, "We're not getting ready to riot. We are going to defend ourselves if you attack us."[34] Rumors of this sort often involved black veterans. In Fayetteville, North Carolina, local whites feared an impending race riot after black people were allegedly observed drilling under an African American officer who had recently returned from service. "We've known these Negroes all their lives," a consternated white resident exclaimed. "If they're drilling, let's go down there and see them and talk with them." A group went to investigate the situation, only to find that the head of a local black fraternal lodge had died and its members were practicing an elaborate burial ceremony.[35]

What white people mistook for an urge to wage race war in fact reflected a heightened sense of self-worth and civic awareness on the part of many African Americans, and black veterans in particular. Reverend Robert McCaslin of Montgomery, Alabama, expressed alarm at "the new feeling of superiority among the negroes" in his community, who "believe they have won the war." Their talk was "having a bad affect among the whites," he observed.[36] The historical fears of black soldiers internalized by many southern whites caused them to interpret a desire to be seen as full citizens and treated as equal human beings as an organized effort to overthrow the region's racial hierarchy.

The Tuskegee establishment attempted to calm white concerns regarding black veterans. The March 1919 issue of the *Southern Workman*, published by Tuskegee's sister institution, the Hampton Institute, included a special section entitled "After the War: A Symposium." The issue included a statement from Emmett J. Scott, who sought to ease the paranoia of white southerners by writing, "The returning soldier will not be a foul wretch from whom to shrink in terror, or a plague from which to flee in fear, as some seem to think. He will return benefited both physically and mentally by reason of his military training and experience, and with a broader vision and appreciation of American citizenship, as well as with new ideas of what liberty and freedom really mean."[37] Ironically, Scott articulated precisely what southern whites most feared, revealing the stark difference in how African Americans viewed and interpreted the experience of black veterans. The *Southern Workman* also reprinted a version of the cautionary, and widely criticized, speech by Tuskegee president Robert R. Moton delivered to black soldiers during his visit to France after the war, as well as a statement by Tuskegee's director of research, Monroe N. Work. Work assured white southerners that African American servicemen had no intention of "returning in a spirit of hostility" and desired only "to become, as civilians, better and more useful men and to help promote the welfare of their respective communities."[38] Both Moton and Work stressed the same point: black soldiers would return to the region free of incident and not challenge the racial status quo.

Black educational and political leaders in the South collaborated with progressive-minded white southerners such as Will Alexander. Alexander, in response to the climate of fear, suspicion, and outright hostility caused by the return of African American soldiers to the South, established the Inter-Racial Committee of the YMCA, which became the Commission on Interracial Cooperation (CIC) in early 1919. The CIC faced many challenges stemming from the middle-class presumptions of its white leadership, suspicion on the part of African American activists, and outright hostility from committed white supremacists. Nevertheless, the CIC received significant financial support from major northern philanthropic foundations and overcame obstacles to become the leading southern interracial reform organization during the 1920s.[39] Its representatives, both black and white, men and women, invested in the evolution of a "New South" predicated upon mutual progress and racial toleration, attempted, as best they could, to diffuse tensions and present a positive image of returning black servicemen and their impact on regional race relations.[40]

DESPITE THESE EFFORTS, the South experienced a dramatic surge in racial violence in the year following the war. Lynching emerged as the most effective weapon in the arsenal of southern whites to restore a sense of normalcy to a regional social order seemingly turned upside down. Reversing a gradual decline, an estimated seventy-six black people fell victim to mob violence and white vigilantism in 1919, the highest total since 1908 and an increase of forty from 1917.[41] African American servicemen had physically and symbolically disrupted the southern color line, and the codes of etiquette that maintained its tenuous stability. Lynching functioned as both a fierce corrective and a warning for black people to remember their place. As a new wave of racial terrorism swept the South after the armistice, African Americans confronted the cruel irony of fighting for their lives against fellow American citizens. This made the lynching of at least eleven African American veterans in 1919 particularly tragic and laden with symbolic meaning.

Following the December 1918 killing of Charles Lewis, the first reported lynching of a returned black serviceman in the new year occurred on March 14, 1919. A mob near Pensacola, Florida, burned Bud Johnson to death for allegedly attacking a well-known white woman. NAACP secretary John R. Shillady demanded that Florida governor Sidney J. Catts punish those responsible for Johnson's gruesome execution. Catts responded by urging the organization to teach black people "not to kill our white officers and disgrace our white women."[42] One week later, the small town of El Dorado, Arkansas, gained a similar notoriety. Twenty-five-year-old Frank Livingston, recently discharged from Camp Pike, Arkansas, and living at the time as a farmer on the property of Robinson Clay, killed him following a quarrel over livestock. In a panicked effort to conceal his crime, Livingston also murdered Clay's wife and then set fire to the farm, with the two bodies inside. A mob of 150 to 200 men, both white and black, captured Livingston and, after he allegedly confessed to the crime, tied the former soldier to a tree and set him aflame.[43] Although Arkansas governor Charles Brough denounced Livingston's lynching, law enforcement officials took no active steps to apprehend those individuals responsible.[44] On May 8, an anonymous veteran was lynched along with a black woman near the town of Pickens in Holmes County, Mississippi. The returned soldier had been accused of hiring the female victim to write a note to a young white woman.[45]

The bloodshed continued into the summer months of 1919. On August 3, Charles Kelley, who had been recently discharged from Camp Gordon, was killed in the small town of Woolsey, Georgia. While driving his father to church, Kelley did not turn his car out of the road quick enough to suit a white boy also driving on the street. The boy informed his father, who confronted Kelley. Kelley tried to run, but was shot in the back.[46] Days later another veteran also lost his life in Georgia, this time in Pope City, a railroad settlement in Wilcox County. On August 14, a lynch mob hung returned serviceman Jim Grant for reportedly killing two white men while they attempted to take another black man in custody. Adding further insult, the crowd publicly whipped Grant's father and told him to leave the area immediately.[47]

The lynching of Lucious McCarthy was particularly heinous. On August 30, Winifred Stewart, a white woman from Bogalusa, Louisiana, a town located on the outskirts of New Orleans, alleged that a black man had entered her home and attempted to assault her. News of the incident quickly spread, and the following morning an intense search ensued to capture the perpetrator. Bloodhounds led a search party to the town's black section, where law enforcement officials arrested McCarthy and six other men. Stewart identified McCarthy as her assailant. But before police officers could take him to jail, a frenzied mob seized the former soldier and shot him to death. Simply killing McCarthy, however, did not suffice. The executioners tied a rope around his bullet-riddled body, attached it to an automobile, and proceeded to drag it through the town's main streets. Acting "with coolness" and "grim, clock-like precision," the procession finally stopped in front of the home of the alleged victim. There, the mob, now numbering an estimated fifteen hundred people, placed McCarthy on a pile of pine branches and set him on fire. An hour later, when local authorities arrived to the scene, all that remained of the former soldier was a pile of smoldering ashes.[48]

The following day, September 1, a mob of thirty white men lynched veteran Clinton Briggs in Star City, Arkansas, for allegedly making "insulting proposals" to the daughter of his employer. Other reports indicate that a white man told Briggs to get off the sidewalk, and he responded by saying, "This is a free country." The mob killed Briggs with three shots—to his face, neck, and groin—and left his body on the roadside.[49] September proceeded with the lynching of L. B. Reed in Clarksdale, Mississippi. A white mob killed the veteran and strung his body across a bridge for allegedly having an "intimate relationship" with a white woman. The *New York Age* asserted that Reed and the woman were "sweethearts" and sarcastically noted that such relationships between white men and black women went unpunished on a daily basis.[50] The month concluded with the September 27 lynching of returned serviceman Robert Crosky in Montgomery, Alabama, who, along with another black man, was shot by a posse of twenty-five white vigilantes for supposedly assaulting a white woman.[51]

The brutal murder of Leroy Johnston the following month represented more than just a singular lynching. It occurred during one of the worst racial massacres in American history. In Phillips County, Arkansas, black sharecroppers, frustrated with continued exploitation by white cotton merchants and plantation owners and emboldened by the expectations of the war, established the "Progressive Farmers and Household Union of America." Federal investigators suspected its lead organizer, twenty-seven-year-old tenant farmer Robert L. Hill, of being "a young soldier in the late war." Although Hill registered for the draft, it is uncertain if he actually served.[52] The union, a bold experiment in rural collective labor organizing, struck a chord with local black sharecroppers and returned servicemen in particular, whose hunger for economic justice prompted them to join in significant numbers.[53] White planters and law enforcement officials, to the contrary, viewed the presence of the union as a source of trouble and possibly as signaling the early stages of an incipient black insurgency. Rumor, fear, and a stern commitment by the white ruling class to suppressing any form of communal African American economic assertiveness climaxed on the night of September 30, 1919. At approximately eleven o'clock, local whites confronted the union as it met in a small church located at Hoop Spur. A shootout ensued that left one white man dead. For the county's white population, suspicions of an insurrectionary plot had been confirmed. Over the course of several subsequent days, white posses, some spilling into Phillips County from neighboring Tennessee and Mississippi, mobilized to hunt down and murder black people at will. White soldiers of the U.S. Army, many recently returned from France and requested by the governor of Arkansas, further abetted the pogrom. Estimates of the number of African Americans slaughtered reached into the hundreds.[54]

Leroy Johnston came from one of the most prestigious and successful African American middle-class families in eastern Arkansas. His father was a prominent Presbyterian minister, his mother a schoolteacher, one of his brothers, Louie, a physician, and another, Elihue, a dentist and owner of a three-story building in their hometown of Helena. Leroy, the youngest of the four Johnston brothers, served as a bugler in the 369th Infantry Regiment and returned to the United States carrying the physical scars of wounds from Chateau-Thierry. They spent October 1 hunting for squirrels, leaving early that morning and oblivious to the violence brewing in the neighboring countryside. While returning from their trip, several white "friends" of the family intercepted the brothers and suggested they return to Helena by train because of the shooting at Hoop Spur and the suspicion four armed black men would inevitably arouse. This warning proved to be a trap. A group of white men boarded the train and confronted the Johnston brothers. What happened next is unclear—one version of events has the posse forcing the brothers off the train at gunpoint to a waiting automobile; another report indicated that after being fed to a larger mob, Louie Johnston grabbed a gun from one of the assailants and killed him. Regardless, the real transgression of the Johnston brothers lay in their affluence and incidental, but nevertheless threatening, brandishing of firearms. The mob opened fire, tearing the four men to pieces and leaving their ravaged bodies on the side of a road. Leroy Johnston had survived combat in France, but he could not overcome the ferocity of white violence and hatred in Phillips County, Arkansas. Because of their social standing and professional success, the *Crisis* described the murders of the Johnston brothers as the "saddest and worst feature of the whole miserable slaughter of Negroes."[55]

The December 27 lynching of twenty-five-year-old veteran Powell Green in Franklington, North Carolina, capped off the bloody year of 1919 in the South. Green had lived his entire life in Franklin County and worked in a local sawmill before entering the military.[56] Long-standing community ties, however, could not prevent his death. Trouble began around nine o'clock that evening when Green, while attending a local movie theater, was told by the white proprietor, R. M. Brown, to abide by the no smoking rule and stop lighting his cigarette. The former soldier took the request as an affront to his right to smoke wherever he pleased. Green and Brown began to argue. Their confrontation spilled outside, where Green whipped out a gun and shot Brown in the chest. A policeman already at the scene apprehended Green and prepared to transport him to the county jail at Raleigh. But vengeance-seeking white residents "clamored for the murderer." A mob overpowered the six officers protecting Green, grabbed their prey, tied a rope around his neck, and fastened it to an automobile. Green was dragged for two miles before the mob, comprising nearly the entire town by estimation of Franklington's mayor, finally hung him on a pine sapling that barely had enough strength to hold his weight. Souvenir hunters hungrily fought over pieces of Green's clothing, his "cheap watch and chain," as well as chips from the tree his battered body hung from.[57] In reporting that Green "had recently been discharged from the army," the *Raleigh News & Observer* concluded, "He was undoubtedly a bad Negro. It seems that he was disposed to think well of himself and was self-assertive, and resented anything that seemed to reflect on him or his conduct."[58] An editorial in the same newspaper blamed the incident on "negro agitators" who had targeted returned soldiers like Green to "assume an attitude of defiance."[59]

What went through the minds of black veterans like Powell Green, forced to confront their mortality in the public spectacle of southern lynching culture? As the mobs descended, as the noose tightened around their neck, as the bullets pierced their body, as the flames licked at their feet, did the cruel irony of risking one's life on behalf of the nation during the war, only to have it brutally extinguished by fellow American citizens during peace, cross their minds? Did their thoughts turn to more personal concerns, such as the loved ones who would now be left without a husband, a father, a brother, or a son? Did they pray to God and try to find a place of solace, peace, and understanding in the face of incomprehensible pain and suffering?

Such questions, and along with them the humanity of African American veterans who lost their lives at the hands of southern lynch mobs, were regularly overshadowed by the extraordinary symbolism of their deaths. Devoting little attention to the context and specific details of each particular lynching, the NAACP and black newspapers implied that the veteran status of these men played a central, if not the determining reason for their deaths. This may well have been true in some cases. But the alleged transgressions of lynched former soldiers and the justifications given for their deaths did not differ from the traditional rationales provided by southern white lynch mobs and their apologists.[60] No definitive causal relationship exists linking the lynching of these men to the fact they had served in the army. In the case of Frank Livingston, for example, he allegedly committed such a heinous crime—killing two white people and subsequently burning the bodies to conceal his actions—that other African Americans apparently approved of his lynching, or at least felt that it was justified, as seen by their participation in the mob. His punishment resulted not simply from being a veteran but because he had committed a serious crime that made him subject to the South's distinctive form of justice.[61]

The black press and the NAACP focused not so much on why these veterans had been lynched but on the fact that they were veterans. They used the symbolic meaning of these incidents as propaganda, demonstrating the hypocrisy of the United States and to force the government to respond to demands for black citizenship rights.[62] Under the headline "Will Uncle Sam Stand for This Cross," the *Chicago Defender* featured a provocative photo in its April 5, 1919, issue, depicting a crooked-looking white man, representing "the South," adorning a line of returned African American veterans with the "croix de lynch."[63] In a June 1919 editorial entitled "Vanishing War Dreams," James Weldon Johnson made specific mention of the Charles Lewis lynching in Kentucky, and added, "Since then, at least, four other colored soldiers have been lynched; some of them wearing their uniforms; one of them because he was wearing his uniform."[64] The lynching of a black veteran represented the ultimate act of contempt for black citizenship. By emphasizing the fact that these men had served in the war, black newspapers employed the symbolism of African American soldiers as embodiments of civic obligation to highlight both the depravity and the fundamental un-Americanness of white lynchers, as well as those who sanctioned their actions. The NAACP employed a similar strategy when it released its annual report on the number of black people lynched in 1919. The list explicitly identified which victims were veterans, while the social backgrounds of the other casualties received no mention.[65] Additionally, the NAACP issued a press release solely devoted to publicizing the names of black veterans killed in 1919, an act designed to position those white southerners guilty of lynching outside the boundaries of American patriotism and civility.[66] The symbolism of the lynched black veteran served a strategic purpose for the NAACP and its antilynching campaign.

But symbolism was often grounded in reality. Many black veterans did, in fact, become targets of white vigilantes specifically because of their veteran status. Fears concerning the region's system of labor relations, interracial sex, and the looming possibility of racial warfare converged around black veterans, rendering them a threat that many white racists confronted with a very real and deadly sense of urgency. On November 2, 1919, a white man in Dadeville, Alabama, attacked Reverend George A. Thomas, a first lieutenant and chaplain during the war, in his words, "for no other reason than that I wore Uncle Sam's uniform." His assailant also assaulted at least one other black ex-soldier for the same reason.[67] For other similarly unsuspecting veterans, the results of such

"Will Uncle Sam Stand for This Cross?," Chicago Defender, *April 5, 1919.*

encounters were even more severe. In Thomson, Georgia, in September 1919, a mob of several white men approached an unnamed recently discharged African American officer while he waited for a train. They threateningly asked him for his rank and demanded to know his reasons for being in town. Sensing trouble, and quite reasonably fearing for his life, the former officer evaded the men and sought police protection. After the mob attempted to abduct him, he received an escort back to the station and boarded a train headed to Harlem, Georgia, where the relatives of his wife lived. Once on board, the former officer was promptly shot by a white man. Several other vigilantes subsequently entered the train to finish the job. The unnamed veteran never arrived in Harlem, Georgia. His ultimate fate remained unknown.[68]

The mere sight of an African American veteran in uniform sometimes proved sufficient to spark violence. Discharged black soldiers, especially those with little means, often returned home with nothing other than their army-issued clothes. More than simply an article of dress, the uniform connoted authority, power, manliness, and respect, a fact not lost on black servicemen and southern whites alike. Wearing the uniform thus constituted a bold act of defiance on the part of black veterans as an assertion of their citizenship and manhood. For these reasons many white southerners insisted that when African American troops returned to the South, they did so out of uniform, a plea that ignored the War Department's policy of allowing soldiers to wear their military fatigues for up to three months after discharge.[69] White vigilantes often took matters into their own hands. In its April 5, 1919, issue, the *Chicago Defender* ran an announcement alerting black veterans of the war to reports of servicemen being stopped at southern railroad stations and "disrobed of their uniforms to keep them from marching through the streets."[70] Alabama sharecropper Ned Cobb similarly recalled stories of discharged African American troops being met at southern train stations and subsequently forced to remove their uniforms by white mobs.[71] In robbing returned soldiers of their uniforms, racist whites attempted to also rob them of their civic value, dignity, and very identity as veterans of the U.S. Army.

Twenty-four-year-old Daniel Mack experienced this pain and humiliation firsthand. Mack worked as a farmer in Shingler, Georgia, before his call into the army. Two years later and after having served overseas with the 365th Infantry Regiment, Mack returned home. On April 5, 1919, Mack, dressed in his army uniform, and a friend ventured into the town of Sylvester, a short distance from Shingler and the nearest commercial district. It was a busy Saturday afternoon, and people from the surrounding countryside crowded the streets. While walking, Mack inadvertently brushed against a white passer-by, Samuel Haman.[72] An aggrieved Haman struck Mack in response to this slight of racial custom, knocking him off the sidewalk. Mack, emboldened by his time in the army, retaliated. A fight ensued, leading to his arrest. At his arraignment the following Monday morning, Mack pleaded not guilty to assault, punctuating his plea with the statement, "I fought for you in France to make the world safe for democracy. I don't think you treated me right in putting me in jail and keeping me there, because I've got as much right as anybody else to walk on the sidewalk." Taken aback by his insolence, the presiding justice of the peace admonished him with the reminder that "this is a white man's country and you don't want to forget it." Mack received a sentence of thirty days on a chain gang and was led away in shackles.

In both the black and white communities, emotions ran high. African Americans were appalled by the miscarriage of justice perpetrated upon a veteran, one of their heroes. Mack's bravado and the subsequent efforts by the black community to secure his release outraged local whites. Tensions climaxed on April 14, nine days after Mack's initial arrest. A mob intent on ridding Sylvester of this troublesome former soldier, whose presence had disrupted the racial order, formed in front of the jail. With the full cooperation of the chief of police, who personally opened the doors to the prison, the mob seized Mack from his cell. They carried him to the outskirts of the town, and, while still shackled, unmercifully beat Mack with sticks, clubs, and revolver butts. After stripping Mack of his clothes, the mob dispersed, leaving him for dead. Mack, however, regained consciousness and, despite multiple skull fractures, miraculously crawled to the home of a nearby black family, who assisted him in fleeing the area. According to a report conducted by the NAACP, the causes of the incident lay primarily in "the very great and very bitter feeling against the colored soldiers because of their supposed friendly treatment shown them by the French people while in Europe."[73]

As Mack's initial assertiveness attests, African American veterans were not merely victims. A number of former soldiers vigorously resisted white supremacy and, in response to real or perceived infringements upon their civic rights and personal freedoms, confronted their white adversaries with sometimes violent results. In Blakely, Georgia, an African American veteran named Henry Bryant, aided by his brother, engaged in a fierce shootout with a white mob after they attempted to storm his home in objection to his relationship with a local white woman. They killed four white men, described as "American Huns" by the *Pittsburgh Courier*, over the course of three hours before running out of ammunition. Henry Bryant managed to escape into the nearby woods, but his brother was less fortunate and died at the hands of the mob.[74] In early March 1919, an unnamed black veteran killed two white men, Bob Bedford and Barney Nance, in Sardis, Mississippi, a small town in the northwest corner of the state. The recently discharged serviceman had intervened in a fight between two white and two black boys. Bedford and Nance jumped in and, as the battle escalated, "the marksmanship of the well trained soldier proved the best." The *St. Louis Argus* remarked that "the white people down here are beginning to realize the folly in trying to treat the Colored returned soldiers as they did before the war."[75]

Ex-soldiers, both formally and informally, occasionally banded together to protect their safety and the rights of other black people. In one instance, a group of African American veterans rushed to the defense of a black chauffeur at a Miami depot after he was attacked by several white chauffeurs and threatened retaliation.[76] In June 1919, veterans in Birmingham, Alabama, displayed a remarkable sense of collective outrage and defiance after a white streetcar conductor shot a black former sergeant, John Green, three times at point-blank range for insisting on his change.[77] The conductor also shot another soldier accompanying Green, leaving him in critical condition. In response to the Green shooting, a local organization made up of black veterans offered a $250 reward for the arrest of the conductor.[78] By all accounts, the police made no effort to pursue an arrest. Nevertheless, the actions of these veterans, as well as others, reflected a spirit of camaraderie and boldness to challenge violence perpetrated upon black southerners and fellow former soldiers in particular.

A shooting on another Alabama streetcar would have even larger national implications. No singular incident of violence involving a black serviceman received more attention and held greater significance in the context of postwar struggles for civil rights than the dramatic and prolonged ordeal of Sergeant Edgar Charles Caldwell. Caldwell was born on May 18, 1892, in Greenville, South Carolina. He served for three years in the Twenty-fourth Infantry before settling in Atlanta, Georgia. Caldwell was drafted into the army and, because of his previous military experience, became a noncommissioned officer in the 157th Depot Brigade stationed at Camp McClellan, located just outside the city of Anniston in Calhoun County, Alabama.[79]

On the afternoon of Sunday, December 15, 1918, Caldwell obtained a pass to leave camp. Accompanied by Lee Bernard, a fellow soldier, he boarded a local streetcar headed for the black enclave of Hobson City. Cecil Linten, the train's white conductor, immediately took note of Caldwell's uniformed presence and determined to make sure that he knew his place. Linten accused the sergeant of not paying his fare and ordered him to exit the train. Insisting that he had indeed paid, Caldwell scoffed at Linten's demand. A heated confrontation ensued. Enraged by his boldness, Linten, aided by motorman Kelsie Morrison, assaulted Caldwell, punching him twice in the face and forcibly throwing him out of the streetcar. While Caldwell lay on the ground, Morrison proceeded to kick him in the stomach, not knowing, however, that Caldwell was armed. A skilled marksman after years of military service, Caldwell drew his pistol and opened fire. A single shot to the head instantly killed Linten. Morrison somehow survived a bullet through his neck. Realizing the gravity of the situation, Caldwell immediately fled the scene, eluded a number of passengers who gave chase, and took refuge in the city's outlying hills. Joseph Omelia, an unarmed military policeman, found and apprehended the officer later that night, hurrying him to the stockade at Camp McClellan before vengeance-seeking white posses could exact retribution.[80]

The shooting and Caldwell's subsequent arrest elicited heated emotions on both sides of the color line. Local whites, many of whom no doubt flashed back to November 24, 1898, and the riot involving black troops of the Third Alabama Volunteers, viewed Caldwell's actions as confirmation of their fears regarding African American soldiers and sought immediate revenge.[81] Civil authorities, quite literally, attempted to strip Caldwell of the manhood and dignity associated with his military stature. They replaced the officer's uniform he proudly wore with a suit of standard overalls, rendering him indistinguishable from any other black prisoner.[82] Many enraged whites, however, had little patience for the criminal justice system and demanded Caldwell's head. Anniston-Hobson City NAACP branch secretary, Thomas Jackson, wrote to John Shillady, "The newspaper accounts of the affair so aroused the race prejudice of the white people of the county that they were talking of lynching him. It was generally stated that a damn yankee Negro soldier had come down south to start trouble."[83] The fact that Caldwell resided in Atlanta, Georgia, before the war mattered little to local whites, whose response to the entire affair was informed by a historical legacy and imaginary of African American soldiers as a violent occupying force.[84] As a result of such sentiment, on December 18, a grand jury under the supervision of Judge Hugh D. Merrill, following a parade of witnesses, spent all of ninety minutes to indict Caldwell for murder in the first degree.[85]

African Americans, both in Calhoun County and throughout the nation, took immediate interest in Caldwell's case, which rapidly became a cause célèbre for the NAACP and the black press. "SOLDIER DEFIES JIM-CROWISM, SHOOTS TWO MEN IN A ROW," the *Cleveland Advocate* dramatically reported.[86] The local Anniston-Hobson City NAACP mobilized around Caldwell's defense, coalescing the support of African American residents who were all too familiar with the farce of southern justice. With the national headquarters hesitant to become involved for fear of further inflaming passions, branch president Reverend R. R. Williams took charge. He solicited Emmett J. Scott for advice and successfully raised enough funds in a short amount of time to secure the counsel of two capable white attorneys, state senator Charles D. Kline and judge Basil M. Allen from Birmingham.[87] As Caldwell's December 17 trial date neared, Reverend Williams continued to push the national leadership of the NAACP into action, stressing to a reticent John Shillady the importance of the moment as a "test case of what is coming [to] us after the war."[88]

Caldwell's legal journey reflected the profound ironies of citizenship and national belonging for African Americans in postwar America. Although Caldwell steadfastly asserted he did not shoot either Linten or Morrison, his legal defense realized its best hopes for victory rested on challenging the local and state jurisdiction. Because, the defense contended, Caldwell at the time of the shooting had not been discharged from the army and the formal armistice ending the war had not been signed, he should never have been turned over to civil authorities following his apprehension but instead warranted trial in a military court. In this reasoning, Caldwell relied upon his military status to stake claim to a fundamental right of citizenship: a fair trial by a jury of one's peers. Local whites of Calhoun County, however, would have none of it. Caldwell's first municipal trial resulted in a guilty verdict of murder in the first degree and a sentence of death, handed down on January 17, 1919, by an all-white jury after only two hours of deliberation. The defense team raised the stakes by filing an appeal to the Alabama State Supreme Court, halting a scheduled February 28 execution, and buying precious time for the NAACP to pressure the federal government to intervene in the fate of one of its soldiers. Upon learning of the Caldwell affair from Secretary of War Newton Baker, President Woodrow Wilson contacted Alabama governor Thomas Kilby and expressed his desire for Attorney General Palmer to review the case.[89] Despite being black, and despite the seriousness of his crime, Caldwell was still a soldier, a fact that in the immediate aftermath of the war even Wilson himself had to acknowledge carried with it an expectation of civic reciprocity on the part of the government.

Edgar Caldwell's saga played out on a national stage. From New York City to San Francisco, Chicago to New Orleans, African Americans followed the drama of the case through constant coverage in periodicals such as the *Cleveland Advocate*, the *Chicago Defender*, and the *Crisis*. Caldwell's fate represented the broader hopes of a race longing for democratic justice following the war. Their hopes suffered a setback on July 7 when the Alabama Supreme Court, not surprisingly, upheld Caldwell's conviction and set a new execution date of August 15.[90] The NAACP, at both the local and national levels, pressed on. With Washington, D.C., branch attorney James C. Cobb now manning the helm, the NAACP, with the assistance of Emmett J. Scott, implored the Justice Department to avert what it saw as a gross miscarriage of justice.[91] The federal government, despite acknowledging that Caldwell should not have been initially turned over to civil authorities, hesitated to reclaim jurisdiction for the case, recognizing that such a decision would be construed as an attack on states' rights and the sovereignty of southern white supremacy. After the Alabama Supreme Court again refused to reconsider the lower court's ruling and, with a new December 5 execution date looming, the Justice Department compromised by submitting an *amicus* brief in support of an appeal on the grounds of reasonable doubt to the Eleventh Circuit Court of Appeals. On December 3, a federal judge in Birmingham ruled that sufficient grounds for reasonable doubt existed, and the case was sent to the U.S. Supreme Court, with oral arguments scheduled for March 1920.

While Cobb's legal team prepared for its milestone appearance before the nation's highest court, and Caldwell sat in a Birmingham jail cell, black support for the former soldier's defense reached a groundswell. "No greater interest has been shown in any case in recent years," the *Cleveland Advocate* noted.[92] Letters condemning Caldwell's conviction and demanding justice flooded the White House and the Alabama governor's office.[93] Describing the affair as "one of the most notable cases involving the legal rights of a colored man, with which we are familiar," the January 1920 issue of the *Crisis* ran an editorial detailing the entire case and the NAACP's efforts to date.[94] The March 1920 issue included a picture of Caldwell, in full uniform, alongside a plea for "500 Negroes who believe in Negro manhood" to contribute at least one dollar to his defense fund.[95] He was no longer a faceless name, but a symbol of broader attacks on black citizenship and the manhood of the race. This strategy bore fruit, as donations poured in from throughout the country, with one contributor asserting his belief in "Negro manhood" along with his pledge for Caldwell's innocence.[96]

On March 4 and 5, 1920, Cobb and his colleagues argued their case before the Supreme Court. Their appearance marked the climax of a remarkable effort to fight for the political rights of all African Americans following the war by saving the life a soldier who came to embody the tortured state of American democracy. Caldwell's defense team forcefully asserted that, because he was a soldier enlisted in the army during a time of war, civil authorities, pursuant to the Articles of War, had no right to detain or prosecute Caldwell, thus warranting trial by court-martial. While the court deliberated, Caldwell sent a pained letter to James Weldon Johnson from his jail cell in Birmingham, requesting "all of the members of that N.A.A.C.P. to please prayer for me," as well as for his "little wife." Fully cognizant that his time was potentially short, Caldwell wrote, "I am asking God to go into president Wilson heart & give me another chance here on earth."[97] That chance would not come. The Court, in a nine-page decision issued on April 9 by former slaveholder and Confederate veteran Chief Justice Edward Douglass White, affirmed the ruling of the Supreme Court of Alabama that the state was within its jurisdiction to try and convict Caldwell for murder.[98] With this final cruel reminder of the depths of white supremacy, the battle to save Caldwell's life came to an end.

The final act in the "legal lynching" of Edgar Caldwell occurred on the night of July 20, 1920, at the Calhoun County prison. There, at four minutes before midnight, authorities sprung a trap door on the floor of the scaffold where Caldwell stood with a noose around his neck. He dropped and hung, neck broken, gasping for breath, for twelve excruciating minutes before physicians finally pronounced him dead. The *Anniston Star* described his death as "cruel and brutal," speculating that "the minutes he spent in dying were as hours to him."[99]

Before Caldwell met his grisly fate, he addressed a crowd of approximately 2,500 spectators who had congregated in front of the jail. By all accounts, he exhibited almost superhuman fortitude and courage. According to the *Crisis*, Caldwell boldly proclaimed moments before his death, "I am being sacrificed today upon the altar of passion and racial hatred that appears to be the bulwark of America's civilization. If it would alleviate the pain and sufferings of my race, I would count myself fortunate in dying, but I am but one of the many victims among my people who are paying the price of America's mockery of law and dishonesty in her profession of world democracy."[100]

But did Caldwell actually utter these words? Other accounts, including that of the local *Anniston Star*, have Caldwell, who underwent a religious conversion while in jail, reading verses from the Bible, singing hymns, and praying before being led to the gallows, eliciting tears of compassion from men and women of both races.[101] Additionally, the letter he wrote to the NAACP in March 1920 lacked the eloquence, race consciousness, and political forcefulness of his purported jailhouse indictment of American democracy.[102] What, then, to make of this extremely moving punctuation?

Whether by witnesses to the execution or perhaps by W. E. B. Du Bois himself, this statement as it appeared in the *Crisis* was certainly crafted to reconstruct Caldwell as a victimized, but yet, even when confronted with imminent death, racially conscious and politically militant black soldier. For the NAACP, and black America more broadly, Caldwell served a utilitarian purpose. Like the thirteen black soldiers executed in the wake of the Houston uprising, Caldwell was now a martyr, a perfect symbolic embodiment of America's betrayal of the race, democracy, and the principles of equal justice before the law. Caldwell could not be seen as humble, passive, or forgiving in death. It was necessary for the NAACP to speak through Caldwell, make use of his symbolism as a soldier, and punctuate his ordeal with an indictment of the nation and its hypocrisy toward African Americans in the wake of the war. As Du Bois wrote of the fallen soldier, "His end means but one more reason for a more unbending and relentless fight on the part of every Negro and every right-minded person of every race to end this farce which allows color prejudice to blind justice and judge man not on his deeds but on the color of his skin."[103]

As violence gripped virtually every corner of the South, Will Alexander of the CIC attempted to find a silver lining and some hope for the future. When he asked an elderly white minister if he had experienced any racial tensions with African Americans in his community after the war, the man replied, "No, we had to kill a few of them, but we didn't have any trouble."[104] Violence for many white southerners functioned as a wholly acceptable corrective to a system of black-white social, economic, and cultural relations in disarray. African American veterans symbolized a breakdown of the very boundaries and codes of racial etiquette that governed relations between the races and breathed life into the idea of white supremacy. Historical fears and perceptions converged with the determination of many African American veterans to assert their rightful place as citizens in the South, defend themselves against racial abuse, and inject democratic meaning into their everyday lives. For black servicemen who returned to the South, the war did not end with the armistice. The torrent of racial violence dramatically revealed the extent to which white southerners were prepared to fight to maintain a way of life they deemed under attack, and the equally determined resolve of a significant number of African American veterans and members of their communities to fight back.

VIOLENCE IN THE SOUTH represented a larger national phenomenon of racial tension and hostility. An estimated twenty-five race "riots" erupted in cities, large and small, in 1919 alone. Most of these incidents were not riots in a formal sense, but instead confrontations of varying size and intensity between white and black citizens. For example, on May 10, 1919, in Charleston, South Carolina, two black people died and seventeen individuals were wounded following clashes between black residents and white sailors. The following month in the city of Longview, a cotton community located in northeast Texas, Samuel Jones, a prominent black businessman and agent for the *Chicago Defender*, seriously injured four white men in a shootout after a mob attempted to run him out of town.[105] Police and African Americans in Norfolk, Virginia, engaged in a shootout on the night of July 21. Two white officers and four black men were wounded. City authorities dispatched sailors and marines from neighboring Newport News to prevent a full-scale riot from occurring.[106]

These outbursts paled in comparison to the violence that took place in Washington, D.C., Chicago, and Tulsa. African American veterans played a significant role in all three riots. Black servicemen, as they returned and relocated to various urban centers, carried with them expectations of democratic rights and fair treatment. Their presence infused the black communities of these cities with a collective spirit of racial pride, as well as an increased willingness to confront white aggression. They also knew how to handle guns. This crucial aspect of their war experience, combined with their organizational skills and cosmopolitanism, elevated black veterans to the role of both communal leaders and defenders.

American cities became hotbeds of social tension and unrest following the armistice. Demands for the institutionalization of industrial democracy by workers and increased resistance by employers fractured any semblance of national cohesion. The end of the war severely weakened the authority and credibility of the National War Labor Board (NWLB) to intervene in labor disputes. An estimated four million workers engaged in strikes in 1919, determined to maintain the high wages, eight-hour days, and union recognition they had successfully garnered during the war.[107] The Russian Revolution loomed large over this period of class conflict. Domestic postwar labor unrest became synonymous with "Bolshevism" and the spread of communist ideology. With patriotism and hypernationalistic fervor still gripping much of the country, the federal government and big business used the negative connotations of Bolshevism to smear unions and other dissident organizations as revolutionary and, at worst, anarchist. The Committee on Public Information and the United States Post Office Department under Albert S. Burleson smoothly transitioned wartime anti-German propaganda into a campaign to attack Bolshevism as a palpable threat to American democracy and domestic tranquillity. Feminists, socialists, the American Federation of Labor (AFL), eastern European immigrants, and African American militants all felt the brunt of the so-called Red Scare, spearheaded by U.S. attorney general A. Mitchell Palmer and government intelligence officials, including a young ambitious agent named J. Edgar Hoover.[108]

Discharged servicemen compounded growing fears of Bolshevism and labor unrest. White veterans became a distinctive social problem. The possibility that soldiers had been exposed to radical ideologies originating in Germany or Russia worried military officials. They encouraged veterans to quietly assimilate back into civilian life by returning to their families, avoiding social agitators, and securing a job through the United States Employment Service, established by the U.S. Department of Labor in January 1918. Nevertheless, frustration with the government and the lack of postwar opportunities ran high. Job competition and rising inflation steered many veterans toward labor unions, which provided returning servicemen with a political voice reflective of their class-specific interests and demands. Calls by veterans for adjusted compensation became increasingly louder and militant. Wartime enthusiasm and patriotism dissipated following the armistice, replaced with a growing disillusionment of the federal government and its commitment to those who had risked their lives on its behalf.[109]

The return of black servicemen further complicated an already unstable social climate in many cities. Working-class black and white urban residents competed for highly sought-after jobs, made even more scarce by discharged soldiers expecting employment. The allure of the city attracted a significant number of black soldiers, who, in the wake of their social and ideologically broadening war experience, rejected the provincialism of small-town or rural life. Their presence not only placed even greater strain on municipal social services and housing markets but also exacerbated already volatile relations between white and black workers. In April 1919 executives of the New York Central Railroad employed some one hundred black veterans as strikebreakers to undermine efforts of the Freight Handlers' Union for better conditions.[110] Moreover, the expectations of social acceptance, political opportunity, and democratic justice that many black servicemen steadfastly clung to as they disembarked from military transport ships and boarded trains back to their homes reflected the larger aspirations of African Americans in cities throughout the nation. "Is it any wonder that Negro soldiers are refusing 'to go back to the cotton fields' and to a condition of half slavery after once tasting real freedom?" the *Daily Herald* (New York) questioned.[111] As white people pondered the implications of such expectations, racial discord continued to mount.

AFRICAN AMERICANS FROM THE Washington, D.C., area made a significant contribution to the war effort. Black people took tremendous pride in the fact that the government mustered the all-black First Separate Battalion of the National Guard into service to guard the city following the April 1917 declaration of war. Howard University proudly stood at the center of organizing efforts to establish and fill the Des Moines officers' training camp, and many graduates hailed from the prestigious institution. Black men from Washington, D.C., and surrounding communities in Maryland and Virginia constituted significant portions of the 372nd Infantry Regiment of the Ninety-third Division and the 368th Infantry Regiment of the Ninety-second Division.[112]

They returned from war to a city steeped in racial tension.[113] Race relations in the district had steadily deteriorated since native southerner Woodrow Wilson assumed office and attempted to transform the capital into a Jim Crow city. Wilson's policy of racial segregation in federal departments and systematic purge of black civil service employees drew heated protest from the district's black community, led by the vociferous William Monroe Trotter.[114] During the war, Washington, D.C.'s black and white populations experienced significant increases, transforming the demographics of the city as well as racial attitudes. The discharge of thousands of servicemen from neighboring Camp Meade in search of employment in the early months of 1919 destabilized conditions even further. White newspapers fanned the flames of racial paranoia. The *Washington Post* ran a series of inflammatory front-page articles throughout late June and early July detailing alleged attacks by black men on white women, suggesting that the city was in the midst of a black crime wave. The sexual criminalization of black men and victimization of white women again functioned as a warning to white residents that African Americans had overstepped their bounds. Black

Washingtonians refuted the baseless accusations but nevertheless prepared for the possibility of violence.

On the night of Saturday, July 18, hundreds of white civilian workers, veterans, and soldiers on pass from nearby Camp Meade gathered to enact revenge for a reported attack on a white woman by a group of black men that occurred the previous evening. They headed directly for the city's black neighborhood. Four days of racial warfare ensued. White mobs, composed mostly of marines and sailors, seized upon and beat, stabbed, and shot black people at will. Howard University professor Carter G. Woodson, who found himself in the midst of the violence, witnessed a black man shot before his very eyes.[115] Vigilantes pummeled two African Americans directly in front of the White House. The city's black newspaper, the *Washington Bee*, reported that one of the first victims of the riot, twenty-two-year-old Randall Neal, had recently returned home from the war and described his killing as "one of the most cowardly murders that was ever perpetrated upon a young man who had been to France to fight for world democracy."[116]

By Monday, July 20, the nature of the violence had changed dramatically. African Americans, with black veterans standing on the front lines, now aggressively defended themselves from the white onslaught, taking up arms and assuming the offensive. Carloads of black men and women sped through the streets of the city, firing upon crowds of white people they identified as potential invaders. Officers at the Howard University ROTC were reportedly prepared to equip black people with guns and ammunition if necessary.[117] Light-skinned black veterans provided intelligence by infiltrating the white mobs.[118]

In describing the "reign of hysteria and terror" that engulfed the city's neighborhoods, the *Washington Bee* emphasized that black residents "armed themselves as best they could." The paper specifically mentioned that there were "colored soldiers among them who had served with distinction in France, some of whom had been wounded 'fighting to make the world safe for democracy.'"[119] These men most likely consisted of recently discharged servicemen from the 372nd and 368th Infantry Regiments. Military intelligence records substantiate that black veterans played a central part in the riot. An intelligence officer reported that members of the 368th, especially embittered from their military experience, participated in the rioting, having "boasted of their ability to handle guns and of their determination to use arms in their possession rather than submit to unjust treatment."[120] By Tuesday evening, July 21, more than one thousand troops ordered into the city by Congress, assisted by a timely rainstorm, had quelled the violence, which counted six people dead and several hundred wounded. The rioting left the nation's capital, America's geographic symbol of democracy, severely scarred, and caused white and black citizens alike to ponder the meaning of the destructive forces unleashed by the war.[121]

The riot also scarred Charles Hamilton Houston. Once he was discharged, Houston returned home to Washington, D.C. After pondering his career options, he decided to follow in the footsteps of his father and become a lawyer. Not one to limit his aspirations, Houston applied to Harvard and other top law schools. The Washington riot erupted while Houston waited to receive word about his educational future. Once the violence calmed, Charles's father, William Houston, broke his rule of practicing only civil law and took the case of twenty-five-year-old T. S. Jones. Jones had been out on the night of July 21 when a mob attacked him. Armed with a revolver, he fired a shot into the angry crowd, which scattered. District police later arrested Jones and charged him with the death of a nineteen-year-old white man. The injustice of the indictment proved too much for William Houston to stand. Charles watched as his father and colleagues pored over the case. To their disappointment, James was convicted of murder in the first degree. When Charles Houston received his acceptance to Harvard Law School, his sense of purpose and determination to fight for racial justice had been steeled by both his frustrating time in the army and the violence he encountered upon his return home.[122]

Less than one week passed after the Washington riot before Chicago exploded. The city's black community experienced a dramatic demographic transformation during the war. Between 1916 and 1920, more than fifty-five thousand southern African American migrants had flooded the city, drawn by the promise of available employment and social freedom, causing the "Black Belt" to burst at the seams.[123] This population increase brought about profound changes in municipal social, political, and economic relations. Neighborhood boundaries between white and black residents became battlegrounds, as did everyday social interactions in the public sphere. Strikes and high unemployment plagued the city immediately following the war, and the presence of black workers, often used as strikebreakers, exacerbated an already tense labor environment.[124]

City leaders feared that the return of black soldiers, emboldened by their war service and expecting job opportunities, would push hostilities past the tipping point. The Chicago branch of the Bureau for Returning Soldiers, Sailors & Marines of the United States Employment Service encountered considerable difficulty incorporating black veterans into the city's labor force. "The colored soldiers offer the greatest problem," remarked a field agent in an April 1919 report, a statement that spoke to the preference of the city's industries to hire white veterans before their black counterparts.[125] Alexander L. Jackson of the YMCA explained to the city's intellectual and business elite that a "new mind among colored soldiers" had the potential to cause trouble, being that they returned with "a consciousness of power hitherto unrealized," combined with a new "sense of manhood." The famed University of Chicago sociologist Robert E. Park, with a sense of foreboding, asked, "What is going to happen when the negro troops return from France?"[126]

The stoning and subsequent drowning on July 27 of young Eugene Williams who errantly crossed an imaginary barrier separating white and black swimmers at Lake Michigan's 29th Street beach on a ninety-six-degree day sparked an inferno of racial violence. The black community reacted to the boy's death with outrage. Threatened whites responded with weapons and their fists. "Athletic clubs" of young white men viciously attacked scores of black people the first day of the riot. Calm temporarily descended upon the city with nightfall, but the following day, with temperatures still sweltering, violence resurfaced. White gangs met black workers at the city's stockyards with clubs, pipes, and hammers. Black Belt residents greeted carloads of invading whites with sniper fire. Atrocities of all sorts swept the city. Seventeen people died on July 28 alone.[127]

Many recently returned African American soldiers could not have imagined a more shocking welcome. On August 22 Stanley B. Norvell, a veteran of the 370th Infantry, wrote to Victor F. Lawson, editor of the *Chicago Daily News* and member of the twelve-person commission established by Illinois governor Frank Lowden to study the causes of the riot. Norvell hoped that his eight-page letter would "be of some little service to you and your worthy commission." In meticulous detail, he informed Lawson of the challenges that lay before him, explaining why black people had become masters at hiding their true thoughts from white people and the "inevitable evolution" of the Negro which lay at the heart of the riot. Norvell, who during the war "commanded a machine gun company throughout the St. Mihiel and Argonne drives, dined with and served on the general staff of the French High Command" and received the French Croix de Guerre, maintained an objective, almost academic tone throughout much of his note. But when he turned to the recent experiences of African American servicemen like himself and their reception following the war, Norvell unleashed his passions. Reflecting on the poor treatment of black officers, the unjust retirement of Charles Young, and the horrors of the recent riot, he implored Lawson:

> Try to imagine, if you can, the feelings of a Negro officer, who clothed in the full panoply of his profession and wearing the decorations for valor of three governments, is forced to the indignity of a jim-crow car and who is refused a seat in a theatre and a bed in a hotel. Think of the feelings of a colored offi-

cer, who after having been graduated from West Point and having worked up step by step to the rank of colonel to be retired on account of blood pressure—and other pressure—in order that he might not automatically succeed to the rank of general officer. Try to imagine the smouldering hatred within the breast of an overseas veteran who is set upon and mercilessly beaten by a gang of young hoodlums simply because he is colored.[128]

Norvell might very well have been referring to fellow 370th veterans, Lieutenant Louis C. Washington and Lieutenant Michael Browning. Before the riot, Washington was barracked at the Camp Grant Demobilization Center for the general court martial of a soldier accused of rape. On July 26, he began a five-day leave from Camp Grant and returned to his Forestville Avenue home. Two days later, July 28, Washington and Browning, accompanied by their wives and another individual, got together for what should have been an enjoyable evening at the theater. The show ended around half past eleven, and on any other night they would have hailed a car for the cross-town journey back home. To their dismay, car service had been discontinued because of the riot, and they began to walk. "After we crossed Grand Boulevard," Washington recounted, "I heard a yell, 'One, two, three, four, five, six,' and then they gave a loud cheer and said, 'Everybody, let's get the niggers! Let's get the niggers.'" A roaming mob of four to six white boys had spotted Washington and his companions. "Just before we got to Forrestville Avenue, about twenty yards, they swarmed in on us." The mob shot Browning in the leg and slashed Washington with a knife. Washington, however, was carrying a blade of his own and in self-defense stabbed one of his assailants, Clarence Metz, to death. The next day, police called Washington to the Stanton Avenue station and asked him to identify a man arrested in the rioting. "Upon arriving at the police station," Washington stated, "they asked me if I was armed. I said no, that the only thing I had with me was a pen knife, which I showed them. They then told me a man had been stabbed and that I would be held as a witness. They then locked me in a cell."[129]

Racial violence seemed to follow Charles Spurgeon Johnson throughout every step of his homecoming. The former sergeant major with the 803rd Pioneer Infantry had remained in France during the spring and early summer months of 1919, engaging in clean-up work along with other black pioneer infantrymen following the armistice. Clashes between white and black soldiers marred his July 5 departure from Brest. Almost two weeks later, on July 18, the steamer *Philippines* carrying the 803rd docked at Newport News, Virginia.[130] Three days after their arrival, while the regiment went through the tedious process of sorting and reclassification, racial violence erupted in Norfolk, where black residents battled the local police. On July 22, in an atmosphere of tension, Johnson and twelve hundred other men from Chicago boarded a train and departed for the Windy City. The journey took them through Washington, D.C., still smoldering from the riots which had been quelled only days earlier. Johnson had traded one war zone for another. The men of the 803rd pulled into Chicago during the early morning hours of July 24 and reveled in homecoming festivities throughout the entire day. "Kissed, feasted, and paraded to the limit," they were the last of Chicago's black soldiers to return from war, a distinction not lost on the men as they marched triumphantly from the train station to Grant Park before thousands of cheering relatives and well-wishers. The heartwarming reception, replete with jazz music, home-cooked meals, and smokes, could not help but restore at least some of Johnson's faith in the potential of American democracy to embrace the patriotic contributions of black people.[131]

Any optimism was short-lived. After final demobilization procedures at Camp Grant, Johnson delved right back into his work at the University of Chicago and the Urban League. While walking to his Urban League office, most likely on the night of July 28, Johnson found himself in the midst of the riot. Before his very eyes, vigilantes stabbed a man to death on the steps of his building. He tried to get home, but the roaming mobs made for a perilous journey. From the Loop to the Midway, Johnson encountered wounded friends, dragging them to safety while dodging bullets fired at him by enraged rioters. He somehow survived and made it back to his quarters at the University of Chicago. As he related to his friend Edwin Embree, Johnson "knew he had been in the midst of one of the great conflicts of modern times, something as significant perhaps as the war he had just come from in Europe." His mind racing, Johnson sat down in his blood-stained clothes and, with social scientific detachment, began to make sense of the madness he had returned home to.[132]

For two weeks the riot continued to rage. Johnson and other former soldiers could expect little assistance from law enforcement officials, who devoted most of their energies to policing the Black Belt, arresting and frequently abusing African American victims. Black and white newspapers reported rumor as fact, adding to the hysteria gripping both sides of the color line. And so it continued, fourteen days of chaos, until the state militia withdrew from the city on August 8. The bloodshed left a total of thirty-eight people dead—twenty-three black and fifteen white—more than five hundred more injured, and the nation in stunned disbelief.[133]

When the riot erupted, black Chicagoans stood prepared to defend themselves from white aggression. This was due in large part to the presence and inspiration of black veterans, particularly those of the 370th Infantry Regiment, still locally called the Eighth Illinois National Guard. Wartime mobilization and the military participation of the "Old Eighth," long the pride of black Chicago, politicized the city's African American community. The patriotic contributions of African Americans in Chicago to the war effort illuminated the power of their citizenship, while, through letters and press coverage, they indirectly participated in the physical, ideological, and emotional battles of their sons, brothers, fathers, and husbands. The *Defender* proved instrumental in preserving and nourishing the connection between the Eighth Illinois and Chicago's black residents. As the voice of Chicago's black community, the *Defender* consistently reported the exploits of the Eighth, from its training at Camp Logan in Houston, Texas, to its service in France, fueling a widespread sense of race pride. The *Defender* marked the February 17, 1919, homecoming parade of the Eighth with extensive praise for their heroism and service not only to the nation but most importantly to the race. In an editorial call to action, the paper told the soldiers of the Eighth what Chicago's African American community expected of them as leaders:

> We are loath to believe that the spirit which "took no prisoners" will tamely and meekly submit to a program of lynching, burning and social ostracism as has obtained in the past. With your help and experience we shall look forward to a new tomorrow, not of subserviency, not of meek and humble obeisance to any class, but with a determination to demand what is our due at all times and in all places. You left home to make the world a safer place for democracy and your work will have been in vain if it does not make your own land a safer place for you and yours. The country that commands your service in times of war owes you protection of life and property in times of peace, and the nation that cannot furnish its citizens with such a guarantee has no right to demand service in time of war.[134]

Many African American veterans took these words to heart. When the riot broke out on July 27, former soldiers, motivated by a combination of race pride, civic consciousness, and military camaraderie, refused to submit to white mob violence. Similar to veterans in Washington, D.C., soldiers of the Eighth protected the black community from white gangs during the two weeks of mayhem. Because they had yet to be officially reorganized, the Eighth Illinois was not one of the National Guard units dispatched by Mayor Thompson to restore order.[135] However, the Chicago Commission on Race Relations, as well as the mainstream Chicago press, noted the important role black ex-soldiers, armed and in uniform, played as "peace guardians" in quelling the riot.[136] The *Chicago Daily Tribune* reported that "many returned soldiers were sworn in at various south side police stations and given rifles," while others "sided with the police in quelling this disturbance."[137]

Several black veterans, however, distrusted the police and took matters into their own hands. The Eighth Illinois armory served as a rallying point and staging ground for organized efforts to defend the African American community from attacks by white mobs. As he returned to Chicago following his latest run as a waiter on the Michigan Central Railroad, Harry Haywood learned of the riot. He immediately feared the worst. A white co-worker cautioned him against entering the city's South Side: "There's a big race riot going on out there, and already this morning a couple of colored soldiers were killed coming in unsuspectingly." While most likely rumor, the warning deepened Haywood's resolve to resist the assault on Chicago's black community. After briefly reuniting with his family, Haywood promptly went to the Eighth Illinois armory and convened with fellow veterans of the regiment to prepare a military defense of their neighborhood from Irish rioters.[138] Equipped with a cache of 1903 Springfield rifles and a Browning submachine gun procured from the armory, Haywood and his comrades established positions in an apartment overlooking 51st Street. There they waited, ready to utilize their military training in anticipation of an impending evening attack.[139] The expected battle never materialized.[140]

Other groups of black veterans set up similar defense posts to counter white ambushes in combat that invoked memories of the French western front. In one incident, a car of former soldiers armed with a machine gun fired upon a truck filled with white rioters.[141] Crouching in stairwells and peering out of windows, black veterans residing at the Wabash Avenue YMCA posted themselves as guards, waiting, if necessary, to unleash a retaliatory strike.[142] The *Chicago Daily Tribune* described a "group of discharged negro soldiers, twelve in number, armed with revolvers," terrifying groups of white people on the South Side. They roamed the streets, frightening the whites into their homes, and "blazed away" at another group of white people "among whom were several women."[143] Even convalescing African American servicemen took to the streets. A military intelligence report indicated that "a considerable number" of black soldiers recovering in the military hospital at Fort Sheridan, located on the outskirts of the city, were absent without leave during the riot.[144]

The Chicago police force tried to control the assertiveness of the city's black veterans. Although some ex-soldiers cooperated with the police during the riot, many were profiled as potential perpetrators of violence and targeted for arrest. A motorcycle policeman on the South Side stopped a carload of six former soldiers of the Eighth Illinois, "one of them decorated for bravery serving his country." The men were detained after a search of the car revealed seven loaded revolvers.[145] Law enforcement officials arrested several black men in uniform, armed with revolvers, who claimed they received authority to go out on riot duty by a discharged army sergeant. They refused to give his name. Police suspected this unnamed sergeant of "urging the men on to violence and then using the uniform as a shield." At the Harrison Street station, police held fourteen suspected rioters in army uniforms, "all claiming to have been discharged." Two of the men wore the French Croix de Guerre with stars, and one had an untreated bullet wound in his arm. The veterans asserted they had been requested to put on their uniforms and were working under the direction of police detectives to help calm the racial turbulence. The actions of the police department, however, did not go unchallenged. In one instance, a volunteer agent of the Chicago Department of Intelligence reported that thirty-five armed ex-soldiers of the Eighth Illinois, "doing police duty without anyone in authority directing their efforts," gathered at the Cottage Grove Avenue station and demanded the release of one of their members.[146] The presence of armed black men in uniform posed a clear threat to the power and legitimacy of the majority-white police force.

While the Chicago police viewed black veterans with trepidation, their presence and influence served as a catalyst and source of inspiration for black residents to defend their communities. From the outset, it was clear the Chicago riot would not be a repetition of the East St. Louis pogrom. The war created a new attitude within Chicago's black community that justified the use of militant self-defense in the face of racial violence. Black veterans embodied this determination. Some African American residents even impersonated soldiers in active service while they patrolled the streets.[147] After the riots, police held Edward Douglas on charges of murder and larceny. "Claims to be discharged soldier, wears uniform of private, refuses to give organization, believed to be imposter," a telegram to the War Department requesting information on his background stated.[148] African American veterans, by virtue of their experience during the war and importance to the black community, functioned as a source of empowerment for black Chicagoans to defend themselves and their homes in the riot.[149] As the *Chicago Defender* remarked following the riot, "A Race that has furnished hundreds of thousands of the best soldiers that the world has ever seen is no longer content to turn the left cheek when smitten upon the right."[150]

More than any other postwar disturbance, the Chicago riot epitomized the "Red Summer" of 1919 and, as the liberal New York–based news magazine the *Outlook* reflected, awakened the North to "the fact that it possesses a race problem of its own."[151] The riot left an indelible mark on Chicago's black community. For the thousands of recently arrived African American southern migrants, it represented a painful message that the city was not the "promised land" they envisioned.[152] For the veterans of the Eighth Illinois, who expected a semblance of democratic treatment upon their return to the United States, the explosion of violence signified a blunt repudiation of their patriotism and disregard of their sacrifice in blood during the war.

Racial violence continued to sweep through the nation's cities during the summer and fall of 1919. On August 30 in Knoxville, Tennessee, white residents attempted to lynch Maurice Mays, a prominent black man, after his arrest for killing a white woman. When their efforts failed, a mob of several thousand ignored the presence of a Tennessee National Guard detachment and began looting local stores for weapons. They directed their fury toward the city's black residents, who responded by aggressively defending themselves. Two white national guardsmen died in the melee.[153] On September 28, in Omaha, Nebraska, rioting targeted both African Americans and white municipal and law enforcement officials. Following the arrest of a local black man, William Brown, for allegedly assaulting a white woman, city officials were determined to prevent the city from slipping into chaos. A mob of more than four thousand men and women, however, demonstrated even greater resolve to punish Brown. They attacked the police, attempted to lynch the city's mayor, Edward Smith, and set the courthouse on fire. Prisoners hoping to save their own lives sacrificed Brown to the mob, which promptly hung its victim on a nearby telephone post. In the frenzy that followed, Brown's lifeless body was filled with hundreds of bullets, tied to an automobile, dragged through the city streets, and finally burned, to the delight of thousands of spectators, some of whom proudly carried away pieces of his charred remains. The mob continued to destroy property and randomly attack any black person unfortunate enough to be on the city's streets until Major General Leonard Wood and sixteen hundred federal troops, ordered to the scene by Secretary of War Newton D. Baker, restored peace the following day.[154]

The violence of 1919 spilled into 1920. Although the number of African American lynchings declined to fifty-three, postwar tensions remained high. The most serious incident occurred in Ocoee, Florida.

Just under 1,000 people—495 of whom were black—lived in Ocoee, a settlement of citrus farmers located roughly twelve miles west of Orlando. In the fall of 1920, two prosperous African American landowners, Mose Norman and Julius Perry, began registering black people in Ocoee to vote. Florida, "redeemed" from Republican control in 1876, remained heavily Democrat and, by 1920, a regenerated Ku Klux Klan had again become an influential force. Norman and Perry's actions carried considerable risk. Three weeks before the election, according to Walter White of the NAACP, "the local Ku Klux Klan sent word to the colored people of Orange County, that no Negroes would be allowed to vote and that if any Negro tried to do so, trouble could be expected." On election day, November 2, Norman and Perry went to cast their ballots. They had paid the poll tax but found their names excluded from the list of registered voters. White officials told the two men, despite their protests, to leave and not to come back. But Mose Norman did return later in the evening, this time armed with a shotgun. He was pistol whipped and driven off. As news of the altercation spread, in seemingly no time at all, hundreds of Ku Klux Klan members from throughout the area descended upon Ocoee. A lynch mob formed to find and dispatch Norman and Perry. In the meantime, Klansmen began terrorizing Ocoee's black community. Homes and churches were set on fire, some with people still inside. A mother and her two-week-old baby burned to death. Fleeing residents were shot down as they desperately sought shelter in the nearby woods. Upwards of fifty black people died in the racial cleansing. The next morning, Perry's corpse was found near the polling site where he had dared to exercise his constitutional rights. The mob had descended on his house, where he and up to eight other armed black men tried to defend themselves. They killed two white men before the vengeful crowd set the house aflame and captured Perry. He was taken to a jail at Orlando, but the sheriff voluntarily gave the keys to the mob, who lynched Perry just outside of the city. Perry's killers brought him back to Ocoee and attached a sign to his broken, mutilated body: "This is what we do to negroes that vote."[155]

The Tulsa, Oklahoma, riot of 1921 marked the climax of this bloody period. An oil-boom city with a population of almost 100,000, Tulsa contained a deep-rooted and prosperous black community. Some 11,000 African Americans called the "Magic City" home and worked diligently to establish a cultural, political, and economic institutional life that made Tulsa one of the most vibrant black communities in the nation. The central thoroughfare of Greenwood Avenue thrived with black businesses—stores, theaters, professional establishments, restaurants, pool halls—thus earning its label the "Negro's Wall Street."

Black Tulsa's parallel development, however, spoke to the realities of racial segregation and white supremacy in a city and state that had many distinctively southern qualities. The color line remained a visible fact in Tulsa, and white residents carefully guarded against any possible incursions—social, economic, political, or otherwise—against their security. They backed their efforts with intimidation and the threat of violence, as the robust local branch of the Ku Klux Klan had a reported thirty-two hundred members in 1921. The hypernationalism of the war era, reflecting nationwide trends, contributed to a general mood of panic among white Tulsans, resulting in the purge of the radical labor union, the Industrial Workers of the World (IWW), from the city and a fear of rising black militancy. Many African Americans from Tulsa served in the war, while others patriotically sacrificed their time, money, and energy to support the war effort. At the very least, they expected equal protection and treatment before the law.[156]

What exactly occurred between nineteen-year-old Dick Rowland, a black man, and Sarah Page, a young white woman, in the elevator of the Drexel Building on Monday morning, May 30, 1921, will never be known. Page claimed that Rowland attempted to assault her. Other accounts support the contention that Rowland innocently stepped on Page's foot, to which she responded hysterically. What is clear is that the subsequent response by white and black Tulsans to the incident and its aftermath led to one of the worst race riots in United States history.

A series of inflammatory articles in the *Tulsa Tribune* describing the alleged attack on Page accompanied Rowland's arrest the following day. The paper also reported that a mob intended to lynch Rowland later that evening. Black Tulsans, upon learning of the imminent violence and convinced of Rowland's innocence, organized to ensure his protection. Rumors circulated throughout the day and into the evening. By half past ten a crowd of up to two thousand white people surrounded the courthouse that held Rowland prisoner. In response, a group of fifty to seventy-five visibly armed black men arrived on the scene and offered to assist the police in their protective efforts. Most of the men were veterans. As police attempted to diffuse the situation, a white man approached one of the veterans, who displayed an army-issued .45-caliber pistol, and attempted to disarm him. Someone fired a shot. A wild exchange of gunfire ensued. When the smoke cleared, a dozen people had been seriously wounded. The race war had begun.

Upon learning of the shootout, black and white residents of Tulsa prepared themselves for battle. The governor authorized the mobilization of the state's National Guard, while groups of hastily deputized white men organized to invade black Tulsa. Black people entrenched themselves. African American veterans, some seasoned in warfare, provided a first line of defense. A former soldier named Seymour Williams, armed with his service revolver, manned a self-made observation post the entire evening to guard against the impending white invasion.[157] Throughout the night, white mobs steadily attempted to enter black Tulsa and African Americans returned fire. With daylight on June 1, the fighting spread and became more intense. Black people continued to defend themselves, but were heavily outnumbered. Whites rioters, abetted by the police, who targeted only African Americans for arrest, began looting and burning black homes and businesses with impunity. At daybreak, the smoke from black Tulsa, consumed by flames, obscured the morning's sunrise. The bodies of murdered black people—men, women, children, the elderly—littered the city. The imposition of martial law entailed police and National Guard forces disarming and interning Tulsa's black survivors in makeshift prisons. Within twenty-four hours, the riot had run its course. Black Tulsa, a once teeming example of prosperity, had been destroyed and its population displaced. Estimates of the number dead ranged from a low of twenty-seven to upwards of three hundred.

From the initial confrontation at the Tulsa courthouse to the resilience of the city's black community, African American veterans played a central role in the riot. The group of armed veterans who boldly confronted the mob on the night of May 31 represented a vanguard of black male leadership. Determined to prevent the lynching of Rowland, they carried with them a rights consciousness and strong commitment to self-defense informed by their war experience. Whereas many whites responded to their assertiveness with fear, black Tulsans relied upon African American veterans to protect their property and lives.

THE FIRST WORLD WAR AND ITS immediate aftermath illuminated the power of racial violence to curtail the spread of true democracy to African Americans. Just as returning black servicemen represented the hope of democracy for African Americans, so too did they represent the threat it posed to white supremacy. The explosion of racial violence following the war forced African Americans to question the meaning of their sacrifice and the best strategy for obtaining social and political equality. For many black veterans, the war transformed how they viewed themselves as soldiers, as well as the nation they fought for. The wave of southern lynchings and nationwide race riots proved that a more protracted struggle, on yet another front, would be required in order to obtain the rewards of their military service. For African American veterans, and black people more broadly, how best to transfer their renewed resistance to white aggression and commitment to achieving racial justice into collective action was the next challenge.

I say this positively: the morale of the New Negro cannot be broken. . . .
The morale of the Negro American soldier in France, the morale of
the Negro West Indian soldier in France, the morale of the Negro African
soldier in France was unbroken and the morale of the soldiers of the bloody
war of 1914 to 1918 is the morale of Negroes throughout the world.

—Marcus Garvey, January 15, 1922

SOLDIERS TO "NEW NEGROES"

African American Veterans and Postwar Racial Militancy

The Chicago riot left Harry Haywood traumatized. His experiences in France, compounded by the violence he encountered upon his return home, caused the former soldier, in his words, to feel "totally disillusioned about being able to find any solution to the racial problem through the help of the government" and convinced that he "could never again adjust to the situation of Black inequality." He had learned valuable lessons in the army about the meaning of democracy, citizenship, manhood, and freedom, making the disconnection between his pre- and postwar life all the more profound. Haywood grappled with the uncertainties of his racial and political identity and struggled to readjust to civilian life in Chicago. Unable to passively submit to white authority, he bounced from job to job. His personal life suffered as well. He married a strong-willed woman in early 1920, only to have the relationship crumble in the span of a few months. White supremacy, Haywood would introspectively recall, had exacted a heavy toll, leading him to realize, "I had to commit myself to struggle against whatever it was that made racism possible."[1] He began to read voraciously—Charles Darwin, H. L. Mencken, Franz Boas, Marx, Engels—hungry to understand the source of his disillusionment, as well as to find a solution. A job with the post office offered an opportunity not only to achieve financial stability but to converse and bond with other black postal employees, many of whom had also served with the Eighth Illinois in the war. He joined a study group comprised of fellow "aspirant intellectuals," where they read about and discussed various dimensions of the "race problem." They considered naming the club the "New Negro Forum." Before disbanding, the meetings further sharpened Haywood's intellect and desire to organize for racial and economic equality. By 1922, after some three years of discussing and studying the politics and economics of race, Haywood considered himself prepared to take the next step in his journey to combating white supremacy. He approached his brother and fellow veteran Otto Hall, and expressed his desire to join the Communist Party, in which Otto was already a member. "In the years since I had mustered out of the Army," Haywood reflected, "I had come from being a disgruntled Black ex-soldier to being a self-conscious revolutionary looking for an organization with which to make revolution."[2]

After this period of intellectual self-discovery, Haywood joined the African Blood Brotherhood (ABB). The ABB was a secret paramilitary organization founded by Cyril Briggs, a native of the Caribbean island of Nevis and editor of the *Crusader*, committed to the defense of the race, the liberation of Africa, and the dismantling of global capitalism. Fusing revolutionary Marxism, black nationalism, and diasporic race consciousness, the ABB reflected the militancy of postwar African American political culture. Based primarily in New York and Chicago, the ABB appealed to radicalized black intellectuals, industrial laborers, and tradesmen. Along with an assortment of dynamic black radicals such as Briggs, Richard Moore, and Edward Doty, Haywood joined other former soldiers who also saw the organization as an attractive political alternative.[3] "I have noted your call for enlistments in the African Blood Brotherhood for the redemption of our fatherland, and hereby rush to enlist," an anonymous veteran wrote to the *Crusader* in December 1919. "Please enroll me and send me any information you care to on the subject," he continued. "I am ready for any call, to the limit or beyond. I fought in the world war for 'democracy' and I am willing to do anything you say for the liberation of my people."[4] Like this veteran, Haywood was drawn to the unabashed militarism of the ABB, its diasporic politics, and appropriation of Wilsonian self-determination. He participated in the ABB for roughly six months before achieving his goal of joining the Communist Party.[5]

The ABB represented just one of several organizations that made up the New Negro movement.[6] The New Negro movement, rooted in the political consciousness and collective racial identity of black people in communities throughout the United States and the African diaspora more broadly, emerged from the domestic and global upheavals of the First World War and its aftermath. While the "New Negro," as a term, was not necessarily new, the vast social, political, and demographic transformations brought about by the war made the New Negro of the war and postwar periods distinct from previous historical epochs.[7] Various factors gave rise to the New Negro: black migration, international revolutionary movements, most notably in Russia and Ireland, the growth of a radical black press, the emergence of a host of new racially militant political organizations, and most significantly a spirit of defiance stemming from the disillusioning experience of black support for and military participation in the war. Combined, these factors inspired an ideologically and geographically diverse political and cultural movement characterized by racial self-organization, international and diasporic consciousness, social identification with the black masses, and a commitment to self-defense against white racial violence. The New Negro rejected the conservative and politically accommodating tactics of the "Old Negro," a characterization of individual leaders and methods of civil rights protest deemed outdated in the context of the postwar period. While in part generational, the men and women who constituted the New Negro movement were the product of a particular historical moment and the social, political, and economic forces that defined it.[8]

Little systematic attention has been paid to the role of African American veterans of the First World War in the history of the New Negro movement. The black veteran, emerging from the crucible of war with renewed self-determination to enact systemic change, signified the development of a spirit of racial militancy that characterized the New Negro. African American veterans embodied a "reconstructed" Negro, radicalized at the levels of racial, gender, and political consciousness by the combination of the war and the ferocity of white supremacy. This symbolic black veteran served a functional purpose for African American journalists and political leaders. Former soldiers represented a renewed vision of black manhood and, most potently, a renewed commitment by black people to translate their war experiences into the achievement of full democracy and equal rights.[9]

The New Negro as African American veteran, however, encompassed more than just a metaphor and rhetorical figure. Many former servicemen, in ways large and small, self-consciously challenged white supremacy after the war and personified the New Negro. Obviously not every African American soldier returned from the war a politically transformed racial militant ready to wage revolution. Most black veterans simply sought to readjust to postwar life as best they could. Others turned to more traditional, even conservative, options of political participation to bring about racial change. But for countless African American soldiers, the contradictions between the promise of democracy and the pain of racial discrimination, of being welcomed as heroes while at the same time facing the threat of racial violence, made accepting a status quo where black people remained second-class citizens a difficult task. Whether defying Jim Crow segregation on public transportation, refusing to move off the sidewalk, proudly wearing one's uniform, or simply being a little less accommodating to everyday racial indignities, many African American servicemen exhibited a newfound intolerance for white supremacy. Conflict in the South and the major urban race riots of the postwar era reflected the conscious determination of many black veterans, emboldened and politicized by their army experience, to resist continued subjugation. These everyday acts of New Negro militancy constitute an important dimension of the history of wartime black social and political activism.[10] Disillusioned black veterans expressed their frustrations in multiple ways, from correspondence with African American newspapers to physically resisting white aggression or leaving the United States altogether. Their actions frequently inspired other African Americans and informed the tenor of the New Negro movement.

African American veterans also organized. Like their counterparts following the Civil War, World War II, and Vietnam, many ex-soldiers of the First World War served as both leaders and foot soldiers in a diverse range of social and political groups that worked for systemic change. Three New Negro groups in particular stand out for their relationship with black veterans: the League for Democracy (LFD), an organization created by and specifically for African American veterans; the *Messenger*, the socialist magazine edited by A. Philip Randolph and Chandler Owen; and the Universal Negro Improvement Association (UNIA), founded and led by the indomitable Marcus Garvey. While political engagement by black veterans was by no means limited to the *Messenger*, the LFD, and the UNIA, they offer clear examples of the ways in which many former soldiers consciously attempted to organize themselves, and, at the same time, how certain postwar groups openly welcomed ex-servicemen into their ranks. African Americans in the wake of the war, and in the face of heightened racial hostility, determined to fight for their rights as citizens and human beings. Black veterans formed an important part of this struggle.

ON FEBRUARY 27, 1920, one year after his discharge from the army, Willis Brown Godwin reflected on his war experience. As a high school student from Smithville, Virginia, Godwin eagerly entered the army. Originally assigned to a depot brigade, Godwin made the most of his training camp experience; he improved physically and mentally and received a promotion to sergeant. After arriving in France he was transferred to Company K of the 370th Infantry Regiment and engaged in fierce combat at St. Michel, Soissons, and in the Argonne. Despite his achievements, something happened to Godwin while overseas. Perhaps like fellow 370th comrade Harry Haywood, the racism he experienced and the clear dichotomy between racial attitudes in the United States and those in

France weighed heavy on his mind. While he did not point to one singular event or moment, Godwin stated that he came away from his experience with a realization of the "task which was here for me in America." With a critical awareness of the personal and collective meanings of American democracy, he returned home to Virginia and became an instructor in agriculture at the Hampton Institute. "After the fighting, and my return to this country U.S.," he reflected, "it made me wonder why can't all men be treated equally. What did we fight for? Democracy. Are we living it?"[11]

Other black veterans like Godwin asked similar questions and likewise searched for answers. Despite returning to the United States bemedaled and exalted, they struggled to reconcile their initial expectations of military service with the harsh realities of their war and immediate postwar experiences.[12] "I feel that I was faithful to my duty and was ready to give all for Democracy," recalled Judge Goodwin, a farmer from Dinwiddie County, Virginia, who served in a veterinary corps. "As a Negro I feel that at least I might have full citizenship rights."[13] The failure of such a basic expectation to occur caused many former soldiers to interpret their service as a breach on the part of the U.S. government, and the military specifically, to fulfill its obligation of upholding the tenets of democracy, both individually and for the race as a whole. Many returned soldiers drew a stark contrast between overseas and home, between the perceived racial egalitarianism of France and the domestic racism of the United States.[14] As a result of his experience, Milton Hughes, a Howard University student who toiled in a stevedore battalion for the duration of the war, came away with "a very poor opinion of existing conditions and the means to check such as a colored citizen of this Republic when I compare this country and her ideals with France."[15] Having performed their civic duty, African American soldiers came home to a nation where they were seen and treated as second-class citizens, a harsh confirmation that their investment in democracy, an investment that inspired so many soldiers during the war, proved decidedly one-sided.

Many African American veterans refused to silently accept any continued denial of their democratic rights and sought out ways to express their disillusionment.[16] In doing so, they frequently invoked "democracy" as a rhetorical device in order to stress its literal absence from their lives. Floyd Bishop, a veteran from Norfolk, Virginia, with a fourth-grade education, poignantly reflected on the status of the race two months after his discharge in August 1919: "Before the war I was passive as the treatment of the common people colored, in particular, but since the war I am constantly reminded that my people (colored) are not getting any of the things that I served in the war to help bring about—democracy."[17]

The black press, which in many ways became the voice of the New Negro, provided an outlet for African American veterans to express their individual and collective frustrations.[18] Disgruntled and radicalized veterans jolted readers with accounts of their wartime experiences. "I regret to say that I have come home from France with a feeling of intense bitterness towards white men," Lieutenant James H. N. Waring, formerly of the 367th Infantry, angrily told the *Baltimore Afro-American* in March 1919. "Perhaps the superior white officers in our Division were not representative white men," Waring continued, "but I am here to tell you that they were the scum of the earth."[19] Former servicemen flooded *Crisis* editor W. E. B. Du Bois with letters detailing their encounters with racial discrimination. A black soldier stationed at Camp Sherman, Ohio, wrote to Du Bois immediately following the armistice, "Me being one of the soldiers of the United States, drafted for the United States Army, to fight for worlds democracy, I think it my duty to ask my people of the United States to appeal to the said government for Democracy of our and my own people." He rhetorically questioned, "Now why cant we have a fair trial, why cant we have law and order at home in other word why cant we have democracy in the United States and under the flag of which I fight."[20] Returned black soldiers also expressed a commitment to ensuring that their military service was not in vain. A letter penned by an African American veteran in the wake of the July 1919 Washington riot and published by the *Washington Bee* captured this attitude: "During the war the Negro put every grievance behind him and dedicated himself whole-heartedly to the common task. . . . Behold him and admire him for that—but mistake not! There is a new thought in the younger minds and, to be plain blunt, perhaps brutally frank, it approximates this":

> We have labored in sweat and tears—we have pleaded and hoped in vain—we have been loyal in every crisis and died in wars without a winking. . . . We are done forever with blind devotion to a mere geographical idea. . . . Henceforth our Loyalty is for sale—and the price thereof is Justice—no compromise—but Justice absolute and complete, without reservation and without restriction.[21]

In the spring of 1919, a new periodical, the *Veteran*, burst onto the scene. Published and edited by William Y. Bell, it boasted of being the "First and Only Colored Soldier's Paper Published in America" and the "Official Organ of the National Colored Soldiers and Citizens Council."[22] Bell offered former soldiers five to ten dollars a day to serve as agents for the *Veteran* and help circulate the paper in their home towns.[23] It is unknown how many ex-servicemen took the *Veteran* up on its offer. Extant copies do not reflect a focus on issues specific to African American veterans, although Mack C. Nance, a sergeant in the Regular Army, authored a recurring section titled "Travelogues of a Fighting Man."[24] The paper's masthead, however, explicitly appropriated the imagery of the militant former soldier, and many of its articles carried an overtly radical tone. In a June 28, 1919, editorial titled "The Remedy for Mob Violence," William Bell asserted, "The Southern mob fears the fighting Colored American. Southern industries and capital fear the running Colored American. Pleas and protests are ineffective, wornout instruments. A general exodus of our oppressed brothers from the South, next to direct action against the mob, is our most potent weapon."[25] Federal authorities saw the *Veteran* as a paper of particular concern. "The paper is bad," remarked postal agent Robert Bowen. Radical black papers had become "especially active since the return of the troops from France," and the *Veteran* was especially problematic.[26] Bowen flagged an August 6 editorial in the *Veteran* as "an encouragement of retaliatory violence if not provocatory violence" and "worth notice as expressive of the undue feeling of triumph the negro is experiencing over the fact that he is fighting back."[27]

For a handful of black soldiers, their disillusionment with American democracy cut so deep that they decided to remain in France following the armistice. Ex-servicemen formed the core of France's postwar black expatriate community centered in the Montmartre section of Paris. French racial egalitarianism, as they experienced it, provided African American veterans with a welcome respite from the racism of the United States. Veterans enjoyed a liberating measure of social freedom and prestige because of their status, in the eyes of the French, as civilized and modernized black people. While only a small fraction of the total number of black soldiers who served in France—their presence most likely numbered less than two dozen—African American servicemen-turned-expatriates held an important symbolic value within a transatlantic dialogue on the meanings of race, nation, and empire.[28] They embodied the idea of France as the singular Western imperialist nation devoid of racial discrimination and open to people of all nationalities, an idea promulgated by the black press to highlight American racism and further promoted by the French government to legitimize colonial rule in Africa and Asia.[29]

Veteran Albert Curtis captured these sentiments in a July 1922 letter to the *Chicago Defender*. Writing from Bordeaux, Curtis, who used to sell copies of the *Defender* in his youth, reassured the newspaper's staff that "I am still alive and in good health." Curtis had "served a few years with the Tenth U.S. cavalry, also a few years with the medical department of the U.S. army as first-class sergeant," and, as he wrote, "did my bit in France." He had spent time in London after the war but now had returned to the nation of *liberté*, *egalité*, and *fraternité*.

"I have some money I have worked hard to save and now I am going to enjoy it in a country that knows no color line, and that is France." He was not alone. "There are seven Colored boys here from the United States including myself," Curtis stated, "and we are here to stay." He painted a romantic picture of French economic opportunity and racial egalitarianism, replete with sexual imagery. "There is plenty of work in France, but you must speak French excellently to get it. It is nice here. Every Colored man you meet is married to a French woman."[30]

In addition to social freedom, France and other European countries offered black veteran expatriates specific material benefits as well. Leon Brooks, a former soldier of the 303rd Stevedore Regiment, remained in France to work as a salesman for the Avenard Wine Company.[31] Ex-soldiers also took advantage of educational opportunities. Thirteen black veterans enrolled in French universities following the war, seven of whom attended branches of the University of Paris. One of these men was William Stuart Nelson, born appropriately enough in Paris, Kentucky. Nelson graduated from the Des Moines officers' training camp and served as a first lieutenant in the 317th Engineers of the Ninety-second Division.[32] After earning his bachelor's degree from Howard University in 1920, he returned to France and from 1921 to 1922 studied at the Sorbonne. He later attended the University of Berlin and the University of Marburg in Germany. Nelson added to his remarkable pedigree after returning to the United States, earning a bachelor of divinity from Yale in 1924 and, one year later, receiving an appointment as professor of religion at Howard University.[33]

After introducing France to jazz during the war, African American musicians remained in high demand. Harlem came to Paris in the aftermath of the war, and former servicemen functioned as conduits for the global spread of black music. The French fetish for jazz, ignited by the Harlem 369th "Hellfighters" and other African American regimental bands during the war, grew in response to a war-torn population drawn to black culture and racial primitivism. Opal Cooper, a member of the 807th Pioneer Infantry band, returned to France and became one of the most popular African American musicians in Paris, creating a group called the "Red Devils," which counted another former soldier, Sammy Richardson, as one of its members.[34] Eugene Bullard, in addition to being a respected prizefighter, decorated French Foreign Legion veteran, and internationally famed fighter-pilot, moonlighted as a jazz drummer, albeit not a very good one, following the war. In 1924 he opened Le Grand Duc, which became one of the most popular clubs in Montmartre, frequented by luminaries such as Josephine Baker, Louis Armstrong, and F. Scott Fitzgerald.[35] For Bullard and other African American servicemen-turned-expatriates, France offered an appealing combination of economic opportunity, cultural freedom, and liberation from American racism.

"My experience in the army left me so bitter against white Americans that I remained an expatriate in Europe," Rayford Logan reflected long after the war.[36] Psychologically wounded from his battles with racial discrimination, Logan could not bear the thought of returning to the United States, where even greater oppression awaited him. He therefore applied for an official discharge in France, which he received on August 21, 1919.[37] The army denied Logan's request to study at a French university, so he instead took advantage of rampant postwar inflation and bounced throughout Europe making a precarious living as a currency speculator. During his travels and encounters with people of various religions, cultures, and nationalities, he increasingly began to view the complexities of race and American white supremacy in a broader international context.

This made Pan-Africanism a particularly attractive ideology. Logan did not attend the seminal 1919 gathering but was at the heart of the even more significant 1921 Pan-African Congress. The former officer had remained in contact with his M Street High School French teacher, Jessie Fauset, who served as literary editor of the *Crisis*. W. E. B. Du Bois had left for Paris to make arrangements for the Congress, Fauset informed her onetime student in early August of 1921, and, considering his poor French, Du Bois needed Logan's assistance. Looking for a man with "a noble head," according to Fauset's description, Logan waited patiently at the Gare Saint-Lazare until Du Bois unexpectedly emerged from the third-class train. Years later, a still star-struck Logan recalled his "surprise and delight when I saw him, walking nonchalantly down the platform."[38]

If not for Rayford Logan and fellow veteran William Stuart Nelson, the Pan-African Congress might not have taken place. Du Bois, with trademark conceit, took charge of organizing the congress and selecting the locations—London, Brussels, and Paris—for its three sessions. The Senegalese deputy and Pan-African Congress president Blaise Diagne, however, had growing concerns. Differences of opinion between Du Bois and Diagne, muted during the 1919 congress, exploded to the surface in 1921. Du Bois wanted to push for a more aggressive condemnation of European colonialism, while Diagne, invested in the project of African colonial citizenship, vigorously resisted. Diagne also feared that Du Bois's increasingly radical agenda would tar the congress with the specter of Bolshevism. To make matters worse, the challenges of translation interceded, as Du Bois could neither speak nor understand French, and Diagne had little grasp of the English language.[39] In stepped Logan and William Stuart Nelson, who at the time was studying at the Sorbonne and had become

Logan's good friend. With the congress hanging in the balance, "Stuart urged me to seek an accommodation between Du Bois and Diagne," Logan remembered. Only days before the August 28 opening of the London proceedings, he played the role of both translator and mediator at a tension-filled meeting between the two Pan-African leaders. "By translating only part of their acerbic remarks to each other, I obtained agreement on what Diagne called 'une formule transactionnelle.'" The temporary compromise allowed the Congress to proceed, but Diagne would resign from the movement after chairing the Brussels and Paris sessions.[40] Logan served as secretary and translator for the entire Congress, which William Stuart Nelson and another veteran, former 369th Infantry Regiment captain Napoleon Bonaparte Marshall, also attended.[41] Logan was instrumental in organizing the 1923 Pan-African Congress, held in Lisbon and London. But lingering tensions between the African American and black Francophone participants, Du Bois's heavy-handed leadership, and a lack of financial support caused Logan to become increasingly disillusioned with the movement and its potential for success.[42]

Rayford Logan's immersion into Pan-African politics spoke to the larger diasporic scope of the New Negro. The forces of war and revolution unleashed dramatic social, political, and economic tensions throughout the black world.[43] The wartime demands of military service and labor facilitated the dispersal of millions of peoples of African descent from their homelands to other regions of the diaspora during the conflict. For these populations, the imperial obligation of sacrifice on behalf of the nation led to a heightened political consciousness and expectation for increased citizenship and economic rights. The European powers, in response to such aspirations, feared a weakening of their legitimacy. In the European metropoles, white workers viewed African, Caribbean, and Asian laborers and discharged soldiers as a source of competition for scarce jobs and social resources, while, in the colonies, subject peoples tested the boundaries of imperial authority with acts of resistance, both small and large.[44] Whereas white people sought to stabilize a racial and social order seemingly turned upside down, men and women of color approached the postwar moment swelled with aspirations for fundamental change.[45]

Veterans of African descent, disillusioned yet emboldened by their war experiences, often became active participants in postwar radical movements. Soldiers of the British West Indies Regiment (BWIR) responded aggressively to their travails with British racism.[46] In the wake of a four-day mutiny at Taranto, Italy, in December 1918, sixty noncommissioned officers of the BWIR secretly met to plan the formation of the "Caribbean League," envisioned as a vehicle for the promotion of Pan-Caribbean political unity and black self-determination.

Although the "Caribbean League" never materialized as a formal organization, the men and ideas behind its conception bore direct correlation to the wave of working-class labor activism that swept the Caribbean following the war. In Paris and other French cities like Marseilles, peoples of African descent, including many ex-soldiers, established vibrant communities of social, cultural, and political exchange.[47] The Communist Party in France attracted a handful of West African veterans, most notably a former *tirailleur* named Lamine Senghor. Senghor became increasingly active in metropole politics and joined the French Communist Party in 1924, an experience that profoundly shaped his future radical activities. A committed Marxist despite leaving the party in 1926, he founded the Comité de Défense de la Race Nègre along with a short-lived newspaper, *La Voix des Nègres*.[48] The war and the sacrifices of *tirailleurs* like himself remained a crucial frame of reference as Senghor stridently advocated for the liberation of "le race nègre" from imperial domination. In the March 1927 issue of *La Voix des Nègres*, Senghor poignantly surmised, "When one needs us to make us kill or make us work, we are of the French; but when it is a question of giving us rights, we are not any more of the French, we are negroes."[49] While small in number, those veterans of African descent whose war experience propelled them into radical politics constituted an important part of a global New Negro movement.[50]

In the United States, many African American veterans also organized themselves. Ideological diversity characterized the New Negro movement. Socialists, communists, nationalists, integrationists, and combinations of each all aggressively vied for the attention of the black masses, and quite often the specific notice of former servicemen. African American veterans reflected this philosophical breadth, and thus had their choice of organizations to support and lend their time, effort, and voices to. A broad range of radical groups allowed former soldiers to make sense of their war service and come to terms with the meaning of their experience, in all of its contradictions. At the same time, black veterans channeled their race, gender, political, and diasporic consciousness into the broader struggles for systemic change the New Negro movement represented.

"INVESTIGATION BY THIS SECTION has disclosed among American negro troops in France the probable existence of a secret organization." A flurry of questions must have raced through the mind of acting Military Intelligence Division (MID) director John M. Dunn upon reading this disconcerting opening sentence of a classified February 18, 1919, memo. What was this "secret organization"? Where did it come from? Who was responsible for its creation? What were its intentions?

Dunn had good reason to be concerned. In Le Mans, France, while awaiting demobilization, black officers of the Ninety-second Division clandestinely held a series of meetings. Most of the officers served in the 367th Infantry Regiment. They met away from the scornful eyes of their white superiors, gathering to reflect upon their experiences and determine a postwar course of action to ensure that their service was not in vain. Enraged and humiliated by their treatment at the hands of the division's white officers, they specifically discussed the creation of an organization for African American veterans to combat racial discrimination, both within and outside of the military. Here was the worst fear of American intelligence officials come true: idle black servicemen fomenting political radicalism and inspiring domestic racial unrest. In a follow-up report, military intelligence suspected the insurgent black officers of corresponding with individuals in the United States in violation of censorship regulations. Several had allegedly married French women, and intelligence officials speculated that they functioned as carriers to communicate with the United States through the French post office. The report concluded with an ominous summation of the organization's professed goals: the "protection of Negro interests, collective combating of a white effort, especially in the South, to reestablish white ascendancy, the securing of equal intellectual and economic opportunity for Negroes and the maintenance of the social equality between the races as established in France."[51]

The meetings convened by the Ninety-second Division officers were not isolated events. A January military intelligence report stated that "officers of the 370 Infantry (all colored) are interested in the formation of a secret organization or society among all colored troops in the A.E.F. whose object is the promotion of social equality between colored and white after demobilization."[52] MID agents also suspected black soldiers of the Ninety-third Division's 371st Infantry Regiment of working to form a secret postwar group of their own named the "Soldier's Association for a Fight for True Democracy." An informant relayed that, "having fought and won the cause overseas," the men of the regiment were committed to achieving their rights as equal citizens, even "if it costs another battle."[53] Acting MID director Dunn hoped that the organization would "fall to pieces and nothing much will come of it" once the men returned to their homes.[54] His assumption proved correct. But it could not soothe the harsh truth of the anger many black soldiers felt and their determination to act.

The organization conceived by the rebellious group of Ninety-second Division officers in Le Mans did materialize. At a March 1919 mass meeting at Harlem's Palace Casino, the League for Democracy made its public debut. The audience most likely consisted of returned soldiers from the New York–based

369th and 367th Infantry Regiments, as well as other black Harlemites curious to learn what this new organization, with its arousing name, had to offer. "Lest We Forget," the LFD's promotional brochure began. The phrase captured the spirit of the LFD and its intention to use the fresh memory of the war as a catalyst for black veteran political activism. The stakes were high, and the costs of forgetting the lessons of the war—the pain, the triumph, the sacrifice, the insult, the brotherhood—even greater. Introducing itself to the black masses, the LFD did not mince words in stating why the organization had been established and its motivations:

> Lest we forget that the Democracy for which our men fought and died to have conferred upon Serbian, Belgian, Armenian and Slav is denied us in our own Republic; lest we forget to strike our enemies the death blow while we have them weakened and on the defensive; . . . lest we forget the vile, insidious propaganda directed against us in France during stress of battle; . . . lest we forget our intense sufferings under appointed, exploiting leadership in the past; lest we forget vows and oaths made and taken to right our wrongs without fear and without compromise after the war; lest we forget lessons in organization learned on the Western front; *lest we forget that the individual cannot win against the system*; lest we forget that only thoroughly coordinated, organized effort can obtain what we merit, deserve and desire; lest we forget our irrecompensatable debt and sacred obligations to our dead upon the battlefields of France, that their supreme sacrifices will not be nullified by our forgetfulness—we have formed the League for Democracy.[55]

The founders of the LFD adopted an unabashedly grandiose vision. They described their group as "the most gigantic scheme of organization ever attempted by the race" and projected that it "can and should become the predominant race organization in the Republic." Most pressing, the LFD committed to combating institutionalized racism within the military and protecting the legacy of black soldiers' historical contributions. The organization also adopted broader objectives, such as eliminating black disfranchisement in the South and fighting Jim Crow. To that end, the LFD boasted, "It will have a local Camp in every town in the United States containing 1,000 or more Colored inhabitants. It will be able to reach directly and personally, within 48 hours, over one million Colored people the first year of its organization, for any concerted movement or propaganda it desires to create." Cognizant of other African American organizations with similar agendas, the LFD pledged to cooperate with the NAACP and the National Negro Business League in order to avoid a duplication of efforts. But as an organization "of soldiers, for soldiers, by soldiers," the LFD was singularly unique in its direct appeal to African American veterans' sense of wartime camaraderie and pride in their service. The LFD's founders saw their group as a vehicle for black veterans to fight for their dreams of a racially just society, to continue the fight for democracy. As the LFD's promotional brochure stated, "Suppose again, again and again you will appreciate as never before, the staggering, immense, wonderful, magic powers of organization and group action, the tremendous potential possibilities and probabilities of the League for Democracy."[56]

The national leadership of the LFD drew from some of the finest African American officers of the war. It was not a coincidence that disillusioned former officers, particularly those from the Ninety-second Division, took the initiative to establish the LFD, considering their accomplished background, race consciousness, and the stark disjuncture between their military status and actual treatment during the war.[57] Harlem attorney and former Ninety-second Division officer Aiken Augustus Pope served as president. A Georgia native, Pope attended college at Lincoln University in Pennsylvania and Yale University, where he excelled.[58] After graduating from Yale in 1915, he moved to Boston and enrolled in Harvard Law School, receiving his degree in 1918.[59] During his college and law school years, Pope became a pioneering member of Alpha Phi Alpha fraternity, reactivating along with eleven other brothers the Yale Zeta chapter in March 1913 and founding the Boston Sigma chapter in November 1915. Louis T. Wright, one of the nation's leading African American physicians, held the position of junior vice president. The son of former slaves, Wright graduated valedictorian from Clark Atlanta University and then went on to Harvard University Medical School. He earned his medical degree in 1915, finishing fourth in his class. When the United States entered the war, Wright left his practice in Atlanta to enlist in the Medical Corps training camp at Fort Des Moines and received his commission on June 27, 1917. He sailed for France as a first lieutenant in the 367th Infantry Regiment. During his service overseas, Wright rose to the rank of captain and became the top officer in the Ninety-second Division's surgical wards. He gained a reputation as one of the best physicians in the entire American Expeditionary Force, saved numerous lives, and perfected a procedure to lessen the effects of smallpox. He returned to the United States with a purple heart for injuries incurred during a gas attack. Despite his prodigious rise, Wright always maintained a strong commitment to racial justice. While at Harvard, he challenged a medical school policy restricting the access of black students to white patients and temporarily interrupted his studies to participate in NAACP protests against *Birth of a Nation*. Further inspired by his war experiences, Wright continued his activism with the LFD.[60]

"Lieutenant McKaine of the 'Buffaloes.'" Portrait painting of Osceola McKaine by Orlando Rouland. Courtesy of Hampton University Archives.

The real driving force behind the LFD was Osceola McKaine. McKaine arrived in France confident that the war would lead to a better day for African Americans. But by the time of the armistice, McKaine's battles with racial discrimination as an officer in the Ninety-second Division had soured him toward the conflict's democratizing potential. A seasoned and disciplined soldier from his time in the Regular Army, he maintained his composure until the war's end, when he played perhaps the central role in the secret meetings held in Le Mans, France. Determined to vindicate his honor and that of other black servicemen, McKaine settled in Harlem following demobilization and immediately got to work establishing the LFD. McKaine held the position of field secretary, the group's only paid officer. He established a newspaper, the *New York Commoner*, which debuted on June 28, 1919, and functioned as the official organ of the LFD.[61]

From his Harlem office on the corner of Seventh Avenue and 135th Street, McKaine vigorously promoted the fledgling organization and made a name for himself among the chorus of New Negro voices.[62]

With McKaine manning the helm, the LFD attracted attention and support among both veterans and nonveterans, in Harlem and beyond. At an April meeting held at the Harlem Palace Casino, presided over by former 367th Infantry officer Ambrose B. Nutt, McKaine energized an "enthusiastic capacity audience" with a "masterly address," resulting in the organization adding three hundred new members to its roster. Participation in the LFD quickly grew, and "camps" sprouted in cities across the country. This caught the attention of federal investigators. Walter Loving reported the formation of branches in at least eleven cities, which included Washington, D.C., Boston, Brooklyn, Patterson, Newark, Providence, Philadelphia, Chicago, Atlanta, St. Louis, and Tallahassee.[63]

Lester Granger was one of several dynamic former officers and enlisted men who led the local LFD camps. It took more than four months after the armistice for Granger to leave France. "At Brest, we were waiting there for two months for a vessel. We shot craps all day. Literally—all day," he recalled. In the spring of 1919, Granger arrived back in the United States, having gambled away all of his money, but nevertheless energized to translate his war service into meaningful racial progress. He began working for the Newark, New Jersey, Urban League, which his father had helped to found, assisting African American veterans find employment. At the same time, the LFD caught his attention and he took charge of the Newark camp.[64]

Former 367th Infantry Regiment lieutenant James H. N. Waring, a prominent Baltimore physician and school principal before the war, headed the influential Washington, D.C., branch. He came to the LFD with organizational experience. In the wake of the 1906 Atlanta riot, Waring and other "representative colored men" in Baltimore established the Colored Law and Order League. The goal of the racial and civic uplift group was "to improve the moral, economic and home conditions among the colored people, and to do whatever would promote good citizenship" by reducing the number of saloons, gambling dens, and houses of prostitution in the predominantly black Druid Hill Avenue district.[65] This commitment to racial progress, combined with an infuriating stint in the Ninety-second Division, informed Waring's service with the LFD.

With camps being established throughout the country, membership growing, and McKaine becoming an increasingly popular figure in Harlem's black radical community, federal investigators focused their attention on the LFD. "Next in importance to the Socialist movement among Negroes is the League for Democracy," Walter Loving began in his August 1919 final report on "Negro

Subversion." "Under ordinary circumstances this organization would have no more significance than any other organization of war veterans," Loving informed his MID superiors. Political conditions and the racial climate of postwar America, however, were far from ordinary. Loving identified the "insidious propaganda carried on in France against Negro troops by white Americans, with its resultant bitter feeling," as the raison d'être of the League for Democracy and its rapid growth. The combination of racist military policy and the actions of white officers had created "a veritable hornets nest of radicals," with Osceola McKaine at the forefront, whom Loving described as, "an able, aggressive young radical" who had "associated with him in his work the highest type of officers and enlisted men who served in the army during the war." Loving learned in conversation with leaders of the LFD that the organization welcomed political alliances with other radical movements, and for this reason he believed "the activities of the League for Democracy will merit the closest scrutiny on the part of the Government."[66] Loving's panicked assessment stemmed not so much from what the LFD, still in its infancy, had accomplished but from its tremendous potential.

The first major campaign the LFD launched, an effort to have Ninety-second Division chief of staff Colonel Allen Greer charged with treason, elicited particular concern. African American officers already despised Greer for his duplicity in the issuance of Bulletin No. 35 and encouraging the wholesale persecution of commissioned black servicemen in France. But with his slanderous letter to Tennessee senator Kenneth McKellar, Greer had gone too far. McKaine and the LFD caught wind of the letter, possibly from war correspondent Ralph Tyler, prior to its publication by W. E. B. Du Bois in the May 1919 issue of the *Crisis*. The young organization now had a clear issue to mobilize its black veteran constituency and attract new support.

Through the black press and several well-attended rallies in New York and Washington, D.C., the LFD pressured the Wilson administration to act. At a Harlem meeting on May 18, 1919, before a large and energetic crowd, McKaine assailed Greer, declaring that he had "stigmatized and insulted our race with more studied villainy than even that peerless Bourbon secessionist, Thomas Dixon did in his traitorous 'Birth of a Nation.' These two documents are in the same class as regards disloyalty to their country and insidious anti-Negro propaganda." The former officer added, "Will black men and women who have given their blood and dollars to make the United States safe for white democrats let this vile insult to the race go unchallenged; or will they rise as one man in their righteous anger and deluge the War Department with petitions to have this scoundrel and liar court martialed?" The crowd of supporters frequently interrupted McKaine with applause and shouts of "Down with Greer!"[67] In an open letter to the secretary of war, the LFD publicized its charges against Greer, demanding that the War Department court-martial the Ninety-second Division colonel on charges of "conduct to the prejudice of good order and military discipline; for attempting to influence legislation; and for aiding the enemy." They made explicit that Greer had "grossly humiliated and insulted" the entire race, making him unfit "to be a citizen of the Republic," and that the War Department itself was on trial. After the letter appeared in several African American newspapers, the War Department took notice and felt compelled to respond. On June 10, 1919, McKaine, along with eight other former officers and black civic leaders, met with Secretary of War Newton Baker in Washington, D.C., to voice their protests against Greer and demand punishment. Baker assured the men that their charges would be taken seriously.[68] Additionally, a delegation from the LFD gained an audience with the Senate and House Committees on Military Affairs on June 16.[69]

While the War Department stalled in taking any definitive action concerning the Greer matter, McKaine and the LFD continued to motivate black veterans and the broader African American public to collective action. The LFD held a successful meeting in June 1919 in Washington, D.C., where its branch membership reportedly consisted of more than three hundred men. Linking the national goals of the organization to the local struggles of black Washingtonians to combat racism, branch president James H. N. Waring assured the crowd, "The League is in this fight and intends to see it through," adding that the organization had "declared war on discrimination in the district." Prominent Washington, D.C., journalist and LFD supporter J. Finley Wilson encouraged black people to become members of the rapidly growing organization, telling the audience, "After the colored people have given their dollars so freely and have subscribed to every Liberty Loan to make the world safe for democracy, a democracy in which colored men have not shared, we would commit a crime against all the ages not to over subscribe the League for Democracy which seeks to make democracy safe for Negroes." But the star of the meeting was its principal speaker, Osceola McKaine, who inspired the crowd to aggressively resist discrimination and racial violence. "No Negroes any where in the United States should ever let white mobs take a black man to lynch him without using all the force possible to prevent it," McKaine exhorted. "The only thing with which to meet force is force." The location and timing of this meeting had particular significance considering the bloody Washington riot occurred just weeks later. McKaine and the LFD emboldened the city's black population, and black veterans in particular, to defend themselves and their community in the face of white violence.[70] The following month, McKaine, speaking on the behalf of the organization, confronted Robert Russa Moton at a July 1919 New York Tuskegee Institute banquet. He accused the Tuskegee principal of disrespecting African American soldiers with his mollifying speeches in France and proclaimed that the "new element of the Race" would now elect its own representatives.[71]

Despite its quick ascendance to the forefront of national racial protest and the confidence of its leaders, the LFD diminished in significance by early 1920. As the heated memories of the war cooled, emotions settled, and the esprit de corps between veterans affiliated with the LFD gradually dissipated, the group's cohesiveness suffered. The LFD also had to compete with a host of other New Negro organizations, as well as more established groups such as the NAACP, that had similar goals. Indeed, former soldiers, especially in the South, contributed to the tremendous postwar growth of the NAACP, which saw its branch membership skyrocket from 9,200 in 1918 to 62,200 in 1919.[72] Additionally, the federal government identified the organization as a key target in its campaign to suppress black radicalism and actively sought ways to undermine its effectiveness.

This included fanning the flames of rivalry between the LFD and another black veteran organization, the more conservative Grand Army of Americans (GAA). It reflected the ideological diversity of African American veterans, and the New Negro movement more broadly. A collection of black officers established the GAA in Washington, D.C., in March 1919 with the goal of "looking after the welfare of the soldiers and sailors who have fought for Uncle Sam in any war." The GAA adopted a much less overtly political agenda and expressed its willingness to cooperate with white veteran organizations.[73] This placed it at odds with the much more radical LFD. Samuel F. Sewall, a former captain in the 368th Infantry Regiment and lead organizer of the GAA, prepared to approach Osceola McKaine and discuss the possibility of combining their two organizations, a suggestion first broached by James Weldon Johnson in a *New York Age* editorial. He decided otherwise after attending a raucous June 15 LFD meeting in Washington, D.C., and instead shared his concerns with the Department of Justice. "Capt. Sewall states that Lt. McKaine advocates meeting force with force, which is, in his opinion, unwise doctrine for the negroes at this time," a government agent reported following a conversation with the former officer. Sewall encouraged federal authorities to investigate the LFD for possible violation of army regulations and promised to provide the names of any African American veterans affiliated with the organization.[74]

More than any other factor, overambition led to the premature demise of the LFD. Militancy and optimism could not overcome the fact that the vision of the LFD was too broad in scope and lacked clarity. James Weldon Johnson offered a prophetic observation in the May 1919 issue of the *New York Age*, where he wrote that "the program of the League for Democracy is too comprehensive, it takes in too much," and suggested that the organization "concentrate all its strength and energy upon those particular objects which by the nature of its being it is best fitted to accomplish." The LFD's sole attempt to do just this, its campaign to charge Greer with treason, made little headway and gradually demoralized the membership. Furthermore, this single issue lacked the resonance to attract and maintain a stable membership base outside of a core of intensely politicized former officers like McKaine. With the LFD faltering, the *Commoner* quickly followed, ceasing production by 1922. While exemplifying the spirit and ideals of the New Negro, the fortitude of the LFD and its leaders surpassed what the group could realistically accomplish.[75]

With a meteoric rise and a similarly rapid descent, the LFD nevertheless stood as the most militant organization of its time created specifically by and for African American veterans. At the local level, the group brought returned black soldiers together, allowing them to take pride in their service and direct their frustrations. Former officers and servicemen found in the LFD an organization that restored their manhood and valued their leadership. While the national campaign against Greer may have failed, it nevertheless put the War Department on notice that African American veterans would not remain silent as racist officers degraded their legacy. In its brief moment on the national stage, the LFD represented the determination of African American servicemen to use their war experience as an opportunity to combat institutionalized racism and inspire militant political resistance among African Americans more broadly.

COMPLEMENTING GROUPS SUCH AS the League for Democracy, a host of black newspapers, journals, and periodicals contributed to Harlem's teeming radical energy and the larger postwar milieu of racial militancy. Most paled in comparison to the *Messenger*. The journal, founded and edited by A. Philip Randolph and Chandler Owen, distinguished itself as the nation's leading radical African American newspaper and self-proclaimed voice of the New Negro in the years following the war. The *Messenger*, however, represented more than just a journal. It functioned as the heart of Harlem's socialist community and brought together a vibrant collection of black radical intellectuals. Randolph and Owen became active Socialist Party members in late 1916, spreading their call for antiracist working-class solidarity on the street corners of Harlem. The Independent Political Council established by Randolph and Owen to advance the interests of the Socialist Party boasted of having four hundred black members. The small, cluttered office of the *Messenger*, located on 132nd Street and Lenox Avenue, functioned as a space for social interaction, political organizing, and critical intellectual exchange, where Randolph, Owen, and individuals such as Wilfred A. Domingo, Wallace Thurman, and George Frazier Miller would converse well into the night. The magazine itself served as a platform for this cadre of leftist black intellectuals to promote a radical vision of interracial democracy and working-class unity.[76]

The influence of the *Messenger* spread well beyond Harlem's black socialist circle. The end of the war intensified the *Messenger's* radicalism and its popularization of the New Negro. Randolph and Owen welcomed the arrival of "New Crowd Negroes" who, unlike preceding generations of black leadership, pledged to wage an uncompromising battle against racial discrimination and working-class exploitation. Dismissing the efforts of "Old Crowd Negroes" such as Emmett Scott, W. E. B. Du Bois, Kelly Miller, and Robert R. Moton during the war, Randolph wrote, "The New Crowd is uncompromising. Its tactics are not defensive but offensive. It would not send notes after a Negro is lynched. It would not appeal to white leaders. It would appeal to the plain working people everywhere. The New Crowd sees that the war came, that the Negro fought, bled and died; that the war has ended, and he is not yet free."[77] Inflammatory rhetoric of this sort earned the *Messenger* a prominent place in the postwar "Red Scare," both domestically and internationally. French military intelligence, monitoring "bolshevism among the Negroes," kept a close eye on the *Messenger*, while A. Mitchell Palmer, the crusading U.S. attorney general, labeled the radical magazine "the most able and the most dangerous of all the Negro publications."[78]

Victor Daly received his army discharge in April 1919. He had served with honor as an officer in the 367th Infantry, receiving the French Croix de Guerre. However, the racism that infected the Ninety-second Division had a profound effect on the once unassuming Cornell University student, who emerged from the war with his racial and political consciousness significantly hardened. He more than likely took part or was at least privy to the secret meetings held by Osceola McKaine and other fellow officers of his regiment. Apparently having little desire to return to the tranquil yet politically languid environs of Ithaca, New York, following his release from service, Daly settled in Harlem. In need of an outlet for his swelling radicalism, as well as a job, he began work as the *Messenger*'s business manager, a crucial position at the always financially strapped newspaper.[79]

During his time with the *Messenger* Daly's political assertiveness swelled. A glimpse of his growing radicalism appeared in the October 1919 issue, where he responded to a letter written by a self-described descendant of "black abolition-

Portrait of Victor Daly. Victor R. Daly Papers, #37-5-3157. Courtesy of the Division of Rare and Manuscript Collections, Cornell University Library.

ists" who accused the *Messenger* of being "the worst enemies of the Negro race" by promoting racial hatred, "bolshevism," and social unrest. Daly, answering in lieu of Randolph and Owen, who were "thoroughly in accord with the entire tenor and substance" of his reply, lashed back. He invoked his military service and decorated veteran status, stating that he wrote not solely on the behalf of the *Messenger* but "as one who served as a 1st Lieutenant in the army for nearly two years and winner of the 'Croix de Guerre' in France." He dismissed the writer's accusations, asserting that while the socialist magazine in fact promoted working-class racial cooperation and opposed armed conflict, it unapologetically did "advocate armed resistance."[80]

More explicitly, Daly linked his identity as a veteran with the radical left and the politics of the *Messenger*. Daly displayed his socialist inclinations, emphasizing the "need for peace between the black and white workingmen in America." Directly addressing the author of the letter, Daly wrote, "You have used the term 'Bolshevism' and 'Bolshevist' several times in your letter. So many and varied meanings have been put upon these words by the prostitute press that I am at a loss to know your interpretation of them; but if you interpret them to apply to the above outlined purpose of the *Messenger*, then classify me, too, a former United States Army Officer, as a Bolshevist." This striking statement, from a young man who before the war expressed no discontent with his life as a Cornell University student and thoroughly embodied the bourgeois social traits of Ithaca's black middle class, reflected how military service informed Daly's radicalism. The *Messenger* provided him with the platform to channel and articulate it.[81]

Veteran William N. Colson became a key contributor to the *Messenger* and one of the most radical voices of the New Negro movement. Described by the magazine's editors as "an especially critical thinker, courageous, and possessed of a rare and pleasing literary style," Colson graduated from Virginia Union University along with Chandler Owen. Politically active before the war, he also served as executive director of the Richmond, Virginia, Urban League. Colson earned a commission at Des Moines, where he befriended Victor Daly, and served as a second lieutenant in the 367th Infantry in France.[82] Although enrolling in Columbia University Law School upon returning to the United States on March 15, 1919, he remained anxious to expose the racist treatment he and his fellow soldiers and officers of the Ninety-second Division faced while overseas.[83] Colson's college friend Chandler Owen presented him with the opportunity to do just this, and he joined the staff of the *Messenger* as a contributing editor.[84]

Colson published several articles in the radical newspaper following his military service, most focusing on the experience of black soldiers during the war. Less than four months after his return to the United States, Colson's first article appeared in the July 1919 issue of the *Messenger* under the title "Propaganda and the Negro Soldier." In it he declared black soldiers "were fighting for France and for their race rather than for a flag which had no meaning." Colson's anger and disillusionment with American democracy virtually leapt from the page. Colson aired a similar theme in subsequent articles that appeared regularly throughout late 1919 and early 1920. Essays such as "An Analysis of Negro Patriotism," "The Failure of the Ninety-Second Division," coauthored with fellow Des Moines officer and LFD affiliate Ambrose B. Nutt, and "The Social Experience of the Negro Soldier Abroad" revealed to readers in vivid detail what black soldiers encountered and endured overseas. Colson's experiences and status as a veteran of the war gave him the firsthand knowledge and credibility to make such claims, ensuring that the reading public took his devastating articles seriously.

At the state and federal levels, investigators flagged Colson as a person of potential danger. "May I call your attention to an article by one William N. Colson," postal investigator Robert Bowen wrote to MID chief Marlborough Churchill after reading "Propaganda and the Negro Soldier." He suspected Churchill had already seen Colson's piece but felt that "it is too vicious for it to be wise to take any chance that those in authority may not have noticed it."[85] The following month Bowen again wrote to Churchill, this time regarding Colson's "offensive" and "disquieting" article "An Analysis of Negro Patriotism."[86] "The Messenger goes from bad to worse," Bowen lamented, "and I hope there is some power that will finally send it to the very worst and have done with it."[87] Colson's activities also came under the watchful eye of local New York agents, who reported their findings to the Joint Legislative Committee to Investigate Seditious Activities chaired by state senator Clayton R. Lusk. Colson spoke at a "Red-Hot Mass Meeting" on June 13, 1919, at the Rush AME Zion Church along with A. Philip Randolph, Chandler Owen, W. A. Domingo, and Elizabeth Gurley Flynn of the Industrial Workers of the World (IWW). Colson's brief but poignant remarks, according to a special agent in the audience, "were mainly a protest against the outrageous attempt by Burleson to suppress the mailing of the 'Messenger.'"[88] Colson's radical political activism complemented his piercing articles.

"The Immediate Function of the Negro Veteran," Colson's most forceful essay, appeared in the December 1919 issue of the *Messenger*. In the article, he asserted that returning black soldiers had a distinctive role to play in the postwar reconstruction of the United States, writing, "The returned Negro veteran, by virtue of his service and experience, has a certain special function which he cannot afford to fail to press to the limit." For Colson, this entailed African American veterans accepting their manly responsibility to actively confront and resist racial prejudice and violence, with force if necessary. "The returned soldier," he continued, "by reason of his military training, can do more to stop lynch-law and discrimination in the United States than many Americans want to see. He is accomplishing it by a resolute demonstration of self-defense and a growing desire to lose his life in a good cause." Along with fighting racial discrimination, black veterans, in Colson's view, had begun to ally themselves with the labor movement, a reflection of his socialist vision more so than a quantifiable reality. Colson proclaimed that African American soldiers returned from France possessing a new self-confidence and appreciation of "social values":

> It is, therefore, the function of the returned soldiers with their new appreciation of social values, straightway to appropriate the desire to either revolutionize or destroy every evil American institution which retards their progress. They must first of all continue their campaign of discontent and

dissatisfaction. Let them neither smile nor sleep until they have burned into the soul of every Negro in the United States an unquenchable desire to tear down every barrier which stops their onward march.

Most potently, Colson encouraged black veterans to actively fight back against discrimination and racial abuse, arguing that "each black soldier, as he travels on jim-crow cars, if he has the desire, can act his disapproval. When he is insulted, he can perform a counter-action. When he is exploited economically, he can strike. . . . With Negro veterans fighting back, and stirring up merited discontent and dissatisfaction on every hand, the attitude of the Bourbon South is bound to become less degenerate." Colson concluded by declaring, "The function of the Negro soldier, who is mentally free, is to act as an imperishable leaven on the mass of those who are still in mental bondage."[89]

Colson's article captured the symbolic relationship between African American veterans, New Negro masculinity, and the broader development of a radicalized postwar political environment. He envisioned black veterans serving as the vanguard of a systemic transformation of American society, with himself as prototype. Military service prepared African American soldiers to serve as the logical leaders of the race following the war. The racism of the U.S. Army and the reprieve of French democracy combined to imbue African American soldiers with a distinctive social and political consciousness. As Colson articulated, African American veterans had no choice but to act upon their wartime experience and share their knowledge with the race. Colson, a veteran himself, constructed a symbolic image of the returned black soldier as the personification of the New Negro.

Compared to Victor Daly and William Colson, George Schuyler traveled a more circuitous route to the *Messenger*, but one similarly informed by the disillusionment of service in the American wartime army. After completing his sentence for desertion at the Governor's Island military prison, Schuyler attempted to restart his life in New York City. Schuyler had little success, floating between various jobs until he eventually went back home to Syracuse in 1921. There he joined the Socialist Party, reflecting that "it was exhilarating, and just the type of stimulation I had been hungering for."[90] He returned to New York City in 1922 and became active in various political and intellectual circles, including the Friends of Negro Freedom, an organization founded by A. Philip Randolph and Chandler Owen in March 1920 to challenge the perceived complacency of conservative civil rights organizations like the NAACP and, later, the racialism of Marcus Garvey. Schuyler befriended the *Messenger* editors, and in early 1923 they offered him a position as office manager for the magazine.[91] He was fascinated with the "idea of being associated with an important publication."[92] By this time he was the only veteran on staff; Victor Daly had departed in 1920 following a dispute over his wages, and Colson unexpectedly passed away in 1922.[93]

During his employment with the magazine, Schuyler effectively ran the *Messenger*, describing it as "a good place for a tireless, versatile young fellow to get plenty of activity and exercise."[94] Applying the discipline learned in the military to his position as office manager, Schuyler increased the *Messenger*'s efficiency and made a name for himself in Harlem Renaissance political and literary circles. Beginning in September 1923, Schuyler contributed a monthly column entitled "Darts and Shafts: A Page of Calumny and Satire," which introduced readers to his iconoclastic and often deliberately inflammatory style of writing. In 1926 he became managing editor, a position he held until the *Messenger* folded in July 1928.[95] Schuyler's brilliant use of satire was undoubtedly informed by his time in the wartime army, itself an ultimately satirical experience. As an experienced soldier and commissioned officer who unglamorously spent the final months of the war imprisoned, Schuyler embodied the farcical, tragic-comic nature of race relations and American democracy. Perhaps not surprisingly, Schuyler, unlike Victor Daly and William Colson, made no mention of his military service in his writings for the *Messenger*. His imprisonment was surely both personally embarrassing and enraging. While he went to great lengths to bury this aspect of his past, it nevertheless shaped his sardonically critical view of American race relations and prolific career as an author and journalist.[96]

The *Messenger* owed its reputation as one of the most radical magazines of the New Negro movement to the participatory and symbolic influence of African American veterans. It served as an outlet for Victor Daly, William Colson, and George Schuyler to express their postwar discontent. The magazine's socialist critique of American democracy and the war itself presented these former officers with an attractive political ideology, one that allowed them to both make sense of their war experience and challenge the debilitating influence of racism on interracial working-class solidarity. The *Messenger* provided the camaraderie, organization, and critical intellectual engagement this small group of veterans clearly sought out and relished.

WHILE IN BALTIMORE ON A late February evening in 1919, Marcus Garvey sensed an opportune moment to promote his fledgling, yet rapidly growing organization, the Universal Negro Improvement Association. Black troops had begun to return in mass from France. Homecoming parades and welcoming celebrations joyously erupted in cities throughout the country. A spirit of intense racial pride filled the streets of black America, coupled with a burning desire for true democracy in the wake of the war. African Americans, and former soldiers in particular, listened intently to the diverse assortment of street-corner soapbox orators and speakers on the lecture circuit, searching for answers as to what the war truly meant and seeking direction for how best to realize the transformative potential of black military service. Garvey, a thirty-two-year-old immigrant from Jamaica and aspiring race leader, was acutely attuned to this mood of political restlessness. He had come to Baltimore to build support for the city's UNIA chapter, giving a series of speeches at local churches. On this particular night, he spoke not only to Baltimore's African American community but to the concerns of black people throughout the country, invoking the recent participation of peoples of African descent in the war to motivate them to collective action. "We Negroes have fought and died enough for white people," the UNIA leader implored his audience. "From 1914 to 1918 two million Negroes fought in Europe for a thing foreign to themselves—Democracy." The time of waiting patiently for a white supremacist government to grant African Americans their full democratic rights had passed with the end of the war and the return of black soldiers to the United States. Black people, as Garvey proclaimed, had a new calling: "Now they must fight for themselves."[97]

In a remarkably short time, the UNIA became the most dominant mass organization of peoples of African descent in the early twentieth century. Just as the evolution of the New Negro movement is inextricably connected with the extraordinary rise of the UNIA, the history of the organization itself cannot be divorced from the experiences and symbolic resonance of African American veterans. Garvey consciously invoked the recent historical memory of black military service as a strategy to popularize the UNIA and promote his vision of a diasporic black empire. At the same time, the nationalist and Pan-Africanist ideologies of the UNIA, with its concomitant militarism, attracted many disillusioned African American veterans to its ranks. Former soldiers, as both leaders and members, played a key role in the UNIA's expansion. As the UNIA made its presence felt throughout postwar America and beyond, black veterans, physically and symbolically, figured prominently in the organization's membership, ideology, and performance.

Having experienced firsthand the inconsistencies of British democracy and colonialism in Jamaica, Marcus Garvey founded the UNIA on August 1, 1914, in his hometown of Kingston. Influenced by the self-help racial philosophy of Booker T. Washington, Garvey set out in early 1916 to visit the Tuskegee Institute and give a series of lectures in the South. He instead spent over a year traveling throughout the United States and meeting prominent African American race leaders such as Ida B. Wells-Barnett and Hubert Harrison, arguably the most important early figure of the New Negro movement.[98] Realizing the tremendous organizing potential of African Americans, Garvey settled in Harlem, and by early 1918 New York had replaced Kingston as headquarters of the UNIA. Joining Harlem's numerous soapbox orators, Garvey quickly began to make a name for himself in advocating for black racial pride, self-determination, and African liberation.[99]

The First World War had a significant impact on Marcus Garvey and the development of the UNIA. Garvey boasted that, at its height, the UNIA had a worldwide membership of some four million supporters, with two million in the United States alone. Although headquartered in New York, the majority of the UNIA's American branches were located in the South and catered to the local struggles of rural working-class black people.[100] While Garvey undoubtedly inflated the true size of the UNIA, the phenomenal growth of the organization was directly linked to the effect of the war in politicizing peoples of African descent and heightening their racial consciousness.[101] Moreover, the hypernationalism of the war and its imperialist underpinnings shaped both the structure and the racial philosophy of the UNIA. As the war destructively demonstrated, race, nation, empire, and militarism formed an inextricable nexus in the development of the modern world. Garvey reinterpreted these connections and, in the context of postwar nationalist and racialist thought, developed a broad organizational ideology, which he later termed "African fundamentalism," that stressed the primacy of black racial distinctiveness, historical achievement, economic uplift, and collective diasporic self-determination. While in significant ways a product of Western imperialism—Garvey's vision of the UNIA functioning as the nation-state of a black empire extending throughout the African diaspora was informed by the British Empire—the UNIA forcefully challenged the moral, ideological, and historical legitimacy of European and American global hegemony. Garvey accomplished this by using the history of the war and its ideological impulses to instill in peoples of African descent a renewed sense of pride in their racial heritage and collective ability to determine their own social, political, and economic destiny.[102] Indeed, the political mood and social conditions of the African diaspora and black America were ripe for Marcus Garvey's arrival.

Garvey had a particularly strong reverence for black soldiers. Although he opposed the war, Garvey deeply admired the heroism, manliness, and militancy of black servicemen. He was one of several thousand cheering spectators lining the streets of Harlem to catch a glimpse of the 369th making its triumphant homecoming on February 17, 1919. The spectacle of the marching soldiers, powerful embodiments of manhood and racial pride, and the adoration they received moved Garvey to tears.[103] He never forgot this moment.

Shortly after the end of the war, Garvey began to regularly invoke the fresh historical memory of soldiers of African descent and their military service to both popularize the UNIA and signal the arrival of a new worldwide conflict between whites and peoples of African descent. White supremacists, ranging from Lothrop Stoddard to the Ku Klux Klan, warned of an impending global clash between the white and darker races stemming from the social and political unrest of the war. In his speeches and writings, Garvey brilliantly rearticulated their rhetoric and, using the recent history of soldiers of African descent in the war, argued that in any future race war, black people would emerge victorious.[104] Because black soldiers throughout the diaspora had not fought for themselves and their race, the full military potential of people of African descent remained unrealized. This fact, according to Garvey, made black people destined to emerge triumphant in an impending racial conflict. "They talk about the New York 15th; that was only an experiment in warfare," Garvey exhorted to a cheering crowd in July 1921. "They talk about the Illinois Eighth; that was only a pastime for the boys. They talk about the prowess of the West Indian regiments; those fellows were only having a picnic; it was a gala day. No man has ever yet seen the Negro fighting at his best, because the Negro has never yet fought for himself." With this the audience burst into loud and prolonged applause.[105]

It would take new men, New Negroes, to fight and win this looming race war. Garvey envisioned the UNIA as the New Negro's army, and black veterans its most important combatants. Garvey therefore explicitly linked the symbol of the New Negro to black servicemen. As peoples of African descent recommitted themselves to self-defense against white racial violence, black soldiers represented the New Negro's willingness to fight back. Garvey said as much in a January 13, 1922, speech, asserting, "The new Negro likes a good fight—a fight like the fight of Needham Roberts—two taking twenty—and I want to say to them and to the white world that if they trifle with this Universal Negro Improvement Association they are going to get what they are looking for."[106] Heroes Needham Roberts and Henry Johnson of the 369th Infantry served as historical racial heroes and individual symbols of the potential ability of black people to combat and defeat white racial aggression. Moreover, Garvey linked African American soldiers and the New Negro to the diasporic dimensions of black military service and a global struggle for democracy. "I say this positively: the morale of the New Negro cannot be broken," Garvey declared before a cheering audience in a January 15, 1922, address recounted by the *Negro World*. "The morale of the

Negro American soldier in France, the morale of the Negro West Indian soldier in France, the morale of the Negro African soldier in France was unbroken and the morale of the soldiers of the bloody war of 1914 to 1918 is the morale of Negroes throughout the world."[107] For Garvey, black soldiers in the United States and throughout the diaspora represented the New Negro in both body and spirit.

The importance of black veterans to the UNIA went beyond symbolism, as Garvey actively solicited their participation and leadership. Constructions of the New Negro largely centered on the question of racial leadership, and Garvey, who consciously distinguished himself from preceding generations of black leadership, idolized black soldiers for their military skills, cosmopolitanism, and diasporic sensibilities.[108] "We are not depending on the statesmanship of fellows like Du Bois to lead this race of ours," exclaimed Garvey in his opening address of the August 1921 International Convention of Negroes of the World, "but we are depending on the statesmanship of fellows like the New York Fifteenth, the West Indian regiments and the Eighth Illinois, who fought their way in France."[109] He looked upon African American veterans as future leaders of the race, embodying a new generation of black manhood, militancy, and mastery that had the ability to directly challenge Western dominance, as well as an earlier generation of ineffective "Old Negro" leadership.

Marcus Garvey's admiration of black soldiers, combined with the pageantry, structure, and broader racial philosophy of the UNIA, apparently made the organization extremely attractive to many African American veterans. Black veterans from various backgrounds joined the UNIA in significant numbers. The allure of the organization proved strongest for returned servicemen disillusioned by their war experience. The black nationalism of the UNIA, rooted in a positive vision of history, culture, and destiny, provided a welcome alternative to the hypocrisy of American nationalism, which proved to be morally and materially bankrupt as experienced by many black soldiers.[110] Vilified by their white officers and the broader American military establishment, black veterans instead found praise in the UNIA and Garvey's rhetoric.

This praise carried an overt gender dimension. The qualities of the New Negro that the UNIA modeled itself after—militancy, physical strength, leadership, aggressive resistance to racial violence—were distinctly masculine traits in the context of early twentieth-century gender conventions. For Garvey, black soldiers, as representations of an ideal black manhood, served as perfect representatives of both the New Negro and the UNIA.[111] In a letter appearing in the *Negro World*, Garvey proclaimed, "The new Negro is no coward. He is a man, and if he can die in France or Flanders for white men, he can die anywhere else, even behind prison bars, fighting for the cause of the race that needs assistance."[112] Having fought and defeated Europeans on the battlefield, African American troops embodied the racial and masculine superiority of black men over white men. Black soldiers and their war experience thus allowed Garvey to skillfully both undermine and appropriate pseudoscientific constructions of black manhood and simultaneously elevate the place of black men on the ladder of human evolution. "Do you still believe in the Darwin theory that [the black] man is a monkey or the missing link between the ape and man?" declared Garvey in a March 1921 speech. "If you think it is, that theory has been exploded in the world war. It was you, the supermen, that brought back victory at the Marne!"[113] Participation in the UNIA therefore provided black veterans with the opportunity to reclaim their manhood and openly express their race consciousness, opportunities they often lacked during the war.

Several African American veterans who joined the UNIA came from impressive backgrounds and held crucial leadership positions. Clarence Benjamin Curley became involved in the UNIA through the Black Star Line (BSL), the main entrepreneurial component of the organization's goal of black economic self-sufficiency and a symbol imperial strength. A graduate of Howard University, Curley successfully graduated from the Des Moines officers' training camp and fought in France with the 368th Infantry.[114] While earning an MBA at New York University after the war, he served on the board of directors for the BSL, holding the key positions of general accountant and secretary.[115] William Clarence Matthews, a former Negro League baseball star, Harvard University alum, and prominent Boston-area attorney, served as an important member of the city's UNIA chapter. His leadership contributed to membership in the Boston division increasing from seven individuals in November 1919 to a robust thirteen hundred by May 1920. He was subsequently elevated to the position of assistant counselor general.[116] J. Austin Norris, a former officer who served alongside Charles Hamilton Houston in France, volunteered his time for the UNIA upon returning to the United States. Norris practiced law in Philadelphia, having graduated from Yale University Law School, and, along with representing the city's UNIA division, served as an elected member of the organization's 1922 League of Nations delegation.[117] Similar to the LFD, some of the most distinguished African American veterans of the war found an ideological home in the UNIA and provided Marcus Garvey with stellar examples of racial progress.

Many former soldiers of the British West Indies Regiment joined the UNIA and became prominent members. Men and women from the various isles of the West Indies provided the core of the UNIA's membership base, both in the Caribbean and, following the establishment of the organization's New York headquarters, in the United States. Almost forty-five thousand individuals migrated to the United States from the Caribbean between 1913 and 1919, settling in major cities across the eastern seaboard and fundamentally reshaping the social, political, and cultural demographics of black America in the process.[118] After founding the UNIA in his home of Jamaica, Garvey forged relationships with a number of men throughout the Caribbean who subsequently entered the British military under the aegis of the BWIR. As the UNIA's influence in the Caribbean grew during the war years, British military intelligence officials expressed deep concern with Garvey's correspondence with black soldiers in the BWIR who promoted the organization and contributed to its expanding membership.[119] Veterans of the BWIR played a key role in the rapid growth of the UNIA following the armistice. Service in the British military radicalized many West Indian troops, who experienced discrimination at the hands of their white superiors that parallel what African American soldiers endured in the AEF. Having initially supported the war effort and willingly offered their service on the behalf of the British motherland, soldiers of the BWIR were rewarded with a torrent of racial discrimination and psychological abuse that left them both embittered and motivated to organize for collective self-determination.[120]

West Indian veterans, many of whom migrated to the United States after the war, occupied a wide variety of key leadership positions within the UNIA.[121] Like their African American counterparts, these men were attracted to the Pan-African racial philosophy of the organization, its unabashed militancy, Garvey's valorization of their service, and the opportunity to utilize their skills developed in the war for the cause of collective racial progress. Hugh Mulzac, a native of Union Island in the Grenadines, British West Indies, served as a deck officer on various British and American vessels during the First World War and later became the chief officer of the Black Star Line's *Yarmouth*.[122] The musical director of the UNIA, Arnold Ford, transferred his experiences as a member of the musical corps of the British Royal Navy during the war to shaping the cultural performance and pageantry of the Garvey movement. Born on the island of Barbados, Ford composed several hymns for the UNIA, the most notable being the "Universal Ethiopian Anthem," which members throughout the diaspora sang at the opening of all organizational meetings and gatherings. Another native of Barbados, Rupert Jemmott, served with the British army in Canada during the war and joined the UNIA in Harlem in 1920. His talents as an engineer, first developed while in the army and later refined as a student, led the UNIA to select him as building engineer for the organization's work in Liberia.[123] Samuel Haynes, a veteran of the BWIR from Honduras, emerged from the war and his battles with imperial racism hungry for racial justice. British Honduras, especially its capital of Belize, was a hotbed of radical working-class protest following the return of black servicemen to the colony, as evidenced by a wave of strikes and riots in 1919. The UNIA fed off of this energy, and Haynes became general secretary of the UNIA's British Honduras chapter. He so impressed Marcus Garvey that in 1921 the UNIA leader recruited Haynes to the United States, where he lent his leadership and passion to the development of chapters in several cities throughout the country.[124]

The Universal African Legions, the paramilitary wing of the UNIA, functioned as the primary avenue for black veterans to join the organization and make use of their military training. Garvey based the structure, organization, and drill regulations of the African Legions, a potent symbol of both racial power and national progress, in large part on the U.S. Army.[125] This made the participation of African American veterans, already familiar with the rules and conventions of military life, extremely valued. Many former soldiers, although disillusioned with the U.S. Army, appreciated the discipline and male camaraderie of military life. Because the army denied African American soldiers the opportunity to reenlist following demobilization, the African Legions allowed black veterans to remain associated with a military structure and its personal benefits. However, unlike in the wartime American army, veterans in the African Legions had the chance to openly express their racial consciousness and use their service to challenge the tenets of white supremacy. With Garvey viewing them as valuable leaders of the movement's paramilitary wing, black veterans again signed up for duty, this time in the name of the race.

The expertise of returned servicemen proved a valuable asset to the development and training of the African Legions. Harry Haywood, who contemplated joining the UNIA, stated in his autobiography, "A key role in the movement [UNIA] was also played by deeply disillusioned Black veterans. . . . Veterans were involved in the setting up of the skeleton army for the future African state, and in such paramilitary organizations as the Universal African Legion."[126] Haywood's observation carries added weight considering his brother, Otto Hall, joined the African Legions in Chicago before becoming involved in the Communist Party through the African Blood Brotherhood.[127] Garvey himself glorified the presence of former soldiers in his army of black liberation. In February 1921, informing a New York crowd of his most recent trip to Chicago where he spoke at the Eighth Illinois armory, Garvey said, "I believed that the Chicago African Legions include half of the famous Eighth Illinois boys . . . and besides that big battalion of African Legions, we have the finest display of Black Cross Nurses I ever saw. The Legions and Black Cross Nurses were ready for action."[128] While Garvey surely exaggerated their presence, as he was prone to do with the size of the UNIA in general, former soldiers of the Chicago Eighth Illinois likely joined the city's African Legions post in significant numbers. On a national level, the military experience of black servicemen catapulted them to positions of leadership in the legions. Emmett L. Gaines, a veteran of the Twenty-fourth Infantry before serving in the AEF during World War I, held the key position of minister of the African Legions. Along with commanding the legions, the widely popular Gaines frequently traveled the country and inspired grass-roots support for the UNIA, particularly in the South.[129]

Thomas W. Harvey's war experience helped catapult the former soldier to prominence within the UNIA. Upon the encouragement of a friend, Harvey joined the UNIA's Philadelphia division in 1920, approximately a year after his discharge from the military. While admittedly knowing little of the UNIA, his commitment to the organization deepened after attending a meeting at which Garvey himself spoke. The rally was "packed to rafters, people all in uniforms, parading up and down like they were somebody," recalled Harvey, captivated by Garvey's commanding presence and the spectacle of the African Legions. This moment marked what would become a lifelong commitment to the Garvey movement. He joined the Philadelphia African Legions and, in his words, "was made a lieutenant because of my previous army service," a position he held until 1930. One of Garvey's closest confidants, he continued to rise through the ranks of the UNIA, becoming president of the influential Philadelphia division in 1933, commissioner of the State of New York, and eventually president-general of the entire organization in 1950.[130] Emblematic of many former soldiers who were attracted to the UNIA, Harvey's marked achievements demonstrate the valued presence and leadership capabilities of African American war veterans to the development of the African Legions and the success of the organization more broadly.

A number of veterans who became legionaries had Caribbean backgrounds. St. Lucia native Wilfred Bazil, formerly of the Fifteenth New York National Guard and a commissioned officer in the Ninety-second Division, led the Brooklyn Division African Legions after the war.[131] James B. Nimmo, born in the Bahamas, migrated to Miami at the age of sixteen with the intent to join the U.S. Army after the British military denied him the opportunity because of his race. Drafted into the army, he found his American war experience in France failed to meet expectations, leaving him embittered. The UNIA appealed to Nimmo's Pan-African sensibilities, and, after joining the organization's robust Miami division, he was placed in charge of the local African Legions and its approximately 150 to 200 uniformed men. Nimmo's military background elevated him to the position of colonel in the Miami African Legions, and by 1923 he served as division vice president.[132]

The African Legions figured prominently in the pageantry of the UNIA, which allowed black veterans to exhibit themselves as prototypes of New Negro manhood and black nationalist militancy. The dramatic and impeccably choreographed UNIA parades, famously photographed by James VanDerZee, characterized the organization and paralleled those held for black soldiers during and after the war, in both appearance and meaning, as political assertions of African American civic nationalism and racial pride. In the case of the UNIA's events, black nationalism supplanted civic nationalism in significance for participants and spectators alike. Attracting huge crowds, the pageants prominently featured the African Legions, crisply uniformed and fiercely disciplined, marching in the military formations characteristic of the U.S. Army. The mass gatherings also included the UNIA's Black Cross Nurses, who Garvey modeled after wartime Red Cross nurses and complemented the soldiers of the African Legions as embodiments of feminine militancy. The UNIA's pageants, as part of a historical tradition of ritual and performance within the contested space of American public culture, constituted powerful assertions of nationhood and racial sovereignty.[133] Within this space, black veterans asserted their role as ambassadors of the New Negro.

On August 1, 1920, Harlem came to a standstill by the grand-opening parade of the International Convention of Negroes of the World. "Not a cloud flecked the sky," as thousands of fascinated onlookers lined the sidewalks of Lenox Avenue from 125th Street to 145th Street to witness Garvey, members of the high command, and representatives from UNIA branches throughout the diaspora on display. The Philadelphia African Legions, "marching nearly 200 strong," stood at the head of the procession, which began promptly at 2:00 P.M. They were followed by the "beautiful women" of the Philadelphia and New York Black Cross Nurses who, "clad in their white costumes, with their flowing white caps and their black crosses," "made a truly inspiring spectacle." Although musical bands from various UNIA branches marched in the parade, they were all upstaged by the New York Fifteenth Infantry ensemble, a regular feature at local UNIA events. Its appearance caused the crowd to go "wild with applause as the Fifteenth Band swung along up Lenox avenue and down Seventh avenue, playing marches, interspersed with popular, jazzy music." The historical and symbolic meaning of the band's presence was enhanced by UNIA members carrying dozens of banners, several of which explicitly invoked the recent memory of black military service in the war. Signs reading "The Negro Fought in Europe;

He Can Fight in Africa," "The Negro Is the Greatest Fighter," and "What of the New African Army?" were proudly thrust into the air. The "thrilling, spectacular scene" lasted for three hours and "was carried out without a hitch." It caused Garvey's popularity to soar and, in the process, added "one more chapter to the history of the New Negro in his strivings for self-determination and freedom."[134]

While many African American veterans embraced Garvey and the UNIA, some viewed him as a detriment to racial progress. James Wormley Jones was a dedicated soldier and loyal American. Unlike other black officers in the 368th Infantry Regiment, the captain had escaped persecution in the aftermath of the Meuse-Argonne offensive. Army officials trusted Jones enough to appoint him as a member of the efficiency board looking into the conduct of his fellow servicemen in the Ninety-second Division. He wanted to remain in the army as a military instructor, but the War Department denied his request. Following his discharge, Jones resumed his employment as a detective with the Washington, D.C., police force.[135]

Working undercover to monitor rising African American militancy in Washington, D.C., Jones played the role of the radical, gun-toting, disgruntled black veteran with convincing flair. On March 14, 1919, Jones and another returned soldier, Lieutenant Charles Shaw, spoke to a crowd at the colored YMCA. MID agent Walter Loving sat in the audience, and, unaware that Jones was a police detective, took careful notes of his words. According to Loving, Jones told the audience:

> I am not a public speaker but a soldier and a fighter. I went to France to fight the Hun and I accomplished that object. To prove that I did, I brought back a German machine gun which I captured single handed; that gun I have now at my home with plenty of ammunition. I also have an Austrian high powered rifle and the best automatic revolver made. After fighting and suffering for democracy abroad, we are told to return to our homes and be calm and unassuming. I am not going around with a chip on my shoulder, but when I am insulted and my rights are denied me, I am here to tell you that I am ready to declare war any minute.[136]

Jones delivered a stellar performance, but he had larger career aspirations. On November 19, 1919, he applied for a position in the Department of Justice and the following month was hired as an agent to monitor black radical activity.[137]

Known by his code number "800," Jones quickly became the government's most prized informant. Using the legitimacy of his veteran status, Jones successfully infiltrated the UNIA. While committed to racial equality, Jones viewed

Garvey, as did many other African Americans of a variety of political persuasions, as a charlatan who posed a distinct threat to future progress. Garvey, however, saw the former officer as a valuable addition to the UNIA. As a result, Jones's stature within the organization grew rapidly. He earned Garvey's personal confidence, became a featured speaker at UNIA meetings, and by June 1920 served as the adjutant general of the African Legions. He assumed a host of duties, which included personally training two hundred members of the Newport News, Virginia, division on the drill regulations of the U.S. Army. Jones did this while supplying the federal government with information about the UNIA in order to build a case against the organization's leader, as well as fomenting tensions between the UNIA and the ABB, which he also infiltrated by virtue of his military background.[138] Jones saw himself as performing a valuable service for the race. Praised as an exceptional officer after the war, he maintained a faith in American democracy, and the federal government specifically, that many veterans did not. He thus approached his position as an opportunity to further demonstrate the patriotic loyalty of African Americans by working to rid the nation of Garvey and his organization, which, in his estimation, only bred increased racial hatred.

As Jones's activities attest, Garvey faced tremendous obstacles in realizing his ultimate goals of racial unity, political autonomy, and economic independence for peoples of African descent throughout the diaspora. The federal government exhaustively investigated Garvey and the UNIA from its inception. Garvey compounded his problems with financial mismanagement of the Black Star Line, failing to control internal organizational conflicts, and engaging in a seemingly endless array of vitriolic feuds with prominent black leaders. W. E. B. Du Bois, lambasted Garvey in the pages of the *Crisis*, disparaging him as "a little, fat, black man, ugly . . . with a big head" and branding him in a 1924 editorial as a "lunatic or a traitor." Garvey shot back, characterizing Du Bois as a "misleader" and a "monstrosity" because of his mixed-race heritage. Cyril Briggs of the *Crusader* and the ABB filed a libel suit after Garvey accused him of being a white man in the pages of the *Negro World* and won a public apology. A. Philip Randolph and Chandler Owen, the class-conscious editors of the *Messenger*, railed against Garvey's racialism and spearheaded the "Garvey Must Go" campaign, even going so far as to work with the Justice Department to have him deported.

The federal government took its first step in silencing Garvey by charging him with mail fraud in 1922. On June 21, 1923, he received a five-year jail sentence and served three months in New York's Tombs Prison before being granted bail. Imprisoned again in 1925 and sent to the Atlanta Federal Penitentiary, Garvey was forced to confront the prospect of deportation following a recommendation by the Immigration and Naturalization Service that he be removed from the country. President Calvin Coolidge commuted Garvey's prison sentence, but it did not change his ultimate fate. On a rain-soaked December 2, 1927, day in New Orleans, Garvey stood on the deck of the SS *Saramacca* and bid an emotional farewell to the United States and the hundreds of followers clamoring for one last glimpse of their deposed hero. The UNIA never recovered from Garvey's deportation, and, combined with other setbacks, it ceased to be the dominant force it once was. Garvey lived out the majority of his remaining years in London, where he died on June 10, 1940. Devoted black veterans surely mourned his passing and the fracturing of the UNIA. But they could take comfort in the fact that the remarkable growth and success of the organization owed much to their participation and legacy in the war.[139]

THE INTENSE BURST OF black militancy and radical activity immediately following the First World War constitutes a unique chapter in African American history. The New Negro movement did not simply represent a fleeting moment in the larger context of black struggles for racial justice, nor did the culturalism of the Harlem Renaissance overshadow its radical political dimensions. Similarly, the activism and political consciousness of many veterans did not disappear during the interwar years and beyond. Some effectively fused politics and art; many continued to play an active role in various organizations that remained viable beyond the 1920s; others used their immediate postwar experiences as motivation to improve the material quality of their lives by acquiring an advanced education, starting a business, or merely maintaining steady employment. Undeniably, however, veterans who participated in the New Negro movement developed a strong racial consciousness and heightened appreciation for the potential of both individual acts of resistance and collective organization to challenge white supremacy and hold the nation accountable for its civic obligations to black people. African American veterans laid a crucial foundation for future generations of freedom fighters with their participation in the New Negro movement, a foundation reflective of their desire for true democracy.

I feel I have a history that I am proud of which is worth while to know.

—Beverly Branch Pollard, Co. G, 367th Infantry Regiment

LEST WE FORGET

The War and African American Soldiers in History and Memory

Paris, July 14, 1919. It was a Bastille Day like no other before it. On this, the most meaningful of national holidays, France celebrated the end of the war and the rebirth of a nation scarred by four years of bloodshed and destruction. French citizens, men and women, the young and the old, soldiers and civilians, had begun pouring into Paris from the outlying provinces days in advance of the celebration. By the morning of the 14th, some two million visitors had swelled the city's population. At 8:12 A.M., the sound of trumpets marked the beginning of the parade from Porte Maillot. Thousands of France's wounded and maimed soldiers, some in wheelchairs, others on crutches, led the procession down the Champs-Elysées, underneath the Arc de Triomphe, and toward the Place de la Concorde. They were followed by the nation's two heroes of the war, Allied Supreme Commander Ferdinand Foch and Marshal Joseph Joffre. The crowd cheered in appreciation of the presence of troops from the various Allied countries—the British and their colonial servicemen, the Italians, the Japanese, the Portuguese, and others. Predictably, they saved their most enthusiastic response for France's soldiers, who concluded the parade.[1] The French contingent included the Algerian and Senegalese *tirailleurs*, who had so distinguished themselves on the battlefield and earned the respect of the nation. It was a momentous day, overflowing with the raw emotional memories of the war, and the entire Allied world was present—all except for African American servicemen.

The United States had a prominent presence in the victory parade. American General John Pershing, displaying his personal flag for the first time, rode triumphantly directly behind Foch and Joffre. A select group of American generals and officers accompanied Pershing, followed by roughly fifteen hundred

American soldiers, comprising men selected from various regiments of the AEF.[2] Perhaps the absence of black servicemen should not have come as a great surprise. After all, white officers like Colonel Allen Greer of the Ninety-second Division had wasted little time in smearing the record of African American combat troops and officers, laying the groundwork for a systematic purge of African Americans from the nation's military. In the *Panthéon de la Guerre*, the grand French mural depicting in panorama the war's central participants and completed only three weeks before the November 11, 1918, armistice, artists represented France's African colonial soldiers, but America's black troops, upon the explicit request of the War Department, remained noticeably absent.[3] In the consecration of this first major site of remembrance, African American soldiers had no place. Their exclusion went beyond mere symbolic representation.. By the time of the victory parade, the Ninety-second and Ninety-third Divisions had been hastily shipped home, leaving no black combat troops in France. Thousands of black stevedores, pioneer infantrymen, and other service troops still remained for Pershing to include in the representative assemblage of America's forces. But they would not and, for military decision makers, could not represent the United States and its victorious army before the rest of the world. Therefore, the marching forces of the AEF in arguably the most significant event of the immediate postwar period remained lily white. The marginalization of African American troops spoke volumes to how Woodrow Wilson, the War Department, and much of white America envisioned a similarly Jim Crowed historical memory of the war and black participation in it.

The historical memory of the war became a field of battle following the armistice. Soldiers and civilians alike struggled to make sense of the war, their place in it, and its impact on their lives and identities. In France, Great Britain, and Germany, the memorialization of the war and its victims became a dominant feature of public culture and everyday life.[4] In contrast, American historical memory of the war has been much more ephemeral, due in large part to the short duration of United States' military involvement, the comparatively small loss of life, and its ambiguous political benefits.[5] Perception of the First World War as a forgotten moment has likewise influenced contemporary historiographical considerations of African American historical memory of the conflict and its aftermath. As the war receded in public consciousness, so the story goes, its legacy and memory for most black people became one of disillusionment and remorse at the failure of the war to live up to its lofty democratic ideals.[6] Moreover, the idea of a lost historical memory of the black war experience has been attributed to the self-conscious decision of black veterans themselves to purge the troubling memory of the war from their collective consciousness.[7]

Assessments of the place of African Americans in World War I as somehow being lost or forgotten were due in no small part to the concerted efforts of racist military officials to construct a master historical narrative and collective national memory of the war that minimized the contributions of black servicemen and deemed their use as a failed experiment. The demeaning accounts of African American soldiers and officers that characterized the "official" memory of the war reflected the use of memory, rooted in relations of power and hierarchy, as a tool of maintaining social and political structures of dominance. In the context of white supremacist backlash following the war, the attempted exclusion of African Americans from a national memory of the war complemented larger attempts to marginalize African Americans as citizens from the polity.[8] The memory of the war, however, was contested terrain. Black people's memories sharply contrasted with those of white military officials, offering a rival account of the war. African Americans consciously pushed back against efforts to distort the legacy of their troops, fully aware of the political stakes associated with the memory of the conflict and black participation in it. Additionally, numerous former servicemen, who saw themselves as contributors to a seminal historical moment, actively sought to preserve and share memories of their experiences.[9] African Americans adopted multiple strategies to articulate a range of countermemories of the war, competing versions of the past, embedded in how African Americans, and black soldiers themselves, lived through and survived the tumultuous years of the war era.[10]

The attempted creation and dissemination of a dominant black countermemory of the war reflected the contentious relationship between history and memory. Black intellectuals such as Emmett Scott, Kelly Miller, and W. E. B. Du Bois responded to the charges of white military officials with their own politics of historical memory, employing "history" as an authoritative practice to assert the patriotic service of black soldiers, their manhood, and their ultimate contribution to the war effort. Their works proved important not only in challenging racist characterizations of black soldiers and officers but also in laying a foundation for future reconsiderations of the place of black people in the war. But engaging in this politics of historical memory also revealed the limitations of written history, and its strategic use, to acknowledge the presence and legitimacy of alternate memories of the war, as well as the human complexity of African American soldiers. A singular collective memory of the black war experience did not exist, despite the attempts of black "historians" to create one.[11] Moreover, African American soldiers constituted more than flat symbols of patriotism and sacrifice. A number of black veterans, as well as other writers who had intimate familiarity with black troops during the war, made this very point, producing written accounts that explicitly eschewed history and privileged memory as a means of demonstrating the human complexity of African American servicemen.

These various approaches reflected how African Americans created and used a diverse range of sites of memory to convey the legacy of the war and express its various meanings.[12] Beyond formal written accounts of the black war experience, memories of the war resonated throughout interwar African American culture, a space conducive to a more democratic expression of memory than official history.[13] In the music, paintings, and literature of the era, black artists of the New Negro movement expressed different memories of the war using different genres, revealing a multivocality characteristic of African American memories of the war more broadly.[14] Some African American veterans even took advantage of the arts to express their memories of the war in ways that were at once political but also highly personal. African Americans did not forget about the war. Its legacy remained vitally important, for individual black veterans, for the race, and for the future of the nation. On the at-times treacherous terrain of memory, African Americans continued to battle over just what this legacy entailed.

WARS ARE WAGED TWICE, first on the battlefield, and then in history. How a conflict is memorialized, how its participants are portrayed in history, how its "winners," "losers," and the honor of their respective causes are constructed, hold just as much, if not more, significance, than formal victory.[15] Even in defeat or disgrace, it is possible through history to shape how the nation remembers war—its collective memory—a process of contention and legitimization reflecting the sociopolitical dynamics of power and authority at a particular historical moment.[16] While the Confederacy may not have won the Civil War, for example, its descendants nevertheless waged a highly effective battle through history to manipulate the memory and meaning of the war, transforming it from a struggle about the future of black people into one between differing, albeit noble conceptions of the American nation.[17] Indeed, throughout American history, the creation and re-creation of historical narratives from the raw materials of memory have been central to the ways in which participants in war, soldiers and civilians alike, make sense of their place in a given conflict and ultimately construct their sense of individual and collective national identity.

Such was the case for African Americans in the wake of the First World War. In the days, months, and years following the war, the experience of African American soldiers emerged as a popular subject of study and literary production. African American intellectuals and activists, from a broad ideological spectrum and range of experiences, understood with prescient clarity that how the nation remembered and etched into history the record of black soldiers would ultimately determine the legacy of the conflict and its potential transformative impact on the status, future and present, of African Americans in the body politic.

Many of the first works in the nascent field of African American history, also written with a sense of immediacy, centered on the exploits of black people in the nation's wars. In 1887 George Washington Williams, a veteran of the Civil War and widely acknowledged as the first professional historian of the black experience, wrote *History of the Negro Troops in the War of Rebellion, 1861–1865*. The same year, Joseph T. Wilson, another veteran, published *Black Phalanx*, a study of African American soldiers in the American War of Independence and the Civil War, while the pioneering self-trained historian John Edward Bruce published a six-part series on the history of African American soldiers in the *Cleveland Gazette* in February and March of 1887.[18] Black writers also addressed the Spanish-Cuban-American War and the battlefield heroics of the "Buffalo Soldiers."[19] Booker T. Washington, in his 1900 book *A New Negro for a New Century*, gave significant attention to African American participation in the recently concluded war. Rooted in the struggle for black social and political rights in the late nineteenth and early twentieth centuries, these texts shared a similar concern with demonstrating the patriotism and historical sacrifice of African Americans, willing to risk their lives in defense of the nation, even when denied effective citizenship. More specifically, African American soldiers functioned for these authors as embodiments of a reconstructed vision of black manhood, unhyphenated Americanism, and collective racial progress. This trope shaped how a host of black intellectuals, activists, and lay writers viewed black participation in the World War, its historical meaning, and its significance to the social and political destiny of the race.[20]

Having asserted himself as the most ardent defender of African American soldiers and their legacy, W. E. B. Du Bois eagerly anticipated his NAACP-sponsored "authentic, scientific and definitive" World War I study joining this proud historiographic tradition. As announced in the December 1918 issue of the *Crisis*, Du Bois envisioned the three-volume project overseen by an editorial board, headed by himself, and composed of a diverse collection of African American intellectuals, political figures, and social leaders.[21] His desired list included luminous names such as George E. Haynes, director of Negro Economics in the United States Department of Labor, Colonel Charles Young,

Jesse E. Moorland, Eva Bowles of the YMCA, Atlanta University president John Hope, Howard University educator Kelly Miller, and fellow historian Benjamin Brawley.[22]

Two names, however, topped Du Bois's list: Carter G. Woodson and Emmett J. Scott. Deeming their participation crucial to the success of the study, Du Bois made securing commitments from both men his first priority. He immediately ran into difficulties. In late October and early November 1918, Woodson and Du Bois engaged in a heated exchange of letters regarding the project and Woodson's envisioned role. In a note responding to Du Bois's invitation, Woodson insisted that he "receive full credit for all of the work," considering anything less "both dishonorable and foolish."[23] While undoubtedly annoyed by Woodson's audacity, Du Bois attempted to stay cordial, suggesting various proposals to bridge their impasse.[24] Woodson remained defiant. He continued to demand complete editorial control, relenting on the condition that the NAACP provide an exorbitant salary of $2,500, supplemented by defrayed research expenses. With this final affront, Du Bois reached his breaking point and did not reply to Woodson's offer.[25] Despite Du Bois's respect for Woodson as the second Ph.D. recipient in history from Harvard and founder of the Association for the Study of Negro Life and History, their incompatible personalities and characteristic stubbornness precluded a close relationship, working or otherwise.[26] A partnership with his longtime Tuskegee adversary Emmett Scott on the war history was even more remote. On November 3, 1918, Du Bois, along with James Weldon Johnson, met with Scott to discuss the possibility of a common postwar political agenda. At the meeting, Du Bois broached the idea of the study and the editorial board to Scott, who informed Du Bois of his intentions to write his own history of the war.[27] Unconvinced, Du Bois again requested Scott's cooperation, which Scott not surprisingly rejected, although amicably, for a second time.[28]

The intense back and forth between Du Bois, Woodson, and Scott revealed the high political and intellectual stakes in claiming the authorial rights to the memory of black soldiers in the war. The tensions between Du Bois and Woodson were primarily academic in nature, as two of the country's leading scholars jockeyed for position as the historical spokesman for African American soldiers. Du Bois's dealings with Emmett Scott, on the other hand, had political undertones. Having little intellectual respect for Scott, Du Bois nevertheless realized that his book would potentially increase his national clout and stature in the eyes of black servicemen in particular.

Unable to make use of their scholarly and political legitimacy, Du Bois instead resorted to sullying the reputations of Woodson and Scott with the NAACP and discrediting them as honorable representatives of black soldiers' historical interests. In a November 16, 1918, memo to the NAACP board of directors updating them on the status of the project, Du Bois attached Emmett Scott's final rejection, remarking somewhat disingenuously, "I have no desire at all to interfere with Mr. Scott's plans, or wishes, but he has been to say the least, lacking in frankness in going ahead with a plan almost identical with that of the N.A.A.C.P., after promising at least, cooperation." "Mr. Woodson," Du Bois noted, "has also apparently acted in the same ungenerous manner." Although Du Bois could not contest the pedigree of his fellow Harvard Ph.D. recipient, he had no qualms in dismissing Booker T. Washington's former secretary, casually noting with trademark elitism, "Mr. Scott is not a historian or a trained writer." The history of the war, Du Bois insinuated, was too important a subject to be entrusted in the hands of amateurs, especially ones with competing political agendas. He therefore determined to press ahead with the project, suggesting "that my contribution to the history be confined to the French side, and that I make a trip to France to collect this matter, and to do what I can at the Peace Conference for the African Colonies."[29]

During his fateful postwar sojourn to France, Du Bois, motivated by the heart-wrenching testimonies of African American soldiers, wasted little time in putting pen to paper. In February 1919 he composed a "preliminary and tentative foreword" to the larger "scientific and exhaustive" history titled "The Black Man in the Revolution of 1914–1918," which appeared in the following month's *Crisis*. As the highly instructive moniker of his essay reflected, Du Bois viewed the historical phenomenon of war as a hypermasculine engine of potential radical social, political, and economic change. A weakened Europe, an emergent Pan-African consciousness, and the heroic legacy of black military service combined to shape Du Bois's initial view of the war as a revolutionary turning point in the future of peoples of African descent and African Americans in particular.[30] African American servicemen functioned as the harbingers of this transformation and embodiments of a self-conscious black manhood. After a "rapid survey" of the conditions in France, Du Bois reached an unequivocal conclusion: "The black soldier saved civilization in 1914–18." He began by praising France's Senegalese soldiers, noted the role of the black stevedores, and emphasized the praise received by the Ninety-third Division from its French commanders. The Ninety-second Division, in contrast, "went through hell." Du Bois reserved judgment on its performance but made a clear effort to stress the "anti-Negro prejudice" the division and its officers endured and overcame. "The black men never wavered," despite often debilitating treatment. African American soldiers, as Du Bois saw them, proved their manhood, asserted the place of black people in modern civilization, and ultimately helped save the democratic world from looming destruction.[31]

Du Bois further whetted the appetite of readers with the appearance of "An Essay toward a History of the Black Man in the Great War," an article in the June issue of the *Crisis* composed from the materials and information he gathered while in France. Du Bois, as in his earlier précis, emphasized the essential contribution of black soldiers to the war effort, coupled with a stinging exposure of the discrimination they experienced overseas. It was a similarly vindicationist tract, systematically rescuing African American soldiers, their manhood, and the honor of the race from historical obfuscation. Black servicemen both anchored Du Bois's historical vision and steered its course through the turbulent waters of memory. African American troops waged a simultaneous battle against German autocracy and American white racism, forging a unique identity in the process. In the essay, Du Bois substituted the gift of double consciousness with the burden of "double disillusion" experienced by African American soldiers, who had to confront both the "murder, maiming and hatred" of war and the "frank realization" of white America's intractable pathology: "to hate 'niggers.'" France functioned as the crucial intermediary between the two fundamentally undemocratic national poles of Germany and the United States. In juxtaposing "American race hatred," "transported bodily" from the United States, with the "purling sea of French sympathy and kindliness," Du Bois, in meticulous detail and fiery prose, contrasted the U.S. Army's racism with French treatment of African American soldiers, declaring that "there is not a black soldier but who is glad he went,—glad to fight for France, the only real white Democracy."[32] Du Bois praised the black stevedores, glorified the fighting men of the Ninety-third Division, and lamented the unjust fate of his dear friend Charles Young. Unlike in his previous essay, Du Bois now turned his attention squarely to the Ninety-second—the "center of the storm" concerning the performance of black troops—and its much maligned black officers, Du Bois's shining representatives of "talented tenth" manhood. He emphatically demonstrated the debilitating effects of race prejudice on the division, in particular the 368th Infantry Regiment, whose actions in the Meuse-Argonne reflected incompetence and neglect on the part of the regiment's white commanders more so than cowardice by its black officers.[33] With the historical legacy of African American soldiers seemingly hanging in the balance, Du Bois presented both a moving vindication of their service and a testament to their collective courage, resilience, and democratic aspirations.

While impressively researched and written with his trademark poeticism, the essay reflected Du Bois's self-acknowledged limitations of his initial foray into the history of the war. "This, then, is a first attempt at the story of the Hell which war in the fateful years of 1914–1919 meant to Black Folk, and particularly to American Negroes," Du Bois wrote at the onset of the essay. Clearly cognizant of debates within the historical profession concerning the goal of objectivity and the perils of immediacy, he continued, "It is only an attempt, full of the mistakes which nearness to the scene and many necessarily missing facts, such as only time can supply, combine to foil in part. And yet, written now in the heat of strong memories and in the place of skulls, it contains truth which cold delay can never alter or bring back."[34] Du Bois's methodological rumination begged the question, what did it mean to publish a book, only months following the signing of the armistice, with the physical and mental wounds of the war still raw, the memories of the conflict still simmering, and call it "history"? Was the "cold delay" of objective scholarly historicism compatible with the inherently subjective "heat" of individual and collective memory? This question did not singularly apply to African American intellectuals like Du Bois, or even the United States, for that matter. On both sides of the Atlantic, scholars produced a number of "histories" of the recently concluded war, while internally questioning their abilities to be objective. Commercial demand and the concomitant desire of writers to financially capitalize on the war moment in part fueled the rush to publish the history of black soldiers. However, the development of an early historiography more aptly reflected the symbolic significance of black soldiers to the political future of the race, and how a number of authors attempted to elevate their place in the postwar hierarchy of racial leadership by appropriating this symbolism and asserting themselves as the authoritative "historian" of the war and protector of African American soldiers' historical legacy.

Three books of note, all presented as "histories" of black participation in the war, appeared in 1919. W. Allison Sweeny, a contributing editor to the *Chicago Defender*, published *A History of the American Negro in the Great World War*. "It is a most notable publication, quite worthy to be draped in the robes that distinguishes History from narrative," read a legitimizing statement in the book's preface, imbuing the study of history with almost regal significance.[35] Relying overwhelmingly on press reports and a limited number of official documents, Sweeny glorified the loyalty, patriotism, and heroism of African Americans, and black soldiers specifically, while making little mention of the systemic racial discrimination practiced by the military.[36] On the heels of Sweeny's tome appeared Kelly Miller's *Authentic History of the Negro in the World War*. As professor of sociology and dean of the College of Arts and Sciences at Howard University, Kelly Miller distinguished himself as an accomplished scholar, effective administrator, and prolific writer on various aspects of the race question.[37] Despite having devoted considerable intellectual energy during the war to its racial politics, Miller produced a text curiously devoid of any substantive discussion of African American soldiers, as the majority of the book's twenty-two chapters focused on the European origins and specifics of the conflict. Moreover, the three chapters that do concern themselves with black participation in the war are rife with inaccuracies.[38] Carter G. Woodson in the *Journal of Negro History* went so far as to describe Miller's book as of "dubious authorship."[39]

Emmett J. Scott thus had a very low scholarly threshold to meet with the publication of his book, *Scott's Official History of the American Negro in the World War*. The book received powerful endorsements, with preface comments from Newton D. Baker, John J. Pershing, and former president Theodore Roosevelt. Offering a detailed chronology, statistics, individual unit records, and personal anecdotes, Scott could be proud of his work. Having ready access to War Department documents and direct correspondence with military officials and soldiers alike, he produced an informative, if self-flattering book, stressing the faithful service of African American troops and the larger contribution of African Americans, an "ever-loyal racial group," to the war effort.[40]

Varying in quality and scope, the histories of Sweeney, Miller, and Scott, along with their similar titles and abundant number of photographs, shared two significant characteristics. The first is the positioning of the authors in the text, who are as much a part of the book as African American soldiers. In the case of Miller and Scott, their names appear before "Negro" in the book's title, reflecting a self-interested positioning of their authorial selves as speaking on the behalf of the race. More specifically, all three writers assert their "authentic" and "official" voice in representing African American servicemen and their legacy. Scott is perhaps most flagrant in this regard, as he makes a cognizant effort to demonstrate the value and effectiveness of his work in the War Department, a preemptive strike of sorts against mounting criticisms of his performance. Second, and most glaring, black soldiers are explicitly and exclusively constructed as symbols of African American loyalty and patriotism. Even in the face of virulent racial discrimination, black soldiers distinguished themselves and epitomized unhyphenated American nationalism. Sweeney makes virtually no mention of racial discrimination in his book, going so far as to exalt Woodrow Wilson as the nation's greatest president next to Abraham Lincoln and George Washington.[41] Scott acknowledges that racism did exist but that black soldiers overcame it and fulfilled their civic obligation without regret or bitterness. In chapter 30 he poses the pressing question of the moment: "Did the Negro Soldier Get a Square Deal?" Proclaiming, ironically, that evasion of this question "would be unworthy of an honest historian whose duty it is to chronicle facts," Scott reaches the conclusion that, "while the victim of racial discrimination and injustice," the black soldier, "by his demonstrated loyalty, valor, and efficiency," unquestionably "*proved his right to be granted a fuller measure of justice, respect, opportunity, and fair play in time of peace!*"[42]

This romanticized portrayal of the black experience in the war had the intended purpose of demonstrating the incontrovertible fitness of African Americans for full inclusion into the American body politic and their worth as equal citizens. But this was not simply a case of amateur historians failing to adhere to scientific standards of objectivity and historical methodology. In fact, professional American historians during the war all but abandoned the chimerical goal of objectivity in lieu of employing history as propaganda to support the war effort by denigrating German culture and extolling American moral and political superiority.[43] History, in this context was explicitly political, and black writers used African American soldiers and their record to advance the mutually intertwined causes of racial uplift and the expansion of American democracy.

At least one former soldier was less than impressed by these efforts. Veteran William N. Colson of the *Messenger* published a scathing review of all three books under the acerbic title "Shoddyism Called History." He began the essay with a perceptively critical reflection on the purposes and limitations of history as an intellectual practice, ultimately viewing it as inherently flawed. However, in Colson's estimation, the works of Sweeny, Miller, and Scott did not even merit consideration in this context because they were "not, in fact, histories at all," but "picture books, containing rambling narratives of some of the principle experiences of the Negro in the great war, at home and abroad." He admonished all three men for their naive "praise of the loyalty of the Negro, whatever the attitude of the government," and accused them of jointly committing "the fallacy of assuming that liberty and freedom are the inevitable rewards of bearing arms in war time."

Colson then thoroughly examined each text and took its respective author to task. He dismissed Sweeny's "sentimental" and "hyperbolic" text as reflective of the fact that he had "no conception whatever of reconstruction and the new Negro" and accused Miller of "a rather bold piece of trickery" by even including the word "Negro" in the title of his book, causing "his fast waning reputation great harm." Colson saved his harshest criticism for Emmett Scott, an implicit acknowledgment of the superior quality of the former Tuskegee secretary's book. In a ruthless denunciation, Colson wrote, "Emmett J. Scott, in seeking to vindicate himself, has exhibited his own servility—how he was recommended for his position by the basest of Negro traitors, Robert Russa Moton, and how acceptable he was to the reactionary forces of the nation." Colson viewed the book as an unforgivable misrepresentation of the truth regarding the experience of black soldiers and officers, asserting that African American servicemen found themselves "in a worse plight at the end of the war than when the author took up his position as special assistant to Secretary Baker." Colson clearly had a bone to pick. The tone of the review is not surprising considering the politics of the *Messenger*, which regularly assailed Scott, Miller, and other bourgeois race spokesmen. Such a damning critique, however, would not have meant as much had it not come from a veteran and former officer. Just as in his earlier *Messenger* essays, which vividly exposed the racism of the army and its particularly egregious treatment of African American officers like himself, Colson's review was informed by his radicalism but most notably his own painful memories of the war. Having lived through the crucible of combat and American white supremacy in the army, Colson felt empowered to challenge the legitimacy of Sweeny, Miller, and Scott and assert that returned soldiers had both the ability and responsibility to speak for themselves. He fittingly ended his review by emphatically stating, "A history of the Negro in the recent war is yet to be written."[44]

Colson may not have read the *Complete History of the Colored Soldiers in the World War*, a book authored by five African American veterans, but he would have likely disparaged it as well. John A. Jamieson, a sergeant in the 369th Infantry Regiment and four other veterans of the Ninety-second and Ninety-third Divisions pieced together the book, hastily published in 1919 with the instructive subtitle, *Authentic Story of the Greatest War of Civilized Times and What the Colored Man Did to Uphold Democracy and Liberty*.[45] The recently returned soldiers offered their book as history, "complete" and "authentic," a decision that provided them with an authorial legitimacy they may not have otherwise earned if they presented their narrative as a collection of personal reflections. Nevertheless, memory has an important function in the book and, as the authors asserted, it is their memories as soldiers that made it unique. While in France they determined that "our people throughout the country should have a true history of what our boys have done right from we men who went through every part of the war." This desire separated their history from others written by African American civilians that "contain only official reports" and do not reveal "the hardships, and privations, nor how the men fought individually."[46] In this sense, the book offered a welcome counterbalance to the histories of Scott, Sweeny, and Miller by privileging the firsthand experiences of African American soldiers themselves.

But like other "histories" produced in the immediate aftermath of the war, the work of Jamieson and his comrades is far from objective and possessed an unmistakable political goal. They unabashedly construct black troops as stalwart patriots who successfully demonstrated their fundamental Americanness. In seven chapters, using personal anecdotes and laudatory statements by French and American military officials, the authors highlight the experiences of black troops, focusing predominantly on the battlefield accomplishments of the Ninety-second and Ninety-third Divisions. Perhaps most glaring is the omission of any mention of racial discrimination practiced against African American troops. When "race superiority" is discussed, Germany stands as the lone national culprit. In castigating Germany, they implicitly criticize American white supremacists as unpatriotic, equating "Race prejudice" with "Germanism."[47] However, these veterans had no intentions of presenting themselves, and constructing their fellow black soldiers, as anything but loyal, one-hundred-percent Americans. To this end, they even take unnamed black spokespersons to task for their endorsement of "self-segregation," making them as much to blame for the legitimization of Jim Crow as white racists.[48] African American soldiers had proved beyond any doubt their fidelity to the nation and, through their service, exposed the irrelevance of the color line. Confident of having etched a triumphant, albeit selective, memory of their service into the annals of history, Jamieson and his fellow veterans closed their book with a ringing pronouncement: "WE ARE FIGHTING TODAY FOR AND AS ONE AMERICAN PEOPLE, ONE AND INSEPARABLE, NOW AND FOREVER!"[49]

Veteran Walker H. Jordan also desired to voice his memories of the war, but free from the constraining filter of history. *With "Old Eph" in the Army (Not a History): A Simple Treatise on the Human Side of the Colored Soldier*, written in 1920, is one of the few individual memoirs published by an African American veteran.[50] Jordan served as an officer in the 351st Field Artillery Regiment of the Ninety-second Division. He tells the story of the regiment, from its training at Camp Meade to its journey across the Atlantic, arrival in Brest, interactions with the French, and combat engagement near Metz. In doing so, Jordan sheds light on the inner thoughts, yearnings, hopes, fears, and frustrations that motivated African American soldiers and shaped their memories of the war, beginning with their initial response to the draft to their return to the United States following the armistice. With this goal, Jordan explicitly states that his book is "not a history" and offers a subtle but undeniable critique of history, writing that "it is generally believed that in the necessarily broad scope of the Historian, with his methodological search for statistics and stereotyped formula for objectives and achievements, much of the charm of the intimate and personal is obscured."

Jordan, as author and conveyor of a particular memory of the war shaped by class and gender, aimed to "illuminate the human side of the Colored Fighter," something history, in his opinion, could not adequately accomplish.[51]

Jordan's book at times mirrors the vindicationist tone of other "histories" by extolling the patriotism and heroic service of African American soldiers. But Jordan moves beyond constructing black troops solely as symbolic embodiments of black citizenship by stressing the centrality of their race consciousness and battles with white supremacy. In appropriating the racial slur "old eph" as a term of endearment and using it to describe African American soldiers, Jordan challenges the power of white racism and its ability to determine black racial identity. He therefore places race at the center of how African American soldiers viewed themselves and their experience, destabilizing the presence of American nationalism, which dominates the works of his contemporaries. Jordan characterizes the war as a "test of social equality" and provides several anecdotal examples of how the U.S Army, in its treatment of African American servicemen, sorely failed to meet this standard.[52] France offered a liberating respite, causing Jordan to wonder, "Why should this most damnable of all human curses—Prejudice—follow us there and attempt to breathe the stench of hate in the garden where the fair flowers of trust and friendship were bursting to blossom?"[53] His personal accounts, enhanced by his evocative prose, have the desired effect of demonstrating the human costs of the racial discrimination black troops endured. Jordan's perspective on race and his broader memory of the war, however, are circumscribed by his bourgeois class consciousness and experience as an officer. He asserts the price of racism was highest for black officers, like himself. Jordan makes his case in a moving chapter devoted to defending the competency and manhood of African American officers in the Ninety-second Division. In doing so, he again takes issue with the writing of history, voicing his skepticism that "current History" could not present a truthful record because "so few of the works on the matter are from the pens of those best qualified by actual contact and experience to do exact justice."[54]

Both William Colson and Walker Jordan may have looked somewhat more approvingly on subsequent books written by individuals who in fact had direct personal contact with African American soldiers during the war and eschewed the bold claims of their predecessors in producing "official" histories of the black war experience. In 1923 Hampton Institute educator Charles Williams published *Sidelights on Negro Soldiers*, based on his experiences investigating conditions of black soldiers under the auspices of the Federal Council of Churches and the Phelps-Stokes Fund.[55] The book, whose title reflected a conscious distancing from history, ironically opens with a glowing preface from

Benjamin Brawly, the distinguished African American historian. "Mr. Williams, it will be observed, has not undertaken to write a history of Negro soldiers in the war," Brawly notes approvingly. He adds that Williams's *Sidelights*, "more unpretentious than a history," proved "of more interest than many a formal work," a not so subtle dig at the books of Sweeny, Miller, and Scott, and offered "a vital contribution to the social history of the Negro people in America."[56] By contemporary standards, Williams's book would rightly be categorized as a social history, as he provides an intimate glimpse into the camp life and everyday activities of black servicemen, as well as the religious, educational, and mental effects of the war on their identities. Driven by his memory, Williams's *Sidelights* conveys a humanity that earlier "histories" of black soldiers sorely lacked. Nevertheless, his book reflects the racial and gender ideological currents of his time. His detailing of racial discrimination is counterbalanced with uncritical praise of the heroism, loyalty, and patriotism of black soldiers, and the race as a whole. Williams is likewise wedded to uplift notions of manhood and womanhood, most prominently evidenced by a chapter titled, "The Lure of the Uniform," examining the "problem" of the black girl in the context of wartime efforts to regulate the moral behavior of black women, while the reformation of black manhood, in the form of the black soldier, is approached in a discernibly less problematic fashion.

Williams would have benefited from a more thoughtful reading of *Two Colored Women with the A.E.F.*, written in 1920 by YMCA secretaries Addie Hunton and Kathryn Johnson. Hunton and Johnson, asserting the place of African American women as both historical and literary agents, position themselves in direct opposition to their male counterparts and challenge their presumptuousness, writing that they had "no desire to attain to an authentic history."[57] Instead, Hunton and Johnson are primarily concerned with the "life and spirit" of black troops and consciously invoke memory to convey and honor their experiences. They write in the book's foreword, "Battle scenes and war adventures were ended, but the memory was yet deeply poignant, and often silences revealed the depths of experiences beyond the power of all words. Because of all this, we strive to humbly recount the heart throbs of our heroes." As such, Hunton and Johnson, eschewing chronology, draw from the rich resources of their individual and shared memories to construct a moving narrative of their time overseas and that of the African American servicemen, overwhelmingly SOS troops, they interacted with. Their gender consciousness informs their racial consciousness, infuses the text, and shapes their narrative. The book is dedicated to "the women of our race, who gave so trustingly and courageously the strength of their young manhood to suffer and to die for the cause of freedom."

Having internalized an ethos of racial motherhood, Hunton and Johnson saw themselves, respectively, as the "trusted guardian" of black soldiers, as well as ambassadors of black womanhood, to "represent in France the womanhood of our race in America—those fine mothers, wives, sisters and friends who so courageously gave the very flower of their young manhood to face the ravages of war." For this reason, it was their duty to "make an effort to interpret with womanly comprehension the loyalty and bravery of their men," which they accomplish with compassion and humility.[58]

But what of Du Bois and his highly anticipated history of the war? The appearance of so many books must have surely stoked Du Bois's competitive fires. Where, then, was Du Bois's much-touted intervention?

Exploring this question necessitates returning to the stunning May 1919 edition of the *Crisis*. In a brief editorial titled "History," Du Bois starkly presented what was at stake, writing, "Most American Negroes do not realize that the imperative duty of the moment is to fix in history the status of our Negro troops. Already subtle influences are preparing a fatal attack. It is repeated openly among influential persons: 'The black laborers did well—the black privates can fight—but the Negro officer is a failure.' This is not true and the facts exist to disprove it, but they must be marshaled with historical vision and scientific accuracy."[59] Du Bois, like a general providing orders to his troops, had a clear plan for how to mobilize the resources of history and memory for the purposes of his study and the larger vindication of the race. The "Documents of the War" exposé concluded with an explicit request: "Will every Negro officer and soldier who reads these documents make himself a committee of one to see that the Editor of The Crisis receives documents, diaries and information such as will enable The Crisis history of the war to be complete, true and unanswerable?"[60] The May 1919 *Crisis* was thus not only a searing indictment of the War Department's racist policies toward African American soldiers but also a historical call to action, a recruitment for returned servicemen to invest their memories of the war in Du Bois and his study.

Heeding Du Bois's request, current and former soldiers flooded the office of the *Crisis* with letters, personal testimonies, memoirs, and official records. The documents they provided constituted the bulk of Du Bois's research materials for the World War I study. Having earned the trust of many black servicemen through his wartime advocacy and postwar writings, Du Bois actively solicited materials for the manuscript, employing former soldiers as proxy research assistants. African American veterans, however, did not enter into their relationship with Du Bois blindly and without clear reciprocal expectations. The soldiers who wrote and sent information to Du Bois fully anticipated the good doctor accurately representing their memories of the war, refuting disparaging characterizations of their service, and ultimately rescuing their legacy. Veterans such as Clarence Lee, deeply concerned with the future historical depiction of African American soldiers like himself, informed Du Bois that since his return from France he had collected all literature pertaining to black participation in the war, good and bad, by both black and white authors. He complimented Du Bois in his efforts to create a history of the war from their perspective, writing, "As compared with you, I believe none have been more concise, more exact in expression of that which really took place in the lives of the Negro soldiers in France."[61] Similarly, De Haven Hinkson, a physician from Philadelphia and former soldier in the Ninety-second Division, congratulated Du Bois on the May *Crisis*, offered his support and assistance for the study, and encouraged Du Bois to continue his "good work," emphasizing that he had the support of "all sensible and non-cringing colored Americans."[62] Other soldiers envisioned Du Bois adopting a much more explicitly vindicationist position in his war history. Samuel Kent, a former corporal in the 365th Infantry wrote to Du Bois, stating, "I sincerely urge that in composing the new history, which we are eagerly awaiting, that you will put special emphasis on the heroism and bravery of our colored officers, for they are unequalled for the time and chance they were given to make good."[63]

While anxious to engage in the production of historical memory, most of the veterans, and officers in particular, who wrote to Du Bois quite simply welcomed the opportunity to vent their pent-up frustrations. These men, echoing William Colson in his *Messenger* book review, had no use for "histories" of the war that sugarcoated their experiences. Many of their letters seethed with anger. Du Bois received a note from Louis Pontlock, a former sergeant in the disgraced 368th Infantry Regiment, who recounted in vivid detail the discrimination he and his fellow officers endured while overseas. "In summing up what I have said, to put it all in a nutshell," Pontlock thundered, "*The American Negro soldier in France was treated with the same contempt and undemocratic spirit as the American Negro citizens is treated in the United States.*"[64] A similarly irate black lieutenant of the Ninety-second Division wrote to Du Bois after the war, proclaiming, "If there was ever a hell on earth the officers of the 92nd Division lived in it for eight months. We only hope that Justice will awaken from her long sleep and that a just measure will be meted out to all the perpetrators of the crimes for the 92nd. The names of Greer and the sychophant Ballou will ever live in history among the other names of infamous traitors to a race. God grant 'an eye for an eye!'"[65] The history of the war, as these enraged veterans determined, could not simply be about vindication but also had to render judgment on American white supremacy. They hoped Du Bois's book would at least be a step in this direction.

Despite the encouragement and enthusiastic support of African American veterans, the odds that Du Bois would ever complete his war history became increasingly slim as the years passed. *Darkwater* appeared in 1920, and monthly essays and editorials continued to highlight the *Crisis*. But the much-ballyhooed World War I study was nowhere to be seen. Du Bois, however, never conceded to abandoning the project in written form, his pride clearly preventing him from doing so. Although lacking formal research assistants and financial support of any kind, Du Bois remained confident that the book would eventually see the light of day. In the January 1924 edition of the *Crisis*, Du Bois published the study's preliminary first chapter, "Interpretations," under the heading "The Black Man and the Wounded World," the first public pronouncement of the project's new title.[66] The revised title of the book from "The Negro in the Revolution of the Twentieth Century" to "The Black Man and the Wounded World" reflected Du Bois's transformed perception of the war and its historical legacy. Domestically, the "Red Summer" of 1919 and, globally, the entrenchment of European imperialism and continued exploitation of African peoples soured him to any positive outcome of the war for black people. He thus no longer conceived of the war as a revolutionary moment but instead constructed it as the darkest chapter in the history of the modern world.[67]

Du Bois occasionally returned to "The Black Man and the Wounded World" over the next twelve years, devoting most of his energies to securing much-needed funding for the dormant project. During the late 1920s and early 1930s, nearly every major philanthropic foundation and publishing house received an inquiry from Du Bois regarding the possibility of providing the necessary financial assistance to finally put the history and its troublesome memory behind him.[68] He even floated the idea to Alfred Harcourt in 1931 of publishing "The Black Man and the Wounded World" as a follow-up volume to *Black Reconstruction*.[69] By 1936, however, Du Bois resigned himself to the fact that his manuscript, consisting at the time of an astonishing 808 pages of twenty-one loosely arranged chapters, the majority most likely written in the years immediately following the war, would never reach the public.

How was it that Du Bois, a scholar and historian of incomparable distinction and sense of purpose, failed to complete a project into which he invested so much time and energy? Clearly, something deeper and more prohibiting than his always busy schedule and a lack of financial support accounts for his inability to bring "The Black Man and the Wounded World" to fruition. Du

Bois himself provided a glimpse into this quandary when he wrote in his 1940 semiautobiography *Dusk of Dawn*, "In my effort to reconstruct in memory my thought and the fight of the National Association for the Advancement of Colored People during the World War, I have difficulty in thinking clearly."[70] This striking statement, coming from a master creator of African American history and countermemory through his various essays, editorials, and books, attests to Du Bois's inability both to find positive meaning in the war and to reconcile the tensions between history and the traumas of his individual memory.[71] While sharing the general mood of disillusionment expressed by American historians after the war, Du Bois possessed a cynicism that was both deeply personal and political. He remained scarred by the intense criticism he endured as a result of the "Close Ranks" controversy and struggled to come to terms with his moral equivocation in supporting the Allied war effort. While clinging to the idealism of his prowar stance, Du Bois nevertheless acknowledged that the war failed to have the desired effect of increasing African American social and political rights, causing him to describe the conflict in the opening chapter of the "Wounded World" manuscript as "a Scourge, an Evil, a retrogression to Barbarism, a waste, a wholesale murder."

Du Bois remained hesitant, however, to completely admit his personal error in supporting the war. He asserted in the manuscript that during its brief but important involvement, the United States momentarily lived up to its creed as the embodiment of democracy, that for this moment the two warring ideals he famously articulated in *The Souls of Black Folk* were one.[72] "The moment passed and is gone, but thank God that it came once," Du Bois wistfully wrote in chapter 8 of the manuscript, titled "The Challenge." "The war that brought slavery to most men (and indeed in the end to us) thus brought to some of us a new vision of freedom."[73] He did not go so far as to apologize for his seeming shortsightedness, reasoning that the desire for true American citizenship made the race, himself included, go temporarily mad, a madness that was not completely disheartening and perhaps, on an existential level, even liberating. Du Bois later wrote in his autobiography, "I felt for a moment as the war progressed that I could be without reservation a patriotic American," and in *Dusk of Dawn* he described himself as becoming "nearer to feeling myself a real and full American than ever before or since."[74] This internal grappling with the meaning of his identity as an American and a person of African descent, as a product of both Western civilization and the African diaspora, effectively prevented Du Bois from mustering the intellectual and moral strength necessary to complete "The Black Man and the Wounded World." The traumatic memory of the war and his place in it continued to haunt the recesses of Du Bois's consciousness, causing what would have been the most comprehensive history of black people and African Americans specifically in the First World War to remain unfinished. In the end, memory triumphed over "official" history, a difficult blow for the social scientist in Du Bois to accept. His struggle, while deeply personal, spoke to larger tensions in the possibilities, but also limitations, of history to effectively convey the variegated and often troubled memories of African Americans in the war.

DU BOIS'S DISILLUSIONMENT AND the challenges he encountered with financial and publishing support for his book spoke to the growing rejection of the war's legacy by the American public following the armistice. Initial enthusiasm for the Allied victory gradually dissipated in the tumult of the postwar years. Cries of "Vive Wilson" from enraptured French citizens greeted the American president upon his arrival in Paris for the Versailles peace proceedings. But Wilson's hero-like reception in France belied domestic, social, and political realities. The closely guarded negotiations occurring across the Atlantic barely registered on the American public's radar. More pressing, labor unrest, economic inflation, "Bolshevik" radicalism, and racial violence all pointed toward a society teetering on the brink of chaos, if not all-out revolt.[75] Conditions in Europe, where new revolutionary movements in Germany and other countries emerged out of the ashes of war, appeared even worse. Woodrow Wilson remained tone-deaf to the domestic and international turmoil. With single-minded determination, Wilson fought for his League of Nations in spite of resistance from skeptical European allies, more interested in punishing Germany and dividing the spoils of war, and resurgent congressional Republicans opposed to any constraints on American diplomatic autonomy.[76] The effort nearly killed him, as he suffered a debilitating stroke on October 3, 1919, in the midst of a national tour to rally support for inclusion of the League covenant in the Treaty of Versailles. Paralyzed on the left side of his body, partially blind, and mentally incapacitated, Wilson kept out of the public light and remained president in name only until the end of his term.[77] As a final blow, on November 21, 1919, Congress rejected the Treaty of Versailles and, with it, the League of Nations.

Americans of varying backgrounds, experiences, and political persuasions increasingly asked, is this what the United States had fought for? The war was indeed seen as a transformative, even epochal moment, but not necessarily for the good. In assessing social and cultural life using the measure of "since the war," Americans struggled to make sense of dramatic transformations in religious values, gender norms, sexual behavior, political militancy, and race consciousness. Reactionary developments such as the "Red Scare," prohibition, the national growth of the Ku Klux Klan, the 1924 Johnson-Reed immigration restriction act, and the 1926 Scopes trial emerged in response to the rise of the New Woman, the New Negro, urban consumer culture and accompanying ideas of leisure and pleasure, ethnic working-class labor radicalism, and other signs of postwar modernity. In this climate, the war and America's participation in it became topics of critique, more so than of celebration. "Lost Generation" writers such as Gertrude Stein, Ernest Hemingway, F. Scott Fitzgerald, and John Dos Passos used the war as their muse to offer critical reassessments of American culture and the place of the individual in the modern world.[78] Their works found receptive audiences. Similarly, many historians, after eschewing any claims to objectivity and engaging in blatant propaganda during the war, expressed a profound sense of disappointment and betrayal that their idealistic vision of the conflict's transformative potential had not been met.[79] The American reading public, by and large, had little appetite for "histories" of a war that left their initially high expectations unfulfilled.

Interest did exist, however, for memoirs and personal accounts of the war. In questioning the relevancy of history, men and women hoping to make sense of the conflict turned to the seeming authenticity of narratives rooted in the memories of the participants themselves. Some anticipation thus surrounded the fall 1925 release of *Personalities and Reminiscences of the War*, the war memoir of Major General Robert Lee Bullard. The white Alabama native was a career soldier, an 1885 graduate of West Point with experience serving in Cuba, the Philippines, and along the Mexican border. He quickly rose through the ranks during the war, culminating with his command of the Second Army in October 1918. Bullard continued to serve following the armistice and eventually retired in 1925. He subsequently became president of the National Security League, the wartime hypernationalist organization founded in 1914 by his close friend General Leonard Wood that had become even more reactionary during the "Red Scare" of the postwar years. With John Pershing's two-volume memoir still six years from reaching the public, Bullard's book would offer a high-profile reflection of the war from an American military commander. For this reason, the *New York Times* included *Personalities and Reminiscences of the War* on its list of the one hundred most notable books slated for fall publication.[80]

Even before its official release, Bullard's reminiscences garnered considerable attention. Drawing largely from his personal wartime diaries, Bullard did not bite his tongue. He exposed the lack of war preparation in the War Department, questioned Secretary of War Newton Baker's manliness, offered only qualified praise for General John Pershing, and charged the French army with lacking discipline and fighting spirit in comparison to the American and British forces.

Bullard, with little apparent regard for the potential consequences of his observations, embraced his self-appointed duty of writing a brutally honest narrative free from any hint of romanticism.

While he was not shy to criticize white troops and his fellow officers in the AEF, Bullard's most explosive statements came at the expense of African American soldiers. Bullard had formerly commanded African American troops of the controversial Third Alabama Volunteer Infantry during the Spanish-Cuban-American War. This experience left him bitter toward the inclusion of black soldiers in the nation's military and the racial politics surrounding their use.[81] As commander of the Second Army in France, Bullard's limited interactions with the Ninety-second Division altogether soured him to the ability of black men to be competent soldiers and officers. Bullard devoted an entire chapter to the Ninety-second Division, the only division to receive its own separate treatment. He recounted his efforts to thoroughly investigate the charges against officers of the 368th Regiment accused of cowardice in the Meuse-Argonne fiasco. In the end, Bullard could find no reason to intervene on their behalf, or so he claimed. Bullard asserted he did everything in his power to give the Ninety-second Division a chance to redeem its good name, to no avail. "I never succeeded even to a slight degree," he wrote in exasperation.[82] Ultimately, he concluded that it was not a matter of poor leadership on the part of the division's white officers—whom he described as "exceptionally good"—or inadequate preparation on the part of the army, but the mental and constitutional inferiority of black men that accounted for their failure.[83] "The Negro," he declared, "it seems, cannot stand bombardment."[84]

Bullard punctuated his attack on the manhood of black soldiers by invoking tales of the Ninety-second as the "raping division." He dismissed the idea that French civilians embraced the presence of black soldiers, pointing to the sexual threat they posed to the population's women. "The Negro is a more sensual man than the white man," Bullard reasoned, "and at the same time he is far more offensive to white women than is a white man." He recalled his conversation with Allied commander Foch shortly after the armistice, when he expressed his inability to control the sexual desires of black soldiers and concern for the safety of Frenchwomen, a warning that led to the return of the Ninety-second Division to the United States before any other division of the AEF. A relieved Bullard could not have been more happy to wash his hands of the division as quickly as possible. Summarizing his experience, Bullard wrote, "Altogether my memories of the 92nd Negro Division are a nightmare. . . . If you need combat soldiers, and especially if you need them in a hurry, don't put your time upon Negroes."[85]

The *New York Times*, in its December 27, 1925, review of Bullard's memoir, noted that while the Ninety-second Division was "the only organization that the author condemns," the book would cause "no 'heart-burnings or controversies.' His candor has no sting."[86] The *Times* could not have been more disingenuous. To the contrary, Bullard's charges against the Ninety-second Division created a firestorm among the black press, black political leaders, and former servicemen in particular. By singling out the Ninety-second Division, Bullard reignited debates about the performance of black troops in the war and their place in both history and memory.

In June 1925 the *Chicago Daily Tribune* previewed Bullard's memoir by printing several advance chapters. On June 9, his chapter on the Ninety-second Division appeared under the provocative heading "Negro Division a Nightmare, Says Bullard." Bullard's words quickly enflamed African Americans in Chicago and beyond. The speed, breadth, and intensity of the response to Bullard's slander demonstrated that African Americans, even six years after the war, remained fiercely protective of the legacy of the Ninety-second Division and the broader memory of African American soldiers. Bullard became a target of vilification. The *Chicago Defender* mocked his background, highlighting that the "Alabama rebel" was named after the Confederate general Robert E. Lee and had never risked his life in battle, thus having the luxury to "keep a diary of 'memoirs'" and "give vent to his inherent hatred of Americans of our Race."[87] The *Pittsburgh Courier* followed with a scathing article, characterizing Bullard's memoirs as "the insipid workings of the prejudiced mind of a white southern 'cracker.'" The *Courier* provided direct rebuttals from W. E. B. Du Bois, General Mariano Goybet of the French 157th "Red Hand" Division, and 369th officer Hamilton Fish, who had written to the *New York Herald Tribune* in response to Bullard's charges. In his letter, quoted extensively by the *Courier*, Fish specifically praised the Ninety-third Division, but also supported the Ninety-second by questioning Bullard's leadership and dismissing his blanket characterizations as the misinformed thoughts of a man with "a degree of animus against the colored soldier which is unusual from an army officer who should be familiar with deeds of heroism performed by Negro soldiers in all our wars."[88] Along with the press, black civil rights organizations aggressively defended the memory of the Ninety-second Division from Bullard's charges. The NAACP passed a resolution at the 1925 annual meeting registering its "solemn protest against General Bullard's action as a hostile gesture, most improper in an army officer, from the element in the South that is still unenlightened and still cave-dwelling, and as a gross, wanton insult to ten percent of the people that pay General Bullard his wages and whose servant he is."[89]

The most vociferous protests came directly from African American veterans, and those of the Ninety-second Division in particular. For many ex-soldiers, Bullard's unprovoked attack stirred painful memories, suppressed but easily awakened, of racial discrimination in the war. Some burned with rage. Levi Southe, a former second lieutenant in the 365th Infantry Regiment commissioned at Fort Des Moines, decried Bullard's "cowardly attack" and asserted, "Official records of the war department will be called upon to refute every statement." An even more embittered officer of the Ninety-second dismissed Bullard's charges as "bunk" and proclaimed, "We learned a whole lot about the white man in the war. He is nothing but a beast and a devil and a hypocrite."[90]

Adam E. Patterson took Bullard's claims as a personal affront. The former major and judge advocate of the Ninety-second Division returned to Chicago after the war and became a major figure in the city's Democratic Party. He also established an organization called "The Committee of One Hundred," composed largely of fellow veterans and race men committed to civic racial uplift. With a deep individual and collective investment in the memory of the Ninety-second Division, Patterson refused to let Bullard's aspersions go unchallenged. On June 13, 1925, he authored a vigorous response to the white officer's claims in the *Chicago Defender*. "There are so many discrepancies and misstatements contained in General Bullard's article that they border on the ridiculous," Patterson authoritatively wrote, noting how the assertions of the "southerner of known anti-Negro feeling" contradicted General John Pershing's praise of the Ninety-second Division. Most important, he systematically refuted Bullard's characterizations of African American officers and their conduct in the Meuse-Argonne offensive, placing blame instead on prejudiced white officers, such as Major Max Elser, who "did everything possible to discourage and discredit the Colored soldiers under his command."[91] Patterson's *Defender* rebuttal was followed by an article in the *Chicago Daily Tribune*, prepared along with two other veterans of the Ninety-second Division, Julian Dawson and former first lieutenant Dr. Clarence H. Payne. Using American and French military records, they methodically employed the tools of history to establish a counter-memory of the Ninety-second Division, from its inception to decorated record in combat, which challenged the veracity of Bullard's "reminiscences." Patterson, invoking his authority as a former judge advocate, directly addressed the overstated charges of rape, noting that in fact only one soldier of the Ninety-second Division was convicted of sexual assault. "We challenge any division of the American Expeditionary force to show a better record in their respect," he asserted.[92] Astutely recognizing the power of history, Patterson and his colleagues used it as a weapon to wage a counteroffensive in their battle over the memory of the Ninety-second Division. The legacy of blacks' participation in the war, their manhood, and their personal honor remained worth fighting for.

Another former soldier expressed his indignation as well. In 1924, after his stint in New York with the *Messenger*, George Schuyler began writing for the *Pittsburg Courier*, penning a recurring column titled "Thrusts and Lunges." In his June 20, 1925, piece, he addressed the swirling controversy surrounding Bullard and the memory of the Ninety-second Division. "Negroes are all wrought up over the charges of General Bullard," Schuyler began. Without making reference to his own disillusioning experience during the war, he continued, "So this is the thanks Negroes get for fighting to make the world safe for democracy. Only in a land of liberty like the United States would a high official dare to slur and slander ten percent of the population in this manner. It gives you an idea of the sort of thing the Negro soldier had to face during the late 'war to end war.'" Schuyler's commentary combined personal bitterness with his trademark iconoclasm. He insisted that African Americans utilize some of the wasted energy devoted to "straightening their hair, whitening their skin, parading and dancing" to ensuring that in the future African American divisions were "commanded by capable Negro officers and not Southern crackers." "Here is a real political issue for Negroes to rally around in the next campaign," Schuyler impressed, "instead of yawpping about Lincoln and Roosevelt."[93]

The furor created by Bullard gradually faded. It did not, despite George Schuyler's encouragement, become an issue African Americans invoked to mobilize political activism around the future of black people in the military. But it was nevertheless a telling moment in demonstrating the contentious relationship between history and memory concerning the legacy of black soldiers. Bullard made no claim to writing an authoritative historical account of the war. "These are my memories of the World War," he asserted in the preface. "They are not made from the records. They are truly memories, memories recalled, as all memories are, by a word, a thought, a chance sound or sight, a whiff of air—anything. They are not offered as history."[94] By acknowledging and understating the function of memory in his book, Bullard attempted to minimize its potential impact as a work of history, rife with inaccuracies and personal bias. Nevertheless, black critics and veterans were quite cognizant of the historical implications of his work and, because of Bullard's stature, the power of his particular memory to shape history. *Personalities of Reminiscences* thus became a contested site of memory, one that African Americans aggressively attempted to delegitimize, using both their own personal countermemories and historical facts, as an accurate reflection of the history of black soldiers in the war. African Americans, and veterans in particular, remained fiercely protective of the memory of the war and its representation in history.

THE SLANDEROUS ACCOUNTS OF white military officials like Robert Bullard demonstrated the need for a serviceable countermemory of the war. History remained vitally important and necessary to protect the legacy of African American soldiers, their manhood, and the broader dignity of the race. However, Du Bois's struggles, the narrow interpretations of other authors, and, as the Bullard controversy demonstrated, the continued reactionary need to challenge white supremacist narratives of the war reflected the limitations of "official" written history to effectively memorialize the experiences of black troops.[95] As was the case throughout the postwar era, history represented only one of many strategies, modes of expression, and venues of representation utilized by African Americans to preserve and disseminate their various memories of the war. African Americans, including many veterans, used organizations as varied as the NAACP and the UNIA, and periodicals ranging from the *Crisis* to the *Messenger*, as sites of memory to express meanings of the war and its centrality to the political future of the race. The New Negro movement, in this sense, functioned as a repository of multiple, and often competing, memories of African American military service and its legacy.

The New Negro movement was a cultural development as well as a political one. Interwar black culture served as an important arena for the cultivation and democratization of a broad array of African American memories and countermemories of the war and black military service. Black culture has historically functioned as a crucial resource for African Americans to simultaneously challenge white supremacist constructions of history and engage in an imaginative process of reinterpreting and re-creating history from the experiential perspectives of black people themselves. Postwar black culture was therefore not merely reactive to racist accounts of the past but in constant conversation with history, drawing from it, invoking it, playing with it, offering criticism, but always posing challenges to its primacy, and at times legitimacy, as a method of conveying the complexities of the past. The dynamic nature of black culture after the war functioned in concert with equally dynamic memories of African American soldiers. Black musicians, novelists, painters, poets, playwrights, and other artists of the interwar period expressed a diverse range of memories of the legacy of African American soldiers, memories that included but were by no means limited to the exaltations of black patriotism and loyalty that characterized so many of the "histories" of the war published after the armistice.[96] Instead, the broad outpouring of cultural production reflected how the experience of black soldiers could be interpreted in different ways, employed for different purposes, and articulated in the form of various overlapping tropes. The works of African American veterans, as well as other individuals who had direct personal engagement with either black troops or the politics surrounding their service, while by no means exhaustive, are of particular significance. They speak to an ability of African American artists to use their memories of the war as a resource to explore the complexities of black identity, the nature of human suffering, the dilemmas of American citizenship, and, most potently, the meaning of democracy. Postwar African American culture provided a vibrant space for memories of black soldiers and their experience to further shape how black people viewed the history of the war, its relationship to their present moment, and significance for the future.

The politics of the New Negro movement complemented and drew resonance from its artistry.[97] Black America in the postwar years teemed with cultural energy. Poets, novelists, painters, and musicians responded to the changing demographic, cultural, and political landscapes of the nation brought about by mass migration, military service, and racial violence. Harlem was a particular hotbed of cultural activity.[98] What came to be known as the "Harlem Renaissance" marked an attempt, albeit by a relatively exclusive group of male and female practitioners, to express, make sense of, and, with any success, reconcile the increasingly conflicted place of peoples of African descent in the modern world using black culture as a source of social, historical, and psychological sustenance.[99] Harlem may have received the most attention, but the New Negro cultural movement was both national and transnational in scope. Cities like Chicago and Washington, D.C., radiated as centers of artistic production and served as home to key figures of the period. Across the Atlantic, black artists, writers, and musicians found both refuge and receptive audiences in major European cities, most notably Paris, where they engaged in dialogues with other peoples of the diaspora.[100] In jazz nightclubs, literary parlors, playhouses, galleries, and street corners from the South Side of Chicago to Marseilles, the artists of the New Negro movement offered America and the world new visions of blackness, freedom, and history.

The memory of the war compelled African American artists to think about and express these issues in new ways. The war was not completely disjunctive, as many of the questions regarding race, nation, democracy, and belonging with which African Americans grappled before the conflict remained relevant in its aftermath. But the meaning of these questions had changed, as had the urgency to make sense of the impact of the war and the legacies of black military service within the context of a transformative moment in the history of black modernity. For many artists, the memory of the war served as both a muse and a source of motivation to express various interpretations of African American identity and the place of black people in the nation.

Memories of black service in the war and the expansion of democracy coursed through the melodies of black musicians and jazz artists. Jazz became an aural and performative site of memory due in no small part to the contributions of veteran musicians of the wartime African American regimental bands. "Since the return of colored military bands from France to these shores," noted the *New York Age*, "the country simply has gone wild about jazz music." Not just America, but much of the world as well had been infected by the "jazz germ" in the wake of the war. Black migration and urbanization during the war era, in the North and the South, created the social and cultural conditions for the emergence of jazz. Musicians from various backgrounds built upon and transformed existing vernacular forms, like the sorrow songs, into a new syncopated sound with the use of the trumpet, trombone, and other Western instruments. The African American regimental bands, which emphasized the use of brass and percussion instruments, perfected this style. They served as global ambassadors of jazz and black music more broadly, a phenomenon that continued after the war as well. What to make of this new music, jazz, that had set after-hours spots and concert halls from New Orleans to Harlem to Paris aflame? For a definition, the *Age* turned to Irene Castle, the iconic stage and film performer who, along with her recently deceased husband and dance partner Vernon Castle, had toured with James Reese Europe before the war and had intimate familiarity with his music. "The colored bands jazz a tune," she observed. "That is to say, they slur the notes they syncopate, and each instrument puts in a world of little fancy bits of its own."[101] But jazz encompassed much more than just a type of musical performance and a growing business enterprise. It was a reflection of African American engagement and wrestling with the complexities of modernity, as well as a dynamic form of democratic expression. Moreover, postwar jazz music functioned as a repository of memory.[102] More than any musical genre of its time, jazz took listeners on an existential journey back to a particular historical moment and situated them within its cultural and social milieu. When the black military bands played, they invoked historical memories of the war and infused them with symbolic and ritual meaning in the context of the present.[103]

African American military bands imparted a lasting legacy on the history of interwar black popular music. Several veterans made important contributions to the evolution of jazz and other genres of musical performance. The 350th

Field Artillery Band, led by James Tim Brymn, returned to the United States to wide acclaim. Brymn refined his wartime band, described as "a military symphony engaged in a battle of jazz," into a seventy-piece ensemble and toured and recorded throughout 1920 and 1921 as the "Black Devil Orchestra."[104] One of the band members, Willie "The Lion" Smith, pioneered the stride style of piano performance and became an underground legend throughout Harlem, dominating the nightclub and rent party circuit. The famed Duke Ellington considered "The Lion" one of his most important musical mentors.[105] The 807th "Pioneers," directed by Will Vodery, did not tour after the war, but Vodery became one of the most prolific African American composers, conductors, and arrangers on Broadway. His most lasting contribution was to the landmark 1927 musical *Show Boat*.[106]

James Reese Europe's 369th band and the collection of professional musicians he assembled left arguably the most enduring imprint on jazz music's popularity after the war. Despite being one of the most influential and best-known African American ragtime musicians before the war, Europe achieved even greater fame with the success of his 369th ensemble. Europe and his orchestra of drummers, trumpeters, trombonists, and singers had conquered France, and now they prepared to conquer the United States by demonstrating the genius of black music and its ability to remake American democracy. Upon their return to New York in February 1919, Europe booked the band for a ten-week national tour that took them through nearly every major eastern and midwestern city, highlighted by performances at the Boston Opera House, a full week of engagements in Chicago, and an appearance at Philadelphia's Academy of Music. Their tour opened at home, on March 16, 1919, at the Manhattan Opera House, where three thousand people, black and white, the elite and working class, filled the famed venue to capacity. Jim Europe, resplendent and commanding in his officer uniform, captivated the audience. The band was in top-notch form, and Europe, as Noble Sissle wrote, "with the willowy motion of his swaying arms and typical bobbing of his head seemed to bring from their instruments a new music—music with strains, movement, rhythm, and harmony as inspiring and thrilling as any that had been played."[107]

At the outset of their tour, between March 3 and May 7, 1919, the band cut twenty-eight songs for Pathé Record Company, a watershed moment in jazz history. Five discs, heavily promoted under the banner of "Lieut. Jim Europe's 'Hell Fighters' Jazz Band," were released on April 20 and found a receptive audience. They featured landmark jazz tunes like "That Moaning Trombone" and "St. Louis Blues," along with songs explicitly inspired by the war, such as "On Patrol in No Man's Land," "All of No Man's Land Is Ours," and the wildly popular "How 'Ya Gonna Keep 'Em Down on the Farm? (After They've Seen Paree)." Their rendition of the 1918 Joe Young and Sam Lewis song took on new meaning when sung by Noble Sissle and performed by a band of African American and Puerto Rican veterans:

> How 'ya gonna keep 'em down on the farm
> After they've seen Paree?
> How 'ya gonna keep them away from Broadway,
> Jazzin' around,
> And paintin' the town?
> How 'ya gonna keep 'em away from harm?
> That's the mystery!
> They'll never want to see a rake or plow,
> And who the deuce can parlez-vous a cow?
> How 'ya gonna keep 'em down on the farm
> After they've seen Paree?

Many anxious white southerners quite literally posed this question, contributing to the image of the returning black soldier as a source of social and economic instability. But this query, when asked by African Americans, possessed a political overtone that made the song threatening, even radical. Countless African American soldiers, especially those who served overseas, returned with a broadened sense of the world and freedom. The 369th "Hellfighters" provided a soundtrack for their hopes and democratic aspirations. The success of the band broke new ground for African American musicians in the recording industry and proclaimed to the world that jazz was here.[108]

James Reese Europe's dream of jazz fostering a revolution in black stage performance and a broader reconfiguration of the place of black people in American culture came to an abrupt end. On May 9, a disgruntled member of the band, drummer Herbert Wright, confronted Europe backstage at a Boston performance and killed him with a stab wound to the neck. African Americans throughout the country reacted to news of his death with stunned disbelief. In an event fit for royalty, on May 13, Europe became the first African American in New York City history to receive a public funeral. Thousands of mourners, white and black, many with tears streaming down their cheeks, lined the streets of Harlem and midtown Manhattan to pay respects to Europe. At the end of the delegation accompanying Europe's body to final services at St. Mark's Episcopal Methodist Church somberly marched original members of Europe's band, wearing black armbands, instruments at their sides.[109] The solemnity of the occasion offered a stark contrast to the jubilance of the 369th's return only three months earlier, but similarly demonstrated the historical significance of the famed regiment and, more specifically, the power of jazz to bring people together and create a moment that would long live in the collective historical memories of black and white New Yorkers alike. Invoking the Civil War–era song "John Brown's Body," the *Chicago Defender* proclaimed, "'Jim' Europe is marching on, on, on, and leading the bands of the world today. His memory will never fade." Like John Brown, Europe, in martyrdom, had provided African Americans, through jazz, a new vision of freedom and democracy. The *Defender* continued, "Assassinated, he has but fired our hearts, that were already filled with his music, to prepare, prepare, thoroughly, and give to the world the lasting, everlasting rebuke to prejudice, and the joy of soul that comes in its fullness in the sweetness of music."[110]

The "Hellfighter" band lost much of its sense of direction and purpose following Europe's death. After giving a number of performances under the orchestration of former bandmaster Eugene Mikell, an accomplished jazz conductor and teacher in his own right, the group disbanded in May 1920.[111] Its memory, however, remained very much alive. A reconstituted band, albeit composed of few original members, performed under the name of the "New York Fifteenth Band" and made appearances at various Harlem events. Noble Sissle could not imagine the group under the stewardship of anyone besides his close friend. But, inspired by Europe's memory, Sissle teamed with Eubie Blake and embarked on what would be an illustrious postwar career in vaudeville and theater performance, highlighted by the hit Broadway musical *Shuffle Along*.[112] Europe and his band transformed American music, in the process demonstrating the potential of white Americans to embrace black people as indispensible members of the nation's democracy.

Inspired by the legacy of the 369th "Hellfighters" and other black regiments, many African Americans continued to cling to a memory of black soldiers as triumphant heroes and harbingers of democratic change. For the artists, veterans among them, who culturally represented this legacy, doing so necessitated considerable faith in the significance of black military service and its potential to bring about interracial democracy. This inclination therefore reflected both the historical context of the postwar period and the politics and particular experiences of the artists in relation to African American soldiers. Despite the devastation of the "Red Summer" and dashed hopes of many African American soldiers, organizations such as the NAACP remained committed to the goal of interracial democracy and demonstrating the capacity of black people for full and equal citizenship.[113]

For this reason, works such as Joseph Seamon Cotter Jr.'s "On the Fields of

France," a work that conveyed a memory of the war rooted in the fallacy of the color line, was ideal for display in the *Crisis*. While less well known than most of his war era contemporaries, Cotter made significant contributions to the literary memorialization of African American soldiers as unquestioned patriots. Cotter was a native of Kentucky who, despite limited education, became a prominent local educator and prolific writer, producing a wide variety of works. He also played an active part in local African American political and civic organizations, including the NAACP.[114] One of his poems, "A Sonnet to Negro Soldiers," appeared in the June 1918 "Soldiers Number" of the *Crisis*, a piece Cotter dedicated to the Ninety-second Division.[115]

The *Crisis* posthumously published "On the Fields of France" in the June 1920 issue. The one-act play is an exchange between two mortally wounded officers, one white and one black, on a battlefield in northern France. "I say there, my good fellow, have you a drop of water to spare? The Boches have about done me, I fear," the white officer pleads. The black officer obliges, and they crawl toward each other, "close enough to touch hands." Both men are on the brink of death. The white officer, his strength fading, asks to hold the hand of his black compatriot. They grasp each other, and a wave of comfort overtakes the black officer. "I feel much better-myself. After all-it isn't so hard-to die when you are dying-for Liberty." With a sense of deathbed guilt, the white officer responds, "Do you feel that way too? I've often wondered how your people felt. We've treated you so badly-mean at home that I've wondered if you could feel that way. I've been as guilty as the rest, maybe more so than some. But that was yesterday . . ." A new day beckons, and both men find common ground through history and the ultimate sacrifice of death for the nation. "What is it that I see? . . . Do you see it? . . . It is Washington," the white officer says. "I see him, I see him. And who is that beside him with his swarthy chest bare and torn? It is Attucks—Crispus Attucks, and he beckons to me," the black officer responds. To this, the white officer says, "They stand hand in hand over there and we die hand in hand here on the fields of France. Why couldn't we have lived like this at home? They beckon to us, to you and to me. It is one country she will some day be, in truth as well as in spirit—the country of Washington and Attucks, (speaks slowly and painfully) of Lee and Carney. The country of the white and the country of the blacks. Our country!" The play ends with the two men, hand in hand, simultaneously uttering their final dying word: "America!"[116] As romanticized by Cotter the total devastation of war on the western front effectively shattered the color line and exposed the raw, fundamental humanity of all combatants, irrespective of race.[117] With an undeniable sentimentalism and explicit theme of patriotic racial reconciliation, the play sought to convey the possibility of democracy and interracial brotherhood through military service and loss of life for the nation.

Jessie Fauset also explored this theme in her 1924 debut novel *There Is Confusion.* Fauset stands as one of the most important figures of the New Negro movement. A Cornell University alumna, Fauset taught at Washington, D.C.'s prestigious M Street High School and worked behind the scenes as an active member of the city's influential NAACP chapter. She also contributed pieces of her developing literature to the *Crisis* and officially joined the magazine in 1919 after completing her master's degree in French at the University of Pennsylvania. As literary editor, she immersed herself in the work of the *Crisis* and provided exposure to many of the best and brightest young African American writers of the day. She also continued to hone a sharp political consciousness through her engagement with the politics of the *Crisis* and the global activism of her mentor, W. E. B. Du Bois. Fauset teamed with Du Bois during the 1921 Pan-African Congress, speaking at the proceedings and chronicling them in the pages of the *Crisis* as a landmark moment in the history of the African diaspora. Her notoriety made the appearance of *There Is Confusion* a much-celebrated occasion. The March 21, 1924, reception organized by war veteran Charles S. Johnson in honor of her book functioned as a "coming out party" for the Harlem Renaissance. Prominent white editors rubbed elbows with a who's who of the black intelligentsia and literati, among them James Weldon Johnson, Alain Locke, Arturo Schomburg, Gwendolyn Bennett, Countee Cullen, Georgia Douglass Johnson, and W. E. B. Du Bois.[118]

There Is Confusion attempts to cover much ground, exploring issues such as miscegenation and the illogic of race, notions of black masculinity and femininity, and the function of class in shaping black family and community life. The war and memories of black military service, however, constitute an important unifying thread throughout these themes. Fauset's close proximity to the experiences of African American troops during her time in Washington, D.C., through her editorial work with the *Crisis*, and internationally as a result of her participation in the Pan-African Congresses, had a clear impact on her artistic and political sensibilities. She situates the conclusion of the novel and its key characters firmly in the context of the war and its complex legacy.[119] Her main protagonist, Joanna Marshall, is a talented, ambitious product of New York's black bourgeoisie who, throughout the course of the book, struggles to reconcile the tensions of her racial, class, and gender identities. She becomes famous during the war as the star performer in *Dance of the Nations*, a theatrical show intended to rally civic patriotism, which functions for Joanna as a means to challenge a racially exclusionary conception of American nationalism, while at the same time to assert her place as a black woman in the public sphere. Fauset invokes memories of the contributions black women like herself made to the war effort and, as a later scene involving Joanna performing especially for a group of returning African American soldiers demonstrates, their importance in lifting the morale of black troops in the face of racist disrespect.[120] "She was indeed for them 'Miss America,'" Fauset writes, "making them forget to-night the ingratitude with which their country would meet them tomorrow."[121] She explores this connection more explicitly in the relationship between Joanna's brother, Phillip, and Maggie Ellersley. Phillip, constructed as a prototypical middle-class "race man" who earns an officer commission at Fort Des Moines, fights overseas, proving both his manhood and his patriotism. Maggie, in contrast, has a more modest, working-class background. While in France, Phillip reencounters Maggie, who has offered her service as a YMCA secretary. The two have loved each other since childhood, but class and Joanna's interference kept them apart. But now, brought together by war, they affirm their long denied feelings and marry upon returning to the United States.[122] A less prominent character is Harley Alexander, a black soldier who serves overseas but, "bitter and cynical," opts to remain in France following the armistice.[123] Alexander seems clearly inspired by Fauset's own personal familiarity with African American veterans such as Rayford Logan who became expatriates, as well as her firsthand awareness of the hardships black troops encountered in the American army.

One of the most dramatic scenes involves Peter Bye, Fauset's central male protagonist, who serves in an African American combat regiment in France. While en route to France, Peter encounters Meriwether Bye, a descendant of the family that held his ancestors in bondage and a relative by blood. Peter arrives in France intensely bitter toward all white people and is deeply resentful of Meriwether. However, in the crucible of military service, Peter develops a strong friendship with Meriwether, compelling him to reconsider his distrust of all things white. Later, the two men are thrown together in a chaotic battle in "No Man's Land." Peter is seriously wounded, but spots Meriwether engaged in hand-to-hand combat with a German soldier. Suddenly, there is an explosion. Peter rushes to Meriwether's aid and finds him with his chest blown open from a grenade. Meriwether struggles to survive, recognizes Peter, and dies in the black soldier's arms. When help finally arrives, Peter is found unconscious, his head "dropped low over the fair one," "his black curly hair," "straight and stringy, caked in the blood which lay in a well above Meriwether's heart."[124] Fauset attempts to reconcile the confusing history of racial lineage through the heroic body of the black soldier. But just as confusing is the memory of African American participation in the war, and the paradoxical relationship between black people and the nation they continue to sacrifice for. Using the physical and imaginative space of "No Man's Land," Fauset challenges the legitimacy of whiteness and presents a memory of the war and black military service as a violent, albeit effective, equalizer of the races. The works of Cotter, Fauset, and others reflected a deep literary tradition of black writers espousing the heroic sacrifices of African American soldiers in the nation's wars and clinging to war as an engine of racial democratization.[125]

Victor Daly offered one of the most insightful, and deeply personal, explorations of this theme in his first and only novel. Daly experienced an eventful, and somewhat contentious, transition into postwar life. While serving as business manager for the *Messenger*, Daly had a nasty falling out with A. Philip Randolph and Chandler Owen. In late 1920 the pair accused Daly of misappropriating $2,000, fired him from the newspaper, and demanded his arrest. He had, in fact, persuaded radical labor unions to withdraw their financial support for the paper, most likely as retribution for not receiving his salary. Undaunted, Daly sued for back wages in New York's Seventh Municipal District Court and won a judgment of $962.75, effectively rendering him persona non grata in Harlem's black radical circles.[126] He nevertheless continued to exhibit a resiliency to protect both his personal civil rights and those of African Americans more broadly.[127] Daly relocated to Washington, D.C., in 1922 and worked as business manager for the *Journal of Negro History*, edited by Carter G. Woodson of the Association for the Study of Negro Life and History (ASNLH). In 1934 he took a position as an interviewer with the Department of Labor, where he spent the rest of his professional career working on matters concerning government and municipal integration in Washington, D.C., gradually rising through the ranks to the position of deputy director of the United States Employment Service.[128]

Along with his commitment to African American racial progress, Daly had a long-standing passion for writing. He was an accomplished writer in high school, but did not pursue his interests at Cornell because of a perceived lack of opportunities for black journalists.[129] Daly's departure from the *Messenger* deprived him of a potentially fruitful vehicle for expressing his literary talents, especially considering the journal's increased focus on cultural production under fellow veteran George Schuyler's management during the Harlem Renaissance.[130] Daly nevertheless published two short stories in the *Crisis*, "Private Walker Goes Patrolling" and "Goats, Wildcats and Buffalo," both informed by his war experience.[131] A third story, "Still Five More," was based on an interview he conducted for the ASNLH with the son of a black Civil War veteran and similarly reflected his interest in the African American military experience.[132]

Despite his association with Carter Woodson and the ASNLH, fiction provided Daly with the creative freedom to channel and invoke his memory in ways that the constraints of written history could not.

Victor Daly had an array of literary imagery and symbolism to pull from in the construction of his own novel, *Not Only War: A Story of Two Great Conflicts*.[133] In a 1985 interview, Daly asserted that no black authors influenced his writing, although this is difficult to believe considering Daly's proximity to the New Negro movement and acquaintance with Harlem Renaissance figures such as James Weldon Johnson and Alain Locke.[134] Regardless, his personal memories of the war provided the foundation for his book, shaped its characters, drove its plot, and defined its message. Published in 1932, *Not Only War* occupies an important place in the American literary cannon as the first novel on the black war experience.[135] It is ultimately a tragic tale, revolving around Montgomery "Montie" Jason, a black man, Robert Lee Casper, a white man, and Miriam Pinckney, a black woman, and offers a highly critical vision of interracial democracy, mediated through the sexualization of female bodies, black and white, and the brutal irony of combat. The first half of the book takes place in the fictional southern town of Spartanburg, Virginia, invoking memories of the 369th's harrowing experience in Spartanburg, South Carolina. Montie, constructed by Daly as an innocent, upstanding exemplar of young black manhood, and Robert, as his name suggests, an embodiment of southern male white supremacy, both fall in love with Miriam, a black grade-school teacher whose claims to black female respectability are seriously challenged by her interracial liaison with Robert. The second half of the book is set in France, where Montie, in the wake of his failed courtship of Miriam, serves as a noncommissioned sergeant in a black combat regiment, while Robert serves as a fully commissioned lieutenant. The first encounter between the two central characters occurs when Robert finds Montie billeted in the home of a white French woman and has him court-martialed. Montie, victimized, demoted, and disillusioned, is nevertheless thrown back into battle and, in the novel's final scene, happens upon Robert, wounded, clinging to life in a trench. Exhibiting a spirit of democratic humanism Robert and other racist white officers failed to reciprocate, Montie enters the trench to rescue his adversary, only to be struck by a German assault.[136] The book ends in a scene similar to that in Fauset's *There Is Confusion* and Cotter's one-act play, with Montie and Robert, "face downward, their arms about each other, side by side."[137]

Daly claimed that the characters of *Not Only War* were entirely fictional. Nevertheless, Daly needed only to invoke his memories of the war as an officer in the 367th Infantry Regiment for inspiration. Like Montie, he had approached his war service with an innocent optimism, only to find acute disappointment. Having survived the racial nightmare of the Ninety-second Division, Daly was more than familiar with the army's unjust treatment of black officers as well as white officers' paranoid obsession with restricting access to French women. *Not Only War* is, from this perspective, a powerful critique of American democracy and its failings during the war. More specifically, Daly engages in a highly gendered and deeply ironic commentary on the nature of interracial democracy and its limitations when bound by the constraints of American racial ideology, but also its potential when cast within the fatalistic humanism of combat and death. Whether as a cadet at the Des Moines officers' training camp, on the staff of the *Messenger*, or in his later work with the Department of Labor, Daly constantly sought ways to express his commitment to interracial democracy and African American social progress. With *Not Only War* and through the creative power of literature, Daly skillfully marshaled the resources of his memory to give new meaning to the black experience in the First World War as a moment of both cruel regret and hopeful optimism.

As Daly's novel reflects, black artists, in often more explicit tones, conveyed a memory of the war as a moment of great disillusionment. Black soldiers represented not solely the promise of racial equality through military service but, more profoundly, the failures of the war to achieve this goal. The war serves as an example of the hardening of the color line, not its transgression. For many African Americans, and veterans in particular, memories of racial violence, discrimination, and dashed expectations of democracy remained viscerally raw. Written history, with its vindicationist inclination, failed to capture this reality. Interwar culture provided the creative space for competing memories of the war to be expressed, including those that challenged the legitimacy of the war and the treatment of African American troops in it.

The war inspired African American painters such as Edwin A. Harleston to depict black soldiers and explore the complexities of their legacy. Harleston was born in Charleston, South Carolina, in 1882, one of six brothers and sisters. A graduate of Atlanta University, he studied under W. E. B. Du Bois and maintained a friendship with the *Crisis* editor. He also developed an interest in art and painting. In 1906 Harleston turned down an opportunity to transfer into Harvard University and instead enrolled in the Boston School of the Museum of Fine Arts. He returned to Charleston, professionally frustrated but imbued with a strong political consciousness honed during his time in Boston. He helped to establish the city's NAACP chapter on February 27, 1917, and served as its first president. Charleston was a hotbed of political activity during the war, and many of the city's black men entered the military, among them Harleston's brother,

Robert. Although Edwin did not serve in the army, he nevertheless enthusiastically promoted African American troops through both his political activism and his artistry. He wrote, directed, and acted in a two-act play called *The War Cross* and produced several paintings honoring the patriotism and contributions of African American soldiers. The return of black troops following the armistice further emboldened Charleston's black residents and Harleston in particular. In 1919 Harleston and the NAACP spearheaded a voter registration drive, an effort with potentially deadly ramifications in the context of postwar southern racial hostilities. Frustrated like so many other black southerners with the war's lack of progress, he turned to a new strategy: "After all methods have been tried, and after all the plans that we have devised have been used—it all reverts back to the ballot for our salvation."[138]

Along with his approach to racial progress, Harleston's representations of African American soldiers and their meaning became more militant as well. At the height of the "Red Summer" of 1919, as returning black veterans in Charleston and other southern communities physically and symbolically challenged racial norms, Harleston painted a striking piece entitled *The Soldier* (1919). It captured the black serviceman as New Negro and, in many respects, offered a visual complement to Du Bois's editorial rallying cry, "We Return Fighting." The painting stands in stark contrast to other wartime representations of African American soldiers, such as the 1918 poster *True Sons of Freedom* by Charles Gustrine, a prominent white wartime propagandist, which depicted black troops as unquestioned patriots. Harleston's soldier, arms boldly crossed, eyes fixed and intently staring ahead, has clearly been hardened by war. Chest adorned with medals, he has proved his valor, asserted his manhood on the battlefield, and earned deserved recognition. But, as his stoic face conveys, the costs have been high. The combined traumas of combat and racism, Harleston suggests, have not made the end of the war cause for celebration. Instead, Harleston presents the returning African American soldier as a self-determined militant, prepared, if necessary, to fight again. The painting reflects both Harleston's political motivations and the particular historical context of its production. With the emergence of the New Negro, African American soldiers increasingly embodied a growing frustration with the impact of the war and a more pointed disillusionment with its democratizing potential.[139]

More so than any other figure of the Harlem Renaissance and New Negro movement, Jamaican writer and radical intellectual Claude McKay saw himself as a product of the war moment. McKay published his first book of poetry in 1912, the same year he left his native island for the United States to enroll as a student at the Tuskegee Institute. A restless soul, he traveled widely before set-

Edwin A. Harleston, The Soldier. *200-HN-HARL-7. Courtesy of National Archives and Record Administration, College Park, Md.*

tling in the black Mecca of Harlem, a place that would test the often-conflicting strands of his identity. The war and its reverberations had a profound impact on McKay, shaping his ideological worldview and specific ideas of race, nation, diaspora, and modernity. While working as a railway dining-car waiter, he witnessed the bloody "Red Summer" of 1919 firsthand, an experience that for McKay confirmed the failings of both the war and the United States. "And now this great catastrophe has come upon the world," McKay reflected, "proving the real hollowness of nationhood, patriotism, racial pride, and most of the things one was taught to respect and reverence."[140] Written in the smoldering aftermath of the Chicago riot, his poem "If We Must Die," first published in the socialist journal the *Liberator* edited by Max Eastman, became a rallying cry for the New Negro and established McKay as the voice of an emergent generation of black radicals. He became increasingly interested in communism as a solution to the problems of black social and economic freedom, participating in the African Blood Brotherhood and traveling to Moscow in 1922 to attend the Fourth Congress of the Third Communist International. This marked the beginning of a period abroad lasting until 1934, when he finally returned to the United States. McKay's international sojourn took him to the Soviet Union, Germany, Spain, Morocco, and most notably France, where he lived for several years.

Time in Paris and the port city of Marseilles exposed McKay to a political and cultural world of other peoples of African descent similarly grappling with the complexities of race, empire, and freedom. He explored these issues in his first three novels, *Home to Harlem*, *Banjo*, and *Banana Bottom*, all written while overseas. *Home to Harlem* debuted in 1928 to both acclaim and derision. Some critics hailed McKay's vivid depiction of Harlem and the exotic grittiness of everyday black life. For others, McKay's graphic portrayals of the black working class and its raw humanity rankled their Victorian sensibilities. W. E. B. Du Bois famously remarked that after reading McKay's novel, he felt the need to take a bath.[141]

The First World War and the memory of black military service frame *Home to Harlem* and operate at the center of the novel.[142] Jake Brown, McKay's protagonist, is an African American veteran of the war who, like so many black servicemen, is relegated to laboring as a stevedore. Unable to tolerate the racism of the U.S. Army, he goes AWOL in France. Jake travels to London after the war, meets other black men from the West Indies, immerses himself in the East End underworld, but eventually returns to Harlem, where he, along with his friend Zeddy, also a veteran, engage in a life of drinking, partying, gambling, and carousing with women. Service on the behalf of the nation, McKay suggests, is ultimately fruitless, as Jake often reflects on his war experience, the "fights between colored and white soldiers in France," the "interracial sex skirmishes in England," and ultimately his failed search to find democracy. The racially circumscribed geographic and metaphorical neighborhood of Harlem in effect replaces the nation, offering a space for the expression of black freedom and humanity. But McKay, informed by his internationalism, pushes against a narrow conception of home and, as reflected in the semiautobiographical Haitian character of Ray and his interactions with Jake, points to the need to transgress nationhood through engagement with a certain culture and politics of the diaspora. From this perspective, Jake's army service and time overseas, while disillusioning, imbue him with a worldliness and robust masculinity that serve him well in the streets of Harlem and provide him with the tools for future diasporic mobility. For McKay, the black soldier and veteran do not represent an embodiment of African American patriotism and respectability but are a transnational working-class symbol of black social, political, cultural, and sexual rebellion.[143]

McKay further explored the global and diasporic implications of the war and black military service in his second novel, *Banjo*, published in 1929 and in many ways a sequel to *Home to Harlem*. Like Jake, Banjo, the central protagonist, is a disillusioned African American veteran. However, unlike Jake, McKay does not merely complicate Banjo's connection to the nation but shatters it altogether. He initially served in the Canadian army, not the AEF. Moreover, Banjo renounces his American citizenship and remains in France, where his rebellion takes him to the "the seaman's dream port" of Marseilles. Banjo continues to lament his war experience and his role fighting for, as he reflects, a "wul' safe foh cracker-ism."[144] But while the war may have exposed the failures of nationhood, it created new opportunities for diasporic mobilization. Banjo decides to put together a musical band, in the process immersing himself in a vagabond community of former servicemen and sailors of African descent. Jake even makes an appearance in the second half of the novel, expressing his frustrations with Harlem and his increasingly domesticated life. For McKay, the black soldier, possessed with a unique worldliness, cosmopolitanism, mobility, and war-born race consciousness, functions as a vector of cultural, political, and sexual exchange and mediation. McKay's work represented both a radical critique of the war and a recognition of the global significance of black servicemen.

The image of the lynched black veteran viscerally represented memories of the war as the failure of American democracy. This became a staple literary and performative trope in postwar black culture. It was, of course, grounded in the historical reality of several lynched African American veterans, as well as untold numbers of former soldiers who endured physical and racial abuse following the war. But this invocation also represented a continuation and rearticulation through performance of efforts by the black press and the NAACP to use the image of the black veteran to highlight southern barbarity, un-Americanness, and the hypocrisy of a nation that could proclaim itself the champion of democracy on an international stage while the very defenders of that democracy hung from tree limbs and smoldered in the bonfires of white mobs.

Carrie Williams Clifford used poetry to mediate the relationship between history, memory, and the abused African American veteran. A pioneering figure in the black women's club movement, she founded the Ohio Federation of Colored Women's Clubs and played a prominent role in the NACW. She was also a leader in the Niagara Movement and its successor organization, the NAACP, most notably as a contributing writer to the *Crisis*. In 1910 she moved to Washington, D.C., and became a gravitating figure in local black literary and political circles. The Sunday evening salons Clifford hosted at her home were frequented by friends such as Alain Locke, Georgia Douglass Johnson, Mary Church Terrell, and W. E. B. Du Bois. Her presence in Washington, D.C., further demonstrated the breadth of the postwar black artistic movement beyond the confines of Harlem.[145] She published two collections of poems, *Race Rhymes*

(1911) and *The Widening Light* (1922). The political tumult and racial conflicts of the First World War informed the tone and content of *The Widening Light*. Clifford's affiliations with the NACW and NAACP placed her at the center of black women's wartime activism, the challenges facing African American servicemen, and the broader democratic hopes of the race. In many ways a poetic historical catalog of the war era, *The Widening Light* includes the pieces titled "Mothers of America," "A Dream of Democracy," "The Goal," "Race-hate," "Silent Protest Parade," and "Our Women of the Canteen."[146]

"The Black Draftee from Dixie" first appeared in Clifford's 1922 collection *The Widening Light*. She prefaced the poem with the parenthetical statement "Twelve Negro soldiers who had served overseas were lynched upon their return to their homes in the South."

Upon his dull ear fell the stern command;
And tho' scarce knowing why or whither, he
Went forth prepared to battle loyally,
And questioned not your faith, O Dixie-land!

And tho' the task assigned were small or grand,—
If toiling at mean tasks ingloriously,
Or in fierce combat fighting valiantly,—
With poise magnificent he took his stand!

What tho' the hero-warrior was black?
His heart was white and loyal to the core;
And when to his loved Dixie land he came back,
Maimed, in the duty done on foreign shore,
Where from the hell of war he never flinched,
Because he cried, "*Democracy*," was lynched.[147]

In propagating the trope of the lynched black veteran, the poem links history and memory, symbolism and reality, hope and disillusionment. Clifford's black draftee is unquestionably patriotic and loyal to the nation. He loves America, even his native "Dixie land," but this love is not reciprocated. When spoken from his mouth, "democracy" becomes a threatening phrase, one that challenges the stability of southern racial hierarchies and the place of black people in the nation. Embedded within the metaphoric body of the lynched veteran are the emptiness of democracy and the victimization of a race.

But as Walter White demonstrated in *The Fire in the Flint*, the trope of the lynched black veteran was often intertwined to the trope of the radicalized, militant black veteran who returned to the South ready to combat white supremacy.

White, in the course of his postwar investigations for the NAACP, had seen first-hand the racial hostility that greeted many black servicemen following their return to the South. The gruesome violence in Arkansas; Ocoee, Florida; and other southern communities left an indelible impression on White and on how he subsequently interpreted the meaning of the war. His first novel drew from these memories of unmet expectations and intense desires for democracy. In *The Fire in the Flint*, published in 1924, Walter White similarly places African American veterans within the trope of the socially and politically transgressive New Negro, but for his purposes dressed in the garb of middle-class respectability and racial propriety. White's central character, Dr. Kenneth Harper, served as a medical officer during the war and returned to the South committed to the cause of racial uplift, first by virtue of an individualistic Washingtonesque dedication to his professional work and ultimately through the collective organization of black sharecroppers. His growing resistance to the injustice of black southern life and the relentless attack on black manhood and womanhood pits him against a resurgent Ku Klux Klan, who takes Harper's life in a scene undoubtedly drawn from the numerous lynchings Walter White witnessed and investigated for the NAACP.[148] In the end, White's black veteran is a militant yet tragic figure, symbolic of both the postwar determination of black people to fight for democracy and the virulence of white supremacy in dashing these hopes.[149]

These symbolic cultural representations of black soldiers—as patriotic Americans, as radical militants, as heroes of democracy, as victims of white supremacy—reflected the breadth of African American memories of the war and the effectiveness of different individual artists to use various genres to express them with both subtle poignancy and vivid imagery. They possessed sometimes-explicit political undertones but did not carry the reductive weight of historical accounts of war and the politics of memory engaged in by their respective authors. Nevertheless, often in creating representations of African American soldiers to fit the model of various cultural tropes, certain artists necessarily minimized the human complexity of black servicemen and the multifaceted impacts of their experiences. Thus, while black culture successfully conveyed an inherent dynamism in African American memories of the war, it also had the potential to neglect the personal and individual nuances of how black soldiers themselves actually experienced and remembered the war.

The artwork of veteran Horace Pippin stands as a grand exception. Pippin returned home to West Chester, Pennsylvania, in 1920 with a steel plate in his shoulder, holding together what was left of his nearly useless right arm, injured in combat during his service with the 369th Infantry Regiment in the Meuse-Argonne offensive. Pippin got by the best he could; he married, had a son, and remained active in local church and fraternal organizations such as the Elks. The $22.50 he received every month from his disability pension, along with extra income from various odd jobs and the money his wife contributed from her laundry work allowed for a comfortable life. Nevertheless, he had difficulty shaking the painful memory of the war. From 1925 to 1927 he served as commander of West Chester's black American Legion post, an opportunity to replicate a semblance of the camaraderie he experienced during his time in the 369th. However, he continued to suffer from "blue spells" of depression and his crippled right arm was a constant reminder of his devastating experience.[150]

After a decade of struggling with the traumatic memories of the war and the physical and psychological damage it caused, Pippin began to paint. Art had been a part of Pippin's life since he won a box of crayons at the age of ten in a local drawing contest. But it was the war that, in Pippin's words, "brought out all of the art in me."[151] His first pieces consisted of wood engravings, created with the use of a hot poker. Pippin eventually turned to painting as a means of emotional, physical, and existential rehabilitation: "But I can never for get suffering, and I will never for get sun set. that is when you could see it, so I came home with all of it in my mind. and I paint from it to Day."[152] Pippin overcame the physical challenges of his war disability by holding the brush in his damaged right hand and then using his functional left hand to guide it across the canvass. In the evenings, on the first floor of his small home, the only illumination provided by a 200-watt lightbulb, Pippin reached into the recesses of his consciousness and used the vivid memories of the war as inspiration to depict with poignant humanism the subtle beauty of everyday black life.[153]

Pippin devoted several of his earliest paintings to his experience in the war, each reflecting various scenes, on and off the battlefield, which remained embedded in his memory. Pippin cannot be narrowly labeled a "primitive" artist, considering that his earliest and perhaps most seminal works reflected his experiences in a profoundly modern moment. He depicted both the chaos of war and the human vulnerability of African American soldiers in pieces such as *Shell Holes and Observation Balloon, Champagne Sector* (1931), *Dogfight over the Trenches* (1935), and *The Barracks* (1945).[154] The most significant work in this series, *The End of the War: Starting Home* (1930–33), marked Pippin's first attempt at painting with oils on canvass. It took Pippin over three years and more than one hundred layers of paint to complete the piece, a dramatic rendering of the announcement of the armistice centered on surrendering German soldiers surrounded by entangled trenches, exploding shells, and dogfighting triplanes. The intensity of the painting is palpable, as the chaos and destructiveness of war literally protrude from the canvass. Working with oil paints for the first time,

Horace Pippin, The End of the War: Starting Home. *Philadelphia Museum of Modern Art: Gift of Robert Carlen, 1941.*

Pippin struggled with the technical challenges of controlling the dark color palate, in part explaining why it took three years to complete the painting.[155] Beyond this, Pippin also struggled to accurately capture the meaning of the war and its personal impact; intended to convey the violence of war, the painting was a traumatic act of remembering that required both physical and emotional fortitude. However, unlike Du Bois and the "Wounded World" project, he did finish the painting, suggesting the healing and communicative powers of art to address war-induced trauma and convey historical memory more effectively than formal history itself. After *The End of the War: Starting Home*, Pippin produced with impressive regularity and established a stunning body of work. But it took the completion of this painting for the war to truly end, for him to come to terms with his memory, and to finally be at peace, to be at home.

Popular painter and illustrator N. C. Wyeth "discovered" Pippin in 1937 after happening upon one of his works, *Cabin in the Cotton*, on display in a shoe-repair shop in West Chester, Pennsylvania. This fortuitous encounter, combined with the current fascination with primitivism and folk art, led to four of Pippin's paintings being featured in a traveling "Masters of Popular Painting" show, which made stops at the New York Museum of Modern Art, among other prominent galleries. Pippin's notoriety quickly grew, and his work appeared in mainstream magazines such as *Vogue*, *Life*, *Time*, and *Newsweek*. In January 1940, Pippin opened his first one-man show at the renowned Carlen Galleries in Philadelphia, where he displayed two of his war-themed pieces, *Shell Holes and Observation Balloon, Champagne Sector* and the moving *The End of the War: Starting Home*.[156] Pippin's World War I artwork, as both sites of memory and acts of remembrance, took readers of popular magazines and visitors to art galleries back to 1918, reminding them that African Americans played an important role in the war, and did so with human dignity.

MEMORIES ARE CONTENTIOUS. Memories are messy. Memories are worth fighting, and frequently dying, for. The legacy of African American soldiers in the First World War proved to be an issue of paramount importance for black intellectuals, activists, artists, everyday folk, and, of course, black servicemen themselves. A combative relationship emerged between history and memory. The writing of history, a privileged and highly political act of intellectual activity, proved necessary to combat racist accounts of African American soldiers and to establish a countermemory of black participation in the war. But at the same time, history possessed limitations in its ability to capture the complexities, vicissitudes, and emotional depths of what African American soldiers experienced during the war. The dynamism and multivocality of memory challenged the intellectual and political boundaries of history and sought alternate venues and sites of expression. In the context of the New Negro movement and the experiences of several artists with deep connections to the war, African American culture fostered a broad range of memories and interpretations on the meaning of black military service. The diverse works of jazz musicians, painters, poets, and novelists demonstrated that although a singular collective memory of the war did not exist, the legacy of African American soldiers remained extremely resonant. As historical subjects, symbolic creations, and human actors, black soldiers and veterans of the war continued to challenge, through memory, the very meanings of democracy and the place of peoples of African descent in the modern world. Often celebrated, sometimes mourned, their contributions exalted, their sacrifices lamented, African American soldiers of the First World War, with all that they stood for, would not be forgotten. Their memory lived on.

Epilogue

On October 30, 1925, the Army War College issued a classified report entitled "The Use of Negro Manpower in War." Major General H. E. Ely prepared the study for the army chief of staff in order to determine the future employment of African American soldiers in the wartime military. The "problem" of the black soldier stemming from the First World War continued to vex army officials. Characterizations by white officers, like Robert Bullard, of African American troops as failures formed the subtext of the War College's study and ultimately dictated its findings. Before offering his recommendations, Ely presented the "facts bearing upon the problem." "The negro is physically qualified for combat duty; He is by nature subservient and believes himself to be inferior to the white man; He is most susceptible to the influence of crowd-psychology; He can not control himself in the fear of danger to the extent the white man can; He has not the initiative and resourcefulness of the white man; He is mentally inferior to the white man." Continuing his stream of pseudoscientific racial logic, Ely additionally asserted, "In the process of evolution the American negro has not progressed as far as the other sub-species of the human family. As a race he has not developed leadership qualities. His mental inferiority and the inherent weaknesses of his character are factors that must be considered with great care in the preparation of any plan for his employment in war."[1]

Ely's "factual" explanation of inherent black inferiority rationalized the continuation of "Jim Crow" segregation in the army. The major general made clear that "Negro soldiers as individuals should not be assigned to white units," discounting even the possibility of racial integration. Moreover, he suggested that African American units be first organized into battalions and assigned to divisions of the Regular Army and the National Guard for training. Only when these battalions demonstrated "satisfactory combat efficiency" would they then be enlarged and possibly reorganized as a separate division. The training experience of the Ninety-second Division, with its various regiments scattered in cantonments across the country, warned against a repetition of this blunder. While couched as an efficiency measure, at the heart of Ely's suggestion rested a pervasive distrust of African American soldiers as effective combatants and a desire to, if at all possible, prevent the creation of another black combat division.

Much of the report centered on the still-explosive issue of African American officers. "Negro combat units should be officered entirely by white officers except in the grade of lieutenant," Ely firmly stated. These officers must be, he argued, "carefully selected," an endorsement of the wartime practice of utilizing white officers skilled in handling Negroes. Ely did offer a role for black officers in the army. However, they "should not be placed over white officers, noncommissioned officers or soldiers," but instead "assigned in general to non-combatant units of negro troops."[2] The recommendations sent a clear message: African American officers had failed during the war and, because of immutable mental and biological deficiencies, would continue to fail in the future.

The blistering "Use of Negro Manpower in War" report shaped military policy toward African Americans throughout much of the interwar period. The military denied African Americans the opportunity to enlist in a drastically downsized postwar army. Large numbers of black troops in the Ninth and Tenth Cavalries and Twenty-fourth and Twenty-fifth Infantries, however, continued to serve in the West and South Pacific, raising concerns among army officials about their disproportionate presence. As a result, the War Department instituted a policy restricting new enlistments in the black Regular Army units but allowing for individuals with prior service to reenlist.[3] The size of the historic "Buffalo Soldier" regiments steadily decreased throughout the interwar years, generating fears among African Americans of their possible disbandment. The NAACP and the black press vigorously insisted they remain intact, attesting to both their historic and symbolic importance.[4] While the black Regular Army units struggled for survival, the number of African American officers consisted of a mere two individuals, John E. Green and Benjamin O. Davis Sr.[5]

This dire picture of the black presence in the interwar army has fed historical and popular assessments of the legacy of the First World War and African American soldiers. But a narrow focus on the racist backlash and retrenchment on the part of the military, and American society more broadly, ignores the tremendous contributions of African American servicemen not just during the war itself but throughout the interwar period as well. Many African American soldiers, as veterans, transferred their war and postwar experiences into sustained commitments to fighting for freedom, civil rights, and the broader historical dignity of peoples of African descent.

Rayford Logan, homesick and unfulfilled, returned to the United States from France in December 1924 and embarked on a career in education. He taught at Virginia Union University before attending Harvard University in 1930, where he ultimately received his Ph.D. in history. Logan became the quintessential black intellectual as scholar-activist. He joined the faculty at Howard University, teaching at the esteemed black institution until 1974. Along with passionately advocating for racial justice in the United States and throughout the African diaspora, he worked with the Association for the Study of Negro Life and History and published the classic texts *The Diplomatic Relations of the United States with Haiti*, *What the Negro Wants*, and *The Negro in American Life and Thought*, subsequently retitled *The Betrayal of the Negro* for its 1965 second edition.[6]

Harry Haywood's star continued to rise in the Communist Party. In 1925 he traveled to Moscow, where he spent more than four years studying at the Communist University of the Toilers of the East and the International Lenin School, as well as playing an instrumental role in crafting the Communist Party's policies toward African Americans. At the 1928 Comintern (Communist International), he advanced the "black belt thesis," which argued that the African American peasantry of the Deep South constituted an oppressed nation and necessitated immediate self-determination. Haywood's plank faced criticism from other black communists, including his own brother and fellow veteran Otto Hall, but was nevertheless adopted as the official position of the Comintern on the American "race question."[7] Upon returning to the United States, he became a prominent figure in the Communist Party (CPUSA), heading the League of Struggle for Negro Rights and leading efforts to free the Scottsboro Boys in the 1930s.

George Schuyler remained as outspoken, and controversial, as ever. Schuyler's journalistic prominence increased during his tenure at the *Pittsburgh Courier*, where he established himself as arguably the foremost critic of the New Negro arts movement. Along with his work for the *Courier*, from 1937 to 1944, he served as business manager of the *Crisis*. Schuyler during this time became a significant novelist in his own right, penning *Black No More*, *Black Empire*, and *Slaves Today: A Story of Liberia*. Despite beginning his career with the *Messenger*, by the 1940s Schuyler had long since abandoned socialism as an effective political alternative for African Americans and associated himself with the conservative right. He embraced his role as black America's leading iconoclast, vigorously denouncing communism and offering pointed commentary on the state and future of black people in the United States and beyond.

Charles Spurgeon Johnson used the war as a springboard to become one of the nation's premier black intellectuals. In the wake of the Chicago riot, an inspired Johnson tirelessly labored as lead researcher and associate executive secretary for the Chicago Commission on Race Relations. Released in 1922 and written primarily by Johnson, *The Negro in Chicago* offered explanations for the root causes of the riot and became a model of African American sociological study. He subsequently relocated to New York and, continuing his work with the National Urban League in the positions of research director and editor of

Opportunity, played an instrumental role in birthing the Harlem Renaissance. In 1927 Johnson's desire to enact racial change led him back to the South, where he joined the faculty of Fisk University and headed the department of social research. His contributions to African American social science, which included *Shadow of the Plantation* and *Growing Up in the Black Belt* not only redefined the field but most importantly offered serviceable evidence to confront racial injustice. Johnson transformed Fisk into a research powerhouse and, in October 1946, became the university's first black president.[8]

Several former members of the League for Democracy used their war and postwar experiences as a springboard for continued activism on the behalf of the race. A disillusioned Osceola McKaine abandoned the United States for Belgium in the early 1920s. After several years abroad, partially spent operating a nightclub named Mac's Place, he returned home to South Carolina in 1940 as Europe became engulfed in another World War. It did not take long for the activist in McKaine to resurface. He promptly revitalized the Sumter branch of the NAACP and became an important organizer in World War II–era southern grass-roots political struggles.[9] Louis T. Wright, who worked with McKaine during the LFD's brief ascendancy, became the first African American on the surgical staff at Harlem Hospital and, over the years, transformed the facility into one of the best in the nation. He also volunteered his time to the NAACP and served as chairman of the board of directors. Former field artillery officer and Newark branch leader Lester Granger became a key leader in the National Urban League and in 1941 rose to the position of executive director.

Granger's fellow field artillery officer Charles Hamilton Houston, keeping true to his pledge made during the war, became arguably the most influential African American attorney in United States history. After receiving his law degree from Harvard University in 1924, he committed himself to eradicating racism through the judicial system. As dean of the Howard University Law School, he trained a cadre of young African American attorneys and, as litigation director for the NAACP, spearheaded the organization's legal attack on Jim Crow and the constitutional validity of separate but equal. Nearly every major civil rights case during the 1930s and 1940s bore his imprint. Houston's efforts paved the way for the landmark 1954 *Brown v. Board of Education* ruling, successfully argued by his former student, star protégé, and future Supreme Court justice, Thurgood Marshall.[10]

Beyond these prominent names, there existed thousands of other black servicemen who, in ways large and small, dramatic and subtle, shaped the social, cultural, and political dynamics of black life after the war. They did so by picking up the pieces, as best they could, of a life disrupted by labor and combat.

Many recognized that they would never be the same. The war made a "very lasting" impression on Robert Lee Cypress, a farmer from Surry, Virginia, and private in the 367th Infantry Regiment of the Ninety-second Division, who recalled that "the horrors of war will have a life-long effect."[11] Lemuel Moody of the Fourth Corps Mobile Veterinary Hospital reflected that his time overseas was "altogether improving and broadening" and that his overall experience "changed my out look on life. I see things now with different eyes."[12] Robert Cypress, Lemuel Moody, and countless other former servicemen represented a new generation, shaped by the war and its impact on the future of the race. But far from being "lost," in history and memory, symbol and reality, African American soldiers were thrust into and remained at the center of discussions on the meaning of American democracy, pushing against its all too constraining boundaries and opening new possibilities for its expansion. They inspired new visions of both domestic and diasporic freedom, reflective of the First World War's importance in shaping how African Americans thought of themselves, their nation, and their relationship to it.

Thus, if the men and women who participated and came of age in the Second World War represent a "greatest generation," they are the progeny of those soldiers and civilians, male and female—an African American generation of 1914—who fought in and survived the military and domestic maelstrom of the First. Discussions of the modern civil rights movement traditionally point to the Second World War as a watershed moment in shaping the racial and political consciousness of the brave individuals who placed themselves on the front lines during the 1950s and 1960s for African American freedom and equal citizenship. While undoubtedly true, the ideological tenor and organizational impulses of black activism during World War II and its aftermath drew from the First World War and the memories of African American military participation in it.[13]

"During the World War the patriotism and devotion of the Negroes in the armed forces were sorely tried by all the devilish insults and discriminations which prejudice could devise," Charles Hamilton Houston wrote in an October 1937 letter to President Franklin D. Roosevelt. "We pray that the Negro population will always remain loyal, but it will not again silently endure the insults and discrimination imposed on its soldiers in the course of the last war."[14] As Houston's unequivocal warning reflected, the famous "Double V" campaign, popularized by the *Pittsburgh Courier* and signifying the dual commitment to defeating fascism abroad and American racism at home, represented not a departure but a continuation of the efforts initiated during the First World War, efforts that remained unfulfilled but vividly resonant. It was not a coincidence that former

Messenger editor and Brotherhood of Sleeping Car Porters founder A. Philip Randolph, who came of political age during the World War I era, organized the March on Washington Movement to pressure President Roosevelt to eliminate racial discrimination in wartime government contracting and hiring.[15] Veterans Rayford Logan, Charles Hamilton Houston, and Lester Granger challenged the Roosevelt administration to enforce racial equality in the armed forces. Houston and Logan testified before Congress in August 1940 during debates on the presence of African Americans in the Selective Service Act, where both men invoked their disillusioning experiences in the previous war to warn against a similar repetition in the new world war. In March 1945 Lester Granger became a civilian adviser to the U.S. Navy concerning its policies toward African American servicemen. His investigations and constant pressure moved the navy, ever so grudgingly, toward a policy of racial integration.[16] The legacies of the First World War and the activism of many black veterans loomed large during World War II and throughout subsequent African American struggles for democratic change.

African Americans have had a long, complicated relationship with war and military service. War has repeatedly exposed the democratic incongruities of the nation, while at the same time expanded its effective and imaginative possibilities. Military service has subjected black men, and now women, to often excruciating forms of institutional discrimination, but at the same time provided invaluable material and intangible opportunities. African Americans have used war and participation in the armed forces to individually and collectively stake claim to their citizenship, assert their fundamental humanity, and force the nation as a whole to grapple with the nature of its democracy. The fact that we can trace the arc of the modern black freedom movement through moments of warfare—the Civil War, World War I, World War II, Korea, Vietnam—attests to the power and potential of war as an engine of social and political change, and African American servicemen as the physical and symbolic driving force behind such an evolution.

A perfect illustration of this historical phenomenon took place on April 24, 1991, when Corporal Freddie Stowers became the first African American soldier of both World War I and World War II to receive the Medal of Honor. Stowers had valiantly rallied the men of Company C of the 371st Infantry Regiment during their assault on Côte 188 on September 28, 1918, giving his life in the effort. He had been recommended for the Distinguished Service Cross, a request that his commanding officer subsequently upgraded to the Medal of Honor. But "somehow the recommendation got misplaced," Undersecretary of the Army John Shannon stated, refusing to concede that its mysterious disappearance had any connection to the army's concerted effort to purge the memory of black valor in the First War World from its historical record. African American soldiers received none of the 127 Medal of Honor awards bestowed to American servicemen during the war, and now, seventy-three years later, a wrong was finally being corrected. "On that September day," President George H. W. Bush said in the East Room of the White House, "Corporal Stowers was alone, far from family and home. He had to be scared; his friends died at his side. But he vanquished his fear and fought not for glory but for a cause larger than himself: the cause of liberty." Stowers's two sisters, eighty-eight-year-old Georgiana Palmer and seventy-seven-year-old Mary Bowens accepted the posthumous award. Other attendees and invited guests at the ceremony provided a living continuum of African American military service and accomplishment, bridging the past with the present. Several members of the famed Tuskegee Airmen sat in attendance, proudly sporting red jackets emblazoned with their logo. Top government and military officials acknowledged the historical occasion, among them the first African American chairman of the Joint Chiefs of Staff, Colin L. Powell, at the time the most celebrated black man in the nation because of his successful leadership in the recently concluded Persian Gulf War. One of the soldiers under Powell's command, Staff Sergeant Douglass Warren of the 101st Airborne Division, flew by special charter to Washington from Saudi Arabia to honor his great-great uncle.[17]

It would seem, as dramatic moments such as Stowers's commendation and other acts of recognition by the federal government suggest, that the military has finally solved its race problem and provided a model for the nation as a whole to emulate. And now, with the presidency of Barack Obama, the commander in chief of the United States military is a man of African descent, a seemingly irrefutable illustration of the achievement of true racial equality concerning the nation's armed forces. But conflicts between race and democracy, in governmental policy and the everyday lives of black people, have proved more difficult to reconcile. Talk of a postracial America, while perhaps soothing, functions to suppress both the painful memories and contemporary realities of white supremacy. African Americans continue to grapple with the historical legacies and modern challenges of their place as citizens within the nation, and its relationship to their multifaceted sense of identity. This struggle is just as relevant in the twenty-first century as it was in the twentieth. Questions of war, race, citizenship, social justice, and the place of the United States in the world continue to shape contemporary political debates and, despite the undeniable fact of progress, show no signs of fading.

These issues are not new, just as debates concerning the meaning of democracy remain very much alive. Democracy is not a static term. It is not just a simple catchphrase. It is a powerful ideal, as well as a historically contingent reality and set of relationships, that cuts to the heart of what it means to be black, and what it means to be American. The history of African American soldiers and veterans during the years of the First World War and beyond offers instructive lessons about the dynamic nature of democracy, its possibilities, its limitations, and, ultimately, its centrality to the social and political futures of black people and the nation.

Notes

Abbreviations

CUOHROC	Columbia University Oral History Research Office Collection, Columbia University, New York, N.Y.
FSAA	*Federal Surveillance of Afro-Americans (1917–1925): The First World War, the Red Scare, and the Garvey Movement*, edited by Theodore Kornweibel Jr. Frederick, Md.: University Publications of America, 1986.
HSSL/NYPL	Humanities and Social Science Library, New York Public Library, New York, N.Y.
LOC	Library of Congress, Washington, D.C.
MIB	Military Intelligence Branch
MID	Military Intelligence Division
MSRC	Moorland-Spingarn Research Center, Howard University, Washington, D.C.
NARA	United States National Archives and Records Administration, College Park, Md.
NYSA	New York State Archives, Albany, N.Y.
OHS	Ohio Historical Society, ⟨http://dbs.ohiohistory.org/africanam/index.stm⟩
RG	Record Group
SAAA	Smithsonian Archives of American Art, Washington, D.C.
SC/NYPL	Schomburg Center for Research in Black Culture, New York Public Library, New York, N.Y.
SHAT	Service Historique de l'Armée de Terre, Château de Vincennes, France
TINCF	Tuskegee Institute News Clippings File, Princeton University, Princeton, N.J.
UMA	University of Massachusetts at Amherst
USAMHI	United States Army Military History Institute, Carlisle, Pa.
VWHC	Virginia War Historical Commission Questionnaire, Library of Virginia, ⟨http://www.lva.lib.va.us⟩

Introduction

1. James Preston Spencer, VWHC.

2. Depot brigades functioned as holding units for soldiers until they received transfer orders to a more specific branch of service.

3. "The Loyal Negro Soldier," *Chicago Daily Tribune*, July 16, 1917.

4. Anonymous to Du Bois, July 28, 1918, box 62, Du Bois World War I Papers, UMA.

5. Rodgers, *Contested Truths*; and "Keywords: A Reply," 671.

6. The numerous works of Robert Dahl offer the most exhaustive examination of the his-

tory and meaning of democracy, as well as debates over its feasibility. See, for example, *Democracy and Its Critics*; *Democracy in the United States*; *On Democracy*; *On Political Equality*.

7. Historical literature on African American social and political life during the World War I era is extensive. Key works include Arnesen, *Black Protest and the Great Migration*; Baldwin, *Chicago's New Negroes*; Brown, *Private Politics and Public Voices*; Dittmer, *Black Georgia in the Progressive Era, 1900–1920*; Ellis, *Race, War, and Surveillance*; Gilmore, *Gender and Jim Crow*; Gregory, *The Southern Diaspora*; Foley, *Spectres of 1919*; Grossman, *Land of Hope*; J. W. Harris, *Deep Souths*; Kelly, *Race, Class, and Power in the Alabama Coalfields, 1908–1921*; Krebs, *Fighting for Rights*; W. James, *Holding Aloft the Banner of Ethiopia*; William Jordan, *Black Newspapers and America's War for Democracy, 1914–1920*; Kornweibel, *"Investigate Everything"*; *No Crystal Stair*; and *"Seeing Red"*; Lewis, *W. E. B. Du Bois*, vols. 1 and 2; McMillen, *Dark Journey*; Ortiz, *Emancipation Betrayed*; Reich, "Soldiers of Democracy"; and "The Great War, Black Workers, and the Rise and Fall of the NAACP in the South"; Rolinson, *Grassroots Garveyism*; Rosenberg, *How Far the Promised Land?*; Schneider, *"We Return Fighting"*; Stein, *The World Of Marcus Garvey*; Stephens, *Black Empire*; Turner, *Caribbean Crusaders and the Harlem Renaissance*; D. White, *Too Heavy a Load*; Woodruff, *American Congo*.

8. For discussion of the relationship between race and democracy, see N. Singh, *Black Is a Country*; Sinha and Von Eschen, *Contested Democracy*; West, *Democracy Matters*.

9. For discussions of the historical experiences and symbolic meanings of African American soldiers in the Civil War and post–Civil War period, see Berlin et al., *Freedom's Soldiers*; E. Foner, *Reconstruction*; Harding, *There Is a River*; Painter, *Exodusters*; C. Williams, "Symbols of Freedom and Defeat."

10. Within liberal democratic nations, military service, and compulsory military service in particular, has traditionally been closely tied to citizenship. It has likewise functioned as an opportunity for racial and ethnic minority populations, marginalized from the formal entitlements of citizenship, to make claims for greater democratic and civic inclusion in the body politic. E. Cohen, *Citizens and Soldiers*; Krebs, *Fighting for Rights*.

11. Arthur Barbeau and Florette Henri's *The Unknown Soldiers: African-American Troops in World War I*, remains the lone monograph of African American soldiers and their history during the war. Without completely divorcing the military experience of black soldiers from its social context, Barbeau and Henri detailed the systematic discrimination faced by black soldiers, both abroad and in the United States. Military policy toward African American troops represented Barbeau and Henri's principal subject of inquiry. As such, they paint a clear and vivid picture of the depths of the army's racism and how it adversely impacted the opportunities for African American servicemen to succeed on and off the battlefield. This stands as the book's strength as well as its largest flaw. Barbeau and Henri focused on military discrimination to the exclusion of the totality of black soldiers' experience. As a result, white supremacy appears triumphant, and black soldiers emerge primarily as victims. Other key works on the experiences of African American soldiers in the First World War include Christian, *Black Soldiers in Jim Crow Texas, 1899–1917*; B. Harris, *The Hellfighters of Harlem*; C. Johnson *African American Soldiers in the National Guard*; Keene, *Doughboys*; Lentz-Smith, "The Great War for Civil Rights"; Nelson, *A More Unbending Battle*; Patton, *War and Race*; Roberts, *The American Foreign Legion*; Scipio, *With the Red Hand Division*; Slotkin, *Lost Battalions*; Whalan, *The Great War and the Culture of the New Negro*; C. Williams, "Torchbearers of Democracy."

12. In general, historians have failed to integrate African American soldiers into the history of American military and political involvement in the war. Traditional works have focused on government policy, military bureaucracy, and the battlefield performance of the American army, largely to the marginalization of black troops. This is particularly true for the significant number of studies on Woodrow Wilson, the war, and American foreign policy. By filtering the war through Wilson, a president who exhibited little positive interest in people of color domestically and internationally, scholars similarly minimize the contribution of black soldiers to the history of the war era. See Coffman, *War to End All Wars*; Fleming, *The Illusion of Victory*; Fredericks, *The Great Adventure*; Harries and Harries, *The Last Days of Innocence*; Link, *Wilson*, vols. 3, 4, and 5; *Woodrow Wilson*; *Woodrow Wilson and a Revolutionary World, 1913–1921*; *The Higher Realism of Woodrow Wilson, and Other Essays*; and *Wilson the Diplomatist*. Also see Clements, *The Presidency of Woodrow Wilson*; Ferrell, *Woodrow Wilson and World War, 1917–1921*; Levin, *Woodrow Wilson and World Politics*. More recent studies of the United States in the war usually contain a separate chapter on African Americans, sometimes combined with discussions of other ethnic groups and women during the war. See R. Zeiger, *America's Great War*; Byerly, *Fever of War*; Bristow, *Making Men Moral*; Farwell, *Over There*; Schaffer, *America in the Great War*. A notable exception to this trend is the work of Jennifer Keene, who incorporates the experiences of African American soldiers more seamlessly. See Keene, *Doughboys*.

13. Some notable recent exceptions include Lentz-Smith, "The Great War for Civil Rights"; Reich, "The Great War, Black Workers, and the Rise and Fall of the NAACP in the South"; and "Soldiers of Democracy"; Whalan, *The Great War and the Culture of the New Negro*.

14. The extent to which war constitutes a disjunctive experience in the lives of participants is highly contested. The work of Eric Leed raises important questions regarding the impact of war on individual identity. While suggestive, Leed's analytical framework, which focuses on the experience of British combatants, does not smoothly accommodate African American troops. Most obvious, the majority of black soldiers did not engage in combat and instead served as laborers, the same status that many held in civilian life. They thus experienced the war in a fundamentally different manner. Moreover, the experience of black soldiers who did see time in the trenches does not compare to that of European troops, who measured their service in years as opposed to months. The distinctiveness of African American soldier's experience led to transformations in identity and consciousness that were wholly unique to the particular circumstances they faced in the U.S. military. Leed, *No Man's Land*. Also see Krebs, *Fighting for Rights*.

15. For discussion of wartime notions of citizenship and obligation, see Capozzola, *Uncle Sam Wants You*.

16. Jensen, "Women, Citizenship, and Civic Sacrifice," 139–59.

Chapter One

1. "Great Meeting of Women's Clubs at Wilberforce, O.," *Chicago Defender*, August 15, 1914.

2. "Oklahoma Welcomes Session of National Negro Business League," *New York Age*, August 20, 1914.

3. "Colored Carnegie Library Dedication Draws Large Crowd," *Savannah Tribune*, August 15, 1914; "Cubans Win in Ninth," *New York Age*, August 27, 1914.

4. "Civil Service Applicants to Furnish Photos," *Chicago Defender*, August 8, 1914.

5. "Louisiana Has Murder Epidemic," *Chicago Defender*, August 15, 1914; "3 Lynched for Murder," *New York Times*, August 8, 1914.

6. Keegan, *The First World War*, 122, 295–99. For discussion of the effect of the Somme offensive on British morale, see Fussell, *The Great War and Modern Memory*, 29–32.

7. Eksteins, *Rites of Spring*.

8. J. Cooper, *Pivotal Decades*, 227–33.

9. Historian John Whiteclay Chambers II argues that the U.S. military has evolved through six distinct structural models since the seventeenth century: the Settlement Model, the Colony Model, the Confederation Model, the New Nation Model, the Nation-State Model, and the World Power Model. The Nation-State Model emerged from American participation in the First World War and lasted until the Vietnam War. Chambers, *To Raise an Army*, 6–8.

10. Gerstle, *American Crucible*; O'Leary, *To Die For*.

11. J. W. Harris, *Deep Souths*; G. Wright, *Old South, New South*.

12. Cell, *The Highest Stage of White Supremacy*; Rabinowitz, *Race Relations in the Urban South*; Woodward, *The Strange Career of Jim Crow*.

13. Cecelski and Tyson, *Democracy Betrayed*.

14. Number based on records compiled by the Tuskegee Institute.

15. Hale, *Making Whiteness*.

16. Meier, *Negro Thought in America*.

17. Norrell, *Up From History*, 224–33, 310–43, 384–401, 421–39; Lewis, *W. E. B. Du Bois*, 1:238–64, 297–342.

18. For key histories of the NAACP, see Berg, *The Ticket to Freedom*; Jonas, *Freedom's Sword*; Kellog, *NAACP*; Schneider, *"We Return Fighting"*; Zangrando, *The NAACP Crusade against Lynching, 1909–1950*.

19. Gaines, *Uplifting the Race*.

20. Higginbotham, *Righteous Discontent*; D. White, *Too Heavy a Load*; Giddings, *When and Where I Enter*.

21. McNeil, *Groundwork*, 15–35.

22. Kelley, "'We Are Not What We Seem.'"

23. Hahn, *A Nation under Our Feet*; J. W. Harris, *Deep Souths*; Hunter, *To 'Joy My Freedom*; Kelly, *Race, Class, and Power in the Alabama Coalfields, 1908–1921*; Lipsitz, *A Life in the Struggle*; McMillen, *Dark Journey*; Woodruff, *American Congo*.

24. Scott, "More Letters of Negro Migrants," 440.

25. Ibid., 439.

26. Ibid., 447–48.

27. Arnesen, *Black Protest and the Great Migration*; Gregory, *The Southern Diaspora*; Griffin, *"Who Set You Flowin'?"*; Grossman, *Land Of Hope*; Marks, *Farewell—We're Good and Gone*; Phillips, *AlabamaNorth*; Trotter, *Black Milwaukee*; and *The Great Migration in Historical Perspective*.

28. Knock, *To End All Wars*, 111–15.

29. Lunardini, "Standing Firm," 260.

30. Patler, *Jim Crow and the Wilson Administration*.

31. Rogers Smith makes a distinction between centrist Progressivism and left Progressiv-

ism. Smith, *Civic Ideals*, 413–24. For a general discussion of Woodrow Wilson and the war, see Ferrell, *Woodrow Wilson and World War I*. Richard Hofstadter, in arguing that American entrance into the war ended the Progressive movement, acknowledges that Wilson and government officials justified the conflict in Progressive terms and rhetoric. Hofstadter, *The Age of Reform*, 275.

32. This point is central to Thomas Knock's study of Woodrow Wilson and the First World War. He describes Wilson's war and postwar foreign policy as "Progressive internationalism," beginning in earnest in 1916, and culminating in the failed effort to establish the League of Nations. Knock, *To End All Wars*.

33. "President Calls for War Declaration, Stronger Navy, New Army of 500,000 Men, Full Co-operation with Germany's Foes," *New York Times*, April 3, 1917.

34. Link, *The Papers of Woodrow Wilson*, 41:520–25.

35. David Kennedy recognizes the "ideological battle" surrounding America's role in the war as framed by Woodrow Wilson and how various groups sought to "turn the crisis to their particular advantage." D. Kennedy, *Over Here*, 53.

36. "Democracy and Human Rights," *Washington Bee*, May 5, 1917.

37. Rodgers, *Contested Truths*, 3–16, 213; E. Foner, *The Story of American Freedom*, 171–75.

38. "Democratic Government," *Baltimore Afro-American*, April 28, 1917.

39. J. Johnson, *Black Manhattan*, 232–33.

40. Perry, *Hubert Harrison*.

41. Kornweibel, *No Crystal Stair*, 3; A. P. Anderson, *A. Philip Randolph*, 98.

42. "Messages from the Messenger," *Messenger*, November 1917. Randolph and Owen were referring to W. E. B. Du Bois, Kelly Miller, William Pickens, and Archibald H. Grimke, whom the *Messenger* regularly criticized for their perceived conservative racial and political philosophies.

43. Capozzola, "The Only Badge Needed Is Your Patriotic Fervor"; Gerstle, "Liberty, Coercion, and the Making of Americans," 530–31; Higham, *Strangers in the Land*, 204–6.

44. Vaughn, *Holding Fast the Inner Lines*.

45. See E. Foner, *Story of American Freedom*, 177; Kornweibel, *"Seeing Red,"* 418; Painter, *Standing at Armageddon*, 335–37. The Military Intelligence Branch was renamed the Military Intelligence Division in August 1918. Kornweibel, *"Investigate Everything,"* 236.

46. "Messages from the Messenger," *Messenger*, November 1917.

47. Report, re: Socialist Meeting, East 9th and Chestnut Streets, August 22, 1918, reel 10, frame 920, FSAA.

48. A. P. Anderson, *A. Philip Randolph*, 104–8.

49. Ellis, *Race, War, and Surveillance*, 9–11; Kornweibel, *"Investigate Everything."*

50. Report, re: Possible Uprising of Negroes (Lancaster, Ky.), July 31, 1917, 10218-2, MID, RG 165, NARA.

51. Report, re: Belge, Caprey, Fla. German Neutrality, September 18, 1917, 10218-20, MID, RG 165, NARA.

52. "A Texas Citizen" to Woodrow Wilson, April 19, 1917, reel 8, frame 256, FSAA.

53. "Negro Loyalty in the Present Crisis," *New York Age*, March 29, 1917.

54. "Richmond Negroes Pledge Loyalty," *Norfolk Journal and Guide*, April 7, 1917.

55. "Preached Loyalty," *Richmond Planet*, April 21, 1917.

56. O'Leary, *To Die For.*

57. "The Duty of the Hour," *New York Age*, April 5, 1917.

58. "National Unity," *Savannah Tribune*, April 14, 1917.

59. Rudwick, *Riot at East St. Louis.*

60. William Jordan, *Black Newspapers and America's War for Democracy*, 88–90.

61. "East St. Louis Riots," *Norfolk Journal and Guide*, July 7, 1917.

62. "Making Democracy Safe," *Cleveland Advocate*, July 14, 1917. The *Advocate* made reference not to Woodrow Wilson's war declaration address, but to a May 12, 1917, speech he delivered in Washington, D.C., where he stated, "We have entered this war to make Democracy safe for humanity."

63. Lorini, *Rituals of Race*, 243–50.

64. Dobak and Phillips, *The Black Regulars, 1866–1898*; Schuyler, *Black and Conservative*, 28.

65. Schuyler, *Black and Conservative*, 32.

66. Ibid., 62.

67. Ibid., 76, 84.

68. Ibid., 84–85.

69. Richards, "Osceola E. McKaine," 1–31; Thompson, *History and Views of Colored Officers Training Camp*, 72.

70. Gatewood, "Black Americans and the Quest for Empire," 546.

71. Kramer, *The Blood of Government.*

72. Painter, *Standing at Armageddon*, 283–92, 310–14; Schoultz, *Beneath the United States*, 240–52.

73. "Some Interesting Facts about Negro Soldiers," *Savannah Tribune*, April 28, 1917.

74. "Colored Troops Honored," *Norfolk Journal and Guide*, April 7, 1917.

75. Gatewood, "Alabama's 'Negro Soldier Experiment.'"

76. Christian, *Black Soldiers in Jim Crow Texas*, 69–91; A. Lane, *The Brownsville Affair*; Leiker, *Racial Borders.*

77. C. Williams, "Symbols of Freedom and Defeat."

78. Holmes, *The White Chief.*

79. *Congressional Record* 55 (August 16, 1917): 6063.

80. J. Keith, *Rich Man's War, Poor Man's Fight*; Woodward, *Origins of the New South.*

81. "The Negro in War," *Atlanta Constitution*, July 12, 1917.

82. See Tindall, *The Emergence of the New South*, 53–61; J. W. Harris, "Etiquette, Lynching, and Racial Boundaries in Southern History," 399.

83. Several officers from the Twenty-fourth Infantry were transferred out of the regiment and assigned to the officers' training camp established by the War Department for African American candidates at Fort Des Moines, Iowa.

84. Christian, *Black Soldiers in Jim Crow Texas.*

85. Haynes, *Night of Violence*; Christian, *Black Soldiers in Jim Crow Texas.*

86. Martha Gruening, "Houston: An N.A.A.C.P. Investigation," *Crisis*, November 1917.

87. Haynes, *Night of Violence*, 99.

88. Singleton, *The Autobiography of George A. Singleton*, 77.

89. Testimonies of Corine Foreman, Flossie Chaney, Edna Tucker, Bessie Chaney, Frances

Smith, *Case of United States v. Sergeant William C. Nesbit, et al.*, 942–58, Entry 1007, RG 153, NARA.

90. Testimony of Snow, *Case of United States v. Sergeant William C. Nesbit, et al.*, 36–40, Entry 1007, RG 153, NARA.

91. Ibid., 71–72.

92. Ibid., 78.

93. Testimony of Bernard Bunnemeyer, *Case of United States v. Sergeant William C. Nesbit, et al.*, 962, Entry 1007, RG 153, NARA.

94. For detailed descriptions of the Houston Riot, see Christian, *Black Soldiers in Jim Crow Texas*, 145–72; Haynes, *Night of Violence*. One of these four individuals was an Illinois national guardsmen.

95. Testimony of Henry H. Peacock, Co. I, 24th Infantry, *Case of United States v. Sergeant William C. Nesbit, et al.*, 1257, Entry 1007, RG 153, NARA. Also see Testimony of Private Jesse Harris, Co. L, 24th Infantry, 983; Testimony of Frank Draper, Co. M, 24th Infantry, 1032.

96. Haynes, *Night of Violence*.

97. House Resolution 131, August 30, 1917, Correspondence of the War College, 1903–1919, 5720-2, RG 165, NARA.

98. *Issue* 10, no. 1 (September 6, 1917).

99. *Issue* 10, no. 2 (September 13, 1917).

100. "Houston," *New York Age*, August 30, 1917.

101. Martha Gruening, "Houston: An N.A.A.C.P. Investigation," *Crisis*, November 1917.

102. "The Rioting of Negro Soldiers," *Messenger*, November 1917.

103. General Court-Martial Order No. 1299, Headquarters Southern Department, Fort Sam Houston, Texas, December 10, 1917, Entry 1007, RG 153, NARA.

104. "Thirteen," *Crisis*, January 1918.

105. The second trial resulted in death sentences for five additional servicemen.

106. W. F. Cozart to Woodrow Wilson, January 10, 1918, Entry 1007, RG 153, NARA.

107. Jean Gabrel O'Neill to Woodrow Wilson, February 26, 1918, 10218-112, reel 19, frame 516, FSAA.

108. Mrs. L. Welch to Woodrow Wilson, February 1, 1918, Entry 1007, RG 153, NARA.

109. "Negro Rioters 'Martyrs,' Says Mrs. Barnett," *Chicago Daily Tribune*, December 23, 1917.

110. McMurry, *To Keep the Waters Troubled*, 318–19; Schechter, *Ida B. Wells-Barnett and American Reform*, 133–34, 147–58.

111. "Negro Rioters 'Martyrs,' Says Mrs. Barnett," *Chicago Daily Tribune*, December 23, 1917.

112. Wells, *Crusade for Justice*, 370.

113. Patton, *War and Race*.

114. B. Ross, *J. E. Spingarn*, 82–84.

115. Barbeau and Henri, *The Unknown Soldiers*, 56–57; Chase, "Struggle for Equality," 299; Joel E. Spingarn Papers, MSRC.

116. "Military Training Camp for Colored Men: An Open Letter from Dr. J. E. Spingarn," February 15, 1917, box 95-8, Joel E. Spingarn Papers, MRSC.

117. Ibid.

118. Editorial, *New York Age*, March 1, 1917.

119. "Military Training Camp for Colored Officers. Dr. J. E. Spingarn Explaining His Reasons in a Nutshell," March 8, 1917, box 95-8, Joel E. Spingarn Papers, MSRC.

120. "'Jim Crow' Training Camp—No!," *Chicago Defender*, April 7, 1917.

121. "The Perpetual Dilemma," *Crisis*, April 1917.

122. Roy Nash to Newton D. Baker, April 19, 1917, box 95-8, Joel E. Spingarn Papers, MSRC.

123. Lewis, *W. E. B. Du Bois*, 2:335–48; Lewis, *W. E. B. Du Bois*, 1:528–32.

124. B. Ross, *J. E. Spingarn*, 92.

125. Chase, "The Struggle for Equality."

126. Biographical information, box 37-1, Thomas Montgomery Gregory Papers, MSRC.

127. Patton, *War and Race*, 40.

128. J. Milton Waldron, President, "The Committee of 100 Citizens on the War," and Thomas Gregory, Chairman, "Central Committee of Negro College Men" to Woodrow Wilson, May 11, 1917, box 37-1, Thomas Montgomery Gregory Papers, MSRC.

129. The *Pittsburgh Courier* published Houston's memoir as a serial in July and August of 1940. Charles H. Houston, "Saving the World for 'Democracy,'" *Pittsburgh Courier*, July 20, 1940.

130. McNeil, *Groundwork*.

131. Patton, *War and Race*, 40; Scott, *Scott's Official History*, 86.

132. Recruitment letter, May 24, 1917, box 37-1, Thomas Montgomery Gregory Papers, MSRC.

133. Scott, *Scott's Official History*, 89; Chase, "The Struggle for Equality," 305–6.

134. Houston, "Saving the World for 'Democracy,'" *Pittsburgh Courier*, September 14, 1940.

135. Houston, "Saving the World for 'Democracy,'" *Pittsburgh Courier*, July 20, 1940.

136. Thompson, *History and Views of Colored Officers Training Camp*, 61.

137. Enrollment information, Victor R. Daly Papers, box 1, Cornell University.

138. James Wormley Jones Papers, MSRC; Thompson, *History and Views of Colored Officers Training Camp*, 67.

139. Thompson, *History and Views of Colored Officers Training Camp*, 84, 96.

140. Schuyler, *Black and Conservative*, 31–35, 86–87; Thompson, *History and Views of Colored Officers Training Camp*, 84.

141. Richards, "Osceola E. McKaine," 11–14; Thompson, *History and Views of Colored Officers Training Camp*, 72.

142. Garvin, "The Negro in the Special Services of the U.S. Army," 337–38.

143. Memoirs of William H. Dyer, SC/NYPL.

144. "Race Leaders in the Making," *Norfolk Journal and Guide*, July 28, 1917.

145. Chase, "The Struggle for Equality," 307; Patton, *War and Race*, 59.

146. Patton, *War and Race*, 57.

147. Cade, *Twenty-two Months with "Uncle Sam,"* 17.

148. "Constitution of the 17th Provisional Training Regiment Association," box 37-1, Thomas Montgomery Gregory Papers, MSRC.

149. Thompson, *History and Views of Colored Officers Training Camp*, 80–81.

150. Shellum, *Black Cadet in a White Bastion*.

151. Lewis, *W. E. B. Du Bois*, 1:176, 517; "Men of the Month," *Crisis*, October 1916.

152. As controversy raged in the black press, Young voiced his support for the camp in a

letter to Harry C. Smith, editor of the *Cleveland Advocate*, much to the delight of Joel Spingarn. Young's endorsement carried considerable weight and was published in several prominent black newspapers, including the *Baltimore Afro-American*, the *New York Age*, and the *Washington Bee*.

153. Special Orders No. 119, May 23, 1917, Colonel Charles Young Collection, OHS; Kilroy, *For Race and Country*, 120.

154. Kilroy, *For Race and Country*, 120–21.

155. Quoted in ibid., 121.

156. Charles Young to W. E. B. Du Bois, June 20, 1917, in Aptheker, *Correspondence of W. E. B. Du Bois*, 222–23.

157. "Young Undergoing Physical Examination," *New York Age*, June 14, 1917.

158. Woodrow Wilson to Newton Baker, June 25, 1917, container 4, reel 3, Newton Diehl Baker Papers, LOC.

159. Woodrow Wilson to Senator John Sharp Williams, June 29, 1917, container 4, reel 3, Newton Diehl Baker Papers, LOC.

160. Du Bois to Young, June 28, 1917, Colonel Charles Young Collection, OHS.

161. "Lieut. Col. Young Is to Be Retired," *Chicago Defender*, June 30, 1917.

162. "May Retire Young from Active Service," *New York Age*, June 28, 1917.

163. Special Orders No. 175, July 30, 1917, Colonel Charles Young Collection, OHS.

164. Charles Young to Adjutant General, August 14, 1917, Colonel Charles Young Collection, OHS.

165. "To General H. P. McCain," *Crisis*, February 1918; Lewis, *W. E. B. Du Bois*, 1:532–34.

166. Charles Young to W. P. Bayless, August 12, 1917, Colonel Charles Young Collection, OHS.

167. W. E. B. Du Bois noted this fact with bitter irony in the February 1922 essay "Colonel Young," written to eulogize his death. Du Bois wrote: "He had been sent to Africa because the Army considered his blood pressure too high to let him go to Europe! They sent him there to die. They sent him there because he was one of the very best officers in the service and if he had gone to Europe he could not have been denied the stars of a General. They could not stand a black American General." "Colonel Young," *Crisis*, February 1922.

168. Schuyler, *Black and Conservative*, 87.

169. Quoted in Kilroy, *For Race and Country*, 125–26.

170. Patton, *War and Race*, 58.

171. Schuyler, *Black and Conservative*, 87.

172. Charles H. Houston, "Saving the World for 'Democracy,'" *Pittsburgh Courier*, July 27, 1940.

173. Webster, *Chums and Brothers*, 148. Webster's correspondence with several officers from Atlanta University throughout their war experience formed the core of his book.

174. Houston, "Saving the World for 'Democracy,'" *Pittsburgh Courier*, July 27, 1940.

175. C. C. Ballou to W. T. Johnston, July 10, 1917, quoted in Chase, "The Struggle for Equality," 308.

176. Houston, "Saving the World for 'Democracy,'" *Pittsburgh Courier*, July 27, 1940.

177. Adjutant General to Secretary of War, September 4, 1917, 8142-20, RG 165, NARA.

178. Reminiscences of George Samuel Schuyler (1960), 45–46, CUOHROC.

179. Cade, *Twenty-two Months with "Uncle Sam,"* 23.

180. Edward C. Micksey to W. E. B. Du Bois, September 14, 1917, box 54, W. E. B. Du Bois World War I Papers, UMA.

181. C. C. Ballou to Dr. George W. Cabaniss, September 14, 1917, box 37-1, Thomas Montgomery Gregory Papers, MSRC.

182. Thomas Montgomery Gregory to Mrs. James Montgomery Gregory, September 14, 1917, box 37-1, Thomas Montgomery Gregory Papers, MSRC.

183. "A Negro's Faith in American Justice," *Southern Workman*, December 1918, 591–92.

184. Thompson, *History and Views of Colored Officers Training Camp.*

185. Grotelueschen, *The AEF Way of War*, 10–25.

186. Capozzola, *Uncle Sam Wants You*, 23–26.

187. Chambers, *To Raise an Army*, 103–24; J. Keith, *Rich Man's War, Poor Man's Fight.*

188. Chambers, *To Raise an Army*, 73–101; Ford, *American's All!.*

189. Chambers, *To Raise an Army*, 262–63, 268–69; Capozzola, *Uncle Sam Wants You*, 21–55; Keene, *Doughboys*, 4; Schaffer, *America in the Great War.*

190. J. Keith, *Rich Man's War, Poor Man's Fight*; Kantrowitz, *Ben Tillman and the Reconstruction of White Supremacy.*

191. Reich, "The Great War, Black Workers, and the Rise and Fall of the NAACP in the South," 149.

192. Office of the Provost Marshal General, *Second Report of the Provost Marshal General*, 191.

193. Capozzola, *Uncle Sam Wants You*, 33.

194. Plan I consisted of raising and organizing white and black troops in the same manner within the sixteen divisional training areas. Plan II suggested the organization of one African American regiment within each cantonment, with any remaining black soldiers serving in stevedore or labor battalions. Plan III proposed dividing African American draftees into sixteen equally sized groups and constructing separate training facilities for them just outside of the regular national army cantonments. Plan IV necessitated the placement of all African Americans drafted from southern states into two cantonments, thus leaving white soldiers to occupy the remaining fourteen. Plan V forwarded the option of creating war-strength infantry regiments composed of black draftees and sending them to France, unattached to a division, eight at a time until the entire draft was disposed of. Tasker H. Bliss to Newton Baker, August 24, 1917, 8142-17, RG 165, NARA.

195. Office of the Provost Marshal General, *Second Report of the Provost Marshal General*, 276.

196. Drafted at a higher percentage, poor and working-class whites received far fewer exemptions than their middle-class counterparts, who controlled the decision-making process. J. Keith, "The Politics of Southern Draft Resistance," 1344.

197. Unnamed soldier to W. E. B. Du Bois, February 25, 1918, box 54, Du Bois World War I Papers, UMA.

198. Office of the Provost Marshal General, *Second Report of the Provost Marshal General*, 276. Barbeau and Henri attribute this discrepancy to explicit racial discrimination (Barbeau and Henri, *The Unknown Soldiers*, 36). However, Jeanette Keith complicates this assertion. She

claims that because African American poverty rates surpassed those of whites, if the draft was colorblind (which it was not) black men in the South still would have been disproportionately conscripted. Keith, "The Politics of Southern Draft Resistance," 1350.

199. Chambers, *To Raise an Army*, 225. Selective Service officials created four physical qualification groups to determine the fitness of draftees and in what capacity they could serve. Group A consisted of men "qualified for general military service," Group B of men with remediable physical defects, Group C of men "qualified for special or limited service," and Group D of men disqualified for any type of military service. African Americans were disproportionately represented in Groups A and D. Office of the Provost Marshal General, *Second Report of the Provost Marshal General*, 150–57, 160.

200. J. Keith, "The Politics of Southern Draft Resistance," 1350.

201. It was one of three local boards removed by the secretary of war. *Crisis*, February 1918; Scott, *Scott's Official History*, 51; Chambers, *To Raise an Army*, 226.

202. J. Keith, "The Politics of Southern Draft Resistance," 1350; Hickel, "War, Region, and Social Welfare."

203. Cornelius Vanderbilt Bridgeforth, VWHC.

204. Office of the Provost Marshal General, *Second Report of the Provost Marshal General*, 205.

205. Platt, *E. Franklin Frazier Reconsidered*, 36.

206. Kornweibel, "Apathy and Dissent," 334; Grossman, "Citizenship and Rights on the Home Front during the First World War," 169–90.

207. Office of the Provost Marshal General, *Second Report of the Provost Marshal General*, 205.

208. Kornweibel, "Apathy and Dissent," 334; J. Keith, *Rich Man's War, Poor Man's Fight*, 180–84.

209. Office of the Provost Marshal General, *Second Report of the Provost Marshal General*, 461.

210. Theodore Kornweibel Jr. estimates that 40 to 50 percent of the black population approached the war with varying degrees of apathy or cynicism. His argument, however, does not account for the specific responses of draft-eligible African Americans. Kornweibel, "Apathy and Dissent," 337–38; J. Keith, "The Politics of Southern Draft Resistance," 1346.

211. Mac Tidsdale, VWHC.

212. George Wesley Wyche, VWHC.

213. George Thomas Clark, VWHC.

214. Howard Garrett, VWHC.

215. Herbert Ulysses White, VWHC.

216. Luther Robinson, VWHC.

217. Moses Randolph, VWHC.

218. Albert Johnson, VWHC.

219. Royal Lee Fleming, VWHC.

220. Ernest Bartee, VWHC.

221. Salyer, "Baptism by Fire," 850–51.

222. Mark Meigs makes a similar observation among African American respondents to the

United States Army Military History Institute World War I Questionnaire and Survey. Meigs, *Optimism at Armageddon*, 15.

223. Thomas Clary, VWHC.

224. Stanley Clary Hammon, VWHC.

225. Tonias Thomas White, VWHC.

226. Charles Pettus Brodnax, VWHC.

227. Schaffer, *America in the Great War*.

228. Hatcher Mack, VWHC.

229. Walter James Lethcoe, VWHC.

230. Earnest Burwell, VWHC.

231. Elija Spencer, VWHC; Clarence Bailey, VWHC.

232. Hickel, "War, Region, and Social Welfare."

233. Solomon David Spady, VWHC.

234. Aaron Andrew Jones, VWHC.

Chapter Two

1. Winn Parish was at the heart of Reconstruction-era racial violence in Louisiana. Most notoriously, white "militias" from Winn crossed over into neighboring Grant Parish to participate in the bloody April 1873 Colfax Massacre, which left upwards of 150 African Americans dead. The White League, although established in Grant Parish in 1874, exerted considerable influence in Winn and other neighboring parishes. L. Keith, *The Colfax Massacre*; C. Lane, *The Day Freedom Died*, 83; Lemann, *Redemption*, 14; "Send Off for Drafted Men in Louisiana," *New York Age*, October 18, 1917.

2. "Colored Citizens Give Boys Send-Off," *Fort Smith Arkansas American*, April 10, 1918, reel 244, frame 326, TINCF.

3. "Fifteen Thousand See Negroes Leave," *Memphis Appeal*, April 29, 1918, reel 244, 366, TINCF.

4. Mennell, "African-Americans and the Selective Service Act of 1917," 275–87.

5. Keene, *Doughboys*, 3.

6. Du Bois, *The Souls of Black Folk*, 363.

7. Beaver, *Newton D. Baker*, 225; Lewis, *W. E. B. Du Bois*, 1:534, 541.

8. Newton Baker to Woodrow Wilson, August 17, 1917, in Link, *The Papers of Woodrow Wilson*, 43:506–7.

9. Scott, *Scott's Official History*, 32.

10. Christian, *Black Soldiers in Jim Crow Texas*.

11. Barbeau and Henri, *The Unknown Soldiers*, 27–28.

12. "Will Fight, But Won't Farm," *Chicago Defender*, July 28, 1917.

13. "The War Department and Negro Soldiers," *New York Age*, August 16, 1917.

14. J. D. Leitch, Colonel, General Staff, to Chief of Staff, October 9, 1917, box 1, 92nd Division—Assgt & Relief, 292-12.8, RG 120, NARA.

15. The organization of the Ninety-second Division was as follows: the 183rd Brigade, made up of the 365th and 366th Infantry Regiments, and the 350th Machine Gun Battalion; the 184th Brigade, made up of the 367th and 368th Infantry Regiments, and the 351st Field Artil-

lery Regiment; the 167th Field Artillery Brigade, composed of the 349th, 350th, and 351st Field Artillery Regiments; the 317th Engineer Regiment; the 325th Field Signal Battalion; the 317th Supply Train; and the 317th Ammunition Train, which included the 349th Machine Gun Battalion. American Battle Monuments Commission, *92d Division*, 1–5.

16. J. D. Leitch, Colonel, General Staff, to Chief of Staff, October 9, 1917, box 1, 92nd Division—Assgt & Relief, 292-12.8, RG 120, NARA.

17. Barbeau and Henri, *The Unknown Soldiers*, 82.

18. C. Johnson, *African American Soldiers in the National Guard*, 99–100.

19. Unpublished autobiography, ch. 5, box 166-32, Rayford Whittingham Logan Papers, MSRC.

20. Rayford Logan, "The Consent of the Governed," June 25, 1917, Williams College commencement address, box 166-5, Rayford Whittingham Logan Papers, MSRC.

21. Unpublished autobiography, ch. 5, box 166-32, Rayford Whittingham Logan Papers, MSRC; Janken, *Rayford W. Logan and the Dilemma of the African-American Intellectual*, 1–33.

22. Summers, *Manliness and Its Discontents*, 25–65.

23. Davis, *Here and There with the Rattlers*, 20–24.

24. Horace Pippin war notebook, SAAA.

25. Haywood, *Black Bolshevik*, 5–42. On the idea of the "race man," see Drake and Cayton, *Black Metropolis*; Carby, *Race Men*.

26. "'Just Let Us Get at Germans,' Is Cry of Black Devils as They Are Held from Front," *Cleveland Advocate*, September 7, 1918.

27. The Twenty-sixth and the Forty-second Divisions, two of the first four combat divisions of the AEF sent to France, were composed of National Guard regiments.

28. Memorandum to Chief of Staff, November 13, 1917, Correspondence of War College, 1903–1919, 8142-46, RG 165, NARA.

29. Henry Jervey, Chairman, Operation Committee to Chief of Staff, January 2, 1918, Correspondence of War College, 1903–1919, 8142-64, RG 165, NARA.

30. Scott, *Scott's Official History*, ch. 3. For more on Scott's appointment, see Ellis, *Race, War, and Surveillance*, 54.

31. "The Right Man for the Place," *Cleveland Advocate*, October 13, 1917; *Richmond Planet*, October 13, 1917. Also see "Mr. Scott's Appointment," *New York Age*, October 11, 1917. For an example of reactions to Scott's appointment by the northern white press, see "The Problem of the Negro Soldier," *Outlook*, October 24, 1917.

32. "War Department Bureau Steadily Growing," August 7, 1918, box 590, RG 4, NARA. Also see Scott, *Scott's Official History*, ch. 4.

33. Scott, *Scott's Official History*, 33.

34. Lewis, *W. E. B. Du Bois*, 1:559–60; Ellis, *Race, War, and Surveillance*, 57–65.

35. Walter Loving to Chief Military Intelligence Section, November 9, 1917, 10218-47, MID, RG 165, NARA.

36. Joel Spingarn to Colonel Marlborough Churchill, June 8, 1918, box 7, folder 5, Joel E. Spingarn Papers, HSSL/NYPL.

37. Emmett J. Scott to George Creel, June 3, 1918, box 3, folder 6, General Correspondence of Carl Byoir, Records of the Committee on Public Information, RG 63, NARA.

38. Joel E. Spingarn to Churchill, June 22, 1918, 10218-154, MID, RG 165, NARA; "Help Us to Help," *Crisis*, August 1918; William Jordan, *Black Newspapers and America's War for Democracy*, 122–28.

39. Ellis, "Joel Spingarn's 'Constructive Programme,'" 134–62.

40. Joel Spingarn testimony before House of Representatives Committee on the Judiciary, June 6, 1918, box 8, folder 2, Joel E. Spingarn Papers, HSSL/NYPL.

41. Newton Baker to Woodrow Wilson, July 17, 1918, box 7, folder 5, Joel E. Spingarn Papers, HSSL/NYPL. On July 1, 1918, following the Washington, D.C., editors conference, Secretary of War Baker wrote to Woodrow Wilson and suggested that he "write to the governor of some State in which a lynching has quite recently taken place a strong letter urging full use of the power of the State to search out and prosecute the offenders, and pointing out the unpatriotic character of these acts of brutality and injustice." Wilson took no such action. Newton Baker to Woodrow Wilson, July 1, 1918, container 8, reel 6, Newton Diehl Baker Papers, LOC.

42. "A Statement to the American People," July 26, 1918, in Link, *The Papers of Woodrow Wilson*, 49:97–98.

43. J. E. Spingarn to Thomas Montgomery Gregory, June 4, 1918, box 37-1, Thomas Montgomery Gregory Papers, MSRC.

44. Thomas M. Gregory, Report: Negro situation in northeast Washington and the activities of Lawyer Emanuel M. Hewlett, box 37-1, Thomas Montgomery Gregory Papers, MSRC.

45. Du Bois, *Dusk of Dawn*, 742.

46. Joel Spingarn to Colonel Churchill, June 8, 1918, box 7, folder 5, Spingarn Papers, HSSL/NYPL.

47. "Close Ranks," *Crisis*, July 1918.

48. "DUBOIS' 'SURRENDER' EDITORIAL CAUSES RUMPUS IN NAACP," *Cleveland Advocate*, July 20, 1918.

49. Hubert Harrison, "The Descent of Dr. Du Bois," *Voice*, July 25, 1918, in Perry, *Hubert Harrison*, 170–72.

50. Lewis, *W. E. B. Du Bois*, 1:555–58.

51. Walter Loving to Major Nicolas Biddle, July 22, 1918, box 113-1, folder 10, Walter Loving Papers, MSRC; Ellis, "'Closing Ranks' and 'Seeking Honors,'" 115–18; Lewis, *W. E. B. Du Bois*, 1:559–60; Perry, *Hubert Harrison*, 385–90.

52. Ellis, "'Closing Ranks' and 'Seeking Honors,'" 108; Lewis, *W. E. B. Du Bois*, 1:552–60; William Jordan, "'The Damnable Dilemma,'" 1562–83; Ellis, "W. E. B. Du Bois and the Formation of Black Opinion in World War I," 1584–90.

53. This position, convincingly argued by Mark Ellis, is also supported by David Levering Lewis in his biographical account of the "Close Ranks" controversy. Conversely, William Jordan asserts that "Close Ranks" was consistent with Du Bois's lifelong proclivity toward racial accommodation in certain contexts and was consistent with his war-era thought.

54. Du Bois most likely deepened the hole he found himself in by ending the September 1918 editorial "Our Special Grievances," in an attempt to rationalize the July "Close Ranks" piece, with the blunt statement: "The CRISIS says, *first* your Country, *then* your Rights!" "Our Special Grievances," *Crisis*, September 1918.

55. Blount, *Reminiscences of Samuel E. Blount*, 1–3.

56. Ibid., 3–4.

57. Scott, *Scott's Official History*, 92–93.

58. Barbeau and Henri, *The Unknown Soldiers*, 38–39; Office of the Provost Marshal General, *Second Report of the Provost Marshal General*, 175.

59. Scott, *Scott's Official History*, 73.

60. Charles Arnold to W. E. B. Du Bois, July 19, 1918, box 54, Du Bois World War I Papers, UMA.

61. Scott, *Scott's Official History*, 108.

62. C. H. Williams, *Sidelights on Negro Soldiers*, 26.

63. Ibid.

64. Ibid.

65. *Issue* 10, no. 1 (September 6, 1917).

66. Joseph Kuhn, Chief of the War College Division, Assistant to the Chief of Staff, to Chief of Staff, July 31, 1917, 8142-12, RG 165, NARA.

67. William A. Mann, Chief, Militia Bureau to Adjutant General, July 18, 1917, 8142-10, RG 165, NARA.

68. Joseph Kuhn, Chief of the War College Division, Assistant to the Chief of Staff, to Chief of Staff, July 31, 1917, 8142-12, RG 165, NARA.

69. Haywood, *Black Bolshevik*, 45.

70. Little, *From Harlem to the Rhine*, 52.

71. Unpublished autobiography, ch. 6, box 166-32, Rayford Whittingham Logan Papers, MSRC.

72. Joseph Kuhn, Chief of the War College Division, Assistant to the Chief of Staff, to Chief of Staff, July 31, 1917, 8142-12, RG 165, NARA.

73. Memorandum of Col. Leitch for the Chief of Staff, October 9, 1917, box 1, 292-12.8, Records of the 92nd Division, RG 120, NARA.

74. Houston, "Saving the World for 'Democracy,'" *Pittsburgh Courier*, August 3, 1940.

75. Schuyler, *Black and Conservative*, 87.

76. Record of Trial by General Court-Martial of 1st Lieut. George S. Schuyler, 368th Regiment of Infantry, file #121521, box 6041, RG 153, NARA.

77. Ibid.

78. James M. Mullen, Camp Judge Advocate to Commanding General, October 16, 1918, file #121521, box 6041, RG 153, NARA. The reduction in sentence to five years was approved on October 12, 1918.

79. Woodrow Wilson to Adjutant General, November 30, 1918, file #121521, box 6041, RG 153, NARA.

80. Adjutant General to Commandant, United States Disciplinary Barracks, Atlantic Branch, Fort Jay, New York, December 5, 1918; E. A. Kreger, Acting Judge Advocate General to the Secretary of War, July 3, 1919, file #121521, box 6041, RG 153, NARA.

81. Ferguson, *The Sage of Sugar Hill*, 11–16; Talalay, *Composition in Black and White*, 67–68; O. Williams, *George S. Schuyler*, 22–23.

82. Apparent Cause Card, May 13, 1919, file #121521, box 6041, RG 153, NARA.

83. Blount, *Reminiscences of Samuel E. Blount*, 4.

84. Walker Jordan, *With "Old Eph" in the Army*, 13.

85. Walter E. D. Robinson, World War I Survey, USAMHI.

86. George Granderson Robinson, VWHC.

87. Orville Webb, "A Rookie's Diary," research materials, box 54, Du Bois World War I Papers, UMA.

88. Cade, *Twenty-two Months with "Uncle Sam,"* 26.

89. Scott, *Scott's Official History*, 73.

90. Webster, *Chums and Brothers*, 156.

91. Unpublished autobiography, ch. 6, box 166-32, Rayford Whittingham Logan Papers, MSRC.

92. Anonymous soldiers to Mr. Simons, November 5, 1918, 10218-201, reel 19, frame 971, FSAA.

93. Haywood, *Black Bolshevik*, 45–49.

94. "Army Officer Jailed; Rode in a Pullman," *New York Age*, March 20, 1918; "Case of Lieut. Tribbett Will Be Investigated," *Chicago Defender*, April 20, 1918; Scott, *Scott's Official History*, 113–14.

95. Bulletin No. 35, Headquarters Ninety-second Division, Camp Funston, Kansas, March 28, 1918, box 50, 322-9, Records of the 92nd Division, RG 120, NARA.

96. "Tear Down Ballou Order; Denied Right to Leave Camp," *New York Age*, April 20, 1918.

97. Walter Loving to Chief Military Intelligence Branch, Subject: Effect of General Bell's Address on Colored Troops, April 20, 1918, box 113-1, folder 10, Walter Loving Papers, MSRC.

98. John Shillady, NAACP to War Department, April 11, 1918, box 50, 322-9, Records of the 92nd Division, RG 120, NARA.

99. "'Don't Insist on Legal Rights,' Ballou Tells Colored Soldiers; Policy Is Put above the Law," *New York Age*, April 13, 1918. Also see "The Time for Men," *New York Age*, April 13, 1918.

100. "General Ballou's Order," *Cleveland Advocate*, April 20, 1918.

101. McMurry, *To Keep the Waters Troubled*, 317–19; Schechter, *Ida B. Wells-Barnett and American Reform*, 207–12.

102. Ida B. Wells-Barnett to Woodrow Wilson, April 26, 1918, box 50, 322-9, Records of the 92nd Division, RG 120, NARA.

103. The Citizens' Forum to War Department, April 30, 1918, box 50, 322-9, Records of the 92nd Division, RG 120, NARA.

104. W. H. Moses, Pastor, Zion Baptist Church, to Secretary of War Newton D. Baker, April 14, 1919, box 50, 322-9, Records of the 92nd Division, RG 120, NARA.

105. Janken, *White*, 27–28.

106. "Negroes Protest against Army Edict," *Brooklyn Eagle*, April 23, 1918, reel 244, frame 403, TINCF.

107. Taylor, *The Black Churches of Brooklyn*, 122–23.

108. George Frazier Miller and Walter White to Newton Baker, n.d., box 50, 322-9, Records of the 92nd Division, RG 120, NARA.

109. E. D. Anderson, Colonel, General Staff, to Chief of Staff, May 22, 1918, box 264, 8142-149, RG 165, NARA.

110. "Negro Army Officer Driven from Home by Southern Crackers," *Cleveland Advocate*, November 17, 1917; "Army Lieutenant Flees for Life When Mob Forms," *Chicago Defender*, November 17, 1917.

111. "Negro Officer Says He Was Ill Treated," *Vicksburg Herald*, November 14, 1917; "Negro Officer Had to Flee Vicksburg," *Vicksburg Herald*, November 18, 1917.

112. "Second Army Officer Is Insulted at Vicksburg," *Cleveland Advocate*, December 8, 1917.

113. Captain Harry A. Taylor to Chief, Military Intelligence Section, re: Assault on Negro soldiers, October 1917, 10218-27, MID, RG 165, NARA.

114. "Memoir of James Reese Europe," 83, James Reese Europe Collection, SC/NYPL.

115. "Memoir of James Reese Europe," 80–83, James Reese Europe Collection, SC/NYPL; Little, *From Harlem to the Rhine*, 68–70.

116. Scott, *Scott's Official History*, 80–81.

117. Fish, *Hamilton Fish*, 26–27.

118. William Lloyd Imes, YMCA secretary, to Emmett J. Scott, August 18, 1918, 10218-209, MID files, RG 165, NARA; Keene, *Doughboys*, 94–96.

119. Bristow, *Making Men Moral*, 1–17, 36.

120. D. W. Ketcham to Chief of Staff, Subject: Segregation of Whites and Negroes in Red Cross Convalescent Houses, March 28, 1918; William Graves to Director of Military Relief, American Red Cross, March 30, 1918, 8142-107, Correspondence of War College, 1903–1919, RG 165, NARA.

121. Bristow, *Making Men Moral*, 8, 151–52.

122. Mjagkij, *Light in the Darkness*, 87.

123. Jesse E. Moorland, "The 'Y' Working with the Colored Troops," February 25, 1919, Papers of Jesse E. Moorland, MSRC.

124. Orville Webb, "A Rookie's Diary," research materials, box 54, Du Bois World War I Papers, UMA.

125. Webster, *Chums and Brothers*, 179.

126. Bristow, *Making Men Moral*, 18–30.

127. The use of institutionalized racial discrimination as the main interpretive framework for analyzing the experiences of African American soldiers is most significantly reflected in Barbeau and Henri, *The Unknown Soldiers*.

128. Beardsley, *A History of Neglect*.

129. A postwar study of venereal disease in the AEF indicated an infection rate of 31 percent among the black draftees from South Carolina, Georgia, and Florida. Walker, *Venereal Disease in the American Expeditionary Forces*, 122.

130. Love and Davenport, "A Comparison of White and Colored Troops," 58–60.

131. Byerly, *Fever of War*, 167.

132. Hezekiah Eugene Walker, VWHC.

133. The army set a daily intake goal of 4,761 calories for soldiers in the training camps. However, as Carol Byerly demonstrates, African American soldiers often received a diet consisting of less protein and calories. Farwell, *Over There*, 63; Byerly, *Fever of War*, 171.

134. Douglass Baskerville, VWHC.

135. Chesleigh Plummer Franklin, VWHC.

136. Willie Anderson Chambers, VWHC.

137. Clarence Carlyle Bailey, VWHC.

138. Kevles, "Testing the Army's Intelligence," 565–81; Barbeau and Henri, *The Unknown Soldiers*, 44–48.

139. Keene, *Doughboys*, 28.

140. Webster, *Chums and Brothers*, 154.

141. Mjagkij, *Light in the Darkness*, 88–91.

142. Cade, *Twenty-two Months with "Uncle Sam,"* 27.

143. Jesse E. Moorland, "The 'Y' Working with the Colored Troops," February 25, 1919, Jesse Moorland Papers, MSRC.

144. Charles Arnold to W. E. B. Du Bois, July 12, 1918, box 54, Du Bois World War I Papers, UMA.

145. Peter Beverley, VWHC.

146. Albert Johnson, VWHC.

147. Page William West, VWHC.

148. Bederman, *Manliness and Civilization*, 5–31.

149. Eules Bracey, VWHC.

150. Walter Winfrey Allen, VWHC.

151. Roy Lee Fleming, VWHC.

152. Waverly Lee Crawford, VWHC.

153. Breen, "Black Women and the Great War"; Brown, *Private Politics and Public Voices.*

154. D. White, *Too Heavy a Load*; Giddings, *When and Where I Enter.*

155. "Women's Auxiliary at Work for Soldiers," *New York Age*, May 17, 1917; "Woman's Auxiliary Mobilized for Service," *New York Age*, May 24, 1917; Scott, *Scott's Official History*, 390.

156. Brown, *Private Politics and Public Voices*, 12.

157. Scott, *Scott's Official History*, 388–89; *Southern Workman*, January 1918; Brown, *Private Politics and Public Voices*, 1–29, 36–40; Circle for Negro War Relief, SC/NYPL.

158. Breen, "Black Women and the Great War," 424–40; Hunter, *To 'Joy My Freedom*; Arnesen, *Black Protest and the Great Migration*, 140–45.

159. Brown, *Private Politics and Public Voices*, 54.

160. The regional nature of American race relations allowed for black women to participate in the Red Cross in northern cities with greater frequency, working alongside white women. In the South, where their presence was needed the most, local chapters largely denied black women the opportunity to work in Red Cross canteens. Hine, "The Call That Never Came," 23–26; Brown, *Private Politics and Public Voices*, 67–72; C. H. Williams, *Sidelights on Negro Soldiers*, 123.

161. Brown, *Private Politics and Public Voices*, 74–75.

162. YWCA, "The Work of Colored Women," 13.

163. Ibid., 132.

164. D. White, *Too Heavy a Load*; Gilmore, *Gender and Jim Crow.*

165. Bristow, *Making Men Moral*, 147.

166. YWCA, "The Work of Colored Women," 14.

167. Ibid., 25.

168. Jensen, "Women, Citizenship, and Sacrifice," 149–50.

169. YWCA, "The Work of Colored Women," 23.

170. Ibid., 18–19.

Chapter Three

1. Silas Bradshaw to Lieut. Graster, June 22, 1918, box 37-1, Thomas Montgomery Gregory Papers, MSRC.

2. Sergt. E. A. Means, "Hindenburg Cave," in *Heroes of 1918*.

3. Sergt. Matthew Jenkins, "Capturing Hindenburg Cave," in *Heroes of 1918*.

4. Ibid.

5. Niles, *Singing Soldiers*, 48–50.

6. Ibid., 69–71.

7. Colonel E. D. Anderson to Chief of Staff, May 16, 1918, box 264, 8142-150, RG 165, NARA.

8. Ibid.

9. Ibid.

10. Orville Webb, "A Rookie's Diary," research materials, box 54, Du Bois World War I Papers, UMA.

11. Colonel E. D. Anderson to Chief of Staff, May 22, 1918, box 264, 8142-149, RG 165, NARA.

12. Summary of Complaints Received at National Office N.A.A.C.P. from Colored Soldiers at Army Camps in United States, by Camps, 1919, Part 9: Discrimination in the U.S. Armed Forces, 1918–1955, Series A: General Office Files on Armed Forces' Affairs, 1918–1955, Group 1, Series C, Administrative Files, box C-374, reel 1, Papers of the NAACP (hereafter Discrimination in the Armed Forces, Papers of the NAACP).

13. For discussion of convict-lease in the antebellum South, see Blackmon, *Slavery by Another Name*.

14. "Experienced Men Wanted," *New York Age*, November 8, 1917.

15. Colonel E. D. Anderson to Chief of Staff, July 25, 1918, 8689-266, RG 165, NARA.

16. Colonel E. D. Anderson to Chief of Staff, May 16, 1918, box 264, 8142-150, RG 165, NARA.

17. Webster, *Chums and Brothers*, 153.

18. Orville Webb, "A Rookie's Diary," research materials, box 54, Du Bois World War I Papers, UMA.

19. Sergeant Bernard O. Henderson to W. E. B. Du Bois, December 18, 1918, reel 1, Discrimination in the Armed Forces, Papers of the NAACP.

20. Miss Hayde Moore to John Shillady, December 30, 1918, reel 1, Discrimination in the Armed Forces, Papers of the NAACP.

21. Anonymous soldier to Emmett J. Scott, October 20, 1918, 10218-201, MID, RG 165, NARA.

22. Anonymous soldier to Emmett J. Scott, October 19, 1918, 10218-201, MID, RG 165, NARA.

23. Anonymous soldier to Simmons, November 5, 1918, 10218-201, MID, RG 165, NARA.

24. War Department, *Organization of the Services of Supply*, 15–24; Hagood, *The Services of Supply*.

25. The Service of Supply also employed 5,586 nurses. Hagood, *The Services of Supply*, 25.

26. Barbeau and Henri, *The Unknown Soldiers*, 103.

27. African American stevedores also served at Base Section No. 3 Liverpool and Southamp-

ton, where American troops passed through England on their way to France. War Department, *Organization of the Services of Supply*, 22.

28. Mjagkij, "Behind the Lines," 86.

29. "Stevedores' Career a Round of Harmony," June 7, 1918, *Stars and Stripes.*

30. "'Taters and Suchlike to Be Grown by A.E.F.," March 8, 1918, *Stars and Stripes.*

31. Braddan, *Under Fire with the 370th Infantry*, 44.

32. C. H. Williams, *Sidelights on Negro Soldiers*, 27.

33. A. R. McAliley to Commanding General, November 18, 1918, box 903, 304th Labor Bn., RG 120, NARA. For information on the inequitable conditions black labor troops endured, see Byerly, *Fever of War*, 171–72.

34. Enoch Dunham to W. E. B. Du Bois, July 14, 1919, box 55, Du Bois World War I Papers, UMA.

35. Dawes, *A Journal of the Great War*, 1:18.

36. U.S. Congress, *Alleged Executions without Trial in France*, 201–4.

37. The African American Pioneer Infantry units consisted of the 801st to 809th, the 811th, and the 813th to 816th Battalions. Scott, *Scott's Official History*, 317.

38. "803d Pioneers, from 4 States, Sail for Home," *Chicago Daily Tribune*, July 6, 1919.

39. Charles Spurgeon Johnson, draft registration card, ⟨http://www.ancestry.com⟩; Gilpin and Gasman, *Charles S. Johnson*, 6; Robbins, *Sidelines Activist*, 33–34; P. Johnson, "Seasons in Hell," 21; Embree, *13 Against the Odds*, 55; C. Johnson, "Charles S. Johnson," 197.

40. C. H. Williams, *Sidelights on Negro Soldiers*, 152–54.

41. Robert Stevens, 801st Pioneer Infantry, USAMHI.

42. War Department, *Historical Report of the Chief Engineer*, 118.

43. Gilpin and Gasman, *Charles S. Johnson*, 6; Embree, *13 Against the Odds*, 69; "803d Pioneers, from 4 States, Sail for Home," *Chicago Daily Tribune*, July 6, 1919; C. Johnson, "Charles S. Johnson," 198.

44. Alfred J. Allen, VWHC.

45. J. A. Toliver to W. E. B. Du Bois, June 27, 1919, box 55, Du Bois World War I Papers, UMA.

46. Jerry Modaws Marton, VWHC.

47. On the "new woman," see Patterson, *Beyond the Gibson Girl.*

48. Brown, *Private Politics and Public Voices*, 90.

49. Ibid., 89.

50. Scott, *Scott's Official History*, 379; Memorandum for the Chief of Staff, Subject: Segregation of Whites and Negroes in Red Cross Convalescent Houses, March 21, 1918, box 264, 8142-107, RG 165, NARA; William S. Graves to Director General of Military Relief, American Red Cross, March 28, 1918, box 264, 8142-107, RG 165, NARA.

51. Mjagkij, "Behind the Lines," 87.

52. Ibid., 88.

53. James Wiley to Jesse E. Moorland, March 11, 1918, WWI Letters, Correspondence w/ soldiers & secretaries in France, 1918–1919, box 2, Colored Work Department Records, Kautz Family YMCA Archives.

54. Hunton and Johnson, *Two Colored Women*, 138–39.

55. Ibid., 152.

56. Ibid., 20.

57. Ibid., 94, 98, 214–16.

58. Byerly, *Fever of War*, 97–124, 172.

59. Hunton and Johnson, *Two Colored Women*, 150–51.

60. Ibid., 97–98.

61. Brown, *Private Politics and Public Voices.*

62. Hunton and Johnson, *Two Colored Women*, 150.

63. Ibid., 156. Meigs notes the adoration overseas servicemen had for American female nurses as a "desirable ideal." Meigs, *Optimism at Armageddon*, 121.

64. This figure is based on the high point of regiment strength of the Ninety-third Division, August 31, 1918, and the high point of divisional strength of the Ninety-second Division, September 30, 1918. American Battle Monuments Commission, *93rd Division*, 36; American Battle Monuments Commission, *92nd Division*, 36.

65. Sissle, "Memoirs of Lieutenant 'Jim' Europe," 111–12, James Reese Europe Collection, SC/NYPL.

66. Little, *From Harlem to the Rhine*, 100.

67. Sissle, "Memoirs of Lieutenant 'Jim' Europe," 113, James Reese Europe Collection, SC/NYPL.

68. Scipio, *With the Red Hand Division*, 39–40.

69. Pershing, *My Experiences in the World War*, 1:291.

70. Little, *From Harlem to the Rhine*, 148–49; James Harbord, Chief of Staff, to Chief of the French Mission, 15 janvier 1918, 17N 76, SHAT; A Monsieur le Général Commandant l'Armée, 6 mars 1918, 16N 203, SHAT.

71. Braddan, *Under Fire with the 370th Infantry*, 51.

72. Charles S. Robinson, World War I Survey, USAMHI.

73. Pershing, *My Experiences in the World War*, 2:45.

74. Ibid., 46. For background on Milner and his role in structuring racial hierarchies in South Africa, see Grant, *A Civilised Savagery*, 79–107.

75. Pershing, *My Experiences in the World War*, 2:49; Grundlingh, "The Impact of the First World War on South African Blacks."

76. For discussion of France's and Great Britain's respective imperial policies toward African servicemen in the war, see Morrow, *The Great War.*

77. Blount, *Reminiscences of Samuel E. Blount*, 23.

78. Ibid., 28.

79. Diary entries, June 25 and 26, 1918, 92nd Division interpreter diary, box 62, Du Bois World War I Papers, UMA.

80. Barbeau and Henri, *The Unknown Soldiers*, 139–42.

81. War Department, *Battle Participation of Organizations of the American Expeditionary Forces*, 38.

82. Blount, *Reminiscences of Samuel E. Blount*, 36.

83. Fussell, *The Great War and Modern Memory*, 36–74.

84. Horace Pippin war notebooks, SAAA.

85. Haywood, *Black Bolshevik*, 58.

86. Walker Jordan, *With "Old Eph" in the Army*, 37.

87. Fussell, *The Great War and Modern Memory*, 36–74; Farwell, *Over There*, 110–12.

88. Meigs, *Optimism at Armageddon*, 36–68.

89. Robert Lee Cypress, VWHC.

90. "How a Hampton Boy Went over the Top," *Southern Workman*, December 1918.

91. For discussion of this tension, see Fussell, *The Great War and Modern Memory*.

92. Oscar Walker, "The Eighth Regiment in France," in *Heroes of 1918*.

93. Erkson Thompson, "Near Chateau Thierry," in *Heroes of 1918*.

94. Little, *From Harlem to the Rhine*, 194–99; "Henry Johnson Greeted by Throng upon Return Home," *New York Age*, March 1, 1919.

95. Little, *From Harlem to the Rhine*, 201.

96. "Bill and Needham," *New York Times*, May 22, 1918.

97. "Henry Johnson and Needham Roberts Rout 24 Germans," *New York Age*, May 25, 1918.

98. "The Two Heroes," *Chicago Defender*, June 1, 1918.

99. "Large Crowd Honors Relatives of War Heroes," *Chicago Defender*, July 6, 1918.

100. Blount, *Reminiscences of Samuel E. Blount*, 51.

101. Emmett Scott professed that black soldiers disregarded the German propaganda. Scott, *Scott's Official History*, 136–39.

102. C. H. Williams, *Sidelights on Negro Soldiers*, 71.

103. Diary entry, June 13, 1943, box 4, Rayford Whittingham Logan Papers, LOC; unpublished autobiography, ch. 6, box 166-32, Rayford Whittingham Logan Papers, MSRC.

104. Unpublished autobiography, ch. 6, box 166-32, Rayford Whittingham Logan Papers, MSRC.

105. Diary entry, June 13, 1943, box 4, Rayford Whittingham Logan Papers, LOC; Mason and Furr, *The American Negro Soldier with the Red Hand of France*, 43.

106. Unpublished autobiography, ch. 6, box 166-32, Rayford Whittingham Logan Papers, MSRC.

107. William Hayward to Adjutant General, June 23, 1920, Subject: Historical facts re 93rd Division and 369th U.S. Infantry, 93rd Division Historical Files (boxes 1–3), Stack Area 290, box 1, folders 293-13.6, 293-11.4, RG 120, NARA.

108. Sissle, "Memoirs of Lieutenant 'Jim' Europe," 184–85, James Reese Europe Collection, SC/NYPL.

109. Henry Plummer Cheathum Collection, SC/NYPL.

110. Braddan, *Under First with the 370th Infantry*, 67.

111. James Preston Spencer, VWHC.

112. L. J. McNair, Brig. Gen., General Staff, to Personnel Officer, October 23, 1918, in *The Colored Soldier in the U.S. Army*, USAMHI.

113. Braddan, *Under First with the 370th Infantry*, 73–74.

114. Ibid., 71, 95.

115. Unpublished autobiography, ch. 6, box 166-32, Rayford Whittingham Logan Papers, MSRC; Diary entry, July 30, 1943, box 4, Rayford Whittingham Logan Papers, LOC.

116. Diary entry, July 31, 1943, box 4, Rayford Whittingham Logan Papers, LOC.

117. Janken, *Rayford W. Logan*, 39–40.

118. Ibid., 76.

119. Colonel Herschel Tupes, 372nd Infantry, to Commanding General, A.E.F., August 24,

1918, in *History of Negro Troops in the World War*, Army War College, Historical Section (1942), USAMHI.

120. Concernant les cadres du 372° R.I.U.S., Général Goybet, 21 août 1918, 16N 204, SHAT.

121. Mason and Furr, *The American Negro Soldier with the Red Hand of France*, 99–103.

122. Barbeau and Henri, *The Unknown Soldiers*, 62; Cunningham, "Black Artillerymen from the Civil War through World War I," 14–16.

123. Houston, "Saving the World for 'Democracy,'" *Pittsburgh Courier*, August 31, 1940.

124. Ibid., September 7, 1940.

125. Reminiscences of Lester B. Granger (1961), 24, CUOHROC.

126. Houston, "Saving the World for 'Democracy,'" *Pittsburgh Courier*, August, 31, 1940.

127. Ibid., August 31, 1940; September 7, 1940.

128. Reminiscences of Lester B. Granger (1961), 25, CUOHROC.

129. Houston, "Saving the World for 'Democracy,'" *Pittsburgh Courier*, September 14, 1940.

130. Ibid., 28.

131. Reminiscences of Lester B. Granger (1961), 28, CUOHROC.

132. Houston, "Saving the World for 'Democracy,'" *Pittsburgh Courier*, September 14, 1940.

133. For the background on Boute, see Hunton and Johnson, *Two Colored Women*, 57–61.

134. Diary entry, June 8, 1918, box 62, Du Bois World War I Papers, UMA.

135. "'We've Got Boche on Run' Writes McKaine," *New York Age*, October 12, 1918.

136. Internal documents within the War Department established that African American officers would be kept at the grade of first and second lieutenant, and the few officers holding the rank of captain would remain at this grade. Moreover, the highest-ranking positions within the division were explicitly set aside for white men. The promotion opportunities of black officers were further limited by the army's constant transference of officers from the Ninety-third Division into the Ninety-second. 92nd Division, RG 120, NARA.

137. Memorandum to Officers from Major General Ballou, July 23, 1918, in Cade, *Twenty-two Months with "Uncle Sam,"* 51.

138. Commanding General to the Adjutant General, September 7, 1918, reel 21, frame 86, FSAA.

139. Barbeau and Henri, *The Unknown Soldiers*, 146–48.

140. William Colson, "The Failure of the 92nd Division," *Messenger*, September 1919.

141. Ferrell, *America's Deadliest Battle*.

142. The 370th participated in the ongoing Oise-Aisne offensive, launched by the French on August 18, as part of the French Fifty-ninth Division of the Tenth Army. They entered the front on September 17 and engaged in intense fighting, taking 512 casualties until the Fifty-ninth Division was relieved on October 13. The French Fifty-ninth Division and the 370th were then reassigned on November 5 to pursue retreating German forces, which they did until the November 11 armistice. All together, the 370th endured 665 casualties, with 90 men killed during the operation. American Battlefield Monuments Commission, *93rd Division*, 25–35.

143. Ibid., 8–24.

144. Horace Pippin war notebooks, SAAA; Slotkin, *Lost Battalions*, 277–79.

145. American Battle Monuments Commission, *93rd Division*, 24.

146. Joseph Pate to American Battle Monument Commission, June 5, 1927, Records of the

American Battle Monument Commission, Correspondence with Former Division Officers, 92d and 93d Divs, box 259, RG 117, NARA; Beattie, "Personality," 74–76.

147. American Battle Monuments Commission, *92nd Division*, 10–12; Barbeau and Henri, *The Unknown Soldiers*, 149–50.

148. Blount, *Reminiscences of Samuel E. Blount*, 45.

149. American Battle Monuments Commission, *92nd Division*, 6–24; Barbeau and Henri, *The Unknown Soldiers*, 152.

150. On the doctrine of open warfare and Pershing's belief in its applicability on the western front, see Grotelueschen, *The AEF Way of War*, 31–35.

151. Byerly, *Fever of War*, 110.

152. D. Kennedy, *Over Here*, 195–205; Bruce, *A Fraternity of Arms*, 266–85.

153. Ferrell, *America's Deadliest Battle*; and *Collapse at Meuse-Argonne*. Grotelueschen offers a less critical assessment of the AEF's performance in the Meuse-Argonne based on its strengths and weaknesses. Grotelueschen, *The AEF Way of War*.

154. Major J. N. Merrill to Commanding Officer, 368th Infantry, October 3, 1918, in *History of Negro Troops in the World War*, Army War College, Historical Section (1942), appendix 33, USAMHI.

155. Charles C. Ballou to Commanding General, IV Army Corps, October 12, 1918, 292-65.1, box 5, 92nd Division, RG 120, NARA.

156. James Wormley Jones Papers, MSRC; Barbeau and Henri provide convincing evidence that Elser's incompetence and unauthorized orders led to the withdrawal of the Second Battalion's black officers. Barbeau and Henri, *The Unknown Soldiers*, 152–57.

157. John P. Bubb, Major 28th Infantry, to Commandant, First Corps Infantry School, Aug. 27, 1918, James Wormley Jones Papers, MSRC.

158. Memo from Elser to commanding officer of the 368th, September 30, 1918, James Wormley Jones Papers, MSRC.

159. Warner Ross, *My Colored Battalion*, 30.

160. American Battle Monuments Commission, *92nd Division*, 32.

161. Cade, *Twenty-two Months with "Uncle Sam,"* 97.

162. American Battle Monuments Commission, *92nd Division*, 31–34; Malvern Hill Barnum to Commanding General, 92nd Division, Subject: Operations, November 19, 1918, box 6, Historical, 183rd Inf. Brigade, 92nd Division, RG 120, NARA; Barbeau and Henri, *The Unknown Soldiers*, 159–60.

163. Malvern Hill Barnum to Commanding General, 92nd Division, Subject: Report on Offensive Operations, November 19, 1918, box 6, Historical, 183rd Inf. Brigade, 92nd Division, RG 120, NARA.

164. Warner Ross of the 365th Infantry Regiment praised the black soldiers under his command. Ross, *My Colored Battalion*.

165. Percy, *Lanterns on the Levee*, 199.

166. Pershing, *My Experiences in the World War*, 2:228–29.

167. Diary entry, October 25, 1918, box 2, Diary Book #9, Robert Lee Bullard Papers, LOC.

168. The secretary of war later commuted their sentences after a review determined that the officers had in fact received orders to withdraw during the Meuse-Argonne engagement.

169. Diary entry, November 1, 1918, box 2, Diary Book #9, Robert Lee Bullard Papers, LOC.

Chapter Four

1. Henry Gilliam, VWHC.

2. Gillespie Garland Lomans, VWHC.

3. Henry Gilliam, VWHC.

4. Gillespie Garland Lomans, VWHC.

5. Morrow, *The Great War.*

6. Spengler, *The Decline of the West*; Lenin, *Imperialism, the Highest Stage of Capitalism.*

7. Anderson, *Imagined Communities*; Lemelle and Kelley, "Introduction: Imagining Home: Pan-Africanism Revisited," in *Imaging Home*, 7–9.

8. Kelley, "'But a Local Phase of a World Problem,'" 1056.

9. I invoke the term "mobilized" from Joseph Harris's characterization of a "mobilized diaspora," comprising an international network of politically active and racially conscious descendant Africans who organized their communities around the future betterment of the race. Harris, "Dynamics of the Global African Diaspora," 15. For a definition of the "modern African diaspora," see Palmer, "Defining and Studying the Modern African Diaspora."

10. Butler, "Defining Diaspora, Refining a Discourse," 189.

11. Palmer, "Defining and Studying the Modern African Diaspora."

12. I take the postulation of diaspora as both process and condition from Tiffany Ruby Patterson and Robin D. G. Kelley's seminal essay. Patterson and Kelley, "Unfinished Migrations." Historian Kim Butler, in her important essay, likewise stresses the need to move away from employing diaspora simply as a descriptive ethnographic label and toward an emphasis on the "social *processes* of diasporization." Butler, "Defining Diaspora, Redefining a Discourse," 193. Paul Tiyambe Zeleza builds on these theoretical assertions by describing diaspora as "a process, a condition, a space and a discourse." Zeleza, "Rewriting the African Diaspora," 41.

13. Edwards, *The Practice of Diaspora*; Fierce, *The Pan-African Idea in the United States*; Kelley, "'But a Local Phase of a World Problem,'" 1056; Makalani, "For the Liberation of Black People Everywhere"; Stephens, *Black Empire*; Stovall, *Paris Noir* and "Harlem-Sur-Seine."

14. Lewis, "To Turn as on a Pivot"; Edwards, *The Practice of Diaspora*; Kelley and Patterson, "Unfinished Migrations," 18–21; Butler, "Defining Diaspora, Redefining a Discourse."

15. On the transatlantic nature of social, political, and economic thought during the Progressive Era, and the years of the First World War more specifically, see Rodgers, *Atlantic Crossings.*

16. Du Bois, "The African Roots of War"; Lewis, *W. E. B. Du Bois*, 1:503–5.

17. William Jordan, *Black Newspapers and America's War for Democracy*, 36–67.

18. "Well Worth Thinking About," *New York Age*, February 10, 1915.

19. "Lusitania," *Crisis*, June 1915.

20. "The After Results of the Great War," *New York Age*, October 15, 1914.

21. *Baltimore Afro-American*, December 25, 1915.

22. Edwards, *The Practice of Diaspora.*

23. See Egerton, *Gabriel's Rebellion*; Sidbury, "Saint Domingue in Virginia."

24. Fabre, *From Harlem to Paris.*

25. "In America and in France," *Baltimore Afro-American*, May 5, 1917.

26. A defining moment in the history of European imperialism in Africa was the 1884–85

Berlin Conference. At the conference, the major European powers parceled the continent among themselves.

27. France declared possession of Algeria, its first and most important African colony, in 1830. France claimed Tunisia in 1882. Aldrich, *Greater France*, 25–30.

28. For discussion of this in the context of French West Africa, see Conklin, *A Mission to Civilize*.

29. Although Great Britain did not allow African and Caribbean soldiers to fight on the western front, it did mobilize some 135,000 Indian soldiers to fight in France, revealing important vicissitudes in British racial logic. Levine, "Battle Colors."

30. Fogerty, *Race and War in France*, 31–39.

31. Employing the Tirailleurs Marocains, who had engaged in a mutiny at Fez in 1912, was not without risks. Gershovich, *French Military Rule in Morocco*, 171. An additional 35,000 Moroccan men served as laborers in various war-related industries. Ibid., 172–74. Andrew and Kanya-Forstner, "France, Africa, and the First World War," 14. For an example of French praise of Moroccan soldiers, see 19N 735, SHAT.

32. Clayton, *France, Soldiers and Africa*, 244–50. More than 206,000 Algerians served in the war for France. Ruedy, *Modern Algeria*, 111.

33. At the beginning of the First World War, the French AOF comprised the colonial possessions of Senegal, Guinea, Côte-d'Ivoire (Ivory Coast), Soudan (Sudan), Haute-Volta (Upper Volta), Togo, and Dahomey.

34. Mangin, *La force noire*.

35. Conklin, *A Mission to Civilize*, 144; and "Colonialism and Human Rights, a Contradiction in Terms?," 423; Fogerty, *Race and War in France*, 11.

36. Lunn, "'Les Races Guerrières,'" 519–25; and *Memoirs of the Maelstrom*.

37. Echenberg, *Colonial Conscripts*, 7–8.

38. For background on the *originaires* in the Four Communes, see Fogerty, *Race and War in France*, 239–41; Lunn, *Memoirs of the Maelstrom*.

39. Sénace du 8 juillet 1915, Annales de la Chambre des Députés, Débats Parlemetaires, 11 Legislature, Session Ordinaire de 1915, Du 11 mai au 30 juillet, vol. 102, 986–92; Annales de la Chambre des Députés, Débats Parlemetaires, 11 Legislature, Session Ordinaire de 1915, Du 11 mai au 30 juillet, vol. 102, 1459, Service des Archives de l'Assemblée Nationale.

40. Conklin, *A Mission to Civilize*, 154–55; Lunn, *Memoirs of the Maelstrom*, 81.

41. This belief flowed from a rationalization of colonialism rooted in an imperial ideology that privileged mastery, as integral to French national identity, and its absence as central in the construction of the colonial African other. Conklin, *A Mission to Civilize*, 145–46.

42. Sujet: de l'organisation d'unites offensives mixtes Sénégalaises, 12 février 1917, 6N 96, SHAT.

43. For discussions regarding the use of West African soldiers and debates concerning casualty rates, see Balesi, *From Adversaries to Comrades-in-Arms*; Echenberg, *Colonial Conscripts*; Fogerty, *Race and War in France*, 83–87; Lunn, *Memoirs of the Maelstrom*; Michel, *Les Africains et la Grande Guerre*.

44. Diagne based his appeal in large part on efforts to make African *tirailleurs* exempt from the *indigenat*, a brutal system of often arbitrary punishment levied against African subjects of the AOF for a wide variety of offenses.

45. Fogerty, *Race and War in France*, 50–53.

46. "African Troops in the War," *New York Age*, September 3, 1914.

47. "Foreign," *Crisis*, September 1916.

48. Stuart Hall considers visual imagery as a site of imaginary reunification of peoples of African descent across temporal and geographic distance. Hall, "Cultural Identity and Diaspora," 224.

49. "French Reinforcements," *Chicago Defender*, April 22, 1916.

50. "French Goumiers," *Chicago Defender*, June 3, 1916.

51. "French African Troops," *Chicago Defender*, October 21, 1916; "Thanksgiving Dinner in the Trenches," *Chicago Defender*, December 2, 1916; "French Soldiers Cooking Mid-day Meal," *Chicago Defender*, March 17, 1917.

52. "Picking Off Germans," *Chicago Defender*, January 27, 1917.

53. "Wounded French Troops," *Chicago Defender*, July 22, 1916.

54. Available lists of African American fighters who served in the French Foreign Legion do not include anyone named Bob Jones. It is possible that the *Chicago Defender* is referring to the African American boxer and Foreign Legion veteran Bob Scanlon. If so, the caption stating that Jones "left America when the state of Georgia refused to let Race men use guns or form military companies in the state" is most likely inaccurate.

55. For discussion of the discourse of diaspora, see Edwards, "The Uses of *Diaspora*." Also see Rowell, "An Interview with Brent Hayes Edwards," 792–93.

56. The French Foreign Legion, created in 1831 by King Louis-Philippe and composed of a motley assemblage of foreign volunteers, national castaways, and dissident renegades, offered an early opportunity for African Americans to fight in the war. Approximately 1,100 American citizens fought in the Foreign Legion for France, including a small number of African Americans. According to legionnaire Eugene Bullard's memoirs, six African Americans served in the Foreign Legion during the war. Carisella and Ryan, *The Black Swallow of Death*, 113; Wellard, *The French Foreign Legion*, 81. For a detailed history of the French Foreign Legion, see Porch, *The French Foreign Legion*. Bob Scanlon was born in Mobile, Alabama, as Bob Lewis in 1886. After leaving home at the age of sixteen and working briefly as a cowboy in Vera Cruz, Mexico, he traveled to the United Kingdom and began his boxing career. He made an international name for himself as a reputable middle heavyweight. On August 22, 1914, he joined the French Foreign Legion along with several other Americans residing in France, among them the poet Alan Seeger, who became Scanlon's close friend. A combat wound to his hand in 1916 led to his discharge from the army. Scanlon, "The Record of a Negro Boxer," 208–9; "With the French Legion," *Chicago Defender*, September 29, 1917. Scanlon was later profiled by the *New York Age* as well. "Chops Off Finger to Stay in the War," *New York Age*, March 9, 1918. Born in Columbus, Georgia, in 1894, Bullard ran away from home in 1902 at the age of eight after a lynch mob threatened to kill his father. At an early age, his father instilled in Bullard an admiration of France and its ideals of racial equality. After stowing away to Liverpool in 1906, Bullard finally reached Paris in 1913, where he made a name for himself as a boxer. Bullard enlisted in the Foreign Legion's Third Marching Battalion when war erupted in 1914. In the spring of 1917, while in Paris recovering from wounds incurred at Verdun, Bullard joined the French Flying Corps. He saw combat action and recorded an unofficial kill of a German triplane fighter. When the United States entered the war, Bullard attempted to enlist in the

nascent United States Flying Corps but was refused on account of his color. He was profiled in the *Crisis* in January 1918. Carisella and Ryan, *The Black Swallow of Death*; "Foreign," *Crisis*, January 1918.

57. *Richmond Planet*, June 9, 1917.

58. Lieutenant Colonel Édouard Réquin, "Emploi des troupes de couleur dans l'armée française," July 15, 1918, 10218-195, MID, NARA; Fogerty, *Race and War in France*, 5–6, 285–86.

59. Joel Spingarn to Colonel Réquin, July 30, 1918; Emmett J. Scott to Joel Spingarn, July 31, 1918, 10218-195, MID, NARA.

60. "Tells of the Employment of Negro Troops by French," *New York Age*, August 10, 1918.

61. For discussions of African American views of Africa before the First World War, see Adeleke, *UnAfrican Americans*; Magubane, *The Ties That Bind*; Moses, *The Golden Age of Black Nationalism, 1850–1925*.

62. For discussion of the French Mission, see Keene, "Uneasy Alliances."

63. L. Linard, "Au sujet des troupes noires américaines," 7 août 1918, 17N 76, SHAT.

64. For an excellent discussion of the centrality of African American soldiers as symbols of French interracial democracy in war and postwar African American literary culture, see Whalen, "'The Only Real White Democracy' and the Language of Liberation."

65. Haywood, *Black Bolshevik*, 23–24, 42.

66. Reminiscences of Lester B. Granger (1961) 25–26, CUOHROC.

67. Walker Jordan, *With "Old Eph" in the Army*, 21.

68. William Ross, *With the 351st in France*, 11.

69. Jeanne DeBarges to Lieutenant George J. Austin, box 56, Du Bois World War I Papers, UMA.

70. Haywood, *Black Bolshevik*, 61.

71. Stovall, "Love, Labor, and Race," 306; Keene, "French and American Racial Stereotypes during the First World War."

72. Walker Jordan, *With "Old Eph" in the Army*, 23.

73. Enoch Dunham to W. E. B. Du Bois, July 14, 1919, box 54. Du Bois World War I Papers, UMA.

74. Louis H. Pontlock to W. E. B. Du Bois, April 26, 1919, reel 8, frame 38, Du Bois Papers, UMA.

75. Cade, *Twenty-two Months with "Uncle Sam,"* 48.

76. Reminiscences of Lester B. Granger (1961) 29, CUOHROC.

77. Richard Hall, 804th Pioneer Infantry Regiment, USAMHI.

78. Robert Stevens, 803rd Pioneer Infantry Regiment, USAMHI.

79. Historian Tyler Stovall demonstrates how issues of gender, class, and labor shaped the presence and virulence of French racism against people of color, and colonial workers specifically. Working-class French citizens viewed colonial laborers with a level of disdain they largely withheld from colonial soldiers, who were buffered from violent expressions of racism by the shield of their military status. See Stovall, "The Color Line behind the Lines," 737–69; W. Cohen, "French Racism and Its African Impact," 305–17.

80. ". . . très émue et s'inquiète de la présence de soldats noirs sur son territorie." Rapport Recapitulatif pour la période du Ier au 31 octobre 1918, Mission Militaire Française près l'Armée Americaine, 17N 47, SHAT.

81. Keene, *Doughboys*, 126–27.

82. Ibid., 118–26.

83. Reminiscences of Lester B. Granger (1961) 31, CUOHROC.

84. Walker Jordan, *With "Old Eph" in the Army*, 24.

85. Charles H. Houston, "Saving the World for 'Democracy,'" *Pittsburgh Courier*, September 21, 1940.

86. Stovall, *Paris Noir*, 16–17. Also see Archer-Shaw, *Negrophilia*, 107.

87. Stovall, *Paris Noir*, 31.

88. For a detailed discussion of this phenomenon and its expression in postwar France, see Archer-Shaw, *Negrophilia*; Sharpley-Whiting, *Black Venus*; Blake, *Le Tumulte Noir*; Ezra, *The Colonial Unconscious.*

89. Shack, *Harlem in Montmartre*, 11–25.

90. James Reese Europe Collection, box 1, SC/NYPL; Scott, *Scott's Official History*, 310.

91. Jones et al., "Alfred Jack Thomas," 61–66.

92. Noble Sissle, "The Memoir of James Reese Europe," 106–7, SC/NYPL.

93. See Badger, *A Life in Ragtime*; Little, *From Harlem to the Rhine*; Noble Sissle, "The Memoir of James Reese Europe," SC/NYPL.

94. Blake, *Le Tumulte Noir*, 59.

95. "'We've Got Boche on Run' Writes McKaine," *New York Age*, October 12, 1918.

96. Gaston, *Green Power*, 30, 39–42.

97. Zieger, *America's Great War*, 105.

98. Memorandum, August 21, 1918, box 44, 92nd Division Headquarters decimal file, RG 120, NARA.

99. Memorandum, R. H. Leavitt to Commanding Generals, 183rd and 184th Brigade, August 22, 1918, box 44, 92nd Division Headquarters decimal file, RG 120, NARA.

100. Ballou's order was followed by a subsequent memo from Brigadier General William H. Hay of the 184th Brigade to the officers of the 367th Infantry, 368th Infantry, and 351st Machine Gun Battalion under his command with the subject "Prevention of rape and assaults with intent to commit rape." William H. Hay, Brigade Commander, to All Officers of the 184th Brigade, August 29, 1918, box 44, 92nd Division Headquarters decimal file, RG 120, NARA.

101. From: Ernest Samusson, Regimental Intelligence Officer, 371st Infantry, To: The Town Mayors of Marat la Grande, Marats la Petit and Rembercourt aux Pots, Dept. Meuse, Subject: Relationship of the Colored and White Races, Aug. 31st, 1918, box 2, 93rd Division Historical Files, RG 120, NARA.

102. Braddan, *Under Fire with the 370th Infantry*, 80. For discussion of American soldiers marrying French women, and efforts by military officials to prevent such relationships, see Meigs, *Optimism at Armageddon*, 125–35, 138.

103. Lloyd Blair, 317th Ammunition Train, USAMHI.

104. On sexual relations between American soldiers and French women, see Meigs, *Optimism at Armageddon*, 107–42.

105. Houston, "Saving the World for 'Democracy,'" *Pittsburgh Courier*, September 21, 1940.

106. Ibid., September 28, 1940.

107. *United States v. William Buckner*, file #121766, box 8942, RG 153, NARA.

108. Ibid.; U.S. Congress, *Alleged Executions without Trial in France*, 44.

109. *United States v. William Buckner*, file #121766, box 8942, RG 153, NARA; Herbert E. Watkins, Captain of Cavalry, Army Artillery Headquarter, First Army, AEF to Chief of Artillery, First Army, AEF, September 6, 1918, box 44, 92nd Division, RG 120, NARA.

110. U.S. Congress, *Alleged Executions without Trial in France*, iv.

111. In December 1921 and January 1922, a five-member special committee of the U.S. Senate conducted hearings on charges of alleged executions without trial in France during the war. The hearings were prompted by Georgia senator Thomas Watson, who raised the issue on October 31, 1921, on the Senate floor. Much of the testimony by former soldiers and other military officials centered on accusations levied against Major Hierome Opie of the 116th Infantry that he improperly shot two soldiers under his command. After reviewing the testimony of dozens of witnesses, many of whom swore to unofficial executions of black and white soldiers, both during the war and after the armistice, Judge Advocate Walter Bethel determined that charges of illegal executions were false and no grounds existed to charge Opie with a crime. U.S. Congress, *Alleged Executions without Trial in France*.

112. Ibid., 914–20.

113. Haywood, *Black Bolshevik*, 61–62.

114. U.S. Congress, *Alleged Executions without Trial in France*, 43.

115. Andrew and Kanya-Forstner, "France, Africa, and the First World War," 16. An estimated 119,000 Algerian laborers, both requisitions and volunteers, arrived in France during the war. Ruedy, *Modern Algeria*, 111.

116. Roberts, *The American Foreign Legion*, 98; American Battlefield Monuments Commission, *93d Division*, 5.

117. Memoir of William H. Dyer, SC/NYPL.

118. Brent Edwards employs the French word *décalage*, strictly translated as "gap," "interval," or "shift," to describe this tension and argues that it occupies a central place in the process of diaspora. He defines *décalage* in the context of diaspora as "the kernel of precisely that which cannot be transferred or exchanged, the received biases that refuse to pass over when one crosses the water." Edwards, *The Practice of Diaspora*, 65. Also see Edwards, "The Uses of *Diaspora*."

119. Bamanankan functioned as a lingua franca of the *tirailleur* corps. Mann, *Native Sons*, 163. Fogerty also describes a form of pidgin French—*langue-tirailleur*—that developed during the war in order to facilitate communication between French officers and West African soldiers. Fogerty, *Race and War in France*, 154–68.

120. "A Study of Anglo-American and Franco-American Relations during World War I," July 1942, Army War College, Historical Section, Miscellaneous Records Relating to World War I Studies, 1942–1943, box 1, RG 165, NARA.

121. "Algerian Didn't Gather Him Closely," *Cleveland Advocate*, September 28, 1918.

122. Karl Bardin, "My Most Unusual Experience with the 371st Inf.," March 30, 1972, 93rd Division Historical Files, box 2, RG 120, NARA.

123. "Learning French," *New York Age*, June 8, 1918.

124. Horace E. Garvin, World War I Questionnaire and Survey, USAMHI.

125. "Europe Writes from Europe," *New York Age*, July 28, 1918.

126. Fogerty, *Race and War in France*, 55–87; Barbeau and Henri, *The Unknown Soldiers*, 141.

127. Memorandum from G. K. Wilson, Assistant Chief of Staff, G-1, Second Army to

French Military Mission, November 2, 1918; Liaison Officer, French Mission to G. K. Wilson, Assistant Chief of Staff, G-1, Second Army, November 3, 1918, 17N 96, SHAT.

128. Dewitte, "La dette du sang," 10; Lunn, *Memoirs of the Maelstrom.*

129. Unnamed soldier to W. E. B. Du Bois, January 10, 1918, box 55, Du Bois World War I Papers, UMA.

130. Horace Pippin war notebooks, ca. 1920, SAAA.

131. See Mann, *Native Sons*, 68–72.

132. Conklin, "Colonialism and Human Rights," 429–30; and *A Mission to Civilize*, 151–55.

133. Lunn, *Memoirs of the Maelstrom*, 162, 167, 182 (n. 50).

134. Horace Pippin war notebooks, ca. 1920, SAAA.

135. Albert Veyrene, in *Men of Bronze*, director, William Miles (1977).

136. Echenberg, *Colonial Conscripts*, 32–38; Keene, "French and American Racial Stereotypes during the First World War," 267–69; Michel, *Les Africains et la Grande Guerre*; Nelson, "The 'Black Horror on the Rhine.'"

137. "'Just Let Us Get at Germans,' Is Cry of Black Devils as They Are Held from Front," *Cleveland Advocate*, September 7, 1918.

138. Mason and Furr, *The American Negro Soldier with the Red Hand of France*, 112–13.

139. Ibid., 114.

140. Ibid., 118.

141. Diagne to Clemenceau, 16 novembre 1918, 6N 97, SHAT. For additional discussion of this memo, see Fogerty, *Race and War in France*, 4–5; Keene, "French and American Racial Stereotypes during the First World War."

142. Lewis, *W. E. B. Du Bois*, 1:574–78; "The Future of Africa," *Crisis*, January 1918.

Chapter Five

1. Greenwald, *Women, War, and Work*; K. Kennedy, *Disloyal Mothers and Scurrilous Citizens*; Steinson, *American Women's Activism in World War I*; S. Zeiger, *In Uncle Sam's Service.*

2. McCartin asserts that this concept was central to the history of organized labor in the years encompassing the First World War. McCartin, *Labor's Great War.* Also see D. Kennedy, *Over Here*, 258–79.

3. Hagedorn, *Savage Peace.*

4. "Letters from Overthere," *Savannah Tribune*, February 8, 1919.

5. "Letters from Overthere," *Savannah Tribune*, January 25, 1919.

6. Cade, *Twenty-two Months with "Uncle Sam,"* 103.

7. Blount, *Reminiscences of Samuel E. Blount*, 53.

8. "Letters From France," *Savannah Tribune*, January 11, 1919; Little, *From Harlem to the Rhine*, 325–26.

9. "The Human Side of the Fighter," in *Heroes of 1918.*

10. Farwell, *Over There*, 262.

11. John R. Williams, "A Trench Letter," box 56, Du Bois World War I Papers, UMA.

12. "Letters from Overthere," *Savannah Tribune*, January 25, 1919.

13. Aldrich R. Burton to William Granger, January 1, 1919, box 2, William R. R. Granger Jr. Letters, SC/NYPL.

14. Little, *From Harlem to the Rhine*, 337–41.

15. Mason and Furr, *The American Negro Soldier with the Red Hand of France*, 141–42.

16. In an attempt to refute charges of widespread rape, W. E. B. Du Bois questioned twenty-one mayors of French towns that quartered African American soldiers regarding their conduct. He published their responses in the May 1919 issue of the *Crisis*. "Rape," *Crisis*, May 1919.

17. For discussion of American soldiers as tourists in France, see Meigs, *Optimism at Armageddon*, ch. 3.

18. Aldrich R. Burton to William Granger, April 17, 1919, box 2, William R. R. Granger Jr. Letters, SC/NYPL.

19. Haywood, *Black Bolshevik*, 69–71.

20. Keene, *Doughboys*, 134.

21. Levenstein, *Seductive Journey*, 23.

22. Haywood, *Black Bolshevik*, 80.

23. Little, *From Harlem to the Rhine*, 351–52.

24. Walter H. Loving to Churchill, November 18, 1918, 10218-256, MID, RG 165, NARA.

25. Churchill to Chief of Staff, November 19, 1918, 10218-256, MID, RG 165, NARA.

26. Pershing to Foch, November 26, 1918, in MacGregor and Nalty, *Blacks in the United States Armed Forces: Basic Documents*, 4:257.

27. Pershing to Foch, November 30, 1918, ibid., 258.

28. Bullard, *Personalities and Reminiscences of the War*, 297.

29. General Order No. 40, in ibid., 280–81; Du Bois, "The Negro Soldier in Service Abroad during the First World War," 326–28.

30. Blount, *Reminiscences of Samuel E. Blount*, 62.

31. Allen J. Greer to Senator Kenneth McKellar, December 6, 1918, in "Documents of War," *Crisis*, May 1919.

32. Charles R. Isum to W. E. B. Du Bois, May 17, 1919, reel 7, frame 980, Du Bois Papers, UMA; Du Bois, "The Negro Soldier in Service Abroad during the First World War," 329–31.

33. Hunton and Johnson, *Two Colored Women*, 24.

34. Ibid., 136–37.

35. Extract of letter to Mrs. S. A. Cash from Wagoner S. Dickinson, January 2, 1919, 10218-300, MID, RG 165, NARA. For a discussion of the reemergence of the Ku Klux Klan in relation to World War I, see MacLean, *Behind the Mask of Chivalry*.

36. "My Mission," *Crisis*, May 1919.

37. Lewis, *W. E. B. Du Bois*, 1:561–64.

38. Moton, *Finding a Way Out*, 250–51.

39. Hill, *Garvey Papers*, 1:305–6, 311–12.

40. Bundles, *On Her Own Ground*, 253–54; Fox, *The Guardian of Boston*, 223–26; Hagedorn, *Savage Peace*, 104–13, 203–4; Lewis, *W. E. B. Du Bois*, 2:58–60; McMurry, *To Keep the Waters Troubled*, 321–25.

41. Moton, *Finding a Way Out*, 253; F. James, "Robert Russa Moton and the Whispering Gallery," 235.

42. Moton, *Finding a Way Out*, 254.

43. "The Black Man in the Revolution of 1914–1918," *Crisis*, March 1919.

44. Louis H. Pontlock to W. E. B. Du Bois, April 26, 1919, reel 8, frame 38, Du Bois Papers, UMA.

45. Bertram I. Lawrence, World War I Questionnaire and Survey, USAMHI.

46. Allied Expeditionary Forces—Intelligence Files of Du Bois, 1917–1919, group #: 312, series no.: 21, box no.: 366, folder no.: 5, Du Bois Papers, UMA.

47. "Our Success and Failure," *Crisis*, July 1919.

48. Official AEF travel pass, issued December 14, 1918, Moton Family Papers, LOC.

49. F. James, "Robert Russa Moton and the Whispering Gallery"; Moton, *Finding a Way Out*.

50. "Head of Tuskegee Sees Colored Units," *Stars and Stripes*, January 3, 1919.

51. Moton, *Finding a Way Out*, 263. On Moton's politics, see Fairclough, "Tuskegee's Robert R. Moton," 94–105.

52. Moton himself states that he "cautioned them against striking the attitude of heroes" in the March 1919 *Southern Workman*. Following criticism of his speech, Moton clearly went to lengths to clarify exactly what he said to the Ninety-second Division's soldiers and qualify its tone.

53. E. Green, *Ely*, 449.

54. Keene, *Doughboys*, 134–35.

55. Haywood, *Black Bolshevik*, 72–74.

56. Barbeau and Henri, *The Unknown Soldiers*, 170.

57. Little, *From Harlem to the Rhine*, 355–56; "Hayward Returns with Negro Troops," *New York Times*, February 13, 1919.

58. Scott, *Scott's Official History*, 163.

59. Meigs, *Optimism at Armageddon*, 178–79.

60. Hunton and Johnson, *Two Colored Women*. 234–35.

61. Diary entry, September 7, 1941, box 3, Rayford Whittingham Logan Papers, LOC.

62. Keene, *Doughboys*, 132.

63. "A Survey of the Social and Religious Conditions as They Effect the Colored Soldiers at Camp Humphreys, Virginia," January 25, 1919, reel 19, frame 61, FSAA.

64. Ibid., frames 61–62.

65. "A Brief Report of Conditions among the Colored Soldiers at Camp Meade," February 8, 1919, reel 19, frame 66, FSAA.

66. "A Brief Report on Conditions among Colored Soldiers at Camp Eustis, Virginia," February 14, 1919, reel 19, frame 70, FSAA.

67. Anonymous soldier to NAACP, December 9, 1918, Part 9: Discrimination in the U.S. Armed Forces, 1918–1955, Series A: General Office Files on Armed Forces' Affairs, 1918–1955, Group 1, Series C, Administrative Files, box C-374, reel 1, Papers of the NAACP (hereafter Discrimination in the Armed Forces, Papers of the NAACP).

68. Anonymous soldier to NAACP, December 4, 1918, reel 1, Discrimination in the Armed Forces, Papers of the NAACP.

69. "Soldiers of America," Co. A, 425th Reserve Labor Battalion, Columbus, Ohio, to NAACP, no date, reel 1, Discrimination in the Armed Forces, Papers of the NAACP.

70. "A Brief Report on Conditions among Colored Soldiers at Camp Meade," February 8, 1919, reel 19, frame 67, FSAA.

71. "A Brief Report on Conditions among Colored Soldiers at Camp Eustis, Virginia," February 14, 1919, reel 19, frame 71, FSAA.

72. "The Black Man in the Revolution of 1914–1918," *Crisis*, March 1919.

73. Lewis, *W. E. B. Du Bois*, 1:574.

74. "Returning Soldiers," *Crisis*, May 1919.

75. "The Outer Pocket," *Crisis*, June 1919.

76. Lewis, *W. E. B. Du Bois*, 1:578.

77. Krebs, *Fighting for Rights*; Rosenberg, "For Democracy, Not Hypocrisy," 592–625; and *How Far the Promised Land?*, ch. 2; Capozzola, *Uncle Sam Wants You*.

78. Manela, *The Wilsonian Moment*.

79. "What of Our Hopes?," *Cleveland Advocate*, November 23, 1918.

80. "Returned Soldiers Tell of Heroism 'Over There,'" *Cleveland Advocate*, January 18, 1919.

81. "First Separate Only Heroes," *Washington Bee*, January 11, 1918.

82. William Jordan, *Black Newspapers and America's War for Democracy*, 134–36.

83. "Refused Service in Y.M.C.A. Restaurant Because of Color," *New York Age*, November 30, 1918.

84. "The Negro's Part in the War for Democracy," *Washington Bee*, January 18, 1919.

85. Lorenz, "Ralph W. Tyler," 2–4.

86. "The Man of the Hour and His Job," *Cleveland Advocate*, September 21, 1918.

87. "Stories of the Daring of Race Troops Still Come in from France," *Cleveland Advocate*, November 23, 1918.

88. "Brothers," *Stars and Stripes*, November 8, 1918.

89. "American Officers Urged Color Line among the French," *New York Age*, December 28, 1918.

90. "Tyler Defends Condemned Officers," *Cleveland Advocate*, February 8, 1919, and "Tyler Exposes More Blunders by Certain Commanding Officers," *Cleveland Advocate*, February 15, 1919.

91. "The Boys Have Not Returned as Moton Advised, 'Modest and Unassuming,' Says Tyler," *Cleveland Advocate*, March 15, 1919.

92. "Our 'Boys' on the Frontier of Freedom," *Cleveland Advocate*, June 14, 1919; Lorenz, "Ralph W. Tyler," 4–12.

93. *What Does the Negro Want?: Fourteen Articles Setting Forth What the American Negro Expects after Helping to Win the War for Democracy*, Professor John R. Hawkins, 10218-302, MID, RG 165, NARA.

94. "Negro Determined to Get Justice in This Country," *Savannah Tribune*, April 5, 1919.

95. D. Kennedy, *Over Here*, 245; McCartin, *Labor's Great War*, 173–98; Rosenberg, "For Democracy, Not Hypocrisy"; "Reconstruction," as a discourse of postwar planning, occurred in the context of a transatlantic political economy. See Rodgers, *Atlantic Crossings*, 290–306.

96. Miller, *The Negro in the New Reconstruction*, 15–16.

97. Ibid., 21.

98. Pickens, *The Negro in the Light of the Great War*; Mary White Ovington, "Reconstruction and the Negro," *Crisis*, February 1919. W. E. B. Du Bois likewise invoked the theme of reconstruction in outlining a political program for African Americans after the war, although he did not explicitly connect it to the military service of black soldiers. Du Bois, "Reconstruction," 130–31.

99. "The Battle Begins," *New York Age*, November 16, 1919; Manela, *The Wilsonian Moment*.

100. Krebs, *Fighting for Rights*, 132–34.

101. Glassberg, *American Historical Pageantry*, 225–26. For historical perspectives on African American civic pageantry, see Blight, *Race and Reunion*; Lorini, *Rituals of Race*.

102. Holt, "Afterword," 327; Baker, "Critical Memory and the Black Public Sphere," 14–15.

103. "Cleveland Greets Old 9th Battalion," *Chicago Defender*, March 1, 1919.

104. Research materials, "The Black Man and the Wounded World," box 59, Du Bois World War I Papers, UMA.

105. "Real Welcome," *Baltimore Afro-American*, March 14, 1919.

106. "Negro Troops Come Back with Glorious Record," *Buffalo Commercial Advertiser*, March 11, 1919, reel 244, frame 921, TINCF.

107. "The War," *Crisis*, November 1919; Office of the Provost Marshal General, *Second Report of the Provost Marshal General*, 459.

108. A. Green, *Selling the Race*, 6.

109. "Cheers Ring Loud When 8th Parades," *Chicago Defender*, February 22, 1919.

110. Noble Sissle, "Memoirs of 'Jim' Europe," 191, James Reese Europe Collection, SC/NYPL; "Fifth Av. Cheers Negro Veterans," *New York Times*, February 18, 1919.

111. "Old 15th Regiment Given Rousing Reception," *New York Age*, February 22, 1919.

112. Little, *From Harlem to the Rhine*, 361.

113. "First under the Victory Arch," *New York Age*, February 22, 1919.

114. For discussion of the racial divisions lurking beneath the surface of the parade, see Slotkin, *Lost Battalions*, 399–400.

115. On this theme, see Dailey, Gilmore, and Simon, *Jumpin' Jim Crow*.

116. Hunter, *To 'Joy My Freedom*.

117. While African American resistance to white supremacy in the Jim Crow South is often characterized as primarily infrapolitical, the postwar homecoming parades constituted openly public transcripts of protest. See Scott, *Domination and the Arts of Resistance*; Kelley, "'We Are Not What We Seem,'" 75–112; J. Keith, *Rich Man's War, Poor Man's Fight*.

118. "Negro Soldiers Given Welcome at Fair Park," *Dallas Morning News*, April 22, 1919.

119. "Negro Soldiers Are Welcomed Home," *Mobile Register*, July 3, 1919, reel 244, frame 916, TINCF.

120. "Richmond Honors Returned Colored Troops," *Savannah Tribune*, July 12, 1919.

121. Ortiz, *Emancipation Betrayed*, 157–59.

122. "Decatur County Welcomes Soldiers," *Savannah Tribune*, April 26, 1919. Henry Lincoln Johnson was born in Atlanta, where he became a prominent attorney and active member of the Republican Party. He met his future wife, Georgia Douglass Johnson, at Atlanta University, and they married in 1903. The couple relocated to Washington, D.C., when Johnson received an appointment as recorder of deeds from President William Howard Taft. He died unexpectedly in 1924. "Georgia Douglass Johnson," in Shockley, *Afro-American Women Writers*, 347–48.

123. Dittmer, *Black Georgia in the Progressive Era*, 9–11, 16–19.

124. Editorial, *Savannah Tribune*, May 3, 1919.

125. Scott, *Scott's Official History*, 480.

126. "Home Coming Parade Commendable," *Savannah Tribune*, May 17, 1919.

127. Elija Spener, VWHC.

128. Thomas Toney, VWHC.

129. Floyd Bishop, VWHC.

Chapter Six

1. Report, re: Charles Lewis, February 3, 1919, 10218-274, MID, NARA; "Mob Batters Down Jail Doors and Hangs Negro," *Louisville Courier-Journal*, December 17, 1918; "Negro Soldier Taken From Jail; Lynched," *Montgomery Advertiser*, December 17, 1918; G. C. Wright, *Racial Violence in Kentucky*, 119.

2. "Hoodlums Lynch Colored Soldier," *Cleveland Advocate*, December 28, 1918.

3. Walter Loving to Director, Military Intelligence, December 23, 1918, 10218-274, MID, NARA.

4. Letter to W. E. B. Du Bois, December 29, 1918, reel 11, frame 918; Press Release, December 17, 1919, reel 11, frames 920–21, Part 7: The Anti-Lynching Campaign, 1912–1955, Series A: Anti-Lynching Investigative Files, 1912–1953, Group 1, Series C, Papers of the NAACP (hereafter Anti-Lynching Files, Papers of the NAACP).

5. "Gov. Stanley Asked to Act as to Lynching," *New York Call*, December 12, 1919, box C-343, reel 6, frame 14, Anti-Lynching Files, Papers of the NAACP.

6. "The Hickman Lynching," *New York Evening Sun*, December 23, 1918, box C-343, reel 6, frame 21, Anti-Lynching Files, Papers of the NAACP.

7. For discussions of postwar racial violence in a larger international and diasporic context, see Fryer, *Staying Power*; Manela, *The Wilsonian Moment*; Mathieu, "Jim Crow Rides This Train," 162–76; Stovall, "The Color Line behind the Lines," 737–69; Tuttle, *Race Riot*, 14–16.

8. J. Johnson, *Along This Way*, 339–44.

9. Painter, *Standing at Armageddon*.

10. Reminiscences of Will Winton Alexander (1952), 162, CUOHROC.

11. J. W. Harris, "Etiquette, Lynching, and Racial Boundaries in Southern History," 387–410; Doyle, *The Etiquette of Race Relations in the South*.

12. Minutes of the Meeting of the Inter-Racial Committee, Atlanta, September 17, 1919, Colored Work Department Records, box 9, Kautz Family YMCA Archives.

13. "Soldiers Returning to Farm Demand Better Conditions," *New York Age*, July 19, 1919.

14. The committee provided no firm data to support this number, which was likely too high. "The Work of the Inter-Racial Committee," Colored Work Department Records, box 9, Kautz Family YMCA Archives.

15. "Returned Soldiers Refuse Farm Work," *New Orleans Times-Picayune*, August 30, 1919. James Grossman notes that Louisiana's labor shortages were compounded by migration to the North. Grossman, *Land of Hope*, 40–41.

16. MacLean, *Behind the Mask of Chivalry*, 28–29.

17. John D. Baker to Col. Arthur Wood, April 22, 1919, Entry 352, Bulletins, Instruction Manuals, etc., 1919–1920, in Grossman, *Black Workers in the Era of the Great Migration, 1916–1929*, reel 21, frame 357.

18. John S. Kendall to Mrs. Lella Stuart Vaughn, January 5, 1919, 10218-301, MID, RG 165, NARA.

19. Reminiscences of Will Winton Alexander (1952), 162, CUOHROC.

20. Ayers, *Vengeance and Justice*, 240–44; J. Hall, *Revolt against Chivalry*, 145; Hoch, *White Hero, Black Beast*; Williamson, *The Crucible of Race*, 116–18.

21. Hodes, "The Sexualization of Reconstruction Politics," 402–17.

22. "Put the Blame Where It Belongs," *Vardaman's Weekly* 11, no. 51 (August 28, 1919).

23. C. Williams, "Symbols of Freedom and Defeat."

24. "Achievements of the Interracial Commission," Colored Work Department Records, box 9, Kautz Family YMCA Archives.

25. M. Churchill, Director of Military Intelligence to intelligence officer, Newport News, Virginia, April 28, 1919, 10218-329, MID, RG 165, NARA; Colonel John M. Dunn to M. Churchill, Director of Military Intelligence, April 25, 1919, 10218-329, MID, RG 165, NARA.

26. Reich, "Soldiers of Democracy," 1498–1500.

27. J. W. Sammons to Newton D. Baker, February 3, 1919, 10218-305, MID, RG 165, NARA.

28. "Achievements of the Interracial Commission," Colored Work Department Records, box 9, Kautz Family YMCA Archives.

29. Report, re: Negro Race Riot Propaganda in Texas, September 13, 1919, reel 10, 25, FSAA.

30. Reminiscences of Will Winton Alexander (1952), 163, CUOHROC.

31. On the power of rumor to fuel southern white fears of insurrection in the aftermath of the Civil War, see Hahn, "'Extravagant Expectations' of Freedom," 122–58.

32. Reich, "Soldiers of Democracy," 1499.

33. Charles Breninan to Jones Marley, August 1, 1919, reel 6, 219, FSAA.

34. Reminiscences of Will Winton Alexander (1952), 164–65, CUOHROC.

35. Ibid., 163–64.

36. Minutes of the Meeting of the Inter-Racial Committee, Atlanta, July 24, 1919, Colored Work Department Records, box 9, Kautz Family YMCA Archives.

37. Emmett J. Scott, "After the War: A Symposium," *Southern Workman*, March 1919, 137.

38. Monroe N. Work, "After the War: A Symposium," *Southern Workman*, March 1919, 139.

39. J. Hall, *Revolt against Chivalry*, 62–65.

40. J. W. Harris, *Deep Souths*, 265–66, 285–89.

41. "Tenth Annual Report of the National Association for the Advancement of Colored People for the Year 1919," 15, Part I, 1909–1950: Meetings of the Board of Directors, Records of Annual Conferences, Major Speeches, and Special Reports, Papers of the NAACP.

42. Deposition of H. A. Bryan, July 31, 1919, reel 8, frame 861, Anti-Lynching Files, Papers of the NAACP. Although the witness submitted to a sworn affidavit, the NAACP had doubts as to the complete veracity of this statement. While possibly exaggerated, many details do coincide with newspaper accounts of the lynching. See Correspondence with Mr. Nathan B. Young, President, Florida A & M College, reel 8, frames 866–68, Anti-Lynching Files, Papers of the NAACP.

43. "Negro Burned Alive by a Mob Near El Dorado," *Arkansas Gazette*, May 22, 1919.

44. "Asks Lynching Probe," *Arkansas Gazette*, May 25, 1919.

45. "Former Negro Soldier and Woman Lynched," *Southern Christian Recorder*, May 8, 1919.

46. G. A. Towns to John R. Shillady, August 6, 1919, box C-354, reel 10, frame 690, Anti-Lynching Files, Papers of the NAACP.

47. "Negro Is Lynched in Wilcox County," *Atlanta Constitution*, August, 15, 1919.

48. "Mob Kills Negro, Bogalusa Woman Brands Assailant," *New Orleans Times-Picayune*, September 1, 1919.

49. "Lynching at Star City Followed by Reprisal Threats," *Arkansas Democrat* (Little Rock), September 3, 1919; *Arkansas Gazette*, September 4, 1919.

50. "Former Colored Soldier Is Lynched for Having a White Sweetheart," *New York Age*, October 4, 1919.

51. "Negro Killed as He Lies in Hospital Bed," *Chicago Daily News*, September 29, 1919; Robert Crosky, draft registration card, ⟨http://www.ancestry.com⟩.

52. Robert Lee Hill, draft registration card, ⟨http://www.ancestry.com⟩; C. M. Walser and C. R. Maxey, re: Negro Insurrection at Hoop Spur and Elaine, in Phillips County, Arkansas, reel 19, frame 20, FSAA.

53. Stockley, *Blood in Their Eyes*, 31.

54. "The Real Cause of Race Riots," *Crisis*, December, 1919. For additional in-depth discussions of the Elaine massacre, see Stockley, *Blood in Their Eyes*; Whitaker, *On the Laps of Gods*; Woodruff, "African American Struggles for Citizenship."

55. "Pays Ransom for Bodies of Lynched Sons," *Chicago Defender*, October 11, 1919; 369th/15th NYNG Abstracts 13721-83, roll 3, box 12, vols. 39–40, New York State Archives; "The Real Cause of Race Riots," *Crisis*, December, 1919.

56. Powell Green, draft registration card, ⟨http://www.ancestry.com⟩.

57. "Lynching Actively Investigated," *News & Observer* (Raleigh, N.C.), December 31, 1919.

58. "Six Witnesses Fail to Implicate Any of Lynching Party," *News & Observer* (Raleigh, N.C.), December 29, 1919.

59. Editorial, *News & Observer* (Raleigh, N.C.), December 30, 1919.

60. J. W. Harris, *Deep Souths*, 272.

61. On black participation in the lynching of other African Americans, see Brundage, *Lynching in the New South*, 45; Beck and Tolnay, "When Race Didn't Matter."

62. Waldrep, "Word and Deed," 229–58.

63. "Will Uncle Sam Stand for This Cross," *Chicago Defender*, April 5, 1919.

64. "Vanishing War Dreams," *New York Age*, June 7, 1919.

65. "Tenth Annual Report of the National Association for the Advancement of Colored People for the Year 1919," 15, Part I, 1909–1950: Meetings of the Board of Directors, Records of Annual Conferences, Major Speeches, and Special Reports, Papers of the NAACP.

66. Press release, December 24, 1919, reel 1, Part 9: Discrimination in the U.S. Armed Forces, 1918–1955, Files on Discrimination in the Military, Group 1, Series C, Administrative Files, box C-374, Papers of the NAACP (hereafter Files on Discrimination in the Military, Papers of the NAACP).

67. Reverend George A. Thomas to Moorfield Story, December 26, 1919, reel 1, Files on Discrimination in the Military, Papers of the NAACP.

68. "Mob Attacks Negro Lieutenant at Thomson, Ga., for No Offense Save His Wearing Uniform of U.S. Army," *Daily Herald*, September 6, 1919, TINCF.

69. War Department, *National Defense Act*, 46; Captain F. Sullens to Major Wrisley Brown, November 30, 1918, 10218-289, MID, RG 165, NARA.

70. "Soldiers, Attention!," *Chicago Defender*, April 5, 1919.

71. Rosengarten, *All God's Dangers*, 161.

72. "Soldier in Uniform Is Beaten in Georgia Town," *Chicago Defender*, May 10, 1919.

73. "Sylvester, Georgia," August 1, 1919, reel 1, Files on Discrimination in the Military, Papers of the NAACP; "Negro Soldier Beat Up in Worth County," *Macon (Ga.) News*, April 20, 1919, reel 222, frame 20, TINCF.

74. "American Huns Meet Stiff Opposition in Midnight Attack on Home of Colored Men in Small Georgia Town," *Pittsburg Courier*, January 18, 1919.

75. "White Men Killed by Colored Soldier," *St. Louis Argus*, March 7, 1919, reel 9, frame 791, TINCF.

76. The Work of the Inter-Racial Committee Interracial Commission Reports, box 9, Kautz Family YMCA Archives.

77. In his chapter "Congested Terrain: Resistance on Public Transportation," Robin Kelley specifically discusses how streetcars in Birmingham were sites of frequent violent confrontation between white and black passengers. Kelley, *Race Rebels*, 55–75.

78. "Bullet Ends Life of Sergt. Green," *Chicago Defender*, June 21, 1919.

79. Edgar Charles Caldwell, draft registration card, ⟨http://www.ancestry.com⟩.

80. "Negro Soldier Kills Conductor and Badly Injures Motorman of Anniston Street Car," *Anniston Star*, December 17, 1918; "Much Excitement Caused by Killing of Anniston Man," *Birmingham News*, December 16, 1918; Thomas Jackson to John Shillady, July 18, 1919, Part 8: Discrimination in the Criminal Justice System, 1910–1955, Series A: Legal Department and Central Office Records, 1910–1939, Group I, box D-49, reel 4, frame 642, Papers of the NAACP (hereafter Caldwell File, Papers of the NAACP); "The Caldwell Case," *Crisis*, January 1920.

81. Gatewood, "Alabama's 'Negro Soldier Experiment.'"

82. "Caldwell Is Held without Bail for Murder," *Anniston Star*, December 19, 1918.

83. Thomas Jackson to John Shillady, July 18, 1919, reel 4, frame 592, Caldwell File, Papers of the NAACP; "Grand Jury Will Look into Killing," *Birmingham News*, December 17, 1918.

84. Edgar Charles Caldwell, draft registration card, ⟨http://www.ancestry.com⟩.

85. "Negro Indicted for Murder in 90 Minutes," *Anniston Star*, December 20, 1918; "Negro Soldier Is Indicted for Murder," *Montgomery Advertiser*, December 20, 1918.

86. "Soldier Defies Jim-Crowism, Shoots Two Men in a Row," *Cleveland Advocate*, December 21, 1918.

87. R. R. Williams to Oswald Garrison Villard, December 24, 1918, reel 4, frame 590; John R. Shillady to R. R. Williams, December 27, 1918, reel 4, frame 592, Caldwell File, Papers of the NAACP.

88. R. R. Williams to John Shillady, January 10, 1919, reel 4, frame 595, Caldwell File, Papers of the NAACP.

89. Newton D. Baker to Woodrow Wilson, February 27, 1919; Woodrow Wilson to Thomas Kilby, February 28, 1919, Series 4: Case Files, no. 4955, Woodrow Wilson Papers.

90. *Edgar C. Caldwell v. State of Alabama*, Appeal from Calhoun Circuit Court, Supreme Court of Alabama, (1919), Caldwell Case File, Anniston Public Library.

91. R. R. Williams to Emmett J. Scott, July 7, 1919; Emmett J. Scott to Joseph P. Tumulty, July 12, 1919, Series 4: Case Files, no. 4955, Woodrow Wilson Papers.

92. "Atty. General May Save Sgt. Caldwell," *Cleveland Advocate*, December 6, 1919.

93. See reel 4, frames 775–77, Caldwell File, Papers of the NAACP.

94. "The Caldwell Case," *Crisis*, January 1920.

95. "A Soldier," *Crisis*, March 1920.

96. T. H. Driskell to Arthur Spingarn, March 26, 1920, reel 4, frame 732, Caldwell File, Papers of the NAACP.

97. Edgar C. Caldwell to James Weldon Johnson, March 26, 1920, reel 4, frames 738–40, Caldwell File, Papers of the NAACP.

98. *Caldwell v. Parker*, 252 U.S. 376 (1920), reel 4, frames 751–54, Caldwell File, Papers of the NAACP.

99. "Edgar Caldwell Dies on Gallows," *Anniston Star*, July 30, 1920; "The Hangman's Noose, a Relic of Barbarism," *Anniston Star*, July 31, 1920.

100. "Sergeant Caldwell Executed," *Crisis*, October 1920.

101. Hoping for a commutation of his sentence, Caldwell reportedly stated, "The Lord had a hand in getting me into trouble in order to save my soul." He added further, "The devil made me kill Linton, and I would have been lost forever if I had been executed immediately after the killing. I was converted on Feb. 28 and God has revealed to me that He would save me from the hangman's rope." "Death Hour Nears; Caldwell Renews Hope," *Chicago Defender*, July 24, 1920; "Edgar Caldwell Dies on Gallows," *Anniston Star*, July 30, 1920.

102. Edgar C. Caldwell to James Weldon Johnson, March 26, 1920, reel 4, frames 738–40, Caldwell File, Papers of the NAACP.

103. "Sergeant Caldwell Executed," *Crisis*, October 1920.

104. Reminiscences of Will Winton Alexander (1952), 176–77, CUOHROC.

105. The presence of national guardsmen and a dozen Texas Rangers, sent to the area on July 12 by the governor succeeded in preventing any further violence. For in-depth discussion of the riot, see Tuttle, "Violence in a 'Heathen' Land," 324–33.

106. "Six Shot in Norfolk Riots," *New York Times*, July 22, 1919.

107. Painter, *Standing at Armageddon*, 346–49, 379.

108. S. Cohen, "A Historical Study in Nativism"; Hagedorn, *Savage Peace*; Kornweibel, *"Seeing Red"*; Murray, *Red Scare*.

109. Keene, *Doughboys*.

110. "Negro Veterans Replace Strikers," *Evening Sun* (New York), April 14, 1919, reel 9, frame 887, TINCF.

111. "Shortage of Farm Labor in the South," *Daily Herald*, February 20, 1919, reel 9, frame 901, TINCF.

112. The 372nd included 480 men from Washington, D.C., 25 of whom received the French Croix de Guerre. C. Green, *The Secret City*, 187.

113. Ibid., 188–90.

114. Dennis, "Looking Backward," 77–104; Patler, *Jim Crow and the Wilson Administration*; Wolgemuth, "Woodrow Wilson and Federal Segregation"; Yellin, "In the Nation's Service."

115. Lewis, *When Harlem Was in Vogue*, 19.

116. "The Rights of the Black Man," *Washington Bee*, August 2, 1919.

117. Waskow, *From Race Riot to Sit-in*, 27.

118. Lewis, *When Harlem Was in Vogue*, 19.

119. "Murdering Negroes at Washington," *Washington Bee*, August 23, 1919.

120. Cutler to Churchill, July 23, 1919, 10218-350, MID, RG 165, NARA.

121. Abernathy, "The Washington Race War of July 1919."

122. McNeil, *Groundwork*, 47–49.

123. Tuttle, *Race Riot*, 75–76.

124. Ibid.; Sandburg, *The Chicago Race Riots*; Chicago Commission on Race Relations, *The Negro in Chicago*.

125. R. J. Ayres to Colonel Arthur Woods, April 14, 1919, War Department, General Staff, Field Reports relating to the employment situation, 1919–1920, in Grossman, *Black Workers in the Era of the Great Migration*, reel 21, frame 171.

126. Waskow, *From Race Riot to Sit-in*.

127. Tuttle, *Race Riot*, 35–44.

128. Stanley B. Norvell to Victor F. Lawson, August 22, 1919, Julius Rosenwald Papers, Department of Special Collections, University of Chicago Library, courtesy of Dr. William M. Tuttle Jr.

129. The Cook County coroner ruled Washington's actions justifiable and recommended that no charges be filed against him. Cook County (Ill.) Coroner, *The Race Riots*, 40; Chicago Commission on Race Relations, *The Negro in Chicago*, 25; Tuttle, *Race Riot*, 42; Report, July 29, 1919, 10218-353, MID, RG 165, NARA.

130. "The Friend of the Solider," *Chicago Daily News*, July 18, 1919.

131. "'E-motional Day' Welcomes 803d to Home Town," *Chicago Daily Tribune*, July 25, 1919.

132. Embree, *13 Against the Odds*, 55–57.

133. Chicago Commission on Race Relations, *The Negro in Chicago*, 1–48; Tuttle, *Race Riot*, 32–66.

134. "Welcome, Eighth!," *Chicago Defender*, February 22, 1919.

135. Chicago Commission on Race Relations, *The Negro in Chicago*, 41.

136. Ibid., 33, 42; "Race Riot Zone, Seen From Taxi, Ominous, Quiet," and "Patton of Old I.N.G., Denies Raid on Armory," *Chicago Daily Tribune*, July 29, 1919.

137. "Veterans of Old 8th I.N.G. Armed to Help Quell Riot," and "20 Slain in Race Riots," *Chicago Daily Tribune*, July 29, 1919.

138. During the riot, rumors circulated that the armory of the Eighth Infantry Regiment had been broken into and weapons stolen. An unverified report from the Chicago branch of the Department of Intelligence stated that black residents had broken into the Eighth Infantry storehouse and procured rifles and ammunition. Although the *Chicago Tribune* and later the Chicago Commission on Race Relations reported that such rumors were false, Haywood's narrative demonstrates that the armory was nevertheless a key point of organization for veterans engaged in protecting the black community. Memorandum, July 29, 1919, 10218-353, MID, RG 165, NARA; Chicago Commission on Race Relations, *The Negro in Chicago*, 21; Haywood, *Black Bolshevik*, 80–81.

139. Haywood, *Black Bolshevik*, 84; Tuttle, *Race Riot*, 3–10.

140. Haywood, *Black Bolshevik*, 80–81.

141. Ibid., 81.

142. Tuttle, *Race Riot*, 40.

143. "Riots Spread, Then Wane," *Chicago Daily Tribune*, July 30, 1919.

144. 1st Lieut. James E. Snider to Intelligence Officer, General Department, August 2, 1919, 10218-353, MID, RG 165, NARA.

145. "Riots Spread, Then Wane," *Chicago Daily Tribune*, July 30, 1919.

146. Report, July 29, 1919, 10218-353, MID, RG 165, NARA.

147. Report, August 4, 1919, 10218-353, MID, RG 165, NARA.

148. Telegram, August 30, 1919, 10218-353, MID, RG 165, NARA. The Adjutant General's Office had no record of Edward Douglass. Report to Intelligence Officer, Central Department, Chicago, September 8, 1919, 10218-353, MID, RG 165, NARA.

149. Tuttle, *Race Riot*, 210, 221–22.

150. "Reaping the Whirlwind," *Chicago Defender*, August 2, 1919.

151. "The Race Problem," *Outlook*, September 10, 1919.

152. Grossman, *Land of Hope*, 179.

153. Waskow, *From Race Riot to Sit-in*, 105–10.

154. Ibid., 111–18.

155. "11 Known Dead in Florida Riot over Election," *Washington Post*, November 4, 1920; "Lynched Man Who Wanted to Vote," *Chicago Defender*, November 6, 1920; Hurston, "The Ocoee Riot," 897–901; Ortiz, *Emancipation Betrayed*, 220–24; W. White, "Election by Terror in Florida," 195–97.

156. Ellsworth, *Death in a Promised Land*, 8–44.

157. Ibid., 24, 52, 99. James Hirsh, while providing several examples of black veteran participation in the riot, is less explicit. He implies that the role and memory of black veterans in the riot has been used to glorify the resistance of black Tulsans. Hirsch, *Riot and Remembrance*, 256–62.

Chapter Seven

1. Haywood, *Black Bolshevik*, 83–84.

2. Ibid., 117.

3. For discussions of the ABB, see Makalani, "For the Liberation of Black People Everywhere"; Hill, introduction to *The Crusader*; Solomon, *The Cry Was Unity*; Wilder, *In the Company of Black Men*, 204–5.

4. The man also indicated his desire to join the UNIA as well. *Crusader*, December 1919, 30, 32.

5. Haywood, *Black Bolshevik*, 131–32.

6. Sociologists Verta Taylor and Nancy Whittier define a social movement community as "a network of individuals and groups loosely linked through an institutional base, multiple goals and actions, and a collective identity that affirms members' common interests in opposition to dominant groups." Taylor and Whittier, "Collective Identity in Social Movement Communities," 107. My conceptualization of the New Negro movement is informed by sociological literature on new social movement theory that broadens the criteria for what constitutes a social movement beyond structuralist models of political opportunity and resource mobilization. See Larana, Johnston, and Gusfield, *New Social Movements*; Morris and Mueller, *Frontiers in Social Movement Theory*; Johnston and Klandermans, *Social Movements and Culture*. I am particularly influenced by the works of Taylor and Whittier, who, in their focus on lesbian feminism, propose a social movement model that takes into account the significance of culture, community, symbols, and collective identity in shaping the ability of social movements

to coalesce. Also see Taylor, "Mobilizing for Change in a Social Movement Society"; Taylor and Whittier, "Analytical Approaches to Social Movement Culture," 163–87.

7. The etymology of the term "new Negro" dates to the post-Reconstruction era, when a new generation of African Americans sought to distance themselves from slavery and its legacy. The phrase gained increased currency during the turn of the century, and was invoked by various writers to signify black racial progress. See Gates, "The Trope of a New Negro."

8. Scholarship on the New Negro movement is vast and spans multiple disciplines. Key works include Allen, "The New Negro"; Arnesen, *Black Protest and the Great Migration*; Baldwin, *Chicago's New Negroes*; Foley, *Spectres of 1919*; Grant, *Negro with a Hat*; W. James, *Holding Aloft the Banner of Ethiopia*; Kornweibel, *No Crystal Stair* and *"Seeing Red"*; Makalani, "For the Liberation of Black People Everywhere"; Maxwell, *New Negro, Old Left*; Nadell, *Enter the New Negroes*; Rolinson, *Grassroots Garveyism*; Schneider, *"We Return Fighting"*; Stein, *The World of Marcus Garvey*; Stephens, *Black Empire*; Turner, *Caribbean Crusaders and the Harlem Renaissance*; Whalan, *The Great War and the Culture of the New Negro*.

9. Gates, "The Trope of a New Negro," 129–31; Stephens, *Black Empire*, 39–47; W. E. B. Du Bois, "Returning Soldiers," *Crisis*, May 1919.

10. Key works linking rural and working-class black political activism with the New Negro include Hahn, *A Nation under Our Feet*; Kelly, *Race, Class, and Power in the Alabama Coal Fields, 1908–1921*; Reich, "The Great War, Black Workers, and the Rise and Fall of the NAACP in the South" and "Soldiers of Democracy"; Rolinson, *Grassroots Garveyism*; Woodruff, *American Congo*.

11. Willis Brown Godwin, VWHC.

12. Black men entered the U.S. military with various and interrelated status dimensions—or identity markers—such as race, citizenship, manhood, education, and occupation. Many African American veterans experienced an acute disjuncture between their level of investment in the war—material and ideological—based on their status dimensions and how they were, or were not, commensurately rewarded for their sacrifices by the government and the nation more broadly. Status inconsistency theory offers an explanation for the disillusionment of many black veterans with American democracy. Status inconsistency theory posits that cognitive dissonance occurs in an individual when, through a particular experience and in a particular context, one's status dimensions fail to reinforce each other, creating a perception of inconsistency. Parker, "War, What Is It Good For?," 20, 32–35; Geschwender, "Continuities in Theories of Status Consistency and Cognitive Dissonance," 160–71.

13. Judge Goodwin, VWHC.

14. Leed, *No Man's Land*, 205.

15. Milton Eugene Hughes, VWHC.

16. Parker, "War, What Is It Good For?," 24.

17. Floyd Bishop, VWHC.

18. William Jordan, *Black Newspapers and America's War for Democracy*, 134–62.

19. "Lieuts. Tell of Raw Deals from Superiors," *Baltimore Afro-American*, March 14, 1919.

20. Anonymous soldier to W. E. B. Du Bois, November 13, 1918, box 58, Du Bois World War I Papers, UMA.

21. "The Bee Commended," *Washington Bee*, August 16, 1919.

22. *Veteran*, June 28, 1919, reel 13, frames 929–30, FSAA. The paper described the National Colored Soldiers and Citizens Council as "an intensely American anti-lynching organization of war-veterans and citizens, working to secure to Colored Americans their just manhood and citizenship rights as guaranteed under the Constitution of the United States" and claimed to have "local councils" in thirty-eight states as well as in Panama. "N.C.S.C.C. Notes and Personals," *Veteran*, June 28, 1919, reel 13, frame 933, FSAA.

23. "A Fine Opportunity," *Veteran*, June 28, 1919, reel 13, frame 933, FSAA.

24. "Travelogues of a Fighting Man," June 28, 1919, *Veteran*, reel 13, frame 944, FSAA.

25. "The Remedy for Mob Violence," June 28, 1919, *Veteran*, reel 13, frame 943, FSAA.

26. Robert A. Bowen to William H. Lamar, June 26, 1919, reel 13, frame 928, FSAA.

27. Robert A. Bowen to William H. Lamar, September 4, 1919, reel 13, frame 926, FSAA.

28. Edwards, *The Practice of Diaspora.*

29. Stovall, *Paris Noir*, 39. For additional background of the African American presence in Paris during the war years, see Fabre, *From Harlem to Paris*, 46–62; Shack, *Harlem in Montmartre*, 1–25.

30. "In France," *Chicago Defender*, July 1, 1922.

31. Shack, *Harlem in Montmartre*, 22; *Baltimore Afro-American*, March 22, 1944.

32. Roster of Officers 92nd Division, box 5, 92nd Division—officers, generals, RG 120, NARA.

33. While in Paris, Nelson published a short history of African Americans, *La Race Noire dans la Démocratie Americaine* (Paris, 1922). He attended Union Theological Seminary in New York and Protestant Theological Seminary. Dunnigan, *The Fascinating Story of Black Kentuckians*, 213–14; Craig, "Nelson, William Stuart," 676.

34. Stovall, *Paris Noir*, 35–38; Shack, *Harlem in Montmartre*, 11–25.

35. Carisella and Ryan, *The Black Swallow of Death.*

36. Janken, *Rayford W. Logan*, 43.

37. Discharge certificate, box 166-2; unpublished autobiography, ch. 6, box 166-32, Rayford W. Logan Papers, MSRC.

38. Unpublished autobiography, ch. 7, box 166-32, Rayford W. Logan Papers, MSRC.

39. For discussion of the relationship between language and translation in postwar diasporic politics, see Edwards, *The Practice of Diaspora.*

40. Unpublished autobiography, ch. 7, box 166-32, Rayford W. Logan Papers, MSRC; Lewis, *W. E. B. Du Bois*, 2:38.

41. Marshall attended the London session, while Nelson attended the Paris session. Lewis, *W. E. B. Du Bois*, 2:39.

42. Janken, *Rayford W. Logan*, 35–61.

43. See Manela, *The Wilsonian Moment.*

44. For discussion of racial tensions in war and postwar France, see Stovall, "The Color Line behind the Lines," 737–69.

45. Morrow, *The Great War*, 299–314.

46. Joseph, "The British West Indies Regiment," 114–17. White soldiers of the Bermuda contingent saw active duty in France.

47. Stovall, *Paris Noir*; Edwards, *The Practice of Diaspora*; Kelley, "'But a Local Phase of a World Problem,'" 1045–77.

48. Dewitte, “La dette du sang”; Edwards, *The Practice of Diaspora*; Conklin, *A Mission to Civilize*, 302; Lunn, *Memoirs of the Maelstrom*, 202–5.

49. “Lorsqu’on a besoin de nous pour nous faire tuer ou nous faire travailler, nous sommes des Français; mais quand il s’agit de nous donner des droits, nous ne sommes plus des Français, nous sommes des nègres.” *La Voix des Nègres*, mars 1927, in Dewitte, “La dette du sang,” 8–11.

50. Minkah Makalani discusses this phenomenon through an examination of the African Blood Brotherhood. See Makalani, “For the Liberation of Black People Everywhere.”

51. D. E. Nolan, Assistant Chief of Staff, G-2, to Acting Director of Military Intelligence, February 18, 1919, 10218-315, MID, RG 165, NARA; John M. Dunn to R. I. B. McKenny, March 3, 1919, 10218-315, MID, RG 165, NARA.

52. Asst. Chief of Staff to Acting Director of Military Intelligence, January 30, 1919, reel 21, frame 231, FSAA.

53. Acting Director of Military Intelligence to Assistant Chief of Staff, March 4, 1919, reel 21, frame 237, FSAA.

54. John M. Dunn to R. I. B. McKenny, March 3, 1919, 10218-315, MID, RG 165, NARA.

55. “Constitution of League for Democracy,” 10218-337, MID, RG 165, NARA.

56. Ibid.

57. Historian Eric Leed describes a similar process of disillusionment for soldiers in the British army during World War I. Their class-based disillusionment was not, however, compounded by racism, as was the case for middle-class African American soldiers and officers. Leed, *No Man’s Land*, 76.

58. *Catalogue of Lincoln University, 1908–1909*, 20.

59. *Harvard Alumni Directory, 1919*, 567.

60. Hayden, *“Mr. Harlem Hospital,”* 1–59; Mead, *Harvard’s Military Record in the World War*, 1048–49. Other national officers included Senior Vice President Horace B. Scroggins, Executive Secretary Charles Fearing, a former first lieutenant in the 365th Infantry, and Arthur M. Curtis, also a lieutenant in the Ninety-second Division. Regiment Roster of Officers 92nd Division, box 5, 92nd Division—officers, generals, RG 120, NARA.

61. *New York Commoner*, June 28, 1919, reel 21, frame, FSAA.

62. “Constitution of League for Democracy,” 10218-337, MID, RG 165, NARA; Richards, “Osceola E. McKaine,” 10–84.

63. Walter Loving to Director of Military Intelligence, April 25, 1919, 10218-337, MID, RG 165, NARA; Walter Loving to Director of Military Intelligence, August 6, 1919, 10218-337, MID, RG 165, NARA.

64. Reminiscences of Lester B. Granger (1961), CUOHROC; “Newark Chapter of the League Holds Meeting,” *New York Commoner*, June 28, 1919.

65. Waring, *Work of the Colored Law and Order League*, 18.

66. Walter Loving to Director of Military Intelligence, August 6, 1919, 10218-337, MID, RG 165, NARA.

67. Walter Loving to Director of Military Intelligence, May 19, 1919, 10218-337, MID, RG 165, NARA.

68. The other individuals representing the LFD at this meeting included former Ninety-second Division officers Frank Coleman, James H. N. Waring, Arthur L. Curtis, West Hamil-

ton, Thomas M. Dent, A. B. Aiken, Osceola McKaine, and local Washington, D.C., leaders J. H. Douglas and J. Finley Wilson. Walter Loving to J. E. Cutler, June 11, 1919, reel 21, frame 13, FSAA.

69. Loving to Captain J. E. Cutler, June 12, 1919, 10218-337, MID, RG 165, NARA; Richards, "Osceola E. McKaine," 66–72.

70. Osceola McKaine, "With the Buffaloes in France," *Crusader*, February 1919; Richards, "Osceola E. McKaine," 74, 78–80; Walter Loving to Director of Military Intelligence, June 17, 1919, 10218-337, MID, RG 165, NARA. J. Finley Wilson was a prominent Washington, D.C., journalist and newspaper editor who became president of the National Negro Press Association in 1920.

71. "Dr. Moton Answers Charges at New York Tuskegee Assn. Banquet," *Chicago Defender*, July 5, 1919.

72. Schneider, "*We Return Fighting*," 17; Reich, "The Great War, Black Workers, and the Rise and Fall of the NAACP in the South," and "Soldiers of Democracy."

73. "War Veterans Unite to Aid Democracy," *New York Age*, March 15, 1919; "Soldiers' Organizations," *New York Age*, May 24, 1919; Memo, Re: "'A League for Democracy' and 'The National Brotherhood Association.' Radical Propaganda, Negro," August 30, 1919, reel 11, frame 907, FSAA.

74. J. E. Cutler to Col. Coxe, subject: Conference with Capt. Samuel F. Sewall, colored, June 18, 1919, reel 21, frames 426–27, FSAA.

75. "Soldiers' Organizations," *New York Age*, May 24, 1919; Walter Loving to Director of Military Intelligence, May 19, 1919, 10218-337, MID, RG 165, NARA; Loving to Captain J. E. Cutler, June 12, 1919, 10218-337, MID, RG 165, NARA; Richards, "Osceola E. McKaine," 66–72, 81.

76. Kornweibel, *No Crystal Stair*, 24–35, 54–61; P. Foner, *American Socialism and Black Americans*, 265–87.

77. "A New Crowd—A New Negro," *Messenger*, May–June 1919.

78. Kornweibel, *No Crystal Stair*, 3–70; J. Anderson, *A. Philip Randolph*, 76, 86; P. Foner, *American Socialism and Black Americans*, 265–87; General Collardet, Attaché Militaire à M. Le Ministre de la Guerre, E. M. A. 2e, Bur. I, 8 avril 1919, 7N 1717, SHAT.

79. Victor R. Daly Papers, box 1; Victor Reginald Daly, box 350, Public Affairs Records, Division of Rare and Manuscript Collections, Cornell University.

80. "Open Forum," *Messenger*, October 1919.

81. Ibid.

82. Photos and notes from Victor Daly's Des Moines experience make specific mention of "Bill" Colson. Victor R. Daly Papers, box 1; Victor Reginald Daly, box 350, Public Affairs Records, Division of Rare and Manuscript Collections, Cornell University.

83. Hill, *Garvey Papers*, 1:481.

84. Kornweibel, *No Crystal Stair*, 64.

85. Robert Bowen to Brig. General M. Churchill, June 30, 1919, 10218-341, MID, RG 165, NARA.

86. William N. Colson, "An Analysis of Negro Patriotism," *Messenger*, August 1919.

87. Memo, June 30, 1919, 10218-341, MID, RG 165, NARA. The MID filed reports on articles

Colson published in the July and August editions of the *Messenger*. Robert Bowen to Brig. General M. Churchill, July 28, 1919, 10218-341, MID, RG 165, NARA.

88. M. J. Driscoll to C. L. Converse, July 13, 1919, L0038, Investigations Files, 1918–1920, Records of the Lusk Committee, NYSA.

89. William N. Colson, "The Immediate Function of the Negro Veteran," *Messenger*, December 1919.

90. Schuyler, *Black and Conservative*, 113.

91. Ibid., 31–93; Ferguson, *The Sage of Sugar Hill*, 11–16.

92. Schuyler, *Black and Conservative*, 134.

93. Kornweibel, *No Crystal Stair*, 63n.

94. Schuyler, *Black and Conservative*, 136.

95. Ibid., 165.

96. Hutchinson, "Mediating 'Race' and 'Nation,'" 533–34; Kornweibel, *No Crystal Stair*, 57–58; Ferguson, *The Sage of Sugar Hill*, 40–41.

97. "Garvey Urges Organization," *Baltimore Afro-American*, February 28, 1919.

98. See Perry, *Hubert Harrison*.

99. Stein, *The World of Marcus Garvey*, 30–37; Martin, *Race First*, 5–10.

100. For discussions of the UNIA in the South, see Hahn, *A Nation under Our Feet*; Harold, *The Rise and Fall of the Garvey Movement in the Urban South, 1918–1942*; Rolinson, *Grassroots Garveyism*.

101. W. James, *Holding Aloft the Banner of Ethiopia*, 136.

102. Lively, "Continuity and Radicalism in American Black Nationalist Thought," 213; Hill, *Garvey Papers*, 1:lx, lxix; Stephens, *Black Empire*, 75–101; Martin, *African Fundamentalism*; Hill, *Marcus Garvey Life and Lessons*, xxxvi–xxxix, 1–25.

103. C. Grant, *Negro with a Hat*, 95–113.

104. Hill, *Garvey Papers*, 1:376. In particular, see Stoddard, *The Rising Tide of Color*; MacLean, *Behind the Mask of Chivalry*; Stein, *The World of Marcus Garvey*, 42; Lively, "Continuity and Radicalism in American Black Nationalist Thought, 1914–1929," 217–18.

105. "Speech by Marcus Garvey," July 24, 1921, in Hill, *Garvey Papers*, 3:551. On the significance of race war in postwar revolutionary black internationalism, see Stephens, *Black Empire*, 37.

106. Speech by Marcus Garvey, January 13, 1922, *Negro World*, January 21, 1922.

107. Speech by Marcus Garvey, January 15, 1922, *Negro World*, January 21, 1922.

108. "Lesson 2: Leadership," in Hill, *Marcus Garvey Life and Lessons*, 199–205.

109. "Opening Speech of the Convention by Marcus Garvey," August 1, 1921, in Hill, *Garvey Papers*, 3:577.

110. Lively, "Continuity and Radicalism in American Black Nationalist Thought, 1914–1929," 219; "Lesson 2: Leadership," in Hill, *Marcus Garvey Life and Lessons*, 199–205.

111. Bair, "True Women, Real Men," 154–66.

112. "Editorial Letter by Marcus Garvey," June 10, 1919, in Hill, *Garvey Papers*, 1:416.

113. "Speech by Marcus Garvey," in Hill, *Garvey Papers*, 3:282.

114. Roster of Officers 92nd Division, box 5, 92nd Division—officers, generals, RG 120, NARA.

115. Stein, *The World of Marcus Garvey*, 64; Hill, *Garvey Papers*, 2:322–23, 329, 465–66.

116. Lindholm, "William Clarence Matthews"; Hill, *Marcus Garvey Life and Lessons*, 389, 404, 408, 424; Hill, *Garvey Papers*, 2:465–66; Hill, *Garvey Papers*, 2:322–23, 329.

117. Norris became disillusioned with Garvey and the UNIA following the murder of his close friend and UNIA member Reverend J. W. Eason. He supplied Chandler Owen information regarding the organization to assist the *Messenger* editor in his "Garvey Must Go" campaign. Hill, *Marcus Garvey Life and Lessons*, 414–15; Hill, *Garvey Papers*, vol. 5.

118. W. James, *Holding Aloft the Banner of Ethiopia*, 358.

119. Lt. Col. H. A. Pakenham to MID Section Four, Attachment, November 5, 1918, in Hill, *Garvey Papers*, 1:314.

120. Elkins, "A Source of Black Nationalism in the Caribbean"; Howe, "In the Crucible of Race"; K. Singh, *Race and Class Struggles in a Colonial State*; Martin, "Revolutionary Upheaval in Trinidad, 1919," 313–26.

121. W. James, *Holding Aloft the Banner of Ethiopia*, 66–69.

122. Hill, *Garvey Papers*, 3:48–49.

123. Ibid., 135–36; W. James, *Holding Aloft the Banner of Ethiopia*, 69.

124. W. James, *Holding Aloft the Banner of Ethiopia*, 56–60, 66–69. For more on Haynes and the participation of other veterans of the BWIR in the UNIA, see Howe, *Race, War and Nationalism*, 188.

125. Historian of the UNIA Barbara Bair likewise asserts that black veterans constituted the majority of the African Legion. Bair, "True Women, Real Men," 158; "Rules and Regulation for Universal African Legions of the U.N.I.A. and A.C.L.," in Hill, *Garvey Papers*, 3:755; Hill, *Marcus Garvey Life and Lessons*, 419.

126. Haywood, *Black Bolshevik*, 105.

127. Martin, *Race First*, 236–37.

128. The Eighth Illinois armory was Garvey's preferred venue when speaking in Chicago. Hill, *Garvey Papers*, 2:41, 51; "Speech by Marcus Garvey," February 6, 1921, in Hill, *Garvey Papers*, 3:164.

129. Rolinson, *Grassroots Garveyism*, 54, 61–63.

130. Smith-Irvin, *Footsoldiers of the Universal Negro Improvement Association*, 23–24.

131. "Report of Brooklyn UNIA Meetings," *Negro World*, February 4, 1922. Bazil's name appeared in the *Negro World* article as Wilfred F. Brazil.

132. Nimmo, along with Miami division president Claude Green, was indicted for the murder of Garvey rival Princess Koffey in Miami after her assassination on March 8, 1928. While admitting his opposition to Koffey, Nimmo denied any involvement in the murder. He was later acquitted of all charges and released from jail on July 12, 1928. Vought, "Racial Stirrings in Colored Town," 56–76; Hill, *Garvey Papers*, 7:167.

133. Lorini, *Rituals of Race*, xii–xiii, 251–56.

134. "Report of UNIA Parade," August 3, 1920, in Hill, *Garvey Papers*, 2:490–94, 647.

135. James Wormley Jones Papers, MSRC; Kornweibel, *"Seeing Red,"* 106–7.

136. Report, Subject: Meeting of Musolit Club at Colored Y.M.C.A., Friday evening, March 14th, March 18, 1919, Walter Loving Papers, MSRC.

137. James Wormley Jones to Secretary of War, November 21, 1918, James Wormley Jones Papers, MSRC; Kornweibel, *"Seeing Red,"* 106–7.

138. Jones earned the confidence of ABB founder Cyril Briggs based on his familiarity with firearms acquired in the war. Kornweibel, *"Seeing Red,"* 107–10, 120–27; Grant, *Negro with a Hat*, 220–21, 322.

139. For an excellent discussion of Garvey's conflicts with various black leaders, the government's efforts to destroy the UNIA, and Garvey's ultimate downfall, see Grant, *Negro with a Hat*, esp. ch. 13–18.

Chapter Eight

1. "Paris Thrilled by Allies' Parade to Mark Victory," *New York Times*, July 15, 1919.

2. Ibid.

3. See Levitch, *Panthéon de la Guerre*. An African American soldier was later painted into the *Panthéon* in anticipation of its 1927 arrival to the United States. Levitch, "The Great War Re-remembered," 99.

4. Winter, *Remembering War* and *Sites of Memory, Sites of Mourning*; Fussell, *The Great War and Modern Memory*.

5. For one of the few critical discussions of the First World War in American memory, see J. Cooper, "The Great War and American Memory."

6. This has remained the standard narrative for most discussions of black participation in the First World War, as well as broader discussion of African American military history. See Buckley, *American Patriots*; Nalty, *Strength for the Fight*.

7. This perception is explicitly reflected in the recent work of Richard Slotkin on the "Harlem Hellfighters." See Slotkin, *Lost Battalions*, 518.

8. John Bodnar specifically examines the use of official memory in shaping repressive notions of national belonging. Bodnar, *Remaking America*.

9. Crane, "Writing the Individual Back into Collective Memory," 1375.

10. Scott, *Domination and the Arts of Resistance*; Blight, "W. E. B. Du Bois and the Struggle for American Historical Memory."

11. Any examination of collective memory must start with the seminal work of Maurice Halbwachs. See Halbwachs, *On Collective Memory*. Alan Confino convincingly argues that scholars have often employed the concept of collective memory too loosely and without sufficient methodological rigor. In discussing the relationship between collective memory and cultural representation, Confino writes, "The crucial issue in the history of memory is not how a past is represented but why it was received or rejected" (1390). Therefore, a collective memory does not emerge solely from representation of a particular historical moment, but, as Confino asserts, "how this representation has been interpreted and perceived" (1392). See Confino, "Collective Memory and Cultural History." Also see Crane, "Writing the Individual Back into Collective Memory."

12. Nora, "Between Memory and History."

13. On the "democratization of social memory," see Le Goff, *History and Memory*, 99.

14. I take the term "multivocality" from Jay Winter's instructive analysis of the study of memory. Winter, *Remembering War*, 277.

15. Lepore, *The Name of War*, ix–xxiii.

16. Le Goff, *History and Memory*, 97–98; Winter, *Remembering War*, 277.

17. Blight, *Race and Reunion*.

18. Wilson served with the Louisiana Native Guards and the famed Massachusetts Fifty-fourth Infantry during the Civil War. He became the first African American member of the National Council of Administration of the Grand Army of the Republic. Wilson, *Black Phalanx*; Crowder, *John Edward Bruce*, 91–133.

19. For an example, see Edward A. Johnson, *History of Negro Soldiers in the Spanish-American War* (1899).

20. For further discussion of this phenomenon, see Gates, "The Trope of a New Negro and the Reconstruction of the Image of the Black."

21. "War History," *Crisis*, December 1918.

22. Research notes, "The Black Man and the Wounded World," reel 84, frame 702, Du Bois Papers, UMA.

23. Carter G. Woodson to W. E. B. Du Bois, October 27, 1918, box 58, Du Bois World War I Papers, UMA.

24. W. E. B. Du Bois to Carter G. Woodson, October 30, 1918, box 58, Du Bois World War I Papers, UMA; Carter G. Woodson to W. E. B. Du Bois, November 9, 1918, box 58, Du Bois World War I Papers, UMA; W. E. B. Du Bois to Carter G. Woodson, November 12, 1918, box 58, Du Bois World War I Papers, UMA.

25. Carter G. Woodson to W. E. B. Du Bois, November 16, 1918, box 58, Du Bois World War I Papers, UMA.

26. Meier and Rudwick, *Black History and the Historical Profession*, 13.

27. Lewis, *W. E. B. Du Bois*, 1:562.

28. W. E. B. Du Bois to Emmett J. Scott, November 8, 1918, box 58, Du Bois World War I Papers, UMA; Emmett J. Scott to W. E. B. Du Bois, November 10, 1918, box 58, Du Bois World War I Papers, UMA.

29. W. E. B. Du Bois to Villard, Peabody, and Wood, November 16, 1918, box 58, Du Bois World War I Papers, UMA.

30. Du Bois similarly invoked the language of revolution to describe the war in a July 1919 article in the *Opinion*. Du Bois, "Reconstruction," 130–31.

31. W. E. B. Du Bois, "The Black Man in the Revolution of 1914–1918," *Crisis*, March 1919.

32. For discussion of this theme in Du Bois's writings about the war, and other postwar literary works, see Whalan, "'The Only Real White Democracy' and the Language of Liberation."

33. W. E. B. Du Bois, "An Essay toward a History of the Black Man in the Great War," *Crisis*, June 1919.

34. Ibid.

35. Sweeny, *History of the American Negro in the Great World War*, xvi.

36. Ibid, 114.

37. Kelly Miller attended Howard University and later received a Ph.D. in mathematics from Johns Hopkins University. He returned to Howard in 1890 as a professor of mathematics. He introduced sociology into the Howard curriculum and served as professor of sociology from 1895 to 1934. He was appointed as dean of the College of Arts and Sciences in 1907.

38. Miller, *The Disgrace of Democracy*; *The Negro in the New Reconstruction*; and *Authentic History of the Negro in the World War.*

39. Woodson, Review of *The American Negro in the World War*, 466–67.

40. Scott, *Scott's Official History*, ch. 2.

41. Sweeny, *History of the American Negro in the Great World War*, 257–58.

42. Scott, *Scott's Official History*, ch. 30.

43. Novick, *That Noble Dream*, 111–32.

44. William N. Colson, "Shoddyism Called History," *Messenger*, December 1919.

45. Along with Jamieson, the other African American veteran coauthors of the book included Sergeant G. I. Williams, Corporal H. White, Private Jack Allen, and Private John Graham.

46. Jamieson et al., *Complete History of the Colored Soldiers in the World War*, foreword.

47. Ibid., 152–53.

48. Ibid., 158.

49. Ibid., 159.

50. Other published memoirs include William S. Braddan, *Under Fire with the 370th Infantry (8th I.N.G.), A.E.F: Memoirs of the World War* (n.d.); John Brother Cade, *Twenty-two Months with "Uncle Sam"* (1929); and Napoleon Bonaparte Marshall, *The Providential Armistice* (1930). Two black soldiers of the 372nd Infantry Regiment, Monroe Mason and Arthur Furr, published *The American Negro Soldier with the Red Hand of France* in 1920. Their informative book is more a unit history of the 372nd than a personal memoir.

51. Walker Jordan, preface to *With "Old Eph" in the Army.*

52. Ibid., 21.

53. Ibid., 24.

54. Ibid., 44.

55. C. H. Williams, *Sidelights on Negro Soldiers.*

56. Ibid., 11–12; Carter G. Woodson made a similar observation in his positive review in the *Journal of Negro History*, writing, "This book is not a history, but it is informing." Woodson, Review of *Sidelights on Negro Soldiers*, 235–36.

57. Woodson recognized this in his review, noting, "While the authors make no pretense to scientific treatment, they have certainly facilitated the task of the historian who must undertake the writing of a definitive history of the Negroes' participation in the World War." Woodson, Review of *Two Colored Women with the American Expeditionary Forces*, 379.

58. Hunton and Johnson, *Two Colored Women.* For scholarly discussions of the book, see Piep, "'Modern Understanding'"; Whalan, *The Great War and the Culture of the New Negro*, 53–65.

59. "History," *Crisis*, May 1919.

60. "Documents of the War," *Crisis*, May 1919.

61. Clarence A. Lee to W. E. B. Du Bois, July 15, 1919, box 58, Du Bois World War I Papers, UMA.

62. De Haven Hinkson to W. E. B. Du Bois, May 5, 1919, box 58, Du Bois World War I Papers, UMA.

63. Samuel Kent to W. E. B. Du Bois, July, 12, 1919, box 56, Du Bois World War I Papers, UMA.

64. Louis Pontlock to W. E. B. Du Bois, April 26, 1919, reel 8, frame 43, Du Bois Papers, UMA.

65. Quoted in W. E. B. Du Bois, "The Black Man and the Wounded World," unpublished manuscript, box 56, Du Bois World War I Papers, UMA.

66. "The Black Man and the Wounded World," *Crisis*, January 1924.

67. This view in many ways paralleled the theme of disillusionment, irony, and cynicism that pervaded postwar literary works on the war, on both sides of the Atlantic. See Fussell, *The Great War and Modern Memory*.

68. The funding sources Du Bois approached included the Macmillan Company in July and September 1925, the Slater Fund in June 1927, the Guggenheim Foundation in August 1928 concerning the possibility of receiving a research fellowship, the American Fund for Public Service in January 1929, the Julius Rosenwald Fund in December 1930, the Carnegie Endowment in January 1936, and the Russell Sage Foundation in March 1936. See Series 1, Du Bois Papers, UMA.

69. W. E. B. Du Bois to Alfred Harcourt, September 23, 1931, in Aptheker, *The Correspondence of W. E. B. Du Bois*, 443.

70. W. E. B. Du Bois, *Dusk of Dawn*.

71. On Du Bois and countermemory, see Blight, "W. E. B. Du Bois and the Struggle for American Historical Memory."

72. W. E. B. Du Bois, *The Souls of Black Folk*, 364.

73. W. E. B. Du Bois, "The Black Man and the Wounded World," unpublished manuscript, ch. 8, box 54, Du Bois World War I Papers, UMA.

74. Du Bois, *The Autobiography of W. E. B. Du Bois*, 274; and *Dusk of Dawn*, 741.

75. Hagedorn, *Savage Peace*; Painter, *Standing at Armageddon*.

76. MacMillan, *Paris 1919*.

77. Painter, *Standing at Armageddon*, 368.

78. Dumenil, *The Modern Temper*.

79. Novick, *That Noble Dream*, 111–32.

80. "One Hundred Books That Will Be Published This Fall," *New York Times*, September 27, 1925.

81. October 25, 1918, diary #9, box 2, Robert Lee Bullard Papers, LOC.

82. Bullard, *Personalities and Reminiscences of the War*, 291.

83. Ibid., 294.

84. Ibid.

85. Ibid., 296–98. Bullard's narrative was not altogether representative. The postwar writings of other white officers who commanded African American troops, while not completely laudatory, contained less harsh assessments of their abilities. For example, in *My Colored Battalion* (1920), Warner Ross offered a sympathetic, albeit highly paternalistic, account of the 365th Infantry Regiment. Warner praised the courage of his men, due in no small part to his steadfast leadership. While less condescending than Ross, Arthur Little in *From Harlem to the Rhine* (1936) offers praise of the 369th Infantry Regiment from the perspective of its white leadership.

86. "General Bullard 'Hopes' Not to Arouse Controversy," *New York Times*, December 27, 1925.

87. "Bullard Was Named for Bob Lee," *Chicago Defender*, June 13, 1925.

88. "'Take Back Lies,' Bullard Is Told," *Pittsburgh Courier*, June 20, 1925.

89. "Resolutions Adopted by the National Ass'n in Recent Conference at Denver," *New York Amsterdam News*, July 22, 1925.

90. "Voice of the People," *Chicago Daily Tribune*, June 11, 1925.

91. "92d Officer Nails Bullard's Lie," *Chicago Defender*, June 13, 1925.

92. "92d's Veterans Answer Attack by Gen. Bullard," *Chicago Daily Tribune*, June 21, 1925.

93. "Thrusts and Lunges," *Pittsburg Courier*, June 20, 1925.

94. Bullard, *Personalities and Reminiscences of the War*, preface.

95. Nora, "Between History and Memory," 8–9.

96. This is most thoroughly discussed by Mark Whalan. See Whalan, *The Great War and the Culture of the New Negro*.

97. Culture and politics did not function independently of one another during the postwar period. As such, the "political" New Negro was not simply co-opted by the "cultural" New Negro and the 1925 publication of *The New Negro* by Alain Locke. For discussions of the confluence of New Negro political radicalism with the New Negro arts movement, see Foley, *Spectres of 1919*; Martin, *Literary Garveyism*; Maxwell, *New Negro, Old Left*; Turner, *Caribbean Crusaders and the Harlem Renaissance*.

98. Literature on the Harlem Renaissance is extensive. Key works include Baker, *Modernism and the Harlem Renaissance*; Carroll, *Word, Image, and the New Negro*; Favor, *Authentic Blackness*; Huggins, *Harlem Renaissance*; Hutchinson, *The Harlem Renaissance in Black and White*; Lewis, *When Harlem Was in Vogue*; Nadell, *Enter the New Negroes*; Sherrard-Johnson, *Portraits of the New Negro Woman*; Turner, *Caribbean Crusaders and the Harlem Renaissance*; Wall, *Women of the Harlem Renaissance*; Wintz, *Black Culture and the Harlem Renaissance*.

99. David Levering Lewis convincingly demonstrates the exclusive and bourgeois nature of the Harlem Renaissance. Lewis, *When Harlem Was in Vogue*.

100. Powell, "Re/Birth of a Nation," 17–18; Baldwin, *Chicago's New Negroes*; Edwards, *The Practice of Diaspora*; Fabre, *From Harlem to Paris*.

101. "Jazz Music Is Now All *the* Rage throughout United States," *New York Age*, May 3, 1919. Eric Porter provides detailed analysis of debates during the 1910s, 1920s, and 1930s among African Americans to define the meaning of jazz. Porter, *What Is This Thing Called Jazz?*

102. Gaines, "Artistic Othering in Black Diaspora Musics," 206–7.

103. Gilroy, *The Black Atlantic*, 211.

104. Scott, *Scott's Official History*, 310.

105. Lawrence, *Duke Ellington and His World*, 19.

106. Badger, "James Reese Europe and the Prehistory of Jazz," 48–67; Badger, *A Life in Ragtime*, 204; Tucker, "In Search of Will Vodery," 123–82.

107. Sissle, "Memoirs of Lieutenant 'Jim' Europe," 218–19, James Reese Europe Collection, SC/NYPL.

108. Brooks, *Lost Sounds*, 280–87.

109. Europe was buried at Arlington National Cemetery with full military honors. Badger, *A Life in Ragtime*, 218–20.

110. "'Jim' Europe Lives," *Chicago Defender*, May 17, 1919.

111. Badger, *A Life in Ragtime*, 223.

112. Kimball and Bolcon, *Reminiscing with Sissle and Blake*, 80, 84–151; Slotkin, *Lost Battalions*, 520.

113. For discussion of the NAACP in the postwar era, see Schneider, *"We Return Fighting."* For more localized discussions, see Reich, "Soldiers of Democracy."

114. Cotter Jr. was born on September 2, 1895, in Louisville, Kentucky. His father, Joseph Cotter Sr., was a prominent educator in Louisville. Cotter Jr. attended Fisk University and later worked as an editor and writer for the *Louisville Leader*. During this time he became an active poet. His lone book, *The Band of Gideon and Other Lyrics*, was published in June 1918. He died on February 3, 1919 after a seven-year battle with tuberculosis. Payne, *Joseph Seamon Cotter, Jr.*, 1–22.

115. Cotter Jr., "A Sonnet to Negro Soldiers," *Crisis*, June 1918.

116. Cotter Jr., "On the Fields of France."

117. Whalan, *The Great War and the Culture of the New Negro*, 74–75.

118. Lewis, *When Harlem Was in Vogue*; Lewis, *W. E. B. Du Bois*, 2:157–58.

119. Jones, *Rereading the Harlem Renaissance*, 28–31.

120. Whalan, *The Great War and the Culture of the New Negro*, 154–60.

121. Fauset, *There Is Confusion*, 269.

122. Ibid., 263–72.

123. Ibid., 272–73.

124. Ibid., 251–53.

125. For further discussion of this literary tradition, see J. James, *A Freedom Bought with Blood*.

126. "New York City Briefs," *Chicago Defender*, October 30, 1920; "Daly Sues Editors to Get Back Salary," *Chicago Defender*, November 29, 1920.

127. Kornweibel, *"Seeing Red,"* 94; Victor R. Daly Papers, box 1; Victor Reginald Daly, Public Affairs Records, box 350, Division of Rare and Manuscript Collections, Cornell University.

128. Payne and Daly, "A MELUS Interview: Victor R. Daly," 92.

129. Ibid., 87–88.

130. Hutchinson, "Mediating 'Race' and 'Nation.'"

131. Daly, "Private Walker Goes Patrolling," *Crisis*, June 1930; Daly, "Goats, Wildcats and Buffalo," *Crisis*, March 1932.

132. "Still Five More," *Crisis*, February 1934.

133. Daly, *Not Only War*.

134. Daly lived in an adjoining apartment to James Weldon Johnson during his time in Harlem after the war. He befriended Alain Locke after moving to Washington, D.C. Payne and Daly, "A MELUS Interview: Victor R. Daly," 88–89.

135. For critical discussions of *Not Only War*, see Piep, "'Modern Understanding'"; J. James, *A Freedom Bought with Blood*.

136. J. James, *A Freedom Bought with Blood*, 174–86.

137. Daly, *Not Only War*, 106.

138. Lau, *Democracy Rising*, 34–35.

139. Powell, *Black Art and Culture in the 20th Century*, 39–40.

140. Quoted in Cooper, "Claude McKay and the New Negro of the 1920's," 302.

141. W. Cooper, *Claude McKay*; W. James, *A Fierce Hatred of Injustice*; McKay, *A Long Way from Home*; Tillery, *Claude McKay*.

142. Several literary scholars have recently acknowledged and offered excellent analysis of the centrality of the First World War and black soldiers in *Home to Harlem*. Key works include Davis, "World War I, Literary Modernism, and the U.S. South"; J. James, *A Freedom Fought with Blood*; Stephens, *Black Empire*; Whalan, *The Great War and the Culture of the New Negro*, 140–47.

143. McKay, *Home to Harlem*.

144. Stephens, *Black Empire*, 177–203; Edwards, *Practice of Diaspora*; McKay, *Banjo*, 11, 193–94.

145. "Carrie Williams Clifford," in Rice, *Witnessing Lynching*, 218.

146. Clifford, *The Widening Light*.

147. "The Black Draftee from Dixie," in Clifford, *The Widening Light*, 22.

148. Janken, *White*, 98–112.

149. Davis, "World War I, Literary Modernism, and the U.S. South."

150. May, "World War Veteran Horace Pippin."

151. Pippin war notebooks, SAAA.

152. Ibid.

153. May, "World War Veteran Horace Pippin."

154. Cornel West offers an excellent analysis of the false dichotomy between Pippin as a "modernist" and "primitivist" artist. He likewise recognizes Pippin's art as "a powerful expression of black spiritual strivings to attain self-conscious humanhood." West, "Horace Pippin's Challenge to Art Criticism."

155. Wilson, "Scenes of War," 59; May, "World War Veteran Horace Pippin."

156. "Primitivist Pippin," *Time*, January 29, 1940.

Epilogue

1. U.S. Army War College, "The Use of Negro Manpower in War," USAMHI.

2. Ibid.

3. War Department Circular No. 365, July 22, 1919, USAMHI; Nalty, *Strength for the Fight*, 128.

4. Nalty, *Strength for the Fight*, 128–30.

5. Benjamin O. Davis Sr. Papers, USAMHI. On the career of Benjamin O. Davis Sr., see Fletcher, *America's First Black General*.

6. Janken, *Rayford W. Logan*.

7. Haywood, *Black Bolshevik*.

8. Gilpin and Gasman, *Charles S. Johnson*; Robbins, *Sidelines Activist*.

9. Sullivan, *Days of Hope*, 196–97, 201–2; Richards, "Osceola E. McKaine."

10. McNeil, *Groundwork*.

11. Robert Lee Cypress, VWHC.

12. Lemuel Moody, VWHC.

13. For further discussion of the First World War and African American civil rights struggles, see Lentz-Smith, "The Great War for Civil Rights." Historians have increasingly

begun to challenge the traditional periodization and geographic focus of the civil rights movement. See J. Hall, "The Long Civil Rights Movement and the Political Uses of the Past"; Gilmore, *Defying Dixie*; Sugrue, *Sweet Land of Liberty*.

14. Charles Hamilton Houston to President Franklin D. Roosevelt, October 8, 1937, in Nalty and MacGregor, *Blacks in the Military: Essential Documents*, 96.

15. On June 25, 1941, one week before the march, Roosevelt issued Executive Order 8802, banning racial discrimination in defense industries and creating the Fair Employment Practices Commission.

16. Nalty, *Strength for the Fight*, 196–210.

17. "At Last, a Black Badge of Courage," *Washington Post*, April 25, 1991.

Bibliography

Primary Sources

MANUSCRIPT COLLECTIONS

Ancestry.com, ⟨http://www.ancestry.com⟩

Anniston Public Library, Anniston, Ala.

Caldwell Case File

Columbia University Oral History Research Office Collection, Columbia University, New York, N.Y.

Reminiscences of Will Winton Alexander (1952)

Reminiscences of Lester B. Granger (1961)

Reminiscences of Asa Philip Randolph (1972)

Reminiscences of George Samuel Schuyler (1960)

Cornell University, Division of Rare and Manuscript Collections, Ithaca, N.Y.

Victor R. Daly Papers

Public Affairs Records

Humanities and Social Sciences Library, New York Public Library, New York, N.Y.

Joel E. Spingarn Papers

Kautz Family YMCA Archives, University of Minnesota, Minneapolis, Minn.

Colored Work Department Records

Library of Congress, Washington, D.C.

Newton Diehl Baker Papers

Robert Lee Bullard Papers

Rayford Whittingham Logan Papers

Moton Family Papers

Library of Virginia, ⟨http://www.lva.lib.va.us⟩

Virginia World War I History Commission Questionnaires

Moorland-Spingarn Research Center, Howard University, Washington, D.C.

Thomas Montgomery Gregory Papers

Charles Hamilton Houston Papers

James Wormley Jones Papers

Rayford Whittingham Logan Papers

Walter Loving Papers

Jesse E. Moorland Papers

Joel E. Spingarn Papers

New York State Archives, Albany, N.Y.

Records of the Lusk Committee

369th/15th New York National Guard Abstracts

Ohio Historical Society, *The African-American Experience in Ohio, 1850–1920*, ⟨http://dbs.ohiohistory.org/africanam/index.stm⟩

Colonel Charles Young Collection

Princeton University, Princeton, N.J.
Papers of the National Association for the Advancement of Colored People
Tuskegee Institute Newsclippings File
Woodrow Wilson Papers
Schomburg Center for Research in Black Culture, New York Public Library, New York, N.Y.
Berry Family Collection
Henry Plummer Cheathum Collection
William H. Dyer Collection
James Reese Europe Collection
William R. R. Granger Jr. Letters
Benjamin F. Seldon Papers
UNIA Central Division Records
Service des Archives de l'Assemblée Nationale, Palais Bourbon, Paris, France
Annales de la Chambre des Députés, Débats Parlementaires
Service Historique de l'Armée de Terre, Château de Vincennes, Paris, France
Série 6N: Fonds Clemenceau
Série 7N: Bureau spécial franco-américain
Série 16N: 2e bureau, Section de renseignements aux armies (SRA), grand quartier général
Série 17N: Mission militaire française près l'armée américaine
Série 19N: Armées du front occidental, 1914–1918, IV Armée, Opérations
Smithsonian Archives of American Art, Washington, D.C.
Horace Pippin War Notebooks
United States Army Military History Institute, Carlisle, Pa.
Benjamin O. Davis Sr. Papers
U.S. Army War College, "The Use of Negro Manpower in War." 1925.
World War I Questionnaire and Survey
United States National Archives and Record Administration, College Park, Md.
Records of the U.S. Food Administration, 1917–1920, Record Group 4
Records of the Committee on Public Information, Record Group 63
Records of the American Expeditionary Forces (World War I), Record Group 120
Records of the Office of the Judge Advocate General (Army), Record Group 153
Records of the Office of the Inspector General (Army), Record Group 159
Records of the War Department General and Special Staffs, Record Group 165
Records of the Adjutant General's Office, Record Group 407
University of Massachusetts, Amherst, Mass.
W. E. B. Du Bois Papers
W. E. B. Du Bois World War I Papers—"The Black Man and the Wounded World" manuscript and research materials (microfilm)

GOVERNMENT PUBLICATIONS

American Battle Monuments Commission. *92d Division, Summary of Operations in the World War*. Washington, D.C.: Government Printing Office, 1944.

———. *93d Division, Summary of Operations in the World War*. Washington, D.C.: U.S. Government Printing Office, 1944.

Congressional Record, 65th Cong., 1st sess., Vol. LV, Part 6. Washington, D.C.: Government Printing Office, 1917.

Office of the Provost Marshal General. *Second Report of the Provost Marshal General to the Secretary of War on the Operations of the Selective Service System to December 20, 1918*. Washington, D.C.: Government Printing Office, 1919.

———. *Final Report of the Provost Marshal General to the Secretary of War on the Operations of the Selective Service System to July 15, 1919*. Washington, D.C.: Government Printing Office, 1920.

U.S. Congress. Senate. *Alleged Executions without Trial in France: Hearings before a Special Committee on Charges of Alleged Executions without Trial in France, Sixty-seventh Congress*. Washington, D.C.: Government Printing Office, 1923.

War Department. *Battle Participation of Organizations of the American Expeditionary Forces in France, Belgium and Italy, 1917–1918*. Washington, D.C.: Government Printing Office, 1920.

———. *Historical Report of the Chief Engineer, American Expeditionary Forces, 1917–1919*. Washington, D.C.: Government Printing Office, 1919.

———. *The National Defense Act*. Washington, D.C.: Government Printing Office, 1921.

———. *Organization of the Services of Supply, American Expeditionary Forces*. Washington, D.C.: Government Printing Office, 1921.

PUBLISHED MICROFILM COLLECTIONS

Grossman, James, ed. *Black Workers in the Era of the Great Migration, 1916–1929*. Frederick, Md.: University Publications of America, 1985.

Kornweibel, Theodore, Jr., ed. *Federal Surveillance of Afro-Americans (1917–1925): The First World War, the Red Scare, and the Garvey Movement*. Frederick, Md.: University Publications of America, 1986.

PUBLISHED PRIMARY SOURCES

Aptheker, Herbert, ed. *The Correspondence of W. E. B. Du Bois*. Vol. 1: *Selections, 1877–1934*. Amherst: University of Massachusetts Press, 1973.

Arnesen, Eric, ed. *Black Protest and the Great Migration: A Brief History with Documents*. New York: Bedford/St. Martin's, 2002.

Bliss, James G. *History of the 805th Pioneer Infantry*. St. Paul: Privately published, 1919.

Blount, Samuel E. *Reminiscences of Samuel E. Blount, Corporal and Company. Clerk, Company B, 367th Infantry, 92nd Division, U.S. National Army*. N.p., 1934.

Braddan, William S. *Under Fire with the 370th Infantry (8th I.N.G.), A.E.F: Memoirs of the World War*. Chicago, n.d.

Bullard, Robert Lee. *Personalities and Reminiscences of the War*. New York: Doubleday, Page, 1925.

Cade, John B. *Twenty-two Months with "Uncle Sam": Being the Experiences and Observations' of a Negro Student Who Volunteered for Military Service against the Central Powers from June, 1917 to April, 1919*. Atlanta: Robinson-Cofer, 1929.

Chicago Commission on Race Relations. *The Negro in Chicago: A Study of Race Relations and a Race Riot*. Chicago: University of Chicago Press, 1922.

Clifford, Carrie Williams. *The Widening Light*. Boston: Walter Reid, 1922.

Cook County (Ill.) Coroner. *The Race Riots: Biennial Report 1918–1919 and Official Records of Inquests on the Victims of the Race Riots of July and August, 1919, Whereby Fifteen White Men and Twenty-three Colored Men Lost Their Lives and Several Hundred Were Injured*. Chicago, 1920.

Cotter, Joseph, Jr. "On the Fields of France." *Crisis*, June 1920.

Daly, Victor R. "Goats, Wildcats and Buffalo." *Crisis*, March 1932.

———. *Not Only War: A Story of Two Great Conflicts*. Boston: Christopher Publishing House, 1932.

———. "Private Walker Goes Patrolling." *Crisis*, June 1930.

———. "Still Five More." *Crisis*, February 1934.

Davis, Arthur P. *Here and There with the Rattlers*. Detroit: Harlo Press, 1979.

Dawes, Charles G. *A Journal of the Great War*. Vol. 1. Boston: Houghton Mifflin, 1921.

Embree, Edwin R. *13 Against the Odds*. New York: Viking Press, 1944.

Fauset, Jessie Redmon. *There Is Confusion*. New York: Boni and Liveright, 1924.

Fish, Hamilton. *Hamilton Fish: Memoir of an American Patriot*. Washington, D.C.: Regnery Gateway, 1991.

Gaston, A. G. *Green Power: The Successful War of A. G. Gaston*. Birmingham: Southern University Press, 1968.

Green, Ely. *Ely: Too Black, Too White*. Amherst: University of Massachusetts Press, 1970.

Hagood, Johnson. *The Services of Supply: A Memoir of the Great War*. Boston: Houghton Mifflin, 1927.

Harvard Alumni Association. *Harvard Alumni Directory, 1919*. Boston: Harvard Alumni Association, 1919.

Haywood, Harry. *Black Bolshevik: Autobiography of an Afro-American Communist*. Chicago: Liberator Press, 1978.

Heroes of 1918: Stories from the Lips of Black Fighters. Chicago, 1919.

Heywood, Chester D. *Negro Combat Troops in the World War: The Story of the 371st Infantry*. Worcester, Mass.: Commonwealth Press, 1928.

Hill, Robert A., ed. *The Marcus Garvey and Universal Negro Improvement Association Papers*. Vols. 1–4. Berkeley: University of California Press, 1983.

Hill, Robert A., and Barbara Bair, eds. *Marcus Garvey Life and Lessons*. Berkeley: University of California Press, 1987.

Houston, Charles H. "Saving the World for 'Democracy.'" *Pittsburgh Courier*, July 20–October 14, 1940.

Hunton, Addie W., and Kathryn M. Johnson. *Two Colored Women with the American Expeditionary Forces*. Brooklyn: Brooklyn Eagle Press, 1920.

Jamieson, J. A., et al. *Complete History of the Colored Soldiers in the World War: Authentic Story of the Greatest War of Civilized Times and What the Colored Man Did to Uphold Democracy and Liberty*. New York: Bennett & Churchill, 1919.

Johnson, Charles S. "Charles S. Johnson." In *American Spiritual Autobiographies: Fifteen Self-Portraits*, ed. Louis Finkelstein. New York: Harper & Brothers, 1948.

Johnson, James Weldon. *Along This Way: The Autobiography of James Weldon Johnson*. New York: Viking Press, 1933.
———. *Black Manhattan*. New York: A. A. Knopf, 1930.
Jordan, Walker H. *With "Old Eph" in the Army (Not a History): A Simple Treatise on the Human Side of the Colored Soldier*. Baltimore: H. E. Houck, 1920.
Lenin, Vladimir. *Imperialism, the Highest Stage of Capitalism*. 1917.
Lincoln University. *Catalogue of Lincoln University, 1908–1909*. Philadelphia, 1909.
Link, Arthur S., ed. *The Papers of Woodrow Wilson*. Vol. 41. Princeton: Princeton University Press, 1983.
Little, Arthur. *From Harlem to the Rhine: The Story of New York's Colored Volunteers*. New York: Covici Friede Publishers, 1936.
Love, A. G., and C. B. Davenport. "A Comparison of White and Colored Troops in Respect to Incidence of Disease." *Proceedings of the National Academy of Sciences of the United States of America* 5 (March 15, 1919): 58–67.
MacGregor, Morris J., and Bernard C. Nalty, eds. *Blacks in the United States Armed Forces: Basic Documents*. Vol. 4. Wilmington, Del.: Scholarly Resources, 1977.
Mangin, Charles. *La force noire*. Paris, 1910.
Marshall, Napoleon Bonaparte. *The Providential Armistice: A Volunteer's Story*. Washington, D.C.: Liberty League, 1930.
Martin, Tony, ed. *African Fundamentalism: A Literary and Cultural Anthology of Garvey's Harlem Renaissance*. Dover, Mass.: Majority Press, 1991.
Mason, Monroe, and Arthur Furr. *The American Negro Soldier with the Red Hand of France*. Boston: Cornhill Company, 1920.
McKay, Claude. *Banjo: A Story without a Plot*. New York: Harper and Brothers, 1929.
———. *Home to Harlem*. New York: Harper and Brothers, 1928.
———. *A Long Way from Home*. New York: L. Furman, 1937.
Mead, Frederick S., ed. *Harvard's Military Record in the World War*. Boston: Harvard Alumni Association, 1921.
Miller, Kelly. *Authentic History of the Negro in the World War*. New York: A. Jenkins, 1919.
———. *The Disgrace of Democracy: Open Letter to President Woodrow Wilson*. Washington, D.C., 1917.
———. *The Negro in the New Reconstruction*. Washington, D.C., n.d.
Moton, Robert Russa. *Finding a Way Out: An Autobiography*. New York: Doubleday, Page, 1921.
Nalty, Bernard C., and Morris J. MacGregor, eds. *Blacks in the Military: Essential Documents*. Wilmington, Del.: Scholarly Resources, 1981.
———. *Blacks in the United States Armed Forces: Basic Documents*. 13 vols. Wilmington, Del.: Scholarly Resources, 1977.
Niles, John J. *Singing Soldiers*. New York: C. Scribner's Sons, 1927.
Percy, William Alexander. *Lanterns on the Levee: Recollections of a Planter's Son*. New York: Knopf, 1941.
Perry, Jeffrey B., ed. *A Hubert Harrison Reader*. Middletown, Conn.: Wesleyan University Press, 2001.

Pershing, John J. *My Experiences in the World War*. Vols. 1 and 2. New York: Frederick A. Stokes, 1931.

Pickens, William. *The Negro in the Light of the Great War: Basis for the New Reconstruction*. Baltimore, 1918[?].

Rosengarten, Theodore. *All God's Dangers: The Life of Nate Shaw*. New York: Vintage Books, 1974.

Ross, Warner A. *My Colored Battalion*. Chicago: Warner A. Ross, 1920.

Ross, William O. *With the 351st in France*. Baltimore: Afro-American Company, 1923.

Sandburg, Carl. *The Chicago Race Riots*. New York: Harcourt, Brace and Howe, 1919.

Scanlon, Bob. "The Record of a Negro Boxer." In *Negro: An Anthology*, ed. Nancy Cunard and Hugh D. Ford. New York: F. Ungar, 1970.

Schuyler, George S. *Black and Conservative: The Autobiography of George S. Schuyler*. New Rochelle, N.Y.: Arlington House Publishers, 1966.

Scott, Emmett J. "More Letters of Negro Migrants of 1916–1918." *Journal of Negro History* 4 (October 1919): 412–65.

———. *Scott's Official History of the American Negro in the World War*. New York: Underwood & Underwood, 1919.

Singleton, George A. *The Autobiography of George A. Singleton*. Boston: Forum, 1964.

Smith-Irvin, Jeanette. *Footsoldiers of the Universal Negro Improvement Association (Their Own Words)*. Trenton: Africa World Press, 1989.

Sweeny, W. Allison. *History of the American Negro in the Great World War*. 1919.

Thompson, John L. *History and Views of Colored Officers Training Camp for 1917 at Fort Des Moines, Iowa*. Des Moines: Bystander, 1917.

Walker, George. *Venereal Disease in the American Expeditionary Forces*. Baltimore: Medical Standard Book, 1922.

Waring, James H. N. *Work of the Colored Law and Order League: Baltimore, Md.* Cheyney, Pa.: Committee of Twelve for the Advancement of the Interests of the Negro Race, 1908.

Webster, Edgar H. *Chums and Brothers: An Interpretation of a Social Group of Our American Citizenry Who Are in the First and Last Analysis "Just Folks."* Boston: Gorham Press, 1922.

Wells, Ida B. *Crusade for Justice: The Autobiography of Ida B. Wells*. Ed. Alfreda M. Duster. Chicago: University of Chicago Press, 1970.

White, Walter. *The Fire in the Flint*. New York: Alfred A. Knopf, 1924.

Williams, Charles H. *Sidelights on Negro Soldiers*. Boston: B. J. Brimmer, 1923.

Woodson, Carter G. Review of *The American Negro in the World War* by Emmett J. Scott. *Journal of Negro History* 4 (October 1919): 466–67.

———. Review of *Sidelights on Negro Soldiers* by Charles H. Williams. *Journal of Negro History* 9 (April 1924): 235–36.

———. Review of *Two Colored Women with the American Expeditionary Forces*, by Addie W. Hunton and Kathryn Johnson. *Journal of Negro History* 6 (July 1921): 378–79.

YWCA, National Board, War Work Council, Colored Work Committee. "The Work of Colored Women." New York, 1919.

NEWSPAPERS AND JOURNALS

Anniston Star
Arkansas Democrat (Little Rock)
Arkansas Gazette
Atlanta Constitution
Atlanta Journal
Baltimore Afro-American
Birmingham News
Chicago Daily News
Chicago Daily Tribune
Chicago Defender
Cleveland Advocate
Crisis
Crusader
Daily Herald
Dallas Morning News
Issue
Louisville Courier-Journal
Macon (Ga.) News
Messenger
Montgomery Advertiser
Negro World
New Orleans Times-Picayune
New York Age
New York Amsterdam News
New York Call
New York Evening Sun
New York Times
News & Observer (Raleigh, N.C.)
Norfolk Journal and Guide
Outlook (N.Y.)
Pittsburgh Courier
Richmond Planet
Savannah Tribune
Southern Christian Recorder
Southern Workman
Stars and Stripes
Vardaman's Weekly
Washington Bee
Washington Post

Secondary Sources

BOOKS

Adeleke, Tunde. *UnAfrican Americans: Nineteenth-Century Black Nationalists and the Civilizing Mission*. Lexington: University Press of Kentucky, 1998.

Aldrich, Robert. *Greater France: A History of French Overseas Expansion*. New York: St. Martin's Press, 1996.

Anderson, Benedict. *Imagined Communities: Reflections on the Origin and Spread of Nationalism*. London: Verso, 1983.

Anderson, Jervis. *A. Philip Randolph: A Biographical Portrait*. New York: Harcourt Brace, 1972.

Archer-Shaw, Petrine. *Negrophilia: Avant-Garde Paris and Black Culture in the 1920s*. London: Thames & Hudson, 2000.

Ayers, Edward L. *Vengeance and Justice: Crime and Punishment in the 19th-Century American South*. New York: Oxford University Press, 1984.

Badger, Reid. *A Life in Ragtime: A Biography of James Reese Europe*. New York: Oxford University Press, 1995.

Baker, Houston A. *Modernism and the Harlem Renaissance*. Chicago: University of Chicago Press, 1987.

Baldwin, Davarian L. *Chicago's New Negroes: Modernity, the Great Migration, and Black Urban Life*. Chapel Hill: University of North Carolina Press, 2007.

Balesi, Charles. *From Adversaries to Comrades-in-Arms: West Africa and the French Military, 1885–1918*. Waltham, Mass.: Crossroads Press, 1979.

Barbeau, Arthur E., and Florette Henri. *The Unknown Soldiers: African-American Troops in World War I*. Philadelphia: Temple University Press, 1974; reprint, New York: Da Capo Press, 1996.

Beardsley, Edward H. *A History of Neglect: Health Care for Blacks and Mill Workers in the Twentieth-Century South*. Knoxville: University of Tennessee Press, 1987.

Beaver, Daniel R. *Newton D. Baker and the American War Effort, 1917–1919*. Lincoln: University of Nebraska Press, 1966.

Bederman, Gail. *Manliness and Civilization: A Cultural History of Gender and Race in the United States, 1880–1917*. Chicago: University of Chicago Press, 1995.

Berg, Manfred. *The Ticket to Freedom: The NAACP and the Struggle for Black Political Integration*. Gainesville: University Press of Florida, 2007.

Berlin, Ira, Joseph P. Reidy, and Leslie S. Rowland, eds. *Freedom's Soldiers: The Black Military Experience in the Civil War*. Cambridge: Cambridge University Press, 1988.

Blackmon, Douglas A. *Slavery by Another Name: The Re-Enslavement of Black Americans from the Civil War to World War II*. New York: Doubleday, 2008.

Blake, Jody. *Le Tumulte Noir: Modernist Art and Popular Entertainment in Jazz-Age Paris, 1900–1930*. University Park: Pennsylvania State University Press, 1999.

Blight, David W. *Race and Reunion: The Civil War in American Memory*. Cambridge, Mass.: Belknap Press of Harvard University Press, 2001.

Bodnar, John E. *Remaking America: Public Memory, Commemoration, and Patriotism in the Twentieth Century*. Princeton: Princeton University Press, 1992.

Bristow, Nancy K. *Making Men Moral: Social Engineering during the Great War*. New York: New York University Press, 1996.

Brooks, Tim. *Lost Sounds: Blacks and the Birth of the Recording Industry, 1890–1919*. Urbana: University of Illinois Press, 2004.

Brown, Nikki. *Private Politics and Public Voices: Black Women's Activism from World War I to the New Deal*. Bloomington: Indiana University Press, 2006.

Bruce, Robert B. *A Fraternity of Arms: America and France in the Great War*. Lawrence: University Press of Kansas, 2003.

Brundage, W. Fitzhugh. *Lynching in the New South: Georgia and Virginia, 1880–1930*. Urbana: University of Illinois Press, 1993.

Buckley, Gail. *American Patriots: The Story of Blacks in the Military from the Revolution to Desert Storm*. New York: Random House, 2001.

Bundles, A'Lelia. *On Her Own Ground: The Life and Times of Madam C. J. Walker*. New York: Scribner, 2001.

Byerly, Carol R. *Fever of War: The Influenza Epidemic in the U.S. Army during World War I*. New York: New York University Press, 2005.

Capozzola, Christopher. *Uncle Sam Wants You: World War I and the Making of the Modern American Citizen*. New York: Oxford University Press, 2008.

Carby, Hazel. *Race Men*. Cambridge, Mass.: Harvard University Press, 1998.

Carisella, P. J., and James W. Ryan. *The Black Swallow of Death: The Incredible Story of Eugene Bullard, the World's First Black Combat Aviator*. Boston: Marlborough House, 1972.

Carroll, Anne Elizabeth. *Word, Image, and the New Negro: Representation and Identity in the Harlem Renaissance*. Bloomington: Indiana University Press, 2005.

Cecelski, David S., and Timothy B. Tyson, eds. *Democracy Betrayed: The Wilmington Race Riot of 1898 and Its Legacy*. Chapel Hill: University of North Carolina Press, 1998.

Cell, John W. *The Highest Stage of White Supremacy: The Origins of Segregation in South Africa and the American South*. Cambridge: Cambridge University Press, 1982.

Chambers, John Whiteclay, II. *To Raise an Army: The Draft Comes to Modern America*. New York: Free Press, 1987.

Christian, Garna L. *Black Soldiers in Jim Crow Texas, 1899–1917*. College Station: Texas A&M University Press, 1995.

Clayton, Anthony. *France, Soldiers and Africa*. London: Brassey's Defence Publishers, 1988.

Clements, Kendrick A. *The Presidency of Woodrow Wilson*. Lawrence: University Press of Kansas, 1992.

Coffman, Edward M. *War to End All Wars: The American Military Experience in World War I*. New York: Oxford University Press, 1968.

Cohen, Eliot A. *Citizens and Soldiers: The Dilemmas and Military Service*. Ithaca: Cornell University Press, 1985.

Conklin, Alice L. *A Mission to Civilize: The Republican Idea of Empire in France and West Africa, 1895–1930*. Stanford: Stanford University Press, 1997.

Cooper, John Milton, Jr. *Pivotal Decades: The United States, 1900–1920*. New York: Norton, 1990.

Cooper, Wayne F. *Claude McKay: Rebel Sojourner in the Harlem Renaissance*. Baton Rouge: Louisiana State University Press, 1987.

Cramer, C. H. *Newton D. Baker: A Biography*. Cleveland: World Publishing, 1961.

Crowder, Ralph L. *John Edward Bruce: Politician, Journalist and Self-trained Historian of the African Diaspora*. New York: New York University Press, 2004.

Dahl, Robert A. *Democracy and Its Critics*. New Haven: Yale University Press, 1989.

———. *Democracy in the United States*. Chicago: Rand McNally, 1972.

———. *On Democracy*. New Haven: Yale University Press, 1998.

———. *On Political Equality*. New Haven: Yale University Press, 2006.

Dailey, Jane, Glenda Elizabeth Gilmore, and Bryant Simon, eds. *Jumpin' Jim Crow: Southern Politics from Civil War to Civil Rights*. Princeton: Princeton University Press, 2000.

Dittmer, John. *Black Georgia in the Progressive Era, 1900–1920*. Urbana: University of Illinois Press, 1977.

Dobak William A., and Thomas D. Phillips. *The Black Regulars, 1866–1898*. Norman: University of Oklahoma Press, 2001.

Doyle, Bertram Wilbur. *The Etiquette of Race Relations in the South: A Study in Social Control*. Chicago: University of Chicago Press, 1937.

Drake, St. Clair, and Horace R. Cayton. *Black Metropolis: A Study of Negro Life in a Northern City*. New York: Harcourt, Brace, 1945.

Du Bois, W. E. B. *Autobiography of W. E. B. Du Bois: A Soliloquy on Viewing My Life from the Last Decade of Its First Century*. New York: International Publishers, 1968.

———. *Darkwater: Voices from within the Veil*. Mineola, N.Y.: Dover Publications, 1999.

———. *Dusk of Dawn: An Essay toward an Autobiography of a Race Concept*. In *W. E. B. Du Bois: Writings*, ed. Nathan Huggins. New York: Library of America, 1986.

———. *The Souls of Black Folk*. In *W. E. B. Du Bois: Writings*, ed. Nathan Huggins. New York: Library of America, 1986.

Dumenil, Lynn. *The Modern Temper: American Culture and Society in the 1920s*. New York: Hill and Wang, 1995.

Dunnigan, Alice Allison. *The Fascinating Story of Black Kentuckians: Their Heritage and Traditions*. Washington, D.C.: Associated, 1982.

Echenberg, Myron. *Colonial Conscripts: The "Tirailleurs Sénégalais" in French West Africa, 1857–1960*. Portsmouth, N.H.: Heinemann, 1991.

Edwards, Brent Hayes. *The Practice of Diaspora: Literature, Translation, and the Rise of Black Internationalism*. Cambridge, Mass.: Harvard University Press, 2003.

Egerton, Douglas R. *Gabriel's Rebellion: The Virginia Slave Conspiracies of 1800 and 1802*. Chapel Hill: University of North Carolina Press, 1993.

Eksteins, Modris. *Rites of Spring: The Great War and the Birth of the Modern Age*. Boston: Houghton Mifflin, 1989.

Ellis, Mark. *Race, War, and Surveillance: African Americans and the United States Government during World War I*. Bloomington: Indiana University Press, 2001.

Ellsworth, Scott. *Death in a Promised Land: The Tulsa Race Riot of 1921*. Baton Rouge: Louisiana State University Press, 1982.

Ezra, Elizabeth. *The Colonial Unconscious: Race and Culture in Interwar France*. Ithaca: Cornell University Press, 2000.

Fabre, Michel. *From Harlem to Paris: Black American Writers in France, 1840–1980*. Urbana: University of Illinois Press, 1991.

Farwell, Byron. *Over There: The United States in the Great War, 1917–1918*. New York: W. W. Norton, 1999.

Favor, J. Martin. *Authentic Blackness: The Folk in the New Negro Renaissance*. Durham: Duke University Press, 1999.

Ferguson, Jeffery B. *The Sage of Sugar Hill: George S. Schuyler and the Harlem Renaissance*. New Haven: Yale University Press, 2005.

Ferrell, Robert H. *America's Deadliest Battle: Meuse-Argonne, 1918*. Lawrence: University Press of Kansas, 2007.

———. *Collapse at Meuse-Argonne: The Failure of the Missouri-Kansas Division*. Columbia: University of Missouri Press, 2004.

———. *Woodrow Wilson and World War I, 1917–1921*. New York: Harper & Row, 1985.

Fierce, Milfred C. *The Pan-African Idea in the United States, 1900–1919: African-American Interest in Africa and Interaction With West Africa*. New York: Garland, 1993.

Fleming, Thomas J. *The Illusion of Victory: America in World War I*. New York: Basic Books, 2003.

Fletcher, Marvin. *America's First Black General: Benjamin O. Davis, Sr., 1880–1970*. Lawrence: University Press of Kansas, 1989.

Fogarty, Richard S. *Race and War in France: Colonial Subjects in the French Army, 1914–1918*. Baltimore: Johns Hopkins University Press, 2008.

Foley, Barbara. *Spectres of 1919: Class and Nation in the Making of the New Negro*. Urbana: University of Illinois Press, 2003.

Foner, Eric. *Reconstruction: America's Unfinished Revolution, 1863–1877*. New York: Harper & Row, 1988.

———. *The Story of American Freedom*. New York: W. W. Norton, 1998.

Foner, Phillip. *American Socialism and Black Americans: From the Age of Jackson to World War II*. Westport, Conn.: Greenwood Press, 1977.

Ford, Nancy Gentile. *Americans All!: Foreign-Born Soldiers in World War I*. College Station: Texas A&M University Press, 2001.

Fox, Stephen R. *The Guardian of Boston: William Monroe Trotter*. New York: Atheneum, 1970.

Fredericks, Pierce G. *The Great Adventure: America in the First World War*. New York: Dutton, 1960.

Fryer, Peter. *Staying Power: The History of Black People in Britain*. London: Pluto Press, 1984.

Fussell, Paul. *The Great War and Modern Memory*. Oxford: Oxford University Press, 1975.

Gaines, Kevin K. *Uplifting the Race: Black Leadership, Politics, and Culture in the Twentieth Century*. Chapel Hill: University of North Carolina Press, 1996.

Gatewood, Willard B., Jr. *"Smoked Yankees" and the Struggle for Empire: Letters from Negro Soldiers, 1898–1902*. Urbana: University of Illinois Press, 1971.

Gershovich, Moshe. *French Military Rule in Morocco: Colonialism and Its Consequences*. London: F. Cass, 2000.

Gerstle, Gary. *American Crucible: Race and Nation in the Twentieth Century*. Princeton: Princeton University Press, 2001.

Giddings, Paula. *When and Where I Enter: The Impact of Black Women on Race and Sex in America*. New York: W. Morrow, 1984.

Gilmore, Glenda Elizabeth. *Defying Dixie: The Radical Roots of Civil Rights, 1919–1950*. New York: W. W. Norton, 2008.

———. *Gender and Jim Crow: Women and the Politics of White Supremacy in North Carolina, 1896–1920*. Chapel Hill: University of North Carolina Press, 1996.

Gilpin, Patrick J., and Marybeth Gasman. *Charles S. Johnson: Leadership beyond the Veil in the Age of Jim Crow*. Albany: State University of New York Press, 2003.

Gilroy, Paul. *The Black Atlantic: Modernity and Double Consciousness*. Cambridge, Mass.: Harvard University Press, 1993.

Glassberg, David. *American Historical Pageantry: The Uses of Tradition in the Early Twentieth Century*. Chapel Hill: University of North Carolina Press, 1990.

Glasser, Ruth. *My Music Is My Flag: Puerto Rican Musicians and Their New York Communities, 1917–1940*. Berkeley: University of California Press, 1995.

Grant, Colin. *Negro with a Hat: The Rise and Fall of Marcus Garvey*. New York: Oxford University Press, 2008.

Grant, Kevin. *A Civilised Savagery: Britain and the New Slaveries in Africa, 1884–1926*. New York: Routledge, 2005.

Green, Adam. *Selling the Race: Culture, Community, and Black Chicago, 1940–1955*. Chicago: University of Chicago Press, 2007.

Green, Constance McLaughlin. *Secret City: A History of Race Relations in the Nation's Capital*. Princeton: Princeton University Press, 1967.

Greenwald, Maurine Weiner. *Women, War, and Work: The Impact of World War I on Women Workers in the United States*. Ithaca: Cornell University Press, 1990.

Gregory, James N. *The Southern Diaspora: How the Great Migrations of Black and White Southerners Transformed America*. Chapel Hill: University of North Carolina Press, 2005.

Griffin, Farah Jasmine. *"Who Set You Flowin'?": The African-American Migration Narrative*. New York: Oxford University Press, 1995.

Grossman, James R. *Land of Hope: Chicago, Black Southerners, and the Great Migration*. Chicago: University of Chicago Press, 1989.

Grotelueschen, Mark Ethan. *The AEF Way of War: The American Army and Combat in World War I*. Cambridge: Cambridge University Press, 2007.

Hagedorn, Ann. *Savage Peace: Hope and Fear in America, 1919*. New York: Simon and Schuster, 2007.

Hahn, Steven. *A Nation under Our Feet: Black Political Struggles in the Rural South from Slavery to the Great Migration*. Cambridge, Mass.: Belknap Press of Harvard University Press, 2005.

Halbwachs, Maurice. *On Collective Memory*. Ed. Lewis A. Coser. Chicago: University of Chicago Press, 1992.

Hale, Grace Elizabeth. *Making Whiteness: The Culture of Segregation in the South, 1890–1940*. New York: Pantheon Books, 1998.

Hall, Jacquelyn Dowd. *Revolt against Chivalry: Jessie Daniel Ames and the Women's Campaign against Lynching*. New York: Columbia University Press, 1979.

Harding, Vincent. *There Is a River: The Black Struggle for Freedom in America*. New York: Harcourt & Brace, 1981.

Harold, Claudrena N. *The Rise and Fall of the Garvey Movement in the Urban South, 1918–1942*. New York: Routledge, 2007.

Harries, Meirion, and Susie Harries. *The Last Days of Innocence: America at War, 1917–1918*. New York: Random House, 1997.

Harris, Bill. *The Hellfighters of Harlem: African-American Soldiers Who Fought for the Right to Fight for Their Country*. New York: Carroll & Graff, 2002.

Harris, J. William. *Deep Souths: Delta, Piedmont, and Sea Island Society in the Age of Segregation*. Baltimore: Johns Hopkins University Press, 2001.

Hayden, Robert C. *"Mr. Harlem Hospital": Dr. Louis T. Wright, a Biography*. Littleton, Mass.: Tapestry Press, 2003.

Haynes, Robert V. *A Night of Violence: The Houston Riot of 1917*. Baton Rouge: Louisiana State University Press, 1976.

Higginbotham, Evelyn Brooks. *Righteous Discontent: The Women's Movement in the Black Baptist Church, 1880–1920*. Cambridge, Mass.: Harvard University Press, 1994.

Higham, John. *Strangers in the Land: Patterns of American Nativism, 1860–1925*. New Brunswick: Rutgers University Press, 1955.

Hirsch, James S. *Riot and Remembrance: The Tulsa Race War and Its Legacy*. Boston: Houghton Mifflin, 2002.

Hoch, Paul. *White Hero, Black Beast: Racism, Sexism and the Mask of Masculinity*. London: Pluto Press, 1979.

Hofstadter, Richard. *The Age of Reform: From Bryan to F.D.R.* New York: Vintage Books, 1955.

Holmes, William F. *The White Chief: James Kimble Vardaman*. Baton Rouge: Louisiana State University Press, 1970.

Howe, Glenford D. *Race, War and Nationalism: A Social History of West Indians in the First World War*. Kingston: Ian Randle, 2002.

Huggins, Nathan Irvin. *Harlem Renaissance*. New York: Oxford University Press, 1971.

Hunter, Tera. *To 'Joy My Freedom: Southern Black Women's Lives and Labors after the Civil War*. Cambridge, Mass.: Harvard University Press, 1997.

Hutchinson, George. *The Harlem Renaissance in Black and White*. Cambridge, Mass.: Belknap Press of Harvard University Press, 1995.

Jacobson, Matthew Frye. *Whiteness of a Different Color: European Immigrants and the Alchemy of Race*. Cambridge, Mass.: Harvard University Press, 1998.

James, Jennifer C. *A Freedom Bought with Blood: African American War Literature from the Civil War to World War II*. Chapel Hill: University of North Carolina Press, 2007.

James, Winston. *A Fierce Hatred of Injustice: Claude McKay's Jamaica and His Poetry of Rebellion*. London: Verso, 2000.

———. *Holding Aloft the Banner of Ethiopia: Caribbean Radicalism in Early Twentieth-Century America*. London: Verso, 1999.

Janken, Kenneth Robert. *Rayford W. Logan and the Dilemma of the African-American Intellectual*. Amherst: University of Massachusetts Press, 1993.

———. *White: The Biography of Walter White, Mr. NAACP*. New York: New Press, 2003.

Johnson, Charles, Jr. *African American Soldiers in the National Guard*. Westport, Conn.: Greenwood Press, 1992.

Johnston, Hank, and Bert Klandermans, eds. *Social Movements and Culture*. Minneapolis: University of Minnesota Press, 1995.

Jonas, Gilbert. *Freedom's Sword: The NAACP and the Struggle against Racism, 1909–1969*. New York: Routledge, 2007.

Jones, Sharon L. *Rereading the Harlem Renaissance: Race, Class, and Gender in the Fiction of Jessie Fauset, Zora Neale Hurston, and Dorothy West*. Westport, Conn.: Greenwood Press, 2002.

Jordan, William G. *Black Newspapers and America's War for Democracy, 1914–1920*. Chapel Hill: University of North Carolina Press, 2001.

Kantrowitz, Stephen. *Ben Tillman and the Reconstruction of White Supremacy*. Chapel Hill: University of North Carolina Press, 2000.

Keegan, John. *The First World War*. New York: Vintage Books, 1998.

Keene, Jennifer D. *Doughboys, the Great War, and the Remaking of America*. Baltimore: Johns Hopkins University Press, 2001.

Keith, Jeanette. *Rich Man's War, Poor Man's Fight*. Chapel Hill: University of North Carolina Press, 2004.

Keith, LeeAnna. *The Colfax Massacre: The Untold Story of Black Power, White Terror, and the Death of Reconstruction*. New York: Oxford University Press, 2008.

Kelley, Robin D. G. *Race Rebels: Culture, Politics, and the Black Working Class*. New York: Free Press, 1994.

Kellog, Charles Flint. *NAACP: A History of the National Association for the Advancement of Colored People*. Baltimore: Johns Hopkins University Press, 1967.

Kelly, Brian. *Race, Class, and Power in the Alabama Coalfields, 1908–1921*. Urbana: University of Illinois Press, 2001.

Kennedy, David M. *Over Here: The First World War and American Society*. New York: Oxford University Press, 1980.

Kennedy, Kathleen. *Disloyal Mothers and Scurrilous Citizens: Women and Subversion during World War I*. Bloomington: Indiana University Press, 1999.

Kilroy, David P. *For Race and Country: The Life and Career of Colonel Charles Young*. Westport, Conn.: Praeger, 2003.

Kimball, Robert, and William Bolcon. *Reminiscing with Sissle and Blake*. New York: Viking Press, 1973.

Klinkner, Phillip A., and Rogers M. Smith. *Unsteady March: The Rise and Decline of Racial Equality in America*. Chicago: University of Chicago Press, 1999.

Knock, Thomas J. *To End All Wars: Woodrow Wilson and the Quest for a New World Order*. Princeton: Princeton University Press, 1992.

Kornweibel, Theodore, Jr. *"Investigate Everything": Federal Efforts to Compel Black Loyalty during World War I*. Bloomington: Indiana University Press, 2001.

———. *No Crystal Stair: Black Life and the* Messenger, *1917–1928*. Westport, Conn.: Greenwood Press, 1975.

———. *"Seeing Red": Federal Campaigns against Black Militancy, 1919–1925*. Bloomington: Indiana University Press, 1998.

Kramer, Paul A. *The Blood of Government: Race, Empire, the United States, and the Philippines*. Chapel Hill: University of North Carolina Press, 2006.

Krebs, Ronald R. *Fighting for Rights: Military Service and the Politics of Citizenship*. Ithaca: Cornell University Press, 2006.

Lane, Ann J. *The Brownsville Affair*. Port Washington, N.Y.: Kennikat Press, 1971.

Lane, Charles. *The Day Freedom Died: The Colfax Massacre, the Supreme Court, and the Betrayal of Reconstruction*. New York: Henry Holt, 2008.

Larana, Enrique, Hank Johnston, and Joseph R. Gusfield, eds. *New Social Movements: From Ideology to Identity*. Philadelphia: Temple University Press, 1994.

Lau, Peter F. *Democracy Rising: South Carolina and the Fight for Black Equality since 1865*. Lexington: University Press of Kentucky, 2006.

Lawrence, A. H. *Duke Ellington and His World*. New York: Routledge, 2001.

Leed, Eric J. *No Man's Land: Combat and Identity in World War I*. Cambridge: Cambridge University Press, 1979.

Le Goff, Jacques. *History and Memory*. New York: Columbia University Press, 1992.

Leiker, James N. *Racial Borders: Black Soldiers along the Rio Grande*. College Station: Texas A&M University Press, 2002.

Lemann, Nicholas. *Redemption: The Last Battle of the Civil War*. New York: Farrar, Straus and Giroux, 2006.

Lemelle, Sidney, and Robin D. G. Kelley, eds. *Imaging Home: Class, Culture and Nationalism in the African Diaspora*. London: Verso, 1994.
Lengel, Edward G. *World War I Memories: An Annotated Bibliography of Personal Accounts Published in English since 1919*. Lanham, Md.: Scarecrow Press, 2004.
Lepore, Jill. *The Name of War: King Phillip's War and the Origins of American Identity*. New York: Vintage Books, 1998.
Levenstein, Harvey. *Seductive Journey: American Tourists in France from Jefferson to the Jazz Age*. Chicago: University of Chicago Press, 1998.
Levin, N. Gordon. *Woodrow Wilson and World Politics: America's Response to War and Revolution*. London: Oxford University Press, 1968.
Levitch, Mark. *Panthéon de la Guerre: Reconfiguring a Panorama of the Great War*. Columbia: University of Missouri Press, 2006.
Lewis, David Levering. *W. E. B. Du Bois*. Vol. 1: *Biography of a Race, 1868–1919*. New York: Henry Holt, 1993.
———. *W. E. B. Du Bois*. Vol. 2: *The Fight for Equality and the American Century, 1919–1963*. New York: Henry Holt, 2000.
———. *When Harlem Was in Vogue*. New York: Penguin Books, 1997.
Link, Arthur S. *The Higher Realism of Woodrow Wilson, and Other Essays*. Nashville: Vanderbilt University Press, 1971.
———. *Wilson*. Vol. 3: *The Struggle for Neutrality, 1914–1915*. Princeton: Princeton University Press, 1960.
———. *Wilson*. Vol. 4: *Confusions and Crises, 1915–1916*. Princeton: Princeton University Press, 1964.
———. *Wilson*. Vol. 5: *Campaigns for Progressivism and Peace, 1916–1917*. Princeton: Princeton University Press, 1965.
———. *Wilson the Diplomatist: A Look at His Major Foreign Policies*. Baltimore: Johns Hopkins University Press, 1957.
———. *Woodrow Wilson: Revolution, War, and Peace*. Arlington Heights, Ill.: AHM, 1979.
———. *Woodrow Wilson and a Revolutionary World, 1913–1921*. Chapel Hill: University of North Carolina Press, 1982.
Lipsitz, George. *A Life in the Struggle: Ivory Perry and the Culture of Opposition*. Philadelphia: Temple University Press, 1988.
Litwack, Leon F. *Trouble in Mind: Black Southerners in the Age of Jim Crow*. New York: Alfred A. Knopf, 1998.
Lorini, Alessandra. *Rituals of Race: American Public Culture and the Search for Racial Democracy*. Charlottesville: University Press of Virginia, 1999.
Lunn, Joe. *Memoirs of the Maelstrom: A Senegalese Oral History of the First World War*. Portsmouth, N.H.: Heinemann, 1999.
MacLean, Nancy. *Behind the Mask of Chivalry: The Making of the Second Ku Klux Klan*. New York: Oxford University Press, 1994.
MacMillan, Margaret. *Paris 1919: Six Months That Changed the World*. New York: Random House, 2003.
Magubane, Bernard Makhosezwe. *The Ties That Bind: African-American Consciousness of Africa*. Trenton, N.J.: Africa World Press, 1987.

Manela, Erez. *The Wilsonian Moment: Self-Determination and the International Origins of Anticolonial Nationalism*. New York: Oxford University Press, 2007.
Mann, Gregory. *Native Sons: West African Veterans and France in the Twentieth Century*. Durham: Duke University Press, 2006.
Marks, Carole. *Farewell—We're Good and Gone: The Great Black Migration*. Bloomington: Indiana University Press, 1989.
Martin, Tony. *Race First: The Ideological and Organizational Struggles of Marcus Garvey and the Universal Negro Improvement Association*. Dover, Mass.: Majority Press, 1976.
———. *Literary Garveyism: Garvey, Black Arts, and the Harlem Renaissance*. Dover, Mass.: Majority Press, 1983.
Maxwell, William J. *New Negro, Old Left: African-American Writing and Communism between the Wars*. New York: Columbia University Press, 1999.
McAdam, Doug. *Political Process and the Development of Black Insurgency, 1930–1970*. Chicago: University of Chicago Press, 1985.
McCartin, Joseph A. *Labor's Great War: The Struggle for Industrial Democracy and the Origins of Modern American Labor Relations, 1912–1921*. Chapel Hill: University of North Carolina Press, 1997.
McMillen, Neil R. *Dark Journey: Black Mississippians in the Age of Jim Crow*. Urbana: University of Illinois Press, 1989.
McMurry, Linda O. *To Keep the Waters Troubled: The Life of Ida B. Wells*. New York: Oxford University Press, 1998.
McNeil, Genna Rae. *Groundwork: Charles Hamilton Houston and the Struggle for Civil Rights*. Philadelphia: University of Pennsylvania Press, 1983.
Meier, August. *Negro Thought in America, 1880–1915: Racial Ideologies in the Age of Booker T. Washington*. Ann Arbor: University of Michigan Press, 1963.
Meier, August, and Elliott Rudwick. *Black History and the Historical Profession, 1915–1980*. Urbana: University of Illinois Press, 1986.
Meigs, Mark. *Optimism at Armageddon: Voices of American Participants in the First World War*. New York: New York University Press, 1997.
Michel, Marc. *Les Africains et la Grande Guerre: L'appel à l'Afrique (1914–1918)*. Paris: Karthala, 2003.
Mjagkij, Nina. *Light in the Darkness: African Americans and the YMCA, 1852–1946*. Lexington: University Press of Kentucky, 1994.
Morris, Aldon D., and Carol McClurg Mueller, eds. *Frontiers in Social Movement Theory*. New Haven: Yale University Press, 1992.
Morrow, John H., Jr. *The Great War: An Imperial History*. New York: Routledge, 2004.
Moses, Wilson J. *The Golden Age of Black Nationalism, 1850–1925*. Hamden, Conn.: Archon Books, 1978.
Murray, Robert K. *Red Scare: A Study in National Hysteria*. Minneapolis: University of Minnesota Press, 1955.
Nadell, Martha Jane. *Enter the New Negroes: Images of Race in American Culture*. Cambridge, Mass.: Harvard University Press, 2004.
Nalty, Bernard C. *Strength for the Fight: A History of Black Americans in the Military*. New York: Free Press, 1986.

Nelson, Peter. *A More Unbending Battle: The Harlem Hellfighter's Struggle for Freedom in WWI and Equality at Home*. New York: Basic Civitas Books, 2009.
Norrell, Robert J. *Up from History: The Life of Booker T. Washington*. Cambridge, Mass.: Belknap Press of Harvard University Press, 2009.
Novick, Peter. *That Noble Dream: The "Objectivity Question" and the American Historical Profession*. New York: Cambridge University Press, 1988.
O'Leary, Cecilia Elizabeth. *To Die For: The Paradox of American Patriotism*. Princeton: Princeton University Press, 1999.
Ortiz, Paul. *Emancipation Betrayed: The Hidden History of Black Organizing and White Violence in Florida from Reconstruction to the Bloody Election of 1920*. Berkeley: University of California Press, 2005.
Painter, Nell Irvin. *Creating Black Americans: African-American History and Its Meanings, 1619 to the Present*. New York: Oxford University Press, 2006.
———. *Exodusters: Black Migration to Kansas after Reconstruction*. New York: Knopf, 1976.
———. *Standing at Armageddon: The United States, 1877–1919*. New York: W. W. Norton, 1987.
Patler, Nicholas. *Jim Crow and the Wilson Administration: Protesting Federal Segregation in the Early Twentieth Century*. Boulder: University of Colorado Press, 2004.
Patterson, Martha H. *Beyond the Gibson Girl: Reimagining the American New Woman, 1895–1915*. Urbana: University of Illinois Press, 2005.
Patton, Gerald W. *War and Race: The Black Officer in the American Military, 1915–1941*. Westport, Conn.: Greenwood Press, 1981.
Payne, Robert James, ed. *Joseph Seamon Cotter, Jr.: Complete Poems*. Athens: University of Georgia Press, 1990.
Pencak, William. *For God and Country: The American Legion, 1919–1941*. Boston: Northeastern University Press, 1989.
Perkins, Kathy A., and Judith L. Stephens, eds. *Strange Fruit: Plays on Lynching by American Women*. Bloomington: Indiana University Press, 1998.
Perry, Jeffrey B. *Hubert Harrison: The Voice of Harlem Radicalism, 1883–1918*. New York: Columbia University Press, 2008.
Phillips, Kimberly L. *AlabamaNorth: African-American Migrants, Community, and Working-Class Activism in Cleveland, 1915–1945*. Urbana: University of Illinois Press, 1999.
Platt, Anthony M. *E. Franklin Frazier Reconsidered*. New Brunswick: Rutgers University Press, 1991.
Porch, Douglas. *The French Foreign Legion: A Complete History of the Legendary Fighting Force*. New York: Harper Collins, 1991.
Porter, Eric. *What Is This Thing Called Jazz?: African American Musicians as Artists, Critics, and Activists*. Berkeley: University of California Press, 2002.
Potts-Campbell, Leila, and Avery Center, comps. *Edwin Augustus Harleston: Artist and Activist in a Changing Era*. Charleston: Avery Research Center for African American History & Culture at the College of Charleston, 2006.
Powell, Richard J. *Black Art and Culture in the 20th Century*. London: Thames and Hudson, 1997.

Rabinowitz, Howard N. *Race Relations in the Urban South, 1865–1890*. New York: Oxford University Press, 1978.

Rampersad, Arnold. *The Art and Imagination of W. E. B. Du Bois*. Cambridge, Mass.: Harvard University Press, 1976.

Rice, Anne P., ed. *Witnessing Lynching: American Writers Respond*. New Brunswick: Rutgers University Press, 2003.

Roberts, Frank E. *The American Foreign Legion: Black Soldiers of the 93d in World War I*. Annapolis, Md.: Naval Institute Press, 2004.

Robbins, Richard. *Sidelines Activist: Charles S. Johnson and the Struggle for Civil Rights*. Jackson: University Press of Mississippi, 1996.

Rodgers, Daniel T. *Atlantic Crossings: Social Politics in a Progressive Age*. Cambridge, Mass.: Belknap Press of Harvard University Press, 1998.

———. *Contested Truths: Keywords in American Politics since Independence*. New York: Basic Books, 1987.

Rolinson, Mary. *Grassroots Garveyism: The Universal Negro Improvement Association in the Rural South, 1920–1927*. Chapel Hill: University of North Carolina Press, 2007.

Rosenberg, Jonathan. *How Far the Promised Land?: World Affairs and the American Civil Rights Movement from the First World War to Vietnam*. Princeton: Princeton University Press, 2005.

Ross, B. Joyce. *J. E. Spingarn and the Rise of the NAACP, 1911–1939*. New York: Atheneum, 1972.

Rudwick, Elliot M. *Riot at East St. Louis, July 2, 1917*. Carbondale: Southern Illinois University Press, 1964.

Ruedy, John. *Modern Algeria: The Origins and Development of a Nation*. Bloomington: Indiana University Press, 1992.

Rumer, Thomas A. *The American Legion: An Official History, 1919–1989*. New York: M. Evans, 1990.

Schaffer, Ronald. *America in the Great War: The Rise of the Welfare State*. Oxford: Oxford University Press, 1991.

Schechter, Patricia A. *Ida B. Wells-Barnett and American Reform, 1880–1930*. Chapel Hill: University of North Carolina Press, 2001.

Schneider, Mark Robert. *"We Return Fighting": The Civil Rights Movement in the Jazz Age*. Boston: Northeastern University Press, 2002.

Schoultz, Lars. *Beneath the United States: A History of U.S. Policy toward Latin America*. Cambridge, Mass.: Harvard University Press, 1998.

Scipio, L. Albert, II. *With the Red Hand Division: The Black American Regiments in the French 157th Division*. Silver Springs, Md.: Roman, 1985.

Scott, James C. *Domination and the Arts of Resistance: Hidden Transcripts*. New Haven: Yale University Press, 1990.

Shack, William. *Harlem in Montmartre: A Paris Jazz Story between the Wars*. Berkeley: University of California Press, 2001.

Sharpley-Whiting, T. Denean. *Black Venus: Sexualized Savages, Primal Fears, and Primitive Narratives in French*. Durham: Duke University Press, 1999.

Shellum, Brian G. *Black Cadet in a White Bastion: Charles Young at West Point*. Lincoln: University of Nebraska Press, 2006.

Sherrard-Johnson, Cherene. *Portraits of the New Negro Woman: Visual and Literary Culture in the Harlem Renaissance*. New Brunswick: Rutgers University Press, 2007.

Shockley, Ann Allen, ed. *Afro-American Women Writers, 1746–1933: An Anthology and Critical Guide*. Boston: G. K. Hall, 1988.

Singh, Kelvin. *Race and Class Struggles in a Colonial State: Trinidad 1917–1945*. Calgary: University of Calgary Press, 1994.

Singh, Nikhil. *Black Is a Country: Race and the Unfinished Struggle for Democracy*. Cambridge, Mass.: Harvard University Press, 2004.

Sinha, Manisha, and Penny Von Eschen. *Contested Democracy: Freedom, Race, and Power in American History*. New York: Columbia University Press, 2007.

Slotkin, Richard. *Lost Battalions: The Great War and the Crisis of American Nationality*. New York: Henry Holt, 2005.

Smith, Rogers M. *Civic Ideals: Conflicting Visions of Citizenship in U.S. History*. New Haven: Yale University Press, 1997.

Solomon, Mark. *The Cry Was Unity: Communists and African Americans, 1917–36*. Jackson: University Press of Mississippi, 1998.

Spengler, Oswald. *The Decline of the West*. New York: A. A. Knopf, 1926.

Stein, Judith. *The World of Marcus Garvey: Race and Class in Modern Society*. Baton Rouge: Louisiana State University Press, 1986.

Steinson, Barbara J. *American Women's Activism in World War I*. New York: Garland, 1982.

Stephens, Michelle Ann. *Black Empire: The Masculine Global Imaginary of Caribbean Intellectuals in the United States, 1914–1962*. Durham: Duke University Press, 2005.

Stockley, Grif. *Blood in Their Eyes: The Elaine Race Massacres of 1919*. Fayetteville: University of Arkansas Press, 2001.

Stoddard, Lothrop. *The Rising Tide of Color against White World-Supremacy*. New York: Charles Scribner's Sons, 1920.

Stovall, Tyler. *Paris Noir: African Americans in the City of Light*. Boston: Mariner Books, 1996.

Sugrue, Thomas J. *Sweet Land of Liberty: The Forgotten Struggle for Civil Rights in the North*. New York: Random House, 2008.

Sullivan, Patricia. *Days of Hope: Race and Democracy in the New Deal Era*. Chapel Hill: University of North Carolina Press, 1996.

Summers, Martin. *Manliness and Its Discontents: The Black Middle Class and the Transformation of Masculinity, 1900–1930*. Chapel Hill: University of North Carolina Press, 2004.

Talalay, Kathryn. *Composition in Black and White: The Life of Philippa Schuyler*. New York: Oxford University Press, 1995.

Taylor, Clarence. *The Black Churches of Brooklyn*. New York: Columbia University Press, 1994.

Tillery, Tyrone. *Claude McKay: A Black Poet's Struggle for Identity*. Amherst: University of Massachusetts Press, 1992.

Tindall, George B. *The Emergence of the New South, 1913–1945*. Baton Rouge: Louisiana State University Press, 1967.

Trotter, Joe William, Jr. *Black Milwaukee: The Making of an Industrial Proletariat*. Urbana: University of Illinois Press, 1985.

———, ed. *The Great Migration in Historical Perspective: New Dimensions of Race, Class, and Gender*. Bloomington: Indiana University Press, 1991.

Turner, Joyce Moore. *Caribbean Crusaders and the Harlem Renaissance*. Urbana: University of Illinois Press, 2005.

Tuttle, William M., Jr. *Race Riot: Chicago in the Red Summer of 1919*. New York: Atheneum, 1978.

Vaughn, Stephen. *Holding Fast the Inner Lines: Democracy, Nationalism, and the Committee on Public Information*. Chapel Hill: University of North Carolina Press, 1980.

Wall, Cheryl A. *Women of the Harlem Renaissance*. Bloomington: Indiana University Press, 1995.

Waskow, Arthur Ocean. *From Race Riot to Sit-in, 1919 and the 1960s: A Study in the Connections between Conflict and Violence*. Garden City, N.Y.: Doubleday, 1966.

Wellard, James. *The French Foreign Legion*. London: André Deutsch, 1974.

Welshe, Peter. *The Rise of African Nationalism in South Africa: The African National Congress 1912–1952*. Berkeley: University of California Press, 1971.

West, Cornel. *Democracy Matters: Winning the Fight against Imperialism*. New York: Penguin Press, 2004.

Whalan, Mark. *The Great War and the Culture of the New Negro*. Gainesville: University Press of Florida, 2008.

Whitaker, Robert. *On the Laps of Gods: The Red Summer of 1919 and the Struggle for Justice That Remade a Nation*. New York: Three Rivers Press, 2009.

White, Deborah Gray. *Too Heavy a Load: Black Women in Defense of Themselves, 1894–1994*. New York: W. W. Norton, 1999.

Wilder, Craig Steven. *In the Company of Black Men: The African Influence on African American Culture in New York City*. New York: New York University Press, 2001.

Williams, Oscar R. *George S. Schuyler: Portrait of a Black Conservative*. Knoxville: University of Tennessee Press, 2007.

Williamson, Joel. *The Crucible of Race: Black-White Relations in the American South since Emancipation*. New York: Oxford University Press, 1984.

Willis-Braithwaite, Deborah. *VanDerZee, Photographer: 1886–1983*. New York: Harry N. Abrams, 1998.

Wilson, Joseph T. *Black Phalanx: A History of the Negro Soldiers of the United States in the Wars of 1775–1812, 1861–65*. Hartford, Conn.: American Publishing Company, 1887.

Winter, Jay. *Remembering War: The Great War between Memory and History in the Twentieth Century*. New Haven: Yale University Press, 2006.

———. *Sites of Memory, Sites of Mourning: The Great War in European Cultural History*. Cambridge: Cambridge University Press, 1995.

Wintz, Cary D. *Black Culture and the Harlem Renaissance*. Houston: Rice University Press, 1988.

Wohl, Robert. *The Generation of 1914*. Cambridge, Mass.: Harvard University Press, 1979.

Woodruff, Nan. *American Congo: The African American Freedom Struggle in the Delta.* Cambridge, Mass.: Harvard University Press, 2003.

Woodson, Carter G. *The Negro in Our History.* Washington, D.C.: Associated Publishers, 1931.

Woodward, C. Vann. *Origins of the New South, 1887–1913.* Baton Rouge: Louisiana State University Press, 1951.

———. *The Strange Career of Jim Crow.* New York: Oxford University Press, 1955.

Wright, Gavin. *Old South, New South: Revolutions in the Southern Economy since the Civil War.* New York: Basic Books, 1986.

Wright, George C. *Racial Violence in Kentucky, 1865–1940: Lynchings, Mob Rule, and "Legal Lynchings."* Baton Rouge: Louisiana State University Press, 1990.

Zangrando, Robert L. *The NAACP Crusade against Lynching, 1909–1950.* Philadelphia: Temple University Press, 1980.

Zeiger, Robert H. *America's Great War: World War I and the American Experience.* Lanham: Rowman & Littlefield, 2000.

Zeiger, Susan. *In Uncle Sam's Service: Women Workers with the American Expeditionary Force, 1917–1919.* Ithaca: Cornell University Press, 1999.

ARTICLES AND ESSAYS

Abdullah, Ibrahim. "Rethinking the Freetown Crowd: The Moral Economy of the 1919 Strikes and Riot in Sierra Leone." *Canadian Journal of African Studies* 28 (1994): 197–218.

Abernathy, Lloyd M. "The Washington Race War of July 1919." *Maryland Historical Magazine* 58 (December 1963): 309–24.

Andrew, C. M., and A. S. Kanya-Forstner. "France, Africa, and the First World War." *Journal of African History* 19 (1978): 11–23.

Allen, Ernest, Jr. "The New Negro: Explorations in Identity and Social Consciousness, 1910–1922." In *1915, The Cultural Moment: The New Politics, the New Woman, the New Psychology, the New Art and the New Theatre in America*, ed. Adele Heller and Lois Rudnick. New Brunswick: Rutgers University Press, 1991.

Aptheker, Herbert. "Du Bois as Historian." In *Afro-American History: The Modern Era.* New York: Citadel Press, 1971.

Badger, R. Reid. "James Reese Europe and the Prehistory of Jazz." *American Music* 7 (Spring 1989): 48–67.

Bair, Barbara. "True Women, Real Men: Gender, Ideology, and Social Roles in the Garvey Movement." In *Gendered Domains: Rethinking Public and Private in Women's History*, ed. Dorothy O. Helly and Susan M. Reverby. Ithaca: Cornell University Press, 1992.

Baker, Houston A., Jr. "Critical Memory and the Black Public Sphere." In *The Black Public Sphere: A Public Culture Book*, ed. The Black Public Sphere Collective. Chicago: University of Chicago Press, 1995.

Beattie, Taylor V. "Personality: Seventy-three Years after His Bayonet Assault on Hill 188, Freddie Stowers Got His Medal of Honor." *Military History* (August 2004): 74–76.

Beck, E. M., and Stewart E. Tolnay. "When Race Didn't Matter: Black and White Mob Violence against Their Own Color." In *Under Sentence of Death: Lynching in the South*, ed. W. Fitzhugh Brundage. Chapel Hill: University of North Carolina Press, 1997.

Blight, David W. "W. E. B. Du Bois and the Struggle for American Historical Memory." In *History and Memory in African-American Culture*, ed. Geneviève Fabre and Robert O'Meally. New York: Oxford University Press, 1994.

Breen, William J. "Black Women and the Great War: Mobilization and Reform in the South." *Journal of Southern History* 44 (August 1978): 421–40.

Butler, Kim D. "Defining Diaspora, Redefining a Discourse." *Diaspora* 10 (2001): 189–219.

Capozzola, Christopher. "The Only Badge Needed Is Your Patriotic Fervor: Vigilance, Coercion, and the Law in World War I America." *Journal of American History* 88 (March 2002): 1354–82.

Chase, Hal S. "Struggle for Equality: Fort Des Moines Training Camp for Colored Officers, 1917." *Phylon* 39, no. 4 (1978): 297–310.

Cohen, Stanley. "A Historical Study in Nativism: The American Red Scare of 1919–1920." In *Causes and Consequences of World War I*, ed. John Milton Cooper Jr. New York: Quadrangle, 1972.

Cohen, William B. "French Racism and Its African Impact." In *Double Impact: France and Africa in the Age of Imperialism*, ed. G. Wesley Johnson. Westport, Conn.: Greenwood Press, 1985.

Confino, Alon. "Collective Memory and Cultural History: Problems of Method." *American Historical Review* 105 (December 1997): 1386–1403.

Conklin, Alice L. "Colonialism and Human Rights, A Contradiction in Terms? The Case of France and West Africa, 1895–1914." *American Historical Review* 103 (April 1998): 419–42.

Cooper, John Milton. "The Great War and American Memory." *Virginia Quarterly Review* (Winter 2003): 70–84.

Cooper, Wayne. "Claude McKay and the New Negro of the 1920's." *Phylon* 25, no. 3 (1964): 297–306.

Craig, Berry. "Nelson, William Stuart." In *The Kentucky Encyclopedia*, ed. John E. Kleber. Lexington: University Press of Kentucky, 1992.

Crane, Susan A. "Writing the Individual Back into Collective Memory." *American Historical Review* 102 (December 1997): 1372–85.

Cunningham, Roger D. "Black Artillerymen from the Civil War through World War I." *Army History* 58 (Spring 2003): 5–19.

Dennis, Michael. "Looking Backward: Woodrow Wilson, the New South and the Question of Race." *American Nineteenth Century History* 3 (Spring 2002): 77–104.

Dewitte, Philippe. "La dette du sang." *Hommes & Migrations* 1148 (November 1991): 8–11.

Du Bois, W. E. B. "The African Roots of War." *Atlantic Monthly* (May 1915): 707–14.

———. "The Negro Soldier in Service Abroad during the First World War." *Journal of Negro Education* 12 (Summer 1943): 324–34.

———. "Reconstruction." *Opinion* 18 (July 1919): 130–31.

Edwards, Brent Hayes. "The Uses of *Diaspora*." *Social Text* 19 (Spring 2001): 45–73.

Elkins, W. F. "A Source of Black Nationalism in the Caribbean: The Revolt of the British West Indies Regiment at Taranto, Italy." *Science & Society* 34 (Spring 1970): 99–103.

Ellis, Mark. "'Closing Ranks' and 'Seeking Honors': W. E. B. Du Bois in World War I." *Journal of American History* 79 (June 1992): 96–124.

———. "Joel Spingarn's 'Constructive Programme' and the Wartime Antilynching Bill of 1918." *Journal of Policy History* 4 (1992): 134–62.

———. "W. E. B. Du Bois and the Formation of Black Opinion in World War I: A Commentary on 'The Damnable Dilemma.'" *Journal of American History* 81 (March 1995): 1584–90.

Fairclough, Adam. "Tuskegee's Robert R. Moton and the Travails of the Early Black College President." *Journal of Blacks in Higher Education* 31 (Spring 2001): 94–105.

Fields, Barbara J. "Ideology and Race in American History." In *Region, Race, and Reconstruction: Essays in Honor of C. Vann Woodward*, ed. J. Morgan Kousser and James M. McPherson. New York: Oxford University Press, 1982.

Gaines, Kevin. "Artistic Othering in Black Diaspora Musics." In *Uptown Conversation: The New Jazz Studies*, ed. Robert G. O'Meally, Brent Hayes Edwards, and Farrah Jasmine Griffin. New York: New York University Press, 2004.

Garvin, Charles Herbert. "The Negro in the Special Services of the U.S. Army: Medical Corps, Dental Corps and Nurses Corps." *Journal of Negro Education* 12 (Summer 1943): 335–44.

Gates, Henry Louis, Jr. "The Trope of a New Negro and the Reconstruction of the Image of the Black." *Representations* 24 (Autumn 1988): 129–55.

Gatewood, Willard B., Jr. "Alabama's 'Negro Soldier Experiment,' 1898–1899." *Journal of Negro History* 57 (October 1972): 333–51.

———. "Black Americans and the Quest for Empire, 1898–1903." *Journal of Southern History* 38 (November 1972): 545–66.

Gerstle, Gary. "Liberty, Coercion, and the Making of Americans." *Journal of American History* 84 (September 1997): 524–58.

Geschwender, James A. "Continuities in Theories of Status Consistency and Cognitive Dissonance." *Social Forces* 46 (December 1967): 160–71.

———. "Status Inconsistency, Social Isolation, and Individual Unrest." *Social Forces* 46 (June 1968): 477–83.

Grossman, James. "Citizenship and Rights on the Home Front during the First World War: The 'Great Migration' and the 'New Negro.'" In *Minorities in Wartime: National and Racial Groupings in Europe, North America and Australia during the Two World Wars*, ed. Panikos Panayi. Oxford: Berg, 1993.

Grundlingh, Albert. "The Impact of the First World War on South African Blacks." In *Africa and the First World War*, ed. Melvin E. Page. New York: St. Martin's Press, 1987.

Hahn, Steven. "'Extravagant Expectations' of Freedom: Rumour, Political Struggle, and the Christmas Insurrection Scare of 1865 in the American South." *Past and Present* 157 (1997): 122–58.

Hall, Jacquelyn Dowd. "The Long Civil Rights Movement and the Political Uses of the Past." *Journal of American History* 91 (March 2005): 1233–63.

Hall, Stuart. "Cultural Identity and Diaspora." In *Identity: Community, Culture, Difference*, ed. Jonathan Rutherford. London: Lawrence & Wishart, 1990.

Harris, J. William. "Etiquette, Lynching, and Racial Boundaries in Southern History: A Mississippi Example." *American Historical Review* 100 (April 1995): 387–410.

Harris, Jerome. "Jazz on the Global Stage." In *The African Diaspora: A Musical Perspective*, ed. Ingrid Monson. New York: Garland, 2000.

Harris, Joseph E. "Dynamics of the Global African Diaspora." In *The African Diaspora*, ed. Alusine Jalloh and Stephen E. Maizlish. College Station: Texas A&M University Press, 1996.

Hickel, K. Walter. "War, Region, and Social Welfare: Federal Aid to Servicemen's Dependents in the South, 1917–1921." *Journal of American History* 87 (March 2001): 1362–91.

Hill, Robert A. Introduction to *The Crusader*. New York: Garland, 1987.

Hine, Darlene Clark. "The Call That Never Came: Black Women Nurses and World War I." *Indiana Military History Journal* 15 (January 1983): 23–26.

Hodes, Martha. "The Sexualization of Reconstruction Politics: White Women and Black Men in the South after the Civil War." *Journal of the History of Sexuality* 3 (January 1993): 402–17.

Holt, Thomas. "Afterword: Mapping the Black Public Sphere." In *The Black Public Sphere: A Public Culture Book*, ed. The Black Public Sphere Collective. Chicago: University of Chicago Press, 1995.

Howe, Glenford D. "In the Crucible of Race: Race, Power, and Military Socialization of West Indian Recruits during the First World War." *Journal of Caribbean Studies* 10 (Summer and Fall 1995): 163–81.

Hurston, Zora Neale. "The Ocoee Riot." In *Zora Neale Hurston: Folklore, Memoirs, and Other Writings*, ed. Cheryl Wall. New York: Library of America, 1995.

Hutchinson, George. "Mediating 'Race' and 'Nation': The Cultural Politics of *The Messenger*." *African American Review* 28 (Winter 1994): 531–48.

James, Felix. "Robert Russa Moton and the Whispering Gallery after World War I." *Journal of Negro History* 62 (July 1977): 235–42.

Jensen, Kimberly. "Women, Citizenship, and Civic Sacrifice: Engendering Patriotism in the First World War." In *Bonds of Affection: Americans Define Their Patriotism*, ed. John Bodnar. Princeton: Princeton University Press, 1996.

Jones, James Nathan, Franklin F. Johnson, and Robert B. Cochrane. "Alfred Jack Thomas: Performer, Composer, Educator." *Black Perspective in Music* 11 (Spring 1983): 61–75.

Jordan, William. "'The Damnable Dilemma': African-American Accommodation and Protest during World War I." *Journal of American History* 81 (March 1995): 1562–83.

Joseph, C. L. "The British West Indies Regiment, 1914–1918." *Journal of Caribbean History* 2 (May 1971): 94–124.

Keene, Jennifer D. "French and American Racial Stereotypes during the First World War." In *National Stereotypes in Perspective: Americans in France, Frenchmen in America*, ed. William L. Chew III. Atlanta: Rodopi, 2001.

———. "Uneasy Alliances: French Military Intelligence and the American Army during the First World War." In *Knowing Your Friends: Intelligence inside Alliances and Coalitions from 1914 to the Cold War*, ed. Martin Alexander. Portland, Ore.: 1998.

———. "W. E. B. Du Bois and the Wounded World: Seeking Meaning in the First World War for African-Americans." *Peace and Change* 26 (April 2001): 135–52.

Keith, Jeanette. "The Politics of Southern Draft Resistance, 1917–1918: Class, Race and Conscription in the Rural South." *Journal of American History* 87 (March 2001): 1335–61.

Kelley, Robin D. G. "'But a Local Phase of a World Problem': Black History's Global Vision, 1883–1950." *Journal of American History* 86 (December 1999): 1045–77.

———. "'We Are Not What We Seem': Rethinking Black Working-Class Opposition in the Jim Crow South." *Journal of American History* 80 (June 1993): 75–112.

Kenny, Michael G. "A Place for Memory: The Interface between Individual and Collective History." *Comparative Studies in Society and History* 41 (July 1999): 420–37.

Kevles, Daniel J. "Testing the Army's Intelligence: Psychologists and the Military in World War I." *Journal of American History* 55 (December 1968): 565–81.

Kornweibel, Theodore, Jr. "Apathy and Dissent: Black American's Negative Responses to World War I." *South Atlantic Quarterly* 80 (Summer 1981): 322–38.

Lang, Anthony. "Voluntary Associations and Black Ethnic Identity." *Phylon* 39, no. 2 (1978): 171–79.

Levine, Phillipa. "Battle Colors: Race, Sex, and Colonial Soldiery in World War I." *Journal of Women's History* 9 (Winter 1998): 104–30.

Levitch, Mark. "The Great War Re-remembered: The Fragmentation of the World's Largest Painting." In *Matters of Conflict: Material Culture, Memory, and the First World War*, ed. Nicholas J. Saunders. New York: Routledge, 2004.

Lewis, Earl. "To Turn as on a Pivot: Writing African Americans into a History of Overlapping Diasporas." *American Historical Review* 100 (June 1995): 765–87.

Lindholm, Karl. "William Clarence Matthews: Brief Life of a Baseball Pioneer." *Harvard Magazine* (September–October 1998): 35–35.

Lively, Adam. "Continuity and Radicalism in American Black Nationalist Thought, 1914–1929." *Journal of American Studies* 18 (August 1984): 207–35.

Lorenz, Alfred Lawrence. "Ralph W. Tyler: The Unknown Correspondent of World War I." *Journalism History* 31 (Spring 2005): 2–12.

Lunardini, Christine A. "Standing Firm: William Monroe Trotter's Meetings with Woodrow Wilson, 1913–1914." *Journal of Negro History* 64 (Summer 1979): 244–64.

Lunn, Joe. "'Les Races Guerrières': Racial Preconceptions in the French Military about West African Soldiers during the First World War." *Journal of Contemporary History* 34 (October 1999): 517–36.

Martin, Tony. "Revolutionary Upheaval in Trinidad, 1919: Views from British and American Sources." *Journal of Negro History* 58 (July 1973): 313–26.

May, Stephen. "World War I Veteran Horace Pippin Used Art to Purge Himself of the Horrors of the Trenches." *Military History* 14 (February 1998): 14 ff.

Mennell, James. "African-Americans and the Selective Service Act of 1917." *Journal of Negro History* 84 (Summer 1999): 275–87.

Nelson, Keith L. "The 'Black Horror on the Rhine': Race as a Factor in Post–World War I Diplomacy." *Journal of Modern History* 42 (December 1970): 606–27.

Nora, Pierre. "Between History and Memory: Les Lieux de Mémoire." *Representations* 26 (Spring 1989): 7–24.

Norvell, Stanley B., and William M. Tuttle Jr. "Views of a Negro during 'The Red Summer' of 1919." *Journal of Negro History* 51 (July 1966): 209–18.

O'Meally, Robert, and Geneviève Fabre. Introduction to *History and Memory in African-American Culture*, ed. Geneviève Fabre and Robert O'Meally. New York: Oxford University Press, 1994.

Palmer, Colin A. "Defining and Studying the Modern African Diaspora." *Perspectives* 36 (September 1998): 22–25.

Patterson, Tiffany Ruby, and Robin D. G. Kelley. "Unfinished Migrations: Reflections on the African Diaspora and the Making of the Modern World." *African Studies Review* 43 (April 2000): 11–45.

Payne, James Robert, and Victor R. Daly. "A MELUS Interview: Victor R. Daly." *MELUS* 12 (Summer 1985): 87–92.

Piep, Karsten H. "'Modern Understanding': Gender and Race Politics in American World War I Writings." *Erfurt Electronic Studies in English*, June 2003. ⟨http://webdoc.sub.gwdg.de/edoc/ia/eese/artic23/piep/6_2003.html⟩.

Powell, Richard J. "Re/Birth of a Nation." In *Rhapsodies in Black: Art of the Harlem Renaissance*, ed. David A. Bailey and Richard J. Powell. Berkeley: University of California Press, 1997.

Reich, Steven A. "The Great War, Black Workers, and the Rise and Fall of the NAACP in the South." In *The Black Worker: A Reader*, ed. Eric Arnesen. Urbana: University of Illinois Press, 2007.

———. "Soldiers of Democracy: Black Texans and the Fight for Citizenship, 1917–1921." *Journal of American History* 82 (March 1996): 1478–1504.

Rodgers, Daniel T. "In Search of Progressivism." *Reviews in American History* 10 (1982): 113–32.

———. "Keywords: A Reply." *Journal of the History of Ideas* 49 (October–December 1988): 669–76.

Rosenberg, Jonathan. "For Democracy, Not Hypocrisy: World War and Race Relations in the United States, 1914–1919." *International History Review* 21 (September 1999): 592–625.

Rowell, Charles H., and Brent Hayes Edwards. "An Interview with Brent Hayes Edwards." *Callaloo* 22 (Autumn 1999): 784–97.

Salyer, Lucy E. "Baptism by Fire: Race, Military Service, and U.S. Citizenship Policy, 1918–1935." *Journal of American History* 91 (December 2004): 847–76.

Sayer, Derek. "British Reaction to the Amritsar Massacre 1919–1920." *Past and Present* 131 (May 1991): 130–64.

Sidbury, James. "Saint Domingue in Virginia: Ideology, Local Meanings, and Resistance to Slavery, 1790–1800." *Journal of Southern History* 63 (August 1997): 531–52.

Stovall, Tyler. "The Color Line behind the Lines: Racial Violence in France during the Great War." *American Historical Review* 103 (June 1998): 737–69.

———. "Harlem-Sur-Seine: Building an African American Diasporic Community in Paris." *Stanford Electronic Humanities Review* 5, no. 2 (1997). ⟨http://www.stanford.edu/group/SHR/5-2/stoval.html⟩.

———. "Love, Labor, and Race: Colonial Men and White Women in France during the Great War." In *French Civilization and Its Discontents: Nationalism, Colonialism, Race*, ed. Tyler Stovall and Georges Van Den Abbeele. Lanham, Md.: Lexington Books, 2003.

Taylor, Verta. "Mobilizing for Change in a Social Movement Society." *Contemporary Sociology* 29 (January 2000): 219–30.

Taylor, Verta, and Nancy E. Whittier. "Analytical Approaches to Social Movement Culture: The Culture of the Women's Movement." In *Social Movements and Culture*, ed. Hank Johnston and Bert Klandermans. Minneapolis: University of Minnesota Press, 1995.

———. "Collective Identity in Social Movement Communities: Lesbian Feminist Mobilization." In *Frontiers in Social Movement Theory*, ed. Aldon D. Morris and Carol McClurg Mueller. New Haven: Yale University Press, 1992.

Tucker, Mark. "In Search of Will Vodery." *Black Music Research Journal* 16 (Spring 1996): 123–82.

Tuttle, William M., Jr. "Violence in a 'Heathen' Land: The Longview Race Riot of 1919." *Phylon* 33, no. 4 (1972): 324–33.

Vought, Kip. "Racial Stirrings in Colored Town: The UNIA in Miami during the 1920s." *TEQUESTA: The Journal of the Historical Association of Southern Florida* 60 (2000): 56–76.

Waldrep, Christopher. "Word and Deed: The Language of Lynching, 1820–1953." In *Lethal Imagination: Violence and Brutality in American History*, ed. Michael A. Bellesiles. New York: New York University Press, 1999.

Wesley, Charles H. "W. E. B. Du Bois: The Historian." In *Black Titan: W. E. B. Du Bois*, ed. John Henrik Clarke, Esther Jackson, Ernest Kaiser, and J. H. O'Dell. Boston: Beacon Press, 1970.

West, Cornel. "Horace Pippin's Challenge to Art Criticism." In *I Tell My Heart: The Art of Horace Pippin*, ed. Judith Stein. New York: Universe, 1993.

Whalan, Mark. "'The Only Real White Democracy' and the Language of Liberation: The Great War, France, and African American Culture in the 1920s." *Modern Fiction Studies* 51 (Winter 2005): 775–800.

White, Walter. "Election by Terror in Florida." *New Republic*, January 12, 1921, 195–97.

Williams, Chad. "Symbols of Freedom and Defeat: Black Troops, White Southerners, and the Christmas Insurrection Scare of 1865." In *Black Flag over Dixie: Racial Atrocities and Reprisals in the Civil War*, ed. Gregory J. W. Urwin. Carbondale: Southern Illinois University Press, 2004.

Wilson, Judith. "Scenes of War." In *I Tell My Heart: The Art of Horace Pippin*, ed. Judith Stein. New York: Universe, 1993.

Wolgemuth, Kathleen L. "Woodrow Wilson and Federal Segregation." *Journal of Negro History* 44 (April 1959): 158–73.

Woodruff, Nan. "African American Struggles for Citizenship in the Arkansas and Mississippi Deltas in the Age of Jim Crow." *Radical History Review* 55 (Winter 1993): 33–52.

Zeleza, Paul Tiyambe. "Rewriting the African Diaspora: Beyond the Black Atlantic." *African Affairs* 104, no. 414 (2005): 35–68.

DISSERTATIONS AND THESES

Davis, David A. "World War I, Literary Modernism, and the U.S. South." Ph.D. dissertation, University of North Carolina, 2006.

Johnson, Phillip James. "Seasons in Hell: Charles S. Johnson and the 1930 Liberian Labor Crisis." Ph.D. dissertation, Louisiana State University, 2004.
Lentz-Smith, Adriane D. "The Great War for Civil Rights." Ph.D. dissertation, Yale University, 2005.
Makalani, Minkah. "For the Liberation of Black People Everywhere: The African Blood Brotherhood, Black Radicalism, and Pan-African Liberation in the New Negro Movement, 1917–1936." Ph.D. dissertation, University of Illinois, Urbana-Champaign, 2004.
Mathieu, Marie Sarah-Jane. "Jim Crow Rides This Train: The Social and Political Impact of African American Sleeping Car Porters in Canada, 1880–1939." Ph.D. dissertation, Yale University, 2001.
Mjagkij, Nina. "Behind the Lines: The Social Experience of Black Soldiers during World War I." M.A. thesis, University of Cincinnati, 1986.
Parker, Christopher S. "War, What Is It Good For: Race, Military Service, and Social Change, 1945–1995." Ph.D. dissertation, University of Chicago, 2001.
Richards, Miles S. "Osceola E. McKaine and the Struggle for Black Civil Rights: 1917–1946." Ph.D. dissertation, University of South Carolina, 1994.
Williams, Chad Louis. "Torchbearers of Democracy: The First World War and the Figure of the African-American Soldier." Ph.D. dissertation, Princeton University, 2004.
Yellin, Eric Steven. "In the Nation's Service: Racism and Federal Employees in Woodrow Wilson's Washington." Ph.D. dissertation, Princeton University, 2007.

Index